26th Edition

Standard Catalog of®

UNITED STATES PAPER MONEY

Edited by George S. Cuhaj
William Brandimore, Market Analyst

Published by

krause publications
An Imprint of F+W Publications

700 East State Street • Iola, WI 54990-0001
715-445-2214 • 888-457-2873
www.krausebooks.com

Our toll-free number to place an order or obtain
a free catalog is (800) 258-0929.

ISSN 1081-5996
ISBN-13: 978-0-89689-573-7
ISBN-10: 0-89689-573-4

Designed by: Sandra Morrison
Edited by: George Cuhaj

Photos courtesy of Stack's, Lyn Knight,
and from the collections of William Brandimore,
Ray Czahor, and Chester L. Krause.

Printed in China

Table of Contents

Introduction

Though paper media representing gold or other intrinsic-value stores of wealth has been issued in the United States and its predecessor colonies and territories since 1690, the widespread acceptance of paper currency by the American people is a comparatively recent development and came only grudgingly.

Paper money emissions by the British colonies in New England, the earliest paper currency within the borders of what is now the United States of America, circulated alongside other untraditional exchange media such as Indian wampum shells and musket balls during chronic periods of shortages of "real" - coined - money.

Even though the first issues of an organized central government, the Continental Congress' currency notes, promised to pay the bearer face value in "Spanish milled dollars, or the value thereof in gold or silver," these notes circulated at a heavy discount - if they were accepted at all. The fledgling government's final solution for the Continental Currency problem, accepting them in 1787 at 1% of face value in exchange for interest bearing bonds, did nothing to bolster public confidence in paper money.

Neither did the often larcenous "banking" practices of the various elements of the private sector to whom the note-issuing prerogative fell. With states denied the power to issue money by the Constitution of the United States, and the powers of the Federal Government to do so left unspecified; various private issues of banks, railroads, utilities, and even individual citizens, cropped up, with varying resources to guarantee their value, until the Government halted the practice in 1863.

By the late 19th Century, U.S.-issued paper money had become a viable part of the nation's commerce as people recognized that such notes were, indeed, redeemable on demand for gold or silver. By 1963, paper currency was such an ingrained part of the American economy that the Government was able to remove all specie-redemption quality from its currency issues, raising only minimal objections from strict interpretationists of the Constitution.

Now, ironically, paper money may be on the way out as a circulating medium of exchange. The growth of demand deposits (checking accounts), electronic fund transfers and the arrival of the home computer age may one day soon put an end for the need for physical symbols of wealth to pass from hand to hand.

Scope of this catalog

It is not the intention of this catalog to provide a reference to every type of official and unofficial paper currency which has circulated in the United States. Indeed, such a project between the covers of one volume represents an impossible, though intriguing challenge.

Rather, this catalog will provide a guide to those paper money issues since 1812 of the Government of the United States of America, along with several related currency issues which are traditionally collected by paper money hobbyists in conjunction with the regular issues of the U.S.

Such a scope is intended, therefore, to provide the collector of U.S. paper money with a catalog reflective of the current state of the hobby.

The reader will be provided with sufficient background information to facilitate and illuminate the building of a collection, without being subjected to fiscal, legislative or historical data that would be of interest to only a small minority of readers.

Numbering System

In using this book, you will immediately notice that "KL" and "FR" numbers are used at the beginning of each entry. This catalog system was invented as a shorthand identification system for use in price lists, advertisements and auction catalogs where space is at a premium. Instead of writing a full description of a $1 Legal Tender Note, series 1923, you can write KL-28. Therefore, many more notes can be listed in an ad for the same cost. The two commonly used numbering systems are Friedberg (FR) numbers, invented by pioneer cataloger Robert Friedberg, and Krause-Lemke (KL) numbers created by Chester L. Krause and Robert F. Lemke as an improvement. Both catalog numbers are given for each listing in this book for your convenience.

History of Pre-Federal Paper Money in the U.S.

To better understand the forces which shaped the United States Government's issues of paper currency since 1861, it is necessary to look backward to the many and varied public and private currency issues which preceded them in this country. The use of paper money in the area which would become the United States actually predates its use in many parts of Western Europe and in most of the rest of the world. While paper currencies had been in use in China since the 7th Century, when it was known as "flying money" because of its light weight and ability to circulate widely with ease, it was not until the late 17th Century that the western world began experiments with non-metallic circulating currencies. Surprisingly quickly, the North American continent had its first "paper money" issues in 1685, when the Intendant of New France (Canada) issued promissory notes hand-printed on pieces of playing cards, to circulate as money until the delayed arrival of the paymaster.

The Massachusetts Bay Colony followed suit soon after, issuing in December, 1690, £7,000 worth of the first publicly authorized paper money notes in the western world to pay expenses of a border war with Canada (previous paper money issues in Europe and North America had been either issued by banks, or were emergency measures not authorized by any public body).

Following that precedent, by the turn of the 18th Century, other colonies were emitting paper currencies as needed to run their specie-short economies. By the end of the War for Independence, all 13 colonies had issued some form of paper currency. Beginning in May, 1775, the Congress of the newly unified former colonies began the issue of Continental Currency to finance its fight for freedom.

The Continental Currency was plagued, though, by increasing public distrust. The Continental paper dollar was able to hold its value at par with a specie dollar only until October, 1777, by which time widespread counterfeiting by British, Tories and opportunists conspired with the natural inflation of a printing press economy and increasing uncertainty as to the outcome of the war to push the exchange ratio of the Continental Currency to $11 in paper for $10 in specie.

After that point, the devaluation accelerated. By the next year, October, 1778, the ratio was 4.66 to 1.

The low point was reached in April, 1780, when a dollar in silver or gold was worth $40 Continental. And these were the *official* exchange ratios adopted by the Congress and many of the states, to offset the rampant inflation. In actual commerce, the Continentals were all but worthless. George Washington lamented that it took a wagonful of Continental Currency to purchase a wagonload of supplies for his army. A truer measure of the value of the Government paper currency could be found in the fact that by October, 1787, amid speculation that the Continental Currency might never be redeemable, it was selling at the rate of $250 paper for $1 specie. Eventually, the Government issued 6% interest bearing bonds at the rate of $1 for every $100 of Continental Currency turned in.

Issued current with the Colonial and Continental currencies were numerous privately-sponsored paper monies produced by banks (as early as 1732 in Connecticut), utilities, merchants, individuals and even churches.

These issues continued after the Revolutionary War, and proliferated in the 19th Century. Today, lumped together under the generic, if not altogether correct, label of "broken bank notes," these colorful, historic notes and their collectible adjuncts make up a significant portion of the paper money hobby's interest.

The tens of thousands of privately-issued bank and scrip notes of the 1800s ranged in denomination from one-half cent to several thousand dollars. While today their collector value depends on a combination of rarity, condition and demand; their value when issued was solely dependent on the reputation of the issuing authority - be it bank, railroad or Main Street apothecarian. In those days, when a note might be worth every cent of its face value or might be worth nothing more than the paper on which it was printed, an entire industry sprang up to supply banks and merchants with accurate, timely information about which notes would pass current, which should be accepted only at a discount, and those from an issuer who had gone "broken." In addition, because of the wealth of larcenous talent available for changing broken bank notes into "good" notes through the alteration of a bank or city name, or raising the denomination of a note from $1 to $10 by deft penmanship; those who handled the dizzying variety of paper money in circulation in the mid 19th Century needed books which listed and described the genuine issues of a particular bank. (It is, incidentally, from the common name of these paper money reporting services that the name *Bank Note Reporter* was derived for the monthly paper money newspaper published by the publisher of this catalog.)

The only restraints on the issue of paper money at that time were those which the individual states cared to apply, and such restraints were infrequent and ineffective.

The Federal Government put an effective end to these halcyon days of currency free-for-all in 1863, by imposing a 10% tax on outstanding notes; and later through the 14th Amendment to the Constitution, forbidding the private issue of circulating media of exchange altogether.

The Government of the United States of America has attained a monopoly on the note-issuing function which it has maintained, except in localized emergency situations, to this day.

Paper Money Grading

Introduction

Grading is the most controversial component of paper money collecting. Small differences in grade can mean significant differences in value.

To facilitate communication between sellers and buyers, it is essential that grading terms and their meanings be as standardized and as widely used as possible. The standardization should reflect common usage as much as practicable.

The grades and definitions as set forth below cannot reconcile all the various systems and grading terminology variants. Rather, the attempt is made here to try and diminish the controversy with some common-sense grades and definitions that aim to give more precise meaning to the grading language of paper money.

Grading Guide

Crisp Uncirculated (CU): A perfectly preserved note, never mishandled by the issuing authority, a bank teller, the public or a collector.

Paper is clean and firm, without discoloration. Corners are sharp and square, without any evidence of rounding. (Rounded corners are often a tell-tale sign of a cleaned or "doctored" note.) An uncirculated note will have its original, natural sheen.

About Uncirculated (AU): A virtually perfect note, with some minor handling. May show evidence of bank counting folds at a corner or one light fold through the center, but not both. An AU note cannot be creased, a crease being a hard fold which has usually "broken" the surface of the note.

Paper is clean and bright with original sheen. Corners are not rounded.

Extremely Fine (XF): very attractive note, with light handling. May have a maximum of three light folds or one strong crease.

Paper is clean and bright with original sheen. Corners may show only the slightest evidence of rounding. There may also be the slightest sign of wear where a fold meets the edge.

Very Fine (VF): An attractive note, but with more evidence of handling and wear. May have a number of folds both vertically and horizontally.

Paper may have minimal dirt, or possible color smudging. Paper itself is still relatively crisp and not floppy.

There are no tears into the border area, although the edges do show slight wear. Corners also show wear but not full rounding.

Fine: A note which shows considerable circulation, with many folds, creases and wrinkling. Paper is not excessively dirty but may have some softness.

Edges may show much handling, with minor tears in the border area. Tears may not extend into the design. There will be no center hole because of excessive folding.

Colors are clear but not very bright. A staple hole or two would not be considered unusual wear in a Fine note. Overall appearance is still on the desirable side.

Very Good (VG): A well-used note, abused but still intact.

Corners may have much wear and rounding, tiny nicks, tears may extend into the design, some discoloration may be present, staining may have occurred, and a small hole may be seen at center from excessive folding.

Staple and pinholes are usually present, and the note itself is quite limp but no pieces of the note are missing. A note in VG condition may still have an overall not unattractive appearance. **Good (G):** A well-worn and heavily-used note. Normal damage from prolonged circulation will include strong multiple folds and creases, stains, pinholes and/or staple holes, dirt, discoloration, edge tears, center hole, rounded corners and an overall unattractive appearance. No large pieces of the note may be missing. Graffiti is commonly seen on notes in Good condition.

Fair: A totally limp, dirty, and very well-used note. Large pieces may be half torn off or missing besides the defects mentioned under the Good category. Tears will be larger, obscured portions of the note will be bigger. **Poor:** A "rag" with severe damage because of wear, staining, pieces missing, graffiti, larger holes. May have tape holding pieces of the note together. Trimming may have taken place to remove rough edges.

The above Introduction and Grading Guide is an adaptation work prepared under the guidance of the Grading Committee of the International Bank Note Society.

How To Look At A Banknote

In order to ascertain the grade of a note, it is essential to examine it out of a holder and under a good light. Move the note around so that light bounces off at different angles. Try holding it up obliquely so that the note is almost even with your eye as you look up at the light. Hard-to-see folds or slight creases will show up under such examination.

Cleaning, Washing, Pressing

Cleaning, washing or pressing paper money is generally harmful and reduces both the grade and the value of a note. At the very least, a washed or pressed note may lose its original sheen and its surface may become lifeless and dull. The defects a note has, such as folds and creases, may not necessarily be completely eliminated and their telltale marks can be detected under a good light. Carelessly washed notes may also have white streaks where the folds or creases were (or still are).

Processing of a note will automatically reduce it at least one full grade.

Other Defects

Glue, tape or pencil marks may sometimes be successfully removed. While such removal will leave a cleaned surface, it will improve the overall appearance of the note without concealing any of its defects. Under such circumstances, the grade of that note may also be improved.

The words "pinholes," "staple holes," "trimmed," "writing on face... tape marks," etc., should always be added to the description of a note.

The Term "Uncirculated"

The word "Uncirculated" is used in this grading guide only as a qualitative measurement of the appearance of a note. It has nothing at all to do with whether or not an issuer has actually released the note to circulation. Either a note is uncirculated in condition or it is not, there can be no degrees of uncirculated. Defects in color, centering and the like may be included in a description but the fact that a note is or is not in uncirculated condition should not be a disputable point.

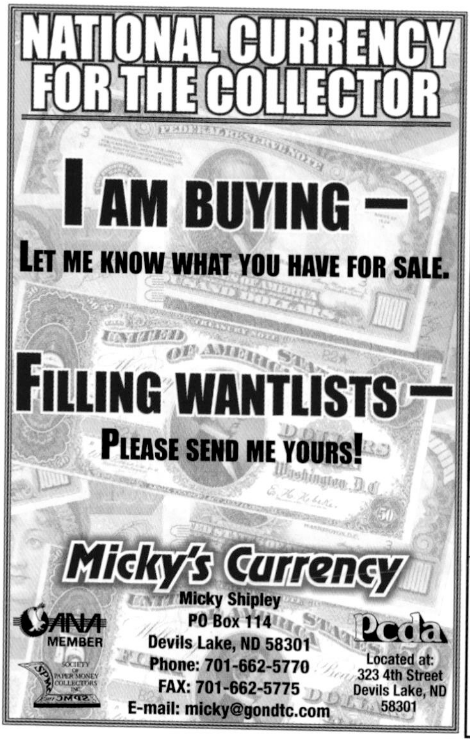
NATIONAL CURRENCY FOR THE COLLECTOR
I AM BUYING —
LET ME KNOW WHAT YOU HAVE FOR SALE.
FILLING WANTLISTS —
PLEASE SEND ME YOURS!
Micky's Currency
Micky Shipley
PO Box 114
Devils Lake, ND 58301
Phone: 701-662-5770
FAX: 701-662-5775
E-mail: micky@gondtc.com
ANA MEMBER
SOCIETY OF PAPER MONEY COLLECTORS INC.
SPMC
Pcda
Located at:
323 4th Street
Devils Lake, ND
58301

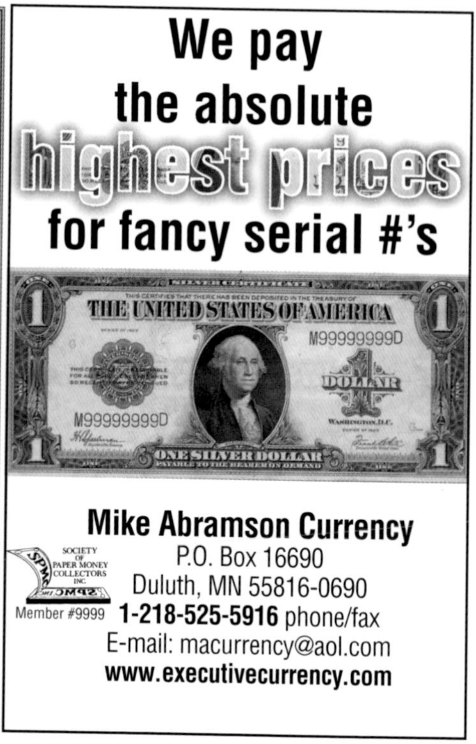
We pay
the absolute
highest prices
for fancy serial #'s
THE UNITED STATES OF AMERICA
M99999999D
ONE SILVER DOLLAR
Mike Abramson Currency
P.O. Box 16690
Duluth, MN 55816-0690
1-218-525-5916 phone/fax
E-mail: macurrency@aol.com
www.executivecurrency.com
SOCIETY OF PAPER MONEY COLLECTORS INC.
SPMC
Member #9999

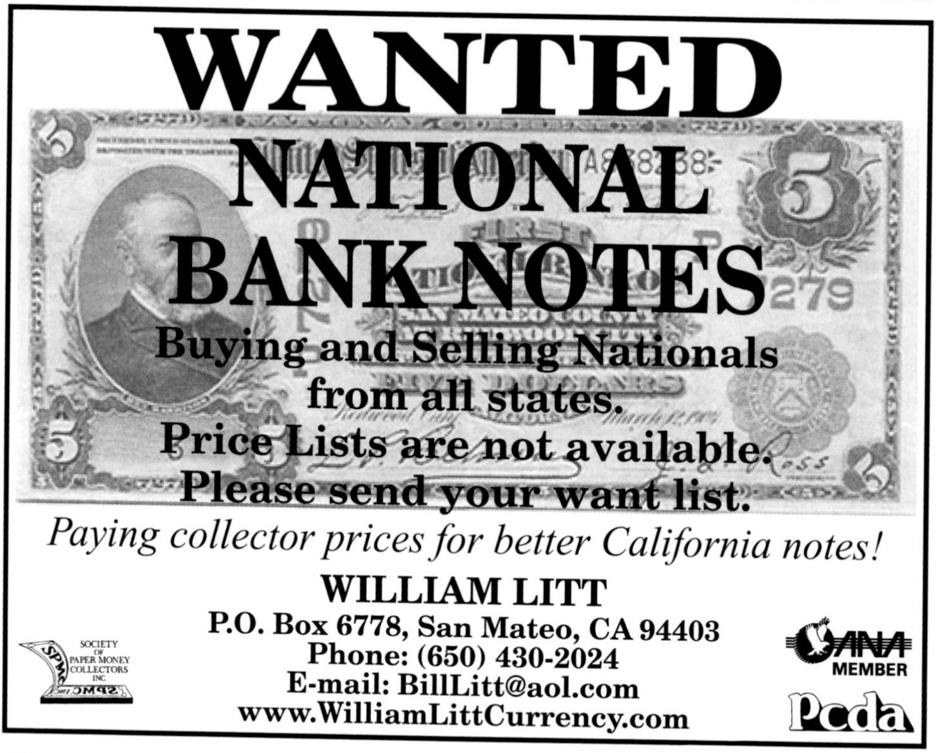
WANTED
NATIONAL
BANK NOTES
Buying and Selling Nationals
from all states.
Price Lists are not available.
Please send your want list.
Paying collector prices for better California notes!
WILLIAM LITT
P.O. Box 6778, San Mateo, CA 94403
Phone: (650) 430-2024
E-mail: BillLitt@aol.com
www.WilliamLittCurrency.com
SOCIETY OF PAPER MONEY COLLECTORS INC.
SPMC
ANA MEMBER
Pcda

A Numismatic Tradition since 1933
Kagin's
Over the last seven decades, we have purchased more currency than any other firm.
Whether it's . . .
the Lowest denomination
On demand I will pay to the bearer ONE MILL on the return of this bottle & label John B. Thompson
No. 161 River Street TROY, N.Y.
One Mill
the Highest
$100,000 Specimen Note
the Most Valuable
$1,000 FR-1218d Gold Certificate
the Earliest
1690 20 Shillings, Mass.
the Most Exotic
Alaskan Seal Money
the Best Condition
$20 The Ohio NB of Columbus
PMG Superb Gem 69 EPQ
or the Rarest
$100 National Gold Bank Note
Santa Barbara - UNIQUE
...We buy it all!
Donald H. Kagin
PhD/Numismatics
Meredith J. Hilton
Currency
Judy Kagin
Currency
www.kagins.com
98 Main Street, #201,
Tiburon,CA 94920
888-8KAGINS or Fax 415-435-1627

Large Size Currency

For the convenience of the reader, brief and basically historical backgrounds have been provided for each of the major types of U.S. currency. No great amount of fiscal or legislative data has been provided, except where it might serve to clarify some aspects of the notes themselves or their collectibility.

Demand Notes

Despite two issues of interest-bearing Treasury notes in 1860-1861, the opening guns of the Civil War found the United States Government short of the necessary funds to put down the rebellion in a protracted war.

Congress moved swiftly in the national emergency to provide legislation authorizing the issue of $60,000,000 by Acts of July 17, and Aug. 5, 1861.

It is generally believed among numismatists today that the Demand Notes were backed by faith in the Government alone; but this was not entirely the case. By the terms of the authorizing legislation, the Demand Notes were not payable in gold. But, in a circular from the Secretary of the Treasury sent out before the suspension of specie payments on Dec. 21, 1861, they were declared payable in coin, and the Government redeemed them as such in order to sustain its credit. Thus, for a short time in 1861, the Demand Notes were quoted on a par with gold. However, as the war progressed, in most parts of the country the Demand Notes - and all other paper money of the U.S. Government - were acceptable only at a discount, even though they were receivable for all payments to the Government, including duties.

The Demand Notes took their famous "Greenback" nickname from the color of their back designs (back designs in themselves were scarce on paper money in the U.S. prior to the Civil War). The name was subsequently applied to virtually every other form of U.S. currency and remains current today.

Because the United States Government was not prepared to be in the note-printing business in 1861, the work of producing the Demand Notes was contracted to the American Bank Note Company and National Bank Note Company. Working with essentially stock currency elements, the private contractors turned out more than 7.25 million $5, $10 and $20 Demand Notes.

The actual "issuing" of the notes required that they be signed by the Treasurer of the United States (Francis E. Spinner) and the Register of the Treasury (Lucius E. Chittenden), or persons designated by them.

Accordingly, platoons of clerks within the Treasury Department were put to work autographing Demand Notes. However, on the very earliest specimens, the engraved blanks on the face of the notes indicated only the office of the signer, and the clerks were required to pen in the words "for the" on each note as they signed it, a most laborious process that was eliminated with the addition of "for the" on the engraved face plates themselves. The Demand Notes which survive today with the hand-signed "for the" on the face are much scarcer than the engraved version, and command a significant price premium.

Rarity and value of the Demand Notes is also affected by the engraved location on the face of the note indicating where the notes were issued and, therefore, payable.

The obligation on the notes reads: "The United States promises to pay to the bearer five dollars (or ten dollars or twenty dollars) on demand ... payable by the Assistant Treasurer of the United States at..."

One of five cities was then engraved. Those notes payable at New York are far and away the most common among the survivors, with Philadelphia second and Boston third. Specimens which promise redemption in Cincinnati and, especially, St. Louis, are extremely rare and seldom encountered.

United States Notes (Legal Tender Notes)

The longest-lived type of U.S. paper money, the United States Notes (called interchangeably Legal Tender Notes because of the wording of the obligation) was first authorized in 1862 and is still current today, though none have been issued since 1969.

The subject of major Constitutional debate at the time of their issue, the notes did much to pave the way for future issues of U.S. currency backed only by the credit of the Government.

While there are five official "issues" of large size Legal Tender Notes, as well as the small size series, they are generally collected today by type (major design) and, occasionally, by signature combination. The First Issue of United States Notes, dated March 10, 1862, was issued in denominations of $5, $10, $20, $50, $100, $500 and $1,000.

Two different varieties of notes, bearing different obligation wording on the backs, are popularly collected among the First Issue notes.

The earliest First Issues bear what is known as the First Obligation on back, reading: "This note is a legal tender for all debts public and private, except duties on imports and interest on the public debt, and is exchangeable for U.S. six per cent twenty year bonds, redeemable at the pleasure of the United States after five years."

The Second Obligation, much rarer, reads as follows: "This note is a legal tender for all debts, public and private, except duties on imports and interest on the public debt, and is receivable in payment of all loans made to the United States."

These First Issue notes do not carry the large face inscriptions "United States Note" or "Treasury Note," which are found on later Legal Tender issues.

Dated Aug. 1, 1862, and issued only in denominations of $1 and $2, the Second Issue U.S. Notes carry the Second Obligation on back.

The Third Issue U.S. Notes, dated March 10, 1863, were issued in denominations from $5 through $1,000, again using the Second Obligation.

Fourth Issue Legal Tenders were authorized by an Act of Congress dated March 3, 1863, and issued in denomination from $1 through $10,000 in the various Series of 1869, 1874, 1878, 1880, 1907, 1917 and 1923. Those notes in Series 1869 bear the label "Treasury Notes" on face, with all later issues carrying the "United States Notes" designation.

Back obligation on all series is the same: "This note is a legal tender at its face value for all debts public and private, except duties on imports and interest on the public debt."

The Fifth Issue Legal Tenders consisted solely of the Series 1901 $10 note (the popular Bison design), issued under the authority of the Legal Tender Acts of 1862-1863. A new face obligation was introduced: "This note is a legal tender for ten dollars subject to the provisions of Section 3588 R.S.," on back, the obligation reads: "This note is a legal tender at its face value for all debts public and private except duties on imports and interest on the public debt."

Compound Interest Treasury Notes

Circulating currency notes which grew in face value each six-month period they remained in circulation were just one of the innovations to which the Federal Government turned to finance the protracted Civil War.

Authorized by Congressional Acts of March 3, 1863, and June 30, 1864, these notes were intended to circulate for three years, bearing interest at the then-attractive rate of six percent a year, compounded semi-annually. The backs of each note carry a table spelling out the actual interest earned and current face value of the note through maturity. Theoretically, a note that was acquired when issued at face value, could be spent a year later as $10.60; although little is known as to whether this theory worked in practice. It is known, though, that those persons holding the notes at maturity generally took their profit, leaving very few surviving specimens for today's collectors.

Neither should it be assumed that the surviving notes continue to earn interest. The interest payments ended at maturity.

The face of each note bears a surcharge in large gold letters, reading "Compound Interest Treasury Note," along with corresponding numerals of issue value. Unfortunately, the gold ink used for these overprints contributed greatly to the demise of the notes themselves, for it is highly acidic and attacks the rather fragile paper to the point where many examples are found with this surcharge "burned" into and through the paper. Additionally, the $50 and $100 notes, the highest values which could practically be said to have circulated, were extensively counterfeited and the Treasury was forced to withdraw them in the face of such "competition."

In any denomination, the Compound Interest Treasury Notes are scarce in better than Fine condition.

Examples are known with a number of different issue dates on the face. The $10-$50 notes with the June 10 or July 15, 1864, dates are the rarest, with dates from Aug. 15, 1864, through Oct. 16, 1865, being more common; while in the $100 notes, the June 10, 1864, date is most common, followed by the Aug. 15, 1864-Sept. 1, 1865, dates. No July 15, 1864-dated $100 Compound Interest Treasury Notes are known, nor are there any reported survivors among the $500 and $1,000 denominations, though the Treasury reports several examples still officially outstanding.

Interest Bearing Notes

As a group, probably the rarest type of U.S. paper money is the Interest Bearing Note issues of the Civil War era. Like the Compound Interest Treasury Notes and the Refunding Certificates (also interest bearing), they were something of a desperation currency issue by the Federal Government to bolster the Union war chest.

The Interest Bearing Notes were issued in a trio of distinctive types, all of which are very rare, or unknown to have survived.

The first issue was a series of One-Year Notes, issued under authority of the Act of March 3, 1863, and paying interest of five percent for one year. Face designs of the one-year issue were similar to the Compound Interest Treasury Notes, without the gold surcharges. Backs were significantly different, lacking the tabular interest-figuring chart. A face inscription reads: "One year after date the United States will pay to the bearer with five per interest - dollars." On back, the obligation was worded: "This note is a legal tender at its face value, excluding interest, for all debts public and private, except duties on imports and interest on the public debt."

Denominations of the One-Year Notes ranged from $10 through $5,000, with no specimens of the $500, $1,000 or $5,000 known. Each note bears an individually stamped date of issue on the face. One year from that date, the notes were redeemable for face value plus interest.

Two-Year Notes were also authorized by the March 3, 1863 Act of Congress. Issued only in the $50, $100, $500 and $1,000 denominations, and paying five percent interest per year for a two-year term, they are naturally much scarcer because of the high return they offered the holder near the end of the Civil War. Designs were completely different from the One-Year Notes, although the face and back inscriptions are similar.

Like the Interest Bearing Notes themselves, the Three-Year Notes are comprised of three separate issues, due to three different authorizing Acts of Congress; July 17, 1861, June 30, 1864, and March 3,1865. Again issued in the higher denominations, from $50 through $5,000, the notes paid interest at the rate of 7-3/10 percent a year; the highest rate the Government paid on circulating notes. Like the Compound Interest Treasury Notes, the actual amount of interest is spelled out on the notes, though in this case it is expressed in terms of interest per day. Thus, the $50 note expresses a promise to pay interest of one cent per day, while the $5,000 bill paid interest at the rate of $1 per day.

That the notes were not intended to circulate widely is indicated by the fact that they are payable to the order, not to the bearer. That is, there is a blank on the face of every Three-Year Interest Bearing Note for the name of the original holder, and a corresponding blank on back for endorsement at the time of maturity.

Another feature which makes the Three-Year Notes unusual among U.S. paper money issues was the original attachment of five coupons to each note. Each coupon indicated the interest payable for a six-month period, and was removed from the note when that interest was collected semi-annually. The final interest payment was made when the note itself was presented for redemption at the end of the three-year period. This arrangement is spelled out on the face of each note.

As mentioned earlier, these notes are of the greatest rarity, most of them unknown to survive, existing only in proof form or existing in a unique, or nearly so, issued example.

Refunding Certificates

More of a government security than circulating medium of exchange, the Refunding Certificates authorized by Congress in the Act of Feb. 26, 1879, brought these interest bearing instruments within the reach of more Americans in that they were denominated at $10.

The authorizing legislation intended that these notes bear interest of four percent annually in perpetuity. However, in 1907 Congress passed a law stopping interest payments as of July 1, forever fixing the "face" value of these notes at $21.30. Presumably at that time the incentive for the public to hold these notes was removed, and their redemption accelerated.

The $10 Refunding Certificates were issued in two different forms, one type payable to the bearer, the other to the order of the original purchaser. Like the Three-Year Interest Bearing Notes, the Refunding Certificates payable to order had spaces on face and back for the owner and endorser. The "pay to order" type is far rarer than the "pay to bearer" variety.

Rather than being redeemable for specie, per se, these notes, in amounts of $50 or more, were convertible into four percent bonds.

Silver Certificates

Among the most popular of U.S. notes due to their wealth of design excellence and challenging, but not impossible rarity, the Silver Certificates of 1878-1963 comprise five major issues of large size notes, and the various series of small size notes.

Authorizing legislation for all issues were the Congressional Act of Feb. 28, 1878, and Aug. 4, 1886.

The First Issue Silver Certificates consist of Series 1878 and 1880 notes in denominations from $10-$1,000. The notes of 1878, besides bearing the engraved signatures of G.W. Scofield, Register of the Treasury, and James Gilfillan, Treasurer of the U.S., have on their face an engraved or autographed countersignature of the Assistant Treasurers in New York, Washington, D.C., and San Francisco, attesting that the requisite amount of silver dollars had been deposited in their offices to cover the face value of the notes. In addition to the Series 1878 countersigned notes, several $20 Series 1880 Silver Certificates are known bearing the engraved countersignature of T. Hillhouse, Assistant Treasurer at New York.

The silver bills' Second Issue was made up of notes from $1 through $1,000 in the Series of 1886, 1891 and 1908, although not all denominations were issued in all series

The "Educational" notes, $1, $2, and $5 Silver Certificates of Series 1896, are the sole component of the Third Issue.

Similarly, the Fourth Issue Silver Certificates are made up of $1, $2 and $5 notes of the Series of 1899.

The Silver Certificates of the Fifth Issue are the Series 1923 $1 and $5 notes.

The obligation on the First Issue notes reads: "This certifies that I there have been deposited with the Treasurer of the U.S. at Washington, D.C. (or Assistant Treasurers at few York and San Francisco) payable at his office to the bearer on demand - silver dollars. This certificate is receivable for customs, taxes and all public dues and when so received may be reissued."

Obligation on the last four issues of silver notes was worded: "This certifies that there have been deposited in the Treasury of the United States - silver dollars payable to the bearer on demand. This certificate is receivable for customs, taxes and all public dues and when so received may be issued."

Treasury or Coin Notes

Pushed through Congress by the silver mining industry, the authorizing legislation of July 14, 1890, which created the Treasury Notes carefully did not specify that they be redeemable in silver; only that they be issued to pay for silver bullion purchased by the Treasury and that they be payable "in Coin" (hence the more commonly encountered name Coin Notes). With the cooperation of Treasury officials, silver sellers were able to turn their bullion in at artificially high official prices, receive the Coin Notes in payment, and redeem them immediately for gold coin and a tidy profit.

In denominations of $1, $2, $5, $10, $20, $100 and $1,000, the Coin Notes were issued in Series 1890 and 1891 form, the 1890 issue bearing ornately engraved green back designs that filled the print area. The $50 was issued only in Series of 1891, and the $500 note, which had been designed and a plate prepared with the portrait of Gen. William T. Sherman, was not issued at all. It was felt that even as late as 25 years after the Civil War, the use of Sherman's portrait on a currency note would inflame passions in the South. The 1890 notes are much scarcer and in greater demand than the Series 1891 issue, especially in new condition.

Face and back obligations of the Coin Notes are interesting and unique. They read: "This United States of America will pay to bearer - dollars in coin." And, "This note is a legal tender at its face value in payment of all debts public and private except when otherwise expressly stipulated in the contract

National Gold Bank Notes

Gold and the American West have been inseparably linked as part of this nation's history since the discovery of gold at Sutter's Mill in 1848. The unique, but short-lived National Gold Bank Note (N.G.B.N.) series was a contemporary part of "The Golden West," and today trades on that romantic image - and the inherent rarity of the notes themselves - as one of the most sought-after types of U.S. paper money.

The National Gold Bank Notes were authorized under the provisions of the Currency Act of July 12, 1870, and are very much analogous to the regular National Currency issue.

The principal difference, besides design, is that the National Gold Bank Notes were payable - and prominently said so - in gold coin. This was a concession to the traditional mistrust of Western America in paper currency and the California area's long history of gold use as the principal medium of exchange, whether in the form of gold dust, nuggets, private-issue coinage or genuine coins of the United States Mint.

Under the general provisions of the National Bank Act of 1863, the National Gold Banks had to secure the issue of their currency with the deposit of bonds with the Treasurer of the United States. However, the conditions for the N.G.B.N. issues were a bit more stringent. The Gold Banks could issue notes only to the value of 80% of their deposited bonds, while the other National banks could issue to 90%. Additionally, the Gold Banks were required to have on hand in their vaults gold coinage equal to 25% of the value of their note issue. The responsibility of redeeming these notes *in gold,* lay with the issuing banks, not the Federal Government, which did not resume specie payments until 1879, nearly a decade after the N.G.B.N. issues began. The Treasury would, of course, redeem National Gold Bank Notes for other lawful currency.

This gold redemption property gave the N.G.B.Ns the necessary credibility, and they circulated at par with the precious metal. They circulated so extensively that surviving notes are generally found in conditions which many collectors would find unacceptable in other U.S. currency types. No strictly uncirculated National Gold Bank Note is known today, and the average condition found is Good to Very Good. Examples in Fine or better condition command attractive premiums in the infrequent times when they become available.

Though authorized in denominations from $5-$1,000, National Gold Bank Notes were issued to circulation only as high as $500. The face of each note was similar to corresponding denominations in the First Charter National Bank Note series, while the backs had as their central feature a photo-like engraving of a stack of U.S. gold pieces, representing $211.50 face value in $1 through $20 denominations.

In all, 10 National Gold Banks were chartered, nine in California and The Kidder National Gold Bank in Boston, Mass. Notes were actually printed for the Kidder N.G.B., and delivered, but the bank eventually returned them all for cancellation, never issuing them to circulation. The Kidder was the only National Gold Bank to have $1,000 notes prepared.

Because of the relatively small size of the issue, much can be determined about the issue and survivability of the National Gold Bank Notes.

In the period 1870-1878, exactly 196,849 notes, with a face value of $3,267,420, were issued.

Treasury records indicate a total of 6,639 notes remain outstanding (including four $500 examples, none of which are known to collectors).

Like the other National Bank Notes, National Gold Bank Notes are known in both Original Series and Series of 1875 issues, although all nine California banks did not issue all denominations in both series. Indeed, the Series 1875 notes are somewhat scarcer than the Original notes.

Federal Reserve Bank Notes

Often confused with the Federal Reserve Notes, which are currency issues of the Federal Reserve System itself, Federal Reserve Bank Notes were issued by the 12 individual Federal Reserve Banks, much like the National Bank Notes. Indeed, Federal Reserve Bank Notes, large and small size, carry the "National Currency" inscription. In the large size note-issuing period, the similarity of Federal Reserve Bank Notes to Federal Reserve Notes extended to nearly identical back designs in the $5-$50 denominations. FRBNs were also issued in $1 and $2 denominations, while the FRNs were issued in value from $5 through $10,000.

Two separate issues of Federal Reserve Bank Notes comprise the large size issue, while there was a single issue in small size.

The Series 1915 FRBNs were authorized under the terms of the Federal Reserve Act of Dec. 23, 1913. Issued only in denominations of $5-$20, only the banks in Atlanta, Chicago, Kansas City, Dallas and San Francisco participated, with the Frisco bank issuing only $5s.

Like the National Bank Notes, the obligation to pay the bearer on the FRBNs is made by the issuing bank, rather than the Fed system or U.S. Government. The security notice on the 1915 issue reads: "Secured by United States bonds deposited with the Treasurer of the United States."

That obligation was changed for the Series 1918 FRBNs, issued under authority of a Congressional Act of April 23, 1918. The modification reads: "Secured by United States certificates of indebtedness or United States one-year gold notes, deposited with the Treasurer of the United States."

The Series 1918 FRBNs consist of all denominations from $1 through $50, though again, not all 12 banks issued all denominations. For instance, only the Atlanta and St. Louis banks issued $20 Series 1918 FRBNs, while only St. Louis issued $50s.

Spurred initially by demand for the attractive "Battleship" back design of the $2, and the defiant eagle on the $1 (symbols of America's defense posture in World War I), all large size FRBNs are actively collected today, especially in new condition. A wealth of combinations of U.S. Government signatures combined with signatures of the various Governors and Cashiers of the individual issuing banks, creates myriad varieties to keep the series challenging.

Also contributing to the challenge is the sheer scarcity of surviving specimens. Treasury sources indicate just over $2 million worth of FRBNs outstanding, from a total issue of more than $760 million.

Federal Reserve Notes

Authorized by the Federal Reserve Act of Dec. 23, 1913 and first issued in 1914, the Federal Reserve Note is the only type of U.S. paper money which continues in production today.

The large size issues of FRNs are in two series, 1914, in denominations from $5-$100, and 1918, in denominations from $500-$10,000. Additionally two distinctive varieties of 1914 notes exist, those with red Treasury Seal and serial number, and those with the elements in blue. The Red Seal 1914 FRNs are considerably scarcer than the blue.

While they are issued to circulation through the twelve Federal Reserve Banks, the FRNs are an obligation of the United States Government, rather than bank named thereon (unlike the Federal Reserve Bank Notes). Neither are Federal Reserve Notes secured by government bonds, precious metals or other reserves. The obligation on FRNs simply states that: "The United States of America will pay to the bearer on demand - dollars."

On back, the redemption qualities of the large size FRNs was spelled out thus: "This note is receivable by all National and member banks and Federal Reserve Banks and for all taxes, customs and other public dues. It is redeemable in gold on demand at the Treasury Department of the United States in the city of Washington, District of Columbia or in gold or lawful money at any Federal Reserve Bank."

This redeemable-in-gold clause continued in use on the Series 1928 small size FRNs, but was revoked with the passage of the Gold Reserve Act of 1933. The obligation, beginning with the Series 1934 notes, was modified to read: "This note is legal tender for all debts, public and private, and is redeemable in lawful money at the United States Treasury, or at any Federal Reserve Bank."

Beginning with Series 1963, the obligation was changed to its present form: "This note is legal tender for all debts, public and private."

Wide variances in the number of notes printed for each bank in any particular series of a denomination have created many challenging issues within the Federal Reserve Note series, both large and small size.

NOTE: Three interesting, if not altogether popular among collectors, varieties exist within the large size FRNs bearing the White-Mellon Federal signature combination, and two within the Burke-McAdoo combination notes. The variations deal with the size and placement of the numeral-letter combination designating the bank through which the notes were issued, and appearing in the lower left corner of the face. The earliest variety has a large size combination, matching that in the upper right corner of the note. The second variety has the combination greatly reduced (compared to that in the upper right). The third reverts to the larger size, but the combination has been moved higher and more to the left, while the Treasury and Fed Bank Seals on each end of this variety have been moved closer to center. Not all three varieties exist on every bank in every combination. While the second and third varieties command some premium from interested collectors, the demand for them is not such as to greatly influence the market for the type as a whole, and they are, therefore, not cataloged individually.

Gold Certificates

With their bright orange back designs (though some early gold notes are uniface), the large size Gold Certificates issued from 1865 through 1928 are a popular and tangible reminder of the days when U.S. paper currency was "as good as gold."

While many of the earlier Gold Certificate issues were not designed to be used in general circulation, due to their high face value, later types did enter the channels of commerce, circulating alongside the myriad other currency issues of the late 19th and early 20th Centuries.

Nine separate issues of Gold Certificates were created in the large size series, several of which were used almost exclusively in inter-bank channels to transfer and settle gold accounts.

The first issue goldbacks were authorized by the Currency Act of March 3, 1863, and consisted of notes in denominations of $20, $100, $500, $1,000, $5,000 and $10,000. While examples of the two lowest denominations survive, they are extremely rare.

No known examples of the second issue Gold Certificates are known today. Issued pursuant to the same act, and countersigned and dated by hand in the 1870-71 period, they were in denominations of $100-$10,000 only.

Third issue gold notes, bearing the impression "Series of 1875," were also issued in limited denominations: $100, $500, and $1,000. Uniface, the issue is represented today by only a few examples of the $100 note.

With the fourth issue, Gold Certificates entered general circulation, and the type begins to be known by its series designation. Ten-dollar goldbacks were issued in Series 1907 and 1922; $20 in Series 1882, 1905,1906 and 1922; $50 in Series 1882,1913 and 1922; $100 in Series 1882 and 1922; $500 in Series 1882; $1,000 in Series 1882, 1907 and 1922; $5,000 in Series 1882 and 1888; and, $10,000 in Series 1882,1888 and 1900. Naturally, the notes in denominations above $100 are very rare, though not unknown.

To correspond the various issues to the series in these post-1875 notes; the fourth issue consisted of the Series 1882 notes; the fifth issue comprises the 1888 Series, the sixth is the 1900 $10,000 notes; the seventh issue Gold Certificates are the Series 1905, 1906 and 1907 $10 and $20 notes; the eighth is the $1,000 of Series 1907; and, the ninth issue of large size Gold Certificates are the Series 1913 ($50 only) and 1922 goldbacks in $10-$1,000 denominations.

United States Notes

One Dollar

Salmon P. Chase at left.

Numerals "1 2 3" vertically in center.

National Bank Note Co. American Bank Note Co. in lower border.
No ABNCo monogram.

KL#	Fr#	Series	Signatures	Seal	Fine	XF	CH CU (63)	Gem CU (65)
1	17	1862	Chittenden-Spinner	Small red	15,000.	20,000.	Rare	—

National Bank Note Co. American Bank Note Co. in lower border.
ABNCo monogram.

2	17a	1862	Chittenden-Spinner	Small red	570.	975.	2750.	3500.

National Bank Note Co. twice in lower border. No ABNCo monogram.

3	16	1862	Chittenden-Spinner	Small red	500.	975.	2600.	5000.

National Bank Note Co. twice in lower border.
ABNCo. monogram upper right.

4	16a	1862	Chittenden-Spinner	Small red	650.	2750.	5000.	8500.

George Washington at center, Columbus' discovery of land at upper left.

Red serial numbers. National Bank Note Co., bottom back.

KL#	Fr#	Series	Signatures	Seal	Fine	XF	CH CU (63)	Gem CU (65)
5	18	1869	Allison-Spinner	Large red	600.	1500.	3250.	10,000.

National Bank Note Co., lower portion back design.

Red serial numbers. Red ornamentation at right, face design.

KL#	Fr#	Series	Signatures	Seal	Fine	XF	CH CU (63)	Gem CU (65)
6	19	1874	Allison-Spinner	Small red	240.	1200.	2500.	3500.

Engraved & Printed at the Bureau Engraving & Printing on face at right.

Columbian Bank Note Co., twice near bottom back.

KL#	Fr#	Series	Signatures	Seal	Fine	XF	CH CU (63)	Gem CU (65)
7	20	1875	Allison-New	Small red	255.	600.	1500.	2500.
			Series A in lower right face.					
8	21	1875	Allison-New	Small red	1000.	2750.	9000.	11,000.
			Series B in lower right face.					
9	22	1875	Allison-New	Small red	1250.	3000.	9500.	11,000.
			Series C in lower right face.					
10	23	1875	Allison-New	Small red	1200.	2000.	4000.	7000.
			Series D in lower right face.					
11	24	1875	Allison-New	Small red	1150.	4000.	8250.	11,000.
			Series E in lower right face.					
12	25	1875	Allison-New	Small red	1875.	7500.	13,000.	18,000.
13	26	1875	Allison-Wyman	Small red	300.	1000.	2000.	2500.

Series 1878 at top margin,
Printed by Bureau of Engraving & Printing at lower margin on back.

KL#	Fr#	Series	Signatures	Seal	Fine	XF	CH CU (63)	Gem CU (65)
14	27	1878	Allison-Gilfillan	Small red	275.	600.	2000.	2500.

KL#	Fr#	Series	Signatures	Seal	Fine	XF	CH CU (63)	Gem CU (65)
			Plain ONE at right. Blue serial number within an ornate panel.					
15	28	1880	Scofield-Gilfillan	Large brown	240.	450.	1250.	3200.
16	29	1880	Bruce-Gilfillan	Large brown	190.	400.	1100.	2400.
17	30	1880	Bruce-Wyman	Large brown	190.	400.	1100.	1500.
18	31	1880	Rosecrans-Huston	Large red	500.	1750.	4000.	6000.
19	32	1880	Rosecrans-Huston	Large brown	570.	1750.	3500.	5000.
20	33	1880	Rosecrans-Nebeker	Large brown	600.	2000.	5000.	7500.
21	34	1880	Rosecrans-Nebeker	Small red	190.	400.	1100.	2000.
22	35	1880	Tillman-Morgan	Small red	190.	400.	1100.	2500.

Serial number panel removed.

KL#	Fr#	Series	Signatures	Seal	Fine	XF	CH CU (63)	Gem CU (65)
23	36	1917	Teehee-Burke	Small red	80.00	200.	550.	800.
24	37	1917	Elliott-Burke	Small red	125.	225.	550.	800.
25	37a	1917	Burke-Elliott	Small red	300.	700.	1500.	2750.
26	38	1917	Elliott-White	Small red	80.00	140.	450.	600.
27	39	1917	Speelman-White	Small red	80.00	175.	450.	600.

George Washington at center.

KL#	Fr#	Series	Signatures	Seal	Fine	XF	CH CU (63)	Gem CU (65)
28	40	1923	Speelman-White	Small red	130.	400.	1000.	1400.

Silver Certificates

Martha Washington at left.

Blue serial number.

KL#	Fr#	Series	Signatures	Seal	Fine	XF	CH CU (63)	Gem CU (65)
29	215	1886	Rosecrans-Jordan	Small red	375.	875.	2000.	3250.
30	216	1886	Rosecrans-Hyatt	Small red	425.	840.	2000.	3500.
31	217	1886	Rosecrans-Hyatt	Large red	375.	850.	2200.	5500.
32	218	1886	Rosecrans-Huston	Large red	375.	850.	2200.	3500.
33	219	1886	Rosecrans-Huston	Large brown	375.	850.	2200.	4750.
34	220	1886	Rosecrans-Nebeker	Large brown	450.	850.	2750.	5500.
35	221	1886	Rosecrans-Nebeker	Small red	475.	1500.	2600.	5500.

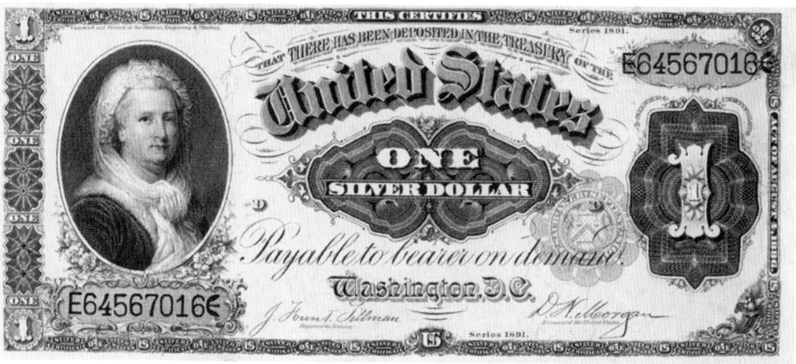

KL#	Fr#	Series	Signatures	Seal	Fine	XF	CH CU (63)	Gem CU (65)
36	222	1891	Rosecrans-Nebeker	Small red	450.	850.	2400.	5200.
37	223	1891	Tillman-Morgan	Small red	425.	775.	2000.	4750.

History instructing youth; Washington D.C. and Constitution at center right. Martha and George Washington on the back.

KL#	Fr#	Series	Signatures	Seal	Fine	XF	CH CU (63)	Gem CU (65)
38	224	1896	Tillman-Morgan	Small red	450.	950.	3000.	5000.
39	225	1896	Bruce-Roberts	Small red	450.	950.	3000.	5000.

Eagle on flag, capitol behind, at center; small portraits of Lincoln and Grant below.

Series date above upper right serial number.

KL#	Fr#	Series	Signatures	Seal	Fine	XF	CH CU (63)	Gem CU (65)
40	226	1899	Lyons-Roberts	Small blue	150.	350.	750.	1000.

Series date below serial number.

KL#	Fr#	Series	Signatures	Seal	Fine	XF	CH CU (63)	Gem CU (65)
41	226a	1899	Lyons-Roberts	Small blue	150.	350.	750.	1000.
42	227	1899	Lyons-Treat	Small blue	150.	350.	750.	1750.
43	228	1899	Vernon-Treat	Small blue	150.	350.	500.	700.
44	229	1899	Vernon-McClung	Small blue	250.	500.	500.	700.

Series date vertical at right.

KL#	Fr#	Series	Signatures	Seal	Fine	XF	CH CU (63)	Gem CU (65)
44A	229a	1899	Vernon-McClung	Small blue	3000.	6000.	11,000.	19,000.
45	230	1899	Napier-McClung	Small blue	135.	250.	500.	700.
46	231	1899	Napier-Thompson	Small blue	500.	1200.	2500.	4000.
47	232	1899	Parker-Burke	Small blue	135.	275.	500.	1000.
48	233	1899	Teehee-Burke	Small blue	135.	275.	500.	700.
49	234	1899	Elliott-Burke	Small blue	135.	275.	500.	700.
50	235	1899	Elliott-White	Small blue	135.	275.	500.	700.
51	236	1899	Speelman-White	Small blue	135.	275.	500.	700.

George Washington at center.

KL#	Fr#	Series	Signatures	Seal	Fine	XF	CH CU (63)	Gem CU (65)
52	237	1923	Speelman-White	Small blue	45.00	75.00	200.	275.
53	238	1923	Woods-White	Small blue	45.00	75.00	200.	275.
54	239	1923	Woods-Tate	Small blue	185.	440.	700.	1200.

Treasury or Coin Notes

Edwin M. Stanton at left.

KL#	Fr#	Series	Signatures	Seal	Fine	XF	CH CU (63)	Gem CU (65)
55	347	1890	Rosecrans-Huston	Large brown	700.	1750.	4100.	6000.
56	348	1890	Rosecrans-Nebeker	Large brown	750.	1750.	6500.	8750.
57	349	1890	Rosecrans-Nebeker	Small red	725.	1750.	6500.	8750.

KL#	Fr#	Series	Signatures	Seal	Fine	XF	CH CU (63)	Gem CU (65)
58	350	1891	Rosecrans-Nebeker	Small red	350.	675.	1500.	2500.
59	351	1891	Tillman-Morgan	Small red	350.	675.	1500.	2500.
60	352	1891	Bruce-Roberts	Small red	350.	675.	1500.	2500.

Federal Reserve Bank Notes

1918

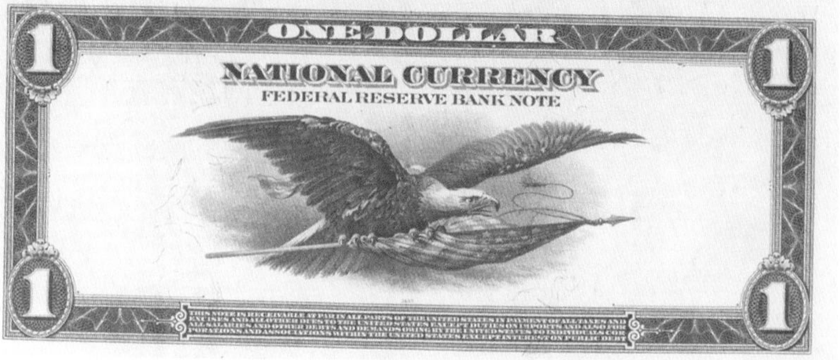

George Washington at left. Eagle on flag on back.

KL#	Fr#	Bank	Federal Sigs.	Bank Sigs.	Fine	XF	CH CU (63)	Gem CU (65)
61	708	Boston	Teehee-Burke	Bullen-Morss	125.	250.	550.	850.
62	709	Boston	Teehee-Burke	Willett-Morss	225.	375.	750.	1400.
63	710	Boston	Elliott-Burke	Willett-Morss	110.	265.	550.	800.
64	711	New York	Teehee-Burke	Sailer-Strong	110.	225.	550.	800.
65	712	New York	Teehee-Burke	Hendricks-Strong	110.	225.	550.	800.
66	713	New York	Elliott-Burke	Hendricks-Strong	110.	225.	550.	600.
67	714	Philadelphia	Teehee-Burke	Hardt-Passmore	160.	275.	550.	1250.
68	715	Philadelphia	Teehee-Burke	Dyer-Passmore	160.	275.	550.	1250.
69	716	Philadelphia	Elliott-Burke	Dyer-Passmore	160.	275.	550.	1250.
70	717	Philadelphia	Elliott-Burke	Dyer-Norris	110.	225.	550.	600.
71	718	Cleveland	Teehee-Burke	Baxter-Fancher	110.	225.	550.	800.
72	719	Cleveland	Teehee-Burke	Davis-Fancher	160.	250.	550.	1300.
73	720	Cleveland	Elliott-Burke	Davis-Fancher	110.	275.	550.	1300.
74	721	Richmond	Teehee-Burke	Keesee-Seay	160.	275.	525.	1250.
75	722	Richmond	Elliott-Burke	Keesee-Seay	110.	225.	550.	1250.
76	723	Atlanta	Teehee-Burke	Pike-McCord	110.	225.	550.	1250.
77	724	Atlanta	Teehee-Burke	Bell-McCord	160.	325.	640.	1500.
78	725	Atlanta	Teehee-Burke	Bell-Wellborn	180.	300.	520.	750.

KL#	Fr#	Bank	Federal Sigs.	Bank Sigs.	Fine	XF	CH CU (63)	Gem CU (65)
79	726	Atlanta	Elliott-Burke	Bell-Wellborn	180.	285.	700.	850.
80	727	Chicago	Teehee-Burke	McCloud-McDougal	105.	210.	425.	700.
81	728	Chicago	Teehee-Burke	Cramer-McDougal	105.	210.	425.	700.
82	729	Chicago	Elliott-Burke	Cramer-McDougal	105.	210.	425.	700.
83	730	St. Louis	Teehee-Burke	Attebery-Wells	160.	325.	500.	1200.
84	731	St. Louis	Teehee-Burke	Attebery-Biggs	160.	325.	640.	1500.
85	732	St. Louis	Elliott-Burke	Attebery-Biggs	240.	400.	725.	1500.
86	733	St. Louis	Elliott-Burke	White-Biggs	110.	220.	825.	1500.
87	734	Minneapolis	Teehee-Burke	Cook-Wold	110.	220.	425.	700.
88	735	Minneapolis	Teehee-Burke	Cook-Young	475.	1250.	3750.	5000.
89	736	Minneapolis	Elliott-Burke	Cook-Young	110.	300.	425.	700.
90	737	Kansas City	Teehee-Burke	Anderson-Miller	110.	220.	475.	700.
91	738	Kansas City	Elliott-Burke	Anderson-Miller	110.	220.	425.	700.
92	739	Kansas City	Elliott-Burke	Helm-Miller	110.	220.	425.	550.
93	740	Dallas	Teehee-Burke	Talley-Van Zandt	110.	220.	425.	700.
94	741	Dallas	Elliott-Burke	Talley-Van Zandt	400.	875.	2400.	3250.
95	742	Dallas	Elliott-Burke	Lawder-Van Zandt	250.	600.	900.	1200.
96	743	San Francisco	Teehee-Burke	Clerk-Lynch	110.	220.	425.	700.
97	744	San Francisco	Teehee-Burke	Clerk-Calkins	110.	220.	425.	700.
98	745	San Francisco	Elliott-Burke	Clerk-Calkins	175.	600.	3000.	5000.
99	746	San Francisco	Elliott-Burke	Ambrose-Calkins	150.	275.	650.	1400.

United States Notes

Two Dollars

Alexander Hamilton at left center.

Red Numerals "1 2 3" vertically in center.

National Bank Note Co. vertically at left;
Patented April 23, 1860, National Bank Note Co., in lower border.

KL#	Fr#	Series	Signatures	Seal	Fine	XF	CH CU (63)	Gem CU (65)
100	41	1862	Chittenden-Spinner	Small red	775.	2200.	4750.	5750.

American Bank Note Co. vertically at left;
Patented April 23, 1860, National Bank Note Co., in lower border.

101	41a	1862	Chittenden-Spinner	Small red	775.	2200.	4750.	5750.

Capitol Building at center, Thomas Jefferson at upper left.

Red serial numbers, red seal at right.

Engraved and printed at the Treasury Department, vertically at left; .American Bank Note Co. Bottom left, face design and twice below on back.

KL#	Fr#	Series	Signatures	Seal	Fine	XF	CH CU (63)	Gem CU (65)
102	42	1869	Allison-Spinner	Large red	1000.	3500.	7500.	20,000.

Red serial numbers. Red ornamentation at right.

KL#	Fr#	Series	Signatures	Seal	Fine	XF	CH CU (63)	Gem CU (65)
103	43	1874	Allison-Spinner	Small red	460.	1450.	3400.	5250.

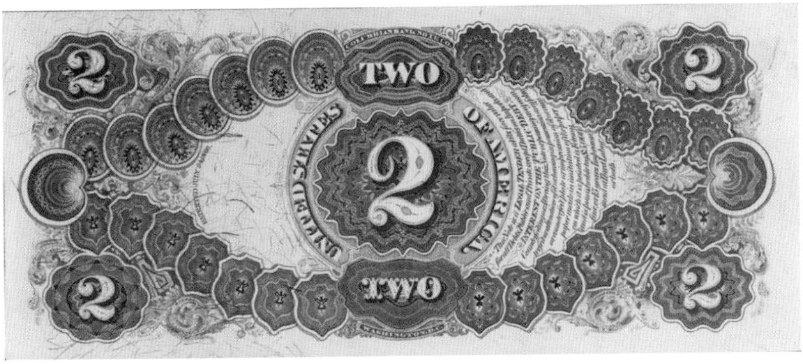

KL#	Fr#	Series	Signatures	Seal	Fine	XF	CH CU (63)	Gem CU (65)
104	44	1875	Allison-New	Small red	480.	1000.	2250.	3000.

Series A at lower right of face design.

KL#	Fr#	Series	Signatures	Seal	Fine	XF	CH CU (63)	Gem CU (65)
105	45	1875	Allison-New	Small red	975.	2400.	5000.	8000.

Series B at lower right of face design.

KL#	Fr#	Series	Signatures	Seal	Fine	XF	CH CU (63)	Gem CU (65)
106	46	1875	Allison-New	Small red	850.	2400.	3500.	5000.
107	47	1875	Allison-Wyman	Small red	480.	1075.	4000.	5500.
108	48	1878	Allison-Gilfillan	Small red	380.	800.	2000.	3500.
109	49	1878	Scofield-Gilfillan	Small red	5000.	7000.	Rare	—

Red serial numbers. Ornamentation removed.

KL#	Fr#	Series	Signatures	Seal	Fine	XF	CH CU (63)	Gem CU (65)
110	50	1880	Scofield-Gilfillan	Large brown	250.	525.	1350.	2000.
111	51	1880	Bruce-Gilfillan	Large brown	285.	600.	1450.	2500.
112	52	1880	Bruce-Wyman	Large brown	240.	600.	1500.	1800.
			Blue serial numbers.					
113	53	1880	Rosecrans-Huston	Large red	1000.	4750.	15,000.	500.
114	54	1880	Rosecrans-Huston	Large brown	3000.	10,000.	20,000.	30,000.
115	55	1880	Rosecrans-Nebeker	Small red	375.	750.	2700.	4750.
116	56	1880	Tillman-Morgan	Small red	285.	600.	1200.	1950.

Red serial numbers.

KL#	Fr#	Series	Signatures	Seal	Fine	XF	CH CU (63)	Gem CU (65)
117	57	1917	Teehee-Burke	Small red	105.	225.	450.	700.

KL#	Fr#	Series	Signatures	Seal	Fine	XF	CH CU (63)	Gem CU (65)
118	58	1917	Elliott-Burke	Small red	105.	225.	450.	700.
119	59	1917	Elliott-White	Small red	105.	225.	450.	700.
120	60	1917	Speelman-White	Small red	105.	225.	500.	700.

Silver Certificates

General Winfield Scott Hancock at left.

KL#	Fr#	Series	Signatures	Seal	Fine	XF	CH CU (63)	Gem CU (65)
121	240	1886	Rosecrans-Jordan	Small red	700.	1750.	3500.	5000.
122	241	1886	Rosecrans-Hyatt	Small red	700.	1800.	3500.	5000.
123	242	1886	Rosecrans-Hyatt	Large red	700.	1750.	4500.	8500.
124	243	1886	Rosecrans-Huston	Large red	700.	2000.	4000.	5000.
125	244	1886	Rosecrans-Huston	Large brown	800.	2000.	4500.	9000.

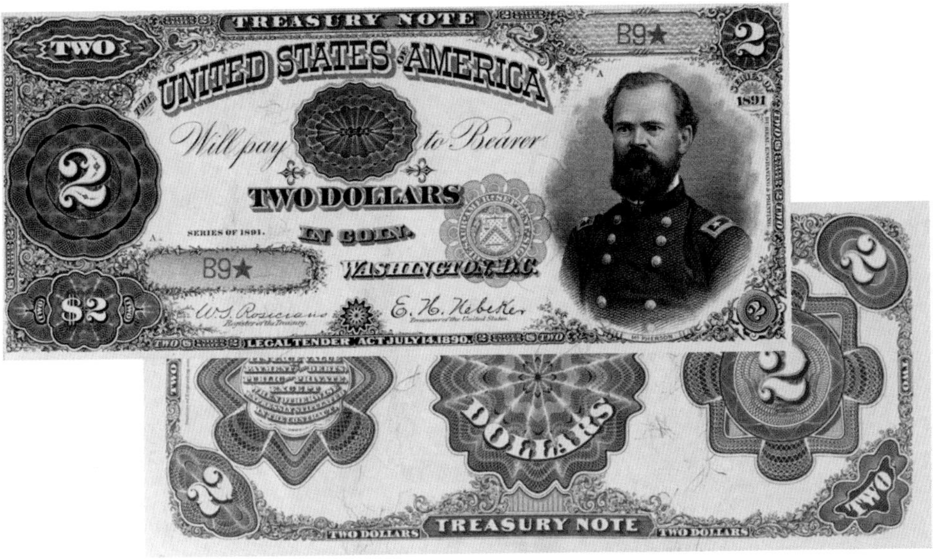

William Windom at center.

KL#	Fr#	Series	Signatures	Seal	Fine	XF	CH CU (63)	Gem CU (65)
126	245	1891	Rosecrans-Nebeker	Small red	900.	2500.	5000.	6500.
127	246	1891	Tillman-Morgan	Small red	900.	2500.	5000.	6500.

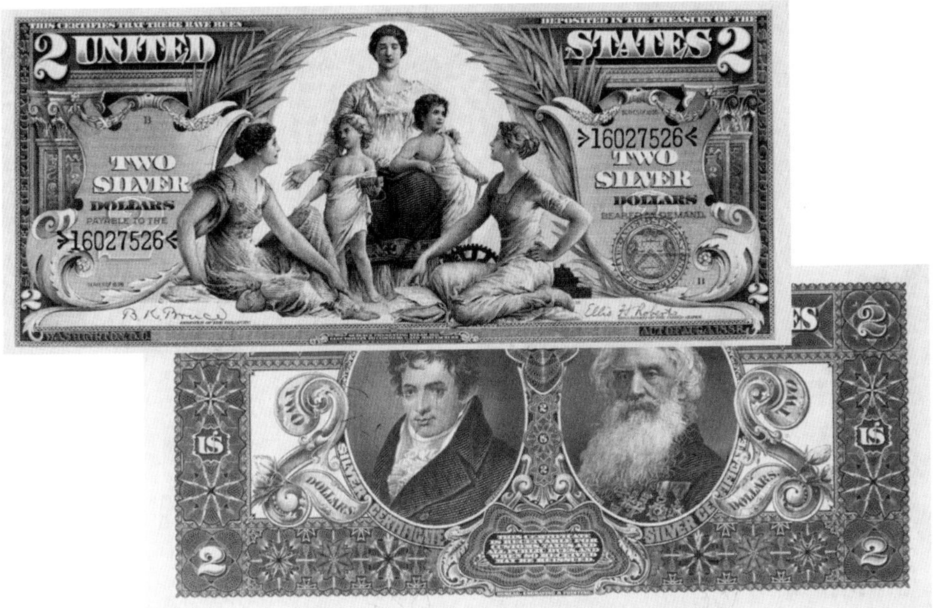

Science presenting Steam and Electricity to Industry and Commerce.
Robert Fulton and Samuel Morse.

KL#	Fr#	Series	Signatures	Seal	Fine	XF	CH CU (63)	Gem CU (65)
128	247	1896	Tillman-Morgan	Small red	950.	4500.	7500.	10,000.
129	248	1896	Bruce-Roberts	Small red	950.	4500.	7500.	10,000.

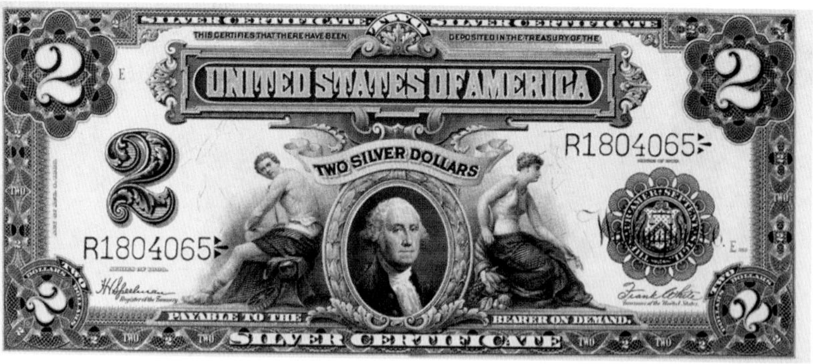

George Washington at center, flanked by Mechanics and Agriculture.

KL#	Fr#	Series	Signatures	Seal	Fine	XF	CH CU (63)	Gem CU (65)
130	249	1899	Lyons-Roberts	Small blue	310.	900.	1500.	3000.
131	250	1899	Lyons-Treat	Small blue	310.	900.	1500.	3000.
132	251	1899	Vernon-Treat	Small blue	310.	900.	1500.	3000.
133	252	1899	Vernon-McClung	Small blue	310.	900.	1500.	3000.
134	253	1899	Napier-McClung	Small blue	310.	900.	1500.	3000.
135	254	1899	Napier-Thompson	Small blue	900.	2000.	3500.	7500.
136	255	1899	Parker-Burke	Small blue	265.	750.	1600.	2500.
137	256	1899	Teehee-Burke	Small blue	265.	750.	1600.	2500.
138	257	1899	Elliott-Burke	Small blue	265.	750.	1600.	2500.
139	258	1899	Speelman-White	Small blue	300.	750.	1600.	2500.

Treasury or Coin Notes

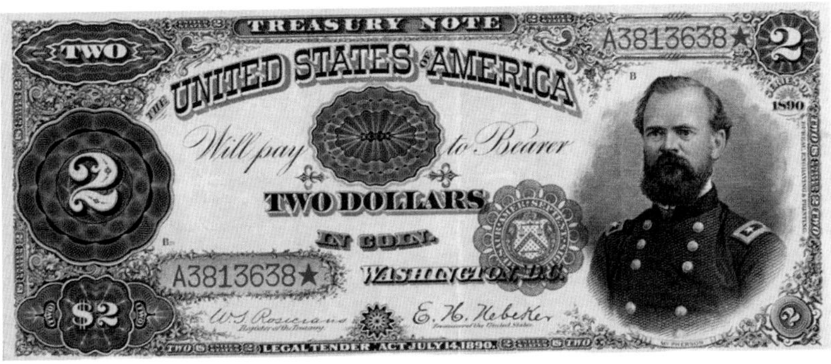

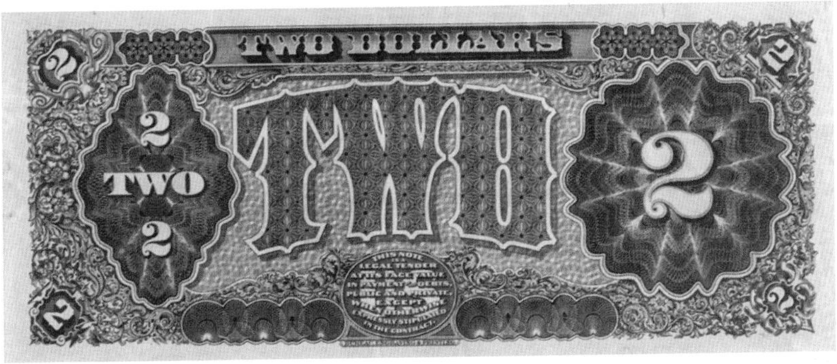

General James B. McPherson at right.

KL#	Fr#	Series	Signatures	Seal	Fine	XF	CH CU (63)	Gem CU (65)
140	353	1890	Rosecrans-Huston	Large brown	1200.	5000.	12,500.	35,000.
141	354	1890	Rosecrans-Nebeker	Large brown	2400.	7000.	16,500.	37,500.
142	355	1890	Rosecrans-Nebeker	Small red	1100.	7000.	15,000.	37,500.

KL#	Fr#	Series	Signatures	Seal	Fine	XF	CH CU (63)	Gem CU (65)
143	356	1891	Rosecrans-Nebeker	Small red	750.	1600.	4500.	5500.
144	357	1891	Tillman-Morgan	Small red	600.	1600.	4500.	9500.
145	358	1891	Bruce-Roberts	Small red	525.	1600.	5000.	7500.

Federal Reserve Bank Notes

1918

Thomas Jefferson at left. Battleship New York.

KL#	Fr#	Bank	Federal Sigs.	Bank Sigs.	Fine	XF	CH CU (63)	Gem CU (65)
146	747	Boston	Teehee-Burke	Bullen-Morss	475.	1250.	2500.	5000.
147	748	Boston	Teehee-Burke	Willett-Morss	475.	1000.	2500.	3750.
148	749	Boston	Elliott-Burke	Willett-Morss	475.	1000.	2500.	3750.
149	750	New York	Teehee-Burke	Sailer-Strong	475.	1000.	2500.	3750.
150	751	New York	Teehee-Burke	Hendricks-Strong	475.	1000.	2500.	3750.
151	752	New York	Elliott-Burke	Hendricks-Strong	475.	1000.	2500.	3750.
152	753	Philadelphia	Teehee-Burke	Hardt-Passmore	475.	1000.	2300.	3500.
153	754	Philadelphia	Teehee-Burke	Dyer-Passmore	475.	1000.	2500.	3750.
154	755	Philadelphia	Elliott-Burke	Dyer-Passmore	800.	4000.	9000.	12,500.
155	756	Philadelphia	Elliott-Burke	Dyer-Norris	535.	1000.	2400.	3750.
156	757	Cleveland	Teehee-Burke	Baxter-Fancher	535.	1000.	2400.	3750.
157	758	Cleveland	Teehee-Burke	Davis-Fancher	535.	1000.	2400.	3750.
158	759	Cleveland	Elliott-Burke	Davis-Fancher	535.	1200.	2400.	3750.
159	760	Richmond	Teehee-Burke	Keesee-Seay	550.	1250.	2500.	4500.
160	761	Richmond	Elliott-Burke	Keesee-Seay	550.	1250.	2500.	2850.
161	762	Atlanta	Teehee-Burke	Pike-McCord	550.	1250.	3000.	4000.
162	763	Atlanta	Teehee-Burke	Bell-McCord	550.	1250.	2500.	4000.
163	764	Atlanta	Elliott-Burke	Bell-Wellborn	1250.	2000.	4000.	6000.

KL#	Fr#	Bank	Federal Sigs.	Bank Sigs.	Fine	XF	CH CU (63)	Gem CU (65)
164	765	Chicago	Teehee-Burke	McCloud-McDougal	525.	1250.	2500.	5100.
165	766	Chicago	Teehee-Burke	Cramer-McDougal	525.	1000.	2500.	3200.
166	767	Chicago	Elliott-Burke	Cramer-McDougal	525.	1000.	2500.	3200.
167	768	St. Louis	Teehee-Burke	Attebery-Wells	525.	1000.	2500.	4000.
168	769	St. Louis	Teehee-Burke	Attebery-Biggs	1000.	4750.	8500.	10,000.
169	770	St. Louis	Elliott-Burke	Attebery-Biggs	1000.	4750.	8500.	10,000.
170	771	St. Louis	Elliott-Burke	White-Biggs	550.	1500.	2500.	3500.
171	772	Minneapolis	Teehee-Burke	Cook-Wold	550.	1750.	3000.	4750.
172	773	Minneapolis	Elliott-Burke	Cook-Young	550.	1150.	2500.	3500.
173	774	Kansas City	Teehee-Burke	Anderson-Miller	550.	1250.	2500.	3500.
174	775	Kansas City	Elliott-Burke	Helm-Miller	550.	1150.	2500.	5750.
175	776	Dallas	Teehee-Burke	Talley-Van Zandt	700.	1150.	4000.	7000.
176	777	Dallas	Elliott-Burke	Talley-Van Zandt	800.	1150.	2500.	3500.
177	778	San Francisco	Teehee-Burke	Clerk-Lynch	475.	1000.	2000.	3250.
178	779	San Francisco	Elliott-Burke	Clerk-Calkins	750.	1250.	4000.	5000.
179	780	San Francisco	Elliott-Burke	Ambrose-Calkins	550.	1000.	2000.	3250.

Demand Notes

Five Dollars

Statue of Freedom at left, Alexander Hamilton at right.

KL#	Fr#	Payable at:	VG	Fine	VF
180	3-A	Boston Unique	—	—	—
181	3	Boston	2300.	3000.	6500.
182	1a	New York	14,000.	35,000.	65,000.
183	1	New York	2000.	3000.	6500.
185	2	Philadelphia	2750.	3300.	8000.
187	5	St. Louis	Very Rare.	Rare	38,000.
189	4	Cincinnati	—	Rare	—

United States Notes

First Obligation inscription on back. Red serial numbers. "Series" on face.

American Bank Note Co. in top border on face.

KL#	Fr#	Series	Signatures	Seal	Fine	XF	CH CU (63)	Gem CU (65)
190	61a	1862	Chittenden-Spinner	Small red	465.	1250.	4000.	6500.

Second Obligation inscription on back. Red serial numbers.

American Bank Note Co. in top border on face.

KL#	Fr#	Series	Signatures	Seal	Fine	XF	CH CU (63)	Gem CU (65)
191	62	1862	Chittenden-Spinner	Small red	500.	1450.	4000.	6500.

American Bank Note Co. and National Bank Note Co. lower border on face.

KL#	Fr#	Series	Signatures	Seal	Fine	XF	CH CU (63)	Gem CU (65)
191A	63	1863	Chittenden-Spinner	Small red	550.	1500.	2750.	3500.

American Bank Note Co. twice in lower border on face. One serial number.

KL#	Fr#	Series	Signatures	Seal	Fine	XF	CH CU (63)	Gem CU (65)
192	63a	1863	Chittenden-Spinner	Small red	550.	1150.	3000.	5100.

American Bank Note Co. twice in border on face. Two serial numbers.

KL#	Fr#	Series	Signatures	Seal	Fine	XF	CH CU (63)	Gem CU (65)
193	63b	1863	Chittenden-Spinner	Small red	500.	875.	2750.	4000.

The Pioneer at center, Andrew Jackson at lower left.

American Bank Note Co. twice in lower border on face. Two red serial numbers.

KL#	Fr#	Series	Signatures	Seal	Fine	XF	CH CU (63)	Gem CU (65)
194	64	1869	Allison-Spinner	Large red	600.	1500.	3500.	26,000.

Bureau, Engraving & Printing, upper left on face.
American Bank Note Co., upper and lower margin on back.

Red serial numbers. Large "V" in red ornamentation at right.

195	65	1875	Allison-New	Small red	600.	1325.	3350.	5200.

Series A in lower right of face design.

196	66	1875	Allison-New		1500.	2500.	6000.	10,000.

Series B in lower right of face design.

197	67	1875	Allison-New		340.	750.	1850.	3500.
198	68	1875	Allison-Wyman	Small red	340.	775.	1500.	3000.
199	69	1878	Allison-Gilfillan	Small red	340.	800.	2000.	3000.

Red serial numbers.

KL#	Fr#	Series	Signatures	Seal	Fine	XF	CH CU (63)	Gem CU (65)
200	70	1880	Scofield-Gilfillan	Large brown	1600.	3000.	7000.	9750.
201	71	1880	Bruce-Gilfillan	Large brown	440.	875.	1900.	2900.
202	72	1880	Bruce-Wyman	Large brown	420.	850.	1900.	3400.

Blue serial numbers.

KL#	Fr#	Series	Signatures	Seal	Fine	XF	CH CU (63)	Gem CU (65)
203	73	1880	Bruce-Wyman	Large red	450.	900.	1700.	2500.
204	74	1880	Rosecrans-Jordan	Large red	375.	900.	1500.	2500.
205	75	1880	Rosecrans-Hyatt	Large red	480.	1000.	4000.	8000.
206	76	1880	Rosecrans-Huston	Large red	900.	1750.	6000.	9000.
207	77	1880	Rosecrans-Huston	Large brown	580.	1750.	6000.	9000.
208	78	1880	Rosecrans-Nebeker	Large brown	800.	2000.	6000.	8000.
209	79	1880	Rosecrans-Nebeker	Small red	215.	400.	1250.	1750.
210	80	1880	Tillman-Morgan	Small red	215.	400.	1250.	1750.
211	81	1880	Bruce-Roberts	Small red	215.	400.	1250.	1750.
212	82	1880	Lyons-Roberts	Small red	370.	1000.	2750.	4000.

Red serial numbers. Ornamental "V" at left.

KL#	Fr#	Series	Signatures	Seal	Fine	XF	CH CU (63)	Gem CU (65)
213	83	1907	Vernon-Treat	Small red	190.	350.	800.	1000.
214	84	1907	Vernon-McClung	Small red	190.	350.	800.	1000.
215	85	1907	Napier-McClung	Small red	190.	350.	800.	1000.
216	86	1907	Napier-Thompson	Small red	600.	1150.	4000.	6000.
217	87	1907	Parker-Burke	Small red	190.	350.	800.	1000.
218	88	1907	Teehee-Burke	Small red	190.	350.	1200.	2000.
219	89	1907	Elliott-Burke	Small red	190.	350.	800.	1000.
220	90	1907	Elliott-White	Small red	190.	350.	800.	1000.
221	91	1907	Speelman-White	Small red	190.	350.	800.	1000.
222	92	1907	Woods-White	Small red	200.	350.	800.	1000.

National Gold Bank Notes

Columbus in Sight of Land at left,
America Presented to the Old World at right.
Various U.S. Gold Coins.

KL#	Fr#	Series	Issuing Bank	Location	Good	Fine	VF
223	1136	Orig.	First Nat'l Gold Bank	San Francisco	1750.	6000.	10,500.
224	1137	Orig.	Nat'l Gold Bank & Trust Co.	San Francisco	4500.	15,000.	—
225	1138	Orig.	Nat'l Gold Bank of D.O. Mills	Sacramento	4000.	6000.	16,500.
226	1139	Orig.	First Nat'l Gold Bank	Stockton	4000.	Rare	—
227	1140	Orig.	First Nat'l Gold Bank	Santa Barbara	7500.	Rare	—
228	1141	Orig.	Farmers' Nat'l Gold Bank	San Jose	2500.	11,500.	—

Silver Certificates

Ulysses S. Grant at right center. Five silver dollars.

Blue serial numbers.

KL#	Fr#	Series	Signatures	Seal	Fine	XF	CH CU (63)	Gem CU (65)
229	259	1886	Rosecrans-Jordan	Small red	1250.	4600.	10,000.	22,000.
230	260	1886	Rosecrans-Hyatt	Small red	1250.	4600.	10,000.	22,000.
231	261	1886	Rosecrans-Hyatt	Large red	1250.	5500.	12,500.	27,000.
232	262	1886	Rosecrans-Huston	Large red	1250.	5000.	14,500.	32,000.
233	263	1886	Rosecrans-Huston	Large brown	1250.	6000.	10,000.	25,000.
234	264	1886	Rosecrans-Nebeker	Large brown	1250.	5000.	11,500.	22,000.
235	265	1886	Rosecrans-Nebeker	Small red	1250.	5000.	13,500.	30,000.

Ulysses S. Grant at right center.

KL#	Fr#	Series	Signatures	Seal	Fine	XF	CH CU (63)	Gem CU (65)
236	266	1891	Rosecrans-Nebeker	Small red	800.	2000.	6000.	8000.
237	267	1891	Tillman-Morgan	Small red	800.	2000.	6000.	10,000.

Electricity presenting light to the world.
Ulysses S. Grant at left and Philip H. Sheridan at right.

KL#	Fr#	Series	Signatures	Seal	Fine	XF	CH CU (63)	Gem CU (65)
238	268	1896	Tillman-Morgan	Small red	2700.	6300.	9000.	20,000.
239	269	1896	Bruce-Roberts	Small red	2700.	6300.	9000.	20,000.
240	270	1896	Lyons-Roberts	Small red	2700.	6300.	9000.	20,000.

Chief Tatoka-Inyanka (Running Antelope)
of the Hunkpapa Sioux at center.

KL#	Fr#	Series	Signatures	Seal	Fine	XF	CH CU (63)	Gem CU (65)
241	271	1899	Lyons-Roberts	Small blue	650.	1900.	3750.	8000.

KL#	Fr#	Series	Signatures	Seal	Fine	XF	CH CU (63)	Gem CU (65)
242	272	1899	Lyons-Treat	Small blue	650.	1900.	3750.	6000.
243	273	1899	Vernon-Treat	Small blue	650.	1900.	3750.	8000.
244	274	1899	Vernon-McClung	Small blue	650.	1900.	3750.	8000.
245	275	1899	Napier-McClung	Small blue	650.	1900.	3750.	8000.
246	276	1899	Napier-Thompson	Small blue	900.	2000.	10,000.	20,000.
247	277	1899	Parker-Burke	Small blue	650.	1900.	3750.	6500.
248	278	1899	Teehee-Burke	Small blue	650.	1900.	3750.	6500.
249	279	1899	Elliott-Burke	Small blue	650.	1900.	3750.	6500.
250	280	1899	Elliott-White	Small blue	650.	1900.	3750.	7500.
251	281	1899	Speelman-White	Small blue	650.	1900.	3750.	6600.

Abraham Lincoln at center.
Obverse of the Great Seal of the United States.

KL#	Fr#	Series	Signatures	Seal	Fine	XF	CH CU (63)	Gem CU (65)
252	282	1923	Speelman-White	Small blue	1750.	2750.	5000.	12,000.

Treasury or Coin Notes

General George H. Thomas at center.

KL#	Fr#	Series	Signatures	Seal	Fine	XF	CH CU (63)	Gem CU (65)
253	359	1890	Rosecrans-Huston	Large brown	1000.	4750.	8500.	12,000.
254	360	1890	Rosecrans-Nebeker	Large brown	3000.	10,000.	52,500.	85,000.
255	361	1890	Rosecrans-Nebeker	Small red	750.	4250.	5000.	9000.
256	362	1891	Rosecrans-Nebeker	Small red	550.	1250.	3250.	4500.
257	363	1891	Tillman-Morgan	Small red	550.	1250.	3250.	4500.
258	364	1891	Bruce-Roberts	Small red	550.	1250.	3250.	4500.
259	365	1891	Lyons-Roberts	Small red	1250.	2400.	9000.	12,000.

Federal Reserve Bank Notes

1915

Abraham Lincoln at left.
Columbus discovery of land at left and Landing of the Pilgrims at right.

KL#	Fr#	Bank	Federal Sigs.	Bank Sigs.	Fine	XF	CH CU (63)	Gem CU (65)
320	788	Atlanta	Teehee-Burke	Bell-Wellborn	375.	750.	1500.	2000.
321	789	Atlanta	Teehee-Burke	Pike-McCord	375.	750.	1500.	2000.
322	793	Chicago	Teehee-Burke	McLallen-McDougal	450.	900.	2500.	3000.
323	800	Kansas City	Teehee-Burke	Anderson-Miller	400.	700.	1400.	2000.
324	801	Kansas City	Teehee-Burke	Cross-Miller	450.	700.	1500.	2200.
325	802	Kansas City	Teehee-Burke	Helm-Miller	450.	700.	1500.	2200.
326	805	Dallas	Teehee-Burke	Hoopes-Van Zandt	450.	1500.	3250.	4250.
327	806	Dallas	Teehee-Burke	Talley-Van Zandt	500.	700.	1750.	2500.
328	808	San Francisco	Teehee-Burke	Clerk-Lynch	500.	1000.	3000.	4000.

1918

KL#	Fr#	Bank	Federal Sigs.	Bank Sigs.	Fine	XF	CH CU (63)	Gem CU (65)
329	781	Boston	Teehee-Burke	Bullen-Morss	700.	1000.	4250.	6000.
330	782	New York	Teehee-Burke	Hendricks-Strong	375.	650.	1450.	2300.
331	783	Philadelphia	Teehee-Burke	Hardt-Passmore	375.	650.	1725.	2100.
332	784	Philadelphia	Teehee-Burke	Dyer-Passmore	375.	650.	1450.	2100.
333	785	Cleveland	Teehee-Burke	Baxter-Fancher	375.	650.	1450.	2300.
334	786	Cleveland	Teehee-Burke	Davis-Fancher	375.	650.	1450.	2100.
335	787	Cleveland	Elliott-Burke	Davis-Fancher	375.	650.	1450.	2100.
336	790	Atlanta	Teehee-Burke	Pike-McCord	375.	650.	1450.	2100.
337	791	Atlanta	Teehee-Burke	Bell-Wellborn	375.	650.	1450.	2100.
338	792	Atlanta	Elliott-Burke	Bell-Wellborn	500.	925.	2500.	3500.

KL#	Fr#	Bank	Federal Sigs.	Bank Sigs.	Fine	XF	CH CU (63)	Gem CU (65)
339	794	Chicago	Teehee-Burke	McCloud-McDougal	375.	650.	1450.	2100.
340	795	Chicago	Teehee-Burke	Cramer-McDougal	600.	1000.	4500.	6500.
341	796	St. Louis	Teehee-Burke	Attebery-Wells	375.	650.	1450.	2100.
342	797	St. Louis	Teehee-Burke	Attebery-Biggs	375.	650.	1450.	2100.
343	798	St. Louis	Elliott-Burke	White-Biggs	375.	650.	1450.	2100.
344	799	Minneapolis	Teehee-Burke	Cook-Wold	375.	850.	1600.	3150.
345	803	Kansas City	Teehee-Burke	Anderson-Miller	375.	850.	1600.	2250.
346	804	Kansas City	Elliott-Burke	Helm-Miller	375.	850.	1600.	2250.
347	807	Dallas	Teehee-Burke	Talley-Van Zandt	375.	900.	3000.	4000.

Dated May 20, 1914.

348	809	San Francisco	Teehee-Burke	Clerk-Lynch	375.	850.	1600.	2250.

Dated May 18, 1914.

348A	809a	San Francisco	Teehee-Burke	Clerk-Lynch	700.	1000.	4500.	6400.

Federal Reserve Notes

1914

Abraham Lincoln at center.
Columbus discovery of land at left and Landing of the Pilgrims at right.

Red Seal

KL#	Fr#	Bank	Signatures	Fine	XF	CH CU (63)	Gem CU (65)
260	832	Boston	Burke-McAdoo	400.	850.	2250.	3250.
261	833	New York	Burke-McAdoo	400.	1100.	2275.	4500.
262	834	Philadelphia	Burke-McAdoo	400.	1100.	2275.	4500.
263	835	Cleveland	Burke-McAdoo	400.	1100.	2275.	4500.
264	836	Richmond	Burke-McAdoo	500.	1600.	3000.	3750.
265	837	Atlanta	Burke-McAdoo	400.	1100.	2275.	3500.

KL#	Fr#	Bank	Signatures	Fine	XF	CH CU (63)	Gem CU (65)
266	838	Chicago	Burke-McAdoo	400.	1100.	2275.	3500.
267	839	St. Louis	Burke-McAdoo	400.	1100.	2275.	3500.
268	840	Minneapolis	Burke-McAdoo	400.	1100.	2275.	3500.
269	841	Kansas City	Burke-McAdoo	400.	1100.	2275.	3500.
270	842	Dallas	Burke-McAdoo	400.	1100.	2275.	3500.
271	843	San Francisco	Burke-McAdoo	400.	1100.	2275.	3500.

Blue seal.

KL#	Fr#	Bank	Signatures	Fine	XF	CH CU (63)	Gem CU (65)
272	844	Boston	Burke-McAdoo	90.00	180.	400.	700.
273	845	Boston	Burke-Glass	90.00	180.	400.	700.
274	846	Boston	Burke-Houston	90.00	180.	400.	700.
275	847	Boston	White-Mellon	90.00	180.	400.	700.
276	848	New York	Burke-McAdoo	90.00	180.	400.	700.
277	849	New York	Burke-Glass	250.	525.	1400.	2000.
278	850	New York	Burke-Houston	90.00	180.	400.	700.
279	851	New York	White-Mellon	90.00	180.	400.	700.
280	852	Philadelphia	Burke-McAdoo	90.00	175.	400.	700.
281	853	Philadelphia	Burke-Glass	100.	210.	400.	650.
282	854	Philadelphia	Burke-Houston	100.	210.	400.	650.
283	855	Philadelphia	White-Mellon	90.00	175.	400.	700.
284	856	Cleveland	Burke-McAdoo	90.00	175.	400.	700.
285	857	Cleveland	Burke-Glass	310.	750.	1500.	2000.
286	858	Cleveland	Burke-Houston	90.00	175.	400.	700.
287	859	Cleveland	White-Mellon	90.00	175.	400.	700.
288	860	Richmond	Burke-McAdoo	90.00	175.	400.	700.
289	861	Richmond	Burke-Glass	230.	1050.	2000.	2750.
290	862	Richmond	Burke-Houston	90.00	175.	400.	700.
291	863	Richmond	White-Mellon	90.00	175.	400.	700.
292	864	Atlanta	Burke-McAdoo	90.00	175.	400.	700.
293	865	Atlanta	Burke-Glass	90.00	175.	400.	700.
294	866	Atlanta	Burke-Houston	90.00	175.	400.	700.
295	867	Atlanta	White-Mellon	90.00	175.	400.	700.
296	868	Chicago	Burke-McAdoo	90.00	175.	400.	700.
297	869	Chicago	Burke-Glass	90.00	175.	400.	700.
298	870	Chicago	Burke-Houston	90.00	175.	400.	700.
299	871	Chicago	White-Mellon	90.00	175.	400.	700.
300	872	St. Louis	Burke-McAdoo	90.00	310.	400.	700.
301	873	St. Louis	Burke-Glass	200.	310.	600.	750.
302	874	St. Louis	Burke-Houston	110.	260.	525.	675.
303	875	St. Louis	White-Mellon	90.00	175.	350.	700.
304	876	Minneapolis	Burke-McAdoo	230.	360.	700.	800.
305	877	Minneapolis	Burke-Glass	90.00	175.	350.	700.
306	878	Minneapolis	Burke-Houston	90.00	175.	350.	700.
307	879	Minneapolis	White-Mellon	90.00	175.	350.	700.
308	880	Kansas City	Burke-McAdoo	225.	465.	775.	1250.
309	881	Kansas City	Burke-Glass	225.	465.	775.	1250.
310	882	Kansas City	Burke-Houston	225.	465.	775.	1250.
311	883	Kansas City	White-Mellon	90.00	175.	350.	850.
312	884	Dallas	Burke-McAdoo	90.00	175.	350.	2000.
313	885	Dallas	Burke-Glass	90.00	175.	350.	800.
314	886	Dallas	Burke-Houston	90.00	175.	350.	800.
315	887	Dallas	White-Mellon	90.00	175.	350.	800.
316	888	San Francisco	Burke-McAdoo	90.00	175.	350.	800.
317	889	San Francisco	Burke-Glass	90.00	175.	350.	800.
318	890	San Francisco	Burke-Houston	90.00	175.	350.	800.
319	891	San Francisco	White-Mellon	90.00	165.	350.	800.

Refunding Certificates

Ten Dollars

Benjamin Franklin at upper left.

KL#	FR#	Signatures	VG	Fine	XF
394	213	Scofield-Gilfillan	—	—	370,000.

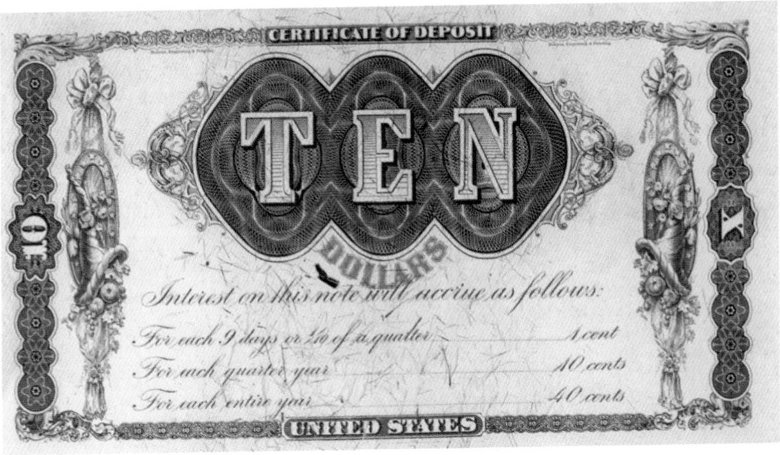

KL#	FR#	Signatures	VG	Fine	XF
395	214	Scofield-Gilfillan	1400.	2250.	5000.

Demand Notes

Abraham Lincoln at left, eagle at top center, Art at right.

KL#	Fr#	Payable at:	VG	Fine	VF
349	8-a	Boston	Very Rare.	—	—
350	8	Boston	3250.	8000.	22,000.
351	6a	New York	—	Rare	—
352	6	New York	3400.	8000.	20,000.
353	7a	Philadelphia	Very Rare.	—	—
354	7	Philadelphia	3450.	8000.	20,000.
356	10	St. Louis	Very Rare.	—	—
357	9a	Cincinnati	Very Rare.	—	—
358	9	Cincinnati	Very Rare.	—	—

United States Notes

First Obligation inscription on back. One red serial number.

KL#	Fr#	Series	Signatures	Seal	Fine	XF	CH CU (63)	Gem CU (65)
359	93	1862	Chittenden-Spinner	Small red	1400.	2500.	12,650.	16,000.

American Bank Note Co. upper border. One red serial number.
Second Obligation inscription on back.

360	94	1862	Chittenden-Spinner	Small red	1300.	2850.	8000.	10,500.

National Bank Note Co. lower border.

360A	95	1863	Chittenden-Spinner	Small red	1400.	3400.	10,000.	12,500.

American Bank Note Co. lower border.

360B	95a	1863	Chittenden-Spinner	Small red	2750.	7500.	15,750.	26,000.

American Bank Note Co. lower border. Two red serial numbers.
Second Obligation inscription on back.

KL#	Fr#	Series	Signatures	Seal	Fine	XF	CH CU (63)	Gem CU (65)
361	95b	1863	Chittenden-Spinner	Small red	1250.	3900.	9000.	16,000.

Daniel Webster at lower left, Small eagle at lower center,
Pocahontas presented at Court at right.

American Bank Note Co. upper and lower borders. Red serial numbers.

KL#	Fr#	Series	Signatures	Seal	Fine	XF	CH CU (63)	Gem CU (65)
362	96	1869	Allison-Spinner	Large red	750.	2500.	7500.	16,000.

Bureau of Engraving and Printing at upper face,
National Bank Note Co. on back.

KL#	Fr#	Series	Signatures	Seal	Fine	XF	CH CU (63)	Gem CU (65)
363	97	1875	Allison-New	Small red	10,000.	22,000.	Rare	—

Series A in lower right face.

KL#	Fr#	Series	Signatures	Seal	Fine	XF	CH CU (63)	Gem CU (65)
364	98	1875	Allison-New		1000.	2000.	6500.	12,500.
365	99	1878	Allison-Gilfillan	Small red	1000.	2250.	6500.	9000.

Red serial numbers.

KL#	Fr#	Series	Signatures	Seal	Fine	XF	CH CU (63)	Gem CU (65)
366	100	1880	Scofield-Gilfillan	Large brown	635.	1500.	3000.	4750.
367	101	1880	Bruce-Gilfillan	Large brown	550.	1300.	2900.	4500.
368	102	1880	Bruce-Wyman	Large brown	565.	1100.	2800.	4500.

Blue serial numbers.

KL#	Fr#	Series	Signatures	Seal	Fine	XF	CH CU (63)	Gem CU (65)
369	103	1880	Bruce-Wyman	Large red	700.	1750.	4500.	5500.
370	104	1880	Rosecrans-Jordan	Large red	550.	1400.	3500.	6250.
371	105	1880	Rosecrans-Hyatt	Large red	550.	1400.	3500.	6250.
372	106	1880	Rosecrans-Hyatt	Red spikes	550.	1400.	3000.	6250.
373	107	1880	Rosecrans-Huston	Red spikes	550.	1400.	3500.	6250.
374	108	1880	Rosecrans-Huston	Large brown	550.	1400.	3500.	5000.
375	109	1880	Rosecrans-Nebeker	Large brown	—	Rare	—	—
376	110	1880	Rosecrans-Nebeker	Small red	600.	1500.	2900.	4500.
377	111	1880	Tillman-Morgan	Small red	600.	1500.	2900.	4500.
378	112	1880	Bruce-Roberts	Small red	850.	2250.	4250.	7750.
379	113	1880	Lyons-Roberts	Small red	500.	1500.	2600.	3500.

American Bison Pablo at center, Meriweather Lewis at left and William Clark at right. Progress standing at center.

Red serial numbers. Large "X TEN" at left.

KL#	Fr#	Series	Signatures	Seal	Fine	XF	CH CU (63)	Gem CU (65)
380	114	1901	Lyons-Roberts	Small red	800.	2250.	4750.	15,000.
381	115	1901	Lyons-Treat	Small red	800.	2250.	4750.	12,000.
382	116	1901	Vernon-Treat	Small red	800.	2250.	4750.	12,000.
383	117	1901	Vernon-McClung	Small red	800.	3200.	4750.	25,000.
384	118	1901	Napier-McClung	Small red	800.	3500.	5000.	12,000.
385	119	1901	Parker-Burke	Small red	750.	1900.	5000.	12,000.
386	120	1901	Teehee-Burke	Small red	750.	2500.	7000.	12,000.
387	121	1901	Elliott-White	Small red	750.	2500.	5000.	12,000.
388	122	1901	Speelman-White	Small red	750.	2500.	5000.	12,000.

Andrew Jackson at center.

Red serial numbers. Large "X DOLLARS" at right.

KL#	Fr#	Series	Signatures	Seal	Fine	XF	CH CU (63)	Gem CU (65)
389	123	1923	Speelman-White	Small red	2000.	5000.	9000.	17,500.

Compound Interest Treasury Notes

Salmon P. Chase at left, Eagle of the Capitol at center, Peace at right.

KL#	FR#	Act	Overprint Date	Signatures	VG	Fine	XF
390	190	1863	June 10, 1864	Chittenden-Spinner	3000.	6000.	12,500.
391	190-A	1864	July 15, 1864	Chittenden-Spinner	3000.	6500.	12,000.

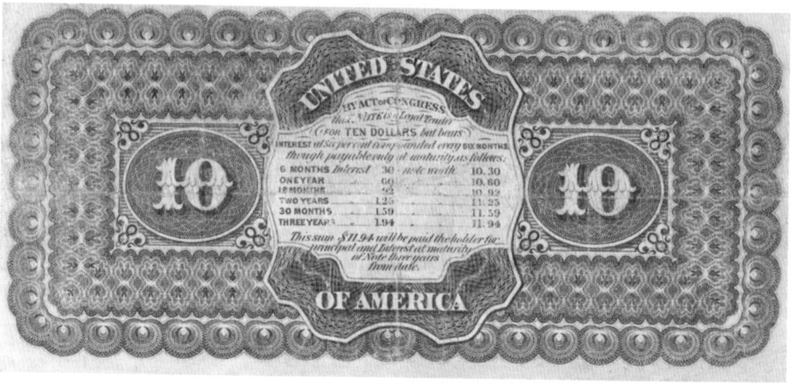

KL#	FR#	Act	Overprint Date	Signatures	VG	Fine	XF
392	190b	1864	Aug. 15-Dec. 15,1864	Colby-Spinner	3000.	6000.	12,500.

Interest Bearing Notes

Salmon P. Chase at left, Eagle of the Capitol at center, Peace at right.

KL#	FR#	Act	Signatures	VG	Fine	XF
393	196	1863	Chittenden-Spinner	4000.	8000.	19,000.
393A	196a	1863	Chittenden-Spinner	4000.	8000.	19,000.

Gold Certificates

Michael Hillegas at center.

Large "X TEN" at left.

KL#	Fr#	Series	Signatures	Fine	XF	CH CU (63)	Gem CU (65)
436	1167	1907	Vernon-Treat	245.	575.	1900.	3600.
437	1168	1907	Vernon-McClung	245.	575.	1900.	3600.
438	1169	1907	Napier-McClung	245.	575.	1900.	3600.
439	1170	1907	Napier-Thompson	390.	1250.	3250.	5500.
440	1171	1907	Parker-Burke	245.	600.	1800.	3600.
441	1172	1907	Teehee-Burke	245.	600.	1800.	3600.

Legal Tender clause and large "X TEN" at left.

KL#	Fr#	Series	Signatures	Fine	XF	CH CU (63)	Gem CU (65)
442	1173	1922	Speelman-White	245.	600.	1800.	4000.

Small serial number.

KL#	Fr#	Series	Signatures	Fine	XF	CH CU (63)	Gem CU (65)
442A	1173a	1922	Speelman-White	245.	600.	1800.	4000.

National Gold Bank Notes

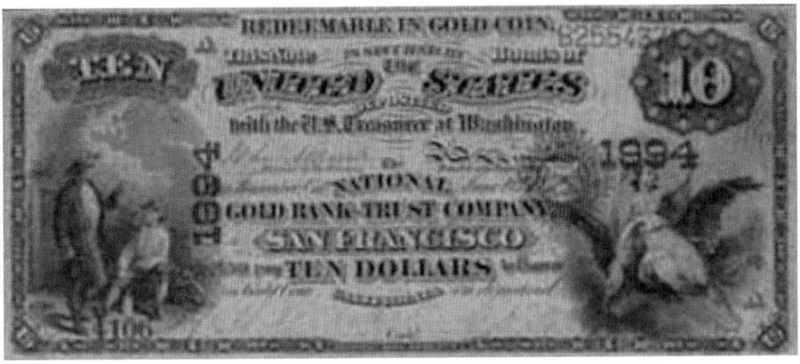

Franklin and Electricity, 1752 at left, America Seizing Lightning at right.
Various U.S. Gold Coins.

KL#	Fr#	Series	Issuing Bank	Location	Good	Fine	VF
403	1150	1875	First Nat'l Gold Bank	Petaluma	4000.	15,000.	—
405	1151a	1875	Union Nat'l Gold Bank	Oakland	—	92,000.	—
406	1147	1875	First Nat'l Gold Bank	Stockton	4000.	15,000.	—
396	1142	Orig.	First Nat'l Gold Bank	San Francisco	2400.	7500.	—
397	1143	Orig.	Nat'l Gold Bank & Trust Co.	San Francisco	4000.	15,000.	—
398	1144	Orig.	Nat'l Gold Bank of D.O. Mills	Sacramento	4000.	15,000.	—
399	1146	Orig.	First Nat'l Gold Bank	Stockton	4000.	15,000.	—
400	1145	Orig.	First Nat'l Gold Bank	Santa Barbara	17,500.	48,900.	—
401	1148	Orig.	Farmers' Nat'l Gold Bank	San Jose	4000.	15,000.	—
402	1149	Orig.	First Nat'l Gold Bank	Petaluma	4000.	18,000.	—
404	1151	Orig.	First Nat'l Gold Bank	Oakland	4000.	15,000.	—

Silver Certificates

Robert Morris at upper left.

KL#	Fr#	Series	CounterSigned by:	Fine	XF	CH CU (63)
			Place of Deposit: New York.			
407	284	1878	J.C. Hopper, Asst. U.S. Treasurer	—	—	89,000.
			Place of Deposit: New York.			
408	283	1878	W.G. White, Asst. U.S. Treasurer	—	253,000.	—
			Place of Deposit: Washington, D.C.			
409	285a	1878	A.U. Wyman, Asst. U.S. Treasurer	—	40,000.	16,000.
			Payable at: New York.			
410	284a	1878	T. Hillhouse, Asst. U.S. Treasurer	—	Rare	—
			Payable at: New York.			
411	286	1880	T. Hillhouse, Asst. U.S. Treasurer	—	10,000.	23,000.

Blue serial numbers, with large "X" below center seal.

KL#	Fr#	Series	Signatures	Seal	Fine	XF	CH CU (63)	Gem CU (65)
412	287	1880	Scofield-Gilfillan	Large brown	3000.	5250.	14,000.	19,000.
413	288	1880	Bruce-Gilfillan	Large brown	1700.	5250.	14,000.	19,000.
414	289	1880	Bruce-Wyman	Large brown	1700.	6500.	17,500.	19,000.

Blue serial numbers, without large "X" below center seal.

KL#	Fr#	Series	Signatures	Seal	Fine	XF	CH CU (63)	Gem CU (65)
415	290	1880	Bruce-Wyman	Large red	3000.	20,000.	35,000.	50,000.

Thomas A. Hendricks at center.

KL#	Fr#	Series	Signatures	Seal	Fine	XF	CH CU (63)	Gem CU (65)
416	291	1886	Rosecrans-Jordan	Small red	1250.	4500.	20,000.	20,000.
417	292	1886	Rosecrans-Hyatt	Small red	1250.	4500.	12,000.	20,000.
418	293	1886	Rosecrans-Hyatt	Large red	1250.	3000.	12,000.	20,000.
419	294	1886	Rosecrans-Huston	Large red	1250.	4500.	12,000.	20,000.
420	295	1886	Rosecrans-Huston	Large brown	1250.	4500.	12,000.	20,000.
421	296	1886	Rosecrans-Nebeker	Large brown	1250.	4500.	12,000.	20,000.
422	297	1886	Rosecrans-Nebeker	Small red	1250.	4500.	12,000.	16,000.
423	298	1891	Rosecrans-Nebeker	Small red	2750.	9000.	20,000.	25,000.
424	299	1891	Tillman-Morgan	Small red	750.	1500.	5000.	7000.
425	300	1891	Bruce-Roberts	Small red	750.	1500.	5000.	10,000.
426	301	1891	Lyons-Roberts	Small red	800.	1850.	5000.	8000.
					800.	1850.	5500.	10,000.

Large "X TEN" at left.

KL#	Fr#	Series	Signatures	Seal	Fine	XF	CH CU (63)	Gem CU (65)
427	302	1908	Vernon-Treat	Small blue	800.	1850.	5500.	7750.
428	303	1908	Vernon-McClung	Small blue	800.	2200.	5500.	7750.
429	304	1908	Parker-Burke	Small blue	800.	1850.	5500.	7750.

Treasury or Coin Notes

General Philip Sheridan at center.

KL#	Fr#	Series	Signatures	Seal	Fine	XF	CH CU (63)	Gem CU (65)
430	366	1890	Rosecrans-Huston	Large brown	1500.	3500.	9000.	25,500.
431	367	1890	Rosecrans-Nebeker	Large brown	1500.	3500.	9000.	25,500.
432	368	1890	Rosecrans-Nebeker	Small red	2000.	3500.	9000.	13,000.
433	369	1891	Rosecrans-Nebeker	Small red	1250.	2500.	4500.	6000.
434	370	1891	Tillman-Morgan	Small red	1250.	2500.	4500.	6000.
435	371	1891	Bruce-Roberts	Small red	1100.	2400.	4500.	8500.

Federal Reserve Bank Notes

1915

Andrew Jackson at center. Farming at left and Industry at right.

KL#	Fr#	Bank	Federal Sigs.	Bank Sigs.	Fine	XF	CH CU (63)	Gem CU (65)
503	811	Atlanta	Teehee-Burke	Bell-Wellborn	2500.	4250.	7750.	10,500.
504	813	Chicago	Teehee-Burke	McLallen-McDougal	1300.	2750.	5000.	6750.
505	816	Kansas City	Teehee-Burke	Anderson-Miller	1300.	2750.	5000.	6750.
506	817	Kansas City	Teehee-Burke	Cross-Miller	2600.	4500.	8000.	11,000.
507	818	Kansas City	Teehee-Burke	Helm-Miller	1750.	3000.	6000.	8250.
508	819	Dallas	Teehee-Burke	Hoopes-Van Zandt	1300.	2750.	5000.	6750.
509	820	Dallas	Teehee-Burke	Gilbert-Van Zandt	2600.	4500.	8000.	11,000.
510	821	Dallas	Teehee-Burke	Talley-Van Zandt	2600.	5000.	8000.	11,000.

1918

KL#	Fr#	Bank	Federal Sigs.	Bank Sigs.	Fine	XF	CH CU (63)	Gem CU (65)
511	810	New York	Teehee-Burke	Hendricks-Strong	1250.	2750.	5000.	6900.
512	812	Atlanta	Elliott-Burke	Bell-Wellborn	1250.	2750.	5000.	6900.
513	814	Chicago	Teehee-Burke	McCloud-McDougal	1250.	4000.	5000.	7500.
514	815	St. Louis	Teehee-Burke	Attebery-Wells	1250.	2750.	5000.	6900.

Federal Reserve Notes

1914

Red Seal.

KL#	Fr#	Bank	Signatures	Fine	XF	CH CU (63)	Gem CU (65)
443	892	Boston	Burke-McAdoo	700.	2000.	3500.	5750.
444	893	New York	Burke-McAdoo	700.	1500.	3500.	5750.
445	894	Philadelphia	Burke-McAdoo	700.	1500.	3500.	5750.
446	895	Cleveland	Burke-McAdoo	700.	1500.	3500.	5750.
447	896	Richmond	Burke-McAdoo	700.	1500.	3500.	5750.
448	897	Atlanta	Burke-McAdoo	700.	1500.	3500.	5750.
449	898	Chicago	Burke-McAdoo	700.	1500.	3500.	5750.
450	899	St. Louis	Burke-McAdoo	700.	1500.	3500.	5750.
451	900	Minneapolis	Burke-McAdoo	700.	1500.	3500.	5750.
452	901	Kansas City	Burke-McAdoo	700.	1500.	3500.	5750.
453	902	Dallas	Burke-McAdoo	700.	1500.	3500.	5750.
454	903	San Francisco	Burke-McAdoo	700.	1500.	3500.	5750.

Blue Seal.

KL#	Fr#	Bank	Signatures	Fine	XF	CH CU (63)	Gem CU (65)
455	904	Boston	Burke-McAdoo	105.	240.	575.	1100.
456	905	Boston	Burke-Glass	150.	420.	800.	1100.
457	906	Boston	Burke-Houston	105.	240.	575.	1100.
458	907	Boston	White-Mellon	105.	240.	575.	1100.
459	908	New York	Burke-McAdoo	105.	240.	575.	1100.
460	909	New York	Burke-Glass	150.	420.	800.	1100.
461	910	New York	Burke-Houston	105.	240.	575.	1100.
462	911	New York	White-Mellon	105.	240.	575.	1100.
463	912	Philadelphia	Burke-McAdoo	105.	320.	575.	1100.
464	913	Philadelphia	Burke-Glass	205.	625.	1800.	2400.
465	914	Philadelphia	Burke-Houston	95.00	240.	575.	1100.
466	915	Philadelphia	White-Mellon	95.00	240.	575.	1100.
467	916	Cleveland	Burke-McAdoo	150.	240.	575.	1100.
468	917	Cleveland	Burke-Glass	250.	420.	875.	1100.
469	918	Cleveland	Burke-Houston	105.	240.	575.	1100.
470	919	Cleveland	White-Mellon	105.	240.	575.	1100.
471	920	Richmond	Burke-McAdoo	95.00	240.	575.	1100.
472	921	Richmond	Burke-Glass	300.	875.	2400.	2750.
473	922	Richmond	Burke-Houston	155.	240.	575.	1100.
474	923	Richmond	White-Mellon	105.	240.	575.	1100.
475	924	Atlanta	Burke-McAdoo	300.	775.	2400.	2750.
476	925	Atlanta	Burke-Glass	105.	240.	575.	1100.
477	926	Atlanta	Burke-Houston	235.	620.	1800.	2400.
478	927	Atlanta	White-Mellon	105.	240.	575.	1100.
479	928	Chicago	Burke-McAdoo	105.	240.	575.	1100.
480	929	Chicago	Burke-Glass	220.	240.	1800.	2400.
481	930	Chicago	Burke-Houston	105.	240.	575.	1100.
482	931	Chicago	White-Mellon	105.	240.	575.	1100.
483	932	St. Louis	Burke-McAdoo	105.	240.	575.	1100.
484	933	St. Louis	Burke-Glass	365.	675.	800.	1100.
485	934	St. Louis	Burke-Houston	105.	240.	575.	1100.
486	935	St. Louis	White-Mellon	150.	420.	750.	1100.
487	936	Minneapolis	Burke-McAdoo	105.	240.	575.	1100.
488	937	Minneapolis	Burke-Glass	105.	240.	575.	1100.
489	938	Minneapolis	Burke-Houston	150.	620.	1200.	1400.
490	939	Minneapolis	White-Mellon	105.	240.	575.	1100.
491	940	Kansas City	Burke-McAdoo	105.	240.	575.	1100.
492	941	Kansas City	Burke-Glass	420.	925.	3000.	3750.
493	942	Kansas City	Burke-Houston	105.	240.	575.	1100.
494	943	Kansas City	White-Mellon	105.	240.	575.	1100.
495	944	Dallas	Burke-McAdoo	105.	420.	575.	1100.
496	945	Dallas	Burke-Glass	825.	5250.	7000.	9000.
497	946	Dallas	Burke-Houston	105.	240.	575.	1100.
498	947	Dallas	White-Mellon	105.	240.	575.	1100.
499	948	San Francisco	Burke-McAdoo	310.	875.	2300.	2500.
500	949	San Francisco	Burke-Glass	285.	875.	2250.	4500.
501	950	San Francisco	Burke-Houston	285.	875.	2250.	4500.
502	951	San Francisco	White-Mellon	105.	240.	575.	1100.

Demand Notes

Twenty Dollars

America at center, standing with sword and shield.

KL#	Fr#	Payable at:	VG	Fine	VF
515	13a	Boston - Type One	Rare	—	—
516	13	Boston	21,000.	—	—
517	11a	New York	Unique	—	—
518	11	New York	21,000.	—	87,500.
520	12	Philadelphia	20,000.	—	100,000.
522	14	Cincinnati	Unique	—	—
522A	15	St. Louis	Unknown in private hands		—

United States Notes

First Obligation inscription on back. One red serial number.

KL#	Fr#	Series	Signatures	Seal	Fine	XF	CH CU (63)	Gem CU (65)
523	124	1862	Chittenden-Spinner	Small red	2000.	8000.	17,500.	—

American Bank Note Co. lower border. One red serial number.
Second Obligation inscription on back.

KL#	Fr#	Series	Signatures	Seal	Fine	XF	CH CU (63)	Gem CU (65)
524	125	1862	Chittenden-Spinner	Small red	2000.	6750.	17,500.	—

National Bank Note Co. American Bank Note Co.

Second Obligation on back. Two red serial numbers.

KL#	Fr#	Series	Signatures	Seal	Fine	XF	CH CU (63)	Gem CU (65)
525	126	1863	Chittenden-Spinner	Small red	2000.	6750.	16,500.	18,000.
525A	126a	1863	Chittenden-Spinner	Small red	3700.	6750.	16,500.	18,000.
525B	126b	1863	Chittenden-Spinner	Small red	3000.	6000.	16,500.	20,000.

Alexander Hamilton at left, Liberty at right.

American Bank Note Co. lower border. Blue serial numbers.

KL#	Fr#	Series	Signatures	Seal	Fine	XF	CH CU (63)	Gem CU (65)
526	127	1869	Allison-Spinner	Large red	2900.	10,000.	12,500.	20,000.

Blue serial numbers. "XX" twice on face of note.

KL#	Fr#	Series	Signatures	Seal	Fine	XF	CH CU (63)	Gem CU (65)
527	128	1875	Allison-New	Small red	1300.	2750.	5000.	7000.
528	129	1878	Allison-Gilfillan	Small red	900.	1800.	4250.	4000.

Blue serial numbers. "XX" removed.

KL#	Fr#	Series	Signatures	Seal	Fine	XF	CH CU (63)	Gem CU (65)
529	130	1880	Scofield-Gilfillan	Large brown	3000.	12,000.	15,000.	—

KL#	Fr#	Series	Signatures	Seal	Fine	XF	CH CU (63)	Gem CU (65)
530	131	1880	Bruce-Gilfillan	Large brown	1500.	3000.	9000.	13,000.
531	132	1880	Bruce-Wyman	Large brown	1000.	2500.	4750.	7500.
532	133	1880	Bruce-Wyman	Large red	2250.	5000.	10,000.	17,000.
533	134	1880	Rosecrans-Jordan	Large red	750.	1750.	5500.	7500.
534	135	1880	Rosecrans-Hyatt	Large red	800.	1750.	5750.	7000.
535	136	1880	Rosecrans-Hyatt	Red spikes	800.	1500.	3000.	5500.
536	137	1880	Rosecrans-Huston	Red spikes	800.	1500.	4500.	6500.
537	138	1880	Rosecrans-Huston	Large brown	1000.	2250.	6000.	7750.
538	139	1880	Rosecrans-Nebeker	Large brown	1250.	3000.	7500.	10,000.
539	140	1880	Rosecrans-Nebeker	Small red	600.	1250.	4500.	6000.
540	141	1880	Tillman-Morgan	Small red	600.	1250.	4500.	6000.
541	142	1880	Bruce-Roberts	Small red	600.	1250.	4500.	6000.
542	143	1880	Lyons-Roberts	Small red	600.	1250.	4500.	6000.
543	144	1880	Vernon-Treat	Small red	600.	1250.	4500.	6000.
544	145	1880	Vernon-McClung	Small red	600.	1250.	4500.	6000.

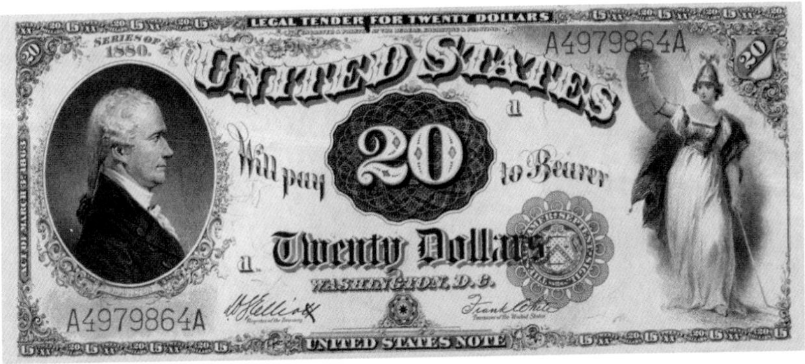

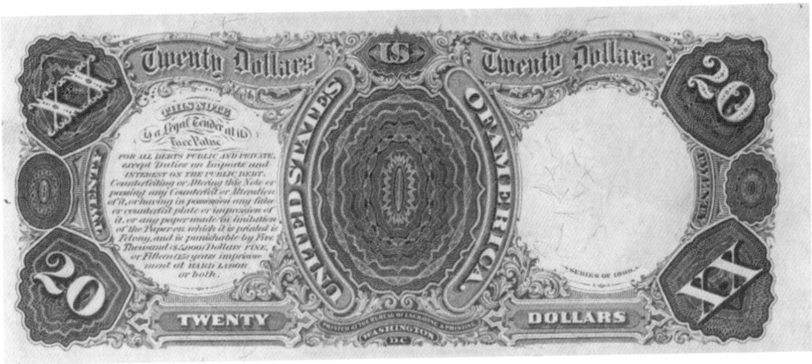

Red serial numbers.

KL#	Fr#	Series	Signatures	Seal	Fine	XF	CH CU (63)	Gem CU (65)
545	146	1880	Teehee-Burke	Small red	400.	1250.	2500.	4000.
546	147	1880	Elliott-White	Small red	400.	1250.	2500.	4000.

Compound Interest Treasury Notes

Victory at left, motor at lower center, Abraham Lincoln at right.

KL#	FR#	Act	Overprint Date	Signatures	VG	Fine	XF
547	191	1864	July 14, 1864	Chittenden-Spinner	—	—	70,000.
548	191a	1864	Aug. 15, 1864-Oct. 16, 1865	Colby-Spinner	5000.	7750.	25,000.

Interest Bearing Notes

KL#	FR#	Act	Signatures	VG	Fine	XF
549	197	1863	Chittenden-Spinner	6500.	74,750.	—
549a	197a		Chittenden-Spinner	5000.	15,000.	45,000.

Gold Certificates

Eagle on shield at left, large "20" in underprint.

KL#	Fr#	Series	Signatures	Fine	XF	CH CU (63)	Gem CU (65)
550	1166b	First/1863	Colby-Spinner	—	500,000.	—	—

James Garfield at right. Eagle on ocean telegraph.

KL#	Fr#	Series	Signatures	Seal	Fine	XF	CH CU (63)	Gem CU (65)
551	1175	1882	Thos. C. Acton, Asst. U.S. Treasurer	Brown	—	8500.	14,750.	
552	1174	1882	Bruce-Gilfillan	Brown	10,500.	—	—	—
553	1176	1882	Bruce-Wyman	Brown	4500.	8500.	44,000.	138,000.
554	1177	1882	Rosecrans-Huston	Large brown	4500.	10,000.	—	—
555	1178	1882	Lyons-Roberts	Small red	700.	2250.	6750.	27,500.
			George Washington at center, "$20" at left. Great Seal.					
556	1179	1905	Lyons-Roberts	Small red	2000.	10,000.	32,000.	80,000.
557	1180	1905	Lyons-Treat	Small red	2000.	8000.	25,000.	75,000.
			George Washington at center, "XX" at left. Great Seal.					
558	1181	1906	Vernon-Treat	Gold	350.	850.	1750.	2500.
559	1182	1906	Vernon-McClung	Gold	300.	1400.	2750.	5500.
560	1183	1906	Napier-McClung	Gold	300.	600.	1750.	4000.
561	1184	1906	Napier-Thompson	Gold	750.	800.	2750.	5500.
562	1185	1906	Parker-Burke	Gold	350.	800.	1750.	2750.
563	1186	1906	Teehee-Burke	Gold	350.	800.	2250.	4500.

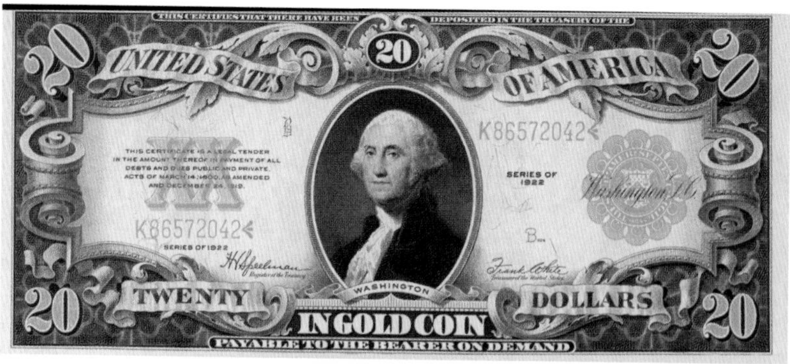

George Washington at center, Legal tender clause and "XX" at left.
Great Seal.

KL#	Fr#	Series	Signatures	Seal	Fine	XF	CH CU (63)	Gem CU (65)
564	1187	1922	Speelman-White	Gold	300.	700.	1750.	2750.

National Gold Bank Notes

Battle of Lexington, 1775 at left, Loyalty at right.
Various U.S. Gold Coins.

KL#	Fr#	Series	Issuing Bank	Location	Good	Fine	VF
566	1152	Orig.	First Nat'l Gold Bank	San Francisco	10,000.	19,000.	—
567	1154	Orig.	Nat'l Gold Bank of D.O. Mills	Sacramento	8000.	30,000.	—
568	1155	Orig.	First Nat'l Gold Bank	Stockton	8000.	25,500.	—
569	1159a	Orig.	First Nat'l Gold Bank	Santa Barbara	10,000.	30,000.	—
570	1156	Orig.	Farmers' Nat'l Gold Bank	San Jose	12,000.	30,000.	—
571	1153	1875	First Nat'l Gold Bank	San Francisco	12,000.	25,000.	—
572	1157	1875	First Nat'l Gold Bank	Petaluma	—	Rare	—
573	1158	Orig.	First Nat'l Gold Bank	Oakland	12,000.	30,000.	—
574	1159	Orig.	Union Nat'l Gold Bank	Oakland	—	Rare	—

Silver Certificates

Stephen Decatur at right.

KL#	Fr#	Series	CounterSigned by:	Fine	XF	CH CU (63)
			Place of Deposit: New York.			
575	305	1878	J.C. Hopper, Asst. U.S. Treasurer	—	Rare	—
			Place of Deposit: Washington, D.C.			
576	306	1878	A.U. Wyman, Asst. U.S. Treasurer	7500.	15,000.	—
			Place of Deposit: New York.			
577	307	1878	T. Hillhouse, Asst. U.S. Treasurer	5000.	18,000.	26,500.
			Place of Deposit: New York.			
578	308	1880	T. Hillhouse, Asst. U.S. Treasurer	7500.	20,000.	47,500.

Large "XX" under seal at center.

KL#	Fr#	Series	Signatures	Seal	Fine	XF	CH CU (63)	Gem CU (65)
579	309	1880	Scofield-Gilfillan	Large brown	5300.	12,500.	—	—
580	310	1880	Bruce-Gilfillan	Large brown	3750.	12,500.	—	—
581	311	1880	Bruce-Wyman	Large brown	3750.	12,500.	—	—
			Large "XX" removed.					
582	312	1880	Bruce-Wyman	Small red	6000.	19,000.	—	—

Daniel Manning at center flanked by Agriculture and Industry.

KL#	Fr#	Series	Signatures	Seal	Fine	XF	CH CU (63)	Gem CU (65)
583	313	1886	Rosecrans-Hyatt	Large red	5000.	20,000.	60,000.	100,000.

KL#	Fr#	Series	Signatures	Seal	Fine	XF	CH CU (63)	Gem CU (65)
584	314	1886	Rosecrans-Huston	Large brown	4000.	10,000.	30,000.	45,000.
585	315	1886	Rosecrans-Nebeker	Large brown	4000.	12,500.	35,000.	46,000.
586	316	1886	Rosecrans-Nebeker	Small red	4000.	10,000.	60,000.	90,000.

"Series 1891" upper right and lower left.

KL#	Fr#	Series	Signatures	Seal	Fine	XF	CH CU (63)	Gem CU (65)
587	317	1891	Rosecrans-Nebeker	Small red	1500.	3750.	12,000.	18,000.
588	318	1891	Tillman-Morgan	Small red	1500.	3750.	12,000.	18,000.
589	319	1891	Bruce-Roberts	Small red	1500.	3750.	12,000.	18,000.
590	320	1891	Lyons-Roberts	Small red	1500.	3750.	12,000.	18,000.

Large blue "XX" at left.

KL#	Fr#	Series	Signatures	Seal	Fine	XF	CH CU (63)	Gem CU (65)
591	321	1891	Parker-Burke	Small blue	1200.	3750.	12,000.	18,000.

Large and small size signature varieties are known.

KL#	Fr#	Series	Signatures	Seal	Fine	XF	CH CU (63)	Gem CU (65)
592	322	1891	Teehee-Burke	Small blue	1500.	3750.	12,000.	18,000.

Treasury or Coin Notes

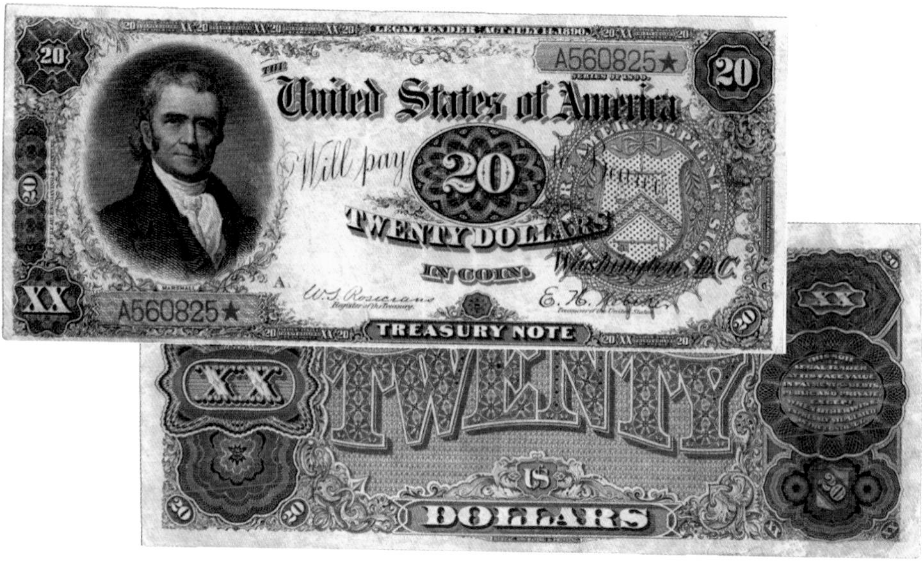

John Marshall at left.

KL#	Fr#	Series	Signatures	Seal	Fine	XF	CH CU (63)	Gem CU (65)
593	372	1890	Rosecrans-Huston	Large brown	4000.	8000.	17,500.	25,000.
594	373	1890	Rosecrans-Nebeker	Large brown	7500.	16,000.	—	—
595	374	1890	Rosecrans-Nebeker	Small red	3000.	10,000.	25,000.	30,000.

KL#	Fr#	Series	Signatures	Seal	Fine	XF	CH CU (63)	Gem CU (65)
596	375	1891	Tillman-Morgan	Small red	2500.	10,000.	17,500.	22,500.
597	375a	1891	Bruce-Roberts	Small red	Rare	—	—	—

Federal Reserve Bank Notes

1915

Grover Cleveland at center.
Auto and steam train at left, tug and ocean liner at right.

KL#	Fr#	Bank	Federal Sigs.	Bank Sigs.	Fine	XF	CH CU (63)	Gem CU (65)
658	822	Atlanta	Teehee-Burke	Bell-Wellborn Unique	—	—	—	—
659	822a	Atlanta	Teehee-Burke	Pike-McCord	—	Rare	—	—
660	824	Chicago	Teehee-Burke	McLallen-McDougal	3000.	7500.	14,500.	25,000.
661	826	Kansas City	Teehee-Burke	Anderson-Miller	2000.	3500.	7500.	10,000.
662	827	Kansas City	Teehee-Burke	Cross-Miller	2000.	3500.	7500.	10,000.
663	828	Dallas	Teehee-Burke	Hoopes-Van Zandt	—	Rare	—	—
664	829	Dallas	Teehee-Burke	Gilbert-Van Zandt	5000.	Rare	—	—
665	830	Dallas	Teehee-Burke	Talley-Van Zandt	—	Rare	—	—

1918

KL#	Fr#	Bank	Federal Sigs.	Bank Sigs.	Fine	XF	CH CU (63)	Gem CU (65)
666	823	Atlanta	Elliott-Burke	Bell-Wellborn	2275.	3750.	8000.	11,000.
667	825	St. Louis	Teehee-Burke	Attebery-Wells	2275.	4500.	8000.	11,000.

Federal Reserve Notes

1914

Grover Cleveland at center.
Auto and steam train at left, tug and ocean liner at right.

KL#	Fr#	Bank	Signatures	Fine	XF	CH CU (63)	Gem CU (65)
598	952	Boston	Burke-McAdoo	725.	4400.	6800.	9000.

KL#	Fr#	Bank	Signatures	Fine	XF	CH CU (63)	Gem CU (65)
599	953	New York	Burke-McAdoo	725.	4400.	6800.	13,500.
600	954	Philadelphia	Burke-McAdoo	725.	4400.	6800.	9000.
601	955	Cleveland	Burke-McAdoo	875.	4400.	6800.	9000.
602	956	Richmond	Burke-McAdoo	725.	4400.	6800.	9000.
603	957	Atlanta	Burke-McAdoo	725.	4400.	6800.	9000.
604	958	Chicago	Burke-McAdoo	725.	4400.	6800.	9000.
605	959	St. Louis	Burke-McAdoo	725.	4400.	6800.	9000.
606	960	Minneapolis	Burke-McAdoo	725.	4400.	6800.	9000.
607	961	Kansas City	Burke-McAdoo	725.	4400.	6800.	9000.
608	962	Dallas	Burke-McAdoo	725.	4400.	6800.	16,000.
609	963	San Francisco	Burke-McAdoo	725.	4400.	6800.	9000.

Blue Seal.

KL#	Fr#	Bank	Signatures	Fine	XF	CH CU (63)	Gem CU (65)
610	964	Boston	Burke-McAdoo	145.	400.	675.	850.
611	965	Boston	Burke-Glass	190.	400.	675.	850.
612	966	Boston	Burke-Houston	215.	400.	675.	850.
613	967	Boston	White-Mellon	145.	400.	675.	850.
614	968	New York	Burke-McAdoo	215.	400.	675.	850.
615	969	New York	Burke-Glass	215.	400.	675.	850.
616	970	New York	Burke-Houston	215.	400.	675.	850.
617	971	New York	White-Mellon	215.	400.	675.	850.
618	972	Philadelphia	Burke-McAdoo	215.	400.	675.	800.
619	973	Philadelphia	Burke-Glass	450.	900.	1750.	2400.
620	974	Philadelphia	Burke-Houston	215.	400.	675.	800.
621	975	Philadelphia	White-Mellon	215.	400.	675.	800.
622	976	Cleveland	Burke-McAdoo	215.	400.	675.	800.
623	977	Cleveland	Burke-Glass	375.	600.	1000.	1250.
624	978	Cleveland	Burke-Houston	215.	400.	675.	800.
625	979	Cleveland	White-Mellon	215.	400.	675.	800.
626	980	Richmond	Burke-McAdoo	400.	750.	2250.	2800.
627	981	Richmond	Burke-Glass	400.	750.	2250.	2800.
628	982	Richmond	Burke-Houston	215.	400.	675.	800.
629	983	Richmond	White-Mellon	215.	400.	675.	800.
630	984	Atlanta	Burke-McAdoo	215.	400.	675.	800.
632	986	Atlanta	Burke-Houston	215.	400.	675.	800.
633	987	Atlanta	White-Mellon	215.	400.	675.	800.
634	988	Chicago	Burke-McAdoo	215.	400.	675.	800.
635	989	Chicago	Burke-Glass	215.	400.	675.	800.
636	990	Chicago	Burke-Houston	215.	400.	675.	800.
637	991	Chicago	White-Mellon	215.	400.	675.	800.
638	992	St. Louis	Burke-McAdoo	215.	400.	675.	800.
639	993	St. Louis	Burke-Glass	375.	750.	1500.	2250.
640	994	St. Louis	Burke-Houston	215.	400.	675.	800.
641	995	St. Louis	White-Mellon	215.	400.	675.	800.
642	996	Minneapolis	Burke-McAdoo	215.	400.	675.	800.
643	997	Minneapolis	Burke-Glass	215.	400.	675.	800.
644	998	Minneapolis	Burke-Houston	215.	400.	675.	800.
645	999	Minneapolis	White-Mellon	250.	500.	1250.	2000.
646	1000	Kansas City	Burke-McAdoo	215.	400.	675.	800.
647	1001	Kansas City	Burke-Glass	215.	400.	675.	800.
648	1002	Kansas City	Burke-Houston	215.	400.	675.	800.
649	1003	Kansas City	White-Mellon	215.	400.	675.	800.
650	1004	Dallas	Burke-McAdoo	215.	400.	675.	800.
651	1005	Dallas	Burke-Glass	215.	400.	675.	800.
652	1006	Dallas	Burke-Houston	250.	575.	1000.	1750.
653	1007	Dallas	White-Mellon	250.	500.	775.	900.
654	1008	San Francisco	Burke-McAdoo	215.	400.	675.	800.
655	1009	San Francisco	Burke-Glass	215.	400.	675.	800.
656	1010	San Francisco	Burke-Houston	215.	400.	675.	800.
657	1011	San Francisco	White-Mellon	215.	400.	675.	800.

United States Notes

Fifty Dollars

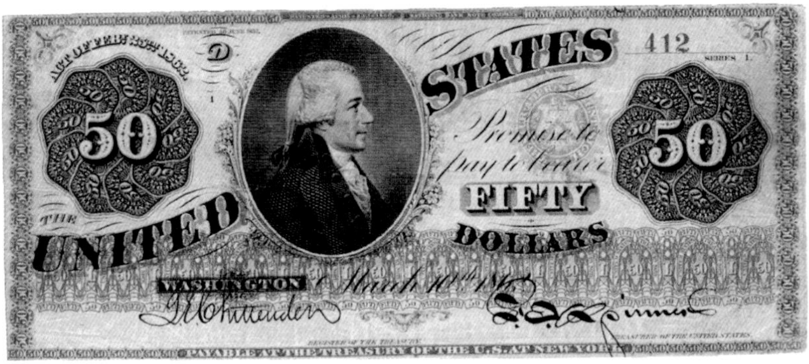

Alexander Hamilton at left. First Obligation inscription.

KL#	Fr#	Series	Signatures	Seal	Fine	XF	CH CU (63)	Gem CU (65)
668	148	1862	Chittenden-Spinner	Small red	23,000.	43,125.	—	—

Alexander Hamilton at left. National Bank Note Co. at top.
Second Obligation inscription.

KL#	Fr#	Series	Signatures	Seal	Fine	XF	CH CU (63)	Gem CU (65)
670	150	1863	Chittenden-Spinner	Small red	12,500.	57,500.	—	—

Peace standing at left, Henry Clay at right.

Blue serial numbers.

KL#	Fr#	Series	Signatures	Seal	Fine	XF	CH CU (63)	Gem CU (65)
671	151	1869	Allison-Spinner	Large red	32,000.	50,000.	150,000.	275,000.

Benjamin Franklin at left, America at right. Ornate "L" twice at center.

Blue serial numbers.

KL#	Fr#	Series	Signatures	Seal	Fine	XF	CH CU (63)	Gem CU (65)
672	152	1874	Allison-Spinner	Small red	15,000.	35,000.	51,750.	120,000.
673	153	1875	Allison-Spinner	Small red	—	Rare	—	—
674	154	1878	Allison-Gilfillan	Small red	5000.	20,000.	42,500.	62,500.

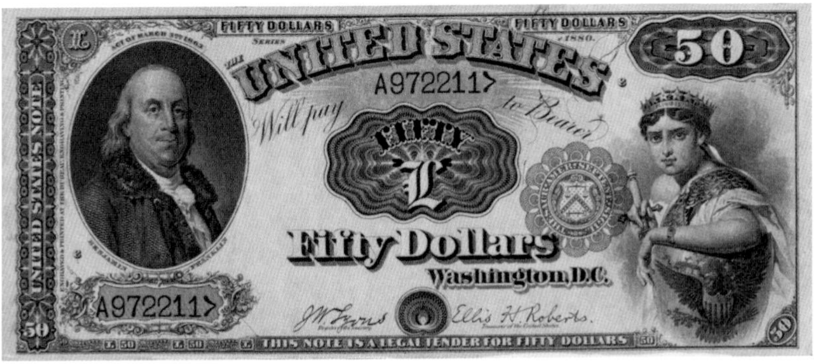

Benjamin Franklin at left, America at right.

KL#	Fr#	Series	Signatures	Seal	Fine	XF	CH CU (63)	Gem CU (65)
675	155	1880	Bruce-Gilfillan	Large brown	7000.	15,750.	32,500.	48,750.
676	156	1880	Bruce-Wyman	Large brown	5000.	30,000.	32,500.	48,750.
677	157	1880	Rosecrans-Jordan	Large red	6000.	14,000.	32,500.	48,750.
678	158	1880	Rosecrans-Hyatt	Large red	10,000.	20,000.	60,000.	67,500.
679	159	1880	Rosecrans-Hyatt	Red spikes	6750.	12,000.	32,500.	47,500.
680	160	1880	Rosecrans-Huston	Red spikes	20,000.	46,000.	Rare	—
681	161	1880	Rosecrans-Huston	Large brown	4500.	9000.	22,500.	30,000.
682	162	1880	Tillman-Morgan	Small red	8000.	12,500.	22,500.	36,000.
683	163	1880	Bruce-Roberts	Small red	18,000.	30,000.	—	—
684	164	1880	Lyons-Roberts	Small red	3000.	8000.	20,000.	32,000.

Compound Interest Treasury Notes

Liberty standing at left, Alexander Hamilton at right.

KL#	FR#	Act	Overprint Date	Signatures	VG	Fine	XF
685	192	1863	June 10, 1864	Chittenden-Spinner	—	—	Rare
686	192-A	1864	July 15, 1864	Chittenden-Spinner Three known.	—	—	—
687	192-B	1864	Aug. 15, 1864-Sept. 1, 1865	Colby-Spinner Two known.	16,000.	30,000.	60,000.

Andrew Jackson at left, Justice seated at center, Salmon P. Chase at right.

687a	202a	1861	March 2, 1861	Chittenden-Spinner	—	—	368,000.

Interest Bearing Notes

Liberty standing at left, Alexander Hamilton at right.

KL#	FR#	Act	Term	Signatures	VG	Fine	XF
688	198	1863	One year	Chittenden-Spinner	10,000.	22,000.	92,000.

Female holding Caduceus at left, Justice seated with shield at center, Loyalty standing at right.

689	203	1863	Two years	Chittenden-Spinner	15,000.	30,000.	65,000.

Eagle at center pearched on rock.

690	207	1861	Three years	Chittenden-Spinner	—	—	172,500.

Eagle at center pearched on shield.

691	212	1864	Three years	Colby-Spinner	—	65,000.	—
692	212d	1865	Three years	Colby-Spinner	—	70,000.	100,000.

Gold Certificates

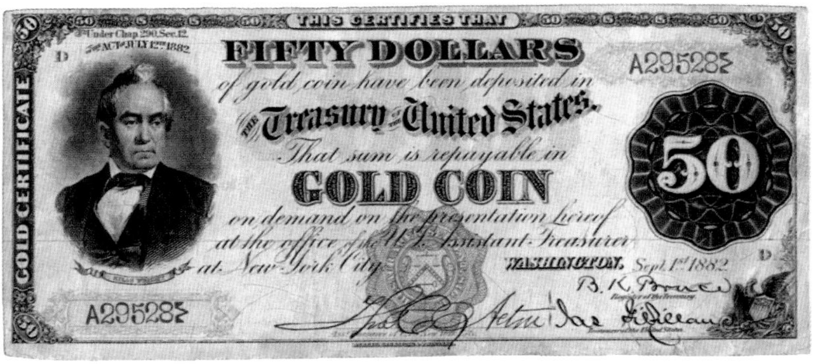

Silas Wright at left.

Countersigned.

KL#	Fr#	Series	Signatures	Seal	Fine	XF	CH CU (63)	Gem CU (65)
693	1189	1882	Bruce-Gilfillan	Brown	—	39,000.	—	—
694	1188	1882	Bruce-Gilfillan	Brown	—	Rare	—	—
695	1190	1882	Bruce-Wyman	Brown	20,000.	70,000.	—	—
696	1191	1882	Rosecrans-Hyatt	Large red	—	Rare	—	—
697	1192	1882	Rosecrans-Huston	Large brown	15,000.	75,000.	—	—
697a	1192a	1882	Rosecrans-Huston	Small red	—	300,000.	—	—
698	1193	1882	Lyons-Roberts	Small red	4500.	6000.	16,500.	22,500.
699	1194	1882	Lyons-Treat	Small red	—	30,000.	—	—
700	1195	1882	Vernon-Treat	Small red	975.	5000.	10,000.	16,500.
701	1196	1882	Vernon-McClung	Small red	2750.	7500.	30,000.	—

KL#	Fr#	Series	Signatures	Seal	Fine	XF	CH CU (63)	Gem CU (65)
702	1197	1882	Napier-McClung	Small red	1750.	5000.	18,500.	40,000.

Ulysses S. Grant at center.

KL#	Fr#	Series	Signatures	Seal	Fine	XF	CH CU (63)	Gem CU (65)
703	1198	1913	Parker-Burke	Gold	900.	3000.	7500.	20,000.
704	1199	1913	Teehee-Burke	Gold	900.	2500.	7500.	22,000.

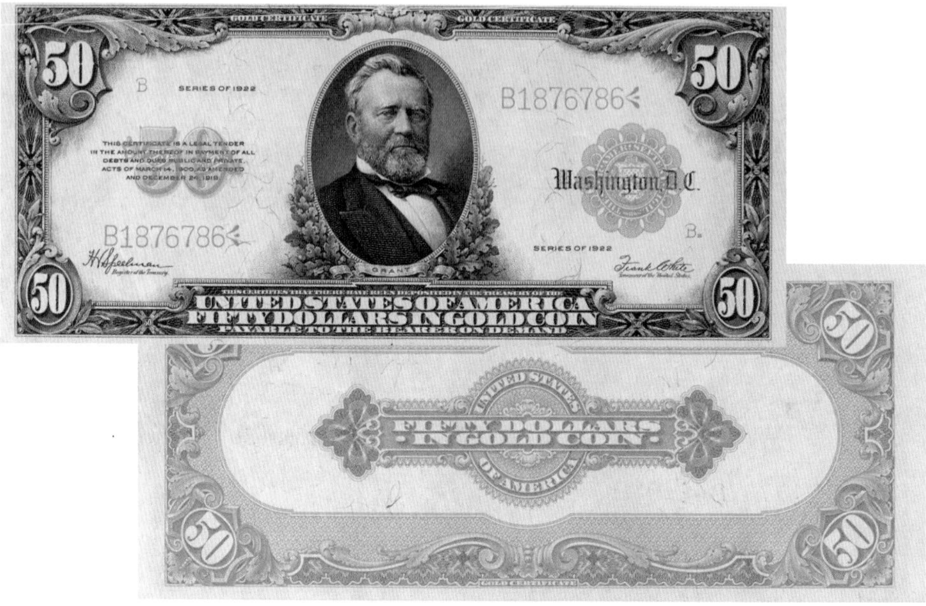

Large and small serial number varieties exist.

KL#	Fr#	Series	Signatures	Seal	Fine	XF	CH CU (63)	Gem CU (65)
705	1200	1922	Speelman-White	Gold	850.	2500.	7500.	22,000.

National Gold Bank Notes

Washington Crossing the Delaware at left, Prayer for Victory at right.
Various U.S. Gold Coins.

KL#	Fr#	Series	Issuing Bank	Location	Good	Fine	VF
706	1160	Orig.	First Nat'l Gold Bank	San Francisco	—	Rare	—
707	1161	Orig.	Farmers' Nat'l Gold Bank	San Jose	—	Rare	—

Silver Certificates

Edward Everett at right.

KL#	Fr#	Series	Signatures	Fine	XF	CH CU (63)
			Payable at: Washington, D.C. Large "FIFTY" below center seal.			
708	324c	1878	A.U. Wyman, Asst. U.S. Treasurer	—	37,000.	—
			Payable at: New York.			
709	324	1878	T. Hillhouse, Asst. U.S. Treasurer	—	Rare	—
			Payable at: San Francisco.			
710	324a	1878	R.M. Anthony, Asst. U.S. Treasurer	—	Rare	—

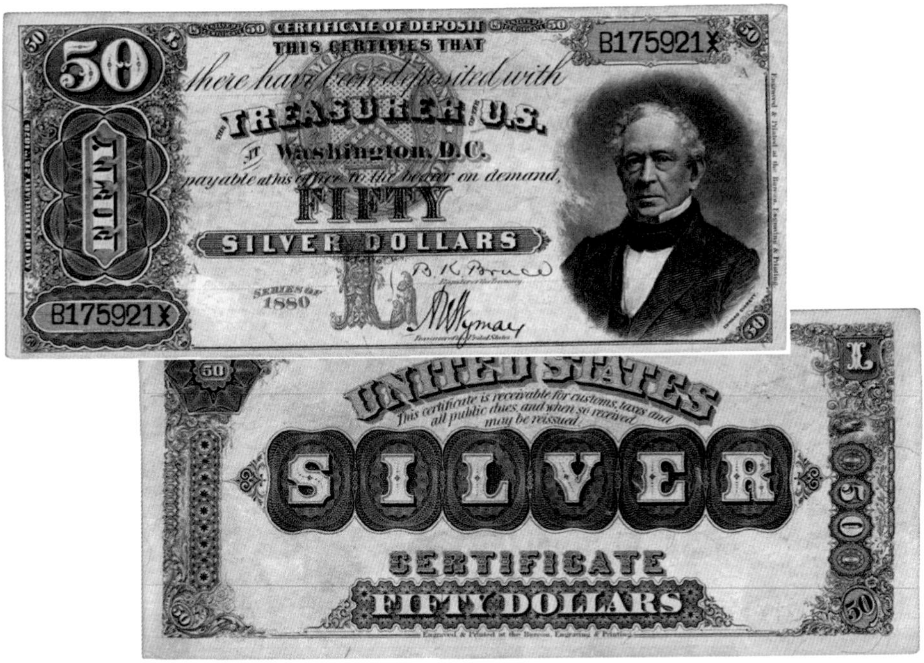

Large "FIFTY" in center, "L" below.

KL#	Fr#	Series	Signatures	Seal	Fine	XF	CH CU (63)	Gem CU (65)
711	325	1880	Scofield-Gilfillan	Large brown	Rare	—	—	—

KL#	Fr#	Series	Signatures	Seal	Fine	XF	CH CU (63)	Gem CU (65)
712	326	1880	Bruce-Gilfillan	Large brown	20,000.	55,000.	—	—
713	327	1880	Bruce-Wyman	Large brown	20,000.	115,000.	—	—

Large "FIFTY" in center.

KL#	Fr#	Series	Signatures	Seal	Fine	XF	CH CU (63)	Gem CU (65)
714	328	1880	Rosecrans-Huston	Large brown	10,000.	30,000.	75,000.	130,000.
715	329	1880	Rosecrans-Nebeker	Small red	20,000.	52,500.	—	—

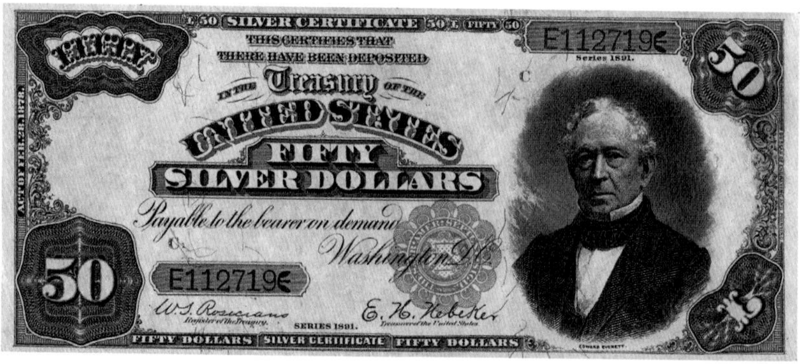

KL#	Fr#	Series	Signatures	Seal	Fine	XF	CH CU (63)	Gem CU (65)
716	330	1891	Rosecrans-Nebeker	Small red	22,500.	45,000.	—	—
717	331	1891	Tillman-Morgan	Small red	4500.	8500.	30,000.	40,000.
718	332	1891	Bruce-Roberts	Small red	4500.	6000.	14,000.	22,500.
719	333	1891	Lyons-Roberts	Small red	4500.	6000.	14,000.	22,500.
720	334	1891	Vernon-Treat	Small red	4500.	7000.	16,000.	25,000.
721	335	1891	Parker-Burke	Blue	2500.	3750.	11,000.	17,000.

Treasury or Coin Notes

William H. Seward at center.

KL#	Fr#	Series	Signatures	Seal	Fine	XF	CH CU (63)	Gem CU (65)
722	376	1891	Rosecrans-Nebeker	Small red	—	125,000.	300,000.	—

Federal Reserve Bank Notes

1918

Ulysses S. Grant at center.
Panama at center, ocean liner and battleship flanking.

KL#	Fr#	Bank	Federal Sigs.	Bank Sigs.	Fine	XF	CH CU (63)	Gem CU (65)
783	831	St. Louis	Teehee-Burke	Attebery-Wells	5000.	10,000.	19,500.	28,500.

Federal Reserve Notes

1914

Red Seals

KL#	Fr#	Bank	Signatures	Fine	XF	CH CU (63)	Gem CU (65)
723	1012	Boston	Burke-McAdoo	2750.	4500.	12,000.	15,000.
724	1013	New York	Burke-McAdoo	2750.	4500.	12,000.	15,000.
725	1014	Philadelphia	Burke-McAdoo	2750.	4500.	12,000.	15,000.
726	1015	Cleveland	Burke-McAdoo	2750.	4500.	12,000.	15,000.
727	1016	Richmond	Burke-McAdoo	2750.	4500.	12,000.	15,000.
728	1017	Atlanta	Burke-McAdoo	2750.	4500.	12,000.	15,000.
729	1018	Chicago	Burke-McAdoo	2750.	4500.	12,000.	15,000.
730	1019	St. Louis	Burke-McAdoo	2750.	4500.	12,000.	15,000.
731	1020	Minneapolis	Burke-McAdoo	2750.	4500.	12,000.	15,000.
732	1021	Kansas City	Burke-McAdoo	2750.	4500.	12,000.	15,000.
733	1022	Dallas	Burke-McAdoo	2750.	4500.	12,000.	15,000.
734	1023	San Francisco	Burke-McAdoo	2750.	4500.	12,000.	15,000.

Blue Seal.

KL#	Fr#	Bank	Signatures	Fine	XF	CH CU (63)	Gem CU (65)
735	1024	Boston	Burke-McAdoo	400.	3000.	2900.	5000.
736	1025	Boston	Burke-Glass	400.	1100.	2900.	5000.
737	1026	Boston	Burke-Houston	580.	3000.	9000.	11,500.
739	1028	New York	Burke-McAdoo	400.	1100.	2900.	5000.
740	1029	New York	Burke-Glass	400.	1100.	2900.	5000.
741	1030	New York	Burke-Houston	400.	700.	1750.	2750.
742	1031	New York	White-Mellon	400.	700.	1750.	2750.
743	1032	Philadelphia	Burke-McAdoo	400.	700.	1750.	2750.
744	1033	Philadelphia	Burke-Glass	3000.	6000.	9000.	11,500.
745	1034	Philadelphia	Burke-Houston	440.	900.	2250.	3500.
746	1035	Philadelphia	White-Mellon	440.	900.	2250.	3500.
747	1036	Cleveland	Burke-McAdoo	440.	900.	2250.	3500.
748	1037	Cleveland	Burke-Glass	3000.	2500.	6000.	9000.
749	1038	Cleveland	Burke-Houston	440.	900.	2250.	3750.
750	1039	Cleveland	White-Mellon	340.	675.	1500.	2400.
751	1040	Richmond	Burke-McAdoo	700.	1250.	3000.	5000.
752	1041	Richmond	Burke-Glass	3000.	6000.	9000.	11,500.
753	1042	Richmond	Burke-Houston	700.	1250.	4000.	5000.
754	1043	Richmond	White-Mellon	700.	1250.	4000.	5000.
755	1044	Atlanta	Burke-McAdoo	480.	1100.	2950.	4750.
756	1045	Atlanta	Burke-Glass	3000.	6000.	9000.	11,500.
757	1046	Atlanta	Burke-Houston	330.	675.	2000.	3750.
758	1047	Atlanta	White-Mellon	480.	1100.	2950.	4750.
759	1048	Chicago	Burke-McAdoo	280.	650.	1450.	2000.
760	1049	Chicago	Burke-Glass	475.	900.	2250.	3750.
761	1050	Chicago	Burke-Houston	475.	900.	2250.	3750.
762	1051	Chicago	White-Mellon	475.	900.	2250.	3750.
763	1052	St. Louis	Burke-McAdoo	475.	1000.	2700.	4500.
764	1053	St. Louis	Burke-Glass	475.	900.	2250.	3750.
765	1054	St. Louis	Burke-Houston	475.	900.	2250.	3750.
767	1056	Minneapolis	Burke-McAdoo	475.	1500.	2250.	3750.
769	1058	Minneapolis	Burke-Houston	800.	1600.	3500.	6000.
771	1060	Kansas City	Burke-McAdoo	475.	900.	2250.	3750.
774	1063	Kansas City	White-Mellon	3000.	6000.	9000.	11,500.
775	1064	Dallas	Burke-McAdoo	580.	1000.	3500.	6000.
777	1066	Dallas	Burke-Houston	3000.	6000.	9000.	11,500.
779	1068	San Francisco	Burke-McAdoo	475.	900.	2250.	3750.
781	1070	San Francisco	Burke-Houston	475.	900.	2250.	3750.
782	1071	San Francisco	White-Mellon	475.	1100.	2950.	4750.

United States Notes

One Hundred Dollars

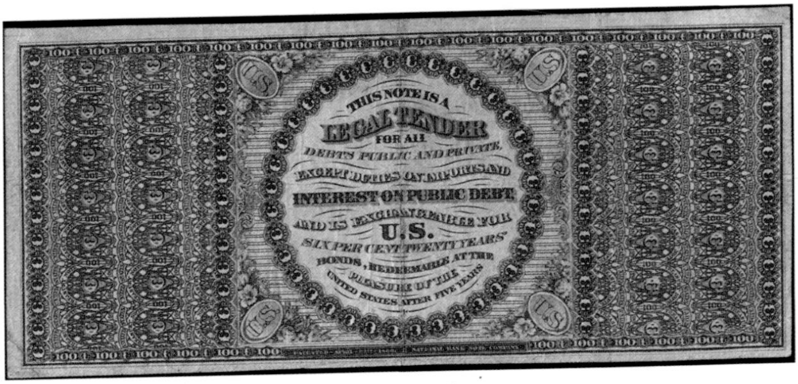

Large Eagle at upper left.

First Obligation inscription on back. Red serial numbers.

KL#	Fr#	Series	Signatures	Seal	Fine	XF	CH CU (63)	Gem CU (65)
784	165	1862	Chittenden-Spinner	Small red	30,000.	50,000.	75,000.	125,000.

American Bank Note Co. or National Bank Note Co. imprint.

Second Obligation inscription on back. Red serial numbers.

KL#	Fr#	Series	Signatures	Seal	Fine	XF	CH CU (63)	Gem CU (65)
785	166	1862	Chittenden-Spinner	Small red	Unique	—	—	—

Second Obligation on back.

KL#	Fr#	Series	Signatures	Seal	Fine	XF	CH CU (63)	Gem CU (65)
786	167	1863	Chittenden-Spinner	Small red	—	—	—	—

Abraham Lincoln at left, Reconstruction vignette at right.

Blue serial numbers.

KL#	Fr#	Series	Signatures	Seal	Fine	XF	CH CU (63)	Gem CU (65)
787	168	1869	Allison-Spinner	Large red	12,500.	45,000.	100,000.	185,000.

Series of 1875 at upper left and lower right face.

KL#	Fr#	Series	Signatures	Seal	Fine	XF	CH CU (63)	Gem CU (65)
788	169	1875	Allison-New	Small red	15,000.	40,000.	65,000.	80,000.
			Series of 1875 at upper left and lower right face.					
789	170	1875	Allison-Wyman	Small red	15,000.	40,000.	65,000.	80,000.

Series 1878 at upper left face.

KL#	Fr#	Series	Signatures	Seal	Fine	XF	CH CU (63)	Gem CU (65)
790	171	1878	Allison-Gilfillan	Small red	15,000.	30,000.	—	—

KL#	Fr#	Series	Signatures	Seal	Fine	XF	CH CU (63)	Gem CU (65)
791	172	1880	Bruce-Gilfillan	Large brown	9000.	30,000.	69,000.	91,000.
792	173	1880	Bruce-Wyman	Large brown	9000.	30,000.	75,000.	91,000.

KL#	Fr#	Series	Signatures	Seal	Fine	XF	CH CU (63)	Gem CU (65)
793	174	1880	Rosecrans-Jordan	Large red	9000.	35,000.	75,000.	91,000.
794	175	1880	Rosecrans-Hyatt	Large red	—	—	—	—
795	176	1880	Rosecrans-Hyatt	Red spikes	9000.	34,000.	65,000.	91,000.
796	177	1880	Rosecrans-Huston	Red spikes	8250.	35,000.	65,000.	80,000.
797	178	1880	Rosecrans-Huston	Large brown	9000.	26,000.	65,000.	80,000.

KL#	Fr#	Series	Signatures	Seal	Fine	XF	CH CU (63)	Gem CU (65)
798	179	1880	Tillman-Morgan	Small red	12,500.	17,500.	35,000.	86,250.
799	180	1880	Bruce-Roberts	Small red	12,500.	17,500.	35,000.	45,000.
800	181	1880	Lyons-Roberts	Small red	12,500.	17,500.	35,000.	45,000.
801	182	1880	Napier-McClung	Small red	Unknown	—	—	—

Compound Interest Treasury Notes

Guardian vignette at lower left, George Washington at center, Justice and shield at lower right.

KL#	FR#	Act	Overprint Date	Signatures	VG	Fine	XF
802	193	1863	June 10, 1864	Chittenden-Spinner	—	41,400.	—
803	193a	1864	July 15, 1864	Chittenden-Spinner	—	—	—
804	193b	1864	Aug. 15, 1864-Sept. 1, 1865	Colby-Spinner	—	34,500.	—

Interest Bearing Notes

KL#	FR#	Act	Term	Signatures	VG	Fine	XF
805	199	1863	One year	Chittenden-Spinner	—	—	—

Farmer and Mechanics at lower left, Treasury Building at upper center, In the Turret at lower right.

KL#	FR#	Act	Term	Signatures	VG	Fine	XF
806	204	1863	Two years	Chittenden-Spinner	—	—	—

General Winfield Scott facing left at top center.

KL#	FR#	Act	Term	Signatures	VG	Fine	XF
807	208	1861	Three years	Chittenden-Spinner	Unknown	—	—
808	212a	1864	Three years	Colby-Spinner	—	45,000.	97,750.

General Winfield Scott facing right at top center.

KL#	FR#	Act	Term	Signatures	VG	Fine	XF
809	212e	1865	Three years	Colby-Spinner	—	—	2,100,000.

Gold Certificates

Eagle on shield at left.

KL#	Fr#	Series	Signatures	Seal	Fine	XF	CH CU (63)	Gem CU (65)
810	1166c	First/1863	Colby-Spinner		Rare	—	—	—

Thomas H. Benton at left.

KL#	Fr#	Series	Signatures	Seal	Fine	XF	CH CU (63)	Gem CU (65)
811	1166h	Second/1870	Allison-Spinner		Unkown in private hands.		—	—
812	1166m	Third/1863/1875	Allison-New		Rare	—	—	—
813	1202	1882	Thos. C. Acton, Asst. U.S. Treasurer	Brown	—	Rare	—	
814	1201	1882	Bruce-Gilfillan	Brown	—	Rare	—	—
815	1203	1882	Bruce-Wyman	Brown	285,000.	—	—	—
816	1204	1882	Rosecrans-Hyatt	Large red	—	Rare	—	—
817	1205	1882	Rosecrans-Huston	Large brown	—	Rare	—	—
818	1206	1882	Lyons-Roberts	Small red	1150.	2750.	9000.	14,500.
819	1207	1882	Lyons-Treat	Small red	3750.	9000.	14,000.	20,000.
820	1208	1882	Vernon-Treat	Small red	3000.	9000.	16,500.	20,000.
821	1209	1882	Vernon-McClung	Small red	1300.	3000.	8750.	24,000.
822	1210	1882	Napier-McClung	Small red	1250.	3000.	10,000.	19,500.
823	1211	1882	Napier-Thompson	Small red	1150.	3000.	9500.	11,500.
824	1212	1882	Napier-Burke	Small red	1150.	3750.	9000.	14,500.
825	1213	1882	Parker-Burke	Small red	1150.	3750.	9000.	14,500.
826	1214	1882	Teehee-Burke	Small red	1150.	3750.	9000.	14,500.

KL#	Fr#	Series	Signatures	Seal	Fine	XF	CH CU (63)	Gem CU (65)
827	1215	1922	Speelman-White	Small red	1000.	8000.	12,000.	15,000.

National Gold Bank Notes

Battle of Lake Erie at left, Union at right. Various U.S. Gold Coins.

KL#	Fr#	Series	Issuing Bank	Location	Good	Fine	VF
829	1163	1875	First Nat'l Gold Bank	San Francisco	—	Rare	—
828	1162	Orig.	First Nat'l Gold Bank	San Francisco	—	Rare	—
830	1164	Orig.	First Nat'l Gold Bank	Santa Barbara	—	Rare	—
831	1165	Orig.	First Nat'l Gold Bank	Petaluma	100,000.	—	—
832	1166	Orig.	Union Nat'l Gold Bank	Oakland	—	Rare	—

Silver Certificates

James Monroe at left.

Place of Deposit: Washington, D.C. Large "100" at bottom center.

KL#	Fr#	Series	CounterSigned by:	Seal	Fine	XF	CH CU (63)	Gem CU (65)
833	337b	1878	A.U. Wyman, Asst. U.S. Treasurer		—	Rare	—	—

Place of Deposit: San Francisco.

KL#	Fr#	Series	CounterSigned by:	Seal	Fine	XF	CH CU (63)	Gem CU (65)
834	337	1878	R.M. Anthony, Asst. U.S. Treasurer		—	Rare	—	—

Note: R.M. Anthony was really the bookkeeper for the Asst. Treasurer.

Place of Deposit: New York.

KL#	Fr#	Series	CounterSigned by:	Seal	Fine	XF	CH CU (63)	Gem CU (65)
835	336	1878	W.G. White, Asst. U.S. Treasurer		—	Rare	—	—
836	338	1880	Scofield-Gilfillan	Large brown		Extremely Rare.	—	—
837	339	1880	Bruce-Gilfillan	Large brown		Extremely Rare.	—	—
838	340	1880	Bruce-Wyman	Large brown	16,000.	45,000.	—	—
839	341	1880	Rosecrans-Huston	Large brown	20,000.	235,000.	—	—
840	342	1880	Rosecrans-Nebeker	Small red	18,000.	125,000.	180,000.	210,000.

KL#	Fr#	Series	Signatures	Seal	Fine	XF	CH CU (63)	Gem CU (65)
841	343	1891	Rosecrans-Nebeker	Small red	5000.	—	—	—
842	344	1891	Tillman-Morgan	Small red	8000.	43,125.	—	—

Treasury or Coin Notes

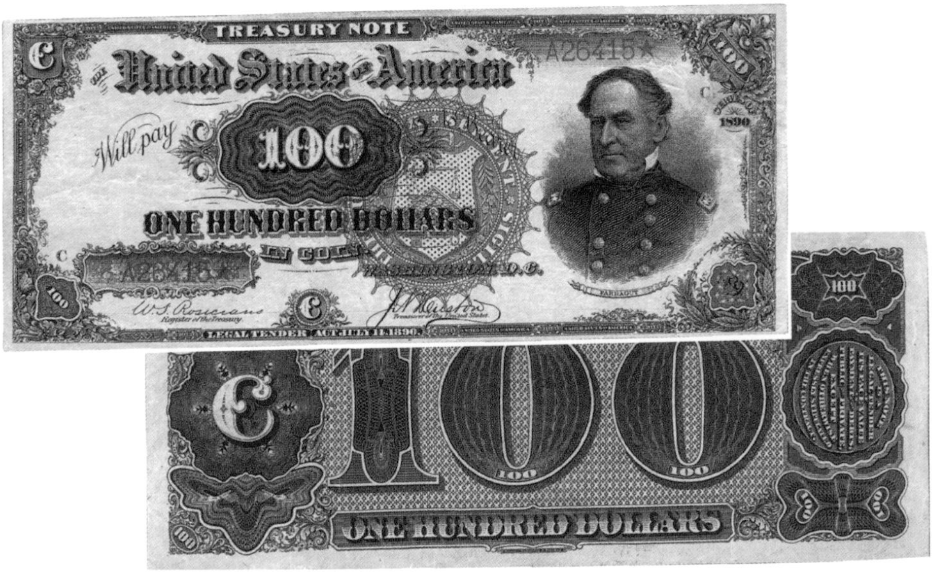

Admiral David G. Farragut at right. Large "100".

KL#	Fr#	Series	Signatures	Seal	Fine	XF	CH CU (63)	Gem CU (65)
843	377	1890	Rosecrans-Huston	Large brown	—	80,500.	356,500.	—

Admiral David G. Farragut at right.

KL#	Fr#	Series	Signatures	Seal	Fine	XF	CH CU (63)	Gem CU (65)
844	378	1891	Rosecrans-Nebeker	Small red	60,000.	140,000.	—	—

Federal Reserve Notes

1914

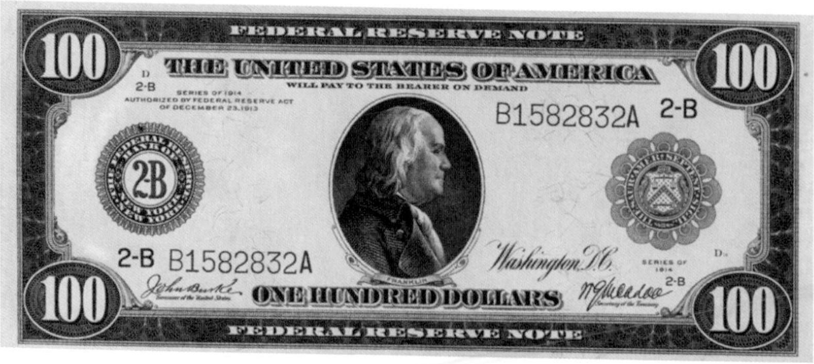

Benjamin Franklin at center.
Vignettes of Labor, Plenty, America, Peace and Commerce.

Red Seal.

KL#	Fr#	Bank	Signatures	Fine	XF	CH CU (63)	Gem CU (65)
845	1072	Boston	Burke-McAdoo	1750.	3750.	15,000.	40,000.
846	1073	New York	Burke-McAdoo	1750.	3750.	15,000.	40,000.
847	1074	Philadelphia	Burke-McAdoo	2500.	5000.	15,000.	40,000.
848	1075	Cleveland	Burke-McAdoo	5000.	7000.	15,000.	40,000.
849	1076	Richmond	Burke-McAdoo	1750.	3750.	15,000.	40,000.
850	1077	Atlanta	Burke-McAdoo	1750.	3750.	15,000.	40,000.
851	1078	Chicago	Burke-McAdoo	3500.	3750.	15,000.	40,000.
852	1079	St. Louis	Burke-McAdoo	1750.	3750.	15,000.	40,000.
853	1080	Minneapolis	Burke-McAdoo	1750.	3750.	15,000.	40,000.
854	1081	Kansas City	Burke-McAdoo	1750.	3750.	15,000.	40,000.
855	1082	Dallas	Burke-McAdoo	1750.	3750.	15,000.	40,000.
856	1083	San Francisco	Burke-McAdoo	1750.	3750.	15,000.	40,000.

Blue Seal.

KL#	Fr#	Bank	Signatures	Fine	XF	CH CU (63)	Gem CU (65)
857	1084	Boston	Burke-McAdoo	700.	1250.	15,000.	40,000.
858	1085	Boston	Burke-Glass	1000.	2250.	4000.	4750.
860	1087	Boston	White-Mellon	800.	1250.	3500.	3750.
861	1088	New York	Burke-McAdoo	700.	1250.	3500.	4500.
862	1089	New York	Burke-Glass	700.	1250.	3500.	4500.
863	1090	New York	Burke-Houston	700.	1250.	3500.	4500.
864	1091	New York	White-Mellon	700.	1250.	3500.	4500.
865	1092	Philadelphia	Burke-McAdoo	700.	1250.	3500.	4500.
868	1095	Philadelphia	White-Mellon	1500.	2500.	5000.	9000.
869	1096	Cleveland	Burke-McAdoo	1000.	2250.	4000.	4750.
870	1097	Cleveland	Burke-Glass	750.	1250.	3500.	4500.
871	1098	Cleveland	Burke-Houston	625.	1250.	3500.	4500.
872	1099	Cleveland	White-Mellon	750.	2000.	3750.	4500.
873	1100	Richmond	Burke-McAdoo	750.	1250.	3500.	4500.
874	1101	Richmond	Burke-Glass	750.	1250.	3500.	4500.
877	1104	Atlanta	Burke-McAdoo	750.	1250.	3500.	4000.
879	1106	Atlanta	Burke-Houston	1000.	2250.	4000.	4750.
880	1107	Atlanta	White-Mellon	750.	1500.	3500.	6000.
881	1108	Chicago	Burke-McAdoo	750.	1250.	3500.	4500.
883	1110	Chicago	Burke-Houston	750.	1250.	3500.	4500.
885	1112	St. Louis	Burke-McAdoo	750.	2500.	3500.	4500.
889	1116	Minneapolis	Burke-McAdoo	750.	1000.	4300.	4500.
892	1119	Minneapolis	White-Mellon	750.	1500.	3500.	6000.
893	1120	Kansas City	Burke-McAdoo	750.	1000.	2750.	4500.
896	1123	Kansas City	White-Mellon	750.	1500.	3500.	6000.
897	1124	Dallas	Burke-McAdoo	750.	1000.	2750.	7500.
900	1127	Dallas	White-Mellon	750.	1500.	3500.	6000.
901	1128	San Francisco	Burke-McAdoo	750.	1500.	3500.	6000.
903	1130	San Francisco	Burke-Houston	625.	1000.	2750.	4500.
904	1131	San Francisco	White-Mellon	1000.	2250.	4000.	4750.

United States Notes

Five Hundred Dollars

Albert Gallatin at center.

First Obligation inscription on back. Red serial number.

KL#	Fr#	Series	Signatures	Seal	Fine	XF	CH CU (63)
904a	183a	1862	Chittenden-Spinner	Small red		Extremely Rare	
			Second Obligation inscription on back. Red serial number.				
905	183b	1862	Chittenden-Spinner	Small red		Extremely Rare	
906	183c	1863	Chittenden-Spinner	Small red	—	540,000.	—
			Justice seated at left, John Quincy Adams at right.				
			Blue serial numbers.				
907	184	1869	Allison-Spinner	Large red		Extremely Rare	
			Victory at left, Brigadier General Joseph K. Mansfield at right.				
908	185a	1874	Allison-Spinner	Small red		Extremely Rare	
909	185b	1875	Allison-New	Small red		Extremely Rare	
910	185c	1875	Allison-Wyman	Small red		Extremely Rare	
911	185d	1878	Allison-Gilfillan	Small red		Extremely Rare	
912	185e	1880	Scofield-Gilfillan	Large brown		Extremely Rare	
913	185f	1880	Bruce-Wyman	Large brown		Extremely Rare	

KL#	Fr#	Series	Signatures	Seal	Fine	XF	CH CU (63)
914	185g	1880	Rosecrans-Jordan	Large red		Extremely Rare	
915	185h	1880	Rosecrans-Hyatt	Large red		Extremely Rare	
916	185-i	1880	Rosecrans-Huston	Large red		Extremely Rare	
917	185j	1880	Rosecrans-Nebeker	Small red		Extremely Rare	
918	185k	1880	Tillman-Morgan	Small red		Extremely Rare	
919	185l	1880	Bruce-Roberts	Small red		Extremely Rare	
920	185m	1880	Lyons-Roberts	Small red	—	150,000.	—
921	185n	1880	Napier-McClung	Small red		Not issued	

Compound Interest Treasury Notes

The Standard Bearer at left, New Ironsides at right.

KL#	FR#	Act	Overprint Date	Signatures	VG	Fine	XF
922	194	1863	June 10, 1864	Chittenden-Spinner		Extremely Rare.	—
923	194a	1864	July 15, 1864	Chittenden-Spinner		Extremely Rare.	—
924	194-B	1864	Aug. 15, 1864-Oct. 1, 1865	Colby-Spinner		Extremely Rare.	—

Interest Bearing Notes

KL#	FR#	Act	Term	Signatures	VG	Fine	XF
925	200	1863	One year	Chittenden-Spinner		Extremely Rare.	—
925A	-	1861	Two years	Chittenden-Spinner		Extremely Rare.	—
			Liberty and Union at left, Eagle on nest at top center.				
926	205	1863	Two years	Chittenden-Spinner		Extremely Rare.	—
			Justice at left, George Washington at top center, Transportation at right.				
927	209	1861	Three years	Chittenden-Spinner		Extremely Rare.	—
			Mortar at lower left, Alexander Hamilton at top center, George Washington at right.				
928	212b	1864	Three years	Colby-Spinner		Extremely Rare.	—
929	212f	1865	Three years	Colby-Spinner		Extremely Rare.	—

Gold Certificates

Abraham Lincoln at left.

KL#	Fr#	Series	Signatures	Fine	XF	CH CU (63)	Gem CU (65)
930	1160d	First/1863	Colby-Spinner	Unknown in private hands			—
931	1166l	Second/1870	Allison-Spinner	Extremely Rare.		—	—

Abraham Lincoln at left. Eagle on flag.

Countersigned.

KL#	Fr#	Series	Signatures	Fine	XF	CH CU (63)	Gem CU (65)
933	1215b	1882	Bruce-Gilfillan	Unknown in private hands			—
934	1215a	1882	Bruce-Gilfillan	Extremely Rare.		—	—
935	1215c	1882	Bruce-Wyman	Extremely Rare.		—	—

KL#	Fr#	Series	Signatures	Fine	XF	CH CU (63)	Gem CU (65)
936	1215d	1882	Rosecrans-Hyatt	Extremely Rare.		—	—
937	1216	1882	Lyons-Roberts	10,500.	25,000.	—	—
938	1216a	1882	Parker-Burke	—	25,000.	—	—
939	1216b	1882	Teehee-Burke	—	25,000.	—	—

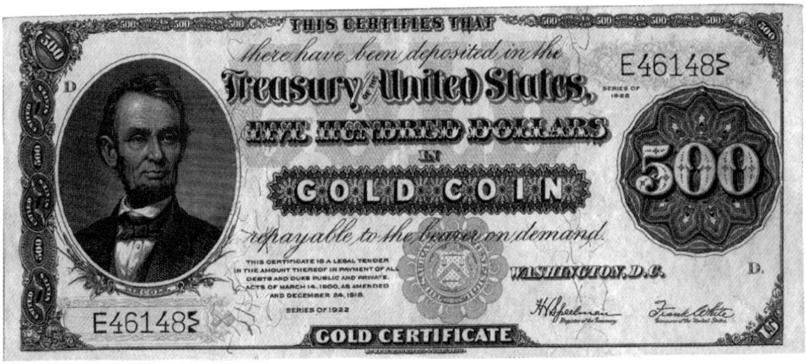

KL#	Fr#	Series	Signatures	Fine	XF	CH CU (63)	Gem CU (65)
940	1217	1922	Speelman-White	—	25,000.	—	—

Abraham Lincoln at left.

KL#	Fr#	Series	Signatures	Fine	XF	CH CU (63)	Gem CU (65)
932	1166n	Third/1863/1875	Allison-New	Unknown in private hands			—

National Gold Bank Notes

Civilization at left, Arrival of the Sirius at right. Various U.S. Gold Coins.

KL#	Fr#	Series	Issuing Bank	Location	Fine
941	-	1875	First Nat'l Gold Bank	San Francisco	Unknown in private hands
942	-	Orig.	Nat'l Gold Bank & Trust Co.	San Francisco	Unknown in private hands
943	-	Orig.	Nat'l Gold Bank of D.O. Mills and Company	Sacramento	Unknown in private hands

Silver Certificates

Charles Sumner at right.

KL#	Fr#	Series	CounterSigned by:	Seal	Fine	XF	CH CU (63)
			Place of Deposit: New York.				
944	345a	1878	W.G. White, Asst. U.S. Treasurer		Unique	—	—
			Place of Deposit: New York.				
945	345a	1878	J.C. Hopper, Asst. U.S. Treasurer		Unknown in private hands		
			Place of Deposit: New York.				
946	345a	1878	T. Hillhouse, Asst. U.S. Treasurer		Not issued	—	—
			Place of Deposit: San Francisco.				
947	345a	1878	R.M. Anthony, Asst. U.S. Treasurer		Unknown in private hands		
			Place of Deposit: Washington, D.C.				
948	345a	1878	A.U. Wyman, Asst. U.S. Treasurer		Unique	—	—
949	345b	1880	Scofield-Gilfillan	Brown	Unknown in private hands		
950	345c	1880	Bruce-Gilfillan	Brown	—	420,000.	—
951	345d	1880	Bruce-Wyman	Brown	Extremely Rare.		

Federal Reserve Notes

1918

John Marshall at center. DeSoto Discovering the Mississippi.

KL#	Fr#	Bank	Signatures	Fine	XF	CH CU (63)
952	1132	Boston	Burke-Glass	16,500.	40,000.	—
953	1132	New York	Burke-Glass	6325.	—	—
954	1132	New York	White-Mellon	—	40,000.	—
955	1132	Philadelphia	Burke-Glass	22,500.	40,000.	—
956	1132	Cleveland	Burke-Glass	10,500.	30,000.	—
957	1132	Richmond	Burke-Glass	Unknown in private hands		—
958	1132	Atlanta	Burke-Glass	—	—	75,000.
960	1132	Chicago	Burke-Glass	8500.	17,250.	—
961	1132	St. Louis	Burke-Glass	30,000.	—	—
962	1132	Minneapolis	Burke-Glass	140,000.	126,500.	—
963	1132	Kansas City	Burke-Glass	15,000.	22,000.	—
964	1132	Dallas	Burke-Glass	—	34,500.	—
965	1132	San Francisco	Burke-Glass	10,750.	—	95,000.
965A	1132	San Francisco	Burke-Houston	Extremely Rare.	—	—
965B	1132	San Francisco	White-Mellon	Extremely Rare.	—	—

United States Notes

One Thousand Dollars

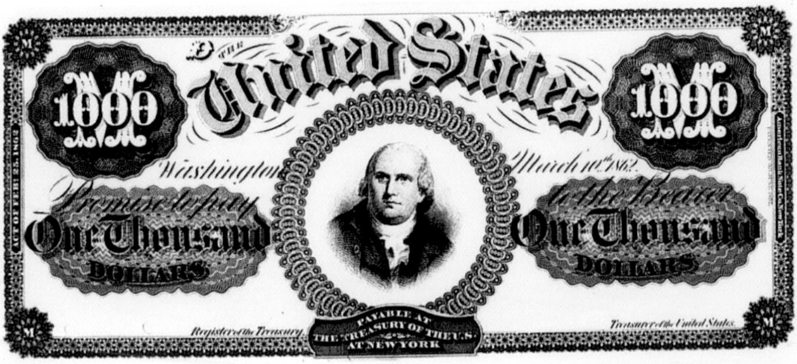

Robert Morris at center.

First Obligation inscription on back. Red serial number.

KL#	Fr#	Series	Signatures	Seal	Fine	XF
966	186a	1862	Chittenden-Spinner	Small red	Unknown in issued form	—
			Second Obligation inscription on back. Red serial number.			
967	186b	1862	Chittenden-Spinner	Small red	Unknown in issued form	—
			Red serial number.			
968	186c	1863	Chittenden-Spinner	Small red	650,000.	—

ABNCo imprint. Blue serial number.

KL#	Fr#	Series	Signatures	Seal	Fine	XF	CH CU (63)
969	186d	1863	Chittenden-Spinner	Small red	Extremely Rare.	—	1,200,000.
			ABNCo imprint.				
969A	186e	1863	Chittenden-Spinner	Small red	Unique	—	—
			Columbus in his study at left, DeWitt Clinton at center.				
969B	186f	1869	Allison-Spinner	Large red	Extremely Rare.	—	—

KL#	Fr#	Series	Signatures	Seal		Fine	XF
970	187a	1878	Allison-Gilfillan	Small red	Extremely Rare.	—	—
971	187b	1880	Bruce-Wyman	Large brown		—	750,000.
972	187c	1880	Rosecrans-Jordan	Large red	Unique	—	—

KL#	Fr#	Series	Signatures	Seal	Fine	XF
973	187d	1880	Rosecrans-Hyatt	Large red	Unique	—
974	187e	1880	Rosecrans-Huston	Large red	Unique	—
975	187f	1880	Rosecrans-Nebeker	Large brown	Unique	—
976	187g	1880	Tillman-Morgan	Small red	Extremely Rare.	—
978	187i	1880	Bruce-Roberts	Small red	Unique	—
979	187j	1880	Lyons-Roberts	Small red	—	75,000.
980	187k	1880	Vernon-Treat	Small red	Extremely Rare.	—
981	187l	1880	Napier-McClung	Small red	Not issued	—

Compound Interest Treasury Notes

KL#	FR#	Act	Overprint Date	Signatures	VG	Fine
982	195	1864	July 15, 1864	Chittenden-Spinner	Unknown	—
983	195a	1864	Aug. 15, 1864-Sept. 15, 1865	Colby-Spinner	Unknown	—

Interest Bearing Notes

Justice at left, eagle with shield at center, Liberty holding flag at right.

KL#	FR#	Act	Term	Signatures	VG	Fine
984	201	1863	One year	Chittenden-Spinner	Unknown	—
984A	-	1861	Two years	Chittenden-Spinner	Unknown	—

Naval engagement between the Guerriere and the Constitution at left, Discovery of the Mississippi by DeSoto at right.

985	206	1863	Two years	Chittenden-Spinner	Unknown	—

Salmon P. Chase at center.

986	210	1861	Three years	Chittenden-Spinner	Unknown	—

Justice with shield at lower center.

987	212c	1864	Three years	Colby-Spinner	Unknown	—
988	212g	1865	Three years	Colby-Spinner	Extremely Rare.	—

Gold Certificates

Eagle on shield at left.

KL#	Fr#	Series	Signatures	Seal	Fine	XF
989	1166e	First/1863	Colby-Spinner		Unique	—

Alexander Hamilton at left.

KL#	Fr#	Series	Signatures	Seal	Fine	XF
990	1166j	Second/1870	Allison-Spinner		Unique	—
991	1166o	Third/1863/1875	Allison-New		Unknown	—

Alexander Hamilton at right. Countersigned.

KL#	Fr#	Series	Signatures	Seal	Fine	XF
992	1218a	1882	Bruce-Gilfillan	Large brown	Extremely Rare.	—

Alexander Hamilton at right.

KL#	Fr#	Series	Signatures	Seal	Fine	XF
993	1218	1882	Bruce-Gilfillan	Large brown	Unknown	—
994	1218b	1882	Bruce-Wyman	Large brown	Unique	—
995	1218c	1882	Rosecrans-Hyatt	Large red	Unique	—
996	1218d	1882	Rosecrans-Huston	Large brown	—	950,000.
997	1218e	1882	Rosecrans-Nebeker	Small red	Extremely Rare.	—
998	1218f	1882	Lyons-Roberts	Small red	97,750.	—
999	1218g	1882	Lyons-Treat	Small red	—	230,000.

Alexander Hamilton at center. Great Seal.

KL#	Fr#	Series	Signatures	Seal	Fine	XF
1000	1219	1907	Vernon-Treat	Small red	Extremely Rare.	—
1001	1219a	1907	Vernon-McClung	Small red	Unknown	—

alexander hamilton Great Seal

KL#	Fr#	Series	Signatures	Seal	Fine	XF
1002	1219b	1907	Napier-McClung	Small red	Unique	241,500.

Alexander Hamilton at center. Great Seal.

KL#	Fr#	Series	Signatures	Seal	Fine	XF
1003	1219c	1907	Napier-Burke	Small red	—	37,500.
1004	1219d	1907	Parker-Burke	Small red	Extremely Rare.	—

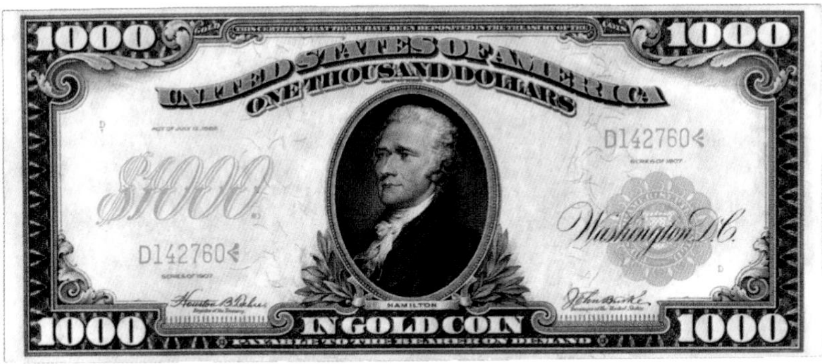

KL#	Fr#	Series	Signatures	Seal	Fine	XF	CH CU (63)
1005	1219e	1907	Teehee-Burke	Small red	—	60,000.	120,000.
1006	1220	1922	Speelman-White	Small red	—	63,250.	—

Silver Certificates

William left. Marcy at left.

Place of Deposit: Washington D.C.

KL#	Fr#	Series	CounterSigned by:	Seal	Fine	XF
1007	346a	1878	A.U. Wyman, Asst. U.S. Treasurer		Unknown	—
			Place of Deposit: San Francisco			
1008	346a	1878	R.M. Anthony, Asst. U.S. Treasurer		Unknown	—
			Place of Deposit: New York			
1009	346a	1878	Unknown signers		Unknown	—
1010	346b	1880	Scofield-Gilfillan	Large brown	Unknown	—
1011	346c	1880	Bruce-Gilfillan	Large brown	Unknown	—
1012	346d	1880	Bruce-Wyman	Large brown	—	580,000.
			Liberty holding shield at left, William left. Marcy at right.			
1013	346e	1891	Tillman-Morgan	Small red	Extremely Rare.	—

Treasury or Coin Notes

Major General George G. Meade at left. Large "1000" on back.

KL#	Fr#	Series	Signatures	Seal	Fine	XF
1014	379a	1890	Rosecrans-Huston	Large brown	—	1,095,000.

Major General George G. Meade at left. Large "1000".

KL#	Fr#	Series	Signatures	Seal	Fine	XF
1015	379b	1890	Rosecrans-Nebeker	Small red	Extremely Rare.	—

Major General George G. Meade at left.

KL#	Fr#	Series	Signatures	Seal	Fine	XF
1016	379d	1891	Rosecrans-Nebeker	Small red	Unknown in private hands	
1017	379c	1891	Tillman-Morgan	Small red	Extremely Rare.	2,100,000.

Federal Reserve Notes

1918

Alexander Hamilton at center. Eagle on flag.

KL#	Fr#	Bank	Signatures	Fine	XF	CH CU (63)	Gem CU (65)
1018	1133	Boston	Burke-Glass	35,000.	—	—	—
1019	1133	New York	Burke-Glass	—	27,600.	—	—
1020	1133	New York	Burke-Houston	17,000.	38,000.	—	—
1022	1133	Philadelphia	Burke-Glass	—	—	45,000.	95,000.
1023	1133	Cleveland	Burke-Glass	—	17,500.	30,000.	95,000.
1024	1133	Richmond	Burke-Glass	Unknown in private hands		—	—
1025	1133	Atlanta	Burke-Glass	11,500.	20,000.	75,000.	—
1026	1133	Atlanta	White-Mellon	—	Rare	—	—
1027	1133	Chicago	Burke-Glass	10,000.	20,000.	—	—
1028	1133	St. Louis	Burke-Glass	17,000.	—	—	—
1029	1133	Minneapolis	Burke-Glass	—	80,000.	—	—
1030	1133	Kansas City	Burke-Glass	—	—	39,000.	45,000.
1031	1133	Dallas	Burke-Glass	—	50,000.	—	—
1032	1133	San Francisco	Burke-Glass	10,000.	35,000.	24,000.	32,500.
1033	1133	San Francisco	White-Mellon	—	—	—	65,000.

Interest Bearing Notes

Five Thousand Dollars

Altar of Liberty vignette at center.

KL#	FR#	Act	Term	Signatures	VG	Fine
1044	202	1863	One year	Chittenden-Spinner	Unknown	—

Justice at left and America at upper center.

KL#	FR#	Act	Term	Signatures	VG	Fine
1045	211	1861	Three years	Chittenden-Spinner	Unknown	—
1045A	211	1865	Three years	Colby-Spinner	Unknown	—

James Madison at left. Large eagle on shield.

KL#	FR#	Act	Term	Signatures	VG	Fine
1045B	188			Scofield-Gilfillan	Unknown	—

Gold Certificates

James Madison at left.

KL#	Fr#	Series	Signatures	Seal	Fine	XF
1046	1166f	First/1863	Colby-Spinner		—	—
1047	1166k	Second/1870	Allison-New		—	—
1048	-	Third/1863/1875	Allison-New		—	—

Other signature varieties were issued in Series 1882 but none are known.

Series 1888 were uniface transfer documents, not intended for general circulation. None are known.

KL#	Fr#	Series	Signatures	Seal	Fine	XF
1059	1221j	1882	Teehee-Burke	Small red	Extremely Rare.	—

Federal Reserve Notes

1918

James Madison at center. Washington Resigning his Commission.

KL#	Fr#	Bank	Signatures	Fine	XF	CH CU (63)
1060	1134	Boston	Burke-Glass	Unknown	—	—
1061	1134	New York	Burke-Glass	Extremely Rare.	—	—
1062	1134	Cleveland	Burke-Glass	Unique	—	—
1063	1134	Richmond	Burke-Glass	Unknown	—	—
1065	1134	Chicago	Burke-Glass	Unique	—	—
1066	1134	St. Louis	Burke-Glass	Unknown	—	—
1067	1134	San Francisco	Burke-Glass	Unique	—	—

Gold Certificates

Ten Thousand Dollars

KL#	Fr#	Series	Signatures	Fine	XF	CH CU (63)	Gem CU (65)
1068	1166g	First/1863	Colby-Spinner		Unknown	—	—
1069	1166l	Second/1870	Allison-New		Unknown	—	—

Andrew Jackson at left. Eagle on flag at right.

KL#	Fr#	Series	Signatures	Fine	XF	CH CU (63)	Gem CU (65)
1079	1225		Lyons-Roberts	1750.	3750.	7000.	8500.
1079A	1225		Lyons-Treat	1750.	3750.	7000.	8500.
1079B	1225		Vernon-Treat	1750.	3750.	7000.	8500.
1079C	1225		Vernon-McClung	1750.	3750.	7000.	8500.
1079D	1225		Napier-McClung	1750.	3750.	7000.	8500.
1079E	1225		Napier-Burke	1750.	3750.	7000.	8500.
1079F	1225		Parker-Burke	1750.	3750.	7000.	8500.

All outstanding 1900 $10,000 Gold Certificates are the result of a 1935 fire in a Treasury storage area in Washington, D.C. While fighting the fire, a quantity of these redeemed and cancelled notes were thrown out into the street, where the scattered notes were picked up by passers-by.

KL#	Fr#	Series	Signatures	Fine	XF	CH CU (63)	Gem CU (65)
1079G	1225		Teehee-Burke	1750.	3750.	7000.	8500.

Andrew Jackson at left.

KL#	Fr#	Series	Signatures	Fine	XF	CH CU (63)	Gem CU (65)
1070	1166q	Third/1863/1875	Allison-New	Unique	—	—	—

Andrew Jackson at left. Eagle on flag at right.

KL#	Fr#	Series	Signatures	Seal	Fine	XF	CH CU (63)
1078	1223g	1882	Teehee-Burke	Small red		Extremely Rare	

Note: Other signature varieties were issued in Series 1882 but, none are known.

Series 1888 were uniface transfer documents, not intended for general circulation.

KL#	Fr#	Series	Signatures	Seal	Fine	XF	CH CU (63)
1078A	1224	1888	Rosecrans-Hyatt	Large red		Unknown	
1078B	1224a	1888	Rosecrans-Nebeker	Small red		Unknown	

Federal Reserve Notes

1918

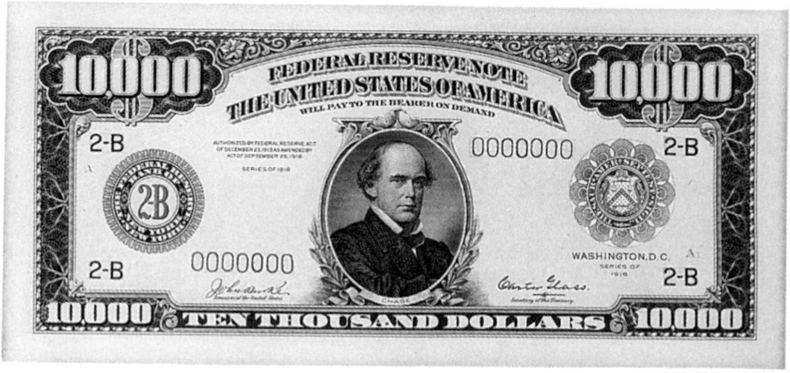

Salmon P. Chase at center. Embarkation of the Pilgrims.

KL#	Fr#	Bank	Signatures	Fine	XF	CH CU (63)
1080	1135	Boston	Burke-Glass	Unknown	—	—
1081	1135	New York	Burke-Glass	Extremely Rare.	—	—
1082	1135	Cleveland	Burke-Glass	Unique	—	—
1083	1135	Richmond	Burke-Glass	Unknown	—	—
1084	1135	St. Louis	Burke-Glass	Unknown	—	—
1085	1135	San Francisco	Burke-Glass	Extremely Rare.	—	—

Small Size Currency

United States Notes

When the switch to the smaller, current size U.S. currency was made in July, 1929, the United States Notes (Legal Tender Notes), bearing red Treasury, seals and serial numbers, were included, although denominations were pared back to only $1, $2, $5 and $100 notes.

The Red Seal $1 is especially popular with collectors in that it was issued only in one series (1928) and in fewer than two million notes. The 1928 $1 Legal Tenders were principally released in Puerto Rico more than 20 years after the notes had been printed. Star notes of the type are especially sought-after and command a strong premium, even in circulated grades.

The small size U.S. Note remained current in the $2 denomination until July, 1965, and in the $5 value until November, 1967. The last issue of Red Seal $100s was in 1968.

The obligation for small size U.S. Notes began in Series 1928 as: "This note is a legal tender at its face value for all debts public and private except duties on imports and interest on the public debt." Under terms of the Act of May 12, 1933, the clause was amended to read: "This note is a legal tender at its face value for all debts public and private." Beginning in Series 1963, it was changed to: "This note is legal tender for all debts, public and private."

Gold Certificates

With the rest of the U.S. currency, the change to smaller notes in 1929 affected the Gold Certificates. Most noticeably, the type lost its distinguishing gold-colored back design as the general configuration of the notes was standardized in all types. The seal and serial numbers continued in gold ink. Among the small size notes, Gold Certificate denominations continued from $10-$10,000, nominally intended for circulation, and even included the $100,000 Gold Certificate of Series 1934, for use in fiscal channels. Like the $100, $1,000 and $10,000 gold notes of Series 1934, the $100,000s were never released to general circulation and may not be legally held by collectors.

Likewise, Series 1928A Gold Certificates were printed in denominations of $10, 20 and $100, though never released.

The small size gold notes were a short series, cut off by the Gold Reserve Act of 1933, which required the surrender of all Gold Certificates (a restriction which was lifted in 1964). For practical purposes the collectibility of the type is thus limited to the Series 1928 notes in the $10, $20, $50 and $100 denominations, which are currently in strong demand in uncirculated condition. Star notes are especially in demand.

Silver Certificates

From the 1929 release date of the small size U.S. currency issues, until Silver Certificate legislation was abolished by a Congressional Act on June 4, 1963, small size Silver Certificates, distinguished by their blue Treasury seal and serial number, were issued in denominations of $1, $5, and $10.

The earliest small size silver notes were redeemable for "One Silver Dollar," (or the appropriate number) as had been the large size issues. A change in the redemption clause, however, was made with the Silver Purchase Act of 1934, which specified the certificates be redeemable for silver dollars or silver bullion. At that time the wording on the notes was changed to read: "One Dollar in Silver." In March, 1964, by order of the Secretary of the Treasury, redemption in silver dollars was halted, and on June 24, 1968, redemption in silver bullion was also discontinued. Like all U.S. currency issued since 1861, Silver Certificates retain their status as legal tender, though today they are convertible only into current U.S. Federal Reserve Notes.

Federal Reserve Notes

Virtually the only type of U.S. paper money encountered in circulation today is the Federal Reserve Note, in denominations of $1-$100. Beginning with the Series 1990 $100 and $50 notes new security features have been added, including a metallic strip and micro-printing. A second printing plant was opened at Fort Worth, Texas in 1990, with the notes identified by a "FW" prefix on the face plate check number. A full redesign of the $5, $10, $20, $50, and $100 notes occured starting in 1995 series with the introduction of the off-centered "big head" notes. With the 2004 series color began to be added to the $10, $20 and $50 notes.

Authorization continued in the small size period for FRNs to be issued in denominations from $5-$10,000. With the demise of the Silver Certificate $1 bill in 1963, that denomination was moved into the FRN realm. The Bicentennial in 1976 led to the re-introduction of the $2 note, which had last been issued as a United States Note in 1966, in the guise of a green-seal Federal Reserve Note.

No Federal Reserve Note of denomination higher than $100 has been printed since 1945, and since 1969 all notes of $500 and higher face value have been actively retired as they are turned into the Federal Reserve System.

Federal Reserve Bank Notes

The small size Federal Reserve Bank Notes were an emergency currency issue authorized March 9, 1933, to inject cash into the economy to combat heavy withdrawals from the Federal Reserve System in the first months of that year.

FRBNs in the small size were printed on currency stock prepared for the regular Series 1929 National Currency. Changes consisted of overprinting several elements. The President (and sometimes Cashier) title at the bottom of the notes was obliterated, and replaced with Governor, and the appropriate signatures of those Federal Reserve Bank officers engraved. There are, however, three exceptions to the Cashier-Governor combination on the small size FRBNs. On the notes of the Chicago bank, the signatures are those of the Assistant Deputy Governor and Governor; for New York, the signature of the Deputy Governor replaces that of the Cashier, and in the St. Louis district, the Controller signed instead of the Cashier.

In the places where the National Bank's charter number would have been imprinted, the proper district letter of the issuing bank appears in heavy black block type. At top of the note, near the obligation, a line was added to read: "or by like deposit of other securities."

Like the regular National Bank Notes of the small size era, the Treasury seal and serial number on the Federal Reserve Bank Notes are in brown ink.

Collector demand for this type has been almost non-existent until recent years. Now, however, the true rarity of some banks and denominations ($5-$100), especially in star notes, is being appreciated.

WWII Emergency Notes

Emergency conditions during World War II brought about several interesting and collectible varieties, of small size U.S. currency.

North African Invasion Notes

When U.S. armed forces hit the beaches of North Africa in 1942 to begin the advance into Axis-held Europe from the south, special currency was issued to the troops which could be easily identified and demonetized in the event of military reverse and the capture of large quantities of the cash.

The notes were normal Silver Certificates, with blue serial numbers, but with Treasury seals printed in yellow. All bearing the Julian-Morgenthau signature combination, the $1 denominations were issued in Series 1935A, the $5s in Series 1934A and $10s in Series 1934 and 1934A. The 1934 $10 notes are quite scarce, especially as star notes.

Hawaii Overprints

As an economic defense precaution against Japanese invasion and occupation of Hawaii, specially marked U.S. currency was issued there in July, 1942, to replace other types in circulation. Distinguished by brown seal and serial numbers, and by "HAWAII" overprints on face and back, such notes could have been declared worthless in the event large numbers of them were captured.

The $1 notes used as emergency currency were Silver Certificates of Series 1935A, while $5s, $10s, and $20s were overprinted examples of San Francisco-district Federal Reserve Notes; the $5s in Series 1934 and '34A, the $10s in Series 1934A only, and the $20s in Series 1934 and '34A. All notes bear the Julian-Morgenthau combination.

By late October, 1944, the emergency monetary conditions were declared ended, and normal currency returned to use in Hawaii, and the Hawaii-overprinted notes went on to do further duty during the occupation of formerly Japanese-held islands in the Pacific.

R & S Experimentals

To test different types of security paper during World War II, when it was not known whether supplies of normal U.S. bank note paper could be maintained, an experimental run of notes was produced using normal, and new special paper.

Notes on the special paper were overprinted with a large red S in the lower right corner, while a control group on regular paper was printed with a large red R in the same location. Exactly 1,184,000 of each type were released to circulation, all Silver Certificates bearing Series 1935A designation and the Julian Morgenthau signature combination. The tests proved to be inconclusive, so no change in bank note paper resulted, but collectors were left with an interesting variety that is especially challenging in uncirculated condition, and truly rare in star note form.

Because unscrupulous persons have applied phony R and S overprints to regular Series 1935A $1 Silver Certificates in an effort to pass them off as the higher-value experimental issue, collectors should be aware of the serial number ranges of the genuine issues. Serial numbers for the genuine R notes run from S70884001C through S72068000C; while those for the S notes are S73884001C through S75068000C.

United States Notes

One Dollar

KL#	Fr#	Series	Signatures	Fine	XF	CH CU (63)	Gem CU (65)
1444	1500	1928	Woods-Woodin	75.00	150.	450.	950.
1444☆	1500	1928☆	Woods-Woodin	5000.	15,000.	—	45,000.

Silver Certificates

KL#	Fr#	Series	Signatures	Fine	XF	CH CU (63)	Gem CU (65)
1445	1600	1928	Tate-Mellon	20.00	35.00	90.00	275.
1445☆	1600	1928☆	Tate-Mellon	75.00	150.	600.	825.
1446	1601	1928A	Woods-Mellon	20.00	30.00	75.00	90.00
1446☆	1601	1928A☆	Woods-Mellon	30.00	100.	500.	675.
1447	1602	1928B	Woods-Mills	20.00	35.00	75.00	100.
1447☆	1602	1928B☆	Woods-Mills	125.	400.	800.	1250.
1448	1603	1928C	Woods-Woodin	200.	400.	775.	1200.
1448☆	1603	1928C☆	Woods-Woodin	3000.	8000.	25,000.	45,000.
1449	1604	1928D	Julian-Woodin	85.00	200.	500.	900.
1449☆	1604	1928D☆	Julian-Woodin	4500.	9000.	18,000.	31,000.
1450	1605	1928E	Julian-Morgenthau	400.	1000.	2000.	2500.
1450☆	1605	1928E☆	Julian-Morgenthau	8000.	12,750.	35,000.	50,000.
1451	1606	1934	Julian-Morgenthau	30.00	60.00	125.	175.
1451☆	1606	1934☆	Julian-Morgenthau	75.00	250.	1000.	1500.

KL#	Fr#	Series	Signatures	Fine	XF	CH CU (63)	Gem CU (65)
1452	1607	1935	Julian-Morgenthau	8.00	15.00	50.00	75.00
1452☆	1607	1935☆	Julian-Morgenthau	50.00	150.	400.	500.
1453	1608	1935A	Julian-Morgenthau	3.00	5.00	18.00	30.00
1453☆	1608	1935A☆	Julian-Morgenthau	3.00	18.00	75.00	115.
1454	1611	1935B	Julian-Vinson	3.00	5.00	20.00	30.00
1454☆	1611	1935B☆	Julian-Vinson	3.00	75.00	275.	400.
1455	1612	1935C	Julian-Snyder	2.00	4.00	18.00	30.00
1455☆	1612	1935C☆	Julian-Snyder	3.00	35.00	65.00	115.
			Wide back, 4 digit plate #5015 or less				
1456	1613	1935D	Clark-Snyder	2.00	5.00	20.00	25.00
			Wide back, 4 digit plate #5015 or less				
1456☆	1613	1935D☆	Clark-Snyder	3.00	25.00	50.00	75.00
			Narrow back, 4 digit plate #5017 or greater				
1456A	1613	1935D	Clark-Snyder	2.50	5.00	15.00	20.00
			Narrow back, 4 digit plate #5017 or greater				
1456A☆	1613	1935D☆	Clark-Snyder	3.00	35.00	75.00	90.00
1457	1614	1935E	Priest-Humphrey	2.50	4.00	15.00	18.00
1457☆	1614	1935E☆	Priest-Humphrey	3.00	10.00	25.00	35.00
1458	1615	1935F	Priest-Anderson	2.50	4.00	15.00	18.00
1458☆	1615	1935F☆	Priest-Anderson	2.50	10.00	35.00	50.00
1459	1616	1935G	Smith-Dillon	2.50	5.00	15.00	20.00
1459☆	1616	1935G☆	Smith-Dillon	3.00	20.00	50.00	60.00
1460	1617	1935G	Smith-Dillon	2.50	7.00	60.00	70.00
1460☆	1617	1935G☆	Smith-Dillon	3.00	35.00	250.	325.
1461	1618	1935H	Granahan-Dillon	2.50	5.00	25.00	50.00
1461☆	1618	1935H☆	Granahan-Dillon	3.00	10.00	45.00	90.00

KL#	Fr#	Series	Signatures	Fine	XF	CH CU (63)	Gem CU (65)
1462	1619	1957	Priest-Anderson	2.50	4.00	10.00	15.00
1462☆	1619	1957☆	Priest-Anderson	3.00	8.00	14.00	16.00
1463	1620	1957A	Smith-Dillon	2.50	4.00	12.00	15.00
1463☆	1620	1957A☆	Smith-Dillon	3.00	6.00	15.00	17.00
1464	1621	1957B	Granahan-Dillon	2.50	4.00	12.00	15.00
1464☆	1621	1957B☆	Granahan-Dillon	3.00	6.00	15.00	17.00

Federal Reserve Notes

Series 1963 Granahan-Dillon

KL#	Fr#		District	Fine	XF	CH CU (63)	Gem CU (65)
1465	1900A		Boston	FV	3.00	9.00	11.00
1465☆	1900A	☆	Boston	FV	4.00	8.00	10.00
1466	1900B		New York	FV	2.00	8.00	10.00
1466☆	1900B	☆	New York	FV	3.00	9.00	11.00
1467	1900C		Philadelphia	FV	2.00	6.00	8.00
1467☆	1900C	☆	Philadelphia	FV	3.00	9.00	11.00
1468	1900D		Cleveland	FV	2.00	7.00	9.00
1468☆	1900D	☆	Cleveland	FV	3.00	8.00	10.00
1469	1900E		Richmond	FV	3.00	8.00	10.00
1469☆	1900E	☆	Richmond	FV	3.00	10.00	12.00
1470	1900F		Atlanta	FV	3.00	8.00	10.00
1470☆	1900F	☆	Atlanta	FV	3.00	10.00	12.00
1471	1900G		Chicago	FV	2.00	7.00	9.00
1471☆	1900G	☆	Chicago	FV	3.00	10.00	12.00
1472	1900H		St. Louis	FV	2.00	8.00	10.00
1472☆	1900H	☆	St. Louis	FV	3.00	10.00	12.00
1473	1900I		Minneapolis	FV	2.00	6.00	8.00
1473☆	1900I	☆	Minneapolis	FV	3.00	12.00	15.00
1474	1900J		Kansas City	FV	2.00	8.00	10.00
1474☆	1900J	☆	Kansas City	FV	3.00	10.00	12.00
1475	1900K		Dallas	FV	2.00	8.00	10.00
1475☆	1900K	☆	Dallas	FV	3.00	12.00	11.00
1476	1900L		San Francisco	FV	2.00	7.00	8.00
1476☆	1900L	☆	San Francisco	2.00	10.00	35.00	43.00

Series 1963A Granahan-Fowler

KL#	Fr#		District	Fine	XF	CH CU (63)	Gem CU (65)
1477	1901A		Boston	FV	2.00	7.00	9.00
1477☆	1901A	☆	Boston	FV	3.00	10.00	12.00
1478	1901B		New York	FV	2.00	7.00	9.00
1478☆	1901B	☆	New York	FV	3.00	10.00	12.00

KL#	Fr#		District	Fine	XF	CH CU (63)	Gem CU (65)
1479	1901C		Philadelphia	FV	2.00	7.00	9.00
1479☆	1901C	☆	Philadelphia	FV	3.00	10.00	12.00
1480	1901D		Cleveland	FV	2.00	7.00	9.00
1480☆	1901D	☆	Cleveland	FV	3.00	10.00	12.00
1481	1901E		Richmond	FV	2.00	7.00	9.00
1481☆	1901E	☆	Richmond	FV	3.00	10.00	12.00
1482	1901F		Atlanta	FV	2.00	7.00	9.00
1482☆	1901F	☆	Atlanta	FV	3.00	10.00	125.
1483	1901G		Chicago	FV	2.00	7.00	9.00
1483☆	1901G	☆	Chicago	FV	3.00	10.00	12.00
1484	1901H		St. Louis	FV	2.00	7.00	9.00
1484☆	1901H	☆	St. Louis	FV	3.00	10.00	12.00
1485	1901I		Minneapolis	FV	2.00	7.00	9.00
1485☆	1901I	☆	Minneapolis	FV	4.00	12.00	15.00
1486	1901J		Kansas City	FV	2.00	8.00	10.00
1486☆	1901J	☆	Kansas City	FV	3.00	10.00	12.00
1487	1901K		Dallas	FV	2.00	8.00	10.00
1487☆	1901K	☆	Dallas	FV	3.00	12.00	15.00
1488	1901L		San Francisco	FV	2.00	8.00	10.00
1488☆	1901L	☆	San Francisco	FV	3.00	10.00	12.00

Series 1963B Granahan-Barr

KL#	Fr#		District	Fine	XF	CH CU (63)	Gem CU (65)
1490	1902B		New York	FV	2.00	10.00	10.00
1490☆	1902B	☆	New York	FV	5.00	17.00	20.00
1493	1902E		Richmond	FV	2.00	8.00	10.00
1493☆	1902E	☆	Richmond	FV	5.00	17.00	20.00
1495	1902G		Chicago	FV	2.00	8.00	10.00
1495☆	1902G	☆	Chicago	FV	5.00	17.00	20.00
1498	1902J		Kansas City	FV	2.00	8.00	10.00
1500	1902L		San Francisco	FV	2.00	8.00	10.00
1500☆	1902L	☆	San Francisco	FV	5.00	17.00	20.00

Series 1969 Elston-Kennedy

KL#	Fr#		District	Fine	XF	CH CU (63)	Gem CU (65)
1501	1903A		Boston	FV	2.00	6.00	8.00
1501☆	1903A	☆	Boston	FV	2.00	10.00	12.00
1502	1903B		New York	FV	2.00	6.00	8.00
1502☆	1903B	☆	New York	FV	3.00	10.00	12.00
1503	1903C		Philadelphia	FV	2.00	6.00	8.00
1503☆	1903C	☆	Philadelphia	FV	3.00	10.00	12.00
1504	1903D		Cleveland	FV	2.00	6.00	8.00
1504☆	1903D	☆	Cleveland	FV	3.00	10.00	12.00
1505	1903E		Richmond	FV	2.00	6.00	8.00
1505☆	1903E	☆	Richmond	FV	4.00	10.00	12.00
1506	1903F		Atlanta	FV	2.00	6.00	8.00
1506☆	1903F	☆	Atlanta	FV	3.00	10.00	12.00
1507	1903G		Chicago	FV	2.00	6.00	8.00
1507☆	1903G	☆	Chicago	FV	3.00	10.00	12.00
1508	1903H		St. Louis	FV	FV	6.00	8.00
1508☆	1903H	☆	St. Louis	FV	3.00	10.00	12.00
1509	1903I		Minneapolis	FV	FV	6.00	8.00
1509☆	1903I	☆	Minneapolis	2.00	10.00	25.00	30.00
1510	1903J		Kansas City	FV	2.00	6.00	8.00
1510☆	1903J	☆	Kansas City	FV	3.00	10.00	12.00
1511	1903K		Dallas	FV	2.00	6.00	8.00
1511☆	1903K	☆	Dallas	FV	3.00	10.00	12.00
1512	1903L		San Francisco	FV	2.00	6.00	8.00
1512☆	1903L	☆	San Francisco	FV	3.00	10.00	12.00

Series 1969A Kabis-Kennedy

KL#	Fr#		District	Fine	XF	CH CU (63)	Gem CU (65)
1513	1904A		Boston	FV	2.00	6.00	8.00
1513☆	1904A	☆	Boston	FV	5.00	10.00	12.00
1514	1904B		New York	FV	2.00	6.00	8.00
1514☆	1904B	☆	New York	FV	5.00	10.00	12.00
1515	1904C		Philadelphia	FV	2.00	6.00	8.00
1515☆	1904C	☆	Philadelphia	FV	3.00	10.00	12.00
1516	1904D		Cleveland	FV	2.00	6.00	8.00
1516☆	1904D	☆	Cleveland	FV	3.00	10.00	12.00
1517	1904E		Richmond	FV	2.00	6.00	8.00
1517☆	1904E	☆	Richmond	FV	3.00	10.00	12.00
1518	1904F		Atlanta	FV	2.00	6.00	8.00
1518☆	1904F	☆	Atlanta	FV	3.00	10.00	12.00
1519	1904G		Chicago	FV	2.00	6.00	8.00
1519☆	1904G	☆	Chicago	FV	4.00	10.00	12.00
1520	1904H		St. Louis	FV	2.00	6.00	8.00
1520☆	1904H	☆	St. Louis	FV	3.00	10.00	12.00
1521	1904I		Minneapolis	FV	2.00	6.00	8.00
1521☆	1904I	☆	Minneapolis	2.00	10.00	35.00	40.00
1522	1904J		Kansas City	FV	2.00	6.00	8.00
1522☆	1904J	☆	Kansas City	FV	3.00	15.00	20.00
1523	1904K		Dallas	FV	2.00	15.00	20.00
1524	1904L		San Francisco	FV	2.00	6.00	8.00
1524☆	1904L	☆	San Francisco	FV	3.00	10.00	12.00

Series 1969B Kabis-Connally

KL#	Fr#		District	Fine	XF	CH CU (63)	Gem CU (65)
1525	1905A		Boston	FV	2.00	6.00	8.00
1525☆	1905A	☆	Boston	FV	3.00	10.00	12.00
1526	1905B		New York	FV	2.00	6.00	8.00
1526☆	1905B	☆	New York	FV	3.00	10.00	12.00
1527	1905C		Philadelphia	FV	2.00	6.00	8.00
1527☆	1905C	☆	Philadelphia	FV	3.00	10.00	12.00
1528	1905D		Cleveland	FV	2.00	6.00	8.00
1528☆	1905D	☆	Cleveland	FV	3.00	10.00	12.00
1529	1905E		Richmond	FV	2.00	6.00	8.00
1529☆	1905E	☆	Richmond	FV	3.00	10.00	12.00
1530	1905F		Atlanta	FV	2.00	6.00	8.00
1530☆	1905F	☆	Atlanta	FV	3.00	10.00	12.00
1531	1905G		Chicago	FV	2.00	6.00	8.00
1531☆	1905G	☆	Chicago	FV	3.00	10.00	12.00
1532	1905H		St. Louis	FV	2.00	6.00	8.00
1532☆	1905H	☆	St. Louis	FV	3.00	10.00	12.00
1533	1905I		Minneapolis	FV	2.00	6.00	8.00
1533☆	1905I	☆	Minneapolis	5.00	15.00	35.00	40.00
1534	1905J		Kansas City	FV	2.00	6.00	8.00

KL#	Fr#		District	Fine	XF	CH CU (63)	Gem CU (65)
1534☆	1905J	☆	Kansas City	FV	3.00	10.00	12.00
1535	1905K		Dallas	FV	2.00	6.00	8.00
1535☆	1905K	☆	Dallas	FV	3.00	10.00	12.00
1536	1905L		San Francisco	FV	2.00	6.00	8.00
1536☆	1905L	☆	San Francisco	FV	3.00	10.00	12.00

Series 1969C Banuelos-Connally

KL#	Fr#		District	Fine	XF	CH CU (63)	Gem CU (65)
1538	1906B		New York	FV	2.00	7.00	9.00
1540	1906D		Cleveland	FV	2.00	7.00	9.00
1540☆	1906D	☆	Cleveland	5.00	15.00	50.00	60.00
1541	1906E		Richmond	FV	2.00	7.00	9.00
1541☆	1906E	☆	Richmond	3.00	20.00	60.00	75.00
1542	1906F		Atlanta	FV	2.00	7.00	9.00
1542☆	1906F	☆	Atlanta	2.00	10.00	25.00	30.00
1543	1906G		Chicago	FV	2.00	7.00	9.00
1543☆	1906G	☆	Chicago	2.00	10.00	25.00	30.00
1544	1906H		St. Louis	FV	2.00	7.00	9.00
1544☆	1906H	☆	St. Louis	3.00	10.00	25.00	30.00
1545	1906I		Minneapolis	FV	2.00	7.00	9.00
1545☆	1906I	☆	Minneapolis	10.00	20.00	40.00	50.00
1546	1906J		Kansas City	FV	2.00	7.00	9.00
1546☆	1906J	☆	Kansas City	2.00	10.00	25.00	30.00
1547	1906K		Dallas	FV	2.00	7.00	9.00
1547☆	1906K	☆	Dallas	5.00	15.00	50.00	60.00
1548	1906L		San Francisco	FV	2.00	7.00	9.00
1548☆	1906L	☆	San Francisco	50.00	120.	225.	300.

Series 1969D Banuelos-Shultz

KL#	Fr#		District	Fine	XF	CH CU (63)	Gem CU (65)
1561	1907A		Boston	FV	2.00	7.00	9.00
1561☆	1907A	☆	Boston	2.00	10.00	25.00	30.00
1562	1907B		New York	FV	2.00	7.00	9.00
1562☆	1907B	☆	New York	FV	5.00	12.00	15.00
1563	1907C		Philadelphia	FV	2.00	7.00	9.00
1563☆	1907C	☆	Philadelphia	FV	5.00	12.00	15.00
1564	1907D		Cleveland	FV	3.00	7.00	9.00
1564☆	1907D	☆	Cleveland	FV	4.00	12.00	15.00
1565	1907E		Richmond	FV	2.00	7.00	9.00
1565☆	1907E	☆	Richmond	FV	5.00	12.00	15.00
1566	1907F		Atlanta	FV	2.00	7.00	9.00
1566☆	1907F	☆	Atlanta	FV	5.00	12.00	15.00
1567	1907G		Chicago	FV	2.00	7.00	9.00
1567☆	1907G	☆	Chicago	FV	5.00	12.00	15.00
1568	1907H		St. Louis	FV	2.00	7.00	9.00
1568☆	1907H	☆	St. Louis	FV	5.00	12.00	15.00
1569	1907I		Minneapolis	FV	2.00	7.00	9.00
1570	1907J		Kansas City	FV	2.00	7.00	9.00
1570☆	1907J	☆	Kansas City	FV	5.00	12.00	15.00
1571	1907K		Dallas	FV	2.00	7.00	9.00
1571☆	1907K	☆	Dallas	FV	5.00	12.00	15.00
1572	1907L		San Francisco	FV	2.00	7.00	9.00
1572☆	1907L	☆	San Francisco	FV	5.00	12.00	15.00

Series 1974 Neff-Simon

KL#	Fr#		District	Fine	XF	CH CU (63)	Gem CU (65)
1573	1908A		Boston	FV	2.00	6.00	8.00
1573☆	1908A	☆	Boston	FV	3.00	10.00	12.00
1574	1908B		New York	FV	2.00	6.00	8.00
1574☆	1908B	☆	New York	FV	3.00	10.00	12.00
1575	1908C		Philadelphia	FV	2.00	6.00	8.00
1575☆	1908C	☆	Philadelphia	FV	3.00	10.00	12.00
1576	1908D		Cleveland	FV	2.00	6.00	8.00
1576☆	1908D	☆	Cleveland	FV	7.00	30.00	40.00
1577	1908E		Richmond	FV	2.00	6.00	8.00
1577☆	1908E	☆	Richmond	FV	5.00	10.00	12.00
1578	1908F		Atlanta	FV	2.00	6.00	8.00
1578☆	1908F	☆	Atlanta	FV	3.00	10.00	12.00
1579	1908G		Chicago	FV	2.00	6.00	8.00
1579☆	1908G	☆	Chicago	FV	3.00	10.00	12.00
1580	1908H		St. Louis	FV	2.00	6.00	8.00
1580☆	1908H	☆	St. Louis	FV	3.00	10.00	12.00
1581	1908I		Minneapolis	FV	2.00	6.00	8.00
1581☆	1908I	☆	Minneapolis	FV	15.00	45.00	55.00
1582	1908J		Kansas City	FV	2.00	6.00	8.00
1582☆	1908J	☆	Kansas City	FV	3.00	10.00	12.00
1583	1908K		Dallas	FV	2.00	6.00	8.00
1583☆	1908K	☆	Dallas	FV	2.00	10.00	12.00
1584	1908L		San Francisco	FV	2.00	6.00	8.00
1584☆	1908L	☆	San Francisco	FV	3.00	10.00	12.00

Series 1977 Morton-Blumenthal

KL#	Fr#		District	Fine	XF	CH CU (63)	Gem CU (65)
1585	1909A		Boston	FV	2.00	6.00	8.00
1585☆	1909A	☆	Boston	FV	3.00	10.00	12.00
1586	1909B		New York	FV	2.00	6.00	8.00
1586☆	1909B	☆	New York	FV	3.00	10.00	12.00
1587	1909C		Philadelphia	FV	2.00	6.00	8.00
1587☆	1909C	☆	Philadelphia	FV	3.00	10.00	12.00
1588	1909D		Cleveland	FV	2.00	6.00	8.00
1588☆	1909D	☆	Cleveland	FV	3.00	10.00	12.00
1589	1909E		Richmond	FV	2.00	6.00	8.00
1589☆	1909E	☆	Richmond	FV	3.00	10.00	12.00
1590	1909F		Atlanta	FV	2.00	6.00	8.00
1590☆	1909F	☆	Atlanta	FV	3.00	10.00	12.00
1591	1909G		Chicago	FV	2.00	6.00	8.00
1591☆	1909G	☆	Chicago	FV	3.00	10.00	12.00
1592	1909H		St. Louis	FV	2.00	6.00	8.00
1592☆	1909H	☆	St. Louis	FV	3.00	10.00	12.00
1593	1909I		Minneapolis	FV	2.00	6.00	8.00
1593☆	1909I	☆	Minneapolis	FV	3.00	10.00	12.00

KL#	Fr#		District	Fine	XF	CH CU (63)	Gem CU (65)
1594	1909J		Kansas City	FV	2.00	6.00	8.00
1594☆	1909J	☆	Kansas City	FV	3.00	10.00	12.00
1595	1909K		Dallas	FV	2.00	6.00	8.00
1595☆	1909K	☆	Dallas	FV	3.00	10.00	12.00
1596	1909L		San Francisco	FV	2.00	6.00	8.00
1596☆	1909L	☆	San Francisco	FV	3.00	10.00	12.00

Series 1977A Morton-Miller

KL#	Fr#		District	Fine	XF	CH CU (63)	Gem CU (65)
1597	1910A		Boston	FV	2.00	6.00	8.00
1597☆	1910A	☆	Boston	FV	5.00	30.00	40.00
1598	1910B		New York	FV	2.00	6.00	8.00
1598☆	1910B	☆	New York	FV	3.00	10.00	12.00
1599	1910C		Philadelphia	FV	2.00	6.00	8.00
1599☆	1910C	☆	Philadelphia	FV	3.00	10.00	12.00
1600	1910D		Cleveland	FV	2.00	6.00	8.00
1600☆	1910D	☆	Cleveland	FV	3.00	10.00	12.00
1601	1910E		Richmond	FV	2.00	6.00	8.00
1601☆	1910E	☆	Richmond	FV	3.00	10.00	12.00
1602	1910F		Atlanta	FV	2.00	6.00	8.00
1602☆	1910F	☆	Atlanta	FV	3.00	10.00	12.00
1603	1910G		Chicago	FV	2.00	6.00	8.00
1603☆	1910G	☆	Chicago	FV	3.00	10.00	12.00
1604	1910H		St. Louis	FV	2.00	6.00	8.00
1604☆	1910H	☆	St. Louis	FV	3.00	10.00	12.00
1605	1910I		Minneapolis	FV	2.00	6.00	8.00
1605☆	1910I	☆	Minneapolis	FV	6.00	10.00	12.00
1606	1910J		Kansas City	FV	2.00	6.00	8.00
1606☆	1910J	☆	Kansas City		3.00	8.00	10.00
1607	1910K		Dallas	FV	2.00	6.00	8.00
1607☆	1910K	☆	Dallas	FV	3.00	10.00	12.00
1608	1910L		San Francisco	FV	2.00	6.00	8.00
1608☆	1910L	☆	San Francisco	FV	3.00	10.00	12.00

Series 1981 Buchanan-Regan

KL#	Fr#		District	Fine	XF	CH CU (63)	Gem CU (65)
3500	1911A		Boston	FV	2.00	6.00	8.00
3500☆	1911A	☆	Boston	FV	5.00	15.00	18.00
3501	1911B		New York	FV	2.00	6.00	8.00
3501☆	1911B	☆	New York	FV	5.00	12.00	15.00
3502	1911C		Philadelphia	FV	2.00	6.00	8.00
3502☆	1911C	☆	Philadelphia	FV	5.00	12.00	15.00
3503	1911D		Cleveland	FV	2.00	6.00	8.00
3503☆	1911D	☆	Cleveland	FV	4.00	12.00	15.00
3504	1911E		Richmond	FV	2.00	6.00	8.00
3504☆	1911E	☆	Richmond	FV	4.00	20.00	25.00
3505	1911F		Atlanta	FV	2.00	6.00	8.00

KL#	Fr#		District	Fine	XF	CH CU (63)	Gem CU (65)
3505☆	1911F	☆	Atlanta	FV	4.00	20.00	25.00
3506	1911G		Chicago	FV	2.00	6.00	8.00
3506☆	1911G	☆	Chicago	FV	4.00	20.00	25.00
3507	1911H		St. Louis	FV	2.00	6.00	8.00
3507☆	1911H	☆	St. Louis	FV	4.00	12.00	15.00
3508	1911I		Minneapolis	FV	2.00	6.00	8.00
3508☆	1911I	☆	Minneapolis	FV	4.00	12.00	15.00
3509	1911J		Kansas City	FV	2.00	6.00	8.00
3509☆	1911J	☆	Kansas City	FV	5.00	12.00	15.00
3510	1911K		Dallas	FV	2.00	6.00	8.00
3510☆	1911K	☆	Dallas	FV	4.00	20.00	25.00
3511	1911L		San Francisco	FV	2.00	6.00	8.00
3511☆	1911L	☆	San Francisco	FV	4.00	12.00	15.00

Series 1981A Ortega-Regan

KL#	Fr#		District	Fine	XF	CH CU (63)	Gem CU (65)
3600	1912A		Boston	FV	2.00	6.00	8.00
3601	1912B		New York	FV	2.00	6.00	8.00
3601☆	1912B	☆	New York	FV	5.00	20.00	25.00
3602	1912C		Philadelphia	FV	2.00	6.00	8.00

Back plate #129 at left.

KL#	Fr#		District	Fine	XF	CH CU (63)	Gem CU (65)
3602A	-		Philadelphia	FV	2.00	8.00	12.00
3603	1912D		Cleveland	FV	2.00	6.00	8.00
3604	1912E		Richmond	FV	2.00	6.00	8.00
3604☆	1912E	☆	Richmond	FV	5.00	20.00	25.00
3605	1912F		Atlanta	FV	2.00	6.00	8.00

Back plate #129 at left.

KL#	Fr#		District	Fine	XF	CH CU (63)	Gem CU (65)
3605A	-		Atlanta	FV	2.00	6.00	8.00
3606	1912G		Chicago	FV	2.00	6.00	8.00
3606☆	1912G	☆	Chicago	FV	5.00	20.00	25.00
3607	1912H		St. Louis	FV	2.00	6.00	8.00

Back plate #129 at left.

KL#	Fr#		District	Fine	XF	CH CU (63)	Gem CU (65)
3607A	-		St. Louis	FV	2.00	6.00	8.00
3608	1912I		Minneapolis	FV	2.00	6.00	8.00

Back plate #129 at left.

KL#	Fr#		District	Fine	XF	CH CU (63)	Gem CU (65)
3608A	-		Minneapolis	FV	2.00	6.00	8.00
3609	1912J		Kansas City	FV	2.00	6.00	8.00
3610	1912K		Dallas	FV	2.00	6.00	8.00
3610☆	1912K	☆	Dallas	250.	400.	1500.	2000.
3611	1912L		San Francisco	FV	2.00	6.00	8.00
3611☆	1912L	☆	San Francisco	FV	5.00	20.00	25.00

Back plate #129 at left.

KL#	Fr#		District	Fine	XF	CH CU (63)	Gem CU (65)
3611A	-		San Francisco	FV	2.00	6.00	8.00

Series 1985 Ortega-Baker

KL#	Fr#	District	Fine	XF	CH CU (63)	Gem CU (65)
3700	1913A	Boston	FV	FV	6.00	9.00

Back plate #129 at left.

KL#	Fr#	District	Fine	XF	CH CU (63)	Gem CU (65)
3700A	-	Boston	FV	FV	6.00	9.00
3701	1913B	New York	FV	FV	6.00	8.00

Back plate #129 at left.

KL#	Fr#		District	Fine	XF	CH CU (63)	Gem CU (65)
3701A	-		New York	FV	FV	6.00	8.00
3702	1913C		Philadelphia	FV	FV	6.00	8.00
3703	1913D		Cleveland	FV	FV	6.00	8.00
			Back plate #129 at left.				
3703A	-		Cleveland	FV	FV	6.00	8.00
3704	1913E		Richmond	FV	FV	6.00	8.00
3704☆	1913E	☆	Richmond	FV	FV	15.00	20.00
			Back plate #129 at left.				
3704A	-		Richmond	FV	FV	6.00	8.00
3705	1913F		Atlanta	FV	FV	6.00	8.00
			Back plate #129 at left.				
3705A	-		Atlanta	FV	FV	6.00	8.00
3706	1913G		Chicago	FV	FV	6.00	8.00
3706☆	1913G	☆	Chicago	200.	750.	1750.	2000.
			Back plate #129 at left.				
3706A	-		Chicago	FV	FV	6.00	8.00
3707	1913H		St. Louis	FV	FV	6.00	8.00
			Back plate #129 at left.				
3707☆	1913H	☆	St. Louis	FV	FV	15.00	20.00
3707A	-		St. Louis	FV	FV	6.00	8.00
3708	1913I		Minneapolis	FV	FV	6.00	8.00
3708☆	1913I	☆	Minneapolis	FV	2.00	15.00	20.00
3709	1913J		Kansas City	FV	FV	6.00	8.00
3710	1913K		Dallas	FV	FV	6.00	8.00
3710☆	1913K	☆	Dallas	FV	2.00	15.00	20.00
3711	1913L		San Francisco	FV	FV	6.00	8.00
3711☆	1913L	☆	San Francisco	FV	2.00	15.00	20.00
			Back plate #129 at left.				
3711A	-		San Francisco	FV	FV	6.00	8.00

Series 1988 Ortega-Brady

KL#	Fr#		District	Fine	XF	CH CU (63)	Gem CU (65)
3772	1914A		Boston	FV	2.00	9.00	11.00
3772☆	1914A	☆	Boston	FV	5.00	30.00	40.00
3773	1914B		New York	FV	2.00	9.00	11.00
3773☆	1914B	☆	New York	FV	5.00	20.00	25.00
3774	1914C		Philadelphia	FV	2.00	9.00	11.00
3775	1914D		Cleveland	FV	2.00	9.00	11.00
3776	1914E		Richmond	FV	2.00	9.00	11.00
3776☆	1914E	☆	Richmond	FV	5.00	20.00	25.00
3777	1914F		Atlanta	FV	2.00	9.00	11.00
3777☆	1914F	☆	Atlanta	250.	700.	1750.	2000.
3778	1914G		Chicago	FV	2.00	9.00	11.00
3779	1914H		St. Louis	FV	2.00	9.00	11.00
3780	1914I		Minneapolis	FV	2.00	9.00	11.00
3781	1914J		Kansas City	FV	2.00	9.00	11.00
3781☆	1914J	☆	Kansas City	FV	5.00	20.00	25.00
3782	1914K		Dallas	FV	2.00	9.00	11.00
3782☆	1914K	☆	Dallas	FV	5.00	45.00	55.00
3783	1914L		San Francisco	FV	2.00	9.00	11.00
3783☆	1914L	☆	San Francisco	FV	5.00	20.00	25.00

Series 1988A Villalpando-Brady - DC

KL#	Fr#	District	Fine	XF	CH CU (63)	Gem CU (65)
3844	1915A	Boston	FV	2.00	6.00	8.00
3845	1915B	New York	FV	2.00	6.00	8.00
3845☆	1915B ☆	New York	FV	3.00	10.00	12.00
3846	1915C	Philadelphia	FV	2.00	6.00	8.00
3847	1915D	Cleveland	FV	2.00	6.00	8.00
3847☆	1915D ☆	Cleveland	FV	4.00	10.00	12.00
3848	1915E	Richmond	FV	2.00	6.00	8.00
3848☆	1915E ☆	Richmond	FV	3.00	10.00	12.00
3849	1915F	Atlanta	FV	2.00	6.00	8.00
3849☆	1915F ☆	Atlanta	FV	3.00	10.00	12.00
3850	1915G	Chicago	FV	2.00	6.00	8.00
3850☆	1915G ☆	Chicago	FV	3.00	15.00	20.00
3851	1915H	St. Louis	FV	2.00	6.00	8.00
3851☆	1915H ☆	St. Louis	FV	2.00	10.00	12.00
3852	1915I	Minneapolis	FV	2.00	6.00	8.00
3852☆	1915I ☆	Minneapolis	FV	4.00	10.00	12.00
3853	1915J	Kansas City	FV	2.00	6.00	8.00
3854	1915K	Dallas	FV	2.00	6.00	8.00
3854☆	1915K ☆	Dallas	FV	4.00	20.00	25.00
3855	1915L	San Francisco	FV	2.00	6.00	8.00
3855☆	1915L ☆	San Francisco	FV	4.00	20.00	25.00
3861	1916F	Atlanta	FV	2.00	6.00	8.00
3862	1916G	Chicago	FV	2.00	6.00	8.00
3862☆	1916G ☆	Chicago	FV	4.00	20.00	25.00
3863	1916H	St. Louis	FV	2.00	6.00	8.00
3864	1916I	Minneapolis	FV	2.00	6.00	8.00
3865	1916J	Kansas City	FV	2.00	6.00	8.00
3866	1916K	Dallas	FV	2.00	6.00	8.00
3867	1916L	San Francisco	FV	2.00	6.00	8.00
3867☆	1916L ☆	San Francisco	FV	4.00	10.00	12.00

Series 1993 Withrow-Bentsen - DC

KL#	Fr#	District	Fine	XF	CH CU (63)	Gem CU (65)
4012	1918A	Boston	FV	2.00	6.00	8.00
4013	1918B	New York	FV	2.00	6.00	8.00
4013☆	1918B ☆	New York	FV	2.00	10.00	12.00
4014	1918C	Philadelphia	FV	2.00	6.00	8.00
4014☆	1918C ☆	Philadelphia	25.00	75.00	250.	300.
4015	1918D	Cleveland	FV	2.00	6.00	8.00
4016	1918E	Richmond	FV	2.00	6.00	8.00
4017	1918F	Atlanta	FV	2.00	6.00	8.00
4017☆	1918F ☆	Atlanta	FV	2.00	10.00	12.00
4018	1918G	Chicago	FV	2.00	6.00	8.00
4023	1918L	San Francisco	FV	2.00	6.00	8.00
4023A	1916G	Chicago	FV	2.00	6.00	8.00

KL#	Fr#		District	Fine	XF	CH CU (63)	Gem CU (65)
4023A☆	1916G	☆	Chicago	FV	2.00	10.00	12.00
4023B	1919H		St. Louis	FV	2.00	6.00	8.00
4023C	1919I		Minneapolis	FV	2.00	6.00	8.00
4023D	1919K		Dallas	FV	2.00	6.00	8.00
4023D☆	1919K	☆	Dallas	FV	4.00	10.00	12.00
4023E	1919L		San Francisco	FV	2.00	6.00	8.00

Series 1995 Withrow-Rubin - DC

KL#	Fr#		District	Fine	XF	CH CU (63)	Gem CU (65)
4235	1921A		Boston	FV	FV	4.00	5.00
4235☆	1921A	☆	Boston	FV	2.00	6.00	7.00
4236	1921B		New York	FV	FV	4.00	5.00
4236☆	1921B	☆	New York	FV	2.00	12.00	15.00
4237	1921C		Philadelphia	FV	FV	4.00	5.00
4237☆	1921C	☆	Philadelphia	FV	2.00	6.00	7.00
4238	1921D		Cleveland	FV	FV	4.00	5.00
4238☆	1921D	☆	Cleveland	FV	2.00	6.00	7.00
4239	1921E		Richmond	FV	FV	4.00	5.00
4239☆	1921E	☆	Richmond	FV	2.00	6.00	7.00
4240	1921F		Atlanta	FV	FV	4.00	5.00
4240☆	1921F	☆	Atlanta	FV	2.00	6.00	7.00
4241	1921G		Chicago	FV	FV	4.00	5.00
4242	1921I		Minneapolis	FV	FV	4.00	5.00
4243	1921J		Kansas City	FV	FV	4.00	5.00
4244	1921L		San Francisco	FV	FV	4.00	5.00
4245	1922D		Cleveland	FV	FV	4.00	5.00
4246	1922F		Atlanta	FV	FV	4.00	5.00
4246☆	1922F	☆	Atlanta	FV	FV	7.00	9.00
4247	1922G		Chicago	FV	FV	4.00	5.00
4247☆	1922G	☆	Chicago	FV	2.00	6.00	7.00
4248	1922H		St. Louis	FV	FV	4.00	5.00
4249	1922I		Minneapolis	FV	FV	4.00	5.00
4249☆	1922I	☆	Minneapolis	FV	2.00	6.00	7.00
4250	1922J		Kansas City	FV	FV	4.00	5.00
4250☆	1922J	☆	Kansas City	FV	2.00	6.00	7.00
4251	1922K		Dallas	FV	FV	4.00	5.00
4251☆	1922K	☆	Dallas	FV	10.00	35.00	50.00
4252	1922L		San Francisco	FV	FV	4.00	5.00
4252☆	1922L	☆	San Francisco	FV	2.00	6.00	7.00

Series 1999 Withrow-Summers - DC

KL#	Fr#		District	Fine	XF	CH CU (63)	Gem CU (65)
4500	1924A		Boston	FV	FV	3.00	4.00
4500☆	1924A	☆	Boston	FV	2.00	6.00	7.00
4501	1924B		New York	FV	FV	3.00	4.00
4501☆	1924B	☆	New York	FV	2.00	6.00	7.00
4502	1924C		Philadelphia	FV	FV	3.00	4.00
4502☆	1924C	☆	Philadelphia	FV	FV	6.00	7.00
4503	1924D		Cleveland	FV	FV	3.00	4.00
4503☆	1924D	☆	Cleveland	FV	10.00	75.00	100.
4504	1924E		Richmond	FV	FV	3.00	4.00
4504☆	1924E	☆	Richmond	FV	2.00	6.00	7.00
4505	1924F		Atlanta	FV	FV	3.00	4.00
4506	1925F		Atlanta	FV	FV	3.00	4.00
4506☆	1925F	☆	Atlanta	5.00	25.00	115.	140.
4507	1925G		Chicago	FV	FV	3.00	4.00
4508	1925H		St. Louis	FV	FV	5.00	6.00
4508☆	1925H	☆	St. Louis	FV	FV	8.00	10.00
4509	1925I		Minneapolis	FV	2.00	6.00	7.00

KL#	Fr#		District	Fine	XF	CH CU (63)	Gem CU (65)
4510	1925J		Kansas City	FV	FV	3.00	4.00
4511	1925K		Dallas	FV	FV	3.00	4.00
4512	1925L		San Francisco	FV	FV	3.00	4.00
4512☆	1925L	☆	San Francisco	FV	2.00	6.00	7.00

Series 2001 Marin-O'Neill - DC

KL#	Fr#		District	Fine	XF	CH CU (63)	Gem CU (65)
4571	1926A		Boston	FV	FV	3.00	4.00
4571☆	1926A	☆	Boston	FV	2.00	6.00	7.00
4572	1926B		New York	FV	FV	3.00	4.00
4573	1926C		Philadelphia	FV	FV	3.00	4.00
4573☆	1926C	☆	Philadelphia	FV	2.00	6.00	7.00
4574	1926D		Cleveland	FV	FV	3.00	4.00
4575	1926E		Richmond	FV	FV	3.00	4.00
4576	1926F		Atlanta	FV	FV	3.00	4.00
4576☆	1926F	☆	Atlanta	FV	FV	6.00	7.00
4577	1926H		St. Louis	FV	FV	3.00	4.00
4577☆	1926H	☆	St. Louis	5.00	25.00	100.	125.
4578	1926I		Minneapolis	FV	FV	3.00	4.00
4579	1926J		Kansas City	FV	FV	3.00	4.00
4580	1927F		Atlanta	FV	FV	3.00	4.00
4581	1927G		Chicago	FV	FV	3.00	4.00
4581☆	1927G	☆	Chicago	FV	2.00	6.00	7.00
4582	1927H		St. Louis	FV	FV	3.00	4.00
4583	1927I		Minneapolis	FV	FV	3.00	4.00
4584	1927J		Kansas City	FV	FV	3.00	4.00
4585	1927K		Dallas	FV	FV	3.00	4.00
4585☆	1927K	☆	Dallas	FV	2.00	5.00	5.00
4586	1927L		San Francisco	FV	FV	3.00	4.00
4586☆	1927L	☆	San Francisco	FV	2.00	6.00	7.00

Series 2003 Marin-Snow - DC

KL#	Fr#		District	Fine	XF	CH CU (63)	Gem CU (65)
4653	1928A		Boston	FV	FV	3.00	4.00
4653☆	1928A	☆	Boston	FV	FV	6.00	7.00
4654	1928B		New York	FV	FV	3.00	4.00
4654☆	1928B	☆	New York	FV	FV	6.00	7.00
4655	1928C		Philadelphia	FV	FV	3.00	4.00
4656	1928D		Cleveland	FV	FV	3.00	4.00
4656☆	1928D	☆	Cleveland	10.00	50.00	125.	150.
4657	1928E		Richmond	FV	FV	3.00	4.00
4657☆	1928E	☆	Richmond	FV	2.00	6.00	7.00
4658	1928F		Atlanta	FV	FV	3.00	4.00
4658☆	1928F	☆	Atlanta	FV	2.00	6.00	7.00

Series 2003 Marin-Snow -FW

KL#	Fr#		District	Fine	XF	CH CU (63)	Gem CU (65)
4659	1929F		Atlanta	FV	FV	3.00	4.00
4660	1929G		Chicago	FV	FV	3.00	4.00
4660☆	1929G	☆	Chicago	FV	2.00	6.00	7.00
4661	1929H		St. Louis	FV	FV	3.00	4.00
4662	1929I		Minneapolis	FV	FV	3.00	4.00
4663	1929J		Kansas City	FV	FV	3.00	4.00
4664	1929K		Dallas	FV	FV	3.00	4.00
4665	1929L		San Francisco	FV	FV	3.00	4.00
4665☆	1929L	☆	San Francisco	FV	2.00	6.00	7.00

Series 2003A Cabral-Snow - DC

KL#	Fr#	District	Fine	XF	CH CU (63)	Gem CU (65)
4666	-	Boston	FV	FV	3.00	4.00
4667	-	New York	FV	FV	3.00	4.00
4667☆	-	New York	5.00	20.00	100.	125.

Series 2003A Cabral-Snow - FW

KL#	Fr#	District	Fine	XF	CH CU (63)	Gem CU (65)
4668	-	Atlanta	FV	FV	3.00	4.00
4669	-	Kansas City	FV	FV	3.00	4.00
4670	-	Dallas	FV	FV	3.00	4.00
4671	-	San Francisco	FV	FV	3.00	4.00

Series 2006 Cabral-Paulson - DC

KL#	Fr#	District	Fine	XF	CH CU (63)	Gem CU (65)
4798	-	New York	FV	FV	3.00	4.00
4799	-	Philadelphia	FV	FV	3.00	4.00
4800	-	Cleveland	FV	FV	3.00	4.00
4801	-	Richmond	FV	FV	3.00	4.00

Series 2006 Cabral-Paulson - FW

KL#	Fr#	District	Fine	XF	CH CU (63)	Gem CU (65)
4804	-	St Louis	FV	FV	3.00	4.00
4805	-	Minneapolis	FV	FV	3.00	4.00
4807	-	Dallas	FV	FV	3.00	4.00
4808	-	San Francisco	FV	FV	3.00	4.00

Federal Reserve Notes - Web Press

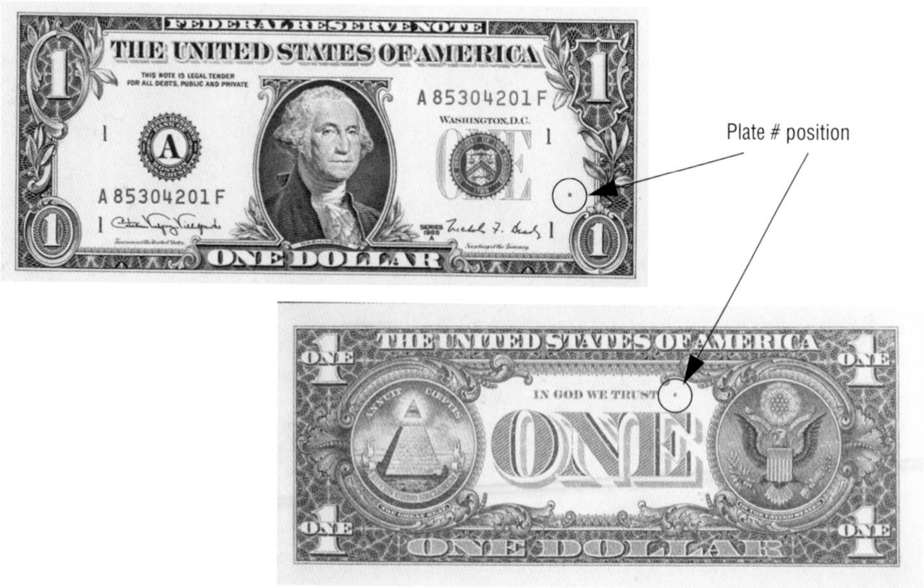

KL#	Series	District Block	Fine	XF	CH CU (63)	Gem CU (65)
WP1	1988A	A - E	10.00	22.50	45.00	65.00
WP2	1988A	A - F	4.00	7.75	40.00	60.00
WP3	1988A	A - G	4.00	7.75	35.00	55.00
WP4	1988A	B - L	100.	400.	2000.	3000.
WP5	1988A	C - A	4.00	10.00	45.00	65.00
WP6	1988A	E - I	4.00	10.00	40.00	60.00
WP7	1988A	E - K	4.00	10.00	45.00	65.00
WP8	1988A	F -	225.	500.	1000.	1250.
WP9	1988A	F - L	15.00	50.00	200.	250.
WP10	1988A	F - M	10.00	40.00	125.	150.
WP11	1988A	F - N	10.00	40.00	125.	150.
WP12	1988A	F - U	4.00	7.75	40.00	60.00
WP13	1988A	F - V	4.00	7.75	40.00	60.00
WP14	1988A	G - P	6.00	25.00	200.	250.
WP15	1988A	G - Q	10.00	30.00	225.	275.
WP16	1993	B - H	5.00	10.00	20.00	30.00
WP17	1993	C - A	4.00	6.00	15.00	25.00
WP18	1995	A - C	4.00	6.00	17.00	27.50
WP19	1995	A - D	4.00	10.00	30.00	40.00
WP20	1995	B - H	4.00	8.00	17.00	27.50
WP21	1995	D - C	5.00	10.00	20.00	30.00
WP22	1995	F - D	5.00	10.00	17.00	27.50

Silver Certificates - Hawaii Emergency

Ovpt: HAWAII on face and back of 1935 A series.

KL#	Fr#	Series	Signatures	Fine	XF	CH CU (63)	Gem CU (65)
1609	2300	1935A	Julian-Morgenthau	40.00	70.00	175.	250.
1609☆	2300	1935A☆	Julian-Morgenthau	275.	550.	2750.	3875.

Silver Certificates - Experimental Issue

Red "R" at lower right.

KL#	Fr#	Series	Fine	XF	CH CU (63)	Gem CU (65)
1611	1609	1935A	75.00	130.	375.	1000.
1611☆	1609	1935A☆	2000.	2700.	6500.	14,000.

Red "S" at lower right.

KL#	Fr#	Series	Fine	XF	CH CU (63)	Gem CU (65)
1612	1610	1935A	75.00	150.	375.	900.
1612☆	1610	1935A☆	2000.	3000.	6500.	13,500.

Silver Certificates - North Africa Emergency

Yellow seal on face.

KL#	Fr#	Series	Signatures	Fine	XF	CH CU (63)	Gem CU (65)
1610	2306	1935A	Julian-Morgenthau	45.00	75.00	240.	325.
1610☆	2306	1935A☆	Julian-Morgenthau	300.	1000.	3000.	4250.

United States Notes

Two Dollars

KL#	Fr#	Series	Signatures	Fine	XF	CH CU (63)	Gem CU (65)
1613	1501	1928	Tate-Mellon	15.00	50.00	125.	425.
1613☆	1501	1928☆	Tate-Mellon	200.	700.	1600.	3750.
1614	1502	1928A	Woods-Mellon	40.00	100.	600.	835.
1614☆	1502	1928A☆	Woods-Mellon	2000.	4750.	10,500.	22,500.
1615	1503	1928B	Woods-Mills	80.00	300.	975.	1300.
1615☆	1503	1928B☆	Woods-Mills	25,000.	30,000.	65,000.	100,000.
1616	1504	1928C	Julian-Morgenthau	20.00	50.00	150.	375.
1616☆	1504	1928C☆	Julian-Morgenthau	500.	1000.	2500.	4000.
1617	1505	1928D	Julian-Morgenthau	15.00	35.00	100.	200.
1617☆	1505	1928D☆	Julian-Morgenthau	75.00	200.	700.	1275.
1618	1506	1928E	Julian-Vinson	20.00	40.00	150.	250.
1618☆	1506	1928E☆	Julian-Vinson	3000.	5000.	12,500.	20,000.
1619	1507	1928F	Julian-Snyder	15.00	25.00	100.	195.
1619☆	1507	1928F☆	Julian-Snyder	50.00	175.	500.	800.
1620	1508	1928G	Clark-Snyder	8.00	15.00	45.00	450.
1620☆	1508	1928G☆	Clark-Snyder	50.00	125.	425.	500.

KL#	Fr#	Series	Signatures	Fine	XF	CH CU (63)	Gem CU (65)
1621	1509	1953	Priest-Humphrey	10.00	15.00	35.00	40.00
1621☆	1509	1953☆	Priest-Humphrey	10.00	35.00	75.00	125.
1622	1510	1953A	Priest-Anderson	6.00	10.00	20.00	25.00
1622☆	1510	1953A☆	Priest-Anderson	10.00	30.00	80.00	100.

KL#	Fr#	Series	Signatures	Fine	XF	CH CU (63)	Gem CU (65)
1623	1511	1953B	Smith-Dillon	6.00	8.00	20.00	28.00
1623☆	1511	1953B☆	Smith-Dillon	15.00	25.00	80.00	100.
1624	1512	1953C	Granahan-Dillon	6.00	8.00	18.00	23.00
1624☆	1512	1953C☆	Granahan-Dillon	13.00	20.00	90.00	110.

KL#	Fr#	Series	Signatures	Fine	XF	CH CU (63)	Gem CU (65)
1625	1513	1963	Granahan-Dillon	5.00	8.00	15.00	20.00
1625☆	1513	1963☆	Granahan-Dillon	7.00	13.00	40.00	50.00
1626	1514	1963A	Granahan-Fowler	5.00	8.00	15.00	20.00

Federal Reserve Notes

Series 1976 Neff-Simon

KL#	Fr#		District	Fine	XF	CH CU (63)	Gem CU (65)
1627	1935A		Boston	3.00	4.00	7.00	8.00
1627☆	1935A	☆	Boston	6.00	10.00	18.00	20.00
1628	1935B		New York	3.00	4.00	7.00	8.00

KL#	Fr#		District	Fine	XF	CH CU (63)	Gem CU (65)
1628☆	1935B	☆	New York	7.00	10.00	18.00	20.00
1629	1935C		Philadelphia	3.00	4.00	7.00	8.00
1629☆	1935C	☆	Philadelphia	6.00	8.00	15.00	20.00
1630	1935D		Cleveland	3.00	4.00	7.00	8.00
1630☆	1935D	☆	Cleveland	5.00	12.00	30.00	35.00
1631	1935E		Richmond	3.00	4.00	6.00	7.00
1631☆	1935E	☆	Richmond	5.00	12.00	30.00	100.
1632	1935F		Atlanta	3.00	4.00	6.00	7.00
1632☆	1935F	☆	Atlanta	6.00	10.00	20.00	50.00
1633	1935G		Chicago	3.00	4.00	6.00	7.00
1633☆	1935G	☆	Chicago	8.00	15.00	45.00	50.00
1634	1935H		St. Louis	3.00	4.00	6.00	7.00
1634☆	1935H	☆	St. Louis	5.00	8.00	15.00	20.00
1635	1935I		Minneapolis	3.00	4.00	6.00	7.00
1635☆	1935I	☆	Minneapolis	25.00	75.00	250.	275.
1636	1935J		Kansas City	3.00	4.00	6.00	7.00
1636☆	1935J	☆	Kansas City	10.00	40.00	100.	150.
1637	1935K		Dallas	3.00	4.00	6.00	7.00
1637☆	1935K	☆	Dallas	7.00	10.00	20.00	25.00
1638	1935L		San Francisco	3.00	4.00	6.00	7.00
1638☆	1935L	☆	San Francisco	8.00	15.00	40.00	50.00

Series 1995 Withrow-Rubin

KL#	Fr#		District	Fine	XF	CH CU (63)	Gem CU (65)
4222☆	1936A	☆	Boston	2.00	10.00	40.00	50.00
4223☆	1936B	☆	New York	2.00	10.00	40.00	50.00
4224☆	1936C	☆	Philadelphia	2.00	10.00	40.00	50.00
4225☆	1936D	☆	Cleveland	2.00	10.00	40.00	50.00
4226☆	1936E	☆	Richmond	2.00	10.00	40.00	50.00
4227	1936F		Atlanta	2.00	4.00	7.00	8.00
4227☆	1936F	☆	Atlanta	2.00	10.00	40.00	50.00
4228☆	1936G	☆	Chicago	2.00	8.00	15.00	20.00
4229☆	1936H	☆	St. Louis	2.00	10.00	40.00	50.00
4230☆	1936I	☆	Minneapolis	2.00	10.00	40.00	50.00
4231☆	1936J	☆	Kansas City	2.00	10.00	40.00	50.00
4232☆	1936K	☆	Dallas	2.00	10.00	40.00	50.00
4233☆	1936L	☆	San Francisco	2.00	10.00	40.00	50.00
4234☆	-	☆		2.00	10.00	40.00	50.00

Series 2003 Marin-Snow - FW

KL#	Fr#		District	Fine	XF	CH CU (63)	Gem CU (65)
4672☆	1937A	☆	Boston	—	—	—	25.00
4673☆	1937B	☆	New York	—	—	—	25.00
4674☆	1937C	☆	Philadelphia	—	—	—	25.00
4675☆	1937D	☆	Cleveland	—	—	—	25.00
4676☆	1937E	☆	Richmond	—	—	—	25.00
4677☆	1937F	☆	Atlanta	—	—	—	25.00

KL#	Fr#		District	Fine	XF	CH CU (63)	Gem CU (65)
4678☆	1937G	☆	Chicago	—	—	—	25.00
4679☆	1937H	☆	St. Louis	—	—	—	25.00
4680	1937I		Minneapolis	—	—	—	6.00
4680☆	1937I	☆	Minneapolis	—	7.50	—	25.00
4681☆	1937J	☆	Kansas City	—	—	—	25.00
4682☆	1937K	☆	Dallas	—	—	—	25.00
4683☆	1937L	☆	San Francisco	—	—	—	25.00

Premium Millennium Federal Reserve Set (12 notes).
In original packaging. Total production 2,000 sets.

Series 2003A Cabral-Snow

KL#	Fr#		District	Fine	XF	CH CU (63)	Gem CU (65)
4684	-		Atlanta	—	—	4.00	6.00
4684☆	-	☆	Atlanta	—	7.50	15.00	25.00

United States Notes

Five Dollars

KL#	Fr#	Series	Signatures	Fine	XF	CH CU (63)	Gem CU (65)
1639	1525	1928	Woods-Mellon	15.00	25.00	100.	155.
1639☆	1525	1928☆	Woods-Mellon	450.	500.	1800.	3000.
1640	1526	1928A	Woods-Mills	15.00	50.00	150.	350.
1640☆	1526	1928A☆	Woods-Mills	900.	2500.	6500.	11,500.
1641	1527	1928B	Julian-Morgenthau	15.00	30.00	85.00	145.
1641☆	1527	1928B☆	Julian-Morgenthau	150.	400.	1250.	2300.
1642	1528	1928C	Julian-Morgenthau	13.00	25.00	65.00	75.00
1642☆	1528	1928C☆	Julian-Morgenthau	70.00	250.	775.	1000.
1643	1529	1928D	Julian-Vinson	35.00	75.00	400.	500.
1643☆	1529	1928D☆	Julian-Vinson	650.	1500.	6000.	7000.
1644	1530	1928E	Julian-Snyder	15.00	25.00	75.00	100.
1644☆	1530	1928E☆	Julian-Snyder	100.	250.	700.	1000.
1645	1531	1928F	Clark-Snyder	10.00	25.00	80.00	100.
1645☆	1531	1928F☆	Clark-Snyder	140.	250.	600.	1250.

KL#	Fr#	Series	Signatures	Fine	XF	CH CU (63)	Gem CU (65)
1646	1532	1953	Priest-Humphrey	10.00	15.00	50.00	60.00
1646☆	1532	1953☆	Priest-Humphrey	30.00	110.	200.	300.
1647	1533	1953A	Priest-Anderson	10.00	18.00	50.00	65.00
1647☆	1533	1953A☆	Priest-Anderson	25.00	75.00	250.	400.
1648	1534	1953B	Smith-Dillon	10.00	15.00	50.00	60.00
1648☆	1534	1953B☆	Smith-Dillon	40.00	75.00	200.	250.
1649	1535	1953C	Granahan-Dillon	10.00	25.00	60.00	75.00
1649☆	1535	1953C☆	Granahan-Dillon	50.00	80.00	300.	500.

KL#	Fr#	Series	Signatures	Fine	XF	CH CU (63)	Gem CU (65)
1650	1536	1963	Granahan-Dillon	8.00	15.00	35.00	50.00
1650☆	1536	1963☆	Granahan-Dillon	10.00	25.00	100.	125.

Silver Certificates

KL#	Fr#	Series	Signatures	Fine	XF	CH CU (63)	Gem CU (65)
1651	1650	1934	Julian-Morgenthau	15.00	40.00	80.00	145.
1651☆	1650	1934☆	Julian-Morgenthau	35.00	150.	450.	550.
1652	1651	1934A	Julian-Morgenthau	15.00	30.00	75.00	100.
1652☆	1651	1934A☆	Julian-Morgenthau	50.00	100.	300.	400.
1653	1652	1934B	Julian-Vinson	10.00	25.00	125.	175.
1653☆	1652	1934B☆	Julian-Vinson	75.00	250.	1200.	2000.
1654	1653	1934C	Julian-Snyder	10.00	30.00	75.00	140.
1654☆	1653	1934C☆	Julian-Snyder	50.00	125.	225.	350.
1655	1654	1934D	Clark-Snyder	10.00	20.00	55.00	100.
1655☆	1654	1934D☆	Clark-Snyder	50.00	100.	300.	400.

KL#	Fr#	Series	Signatures	Fine	XF	CH CU (63)	Gem CU (65)
1656	1655	1953	Priest-Humphrey	10.00	25.00	65.00	75.00
1656☆	1655	1953☆	Priest-Humphrey	20.00	40.00	100.	150.
1657	1656	1953A	Priest-Anderson	8.00	15.00	40.00	60.00
1657☆	1656	1953A☆	Priest-Anderson	15.00	35.00	75.00	110.
1658	1657	1953B	Smith-Dillon	8.00	15.00	40.00	60.00
1658☆	1657	1953B☆	Smith-Dillon	2300.	4500.	8000.	12,000.

Federal Reserve Bank Notes

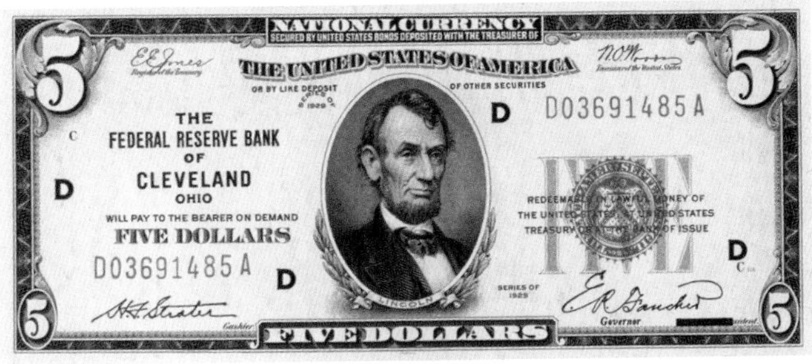

KL#	Fr#	Series	District	Fine	XF	CH CU (63)	Gem CU (65)
1659	1850A	1929	Boston	25.00	60.00	275.	325.
1659☆	1850A	1929☆	Boston	1000.	4000.	10,500.	12,500.
1660	1850B	1929	New York	20.00	50.00	200.	250.
1660☆	1850B	1929☆	New York	1000.	1750.	3000.	4000.
1661	1850C	1929	Philadelphia	20.00	75.00	250.	300.
1661☆	1850C	1929☆	Philadelphia	500.	1000.	3000.	4000.
1662	1850D	1929	Cleveland	20.00	50.00	250.	300.
1662☆	1850D	1929☆	Cleveland	400.	650.	3000.	4000.
1664	1850F	1929	Atlanta	35.00	50.00	450.	550.
1664☆	1850F	1929☆	Atlanta	400.	650.	2700.	3750.
1665	1850G	1929	Chicago	20.00	50.00	200.	250.
1665☆	1850G	1929☆	Chicago	350.	500.	2000.	3500.
1666	1850H	1929	St. Louis	300.	1500.	3500.	4500.
1666☆	1850H	1929☆	St. Louis	3000.	8000.	15,000.	20,000.
1667	1850I	1929	Minneapolis	75.00	225.	900.	1250.
1667☆	1850I	1929☆	Minneapolis	2000.	3500.	8000.	10,000.
1668	1850J	1929	Kansas City	75.00	225.	650.	750.
1668☆	1850J	1929☆	Kansas City	1500.	550.	3500.	5000.
1669	1850K	1929	Dallas	55.00	75.00	300.	400.
1669☆	1850K	1929☆	Dallas	4500.	11,000.	—	—
1670	1850L	1929	San Francisco	1000.	4500.	10,000.	12,000.
1670☆	1850L	1929☆	San Francisco	—	—	—	—

Federal Reserve Notes

Series 1928 Tate-Mellon

KL#	Fr#		District	Fine	XF	CH CU (63)	Gem CU (65)
1671	1950A		Boston	35.00	85.00	350.	400.
1671☆	1950A	☆	Boston	100.	200.	1250.	2000.
1672	1950B		New York	20.00	35.00	150.	250.
1672☆	1950B	☆	New York	60.00	125.	1000.	1250.
1673	1950C		Philadelphia	20.00	35.00	150.	200.
1673☆	1950C	☆	Philadelphia	50.00	125.	1000.	2000.
1674	1950D		Cleveland	20.00	35.00	150.	225.
1674☆	1950D	☆	Cleveland	60.00	125.	600.	1500.
1675	1950E		Richmond	20.00	35.00	150.	250.
1675☆	1950E	☆	Richmond	75.00	300.	1250.	3000.
1676	1950F		Atlanta	20.00	35.00	150.	250.
1676☆	1950F	☆	Atlanta	75.00	250.	1000.	1500.
1677	1950G		Chicago	15.00	55.00	325.	375.
1677☆	1950G	☆	Chicago	75.00	360.	800.	1000.
1678	1950H		St. Louis	40.00	60.00	150.	250.
1678☆	1950H	☆	St. Louis	75.00	250.	1000.	3000.
1679	1950I		Minneapolis	125.	300.	800.	1200.
1679☆	1950I	☆	Minneapolis	300.	750.	2000.	6000.
1680	1950J		Kansas City	25.00	50.00	200.	400.
1680☆	1950J	☆	Kansas City	200.	500.	1500.	2500.
1681	1950K		Dallas	20.00	40.00	125.	200.
1681☆	1950K	☆	Dallas	150.	300.	900.	3000.
1682	1950L		San Francisco	20.00	40.00	150.	300.
1682☆	1950L	☆	San Francisco	150.	300.	1250.	4000.

Series 1928A Woods-Mellon

KL#	Fr#		District	Fine	XF	CH CU (63)	Gem CU (65)
1683	1951A		Boston	100.	300.	1000.	1500.
1683☆	1951A	☆	Boston	250.	500.	1500.	2000.
1684	1951B		New York	12.00	25.00	300.	525.
1684☆	1951B	☆	New York	250.	450.	800.	2000.
1685	1951C		Philadelphia	12.00	25.00	175.	225.
1685☆	1951C	☆	Philadelphia	100.	250.	800.	2000.
1686	1951D		Cleveland	12.00	50.00	175.	200.
1686☆	1951D	☆	Cleveland	100.	250.	800.	2000.
1687	1951E		Richmond	15.00	50.00	250.	300.
1687☆	1951E	☆	Richmond	100.	300.	1000.	2000.
1688	1951F		Atlanta	25.00	75.00	350.	500.
1688☆	1951F	☆	Atlanta	200.	550.	2000.	4000.
1689	1951G		Chicago	15.00	35.00	100.	150.
1689☆	1951G	☆	Chicago	125.	350.	1000.	1500.
1690	1951H		St. Louis	17.00	50.00	225.	250.
1690☆	1951H	☆	St. Louis	200.	550.	2000.	4000.

KL#	Fr#		District	Fine	XF	CH CU (63)	Gem CU (65)
1691	1951I		Minneapolis	90.00	200.	500.	2000.
1691☆	1951I	☆	Minneapolis	—	—	—	—
1692	1951J		Kansas City	15.00	40.00	200.	500.
1692☆	1951J	☆	Kansas City	—	—	—	—
1693	1951K		Dallas	20.00	75.00	250.	500.
1693☆	1951K	☆	Dallas	200.	625.	1500.	6000.
1694	1951L		San Francisco	12.00	35.00	100.	250.
1694☆	1951L	☆	San Francisco	100.	350.	1000.	3000.

Series 1928B Woods-Mellon

KL#	Fr#		District	Fine	XF	CH CU (63)	Gem CU (65)
1695	1952A		Boston	12.00	25.00	75.00	150.
1695☆	1952A	☆	Boston	100.	400.	1000.	2000.
1696	1952B		New York	12.00	25.00	75.00	150.
1696☆	1952B	☆	New York	75.00	400.	800.	1500.
1697	1952C		Philadelphia	15.00	30.00	85.00	100.
1697☆	1952C	☆	Philadelphia	100.	300.	1000.	1350.
1698	1952D		Cleveland	12.00	25.00	75.00	150.
1698☆	1952D	☆	Cleveland	100.	400.	1000.	2000.
1699	1952E		Richmond	12.00	25.00	90.00	150.
1699☆	1952E	☆	Richmond	100.	400.	1000.	1500.
1700	1952F		Atlanta	12.00	25.00	90.00	150.
1700☆	1952F	☆	Atlanta	100.	400.	800.	2000.
1701	1952G		Chicago	12.00	25.00	75.00	150.
1701☆	1952G	☆	Chicago	100.	400.	1000.	2000.
1702	1952H		St. Louis	12.00	25.00	75.00	150.
1702☆	1952H	☆	St. Louis	125.	400.	800.	1600.
1703	1952I		Minneapolis	25.00	75.00	200.	400.
1703☆	1952I	☆	Minneapolis	100.	500.	1000.	2000.
1704	1952J		Kansas City	12.00	25.00	75.00	150.
1704☆	1952J	☆	Kansas City	100.	500.	1000.	2000.
1705	1952K		Dallas	14.00	40.00	125.	200.
1705☆	1952K	☆	Dallas	100.	500.	1000.	2000.
1706	1952L		San Francisco	12.00	25.00	75.00	150.
1706☆	1952L	☆	San Francisco	100.	500.	1000.	2000.

Series 1928C Woods-Mills

KL#	Fr#	District	Fine	XF	CH CU (63)	Gem CU (65)
1710	1953D	Cleveland	Unknown	—	—	—
1712	1953F	Atlanta	400.	1500.	3000.	4500.
1718	1953L	San Francisco	Unknown	—	—	—

Series 1928D Woods-Woodin

KL#	Fr#	District	Fine	XF	CH CU (63)	Gem CU (65)
1724	1954F	Atlanta	1700.	3000.	4000.	5500.

Series 1934 Julian-Morgenthau

KL#	Fr#	District	Fine	XF	CH CU (63)	Gem CU (65)
1731	1955A	Boston	10.00	20.00	90.00	125.
1731☆	1955A ☆	Boston	150.	750.	1400.	1600.
1732	1955B	New York	10.00	20.00	80.00	100.
1732☆	1955B ☆	New York	100.	400.	850.	1000.
1733	1955C	Philadelphia	10.00	20.00	80.00	100.
1733☆	1955C ☆	Philadelphia	125.	550.	900.	1250.
1734	1955D	Cleveland	10.00	20.00	80.00	100.
1734☆	1955D ☆	Cleveland	125.	550.	900.	1250.
1735	1955E	Richmond	10.00	20.00	90.00	125.
1735☆	1955E ☆	Richmond	125.	550.	900.	1250.
1736	1955F	Atlanta	10.00	20.00	100.	125.
1736☆	1955F ☆	Atlanta	125.	550.	900.	1250.
1737	1955G	Chicago	10.00	25.00	90.00	140.
1737☆	1955G ☆	Chicago	130.	275.	700.	1125.
1738	1955H	St. Louis	10.00	20.00	80.00	120.
1738☆	1955H ☆	St. Louis	125.	550.	900.	1250.
1739	1955I	Minneapolis	12.00	35.00	130.	175.
1739☆	1955I ☆	Minneapolis	125.	500.	1000.	1750.
1740	1955J	Kansas City	10.00	20.00	70.00	100.
1740☆	1955J ☆	Kansas City	125.	550.	900.	1250.
1741	1955K	Dallas	10.00	20.00	100.	125.
1741☆	1955K ☆	Dallas	125.	750.	1500.	2000.
1742	1955L	San Francisco	10.00	20.00	80.00	120.
1742☆	1955L ☆	San Francisco	125.	550.	1250.	1750.

Series 1934A Julian-Morgenthau

KL#	Fr#	District	Fine	XF	CH CU (63)	Gem CU (65)
1743	1957A	Boston	10.00	20.00	40.00	50.00
1743☆	1957A ☆	Boston	30.00	80.00	350.	450.
1744	1957B	New York	10.00	20.00	40.00	50.00
1744☆	1957B ☆	New York	25.00	75.00	350.	400.
1745	1957C	Philadelphia	10.00	15.00	45.00	80.00
1745☆	1957C ☆	Philadelphia	30.00	80.00	350.	650.
1746	1957D	Cleveland	12.00	50.00	300.	350.
1747	1957E	Richmond	10.00	20.00	40.00	125.
1747☆	1957E ☆	Richmond	30.00	100.	500.	600.
1748	1957F	Atlanta	15.00	40.00	75.00	100.
1748☆	1957F ☆	Atlanta	40.00	150.	500.	600.
1749	1957G	Chicago	10.00	20.00	40.00	60.00
1749☆	1957G ☆	Chicago	20.00	75.00	350.	400.
1750	1957H	St. Louis	10.00	20.00	50.00	75.00

KL#	Fr#		District	Fine	XF	CH CU (63)	Gem CU (65)
1750☆	1957H	☆	St. Louis	20.00	75.00	350.	400.
1754	1957L		San Francisco	10.00	20.00	40.00	60.00
1754☆	1957L	☆	San Francisco	20.00	75.00	350.	400.

Series 1934B Julian-Vinson

KL#	Fr#		District	Fine	XF	CH CU (63)	Gem CU (65)
1755	1958A		Boston	10.00	20.00	60.00	125.
1755☆	1958A	☆	Boston	75.00	200.	1500.	1750.
1756	1958B		New York	10.00	20.00	50.00	80.00
1756☆	1958B	☆	New York	60.00	150.	1000.	1250.
1757	1958C		Philadelphia	10.00	20.00	50.00	80.00
1757☆	1958C	☆	Philadelphia	75.00	200.	1000.	1250.
1758	1958D		Cleveland	10.00	25.00	75.00	145.
1758☆	1958D	☆	Cleveland	75.00	225.	650.	1000.
1759	1958E		Richmond	10.00	20.00	70.00	85.00
1759☆	1958E	☆	Richmond	75.00	200.	1500.	1750.
1760	1958F		Atlanta	10.00	20.00	70.00	100.
1760☆	1958F	☆	Atlanta	100.	250.	1600.	1800.
1761	1958G		Chicago	10.00	20.00	70.00	100.
1761☆	1958G	☆	Chicago	75.00	200.	1500.	1800.
1762	1958H		St. Louis	12.00	25.00	80.00	125.
1762☆	1958H	☆	St. Louis	75.00	200.	1000.	1250.
1763	1958I		Minneapolis	15.00	30.00	100.	150.
1763☆	1958I	☆	Minneapolis	75.00	200.	1600.	1800.
1764	1958J		Kansas City	200.	750.	3000.	3750.
1766	1958L		San Francisco	10.00	20.00	70.00	95.00
1766☆	1958L	☆	San Francisco	75.00	200.	1800.	2250.

Series 1934C Julian-Snyder

KL#	Fr#		District	Fine	XF	CH CU (63)	Gem CU (65)
1767	1959A		Boston	10.00	20.00	60.00	75.00
1767☆	1959A	☆	Boston	50.00	250.	800.	1000.
1768	1959B		New York	20.00	50.00	90.00	125.
1768☆	1959B	☆	New York	50.00	250.	600.	800.
1769	1959C		Philadelphia	10.00	20.00	60.00	75.00
1769☆	1959C	☆	Philadelphia	50.00	250.	800.	1000.
1770	1959D		Cleveland	10.00	20.00	80.00	140.
1770☆	1959D	☆	Cleveland	50.00	250.	800.	1250.
1771	1959E		Richmond	10.00	20.00	60.00	75.00
1771☆	1959E	☆	Richmond	50.00	250.	800.	1000.
1772	1959F		Atlanta	10.00	20.00	60.00	75.00
1772☆	1959F	☆	Atlanta	50.00	250.	1000.	1250.
1773	1959G		Chicago	10.00	20.00	60.00	75.00
1773☆	1959G	☆	Chicago	50.00	250.	600.	800.
1774	1959H		St. Louis	10.00	20.00	60.00	75.00
1774☆	1959H	☆	St. Louis	50.00	250.	800.	1000.
1775	1959I		Minneapolis	15.00	40.00	125.	150.

KL#	Fr#		District	Fine	XF	CH CU (63)	Gem CU (65)
1775☆	1959I	☆	Minneapolis	100.	350.	1500.	2000.
1776	1959J		Kansas City	20.00	20.00	75.00	90.00
1776☆	1959J	☆	Kansas City	50.00	250.	750.	1000.
1777	1959K		Dallas	14.00	35.00	75.00	100.
1777☆	1959K	☆	Dallas	100.	250.	1000.	1500.
1778	1959L		San Francisco	10.00	20.00	60.00	85.00
1778☆	1959L	☆	San Francisco	50.00	150.	750.	1000.

Series 1934D Clark-Snyder

KL#	Fr#		District	Fine	XF	CH CU (63)	Gem CU (65)
1779	1960A		Boston	10.00	20.00	60.00	75.00
1779☆	1960A	☆	Boston	40.00	250.	650.	900.
1780	1960B		New York	10.00	25.00	90.00	140.
1780☆	1960B	☆	New York	75.00	300.	700.	1100.
1781	1960C		Philadelphia	10.00	20.00	60.00	75.00
1781☆	1960C	☆	Philadelphia	50.00	250.	550.	700.
1782	1960D		Cleveland	10.00	20.00	60.00	75.00
1782☆	1960D	☆	Cleveland	50.00	300.	900.	1250.
1783	1960E		Richmond	10.00	20.00	60.00	75.00
1783☆	1960E	☆	Richmond	50.00	500.	1500.	2000.
1784	1960F		Atlanta	10.00	20.00	60.00	75.00
1784☆	1960F	☆	Atlanta	50.00	800.	3000.	4000.
1785	1960G		Chicago	10.00	20.00	60.00	75.00
1785☆	1960G	☆	Chicago	50.00	200.	500.	700.
1786	1960H		St. Louis	10.00	20.00	60.00	75.00
1786☆	1960H	☆	St. Louis	50.00	250.	600.	1000.
1787	1960I		Minneapolis	15.00	40.00	100.	150.
1787☆	1960I	☆	Minneapolis	100.	600.	1400.	1900.
1788	1960J		Kansas City	10.00	20.00	75.00	90.00
1788☆	1960J	☆	Kansas City	50.00	350.	750.	1000.
1789	1960K		Dallas	15.00	35.00	75.00	100.
1789☆	1960K	☆	Dallas	50.00	250.	600.	900.
1790	1960L		San Francisco	10.00	20.00	65.00	100.
1790☆	1960L	☆	San Francisco	50.00	250.	650.	900.

Series 1950 Clark-Snyder

KL#	Fr#		District	Fine	XF	CH CU (63)	Gem CU (65)
1791	1961A		Boston	8.00	12.00	50.00	60.00
1791☆	1961A	☆	Boston	35.00	75.00	350.	400.
1792	1961B		New York	8.00	12.00	40.00	50.00
1792☆	1961B	☆	New York	—	60.00	250.	300.
1793	1961C		Philadelphia	10.00	12.00	40.00	50.00
1793☆	1961C	☆	Philadelphia	25.00	75.00	350.	400.
1794	1961D		Cleveland	8.00	12.00	40.00	50.00
1794☆	1961D	☆	Cleveland	25.00	75.00	400.	750.
1795	1961E		Richmond	8.00	12.00	40.00	50.00
1795☆	1961E	☆	Richmond	30.00	100.	300.	500.
1796	1961F		Atlanta	8.00	12.00	50.00	60.00

KL#	Fr#		District	Fine	XF	CH CU (63)	Gem CU (65)
1796☆	1961F	☆	Atlanta	30.00	75.00	300.	400.
1797	1961G		Chicago	8.00	12.00	45.00	60.00
1797☆	1961G	☆	Chicago	30.00	110.	350.	475.
1798	1961H		St. Louis	8.00	12.00	40.00	60.00
1798☆	1961H	☆	St. Louis	30.00	75.00	250.	300.
1799	1961I		Minneapolis	9.00	20.00	60.00	85.00
1799☆	1961I	☆	Minneapolis	40.00	100.	400.	600.
1800	1961J		Kansas City	8.00	15.00	40.00	60.00
1800☆	1961J	☆	Kansas City	30.00	75.00	200.	300.
1801	1961K		Dallas	8.00	12.00	40.00	80.00
1801☆	1961K	☆	Dallas	40.00	100.	300.	500.
1802	1961L		San Francisco	8.00	12.00	40.00	70.00
1802☆	1961L	☆	San Francisco	40.00	100.	300.	400.

Series 1950A Priest-Humphrey

KL#	Fr#		District	Fine	XF	CH CU (63)	Gem CU (65)
1803	1962A		Boston	10.00	18.00	25.00	35.00
1803☆	1962A	☆	Boston	10.00	20.00	60.00	75.00
1804	1962B		New York	10.00	18.00	25.00	35.00
1804☆	1962B	☆	New York	10.00	20.00	60.00	80.00
1805	1962C		Philadelphia	10.00	18.00	25.00	35.00
1805☆	1962C	☆	Philadelphia	10.00	20.00	60.00	75.00
1806	1962D		Cleveland	10.00	18.00	25.00	35.00
1806☆	1962D	☆	Cleveland	10.00	20.00	60.00	75.00
1807	1962E		Richmond	10.00	18.00	25.00	35.00
1807☆	1962E	☆	Richmond	10.00	20.00	60.00	75.00
1808	1962F		Atlanta	10.00	18.00	25.00	35.00
1808☆	1962F	☆	Atlanta	—	—	60.00	75.00
1809	1962G		Chicago	9.00	15.00	20.00	30.00
1809☆	1962G	☆	Chicago	10.00	20.00	60.00	75.00
1810	1962H		St. Louis	10.00	18.00	25.00	35.00
1810☆	1962H	☆	St. Louis	25.00	50.00	150.	200.
1811	1962I		Minneapolis	15.00	20.00	40.00	50.00
1811☆	1962I	☆	Minneapolis	25.00	100.	300.	350.
1812	1962J		Kansas City	10.00	18.00	25.00	35.00
1812☆	1962J	☆	Kansas City	15.00	30.00	100.	125.
1813	1962K		Dallas	15.00	20.00	40.00	60.00
1813☆	1962K	☆	Dallas	25.00	50.00	150.	200.
1814	1962L		San Francisco	10.00	18.00	25.00	35.00
1814☆	1962L	☆	San Francisco	15.00	25.00	75.00	125.

Series 1950B Priest-Anderson

KL#	Fr#		District	Fine	XF	CH CU (63)	Gem CU (65)
1815	1963A		Boston	12.00	20.00	30.00	40.00
1815☆	1963A	☆	Boston	10.00	20.00	60.00	75.00
1816	1963B		New York	10.00	15.00	20.00	30.00
1816☆	1963B	☆	New York	15.00	22.00	65.00	85.00
1817	1963C		Philadelphia	12.00	20.00	30.00	40.00
1817☆	1963C	☆	Philadelphia	10.00	20.00	60.00	75.00
1818	1963D		Cleveland	15.00	30.00	100.	125.
1818☆	1963D	☆	Cleveland	15.00	22.00	50.00	65.00
1820	1963F		Atlanta	12.00	20.00	30.00	40.00
1820☆	1963F	☆	Atlanta	10.00	20.00	60.00	75.00
1821	1963G		Chicago	12.00	20.00	30.00	40.00
1821☆	1963G	☆	Chicago	10.00	20.00	60.00	80.00
1822	1963H		St. Louis	12.00	20.00	30.00	40.00
1822☆	1963H	☆	St. Louis	10.00	20.00	60.00	75.00
1823	1963I		Minneapolis	12.00	20.00	35.00	50.00
1823☆	1963I	☆	Minneapolis	20.00	50.00	125.	175.
1824	1963J		Kansas City	12.00	20.00	30.00	40.00
1824☆	1963J	☆	Kansas City	15.00	22.00	50.00	85.00
1825	1963K		Dallas	12.00	20.00	30.00	45.00

KL#	Fr#		District	Fine	XF	CH CU (63)	Gem CU (65)
1825☆	1963K	☆	Dallas	18.00	30.00	80.00	100.
1826	1963L		San Francisco	12.00	20.00	30.00	45.00
1826☆	1963L	☆	San Francisco	18.00	30.00	80.00	100.

Series 1950C Smith-Dillon

KL#	Fr#		District	Fine	XF	CH CU (63)	Gem CU (65)
1827	1964A		Boston	8.00	10.00	15.00	20.00
1827☆	1964A	☆	Boston	15.00	30.00	75.00	125.
1828	1964B		New York	8.00	10.00	15.00	20.00
1828☆	1964B	☆	New York	10.00	18.00	40.00	60.00
1829	1964C		Philadelphia	8.00	10.00	15.00	20.00
1829☆	1964C	☆	Philadelphia	10.00	18.00	40.00	60.00
1830	1964D		Cleveland	8.00	10.00	15.00	20.00
1830☆	1964D	☆	Cleveland	10.00	18.00	40.00	60.00
1831	1964E		Richmond	8.00	10.00	15.00	20.00
1831☆	1964E	☆	Richmond	18.00	30.00	75.00	125.
1832	1964F		Atlanta	8.00	10.00	15.00	20.00
1832☆	1964F	☆	Atlanta	15.00	25.00	60.00	75.00
1833	1964G		Chicago	10.00	12.00	25.00	35.00
1833☆	1964G	☆	Chicago	25.00	35.00	100.	135.
1834	1964H		St. Louis	8.00	10.00	15.00	25.00
1834☆	1964H	☆	St. Louis	25.00	35.00	100.	140.
1835	1964I		Minneapolis	10.00	12.00	25.00	40.00
1835☆	1964I	☆	Minneapolis	30.00	50.00	150.	175.
1836	1964J		Kansas City	8.00	10.00	15.00	20.00
1836☆	1964J	☆	Kansas City	20.00	30.00	75.00	100.
1837	1964K		Dallas	15.00	25.00	50.00	75.00
1837☆	1964K	☆	Dallas	25.00	50.00	150.	225.
1838	1964L		San Francisco	8.00	10.00	15.00	20.00
1838☆	1964L	☆	San Francisco	20.00	40.00	120.	150.

Series 1950D Granahan-Dillon

KL#	Fr#		District	Fine	XF	CH CU (63)	Gem CU (65)
1839	1965A		Boston	8.00	10.00	15.00	25.00
1839☆	1965A	☆	Boston	15.00	30.00	75.00	100.
1840	1965B		New York	8.00	10.00	15.00	20.00
1840☆	1965B	☆	New York	15.00	20.00	40.00	60.00
1841	1965C		Philadelphia	8.00	10.00	15.00	20.00
1841☆	1965C	☆	Philadelphia	15.00	25.00	50.00	70.00
1842	1965D		Cleveland	8.00	10.00	15.00	20.00
1842☆	1965D	☆	Cleveland	15.00	25.00	50.00	70.00
1843	1965E		Richmond	8.00	10.00	15.00	20.00
1843☆	1965E	☆	Richmond	15.00	30.00	60.00	80.00
1844	1965F		Atlanta	8.00	10.00	15.00	25.00
1844☆	1965F	☆	Atlanta	15.00	30.00	70.00	90.00
1845	1965G		Chicago	8.00	10.00	15.00	20.00
1845☆	1965G	☆	Chicago	10.00	20.00	45.00	60.00
1846	1965H		St. Louis	8.00	10.00	15.00	20.00

KL#	Fr#		District	Fine	XF	CH CU (63)	Gem CU (65)
1846☆	1965H	☆	St. Louis	15.00	30.00	70.00	90.00
1847	1965I		Minneapolis	10.00	12.00	25.00	35.00
1847☆	1965I	☆	Minneapolis	30.00	70.00	140.	165.
1848	1965J		Kansas City	8.00	10.00	15.00	20.00
1848☆	1965J	☆	Kansas City	15.00	30.00	60.00	75.00
1849	1965K		Dallas	8.00	10.00	15.00	20.00
1849☆	1965K	☆	Dallas	25.00	50.00	100.	125.
1850	1965L		San Francisco	15.00	25.00	50.00	70.00
1850☆	1965L	☆	San Francisco	30.00	70.00	150.	200.

Series 1950E Granahan-Fowler

KL#	Fr#		District	Fine	XF	CH CU (63)	Gem CU (65)
1852	1966B		New York	9.00	12.00	25.00	35.00
1852☆	1966B	☆	New York	15.00	30.00	75.00	90.00
1853	1966G		Chicago	20.00	40.00	90.00	125.
1853☆	1966G	☆	Chicago	75.00	150.	325.	450.
1854	1966L		San Francisco	15.00	25.00	40.00	50.00
1854☆	1966L	☆	San Francisco	20.00	45.00	100.	200.

Series 1963 Granahan-Dillon

KL#	Fr#		District	Fine	XF	CH CU (63)	Gem CU (65)
1855	1967A		Boston	8.00	10.00	28.00	30.00
1855☆	1967A	☆	Boston	20.00	45.00	70.00	75.00
1856	1967B		New York	8.00	10.00	28.00	30.00
1856☆	1967B	☆	New York	20.00	45.00	60.00	65.00
1857	1967C		Philadelphia	8.00	10.00	28.00	30.00
1857☆	1967C	☆	Philadelphia	20.00	45.00	60.00	65.00
1858	1967D		Cleveland	8.00	10.00	28.00	30.00
1858☆	1967D	☆	Cleveland	20.00	45.00	60.00	65.00
1859	1967F		Atlanta	8.00	10.00	28.00	30.00
1859☆	1967F	☆	Atlanta	20.00	45.00	70.00	75.00
1860	1967G		Chicago	8.00	10.00	28.00	30.00
1860☆	1967G	☆	Chicago	15.00	35.00	60.00	65.00
1861	1967H		St. Louis	8.00	10.00	28.00	30.00
1861☆	1967H	☆	St. Louis	15.00	45.00	60.00	70.00
1861A	1967J		Kansas City	8.00	10.00	28.00	30.00
1861A☆	1967J	☆	Kansas City	15.00	45.00	70.00	75.00
1862	1967K		Dallas	8.00	10.00	28.00	30.00

KL#	Fr#		District	Fine	XF	CH CU (63)	Gem CU (65)
1862☆	1967K	☆	Dallas	15.00	45.00	70.00	75.00
1863	1967L		San Francisco	8.00	10.00	28.00	30.00
1863☆	1967L	☆	San Francisco	15.00	45.00	60.00	65.00

Series 1963A Granahan-Fowler

KL#	Fr#		District	Fine	XF	CH CU (63)	Gem CU (65)
1864	1968A		Boston	8.00	10.00	23.00	25.00
1864☆	1968A	☆	Boston	10.00	25.00	40.00	43.00
1865	1968B		New York	8.00	10.00	23.00	25.00
1865☆	1968B	☆	New York	15.00	30.00	40.00	43.00
1866	1968C		Philadelphia	8.00	10.00	23.00	25.00
1866☆	1968C	☆	Philadelphia	15.00	30.00	40.00	43.00
1867	1968D		Cleveland	8.00	10.00	23.00	25.00
1867☆	1968D	☆	Cleveland	15.00	30.00	40.00	43.00
1868	1968E		Richmond	8.00	10.00	23.00	25.00
1868☆	1968E	☆	Richmond	15.00	30.00	40.00	43.00
1869	1968F		Atlanta	8.00	10.00	23.00	25.00
1869☆	1968F	☆	Atlanta	15.00	40.00	60.00	65.00
1870	1968G		Chicago	8.00	10.00	23.00	25.00
1870☆	1968G	☆	Chicago	15.00	40.00	60.00	65.00
1871	1968H		St. Louis	7.00	10.00	23.00	25.00
1871☆	1968H	☆	St. Louis	15.00	25.00	35.00	45.00
1872	1968I		Minneapolis	8.00	15.00	30.00	35.00
1872☆	1968I	☆	Minneapolis	15.00	40.00	80.00	90.00
1873	1968J		Kansas City	8.00	10.00	23.00	25.00
1873☆	1968J	☆	Kansas City	15.00	30.00	60.00	65.00
1874	1968K		Dallas	8.00	10.00	23.00	25.00
1874☆	1968K	☆	Dallas	15.00	22.00	35.00	40.00
1875	1968L		San Francisco	8.00	10.00	23.00	25.00
1875☆	1968L	☆	San Francisco	15.00	22.00	35.00	40.00

Series 1969 Elston-Kennedy

KL#	Fr#		District	Fine	XF	CH CU (63)	Gem CU (65)
1876	1969A		Boston	6.00	7.00	20.00	23.00
1876☆	1969A	☆	Boston	10.00	30.00	50.00	53.00
1877	1969B		New York	6.00	7.00	20.00	23.00
1877☆	1969B	☆	New York	10.00	20.00	40.00	45.00
1878	1969C		Philadelphia	6.00	7.00	20.00	23.00
1878☆	1969C	☆	Philadelphia	10.00	30.00	50.00	55.00
1879	1969D		Cleveland	6.00	7.00	20.00	23.00
1879☆	1969D	☆	Cleveland	10.00	20.00	40.00	45.00
1880	1969E		Richmond	6.00	7.00	20.00	23.00
1880☆	1969E	☆	Richmond	10.00	30.00	50.00	55.00
1881	1969F		Atlanta	6.00	7.00	20.00	23.00
1881☆	1969F	☆	Atlanta	10.00	25.00	40.00	45.00
1882	1969G		Chicago	6.00	7.00	20.00	23.00
1882☆	1969G	☆	Chicago	10.00	25.00	40.00	45.00
1883	1969H		St. Louis	6.00	7.00	20.00	23.00
1883☆	1969H	☆	St. Louis	15.00	35.00	60.00	65.00
1884	1969I		Minneapolis	10.00	25.00	40.00	45.00
1884☆	1969I	☆	Minneapolis	15.00	45.00	75.00	80.00
1885	1969J		Kansas City	6.00	7.00	20.00	23.00
1885☆	1969J	☆	Kansas City	15.00	30.00	50.00	55.00
1886	1969K		Dallas	6.00	7.00	20.00	23.00
1886☆	1969K	☆	Dallas	15.00	30.00	50.00	55.00
1887	1969L		San Francisco	6.00	7.00	20.00	23.00
1887☆	1969L	☆	San Francisco	15.00	30.00	50.00	55.00

Series 1969A Kabis-Connally

KL#	Fr#		District	Fine	XF	CH CU (63)	Gem CU (65)
1888	1970A		Boston	6.00	8.00	22.00	25.00
1888☆	1970A	☆	Boston	10.00	30.00	65.00	70.00
1889	1970B		New York	6.00	8.00	25.00	—
1889☆	1970B	☆	New York	15.00	32.00	65.00	70.00
1890	1970C		Philadelphia	6.00	8.00	22.00	25.00
1890☆	1970C	☆	Philadelphia	15.00	32.00	70.00	75.00
1891	1970D		Cleveland	6.00	8.00	22.00	25.00
1891☆	1970D	☆	Cleveland	15.00	32.00	75.00	80.00
1892	1970E		Richmond	6.00	8.00	22.00	25.00
1892☆	1970E	☆	Richmond	15.00	32.00	75.00	80.00
1893	1970F		Atlanta	6.00	8.00	22.00	25.00
1893☆	1970F	☆	Atlanta	15.00	32.00	75.00	80.00
1894	1970G		Chicago	6.00	8.00	22.00	25.00
1894☆	1970G	☆	Chicago	15.00	32.00	65.00	70.00
1895	1970H		St. Louis	6.00	8.00	22.00	25.00
1895☆	1970H	☆	St. Louis	15.00	30.00	70.00	75.00
1896	1970I		Minneapolis	6.00	10.00	28.00	30.00
1896☆	1970I	☆	Minneapolis	20.00	40.00	85.00	90.00
1897	1970J		Kansas City	6.00	8.00	23.00	25.00
1897☆	1970J	☆	Kansas City	15.00	35.00	75.00	80.00
1898	1970K		Dallas	6.00	8.00	28.00	30.00
1898☆	1970K	☆	Dallas	20.00	40.00	80.00	85.00
1899	1970L		San Francisco	6.00	8.00	23.00	25.00
1899☆	1970L	☆	San Francisco	15.00	35.00	75.00	80.00

Series 1969B Banuelos-Connally

KL#	Fr#		District	Fine	XF	CH CU (63)	Gem CU (65)
1900	1971A		Boston	15.00	30.00	75.00	80.00
1901	1971B		New York	10.00	30.00	75.00	80.00
1901☆	1971B	☆	New York	50.00	100.	225.	235.
1902	1971C		Philadelphia	10.00	30.00	75.00	80.00
1903	1971D		Cleveland	10.00	30.00	75.00	80.00
1904	1971E		Richmond	10.00	30.00	75.00	80.00
1904☆	1971E	☆	Richmond	50.00	100.	225.	235.
1905	1971F		Atlanta	10.00	30.00	75.00	80.00
1905☆	1971F	☆	Atlanta	50.00	125.	240.	250.
1906	1971G		Chicago	10.00	30.00	75.00	80.00
1906☆	1971G	☆	Chicago	50.00	125.	240.	250.
1907	1971H		St. Louis	10.00	30.00	75.00	80.00
1908	1971I		Minneapolis	20.00	60.00	150.	155.
1909	1971J		Kansas City	10.00	30.00	75.00	80.00
1909☆	1971J	☆	Kansas City	30.00	100.	225.	230.
1910	1971K		Dallas	10.00	30.00	75.00	80.00
1911	1971L		San Francisco	10.00	30.00	75.00	80.00
1911☆	1971L	☆	San Francisco	30.00	100.	225.	230.

Series 1969C Banuelos-Shultz

KL#	Fr#		District	Fine	XF	CH CU (63)	Gem CU (65)
1912	1972A		Boston	5.00	7.00	20.00	23.00
1912☆	1972A	☆	Boston	15.00	30.00	60.00	65.00
1913	1972B		New York	5.00	7.00	20.00	23.00
1913☆	1972B	☆	New York	15.00	30.00	60.00	65.00
1914	1972C		Philadelphia	5.00	7.00	20.00	23.00
1914☆	1972C	☆	Philadelphia	15.00	30.00	60.00	65.00
1915	1972D		Cleveland	5.00	7.00	20.00	23.00
1915☆	1972D	☆	Cleveland	15.00	35.00	65.00	70.00
1916	1972E		Richmond	5.00	7.00	20.00	23.00
1916☆	1972E	☆	Richmond	15.00	35.00	70.00	75.00

KL#	Fr#		District	Fine	XF	CH CU (63)	Gem CU (65)
1917	1972F		Atlanta	5.00	7.00	20.00	23.00
1917☆	1972F	☆	Atlanta	15.00	35.00	65.00	70.00
1918	1972G		Chicago	5.00	7.00	20.00	23.00
1919	1972H		St. Louis	5.00	7.00	20.00	23.00
1919☆	1972H	☆	St. Louis	10.00	35.00	65.00	70.00
1920	1972I		Minneapolis	5.00	7.00	25.00	30.00
1921	1972J		Kansas City	5.00	7.00	20.00	23.00
1921☆	1972J	☆	Kansas City	15.00	35.00	65.00	70.00
1922	1972K		Dallas	5.00	7.00	20.00	23.00
1922☆	1972K	☆	Dallas	15.00	35.00	65.00	70.00
1923	1972L		San Francisco	5.00	7.00	20.00	23.00
1923☆	1972L	☆	San Francisco	15.00	35.00	65.00	70.00

Series 1974 Neff-Simon

KL#	Fr#		District	Fine	XF	CH CU (63)	Gem CU (65)
1924	1973A		Boston	5.00	7.00	15.00	18.00
1924☆	1973A	☆	Boston	6.00	25.00	40.00	43.00
1925	1973B		New York	5.00	7.00	15.00	18.00
1925☆	1973B	☆	New York	6.00	25.00	40.00	43.00
1926	1973C		Philadelphia	5.00	7.00	15.00	18.00
1926☆	1973C	☆	Philadelphia	6.00	20.00	35.00	38.00
1927	1973D		Cleveland	5.00	7.00	15.00	18.00
1927☆	1973D	☆	Cleveland	6.00	25.00	40.00	43.00
1928	1973E		Richmond	5.00	7.00	15.00	18.00
1928☆	1973E	☆	Richmond	6.00	25.00	40.00	43.00
1929	1973F		Atlanta	5.00	7.00	15.00	18.00
1929☆	1973F	☆	Atlanta	6.00	20.00	35.00	38.00
1930	1973G		Chicago	5.00	7.00	15.00	18.00
1930☆	1973G	☆	Chicago	6.00	20.00	35.00	38.00
1931	1973H		St. Louis	5.00	7.00	15.00	18.00
1931☆	1973H	☆	St. Louis	8.00	40.00	75.00	80.00
1932	1973I		Minneapolis	5.00	7.00	15.00	18.00
1932☆	1973I	☆	Minneapolis	6.00	20.00	35.00	38.00
1933	1973J		Kansas City	5.00	7.00	15.00	18.00
1933☆	1973J	☆	Kansas City	6.00	20.00	35.00	38.00
1934	1973K		Dallas	5.00	7.00	15.00	18.00
1934☆	1973K	☆	Dallas	6.00	25.00	40.00	45.00
1935	1973L		San Francisco	5.00	7.00	15.00	18.00
1935☆	1973L	☆	San Francisco	6.00	20.00	35.00	38.00

Series 1977 Morton-Blumenthal

KL#	Fr#		District	Fine	XF	CH CU (63)	Gem CU (65)
1936	1974A		Boston	5.00	7.00	15.00	18.00
1936☆	1974A	☆	Boston	6.00	20.00	40.00	43.00
1937	1974B		New York	5.00	7.00	15.00	18.00
1937☆	1974B	☆	New York	6.00	20.00	40.00	43.00
1938	1974C		Philadelphia	5.00	7.00	15.00	18.00

KL#	Fr#		District	Fine	XF	CH CU (63)	Gem CU (65)
1938☆	1974C	☆	Philadelphia	6.00	20.00	40.00	43.00
1939	1974D		Cleveland	5.00	7.00	15.00	18.00
1939☆	1974D	☆	Cleveland	6.00	20.00	40.00	43.00
1940	1974E		Richmond	5.00	7.00	15.00	18.00
1940☆	1974E	☆	Richmond	6.00	20.00	40.00	43.00
1941	1974F		Atlanta	5.00	7.00	15.00	18.00
1941☆	1974F	☆	Atlanta	6.00	20.00	40.00	43.00
1942	1974G		Chicago	5.00	7.00	15.00	18.00
1942☆	1974G	☆	Chicago	6.00	20.00	40.00	43.00
1943	1974H		St. Louis	5.00	7.00	15.00	18.00
1943☆	1974H	☆	St. Louis	7.00	35.00	70.00	75.00
1944	1974I		Minneapolis	5.00	7.00	15.00	18.00
1945	1974J		Kansas City	5.00	7.00	15.00	18.00
1945☆	1974J	☆	Kansas City	6.00	23.00	45.00	48.00
1946	1974K		Dallas	5.00	7.00	15.00	18.00
1946☆	1974K	☆	Dallas	6.00	20.00	40.00	43.00
1947	1974L		San Francisco	5.00	7.00	15.00	18.00
1947☆	1974L	☆	San Francisco	6.00	20.00	40.00	43.00

Series 1977A Morton-Miller

KL#	Fr#		District	Fine	XF	CH CU (63)	Gem CU (65)
1948	1975A		Boston	7.00	10.00	35.00	38.00
1948☆	1975A	☆	Boston	20.00	60.00	135.	140.
1949	1975B		New York	7.00	10.00	35.00	38.00
1949☆	1975B	☆	New York	10.00	30.00	60.00	65.00
1950	1975C		Philadelphia	7.00	10.00	35.00	38.00
1950☆	1975C	☆	Philadelphia	10.00	30.00	60.00	65.00
1951	1975D		Cleveland	7.00	10.00	35.00	38.00
1951☆	1975D	☆	Cleveland	18.00	50.00	125.	130.
1952	1975E		Richmond	7.00	10.00	35.00	38.00
1952☆	1975E	☆	Richmond	18.00	50.00	125.	130.
1953	1975F		Atlanta	7.00	10.00	35.00	38.00
1953☆	1975F	☆	Atlanta	10.00	30.00	60.00	65.00
1954	1975G		Chicago	7.00	10.00	35.00	38.00
1954☆	1975G	☆	Chicago	20.00	30.00	60.00	65.00
1955	1975H		St. Louis	7.00	10.00	35.00	38.00
1955☆	1975H	☆	St. Louis	20.00	60.00	150.	155.
1956	1975I		Minneapolis	7.00	10.00	35.00	38.00
1956☆	1975I	☆	Minneapolis	18.00	60.00	125.	130.
1957	1975J		Kansas City	7.00	10.00	35.00	38.00
1957☆	1975J	☆	Kansas City	18.00	50.00	125.	130.
1958	1975K		Dallas	7.00	10.00	35.00	38.00
1958☆	1975K	☆	Dallas	15.00	40.00	80.00	85.00
1959	1975L		San Francisco	7.00	10.00	35.00	38.00
1959☆	1975L	☆	San Francisco	10.00	30.00	60.00	65.00

Series 1981 Buchanan-Regan

KL#	Fr#		District	Fine	XF	CH CU (63)	Gem CU (65)
3512	1976A		Boston	5.00	8.00	25.00	28.00
3513	1976B		New York	5.00	8.00	25.00	28.00
3513☆	1976B	☆	New York	7.00	20.00	50.00	53.00
3514	1976C		Philadelphia	5.00	8.00	25.00	28.00
3514☆	1976C	☆	Philadelphia	7.00	20.00	50.00	53.00
3515	1976D		Cleveland	5.00	8.00	25.00	28.00
3515☆	1976D	☆	Cleveland	7.00	20.00	50.00	53.00
3516	1976E		Richmond	5.00	8.00	25.00	28.00
3516☆	1976E	☆	Richmond	7.00	20.00	50.00	53.00
3517	1976F		Atlanta	5.00	8.00	25.00	28.00
3517☆	1976F	☆	Atlanta	7.00	20.00	50.00	53.00

KL#	Fr#		District	Fine	XF	CH CU (63)	Gem CU (65)
3518	1976G		Chicago	5.00	8.00	25.00	28.00
3518☆	1976G	☆	Chicago	7.00	20.00	50.00	53.00
3519	1976H		St. Louis	5.00	8.00	25.00	28.00
3519☆	1976H	☆	St. Louis	10.00	35.00	70.00	75.00
3520	1976I		Minneapolis	5.00	8.00	25.00	28.00
3520☆	1976I	☆	Minneapolis	10.00	50.00	100.	110.
3521	1976J		Kansas City	5.00	8.00	25.00	28.00
3521☆	1976J	☆	Kansas City	10.00	35.00	70.00	75.00
3522	1976K		Dallas	5.00	8.00	25.00	28.00
3522☆	1976K	☆	Dallas	7.00	20.00	50.00	53.00
3523	1976L		San Francisco	5.00	8.00	25.00	28.00
3523☆	1976L	☆	San Francisco	7.00	20.00	50.00	53.00

Series 1981A Ortega-Regan

KL#	Fr#		District	Fine	XF	CH CU (63)	Gem CU (65)
3612	1977A		Boston	7.00	15.00	30.00	33.00
3613	1977B		New York	7.00	15.00	30.00	33.00
3613☆	1977B	☆	New York	8.00	25.00	75.00	78.00
3614	1977C		Philadelphia	7.00	15.00	30.00	33.00
3615	1977D		Cleveland	7.00	15.00	30.00	33.00
3616	1977E		Richmond	7.00	15.00	30.00	33.00
3617	1977F		Atlanta	7.00	15.00	30.00	33.00
3618	1977G		Chicago	7.00	15.00	30.00	33.00
3619	1977H		St. Louis	7.00	15.00	30.00	33.00
3620	1977I		Minneapolis	7.00	15.00	30.00	33.00
3621	1977J		Kansas City	7.00	15.00	30.00	33.00
3622	1977K		Dallas	7.00	15.00	30.00	33.00
3623	1977L		San Francisco	7.00	15.00	30.00	33.00
3623☆	1977L	☆	San Francisco	7.00	25.00	75.00	78.00

Series 1985 Ortega-Baker

KL#	Fr#		District	Fine	XF	CH CU (63)	Gem CU (65)
3712	1978A		Boston	5.00	7.00	15.00	18.00
3713	1978B		New York	5.00	7.00	15.00	18.00
3713☆	1978B	☆	New York	6.00	30.00	60.00	63.00
3714	1978C		Philadelphia	5.00	7.00	15.00	18.00
3714☆	1978C	☆	Philadelphia	6.00	25.00	75.00	80.00
3715	1978D		Cleveland	5.00	7.00	15.00	18.00
3716	1978E		Richmond	5.00	7.00	15.00	18.00
3716☆	1978E	☆	Richmond	6.00	30.00	60.00	63.00
3717	1978F		Atlanta	5.00	7.00	15.00	18.00
3717☆	1978F	☆	Atlanta	6.00	30.00	60.00	63.00
3718	1978G		Chicago	5.00	7.00	15.00	18.00
3718☆	1978G	☆	Chicago	6.00	30.00	60.00	63.00
3719	1978H		St. Louis	5.00	7.00	15.00	18.00
3720	1978I		Minneapolis	5.00	7.00	15.00	18.00
3721	1978J		Kansas City	5.00	7.00	15.00	18.00

KL#	Fr#		District	Fine	XF	CH CU (63)	Gem CU (65)
3722	1978K		Dallas	5.00	7.00	15.00	18.00
3722☆	1978K	☆	Dallas	6.00	30.00	60.00	63.00
3723	1978L		San Francisco	5.00	7.00	15.00	18.00
3723☆	1978L	☆	San Francisco	6.00	30.00	60.00	63.00

Series 1988 Ortega-Brady

KL#	Fr#		District	Fine	XF	CH CU (63)	Gem CU (65)
3784	1979A		Boston	5.00	7.00	15.00	18.00
3784☆	1979A	☆	Boston	6.00	30.00	70.00	75.00
3785	1979B		New York	5.00	7.00	15.00	18.00
3785☆	1979B	☆	New York	6.00	25.00	50.00	53.00
3786	1979C		Philadelphia	5.00	7.00	15.00	18.00
3787	1979D		Cleveland	5.00	7.00	15.00	18.00
3788	1979E		Richmond	5.00	7.00	15.00	18.00
3789	1979F		Atlanta	5.00	7.00	15.00	18.00
3789☆	1979F	☆	Atlanta	—	25.00	50.00	53.00
3790	1979G		Chicago	5.00	7.00	15.00	18.00
3791	1979H		St. Louis	5.00	7.00	15.00	18.00
3792	1979I		Minneapolis	5.00	15.00	40.00	43.00
3793	1979J		Kansas City	5.00	7.00	15.00	18.00
3794	1979K		Dallas	5.00	7.00	15.00	18.00
3795	1979L		San Francisco	5.00	7.00	15.00	18.00

Series 1988A Villalpando-Brady

KL#	Fr#		District	Fine	XF	CH CU (63)	Gem CU (65)
3856	1980A		Boston	5.00	7.00	15.00	18.00
3856☆	1980A	☆	Boston	6.00	15.00	40.00	43.00
3857	1980B		New York	5.00	7.00	15.00	18.00
3857☆	1980B	☆	New York	6.00	15.00	40.00	43.00
3858	1980C		Philadelphia	5.00	7.00	15.00	18.00
3859	1980D		Cleveland	5.00	7.00	15.00	18.00
3859☆	1980D	☆	Cleveland	6.00	15.00	40.00	43.00
3860	1980E		Richmond	5.00	7.00	15.00	18.00
3860☆	1980E	☆	Richmond	6.00	15.00	40.00	43.00
3860A	1980F		Atlanta	5.00	7.00	15.00	18.00
3860A☆	1980F	☆	Atlanta	6.00	15.00	40.00	43.00
3860B	1980G		Chicago	5.00	7.00	15.00	18.00
3860B☆	1980G	☆	Chicago	6.00	15.00	40.00	43.00
3860C	1980H		St. Louis	5.00	7.00	15.00	18.00
3860C☆	1980H	☆	St. Louis	6.00	15.00	40.00	43.00
3860D	1980I		Minneapolis	5.00	7.00	15.00	18.00
3860D☆	1980I	☆	Minneapolis	6.00	15.00	40.00	43.00
3860E	1980J		Kansas City	5.00	7.00	15.00	18.00
3860F	1980K		Dallas	5.00	7.00	15.00	18.00
3860F☆	1980K	☆	Dallas	6.00	15.00	40.00	43.00
3860G	1980L		San Francisco	5.00	7.00	15.00	18.00

Series 1993 Withrow-Bentsen

KL#	Fr#		District	Fine	XF	CH CU (63)	Gem CU (65)
4024	1982A		Boston	5.00	7.00	15.00	18.00
4025	1982B		New York	5.00	7.00	15.00	18.00
4025☆	1982B	☆	New York	6.00	10.00	40.00	50.00
4026	1982C		Philadelphia	5.00	7.00	15.00	18.00
4026☆	1982C	☆	Philadelphia	6.00	7.00	15.00	18.00
4029	1982F		Atlanta	5.00	7.00	15.00	18.00
4030	1982G		Chicago	5.00	7.00	15.00	18.00
4030☆	1982G	☆	Chicago	6.00	10.00	40.00	50.00
4031	1982H		St. Louis	5.00	7.00	15.00	18.00
4031☆	1982H	☆	St. Louis	6.00	10.00	40.00	50.00

KL#	Fr#	District	Fine	XF	CH CU (63)	Gem CU (65)
4032	1982I	Minneapolis	5.00	7.00	200.	225.
4033	1982J	Kansas City	5.00	7.00	15.00	18.00
4034	1982K	Dallas	5.00	7.00	15.00	18.00
4035	-	San Francisco	5.00	7.00	15.00	18.00
4035☆	-	San Francisco	6.00	10.00	40.00	50.00

Series 1995 Withrow-Rubin

KL#	Fr#	District	Fine	XF	CH CU (63)	Gem CU (65)
4096	1984A	Boston	5.00	6.00	10.00	13.00
4096☆	1984A ☆	Boston	6.00	10.00	35.00	40.00
4097	1984B	New York	5.00	6.00	10.00	13.00
4097☆	1984B ☆	New York	6.00	10.00	30.00	35.00
4098	1984C	Philadelphia	5.00	6.00	10.00	13.00
4099	1984D	Cleveland	5.00	6.00	10.00	13.00
4099☆	1984D ☆	Cleveland	6.00	10.00	30.00	35.00
4100	1984E	Richmond	5.00	6.00	10.00	13.00
4101	1984F	Atlanta	5.00	6.00	10.00	13.00
4101☆	1984F ☆	Atlanta	6.00	10.00	50.00	55.00
4102	1984G	Chicago	5.00	6.00	10.00	13.00
4102☆	1984G ☆	Chicago	6.00	10.00	25.00	28.00
4103	1984H	St. Louis	5.00	6.00	10.00	13.00
4104	1984I	Minneapolis	5.00	6.00	10.00	13.00
4105	1984J	Kansas City	5.00	6.00	10.00	13.00
4106	1984K	Dallas	5.00	6.00	10.00	—
4107	1984L	San Francisco	5.00	6.00	10.00	—

Series 1999 Withrow-Summers - DC

KL#	Fr#	District	Fine	XF	CH CU (63)	Gem CU (65)
4513	1986A	Boston	5.00	6.00	10.00	13.00
4514	1986B	New York	5.00	6.00	10.00	13.00
4515	1986C	Philadelphia	5.00	6.00	10.00	13.00
4516	1986D	Cleveland	5.00	6.00	10.00	13.00
4517	1986E	Richmond	5.00	6.00	10.00	13.00
4517☆	1986E ☆	Richmond	6.00	10.00	20.00	23.00
4518	1987A	Boston	5.00	6.00	10.00	13.00
4518☆	1987A ☆	Boston	6.00	10.00	20.00	23.00
4519	1987B	New York	5.00	6.00	10.00	13.00
4519☆	1987B ☆	New York	6.00	10.00	20.00	23.00
4520	1987C	Philadelphia	5.00	6.00	10.00	13.00
4521	1987D	Cleveland	5.00	6.00	10.00	13.00
4522	1987E	Richmond	5.00	6.00	10.00	13.00
4522☆	1987E ☆	Richmond	6.00	10.00	20.00	23.00
4523	1987F	Atlanta	5.00	6.00	10.00	13.00
4523☆	1987F ☆	Atlanta	6.00	8.00	20.00	23.00
4524	1987G	Chicago	5.00	6.00	10.00	13.00
4524☆	1987G ☆	Chicago	6.00	8.00	20.00	23.00
4525	1987H	St. Louis	5.00	6.00	10.00	13.00

KL#	Fr#	District	Fine	XF	CH CU (63)	Gem CU (65)
4526	1987I	Minneapolis	5.00	6.00	10.00	13.00
4527	1987J	Kansas City	5.00	6.00	10.00	13.00
4527☆	1987J ☆	Kansas City	6.00	8.00	20.00	23.00
4528	1987K	Dallas	5.00	6.00	10.00	13.00
4528☆	1987K ☆	Dallas	6.00	6.00	10.00	13.00
4529	1987L	San Francisco	5.00	6.00	10.00	13.00

Series 2001 Marin-O'Neill

KL#	Fr#	District	Fine	XF	CH CU (63)	Gem CU (65)
4587	1989A	Boston	5.00	7.00	15.00	18.00
4588	1989B	New York	5.00	7.00	15.00	18.00
4589	1989C	Philadelphia	5.00	7.00	15.00	18.00
4590	1989D	Cleveland	5.00	7.00	15.00	18.00
4591	1989E	Richmond	5.00	7.00	15.00	18.00
4592	1989F	Atlanta	5.00	7.00	15.00	18.00
4593	1989G	Chicago	5.00	7.00	15.00	18.00
4594	1989H	St. Louis	5.00	7.00	15.00	18.00
4595	1989I	Minneapolis	5.00	7.00	15.00	18.00
4596	1989J	Kansas City	5.00	7.00	15.00	18.00
4597	1989K	Dallas	5.00	7.00	15.00	18.00
4597☆	1989K ☆	Dallas	6.00	10.00	35.00	38.00
4598	1989L	San Francisco	5.00	7.00	15.00	18.00

Series 2003 Marin-Snow - DC

KL#	Fr#	District	Fine	XF	CH CU (63)	Gem CU (65)
4685	-	Cleveland	5.00	7.00	15.00	18.00
4686	-	Atlanta	5.00	7.00	15.00	18.00
4687	-	Chicago	5.00	7.00	15.00	18.00
4687☆	-	Chicago	6.00	10.00	35.00	38.00

Series 2003 Marin-Snow - FW

KL#	Fr#	District	Fine	XF	CH CU (63)	Gem CU (65)
4688	1990A	Boston	5.00	7.00	15.00	18.00
4689	1990B	New York	5.00	7.00	15.00	18.00
4690	1990C	Philadelphia	5.00	7.00	15.00	18.00
4691	1990D	Cleveland	5.00	7.00	15.00	18.00
4692	1990E	Richmond	5.00	7.00	15.00	18.00
4693	1990F	Atlanta	5.00	7.00	15.00	18.00
4694	1990G	Chicago	5.00	7.00	15.00	18.00
4695	1990H	St. Louis	5.00	7.00	15.00	18.00
4696	1990I	Minneapolis	5.00	7.00	15.00	18.00
4697	1990J	Kansas City	5.00	7.00	15.00	18.00
4698	1990K	Dallas	5.00	7.00	15.00	18.00
4699	1990L	San Francisco	5.00	7.00	15.00	18.00
4699☆	1990L ☆	San Francisco	6.00	10.00	35.00	38.00

Federal Reserve Notes - Hawaii Emergency

KL#	Fr#	Series	DistrictSignatures	Fine	XF	CH CU (63)	Gem CU (65)
1960	2301	1934	Julian-Morgenthau	75.00	200.	575.	1100.

Silver Certificates - North Africa Emergency

KL#	Fr#	Series	Signatures	Fine	XF	CH CU (63)	Gem CU (65)
1962	2307	1935A	Julian-Morgenthau	50.00	150.	250.	500.
1962☆	2307	1935A☆	Julian-Morgenthau	325.	1000.	3000.	3700.

Gold Certificates

Ten Dollars

KL#	Fr#	Series	Signatures	VF	XF	CH CU (63)	Gem CU (65)
1963	2400	1928	Woods-Mellon	200.	350.	700.	1000.
1963☆	2400	1928☆	Woods-Mellon	500.	1250.	5000.	7000.

Silver Certificates

KL#	Fr#	Series	Signatures	Fine	XF	CH CU (63)	Gem CU (65)
1964	1700	1933	Julian-Woodin	5000.	8000.	20,000.	30,000.
1964☆	1700	1933☆	Julian-Woodin	—	—	Rare	—
1966	1701	1934	Julian-Morgenthau	30.00	75.00	250.	325.
1966☆	1701	1934☆	Julian-Morgenthau	150.	500.	2250.	2750.

KL#	Fr#	Series	Signatures	Fine	XF	CH CU (63)	Gem CU (65)
1967	1702	1934A	Julian-Morgenthau	35.00	125.	375.	500.
1967☆	1702	1934A☆	Julian-Morgenthau	—	—	—	2500.
1968	1703	1934B	Julian-Vinson	150.	500.	2500.	3750.
1968☆	1703	1934B☆	Julian-Vinson	2000.	4000.	15,000.	20,000.
1969	1704	1934C	Julian-Snyder	20.00	50.00	150.	500.
1969☆	1704	1934C☆	Julian-Snyder	70.00	200.	750.	1000.
1970	1705	1934D	Clark-Snyder	30.00	40.00	275.	325.
1970☆	1705	1934D☆	Clark-Snyder	200.	1000.	4500.	5500.
1971	1706	1953	Priest-Humphrey	30.00	65.00	250.	450.
1971☆	1706	1953☆	Priest-Humphrey	75.00	300.	900.	1250.
1972	1707	1953A	Priest-Anderson	40.00	125.	400.	725.
1972☆	1707	1953A☆	Priest-Anderson	100.	400.	1600.	2200.
1973	1708	1953B	Smith-Dillon	25.00	75.00	250.	425.

Federal Reserve Bank Notes

KL#	Fr#	Series	District	Fine	XF	CH CU (63)	Gem CU (65)
1974	1860A	1929	Boston	30.00	75.00	250.	375.
1974☆	1860A	1929☆	Boston	2500.	5000.	10,000.	13,400.
1975	1860B	1929	New York	30.00	60.00	175.	275.
1975☆	1860B	1929☆	New York	200.	750.	2000.	3250.
1976	1860C	1929	Philadelphia	20.00	65.00	225.	335.
1976☆	1860C	1929☆	Philadelphia	350.	1250.	2500.	3350.
1977	1860D	1929	Cleveland	20.00	100.	500.	275.
1977☆	1860D	1929☆	Cleveland	350.	550.	2500.	3500.
1978	1860E	1929	Richmond	25.00	100.	400.	750.
1978☆	1860E	1929☆	Richmond	500.	2000.	9000.	11,400.
1979	1860F	1929	Atlanta	20.00	75.00	200.	500.
1979☆	1860F	1929☆	Atlanta	1500.	3000.	—	—
1980	1860G	1929	Chicago	30.00	70.00	200.	275.
1980☆	1860G	1929☆	Chicago	900.	2750.	—	—
1981	1860H	1929	St. Louis	20.00	60.00	200.	300.
1981☆	1860H	1929☆	St. Louis	300.	900.	3500.	3350.
1982	1860I	1929	Minneapolis	25.00	75.00	300.	650.
1982☆	1860I	1929☆	Minneapolis	1200.	1500.	3500.	4700.
1983	1860J	1929	Kansas City	25.00	50.00	200.	335.
1983☆	1860J	1929☆	Kansas City	200.	700.	2600.	3700.
1984	1860K	1929	Dallas	325.	750.	2500.	3500.
1984☆	1860K	1929☆	Dallas	5000.	—	—	—
1985	1860L	1929	San Francisco	200.	500.	1500.	1800.
1985☆	1860L	1929☆	San Francisco	1000.	1500.	—	—

Federal Reserve Notes

Series 1928 Tate-Mellon

KL#	Fr#		District	Fine	XF	CH CU (63)	Gem CU (65)
1986	2000A		Boston	35.00	60.00	350.	450.
1986☆	2000A	☆	Boston	150.	450.	2000.	2500.
1987	2000B		New York	35.00	45.00	250.	350.
1987☆	2000B	☆	New York	150.	450.	1000.	1250.
1988	2000C		Philadelphia	40.00	60.00	300.	450.
1988☆	2000C	☆	Philadelphia	150.	450.	1200.	1400.
1989	2000D		Cleveland	35.00	50.00	250.	350.
1989☆	2000D	☆	Cleveland	150.	450.	1250.	1500.
1990	2000E		Richmond	40.00	60.00	450.	600.
1990☆	2000E	☆	Richmond	250.	750.	3000.	3000.
1991	2000F		Atlanta	40.00	60.00	300.	350.
1991☆	2000F	☆	Atlanta	200.	750.	3250.	3750.
1992	2000G		Chicago	40.00	60.00	250.	350.
1992☆	2000G	☆	Chicago	150.	450.	1500.	2000.
1993	2000H		St. Louis	50.00	110.	250.	400.
1993☆	2000H	☆	St. Louis	300.	625.	1250.	1850.
1994	2000I		Minneapolis	30.00	100.	600.	850.
1994☆	2000I	☆	Minneapolis	400.	750.	1250.	2500.
1995	2000J		Kansas City	35.00	60.00	300.	400.
1995☆	2000J	☆	Kansas City	225.	450.	1500.	2000.
1996	2000K		Dallas	35.00	60.00	500.	600.
1996☆	2000K	☆	Dallas	800.	1750.	5000.	6500.
1997	2000L		San Francisco	35.00	60.00	300.	400.
1997☆	2000L	☆	San Francisco	700.	1500.	4000.	5000.

Series 1928A Woods-Mellon

KL#	Fr#		District	Fine	XF	CH CU (63)	Gem CU (65)
1998	2001A		Boston	35.00	60.00	500.	700.
1998☆	2001A	☆	Boston	250.	450.	1500.	2000.
1999	2001B		New York	25.00	100.	250.	300.
1999☆	2001B	☆	New York	400.	800.	1250.	1500.
2000	2001C		Philadelphia	35.00	60.00	300.	350.
2000☆	2001C	☆	Philadelphia	300.	650.	2500.	4000.
2001	2001D		Cleveland	35.00	60.00	250.	300.
2001☆	2001D	☆	Cleveland	175.	350.	1000.	1500.
2002	2001E		Richmond	50.00	100.	750.	900.
2002☆	2001E	☆	Richmond	300.	750.	1650.	2000.
2003	2001F		Atlanta	35.00	60.00	350.	450.
2003☆	2001F	☆	Atlanta	250.	650.	1500.	2000.
2004	2001G		Chicago	35.00	60.00	275.	300.
2004☆	2001G	☆	Chicago	200.	500.	900.	1100.
2005	2001H		St. Louis	50.00	100.	250.	300.
2005☆	2001H	☆	St. Louis	250.	500.	800.	1100.
2006	2001I		Minneapolis	450.	950.	2000.	3000.
2007	2001J		Kansas City	200.	400.	800.	1000.
2008	2001K		Dallas	200.	400.	1100.	2000.
2009	2001L		San Francisco	65.00	100.	350.	400.
2009☆	2001L	☆	San Francisco	250.	400.	1250.	1600.

Series 1928B Woods-Mellon

KL#	Fr#		District	Fine	XF	CH CU (63)	Gem CU (65)
2010	2002A		Boston	—	30.00	80.00	100.
2010☆	2002A	☆	Boston	—	150.	700.	900.
2011	2002B		New York	18.00	30.00	100.	100.
2011☆	2002B	☆	New York	75.00	250.	900.	900.
2012	2002C		Philadelphia	18.00	35.00	90.00	100.
2012☆	2002C	☆	Philadelphia	75.00	200.	1100.	1100.
2013	2002D		Cleveland	18.00	50.00	100.	100.
2013☆	2002D	☆	Cleveland	75.00	175.	1000.	900.
2014	2002E		Richmond	18.00	30.00	100.	120.
2014☆	2002E	☆	Richmond	65.00	150.	900.	1000.
2015	2002F		Atlanta	18.00	30.00	120.	120.
2015☆	2002F	☆	Atlanta	—	200.	800.	1000.
2016	2002G		Chicago	18.00	30.00	120.	140.
2016☆	2002G	☆	Chicago	75.00	200.	1100.	875.
2017	2002H		St. Louis	18.00	30.00	85.00	1000.
2017☆	2002H	☆	St. Louis	60.00	200.	600.	1000.
2018	2002I		Minneapolis	18.00	30.00	100.	120.
2018☆	2002I	☆	Minneapolis	75.00	200.	1100.	1100.
2019	2002J		Kansas City	18.00	30.00	90.00	90.00
2019☆	2002J	☆	Kansas City	125.	450.	2400.	2400.
2020	2002K		Dallas	35.00	30.00	250.	150.
2021	2002L		San Francisco	18.00	25.00	90.00	90.00
2021☆	2002L	☆	San Francisco	60.00	175.	1100.	1100.

Series 1928C Woods-Mills

KL#	Fr#		District	Fine	XF	CH CU (63)	Gem CU (65)
2022	2003B		New York	75.00	250.	600.	750.
2023	2003D		Cleveland	550.	2000.	4500.	6750.
2023☆	2003D	☆	Cleveland	10,000.	20,000.	45,000.	50,000.
2024	2003E		Richmond	1250.	2500.	10,500.	12,500.
2026	2003G		Chicago	50.00	200.	625.	750.

Series 1934 Julian-Morgenthau

KL#	Fr#		District	Fine	XF	CH CU (63)	Gem CU (65)
2027	2004A		Boston	15.00	25.00	100.	150.
2027☆	2004A	☆	Boston	35.00	75.00	800.	1000.
2028	2004B		New York	15.00	30.00	75.00	100.
2028☆	2004B	☆	New York	45.00	125.	650.	800.
2029	2004C		Philadelphia	15.00	30.00	100.	150.
2029☆	2004C	☆	Philadelphia	45.00	70.00	800.	1000.
2030	2004D		Cleveland	15.00	30.00	100.	150.
2030☆	2004D	☆	Cleveland	45.00	150.	900.	1100.
2031	2004E		Richmond	15.00	35.00	120.	150.
2031☆	2004E	☆	Richmond	150.	400.	1500.	1750.
2032	2004F		Atlanta	25.00	40.00	150.	200.
2032☆	2004F	☆	Atlanta	100.	350.	1100.	1400.
2033	2004G		Chicago	15.00	40.00	120.	150.
2033☆	2004G	☆	Chicago	50.00	175.	800.	1000.
2034	2004H		St. Louis	15.00	50.00	150.	200.
2034☆	2004H	☆	St. Louis	175.	400.	1200.	1500.
2035	2004I		Minneapolis	15.00	40.00	100.	150.
2035☆	2004I	☆	Minneapolis	45.00	275.	1200.	1500.
2036	2004J		Kansas City	15.00	40.00	100.	150.
2036☆	2004J	☆	Kansas City	45.00	350.	900.	1100.
2037	2004K		Dallas	15.00	75.00	400.	550.
2037☆	2004K	☆	Dallas	170.	450.	1800.	2250.
2038	2004L		San Francisco	15.00	40.00	100.	150.
2038☆	2004L	☆	San Francisco	95.00	450.	1500.	1800.

Series 1934A Julian-Morgenthau

KL#	Fr#		District	Fine	XF	CH CU (63)	Gem CU (65)
2039	2006A		Boston	—	11.00	40.00	50.00
2039☆	2006A	☆	Boston	20.00	40.00	250.	300.
2040	2006B		New York	—	11.00	40.00	50.00
2040☆	2006B	☆	New York	20.00	40.00	200.	250.
2041	2006C		Philadelphia	—	11.00	40.00	50.00
2041☆	2006C	☆	Philadelphia	20.00	35.00	250.	300.
2042	2006D		Cleveland	—	11.00	40.00	50.00
2042☆	2006D	☆	Cleveland	20.00	40.00	250.	300.
2043	2006E		Richmond	—	11.00	40.00	50.00
2043☆	2006E	☆	Richmond	25.00	50.00	250.	300.
2044	2006F		Atlanta	—	11.00	40.00	50.00

KL#	Fr#		District	Fine	XF	CH CU (63)	Gem CU (65)
2044☆	2006F	☆	Atlanta	20.00	75.00	400.	500.
2045	2006G		Chicago	—	11.00	25.00	40.00
2045☆	2006G	☆	Chicago	25.00	45.00	200.	250.
2046	2006H		St. Louis	—	11.00	40.00	50.00
2046☆	2006H	☆	St. Louis	25.00	60.00	200.	250.
2047	2006I		Minneapolis	—	15.00	50.00	60.00
2047☆	2006I	☆	Minneapolis	30.00	75.00	400.	500.
2048	2006J		Kansas City	—	11.00	45.00	60.00
2048☆	2006J	☆	Kansas City	25.00	50.00	250.	300.
2049	2006K		Dallas	—	11.00	45.00	60.00
2049☆	2006K	☆	Dallas	40.00	100.	400.	500.
2050	2006L		San Francisco	—	15.00	45.00	60.00
2050☆	2006L	☆	San Francisco	35.00	80.00	350.	400.

Series 1934B Julian-Vinson

KL#	Fr#		District	Fine	XF	CH CU (63)	Gem CU (65)
2051	2007A		Boston	—	25.00	100.	150.
2051☆	2007A	☆	Boston	30.00	150.	700.	700.
2052	2007B		New York	—	25.00	75.00	75.00
2052☆	2007B	☆	New York	—	85.00	450.	500.
2053	2007C		Philadelphia	—	25.00	100.	100.
2053☆	2007C	☆	Philadelphia	—	150.	500.	700.
2054	2007D		Cleveland	—	40.00	150.	200.
2054☆	2007D	☆	Cleveland	—	250.	900.	1250.
2055	2007E		Richmond	—	25.00	50.00	175.
2055☆	2007E	☆	Richmond	—	150.	700.	900.
2056	2007F		Atlanta	—	25.00	50.00	100.
2056☆	2007F	☆	Atlanta	—	150.	700.	1000.
2057	2007G		Chicago	—	35.00	75.00	125.
2057☆	2007G	☆	Chicago	90.00	225.	450.	650.
2058	2007H		St. Louis	—	25.00	50.00	100.
2058☆	2007H	☆	St. Louis	—	150.	500.	700.
2059	2007I		Minneapolis	—	45.00	100.	150.
2059☆	2007I	☆	Minneapolis	—	300.	1200.	1500.
2060	2007J		Kansas City	—	25.00	50.00	125.
2060☆	2007J	☆	Kansas City	—	250.	500.	700.
2061	2007K		Dallas	—	25.00	150.	150.
2061☆	2007K	☆	Dallas	—	300.	1250.	1500.
2062	2007L		San Francisco	—	25.00	50.00	100.
2062☆	2007L	☆	San Francisco	—	150.	700.	700.

Series 1934C Julian-Snyder

KL#	Fr#		District	Fine	XF	CH CU (63)	Gem CU (65)
2063	2008A		Boston	11.00	15.00	50.00	50.00
2063☆	2008A	☆	Boston	35.00	75.00	400.	400.
2064	2008B		New York	11.00	15.00	40.00	40.00
2064☆	2008B	☆	New York	25.00	50.00	300.	300.
2065	2008C		Philadelphia	11.00	15.00	40.00	40.00
2065☆	2008C	☆	Philadelphia	30.00	60.00	400.	400.
2066	2008D		Cleveland	11.00	15.00	45.00	45.00
2066☆	2008D	☆	Cleveland	35.00	75.00	400.	400.
2067	2008E		Richmond	11.00	15.00	50.00	50.00
2067☆	2008E	☆	Richmond	35.00	80.00	500.	400.
2068	2008F		Atlanta	11.00	15.00	50.00	50.00
2068☆	2008F	☆	Atlanta	35.00	80.00	500.	400.
2069	2008G		Chicago	—	30.00	50.00	75.00
2069☆	2008G	☆	Chicago	25.00	160.	300.	450.
2070	2008H		St. Louis	11.00	15.00	50.00	50.00
2070☆	2008H	☆	St. Louis	35.00	75.00	400.	400.
2071	2008I		Minneapolis	11.00	15.00	75.00	75.00

KL#	Fr#		District	Fine	XF	CH CU (63)	Gem CU (65)
2071☆	2008I	☆	Minneapolis	100.	250.	1000.	900.
2072	2008J		Kansas City	11.00	15.00	50.00	50.00
2072☆	2008J	☆	Kansas City	20.00	45.00	400.	400.
2073	2008K		Dallas	11.00	15.00	50.00	50.00
2073☆	2008K	☆	Dallas	40.00	85.00	450.	450.
2074	2008L		San Francisco	11.00	15.00	40.00	40.00
2074☆	2008L	☆	San Francisco	35.00	75.00	500.	400.

Series 1934D Clark-Snyder

KL#	Fr#		District	Fine	XF	CH CU (63)	Gem CU (65)
2075	2009A		Boston	12.00	20.00	60.00	60.00
2075☆	2009A	☆	Boston	65.00	125.	700.	700.
2076	2009B		New York	11.00	15.00	60.00	50.00
2076☆	2009B	☆	New York	25.00	70.00	450.	450.
2077	2009C		Philadelphia	11.00	20.00	60.00	75.00
2077☆	2009C	☆	Philadelphia	30.00	90.00	500.	650.
2078	2009D		Cleveland	11.00	17.00	50.00	75.00
2078☆	2009D	☆	Cleveland	30.00	86.00	550.	650.
2079	2009E		Richmond	11.00	15.00	60.00	75.00
2079☆	2009E	☆	Richmond	65.00	250.	1000.	1650.
2080	2009F		Atlanta	12.00	15.00	60.00	75.00
2080☆	2009F	☆	Atlanta	65.00	90.00	900.	1000.
2081	2009G		Chicago	11.00	30.00	90.00	100.
2081☆	2009G	☆	Chicago	90.00	225.	450.	700.
2082	2009H		St. Louis	12.00	15.00	75.00	100.
2082☆	2009H	☆	St. Louis	65.00	100.	800.	900.
2083	2009I		Minneapolis	20.00	45.00	125.	150.
2083☆	2009I	☆	Minneapolis	100.	300.	1400.	1500.
2084	2009J		Kansas City	15.00	15.00	100.	125.
2084☆	2009J	☆	Kansas City	65.00	125.	800.	900.
2085	2009K		Dallas	12.00	20.00	100.	150.
2085☆	2009K	☆	Dallas	125.	200.	1400.	1500.
2086	2009L		San Francisco	11.00	20.00	75.00	110.
2086☆	2009L	☆	San Francisco	125.	200.	1200.	1350.

Series 1950 Clark-Snyder

KL#	Fr#		District	Fine	XF	CH CU (63)	Gem CU (65)
2087	2010A		Boston	11.00	20.00	80.00	125.
2087☆	2010A	☆	Boston	25.00	110.	500.	800.
2088	2010B		New York	11.00	20.00	75.00	100.
2088☆	2010B	☆	New York	20.00	100.	400.	750.
2089	2010C		Philadelphia	11.00	25.00	75.00	100.
2089☆	2010C	☆	Philadelphia	25.00	100.	500.	750.
2090	2010D		Cleveland	11.00	20.00	75.00	100.
2090☆	2010D	☆	Cleveland	25.00	125.	500.	750.
2091	2010E		Richmond	11.00	20.00	75.00	100.
2091☆	2010E	☆	Richmond	35.00	125.	500.	750.
2092	2010F		Atlanta	11.00	25.00	75.00	100.
2092☆	2010F	☆	Atlanta	35.00	125.	500.	750.
2093	2010G		Chicago	11.00	20.00	70.00	100.
2093☆	2010G	☆	Chicago	20.00	125.	500.	750.
2094	2010H		St. Louis	11.00	20.00	75.00	100.
2094☆	2010H	☆	St. Louis	25.00	150.	600.	750.
2095	2010I		Minneapolis	11.00	20.00	90.00	100.
2095☆	2010I	☆	Minneapolis	50.00	250.	900.	1000.
2096	2010J		Kansas City	11.00	20.00	75.00	100.
2096☆	2010J	☆	Kansas City	35.00	125.	600.	750.
2097	2010K		Dallas	11.00	20.00	75.00	100.
2097☆	2010K	☆	Dallas	35.00	125.	600.	750.
2098	2010L		San Francisco	11.00	15.00	75.00	100.
2098☆	2010L	☆	San Francisco	25.00	125.	600.	750.

Series 1950A Priest-Humphrey

KL#	Fr#		District	Fine	XF	CH CU (63)	Gem CU (65)
2099	2011A		Boston	—	30.00	70.00	90.00
2099☆	2011A	☆	Boston	25.00	115.	250.	275.
2100	2011B		New York	—	30.00	70.00	90.00
2100☆	2011B	☆	New York	25.00	90.00	150.	275.
2101	2011C		Philadelphia	—	30.00	70.00	90.00
2101☆	2011C	☆	Philadelphia	25.00	30.00	300.	90.00
2102	2011D		Cleveland	—	30.00	70.00	90.00
2102☆	2011D	☆	Cleveland	25.00	125.	300.	375.
2103	2011E		Richmond	—	30.00	70.00	90.00
2103☆	2011E	☆	Richmond	25.00	125.	300.	375.
2104	2011F		Atlanta	—	30.00	70.00	90.00
2104☆	2011F	☆	Atlanta	25.00	125.	300.	375.
2105	2011G		Chicago	—	30.00	70.00	90.00
2105☆	2011G	☆	Chicago	25.00	150.	250.	375.
2106	2011H		St. Louis	—	30.00	100.	90.00
2106☆	2011H	☆	St. Louis	25.00	150.	250.	375.
2107	2011I		Minneapolis	—	30.00	100.	110.
2107☆	2011I	☆	Minneapolis	25.00	150.	300.	475.
2108	2011J		Kansas City	—	30.00	70.00	90.00
2108☆	2011J	☆	Kansas City	25.00	150.	300.	375.
2109	2011K		Dallas	—	30.00	70.00	90.00
2109☆	2011K	☆	Dallas	25.00	150.	275.	325.
2110	2011L		San Francisco	—	30.00	60.00	90.00
2110☆	2011L	☆	San Francisco	25.00	100.	200.	275.

Series 1950B Priest-Anderson

KL#	Fr#		District	Fine	XF	CH CU (63)	Gem CU (65)
2111	2012A		Boston	—	20.00	40.00	45.00
2111☆	2012A	☆	Boston	15.00	75.00	150.	160.
2112	2012B		New York	—	20.00	35.00	45.00
2112☆	2012B	☆	New York	15.00	75.00	125.	160.
2113	2012C		Philadelphia	—	20.00	35.00	45.00
2113☆	2012C	☆	Philadelphia	15.00	75.00	150.	160.
2114	2012D		Cleveland	—	20.00	40.00	45.00
2114☆	2012D	☆	Cleveland	15.00	75.00	150.	160.
2115	2012E		Richmond	—	20.00	35.00	45.00
2115☆	2012E	☆	Richmond	15.00	75.00	150.	160.
2116	2012F		Atlanta	—	15.00	35.00	40.00
2116☆	2012F	☆	Atlanta	15.00	75.00	150.	160.
2117	2012G		Chicago	—	15.00	35.00	40.00
2117☆	2012G	☆	Chicago	15.00	65.00	125.	150.
2118	2012H		St. Louis	—	12.00	35.00	40.00
2118☆	2012H	☆	St. Louis	15.00	75.00	170.	180.
2119	2012I		Minneapolis	—	20.00	40.00	45.00
2120	2012J		Kansas City	—	20.00	40.00	45.00
2120☆	2012J	☆	Kansas City	15.00	70.00	175.	200.

KL#	Fr#		District	Fine	XF	CH CU (63)	Gem CU (65)
2121	2012K		Dallas	—	20.00	40.00	45.00
2121☆	2012K	☆	Dallas	15.00	60.00	150.	325.
2122	2012L		San Francisco	11.00	20.00	40.00	45.00
2122☆	2012L	☆	San Francisco	15.00	75.00	150.	160.

Series 1950C Smith-Dillon

KL#	Fr#		District	Fine	XF	CH CU (63)	Gem CU (65)
2123	2013A		Boston	11.00	25.00	50.00	65.00
2123☆	2013A	☆	Boston	80.00	150.	300.	375.
2124	2013B		New York	11.00	25.00	50.00	65.00
2124☆	2013B	☆	New York	65.00	120.	300.	300.
2125	2013C		Philadelphia	11.00	25.00	50.00	65.00
2125☆	2013C	☆	Philadelphia	100.	125.	300.	475.
2126	2013D		Cleveland	11.00	30.00	75.00	75.00
2126☆	2013D	☆	Cleveland	90.00	175.	300.	430.
2127	2013E		Richmond	11.00	30.00	55.00	85.00
2127☆	2013E	☆	Richmond	90.00	125.	300.	425.
2128	2013F		Atlanta	11.00	30.00	50.00	70.00
2128☆	2013F	☆	Atlanta	90.00	125.	350.	425.
2129	2013G		Chicago	11.00	30.00	50.00	70.00
2129☆	2013G	☆	Chicago	60.00	125.	350.	275.
2130	2013H		St. Louis	11.00	40.00	75.00	90.00
2130☆	2013H	☆	St. Louis	65.00	75.00	150.	325.
2131	2013I		Minneapolis	11.00	45.00	85.00	100.
2131☆	2013I	☆	Minneapolis	80.00	90.00	250.	375.
2132	2013J		Kansas City	11.00	45.00	75.00	110.
2132☆	2013J	☆	Kansas City	65.00	100.	300.	325.
2133	2013K		Dallas	11.00	40.00	75.00	90.00
2133☆	2013K	☆	Dallas	65.00	85.00	250.	325.
2134	2013L		San Francisco	11.00	45.00	85.00	100.
2134☆	2013L	☆	San Francisco	65.00	—	250.	325.

Series 1950D Granahan-Dillon

KL#	Fr#		District	Fine	XF	CH CU (63)	Gem CU (65)
2135	2014A		Boston	11.00	20.00	50.00	70.00
2135☆	2014A	☆	Boston	11.00	45.00	200.	225.
2136	2014B		New York	11.00	20.00	45.00	65.00
2136☆	2014B	☆	New York	20.00	50.00	150.	275.
2137	2014C		Philadelphia	11.00	20.00	55.00	75.00
2137☆	2014C	☆	Philadelphia	11.00	45.00	200.	275.
2138	2014D		Cleveland	11.00	20.00	55.00	75.00
2138☆	2014D	☆	Cleveland	11.00	45.00	200.	275.
2139	2014E		Richmond	11.00	20.00	50.00	75.00
2139☆	2014E	☆	Richmond	15.00	60.00	250.	325.
2140	2014F		Atlanta	11.00	20.00	50.00	70.00
2140☆	2014F	☆	Atlanta	15.00	60.00	250.	325.
2141	2014G		Chicago	11.00	20.00	55.00	70.00
2141☆	2014G	☆	Chicago	15.00	65.00	250.	325.
2142	2014H		St. Louis	—	—	—	—
2142☆	2014H	☆	St. Louis	—	—	—	325.
2144	2014J		Kansas City	11.00	20.00	50.00	70.00
2144☆	2014J	☆	Kansas City	15.00	30.00	250.	325.
2145	2014K		Dallas	11.00	20.00	50.00	80.00
2145☆	2014K	☆	Dallas	15.00	50.00	275.	325.
2146	2014L		San Francisco	11.00	20.00	50.00	70.00
2146☆	2014L	☆	San Francisco	11.00	30.00	240.	325.

Series 1950E Granahan-Fowler

KL#	Fr#		District	Fine	XF	CH CU (63)	Gem CU (65)
2147	2015B		New York	15.00	55.00	100.	135.
2147☆	2015B	☆	New York	35.00	160.	300.	400.

KL#	Fr#		District	Fine	XF	CH CU (63)	Gem CU (65)
2148	2015G		Chicago	15.00	55.00	125.	135.
2148☆	2015G	☆	Chicago	35.00	160.	300.	400.
2149	2015L		San Francisco	20.00	65.00	150.	175.
2149☆	2015L	☆	San Francisco	110.	200.	425.	500.

Series 1963 Granahan-Dillon

KL#	Fr#		District	Fine	XF	CH CU (63)	Gem CU (65)
2150	2016A		Boston	—	15.00	50.00	55.00
2150☆	2016A	☆	Boston	25.00	75.00	120.	150.
2151	2016B		New York	—	15.00	50.00	55.00
2151☆	2016B	☆	New York	25.00	35.00	60.00	80.00
2152	2016C		Philadelphia	—	15.00	50.00	55.00
2152☆	2016C	☆	Philadelphia	15.00	40.00	80.00	110.
2153	2016D		Cleveland	—	15.00	50.00	55.00
2153☆	2016D	☆	Cleveland	15.00	50.00	100.	135.
2154	2016E		Richmond	—	15.00	50.00	55.00
2154☆	2016E	☆	Richmond	15.00	50.00	120.	150.
2155	2016F		Atlanta	—	15.00	50.00	55.00
2155☆	2016F	☆	Atlanta	15.00	40.00	80.00	110.
2156	2016G		Chicago	—	15.00	50.00	50.00
2156☆	2016G	☆	Chicago	15.00	40.00	80.00	110.
2157	2016H		St. Louis	—	15.00	50.00	55.00
2157☆	2016H	☆	St. Louis	15.00	40.00	80.00	110.
2159	2016J		Kansas City	11.00	25.00	70.00	75.00
2159☆	2016J	☆	Kansas City	15.00	50.00	120.	150.
2160	2016K		Dallas	11.00	25.00	60.00	75.00
2160☆	2016K	☆	Dallas	15.00	50.00	120.	150.
2161	2016L		San Francisco	—	15.00	50.00	53.00
2161☆	2016L	☆	San Francisco	15.00	50.00	100.	110.

Series 1963A Granahan-Fowler

KL#	Fr#		District	Fine	XF	CH CU (63)	Gem CU (65)
2162	2017A		Boston	—	20.00	50.00	47.00
2162☆	2017A	☆	Boston	11.00	40.00	120.	85.00
2163	2017B		New York	—	20.00	50.00	47.00
2163☆	2017B	☆	New York	11.00	40.00	80.00	85.00
2164	2017C		Philadelphia	—	20.00	50.00	47.00
2164☆	2017C	☆	Philadelphia	11.00	40.00	80.00	85.00

KL#	Fr#		District	Fine	XF	CH CU (63)	Gem CU (65)
2165	2017D		Cleveland	—	20.00	50.00	47.00
2165☆	2017D	☆	Cleveland	11.00	40.00	120.	85.00
2166	2017E		Richmond	—	20.00	50.00	47.00
2166☆	2017E	☆	Richmond	11.00	40.00	120.	85.00
2167	2017F		Atlanta	—	20.00	50.00	47.00
2167☆	2017F	☆	Atlanta	11.00	40.00	80.00	85.00
2168	2017G		Chicago	—	20.00	50.00	47.00
2168☆	2017G	☆	Chicago	11.00	40.00	80.00	85.00
2169	2017H		St. Louis	—	20.00	75.00	47.00
2169☆	2017H	☆	St. Louis	11.00	40.00	80.00	85.00
2170	2017I		Minneapolis	—	—	—	—
2170☆	2017I	☆	Minneapolis	—	—	—	—
2171	2017J		Kansas City	—	20.00	70.00	47.00
2171☆	2017J	☆	Kansas City	11.00	40.00	120.	85.00
2172	2017K		Dallas	—	20.00	70.00	47.00
2172☆	2017K	☆	Dallas	11.00	40.00	120.	85.00
2173	2017L		San Francisco	—	20.00	60.00	47.00
2173☆	2017L	☆	San Francisco	11.00	40.00	100.	85.00

Series 1969 Elston-Kennedy

KL#	Fr#		District	Fine	XF	CH CU (63)	Gem CU (65)
2174	2018A		Boston	—	15.00	38.00	42.00
2174☆	2018A	☆	Boston	11.00	40.00	70.00	77.00
2175	2018B		New York	—	15.00	38.00	42.00
2175☆	2018B	☆	New York	11.00	40.00	70.00	77.00
2176	2018C		Philadelphia	—	15.00	38.00	42.00
2176☆	2018C	☆	Philadelphia	11.00	40.00	70.00	77.00
2177	2018D		Cleveland	—	15.00	38.00	42.00
2177☆	2018D	☆	Cleveland	11.00	40.00	100.	77.00
2178	2018E		Richmond	—	15.00	38.00	42.00
2178☆	2018E	☆	Richmond	11.00	40.00	100.	77.00
2179	2018F		Atlanta	—	15.00	38.00	42.00
2179☆	2018F	☆	Atlanta	11.00	40.00	70.00	77.00
2180	2018G		Chicago	—	15.00	38.00	42.00
2180☆	2018G	☆	Chicago	11.00	40.00	70.00	77.00
2181	2018H		St. Louis	—	15.00	38.00	42.00
2181☆	2018H	☆	St. Louis	50.00	100.	200.	225.
2182	2018I		Minneapolis	—	15.00	38.00	42.00
2182☆	2018I	☆	Minneapolis	11.00	40.00	70.00	77.00
2183	2018J		Kansas City	—	15.00	38.00	42.00
2183☆	2018J	☆	Kansas City	11.00	40.00	70.00	77.00
2184	2018K		Dallas	—	15.00	38.00	42.00
2184☆	2018K	☆	Dallas	11.00	40.00	70.00	77.00
2185	2018L		San Francisco	—	15.00	38.00	42.00
2185☆	2018L	☆	San Francisco	11.00	40.00	70.00	77.00

Series 1969A Kabis-Connally

KL#	Fr#		District	Fine	XF	CH CU (63)	Gem CU (65)
2186	2019A		Boston	11.00	15.00	35.00	37.00
2186☆	2019A	☆	Boston	11.00	20.00	60.00	62.00
2187	2019B		New York	—	15.00	35.00	37.00
2187☆	2019B	☆	New York	—	20.00	60.00	62.00
2188	2019C		Philadelphia	—	15.00	35.00	37.00
2188☆	2019C	☆	Philadelphia	11.00	20.00	60.00	62.00
2189	2019D		Cleveland	—	15.00	45.00	37.00
2189☆	2019D	☆	Cleveland	11.00	20.00	60.00	62.00
2190	2019E		Richmond	—	15.00	40.00	37.00
2190☆	2019E	☆	Richmond	11.00	20.00	60.00	95.00
2191	2019F		Atlanta	—	15.00	45.00	37.00
2191☆	2019F	☆	Atlanta	11.00	20.00	75.00	95.00
2192	2019G		Chicago	—	15.00	35.00	37.00
2192☆	2019G	☆	Chicago	11.00	20.00	75.00	85.00
2193	2019H		St. Louis	—	15.00	35.00	37.00
2193☆	2019H	☆	St. Louis	11.00	20.00	60.00	95.00
2194	2019I		Minneapolis	—	15.00	45.00	47.00
2195	2019J		Kansas City	—	15.00	40.00	37.00
2196	2019K		Dallas	—	15.00	45.00	37.00
2196☆	2019K	☆	Dallas	11.00	20.00	60.00	95.00
2197	2019L		San Francisco	—	15.00	40.00	37.00
2197☆	2019L	☆	San Francisco	11.00	20.00	75.00	95.00

Series 1969B Banuelos-Connally

KL#	Fr#		District	Fine	XF	CH CU (63)	Gem CU (65)
2198	2020A		Boston	25.00	75.00	175.	200.
2199	2020B		New York	11.00	50.00	150.	165.
2199☆	2020B	☆	New York	25.00	100.	200.	220.
2200	2020C		Philadelphia	11.00	50.00	150.	165.
2201	2020D		Cleveland	11.00	50.00	150.	165.
2202	2020E		Richmond	11.00	50.00	150.	165.
2202☆	2020E	☆	Richmond	25.00	75.00	350.	375.
2203	2020F		Atlanta	11.00	50.00	150.	165.
2203☆	2020F	☆	Atlanta	25.00	75.00	300.	325.
2204	2020G		Chicago	11.00	50.00	150.	165.
2204☆	2020G	☆	Chicago	11.00	50.00	250.	275.
2205	2020H		St. Louis	20.00	75.00	175.	200.
2205☆	2020H	☆	St. Louis	25.00	75.00	250.	275.
2206	2020I		Minneapolis	25.00	75.00	350.	375.
2207	2020J		Kansas City	25.00	75.00	175.	200.
2207☆	2020J	☆	Kansas City	25.00	75.00	350.	375.
2208	2020K		Dallas	11.00	50.00	150.	165.
2209	2020L		San Francisco	25.00	75.00	350.	375.
2209☆	2020L	☆	San Francisco	11.00	50.00	150.	200.

Series 1969C Banuelos-Shultz

KL#	Fr#	District	Fine	XF	CH CU (63)	Gem CU (65)
2210	2021A	Boston	—	20.00	40.00	42.00

KL#	Fr#		District	Fine	XF	CH CU (63)	Gem CU (65)
2210☆	2021A	☆	Boston	12.00	50.00	125.	105.
2211	2021B		New York	—	20.00	40.00	42.00
2211☆	2021B	☆	New York	—	25.00	75.00	90.00
2212	2021C		Philadelphia	—	25.00	50.00	60.00
2212☆	2021C	☆	Philadelphia	12.00	35.00	80.00	90.00
2213	2021D		Cleveland	—	20.00	40.00	42.00
2213☆	2021D	☆	Cleveland	12.00	30.00	80.00	90.00
2214	2021E		Richmond	—	20.00	40.00	42.00
2214☆	2021E	☆	Richmond	15.00	35.00	75.00	80.00
2215	2021F		Atlanta	—	20.00	40.00	42.00
2215☆	2021F	☆	Atlanta	12.00	35.00	80.00	90.00
2216	2021G		Chicago	—	20.00	40.00	42.00
2216☆	2021G	☆	Chicago	12.00	35.00	100.	120.
2217	2021H		St. Louis	—	20.00	40.00	42.00
2217☆	2021H	☆	St. Louis	12.00	35.00	100.	120.
2218	2021I		Minneapolis	—	20.00	40.00	42.00
2218☆	2021I	☆	Minneapolis	15.00	60.00	140.	160.
2219	2021J		Kansas City	—	20.00	40.00	42.00
2219☆	2021J	☆	Kansas City	15.00	60.00	120.	150.
2220	2021K		Dallas	—	20.00	40.00	42.00
2220☆	2021K	☆	Dallas	15.00	50.00	120.	150.
2221	2021L		San Francisco	—	20.00	40.00	45.00
2221☆	2021L	☆	San Francisco	15.00	50.00	120.	150.

Series 1974 Neff-Simon

KL#	Fr#		District	Fine	XF	CH CU (63)	Gem CU (65)
2222	2022A		Boston	—	15.00	35.00	42.00
2222☆	2022A	☆	Boston	11.00	25.00	70.00	75.00
2223	2022B		New York	—	15.00	35.00	40.00
2223☆	2022B	☆	New York	11.00	25.00	70.00	62.00
2224	2022C		Philadelphia	—	15.00	40.00	42.00
2224☆	2022C	☆	Philadelphia	11.00	25.00	70.00	75.00
2225	2022D		Cleveland	—	15.00	35.00	42.00
2225☆	2022D	☆	Cleveland	11.00	30.00	70.00	75.00
2226	2022E		Richmond	—	15.00	40.00	42.00
2226☆	2022E	☆	Richmond	11.00	25.00	60.00	65.00
2227	2022F		Atlanta	—	15.00	35.00	42.00
2227☆	2022F	☆	Atlanta	11.00	25.00	65.00	55.00
2228	2022G		Chicago	—	15.00	35.00	42.00
2228☆	2022G	☆	Chicago	11.00	25.00	55.00	60.00
2229	2022H		St. Louis	—	15.00	35.00	42.00
2229☆	2022H	☆	St. Louis	11.00	25.00	85.00	95.00
2230	2022I		Minneapolis	—	15.00	35.00	42.00
2230☆	2022I	☆	Minneapolis	11.00	25.00	120.	140.
2231	2022J		Kansas City	—	15.00	35.00	42.00
2231☆	2022J	☆	Kansas City	11.00	25.00	60.00	65.00
2232	2022K		Dallas	—	15.00	35.00	42.00
2232☆	2022K	☆	Dallas	11.00	25.00	60.00	65.00
2233	2022L		San Francisco	—	15.00	35.00	42.00
2233☆	2022L	☆	San Francisco	11.00	25.00	60.00	65.00

Series 1977 Morton-Blumenthal

KL#	Fr#		District	Fine	XF	CH CU (63)	Gem CU (65)
2234	2023A		Boston	—	15.00	35.00	42.00
2234☆	2023A	☆	Boston	—	25.00	70.00	75.00
2235	2023B		New York	—	15.00	35.00	42.00
2235☆	2023B	☆	New York	11.00	25.00	70.00	75.00
2236	2023C		Philadelphia	—	15.00	35.00	42.00
2236☆	2023C	☆	Philadelphia	11.00	25.00	70.00	75.00
2237	2023D		Cleveland	—	15.00	35.00	42.00

KL#	Fr#		District	Fine	XF	CH CU (63)	Gem CU (65)
2237☆	2023D	☆	Cleveland	11.00	25.00	70.00	75.00
2238	2023E		Richmond	—	15.00	40.00	42.00
2238☆	2023E	☆	Richmond	11.00	25.00	60.00	65.00
2239	2023F		Atlanta	—	15.00	35.00	42.00
2239☆	2023F	☆	Atlanta	11.00	25.00	65.00	70.00
2240	2023G		Chicago	—	15.00	35.00	42.00
2240☆	2023G	☆	Chicago	11.00	20.00	55.00	65.00
2241	2023H		St. Louis	—	15.00	35.00	42.00
2241☆	2023H	☆	St. Louis	11.00	25.00	85.00	95.00
2242	2023I		Minneapolis	—	15.00	35.00	45.00
2242☆	2023I	☆	Minneapolis	15.00	50.00	120.	140.
2243	2023J		Kansas City	—	15.00	35.00	42.00
2243☆	2023J	☆	Kansas City	11.00	25.00	60.00	65.00
2244	2023K		Dallas	—	15.00	35.00	42.00
2244☆	2023K	☆	Dallas	11.00	25.00	60.00	65.00
2245	2023L		San Francisco	—	15.00	35.00	42.00
2245☆	2023L	☆	San Francisco	11.00	25.00	60.00	65.00

Series 1977A Morton-Miller

KL#	Fr#		District	Fine	XF	CH CU (63)	Gem CU (65)
2246	2024A		Boston	—	15.00	35.00	37.00
2246☆	2024A	☆	Boston	11.00	20.00	100.	125.
2247	2024B		New York	—	15.00	35.00	40.00
2247☆	2024B	☆	New York	11.00	20.00	60.00	70.00
2248	2024C		Philadelphia	—	15.00	35.00	40.00
2248☆	2024C	☆	Philadelphia	11.00	20.00	70.00	85.00
2249	2024D		Cleveland	—	15.00	35.00	40.00
2249☆	2024D	☆	Cleveland	11.00	20.00	70.00	85.00
2250	2024E		Richmond	—	15.00	35.00	40.00
2250☆	2024E	☆	Richmond	11.00	20.00	80.00	90.00
2251	2024F		Atlanta	—	15.00	35.00	35.00
2251☆	2024F	☆	Atlanta	11.00	20.00	150.	175.
2252	2024G		Chicago	—	15.00	35.00	40.00
2252☆	2024G	☆	Chicago	11.00	20.00	65.00	75.00
2253	2024H		St. Louis	—	15.00	35.00	40.00
2253☆	2024H	☆	St. Louis	11.00	20.00	100.	125.
2254	2024I		Minneapolis	—	15.00	50.00	60.00
2254☆	2024I	☆	Minneapolis	11.00	20.00	135.	115.
2255	2024J		Kansas City	—	15.00	35.00	40.00
2255☆	2024J	☆	Kansas City	11.00	20.00	90.00	115.
2256	2024K		Dallas	—	15.00	35.00	40.00
2256☆	2024K	☆	Dallas	11.00	20.00	60.00	40.00
2257	2024L		San Francisco	—	15.00	35.00	40.00
2257☆	2024L	☆	San Francisco	11.00	20.00	70.00	80.00

Series 1981 Buchanan-Regan

KL#	Fr#	District	Fine	XF	CH CU (63)	Gem CU (65)
3524	2025A	Boston	11.00	20.00	40.00	42.00

KL#	Fr#		District	Fine	XF	CH CU (63)	Gem CU (65)
3524☆	2025A	☆	Boston	15.00	30.00	100.	105.
3525	2025B		New York	11.00	20.00	40.00	42.00
3525☆	2025B	☆	New York	15.00	50.00	125.	135.
3526	2025C		Philadelphia	11.00	20.00	40.00	42.00
3526☆	2025C	☆	Philadelphia	15.00	50.00	125.	135.
3527	2025D		Cleveland	11.00	20.00	40.00	42.00
3527☆	2025D	☆	Cleveland	15.00	50.00	120.	125.
3528	2025E		Richmond	11.00	20.00	40.00	42.00
3528☆	2025E	☆	Richmond	15.00	50.00	100.	110.
3529	2025F		Atlanta	11.00	20.00	40.00	42.00
3529☆	2025F	☆	Atlanta	15.00	50.00	100.	120.
3530	2025G		Chicago	11.00	20.00	50.00	55.00
3530☆	2025G	☆	Chicago	15.00	50.00	100.	105.
3531	2025H		St. Louis	11.00	20.00	50.00	55.00
3532	2025I		Minneapolis	11.00	20.00	50.00	55.00
3532☆	2025I	☆	Minneapolis	15.00	50.00	150.	160.
3533	2025J		Kansas City	11.00	20.00	50.00	55.00
3534	2025K		Dallas	11.00	20.00	40.00	42.00
3535	2025L		San Francisco	11.00	20.00	40.00	42.00
3535☆	2025L	☆	San Francisco	15.00	50.00	100.	105.

Series 1981A Ortega-Regan

KL#	Fr#		District	Fine	XF	CH CU (63)	Gem CU (65)
3624	2026A		Boston	11.00	20.00	45.00	47.00
3625	2026B		New York	11.00	20.00	45.00	47.00
3625☆	2026B	☆	New York	15.00	45.00	200.	100.
3626	2026C		Philadelphia	11.00	20.00	45.00	47.00
3627	2026D		Cleveland	11.00	20.00	45.00	47.00
3628	2026E		Richmond	11.00	20.00	40.00	47.00
3628☆	2026E	☆	Richmond	15.00	45.00	80.00	100.
3629	2026F		Atlanta	11.00	20.00	40.00	47.00
3629☆	2026F	☆	Atlanta	15.00	45.00	100.	100.
3630	2026G		Chicago	11.00	20.00	40.00	47.00
3631	2026H		St. Louis	11.00	20.00	65.00	47.00
3632	2026I		Minneapolis	11.00	20.00	40.00	47.00
3633	2026J		Kansas City	11.00	20.00	40.00	47.00
3634	2026K		Dallas	11.00	20.00	40.00	47.00
3635	2026L		San Francisco	11.00	20.00	45.00	47.00

Series 1985 Ortega-Baker

KL#	Fr#		District	Fine	XF	CH CU (63)	Gem CU (65)
3724	2027A		Boston	—	20.00	35.00	42.00
3724☆	2027A	☆	Boston	11.00	35.00	60.00	75.00
3725	2027B		New York	—	20.00	35.00	72.00
3725☆	2027B	☆	New York	11.00	35.00	60.00	75.00
3726	2027C		Philadelphia	—	20.00	35.00	42.00
3727	2027D		Cleveland	—	20.00	35.00	42.00
3727☆	2027D	☆	Cleveland	11.00	40.00	95.00	105.
3728	2027E		Richmond	—	20.00	35.00	42.00
3729	2027F		Atlanta	—	20.00	35.00	42.00
3729☆	2027F	☆	Atlanta	11.00	45.00	150.	165.
3730	2027G		Chicago	—	20.00	35.00	42.00
3731	2027H		St. Louis	—	20.00	35.00	42.00
3731☆	2027H	☆	St. Louis	11.00	30.00	70.00	75.00
3732	2027I		Minneapolis	—	20.00	40.00	42.00
3733	2027J		Kansas City	—	20.00	35.00	42.00
3734	2027K		Dallas	—	20.00	35.00	42.00
3734☆	2027K	☆	Dallas	11.00	30.00	60.00	70.00
3735	2027L		San Francisco	—	20.00	35.00	42.00
3735☆	2027L	☆	San Francisco	11.00	30.00	80.00	85.00

Series 1988A Villalpando-Brady

KL#	Fr#		District	Fine	XF	CH CU (63)	Gem CU (65)
3868	2029A		Boston	11.00	20.00	35.00	42.00
3868☆	2029A	☆	Boston	15.00	50.00	100.	105.
3869	2029B		New York	11.00	20.00	35.00	42.00
3869☆	2029B	☆	New York	15.00	50.00	100.	105.
3870	2029C		Philadelphia	11.00	20.00	35.00	42.00
3871	2029D		Cleveland	11.00	20.00	35.00	42.00
3871☆	2029D	☆	Cleveland	11.00	50.00	100.	105.
3872	2029E		Richmond	11.00	20.00	35.00	42.00
3873	2029F		Atlanta	11.00	20.00	35.00	42.00
3874	2029G		Chicago	11.00	20.00	35.00	42.00
3875	2029H		St. Louis	11.00	20.00	35.00	42.00
3876	2029I		Minneapolis	11.00	20.00	35.00	42.00
3877	2029J		Kansas City	11.00	20.00	35.00	42.00
3878	2029K		Dallas	11.00	20.00	35.00	42.00
3879	2029L		San Francisco	11.00	20.00	35.00	42.00
3879☆	2029L	☆	San Francisco	15.00	50.00	100.	105.

Series 1990 Villalpando-Brady

KL#	Fr#		District	Fine	XF	CH CU (63)	Gem CU (65)
4000	2030A		Boston	—	11.00	20.00	27.00
4001	2030B		New York	—	11.00	20.00	27.00
4001☆	2030B	☆	New York	—	15.00	60.00	42.00
4002	2030C		Philadelphia	—	11.00	20.00	27.00
4002☆	2030C	☆	Philadelphia	—	15.00	60.00	42.00
4003	2030D		Cleveland	—	11.00	20.00	27.00
4004	2030E		Richmond	—	11.00	20.00	27.00
4005	2030F		Atlanta	—	11.00	20.00	27.00
4006	2030G		Chicago	—	11.00	20.00	27.00
4006☆	2030G	☆	Chicago	—	15.00	65.00	42.00
4007	2030H		St. Louis	—	11.00	20.00	27.00
4007☆	2030H	☆	St. Louis	—	15.00	75.00	42.00
4008	2030I		Minneapolis	—	11.00	20.00	27.00
4009	2030J		Kansas City	—	11.00	20.00	27.00
4010	2030K		Dallas	—	11.00	20.00	27.00
4011	2030L		San Francisco	—	11.00	20.00	27.00

Series 1993 Withrow-Bentsen

KL#	Fr#		District	Fine	XF	CH CU (63)	Gem CU (65)
4036	2031A		Boston	—	—	20.00	22.00
4037	2031B		New York	—	—	20.00	22.00
4037☆	2031B	☆	New York	11.00	25.00	55.00	52.00
4038	2031C		Philadelphia	—	—	20.00	22.00
4038☆	2031C	☆	Philadelphia	11.00	25.00	60.00	52.00
4039	2031D		Cleveland	—	—	20.00	22.00
4041	2031F		Atlanta	—	—	20.00	22.00
4042	2031G		Chicago	—	—	20.00	22.00

KL#	Fr#		District	Fine	XF	CH CU (63)	Gem CU (65)
4042☆	2031G	☆	Chicago	11.00	25.00	65.00	52.00
4043	2031H		St. Louis	—	—	20.00	22.00
4045	2031J		Kansas City	—	—	20.00	22.00
4047	2031L		San Francisco	—	—	20.00	22.00

Series 1995 Withrow-Rubin

KL#	Fr#		District	Fine	XF	CH CU (63)	Gem CU (65)
4108	2032A		Boston	—	—	25.00	27.00
4109	2032B		New York	—	11.00	25.00	27.00
4109☆	2032B	☆	New York	—	—	—	—
4110	2032C		Philadelphia	—	11.00	25.00	27.00
4111	2032D		Cleveland	—	11.00	25.00	27.00
4111☆	2032D	☆	Cleveland	11.00	25.00	50.00	52.00
4112	2032E		Richmond	—	11.00	20.00	22.00
4112☆	2032E	☆	Richmond	11.00	25.00	60.00	65.00
4113	2032F		Atlanta	—	11.00	20.00	22.00
4113☆	2032F	☆	Atlanta	11.00	25.00	75.00	65.00
4114	2032G		Chicago	—	11.00	20.00	22.00
4114☆	2032G	☆	Chicago	11.00	25.00	40.00	52.00
4115	2032H		St. Louis	—	15.00	35.00	22.00
4115☆	2032H	☆	St. Louis	11.00	25.00	45.00	42.00
4116	2032I		Minneapolis	—	11.00	20.00	22.00
4117	2032J		Kansas City	—	11.00	20.00	22.00
4118	2032K		Dallas	—	11.00	20.00	22.00
4119	2032L		San Francisco	—	11.00	20.00	22.00
4119☆	2032L	☆	San Francisco	11.00	20.00	50.00	42.00

Series 1999 Withrow-Summers - DC

KL#	Fr#		District	Fine	XF	CH CU (63)	Gem CU (65)
4530	2033A		Boston	—	—	20.00	22.00
4531	2033B		New York	—	—	20.00	22.00
4532	2033C		Philadelphia	—	—	20.00	22.00
4532☆	2033C	☆	Philadelphia	—	—	45.00	47.00
4533	2033D		Cleveland	—	—	25.00	27.00
4533☆	2033D	☆	Cleveland	—	—	45.00	47.00
4534	2033E		Richmond	—	—	25.00	27.00
4534☆	2033E	☆	Richmond	—	—	45.00	47.00
4535	2033F		Atlanta	—	—	25.00	27.00
4536	2033G		Chicago	—	—	25.00	27.00
4537	2033H		St. Louis	—	—	25.00	27.00
4538	2033I		Minneapolis	—	—	25.00	27.00
4539	2033J		Kansas City	—	—	25.00	27.00
4540	2033K		Dallas	—	—	25.00	27.00
4541	2033L		San Francisco	—	—	25.00	27.00

Series 1999 Withrow-Summers - FW

KL#	Fr#		District	Fine	XF	CH CU (63)	Gem CU (65)
4542☆	2034A	☆	Boston	—	—	45.00	47.00
4543☆	2034B	☆	New York	—	—	45.00	47.00
4544	2034F		Atlanta	—	—	20.00	22.00
4544☆	2034F	☆	Atlanta	—	—	30.00	32.00
4545	2034G		Chicago	—	—	20.00	22.00
4546	2034J		Kansas City	—	—	20.00	22.00
4547	2034K		Dallas	—	—	20.00	22.00
4547☆	2034K	☆	Dallas	—	—	30.00	32.00
4548	2034L		San Francisco	—	—	20.00	22.00

Series 2001 Marin-O'Neill - DC

KL#	Fr#	District	Fine	XF	CH CU (63)	Gem CU (65)
4599	2035A	Boston	—	—	20.00	22.00
4600	2035B	New York	—	—	20.00	22.00
4600☆	2035B ☆	New York	—	40.00	110.	115.
4601	2035C	Philadelphia	—	—	20.00	22.00
4602	2035D	Cleveland	—	—	20.00	22.00
4602☆	2035D ☆	Cleveland	—	—	35.00	37.00
4603	2035E	Richmond	—	—	20.00	22.00
4604	2035F	Atlanta	—	—	20.00	22.00
4605☆	2035G ☆	Chicago	—	—	35.00	37.00
4606	2035H	St. Louis	—	—	20.00	22.00
4607	2035I	Minneapolis	—	—	20.00	22.00

Series 2001 Marin-O'Neill - FW

KL#	Fr#	District	Fine	XF	CH CU (63)	Gem CU (65)
4608	2036A	Boston	—	—	20.00	22.00
4609	2036B	New York	—	—	20.00	22.00
4610	2036E	Richmond	—	—	20.00	22.00
4611	2036F	Atlanta	—	—	20.00	22.00
4612	2036G	Chicago	—	—	20.00	22.00
4613	2036H	St. Louis	—	—	20.00	22.00
4614	2036I	Minneapolis	—	—	20.00	22.00
4615	2036K	Dallas	—	—	25.00	27.00
4615☆	2036K ☆	Dallas	—	—	35.00	37.00
4616	2036L	San Francisco	—	—	20.00	22.00

Series 2003 Marin-Snow - DC

KL#	Fr#	District	Fine	XF	CH CU (63)	Gem CU (65)
4700	2037A	Boston	—	—	15.00	17.00
4701	2037B	New York	—	—	15.00	17.00
4702	2037C	Philadelphia	—	—	15.00	17.00
4703	2037D	Cleveland	—	—	15.00	17.00
4703☆	2037D ☆	Cleveland	—	—	35.00	37.00

KL#	Fr#	District	Fine	XF	CH CU (63)	Gem CU (65)
4704	2037E	Richmond	—	—	15.00	17.00
4705	2037F	Atlanta	—	—	15.00	17.00
4706	2037G	Chicago	—	—	15.00	17.00
4707	2037H	St. Louis	—	—	15.00	17.00
4707☆	2037H ☆	St. Louis	—	—	35.00	37.00
4708	2037I	Minneapolis	—	—	15.00	17.00
4709	2037J	Kansas City	—	—	15.00	17.00
4710	2037K	Dallas	—	—	15.00	17.00
4711	2037L	San Francisco	—	—	15.00	17.00

Series 2003 Marin-Snow - FW

KL#	Fr#	District	Fine	XF	CH CU (63)	Gem CU (65)
4712	-	Boston	—	—	15.00	17.00
4713	-	New York	—	—	15.00	17.00
4714	-	Philadelphia	—	—	15.00	17.00
4715	-	Cleveland	—	—	15.00	17.00
4716	-	Richmond	—	—	15.00	17.00
4717	-	Atlanta	—	—	15.00	17.00
4718	-	Chicago	—	—	15.00	17.00
4719	-	Minneapolis	—	—	15.00	17.00

Series 2004A Cabral-Paulson - FW

KL#	Fr#	District	Fine	XF	CH CU (63)	Gem CU (65)
4770	-	Boston	—	—	15.00	17.00
4770☆	-	Boston	—	—	35.00	37.00
4771	-	New York	—	—	15.00	17.00
4771☆	-	New York	—	—	35.00	37.00
4772	-	Philadephia	—	—	15.00	17.00
4773	-	Cleveland	—	—	15.00	17.00
4774	-	Richmond	—	—	15.00	17.00
4775	-	Atlanta	—	—	15.00	17.00
4775☆	-	Atlanta	—	—	35.00	37.00
4776	-	Chicago	—	—	15.00	17.00
4777	-	St. Louis	—	—	15.00	17.00
4778	-	Minneapolis	—	—	15.00	17.00
4779	-	Kansas City	—	—	15.00	17.00
4780	-	Dallas	—	—	15.00	17.00
4781	-	San Francisco	—	—	15.00	17.00

Federal Reserve Notes - Hawaii Emergency

KL#	Fr#	Series	Signatures	Fine	XF	CH CU (63)	Gem CU (65)
2258	2303	1934A	Julian-Morgenthau	100.	275.	750.	1800.

Silver Certificates - North Africa Emergency

KL#	Fr#	Series	Signatures	Fine	XF	CH CU (63)	Gem CU (65)
2259	2308	1934	Julian-Morgenthau	—	—	—	—
2259☆	2308	1934☆	Julian-Morgenthau	—	—	Rare	—
2260	2309	1934A	Julian-Morgenthau	60.00	100.	300.	450.
2260☆	2309	1934A☆	Julian-Morgenthau	150.	500.	2250.	2750.

Gold Certificates

Twenty Dollars

KL#	Fr#	Series	Signatures	VF	XF	CH CU (63)	Gem CU (65)
2261	2402	1928	Woods-Mellon	175.	300.	900.	1250.
2261☆	2402	1928☆	Woods-Mellon	850.	2500.	9000.	11,000.

Federal Reserve Bank Notes

KL#	Fr#	Series	District	Fine	XF	CH CU (63)	Gem CU (65)
2262	1870A	1929	Boston	30.00	75.00	375.	450.
2262☆	1870A	1929☆	Boston	1250.	2500.	—	—
2263	1870B	1929	New York	35.00	50.00	200.	375.
2263☆	1870B	1929☆	New York	250.	600.	—	—
2264	1870C	1929	Philadelphia	35.00	100.	250.	450.
2264☆	1870C	1929☆	Philadelphia	200.	500.	—	—
2265	1870D	1929	Cleveland	30.00	70.00	350.	500.

KL#	Fr#	Series	District	Fine	XF	CH CU (63)	Gem CU (65)
2265☆	1870D	1929☆	Cleveland	2750.	4000.	—	—
2266	1870E	1929	Richmond	30.00	175.	400.	800.
2266☆	1870E	1929☆	Richmond	400.	900.	3500.	6000.
2267	1870F	1929	Atlanta	35.00	150.	650.	800.
2267☆	1870F	1929☆	Atlanta	1250.	3500.	—	—
2268	1870G	1929	Chicago	30.00	60.00	200.	250.
2268☆	1870G	1929☆	Chicago	1000.	2500.	—	—
2269	1870H	1929	St. Louis	30.00	100.	300.	375.
2269☆	1870H	1929☆	St. Louis	300.	800.	3000.	5000.
2270	1870I	1929	Minneapolis	30.00	100.	250.	350.
2270☆	1870I	1929☆	Minneapolis	575.	1750.	5000.	8200.
2271	1870J	1929	Kansas City	35.00	150.	650.	800.
2271☆	1870J	1929☆	Kansas City	350.	900.	1750.	2900.
2272	1870K	1929	Dallas	300.	750.	2000.	4600.
2272☆	1870K	1929☆	Dallas	5000.	10,000.	—	—
2273	1870L	1929	San Francisco	100.	200.	750.	950.
2273☆	1870L	1929☆	San Francisco	3000.	4250.	—	—

Federal Reserve Notes

Series 1928 Tate-Mellon

KL#	Fr#		District	Fine	XF	CH CU (63)	Gem CU (65)
2274	2050A		Boston	75.00	175.	250.	450.
2274☆	2050A	☆	Boston	100.	700.	3000.	3500.
2275	2050B		New York	50.00	75.00	250.	300.
2275☆	2050B	☆	New York	75.00	400.	1300.	1500.
2276	2050C		Philadelphia	50.00	75.00	300.	375.
2276☆	2050C	☆	Philadelphia	100.	450.	2000.	2500.
2277	2050D		Cleveland	40.00	75.00	200.	250.
2277☆	2050D	☆	Cleveland	75.00	350.	1500.	2000.
2278	2050E		Richmond	50.00	90.00	250.	300.
2278☆	2050E	☆	Richmond	175.	1000.	3000.	3000.
2279	2050F		Atlanta	55.00	100.	300.	350.
2279☆	2050F	☆	Atlanta	175.	750.	3000.	3000.
2280	2050G		Chicago	35.00	75.00	200.	225.
2280☆	2050G	☆	Chicago	75.00	500.	1650.	1800.
2281	2050H		St. Louis	40.00	75.00	225.	250.
2281☆	2050H	☆	St. Louis	100.	800.	2600.	2950.

KL#	Fr#		District	Fine	XF	CH CU (63)	Gem CU (65)
2282	2050I		Minneapolis	40.00	125.	250.	495.
2282☆	2050I	☆	Minneapolis	200.	1400.	2750.	5300.
2283	2050J		Kansas City	40.00	75.00	200.	225.
2283☆	2050J	☆	Kansas City	100.	600.	2000.	2000.
2284	2050K		Dallas	55.00	150.	400.	400.
2284☆	2050K	☆	Dallas	1000.	3000.	6500.	6500.
2285	2050L		San Francisco	40.00	75.00	250.	250.
2285☆	2050L	☆	San Francisco	100.	600.	2000.	2000.

Series 1928A Woods-Mellon

KL#	Fr#		District	Fine	XF	CH CU (63)	Gem CU (65)
2286	2051A		Boston	60.00	150.	500.	1000.
2286☆	2051A	☆	Boston	600.	1200.	4000.	7000.
2287	2051B		New York	60.00	150.	500.	800.
2287☆	2051B	☆	New York	600.	1200.	4000.	7000.
2288	2051C		Philadelphia	60.00	150.	500.	1000.
2288☆	2051C	☆	Philadelphia	600.	1200.	4000.	7700.
2289	2051D		Cleveland	60.00	150.	600.	700.
2289☆	2051D	☆	Cleveland	600.	1200.	4000.	7000.
2290	2051E		Richmond	60.00	150.	500.	700.
2290☆	2051E	☆	Richmond	600.	1200.	4000.	7000.
2291	2051F		Atlanta	60.00	150.	500.	700.
2291☆	2051F	☆	Atlanta	600.	1200.	4000.	7000.
2292	2051G		Chicago	60.00	150.	500.	600.
2292☆	2051G	☆	Chicago	600.	1200.	4000.	7000.
2293	2051H		St. Louis	75.00	175.	600.	800.
2293☆	2051H	☆	St. Louis	600.	1200.	4000.	7000.
2294	2051J		Kansas City	75.00	200.	600.	1200.
2294☆	2051J	☆	Kansas City	600.	1200.	4000.	9000.
2295	2051K		Dallas	60.00	150.	300.	600.
2295☆	2051K	☆	Dallas	600.	1200.	4000.	8000.

Series 1928B Woods-Mellon

KL#	Fr#		District	Fine	XF	CH CU (63)	Gem CU (65)
2296	2052A		Boston	30.00	50.00	150.	250.
2296☆	2052A	☆	Boston	140.	600.	1200.	2250.
2297	2052B		New York	30.00	50.00	140.	275.
2297☆	2052B	☆	New York	140.	300.	1000.	1600.
2298	2052C		Philadelphia	30.00	50.00	150.	300.
2298☆	2052C	☆	Philadelphia	140.	300.	1500.	3000.
2299	2052D		Cleveland	30.00	50.00	150.	300.
2299☆	2052D	☆	Cleveland	140.	300.	1500.	3000.
2300	2052E		Richmond	30.00	50.00	240.	500.
2300☆	2052E	☆	Richmond	140.	350.	1500.	3500.
2301	2052F		Atlanta	60.00	150.	500.	800.
2301☆	2052F	☆	Atlanta	140.	350.	1500.	3500.
2302	2052G		Chicago	30.00	50.00	100.	300.
2302☆	2052G	☆	Chicago	140.	350.	1000.	2100.

2303	2052H		St. Louis	30.00	60.00	150.	300.
2303☆	2052H	☆	St. Louis	140.	350.	1500.	3000.
2304	2052I		Minneapolis	30.00	60.00	160.	500.
2304☆	2052I	☆	Minneapolis	140.	750.	2000.	4500.
2305	2052J		Kansas City	30.00	50.00	125.	250.
2305☆	2052J	☆	Kansas City	140.	750.	1500.	3000.
2306	2052K		Dallas	30.00	60.00	200.	400.
2306☆	2052K	☆	Dallas	140.	750.	1500.	3500.
2307	2052L		San Francisco	30.00	50.00	170.	350.
2307☆	2052L	☆	San Francisco	140.	600.	1500.	3500.

Series 1928C Woods-Mills

KL#	Fr#	District	Fine	XF	CH CU (63)	Gem CU (65)
2308	2053G	Chicago	345.	800.	2000.	2500.
2309	2053L	San Francisco	500.	1500.	5000.	6000.

Series 1934 Julian-Morgenthau

KL#	Fr#		District	Fine	XF	CH CU (63)	Gem CU (65)
2310	2054A		Boston	25.00	40.00	85.00	125.
2310☆	2054A	☆	Boston	50.00	100.	600.	1000.
2311	2054B		New York	25.00	40.00	75.00	105.
2311☆	2054B	☆	New York	50.00	100.	600.	1000.
2312	2054C		Philadelphia	25.00	40.00	85.00	100.
2312☆	2054C	☆	Philadelphia	50.00	100.	600.	1000.
2313	2054D		Cleveland	25.00	40.00	85.00	100.
2313☆	2054D	☆	Cleveland	50.00	100.	600.	1000.
2314	2054E		Richmond	25.00	40.00	85.00	100.
2314☆	2054E	☆	Richmond	70.00	150.	800.	1000.
2315	2054F		Atlanta	25.00	40.00	85.00	100.
2315☆	2054F	☆	Atlanta	70.00	150.	800.	1000.
2316	2054G		Chicago	25.00	40.00	85.00	100.
2316☆	2054G	☆	Chicago	50.00	100.	600.	1000.
2317	2054H		St. Louis	25.00	40.00	85.00	100.
2317☆	2054H	☆	St. Louis	50.00	100.	600.	1000.
2318	2054I		Minneapolis	25.00	40.00	85.00	100.
2318☆	2054I	☆	Minneapolis	50.00	100.	700.	1000.
2319	2054J		Kansas City	25.00	40.00	85.00	100.
2319☆	2054J	☆	Kansas City	50.00	100.	600.	1000.
2320	2054K		Dallas	25.00	40.00	85.00	100.
2320☆	2054K	☆	Dallas	70.00	180.	800.	1000.
2321	2054L		San Francisco	25.00	40.00	85.00	100.
2321☆	2054L	☆	San Francisco	70.00	150.	800.	1000.

Series 1934A Julian-Morgenthau

KL#	Fr#		District	Fine	XF	CH CU (63)	Gem CU (65)
2322	2055A		Boston	25.00	40.00	75.00	135.
2322☆	2055A	☆	Boston	70.00	125.	500.	875.
2323	2055B		New York	20.00	30.00	60.00	135.
2323☆	2055B	☆	New York	50.00	75.00	600.	875.
2324	2055C		Philadelphia	22.00	30.00	75.00	135.
2324☆	2055C	☆	Philadelphia	55.00	90.00	500.	875.
2325	2055D		Cleveland	22.00	30.00	75.00	135.
2325☆	2055D	☆	Cleveland	55.00	90.00	500.	875.
2326	2055E		Richmond	22.00	30.00	75.00	135.
2326☆	2055E	☆	Richmond	50.00	90.00	500.	875.
2327	2055F		Atlanta	25.00	35.00	75.00	135.
2327☆	2055F	☆	Atlanta	50.00	85.00	500.	875.
2328	2055G		Chicago	22.00	30.00	60.00	135.
2328☆	2055G	☆	Chicago	55.00	80.00	500.	875.

KL#	Fr#		District	Fine	XF	CH CU (63)	Gem CU (65)
2329	2055H		St. Louis	25.00	35.00	75.00	135.
2329☆	2055H	☆	St. Louis	55.00	90.00	500.	875.
2330	2055I		Minneapolis	25.00	45.00	100.	200.
2330☆	2055I	☆	Minneapolis	70.00	125.	550.	1000.
2331	2055J		Kansas City	25.00	35.00	75.00	135.
2331☆	2055J	☆	Kansas City	55.00	90.00	500.	875.
2332	2055K		Dallas	25.00	35.00	75.00	135.
2332☆	2055K	☆	Dallas	70.00	125.	650.	1000.
2333	2055L		San Francisco	22.00	30.00	75.00	135.
2333☆	2055L	☆	San Francisco	40.00	80.00	500.	900.

Series 1934B Julian-Vinson

KL#	Fr#		District	Fine	XF	CH CU (63)	Gem CU (65)
2334	2056A		Boston	25.00	35.00	80.00	185.
2334☆	2056A	☆	Boston	75.00	200.	900.	1550.
2335	2056B		New York	22.00	32.00	100.	185.
2335☆	2056B	☆	New York	65.00	100.	750.	1250.
2336	2056C		Philadelphia	25.00	35.00	125.	185.
2336☆	2056C	☆	Philadelphia	80.00	150.	750.	1400.
2337	2056D		Cleveland	25.00	40.00	100.	185.
2337☆	2056D	☆	Cleveland	75.00	200.	750.	1400.
2338	2056E		Richmond	25.00	32.00	100.	185.
2338☆	2056E	☆	Richmond	80.00	150.	900.	1400.
2339	2056F		Atlanta	25.00	35.00	70.00	185.
2339☆	2056F	☆	Atlanta	80.00	150.	700.	1550.
2340	2056G		Chicago	25.00	32.00	100.	185.
2340☆	2056G	☆	Chicago	65.00	100.	750.	1250.
2341	2056H		St. Louis	25.00	35.00	100.	185.
2341☆	2056H	☆	St. Louis	80.00	150.	750.	1400.
2342	2056I		Minneapolis	25.00	40.00	100.	185.
2342☆	2056I	☆	Minneapolis	75.00	200.	900.	1550.
2343	2056J		Kansas City	25.00	35.00	100.	185.
2343☆	2056J	☆	Kansas City	75.00	200.	900.	1550.
2344	2056K		Dallas	25.00	40.00	100.	185.
2344☆	2056K	☆	Dallas	75.00	200.	1000.	2000.
2345	2056L		San Francisco	25.00	40.00	100.	185.
2345☆	2056L	☆	San Francisco	75.00	200.	900.	1550.

Series 1934C Julian-Snyder

KL#	Fr#		District	Fine	XF	CH CU (63)	Gem CU (65)
2346	2057A		Boston	25.00	40.00	100.	135.
2346☆	2057A	☆	Boston	65.00	150.	750.	1000.
2347	2057B		New York	25.00	35.00	70.00	135.
2347☆	2057B	☆	New York	85.00	150.	550.	1000.
2348	2057C		Philadelphia	25.00	40.00	100.	135.
2348☆	2057C	☆	Philadelphia	55.00	150.	650.	1000.
2349	2057D		Cleveland	25.00	40.00	100.	135.
2349☆	2057D	☆	Cleveland	85.00	125.	650.	1000.

KL#	Fr#		District	Fine	XF	CH CU (63)	Gem CU (65)
2350	2057E		Richmond	30.00	40.00	100.	135.
2350☆	2057E	☆	Richmond	85.00	125.	650.	1000.
2351	2057F		Atlanta	25.00	40.00	100.	135.
2351☆	2057F	☆	Atlanta	55.00	150.	700.	1250.
2352	2057G		Chicago	25.00	40.00	100.	135.
2352☆	2057G	☆	Chicago	55.00	120.	500.	1000.
2353	2057H		St. Louis	25.00	40.00	100.	135.
2353☆	2057H	☆	St. Louis	80.00	150.	650.	1000.
2354	2057I		Minneapolis	25.00	45.00	100.	135.
2354☆	2057I	☆	Minneapolis	100.	250.	1000.	1250.
2355	2057J		Kansas City	25.00	40.00	100.	135.
2355☆	2057J	☆	Kansas City	100.	200.	750.	1000.
2356	2057K		Dallas	25.00	40.00	100.	135.
2356☆	2057K	☆	Dallas	100.	200.	800.	1000.
2357	2057L		San Francisco	25.00	40.00	100.	135.
2357☆	2057L	☆	San Francisco	100.	125.	800.	1000.

Series 1934D Clark-Snyder

KL#	Fr#		District	Fine	XF	CH CU (63)	Gem CU (65)
2358	2058A		Boston	—	30.00	75.00	150.
2358☆	2058A	☆	Boston	—	400.	1350.	1375.
2359	2058B		New York	—	30.00	75.00	150.
2359☆	2058B	☆	New York	—	—	—	1000.
2360	2058C		Philadelphia	—	30.00	95.00	150.
2360☆	2058C	☆	Philadelphia	—	100.	—	1000.
2361	2058D		Cleveland	25.00	30.00	95.00	175.
2361☆	2058D	☆	Cleveland	100.	450.	1100.	1375.
2362	2058E		Richmond	—	30.00	95.00	150.
2362☆	2058E	☆	Richmond	—	200.	1000.	1375.
2363	2058F		Atlanta	—	30.00	95.00	150.
2363☆	2058F	☆	Atlanta	—	—	—	1375.
2364	2058G		Chicago	—	25.00	75.00	150.
2364☆	2058G	☆	Chicago	—	200.	750.	1000.
2365	2058H		St. Louis	—	25.00	95.00	150.
2365☆	2058H	☆	St. Louis	—	—	—	1000.
2366	2058I		Minneapolis	—	40.00	120.	150.
2366☆	2058I	☆	Minneapolis	—	—	—	1250.
2367	2058J		Kansas City	—	30.00	95.00	150.
2367☆	2058J	☆	Kansas City	—	—	—	1000.
2368	2058K		Dallas	—	35.00	95.00	150.
2368☆	2058K	☆	Dallas	—	—	—	1250.
2369	2058L		San Francisco	—	35.00	95.00	150.
2369☆	2058L	☆	San Francisco	—	200.	900.	1000.

Series 1950 Clark-Snyder

KL#	Fr#		District	Fine	XF	CH CU (63)	Gem CU (65)
2370	2059A		Boston	22.00	35.00	70.00	90.00
2370☆	2059A	☆	Boston	40.00	250.	450.	625.
2371	2059B		New York	22.00	35.00	70.00	90.00
2371☆	2059B	☆	New York	40.00	250.	400.	625.
2372	2059C		Philadelphia	22.00	35.00	70.00	90.00
2372☆	2059C	☆	Philadelphia	40.00	250.	400.	625.
2373	2059D		Cleveland	22.00	35.00	70.00	90.00
2373☆	2059D	☆	Cleveland	40.00	250.	450.	625.
2374	2059E		Richmond	22.00	35.00	70.00	90.00
2374☆	2059E	☆	Richmond	40.00	250.	450.	625.
2375	2059F		Atlanta	22.00	35.00	70.00	90.00
2375☆	2059F	☆	Atlanta	45.00	250.	700.	625.
2376	2059G		Chicago	22.00	35.00	70.00	90.00
2376☆	2059G	☆	Chicago	40.00	250.	400.	625.

KL#	Fr#		District	Fine	XF	CH CU (63)	Gem CU (65)
2377	2059H		St. Louis	22.00	35.00	70.00	90.00
2377☆	2059H	☆	St. Louis	40.00	250.	550.	625.
2378	2059I		Minneapolis	22.00	35.00	70.00	90.00
2378☆	2059I	☆	Minneapolis	40.00	300.	700.	850.
2379	2059J		Kansas City	22.00	35.00	70.00	90.00
2379☆	2059J	☆	Kansas City	40.00	250.	550.	625.
2380	2059K		Dallas	22.00	35.00	90.00	90.00
2380☆	2059K	☆	Dallas	40.00	300.	700.	750.
2381	2059L		San Francisco	22.00	35.00	65.00	90.00
2381☆	2059L	☆	San Francisco	40.00	250.	450.	625.

Series 1950A Priest-Humphrey

KL#	Fr#		District	Fine	XF	CH CU (63)	Gem CU (65)
2382	2060A		Boston	—	30.00	75.00	85.00
2382☆	2060A	☆	Boston	75.00	150.	250.	375.
2383	2060B		New York	—	30.00	50.00	75.00
2383☆	2060B	☆	New York	75.00	150.	200.	375.
2384	2060C		Philadelphia	—	30.00	75.00	85.00
2384☆	2060C	☆	Philadelphia	75.00	150.	250.	375.
2385	2060D		Cleveland	—	30.00	60.00	75.00
2385☆	2060D	☆	Cleveland	75.00	150.	250.	375.
2386	2060E		Richmond	—	30.00	75.00	85.00
2386☆	2060E	☆	Richmond	75.00	150.	250.	375.
2387	2060F		Atlanta	—	30.00	75.00	85.00
2387☆	2060F	☆	Atlanta	75.00	150.	250.	375.
2388	2060G		Chicago	—	30.00	50.00	70.00
2388☆	2060G	☆	Chicago	75.00	150.	200.	375.
2389	2060H		St. Louis	—	30.00	65.00	75.00
2389☆	2060H	☆	St. Louis	75.00	150.	250.	375.
2390	2060I		Minneapolis	—	30.00	75.00	85.00
2390☆	2060I	☆	Minneapolis	75.00	175.	300.	425.
2391	2060J		Kansas City	—	30.00	65.00	75.00
2391☆	2060J	☆	Kansas City	75.00	160.	275.	400.
2392	2060K		Dallas	—	30.00	75.00	85.00
2392☆	2060K	☆	Dallas	75.00	160.	275.	400.
2393	2060L		San Francisco	—	30.00	65.00	75.00
2393☆	2060L	☆	San Francisco	75.00	160.	275.	400.

Series 1950B Priest-Anderson

KL#	Fr#		District	Fine	XF	CH CU (63)	Gem CU (65)
2394	2061A		Boston	—	30.00	60.00	75.00
2394☆	2061A	☆	Boston	50.00	175.	500.	550.
2395	2061B		New York	—	30.00	50.00	75.00
2395☆	2061B	☆	New York	35.00	125.	250.	325.
2396	2061C		Philadelphia	—	30.00	60.00	75.00
2396☆	2061C	☆	Philadelphia	35.00	175.	350.	425.
2397	2061D		Cleveland	—	30.00	60.00	75.00

KL#	Fr#		District	Fine	XF	CH CU (63)	Gem CU (65)
2397☆	2061D	☆	Cleveland	35.00	150.	300.	375.
2398	2061E		Richmond	—	30.00	60.00	75.00
2398☆	2061E	☆	Richmond	35.00	175.	350.	425.
2399	2061F		Atlanta	—	30.00	60.00	75.00
2399☆	2061F	☆	Atlanta	35.00	175.	350.	425.
2400	2061G		Chicago	—	30.00	50.00	75.00
2400☆	2061G	☆	Chicago	35.00	150.	250.	375.
2401	2061H		St. Louis	—	30.00	60.00	75.00
2401☆	2061H	☆	St. Louis	35.00	150.	300.	375.
2402	2061I		Minneapolis	—	30.00	60.00	75.00
2402☆	2061I	☆	Minneapolis	35.00	150.	300.	375.
2403	2061J		Kansas City	—	30.00	60.00	75.00
2403☆	2061J	☆	Kansas City	35.00	175.	350.	425.
2404	2061K		Dallas	—	30.00	60.00	75.00
2404☆	2061K	☆	Dallas	35.00	175.	350.	425.
2405	2061L		San Francisco	—	30.00	60.00	75.00
2405☆	2061L	☆	San Francisco	35.00	175.	350.	435.

Series 1950C Smith-Dillon

KL#	Fr#		District	Fine	XF	CH CU (63)	Gem CU (65)
2406	2062A		Boston	22.00	40.00	65.00	90.00
2406☆	2062A	☆	Boston	30.00	125.	350.	500.
2407	2062B		New York	22.00	35.00	55.00	80.00
2407☆	2062B	☆	New York	30.00	125.	350.	650.
2408	2062C		Philadelphia	22.00	45.00	65.00	90.00
2408☆	2062C	☆	Philadelphia	30.00	125.	350.	500.
2409	2062D		Cleveland	22.00	35.00	55.00	80.00
2409☆	2062D	☆	Cleveland	30.00	125.	350.	500.
2410	2062E		Richmond	22.00	35.00	55.00	80.00
2410☆	2062E	☆	Richmond	30.00	125.	350.	500.
2411	2062F		Atlanta	22.00	35.00	55.00	80.00
2411☆	2062F	☆	Atlanta	30.00	125.	350.	500.
2412	2062G		Chicago	22.00	35.00	65.00	80.00
2412☆	2062G	☆	Chicago	30.00	125.	300.	450.
2413	2062H		St. Louis	22.00	35.00	55.00	80.00
2413☆	2062H	☆	St. Louis	30.00	125.	350.	500.
2414	2062I		Minneapolis	22.00	35.00	55.00	80.00
2414☆	2062I	☆	Minneapolis	30.00	125.	350.	450.
2415	2062J		Kansas City	22.00	35.00	55.00	80.00
2415☆	2062J	☆	Kansas City	30.00	125.	350.	450.
2416	2062K		Dallas	22.00	40.00	65.00	90.00
2416☆	2062K	☆	Dallas	75.00	125.	650.	750.
2417	2062L		San Francisco	22.00	35.00	65.00	80.00
2417☆	2062L	☆	San Francisco	30.00	125.	450.	500.

Series 1950D Granahan-Dillon

KL#	Fr#		District	Fine	XF	CH CU (63)	Gem CU (65)
2418	2063A		Boston	22.00	35.00	75.00	90.00
2418☆	2063A	☆	Boston	35.00	140.	225.	325.
2419	2063B		New York	22.00	35.00	60.00	90.00
2419☆	2063B	☆	New York	45.00	140.	175.	325.
2419A	2063C		Philadelphia	22.00	35.00	75.00	90.00
2419A☆	2063C	☆	Philadelphia	65.00	125.	200.	300.
2420	2063D		Cleveland	22.00	35.00	75.00	90.00
2420☆	2063D	☆	Cleveland	65.00	125.	200.	300.
2421	2063E		Richmond	22.00	35.00	75.00	90.00
2421☆	2063E	☆	Richmond	45.00	140.	225.	325.
2422	2063F		Atlanta	22.00	35.00	75.00	90.00
2422☆	2063F	☆	Atlanta	40.00	125.	200.	300.
2423	2063G		Chicago	22.00	35.00	60.00	90.00

KL#	Fr#		District	Fine	XF	CH CU (63)	Gem CU (65)
2423☆	2063G	☆	Chicago	40.00	125.	150.	300.
2424	2063H		St. Louis	22.00	35.00	75.00	90.00
2424☆	2063H	☆	St. Louis	45.00	150.	250.	350.
2424A	2063I		Minneapolis	22.00	35.00	125.	90.00
2424A☆	2063I	☆	Minneapolis	55.00	175.	750.	900.
2425	2063J		Kansas City	22.00	35.00	75.00	90.00
2425☆	2063J	☆	Kansas City	40.00	125.	250.	300.
2426	2063K		Dallas	22.00	35.00	75.00	90.00
2426☆	2063K	☆	Dallas	40.00	125.	200.	300.
2427	2063L		San Francisco	22.00	35.00	75.00	90.00
2427☆	2063L	☆	San Francisco	40.00	125.	200.	300.

Series 1950E Granahan-Fowler

KL#	Fr#		District	Fine	XF	CH CU (63)	Gem CU (65)
2428	2064B		New York	25.00	55.00	100.	125.
2428☆	2064B	☆	New York	200.	300.	750.	1000.
2429	2064G		Chicago	25.00	70.00	175.	225.
2429☆	2064G	☆	Chicago	200.	400.	1000.	1250.
2430	2064L		San Francisco	25.00	70.00	175.	225.
2430☆	2064L	☆	San Francisco	200.	400.	800.	1000.

Series 1963 Granahan-Dillon

KL#	Fr#		District	Fine	XF	CH CU (63)	Gem CU (65)
2431	2065A		Boston	22.00	35.00	100.	77.00
2431☆	2065A	☆	Boston	40.00	100.	200.	225.
2432	2065B		New York	22.00	35.00	75.00	77.00
2432☆	2065B	☆	New York	40.00	75.00	125.	175.
2433	2065D		Cleveland	22.00	35.00	100.	77.00
2433☆	2065D	☆	Cleveland	40.00	100.	175.	225.
2434	2065E		Richmond	22.00	35.00	75.00	77.00
2434☆	2065E	☆	Richmond	40.00	100.	200.	225.
2435	2065F		Atlanta	22.00	35.00	100.	77.00
2435☆	2065F	☆	Atlanta	70.00	100.	200.	225.
2436	2065G		Chicago	22.00	35.00	125.	77.00
2436☆	2065G	☆	Chicago	40.00	75.00	200.	175.
2437	2065H		St. Louis	22.00	35.00	100.	77.00

KL#	Fr#		District	Fine	XF	CH CU (63)	Gem CU (65)
2437☆	2065H	☆	St. Louis	40.00	100.	180.	225.
2438	2065J		Kansas City	22.00	35.00	125.	77.00
2438☆	2065J	☆	Kansas City	40.00	100.	200.	225.
2439	2065K		Dallas	22.00	35.00	100.	77.00
2439☆	2065K	☆	Dallas	40.00	100.	200.	225.
2440	2065L		San Francisco	22.00	35.00	100.	77.00
2440☆	2065L	☆	San Francisco	40.00	100.	150.	225.

Series 1963A Granahan-Fowler

KL#	Fr#		District	Fine	XF	CH CU (63)	Gem CU (65)
2441	2066A		Boston	22.00	30.00	60.00	62.00
2441☆	2066A	☆	Boston	35.00	75.00	150.	160.
2442	2066B		New York	22.00	30.00	60.00	62.00
2442☆	2066B	☆	New York	35.00	75.00	150.	160.
2443	2066C		Philadelphia	22.00	30.00	60.00	62.00
2443☆	2066C	☆	Philadelphia	35.00	75.00	150.	160.
2444	2066D		Cleveland	22.00	30.00	60.00	62.00
2444☆	2066D	☆	Cleveland	35.00	75.00	150.	160.
2445	2066E		Richmond	22.00	30.00	60.00	62.00
2445☆	2066E	☆	Richmond	35.00	75.00	150.	160.
2446	2066F		Atlanta	22.00	30.00	60.00	62.00
2446☆	2066F	☆	Atlanta	35.00	75.00	150.	62.00
2447	2066G		Chicago	22.00	30.00	60.00	62.00
2447☆	2066G	☆	Chicago	35.00	75.00	150.	160.
2448	2066H		St. Louis	22.00	30.00	60.00	62.00
2448☆	2066H	☆	St. Louis	35.00	75.00	150.	160.
2449	2066I		Minneapolis	22.00	30.00	60.00	62.00
2449☆	2066I	☆	Minneapolis	35.00	75.00	175.	200.
2450	2066J		Kansas City	22.00	30.00	60.00	62.00
2450☆	2066J	☆	Kansas City	35.00	75.00	150.	160.
2451	2066K		Dallas	22.00	30.00	60.00	62.00
2451☆	2066K	☆	Dallas	35.00	75.00	150.	160.
2452	2066L		San Francisco	22.00	30.00	60.00	62.00
2452☆	2066L	☆	San Francisco	35.00	75.00	150.	160.

Series 1969 Elston-Kennedy

KL#	Fr#		District	Fine	XF	CH CU (63)	Gem CU (65)
2453	2067A		Boston	22.00	30.00	60.00	62.00
2453☆	2067A	☆	Boston	35.00	70.00	140.	150.
2454	2067B		New York	22.00	30.00	60.00	62.00
2454☆	2067B	☆	New York	30.00	65.00	120.	135.
2455	2067C		Philadelphia	22.00	30.00	60.00	62.00
2455☆	2067C	☆	Philadelphia	35.00	70.00	140.	150.
2456	2067D		Cleveland	22.00	30.00	60.00	62.00
2456☆	2067D	☆	Cleveland	30.00	65.00	140.	135.
2457	2067E		Richmond	22.00	30.00	60.00	62.00
2457☆	2067E	☆	Richmond	30.00	65.00	140.	135.
2458	2067F		Atlanta	22.00	30.00	60.00	62.00
2458☆	2067F	☆	Atlanta	35.00	70.00	140.	150.
2459	2067G		Chicago	22.00	30.00	60.00	62.00
2459☆	2067G	☆	Chicago	35.00	65.00	125.	135.
2460	2067H		St. Louis	22.00	30.00	60.00	62.00
2461	2067I		Minneapolis	22.00	30.00	60.00	62.00
2461☆	2067I	☆	Minneapolis	35.00	70.00	150.	150.
2462	2067J		Kansas City	22.00	30.00	60.00	62.00
2462☆	2067J	☆	Kansas City	35.00	70.00	140.	150.
2463	2067K		Dallas	22.00	30.00	60.00	62.00
2463☆	2067K	☆	Dallas	35.00	70.00	140.	150.
2464	2067L		San Francisco	22.00	30.00	60.00	62.00
2464☆	2067L	☆	San Francisco	35.00	65.00	125.	135.

Series 1969A Kabis-Connally

KL#	Fr#		District	Fine	XF	CH CU (63)	Gem CU (65)
2465	2068A		Boston	22.00	40.00	80.00	90.00
2466	2068B		New York	22.00	40.00	70.00	85.00
2466☆	2068B	☆	New York	35.00	70.00	125.	150.
2467	2068C		Philadelphia	22.00	40.00	80.00	90.00
2468	2068D		Cleveland	22.00	40.00	75.00	85.00
2468☆	2068D	☆	Cleveland	35.00	75.00	150.	160.
2469	2068E		Richmond	22.00	40.00	80.00	85.00
2469☆	2068E	☆	Richmond	35.00	70.00	140.	150.
2470	2068F		Atlanta	22.00	40.00	80.00	90.00
2471	2068G		Chicago	22.00	40.00	80.00	85.00
2471☆	2068G	☆	Chicago	35.00	70.00	140.	150.
2472	2068H		St. Louis	22.00	40.00	70.00	90.00
2472☆	2068H	☆	St. Louis	35.00	70.00	140.	150.
2473	2068I		Minneapolis	22.00	40.00	70.00	90.00
2473☆	2068I	☆	Minneapolis	45.00	90.00	160.	190.
2474	2068J		Kansas City	22.00	40.00	90.00	90.00
2475	2068K		Dallas	22.00	40.00	80.00	95.00
2475☆	2068K	☆	Dallas	35.00	70.00	140.	150.
2476	2068L		San Francisco	22.00	40.00	75.00	85.00
2476☆	2068L	☆	San Francisco	35.00	70.00	160.	175.

Series 1969B Banuelos-Connally

KL#	Fr#		District	Fine	XF	CH CU (63)	Gem CU (65)
2477	2069B		New York	35.00	45.00	200.	220.
2477☆	2069B	☆	New York	125.	250.	500.	550.
2478	2069D		Cleveland	50.00	105.	250.	275.
2479	2069E		Richmond	50.00	100.	200.	220.
2480	2069F		Atlanta	50.00	100.	200.	220.
2480☆	2069F	☆	Atlanta	175.	350.	700.	750.
2481	2069G		Chicago	50.00	100.	200.	220.
2481☆	2069G	☆	Chicago	125.	250.	600.	650.
2482	2069H		St. Louis	50.00	105.	250.	275.
2483	2069I		Minneapolis	60.00	125.	400.	450.
2484	2069J		Kansas City	60.00	125.	300.	325.
2484☆	2069J	☆	Kansas City	140.	275.	800.	900.
2485	2069K		Dallas	45.00	105.	200.	230.
2486	2069L		San Francisco	45.00	100.	175.	220.
2486☆	2069L	☆	San Francisco	140.	275.	800.	900.

Series 1969C Banuelos-Shultz

KL#	Fr#		District	Fine	XF	CH CU (63)	Gem CU (65)
2487	2070A		Boston	22.00	30.00	60.00	62.00
2487☆	2070A	☆	Boston	30.00	60.00	135.	145.
2488	2070B		New York	22.00	30.00	60.00	62.00
2488☆	2070B	☆	New York	30.00	60.00	120.	130.

KL#	Fr#		District	Fine	XF	CH CU (63)	Gem CU (65)
2489	2070C		Philadelphia	22.00	30.00	60.00	62.00
2489☆	2070C	☆	Philadelphia	30.00	60.00	135.	140.
2490	2070D		Cleveland	22.00	30.00	60.00	70.00
2490☆	2070D	☆	Cleveland	30.00	60.00	140.	145.
2491	2070E		Richmond	22.00	30.00	60.00	62.00
2491☆	2070E	☆	Richmond	30.00	60.00	120.	130.
2492	2070F		Atlanta	22.00	30.00	60.00	62.00
2492☆	2070F	☆	Atlanta	30.00	60.00	135.	145.
2493	2070G		Chicago	22.00	30.00	60.00	62.00
2493☆	2070G	☆	Chicago	30.00	60.00	135.	145.
2494	2070H		St. Louis	22.00	30.00	60.00	62.00
2494☆	2070H	☆	St. Louis	40.00	80.00	170.	185.
2495	2070I		Minneapolis	22.00	30.00	60.00	62.00
2495☆	2070I	☆	Minneapolis	30.00	60.00	135.	145.
2496	2070J		Kansas City	22.00	30.00	60.00	62.00
2496☆	2070J	☆	Kansas City	40.00	80.00	170.	185.
2497	2070K		Dallas	22.00	30.00	60.00	62.00
2497☆	2070K	☆	Dallas	35.00	70.00	120.	130.
2498	2070L		San Francisco	22.00	30.00	60.00	62.00
2498☆	2070L	☆	San Francisco	35.00	70.00	140.	150.

Series 1974 Neff-Simon

KL#	Fr#		District	Fine	XF	CH CU (63)	Gem CU (65)
2499	2071A		Boston	22.00	30.00	60.00	52.00
2499☆	2071A	☆	Boston	25.00	40.00	115.	90.00
2500	2071B		New York	22.00	30.00	60.00	52.00
2500☆	2071B	☆	New York	25.00	40.00	125.	80.00
2501	2071C		Philadelphia	22.00	30.00	60.00	52.00
2501☆	2071C	☆	Philadelphia	25.00	40.00	125.	52.00
2502	2071D		Cleveland	22.00	30.00	60.00	52.00
2502☆	2071D	☆	Cleveland	25.00	40.00	125.	85.00
2503	2071E		Richmond	22.00	30.00	60.00	52.00
2503☆	2071E	☆	Richmond	25.00	40.00	125.	85.00
2504	2071F		Atlanta	22.00	30.00	50.00	52.00
2504☆	2071F	☆	Atlanta	25.00	40.00	80.00	90.00
2505	2071G		Chicago	22.00	30.00	60.00	52.00
2505☆	2071G	☆	Chicago	25.00	40.00	110.	85.00
2506	2071H		St. Louis	22.00	30.00	60.00	52.00
2506☆	2071H	☆	St. Louis	25.00	40.00	110.	85.00
2507	2071I		Minneapolis	22.00	30.00	60.00	52.00
2507☆	2071I	☆	Minneapolis	25.00	40.00	110.	85.00
2508	2071J		Kansas City	22.00	30.00	60.00	52.00
2508☆	2071J	☆	Kansas City	25.00	40.00	110.	85.00
2509	2071K		Dallas	22.00	30.00	60.00	52.00
2509☆	2071K	☆	Dallas	25.00	40.00	110.	90.00
2510	2071L		San Francisco	22.00	30.00	60.00	52.00
2510☆	2071L	☆	San Francisco	25.00	40.00	105.	85.00

Series 1977 Morton-Blumenthal

KL#	Fr#		District	Fine	XF	CH CU (63)	Gem CU (65)
2511	2072A		Boston	22.00	30.00	60.00	62.00
2511☆	2072A	☆	Boston	25.00	50.00	100.	110.
2512	2072B		New York	22.00	30.00	60.00	62.00
2512☆	2072B	☆	New York	25.00	50.00	100.	110.
2513	2072C		Philadelphia	22.00	30.00	60.00	62.00
2513☆	2072C	☆	Philadelphia	25.00	50.00	100.	110.
2514	2072D		Cleveland	22.00	30.00	60.00	62.00
2514☆	2072D	☆	Cleveland	25.00	50.00	100.	110.
2515	2072E		Richmond	22.00	30.00	60.00	62.00

KL#	Fr#		District	Fine	XF	CH CU (63)	Gem CU (65)
2515☆	2072E	☆	Richmond	25.00	50.00	100.	110.
2516	2072F		Atlanta	22.00	30.00	60.00	62.00
2516☆	2072F	☆	Atlanta	25.00	50.00	100.	110.
2517	2072G		Chicago	22.00	30.00	60.00	62.00
2517☆	2072G	☆	Chicago	25.00	50.00	100.	110.
2518	2072H		St. Louis	22.00	30.00	60.00	62.00
2518☆	2072H	☆	St. Louis	25.00	50.00	100.	110.
2519	2072I		Minneapolis	22.00	30.00	65.00	67.00
2519☆	2072I	☆	Minneapolis	25.00	50.00	110.	130.
2520	2072J		Kansas City	22.00	30.00	60.00	62.00
2520☆	2072J	☆	Kansas City	25.00	50.00	100.	110.
2521	2072K		Dallas	22.00	30.00	60.00	62.00
2521☆	2072K	☆	Dallas	25.00	50.00	100.	110.
2522	2072L		San Francisco	22.00	30.00	60.00	62.00
2522☆	2072L	☆	San Francisco	25.00	50.00	100.	110.

Series 1981 Buchanan-Regan

KL#	Fr#		District	Fine	XF	CH CU (63)	Gem CU (65)
3536	2073A		Boston	22.00	35.00	75.00	80.00
3536☆	2073A	☆	Boston	35.00	90.00	125.	130.
3537	2073B		New York	22.00	35.00	60.00	77.00
3537☆	2073B	☆	New York	35.00	90.00	125.	185.
3538	2073C		Philadelphia	22.00	35.00	75.00	77.00
3538☆	2073C	☆	Philadelphia	45.00	90.00	150.	185.
3539	2073D		Cleveland	22.00	35.00	75.00	77.00
3539☆	2073D	☆	Cleveland	45.00	90.00	150.	185.
3540	2073E		Richmond	22.00	35.00	75.00	77.00
3540☆	2073E	☆	Richmond	45.00	90.00	150.	185.
3541	2073F		Atlanta	22.00	35.00	75.00	77.00
3541☆	2073F	☆	Atlanta	45.00	90.00	140.	185.
3542	2073G		Chicago	22.00	35.00	75.00	77.00
3542☆	2073G	☆	Chicago	45.00	90.00	140.	185.
3543	2073H		St. Louis	22.00	35.00	75.00	77.00
3543☆	2073H	☆	St. Louis	45.00	90.00	140.	185.
3544	2073I		Minneapolis	22.00	35.00	95.00	115.
3544☆	2073I	☆	Minneapolis	45.00	90.00	200.	220.
3545	2073J		Kansas City	22.00	35.00	75.00	77.00
3545☆	2073J	☆	Kansas City	45.00	90.00	150.	185.
3546	2073K		Dallas	22.00	35.00	75.00	77.00
3546☆	2073K	☆	Dallas	45.00	90.00	175.	185.
3547	2073L		San Francisco	22.00	35.00	75.00	77.00
3547☆	2073L	☆	San Francisco	45.00	90.00	150.	185.

Series 1981A Ortega-Regan

KL#	Fr#		District	Fine	XF	CH CU (63)	Gem CU (65)
3636	2074A		Boston	22.00	30.00	60.00	62.00
3637	2074B		New York	22.00	30.00	50.00	62.00
3638	2074C		Philadelphia	22.00	30.00	60.00	62.00
3638☆	2074C	☆	Philadelphia	35.00	70.00	100.	105.
3639	2074D		Cleveland	22.00	30.00	60.00	62.00
3639☆	2074D	☆	Cleveland	35.00	70.00	100.	105.
3640	2074E		Richmond	22.00	30.00	60.00	62.00
3641	2074F		Atlanta	22.00	30.00	60.00	62.00
3641☆	2074F	☆	Atlanta	35.00	70.00	100.	105.
3642	2074G		Chicago	22.00	30.00	50.00	62.00
3643	2074H		St. Louis	22.00	30.00	50.00	62.00
3644	2074I		Minneapolis	22.00	30.00	60.00	62.00
3645	2074J		Kansas City	22.00	30.00	60.00	62.00
3646	2074K		Dallas	22.00	30.00	60.00	62.00
3647	2074L		San Francisco	22.00	30.00	60.00	62.00
3647☆	2074L	☆	San Francisco	35.00	70.00	100.	105.

Series 1985 Ortega-Baker

KL#	Fr#		District	Fine	XF	CH CU (63)	Gem CU (65)
3736	2075A		Boston	—	25.00	50.00	52.00
3736☆	2075A	☆	Boston	22.00	35.00	75.00	77.00
3737	2075B		New York	—	25.00	40.00	52.00
3737☆	2075B	☆	New York	22.00	35.00	75.00	77.00
3738	2075C		Philadelphia	—	25.00	50.00	52.00
3738☆	2075C	☆	Philadelphia	22.00	35.00	75.00	77.00
3739	2075D		Cleveland	—	25.00	50.00	52.00
3739☆	2075D	☆	Cleveland	22.00	35.00	75.00	77.00
3740	2075E		Richmond	—	25.00	50.00	52.00
3740☆	2075E	☆	Richmond	22.00	35.00	75.00	77.00
3741	2075F		Atlanta	—	25.00	50.00	52.00
3742	2075G		Chicago	—	25.00	50.00	52.00
3742☆	2075G	☆	Chicago	22.00	35.00	70.00	77.00
3743	2075H		St. Louis	—	25.00	50.00	52.00
3744	2075I		Minneapolis	—	25.00	50.00	52.00
3745	2075J		Kansas City	—	25.00	50.00	52.00
3745☆	2075J	☆	Kansas City	22.00	35.00	75.00	77.00
3746	2075K		Dallas	—	25.00	50.00	52.00
3746☆	2075K	☆	Dallas	22.00	35.00	75.00	77.00
3747	2075L		San Francisco	—	25.00	50.00	52.00
3747☆	2075L	☆	San Francisco	22.00	35.00	75.00	77.00

Series 1988A Villalpando-Brady

KL#	Fr#		District	Fine	XF	CH CU (63)	Gem CU (65)
3880	2076A		Boston	22.00	30.00	60.00	62.00
3881	2076B		New York	22.00	30.00	60.00	62.00
3881☆	2076B	☆	New York	25.00	50.00	100.	105.
3882	2076C		Philadelphia	22.00	30.00	60.00	62.00
3882☆	2076C	☆	Philadelphia	22.00	30.00	60.00	62.00
3883	2076D		Cleveland	22.00	30.00	60.00	62.00
3884	2076E		Richmond	22.00	30.00	60.00	62.00
3885	2076F		Atlanta	22.00	30.00	60.00	62.00
3885☆	2076F	☆	Atlanta	25.00	50.00	100.	105.
3886	2076G		Chicago	22.00	30.00	60.00	62.00
3886☆	2076G	☆	Chicago	22.00	50.00	100.	105.
3887	2076H		St. Louis	22.00	30.00	60.00	62.00
3888	2076I		Minneapolis	22.00	30.00	60.00	62.00
3889	2076J		Kansas City	22.00	30.00	60.00	62.00
3890	2076K		Dallas	22.00	30.00	60.00	62.00
3890☆	2076K	☆	Dallas	25.00	50.00	100.	105.
3891	2076L		San Francisco	22.00	30.00	60.00	62.00

Series 1990 Villalpando-Brady

KL#	Fr#		District	Fine	XF	CH CU (63)	Gem CU (65)
3952	2077A		Boston	—	25.00	45.00	47.00
3952☆	2077A	☆	Boston	22.00	35.00	70.00	72.00

KL#	Fr#		District	Fine	XF	CH CU (63)	Gem CU (65)
3953	2077B		New York	—	25.00	45.00	47.00
3953☆	2077B	☆	New York	22.00	35.00	70.00	72.00
3954	2077C		Philadelphia	—	25.00	45.00	47.00
3955	2077D		Cleveland	—	25.00	45.00	47.00
3955☆	2077D	☆	Cleveland	22.00	35.00	70.00	72.00
3956	2077E		Richmond	—	25.00	45.00	47.00
3956☆	2077E	☆	Richmond	22.00	35.00	70.00	72.00
3957	2077F		Atlanta	—	25.00	45.00	47.00
3957☆	2077F	☆	Atlanta	22.00	35.00	70.00	72.00
3958	2077G		Chicago	—	25.00	45.00	47.00
3958☆	2077G	☆	Chicago	22.00	35.00	70.00	72.00
3959	2077H		St. Louis	—	25.00	45.00	47.00
3959☆	2077H	☆	St. Louis	22.00	40.00	80.00	85.00
3960	2077I		Minneapolis	—	25.00	45.00	47.00
3960☆	2077I	☆	Minneapolis	22.00	40.00	80.00	85.00
3961	2077J		Kansas City	—	25.00	45.00	47.00
3962	2077K		Dallas	—	25.00	45.00	47.00
3963	2077L		San Francisco	—	25.00	45.00	47.00

Series 1993 Withrow-Bentsen

KL#	Fr#		District	Fine	XF	CH CU (63)	Gem CU (65)
4048	2079A		Boston	—	22.00	40.00	42.00
4048☆	2079A	☆	Boston	—	25.00	60.00	52.00
4049	2079B		New York	—	22.00	45.00	42.00
4049☆	2079B	☆	New York	—	25.00	50.00	52.00
4050	2079C		Philadelphia	—	22.00	40.00	42.00
4051	2079D		Cleveland	—	22.00	40.00	42.00
4051☆	2079D	☆	Cleveland	—	25.00	60.00	52.00
4052	2079E		Richmond	—	22.00	40.00	42.00
4052☆	2079E	☆	Richmond	22.00	30.00	70.00	52.00
4053	2079F		Atlanta	—	22.00	45.00	42.00
4054	2079G		Chicago	—	22.00	40.00	42.00
4055	2079H		St. Louis	—	22.00	45.00	42.00
4057	2079J		Kansas City	—	22.00	40.00	42.00
4058	2079K		Dallas	—	22.00	45.00	42.00
4059	2079L		San Francisco	—	22.00	40.00	42.00
4059☆	2079L	☆	San Francisco	—	25.00	60.00	52.00

Series 1995 Withrow-Rubin

KL#	Fr#		District	Fine	XF	CH CU (63)	Gem CU (65)
4121	2081B		New York	—	22.00	40.00	42.00
4121☆	2081B	☆	New York	—	22.00	50.00	52.00
4122	2081C		Philadelphia	—	22.00	45.00	47.00
4123	2081D		Cleveland	—	22.00	45.00	47.00
4123☆	2081D	☆	Cleveland	—	25.00	70.00	75.00
4124	2081E		Richmond	—	22.00	45.00	47.00
4125	2081F		Atlanta	—	22.00	45.00	47.00
4125☆	2081F	☆	Atlanta	—	25.00	60.00	62.00

4126	2081G	Chicago	—	22.00	40.00	42.00
4127	2081H	St. Louis	—	22.00	45.00	47.00
4128	2081I	Minneapolis	—	22.00	45.00	47.00
4129	2081J	Kansas City	—	22.00	45.00	47.00
4130	2081K	Dallas	—	22.00	45.00	47.00
4131	2081L	San Francisco	—	22.00	40.00	42.00

Series 1996 Withrow-Rubin

KL#	Fr#	District	Fine	XF	CH CU (63)	Gem CU (65)
4162	2083A	Boston	—	—	30.00	37.00
4162☆	2083A ☆	Boston	—	22.00	35.00	52.00
4163	2083B	New York	—	—	30.00	37.00
4163☆	2083B ☆	New York	—	—	35.00	52.00
4164	2083C	Philadelphia	—	—	30.00	37.00
4164☆	2083C ☆	Philadelphia	—	22.00	40.00	37.00
4165	2083D	Cleveland	—	—	30.00	37.00
4165☆	2083D ☆	Cleveland	—	22.00	40.00	52.00
4166	2083E	Richmond	—	—	30.00	37.00
4166☆	2083E ☆	Richmond	—	22.00	40.00	52.00
4167	2083F	Atlanta	—	22.00	40.00	37.00
4167☆	2083F ☆	Atlanta	—	22.00	40.00	52.00
4168	2083G	Chicago	—	—	30.00	37.00
4168☆	2083G ☆	Chicago	—	—	30.00	52.00
4169	2083H	St. Louis	—	—	30.00	37.00
4169☆	2083H ☆	St. Louis	22.00	45.00	150.	90.00
4170	2083I	Minneapolis	—	—	35.00	37.00
4171	2083J	Kansas City	—	—	35.00	37.00
4172	2083K	Dallas	—	—	35.00	37.00
4173	2083L	San Francisco	—	—	35.00	37.00
4173☆	2083L ☆	San Francisco	—	25.00	50.00	52.00

Series 1999 Withrow-Summers - DC

KL#	Fr#	District	Fine	XF	CH CU (63)	Gem CU (65)
4549	2085A	Boston	—	—	30.00	32.00
4549☆	2085A ☆	Boston	—	22.00	60.00	62.00
4550	2085B	New York	—	—	30.00	32.00
4550☆	2085B ☆	New York	—	22.00	45.00	62.00
4551	2085C	Philadelphia	—	—	30.00	32.00
4552	2085D	Cleveland	—	—	30.00	32.00
4552☆	2085D ☆	Cleveland	—	22.00	60.00	62.00
4553	2085E	Richmond	—	—	30.00	32.00
4554	2085F	Atlanta	—	—	30.00	32.00
4555	2085G	Chicago	—	—	30.00	32.00
4555☆	2085G ☆	Chicago	—	22.00	40.00	62.00
4556	2085H	St. Louis	—	—	30.00	32.00
4557	2085I	Minneapolis	—	—	30.00	32.00
4558	2085J	Kansas City	—	—	30.00	32.00
4559	2085L	San Francisco	—	—	30.00	32.00
4559☆	2085L ☆	San Francisco	—	22.00	60.00	62.00

Series 2001 Marin-O'Neill - DC

KL#	Fr#	District	Fine	XF	CH CU (63)	Gem CU (65)
4617	2087B	New York	—	—	30.00	32.00
4617☆	2087B ☆	New York	25.00	65.00	125.	130.
4618	2087D	Cleveland	—	—	30.00	32.00
4619	2087E	Richmond	—	—	30.00	32.00
4620	2088B	New York	—	—	30.00	32.00
4621	2088E	Richmond	—	—	30.00	32.00
4622	2088F	Atlanta	—	—	30.00	32.00
4623	2088G	Chicago	—	—	30.00	32.00
4623☆	2088G ☆	Chicago	—	25.00	50.00	52.00

KL#	Fr#		District	Fine	XF	CH CU (63)	Gem CU (65)
4624	2088H		St. Louis	—	—	30.00	32.00
4625	2088I		Minneapolis	—	—	30.00	32.00
4626	2088J		Kansas City	—	—	30.00	32.00
4627	2088K		Dallas	—	—	30.00	32.00
4628	2088L		San Francisco	—	—	30.00	32.00
4628☆	2088L	☆	San Francisco	—	25.00	50.00	42.00

Series 2004 Marin-Snow - DC

Colored underprint.

KL#	Fr#		District	Fine	XF	CH CU (63)	Gem CU (65)
4733	2089A		Boston	—	—	30.00	32.00
4733☆	2089A	☆	Boston	—	22.00	50.00	52.00
4734	2089B		New York	—	—	30.00	32.00
4734☆	2089B	☆	New York	22.00	40.00	150.	165.
4735	2089C		Philadelphia	—	—	30.00	32.00
4735☆	2089C	☆	Philadelphia	—	22.00	50.00	52.00
4736	2089D		Cleveland	—	—	30.00	32.00
4737	2089E		Richmond	—	—	30.00	32.00
4737☆	2089E	☆	Richmond	—	25.00	100.	32.00
4738	2089F		Atlanta	—	—	30.00	32.00

Series 2004 Marin-Snow - FW

Colored underprint.

KL#	Fr#		District	Fine	XF	CH CU (63)	Gem CU (65)
4739	2090D		Cleveland	—	—	30.00	32.00
4740	2090E		Richmond	—	—	30.00	32.00
4741	2090F		Atlanta	—	—	30.00	32.00
4741☆	2090F	☆	Atlanta	—	22.00	50.00	52.00
4742	2090G		Chicago	—	—	30.00	32.00
4742☆	2090G	☆	Chicago	—	22.00	50.00	52.00
4743	2090H		St. Louis	—	—	30.00	32.00
4744	2090I		Minneapolis	—	—	30.00	32.00

KL#	Fr#		District	Fine	XF	CH CU (63)	Gem CU (65)
4745	2090J		Kansas City	—	—	30.00	32.00
4745☆	2090J	☆	Kansas City	—	22.00	50.00	52.00
4746	2090K		Dallas	—	—	30.00	32.00
4747	2090L		San Francisco	—	—	30.00	32.00
4747☆	2090L	☆	San Francisco	—	22.00	50.00	52.00

Series 2004A Cabral-Snow - DC

KL#	Fr#	District	Fine	XF	CH CU (63)	Gem CU (65)
4782	-	Boston	—	—	30.00	32.00
4782☆	-	Boston	—	22.00	50.00	52.00
4783	-	New York	—	—	30.00	32.00
4783☆	-	New York	—	22.00	50.00	52.00
4784	-	Philadelphia	—	—	30.00	32.00
4785	-	Cleveland	—	—	30.00	32.00
4786	-	Richmond	—	—	30.00	32.00
4786☆	-	Richmond	—	22.00	50.00	52.00
4787	-	Atlanta	—	—	30.00	32.00
4787☆	-	Atlanta	—	22.00	50.00	52.00
4788	-	Chicago	—	—	30.00	32.00
4789	-	Minneapolis	—	—	30.00	32.00
4790	-	Kansas City	—	—	30.00	32.00

Series 2004A Cabral-Snow - FW

KL#	Fr#	District	Fine	XF	CH CU (63)	Gem CU (65)
4791	-	Atlanta	—	—	30.00	32.00
4792	-	St. Louis	—	—	30.00	32.00
4793	-	Minneapolis	—	—	30.00	32.00
4794	-	Kansas City	—	—	30.00	32.00
4795	-	Dallas	—	—	30.00	32.00
4795☆	-	Dallas	—	22.00	50.00	52.00
4796	-	San Francisco	—	—	30.00	32.00

Series 2006 Cabral-Paulson - DC

KL#	Fr#	District	Fine	XF	CH CU (63)	Gem CU (65)
4810	-	Boston	—	—	30.00	32.00
4811	-	New York	—	—	30.00	32.00
4812	-	Philadelphia	—	—	30.00	32.00
4813	-	Richmond	—	—	30.00	32.00

Series 2006 Cabral-Paulson - FW

KL#	Fr#	District	Fine	XF	CH CU (63)	Gem CU (65)
4821	-	San Francisco	—	—	30.00	32.00

Federal Reserve Notes - Hawaii Emergency

KL#	Fr#	Series	DistrictSignatures	Fine	XF	CH CU (63)	Gem CU (65)
2523	2304	1934	Julian-Morgenthau	200.	300.	6000.	3350.

Gold Certificates

Fifty Dollars

KL#	Fr#	Series	Signatures	VF	XF	CH CU (63)	Gem CU (65)
2525	2404	1928	Woods-Mellon	—	1250.	3000.	4750.
2525☆	2404	1928☆	Woods-Mellon	4000.	9000.	15,500.	24,750.

Federal Reserve Bank Notes

Fifty Dollars

KL#	Fr#	Series	District	Fine	XF	CH CU (63)	Gem CU (65)
2526	1880B	1929	New York	75.00	150.	225.	450.
2526☆	1880B	1929☆	New York	300.	920.	3000.	5700.
2527	1880D	1929	Cleveland	70.00	115.	300.	600.
2527☆	1880D	1929☆	Cleveland	345.	1100.	4000.	7500.
2528	1880G	1929	Chicago	85.00	150.	400.	350.
2528☆	1880G	1929☆	Chicago	3000.	7000.	—	—
2529	1880I	1929	Minneapolis	65.00	250.	500.	950.
2529☆	1880I	1929☆	Minneapolis	8000.	—	—	—
2530	1880J	1929	Kansas City	75.00	160.	375.	700.
2530☆	1880J	1929☆	Kansas City	550.	1250.	2500.	4750.
2531	1880K	1929	Dallas	375.	1725.	5200.	9800.
2531☆	1880K	1929☆	Dallas	—	—	—	—
2532	1880L	1929	San Francisco	100.	300.	475.	550.
2532☆	1880L	1929☆	San Francisco	—	4500.	—	—

Federal Reserve Notes

Series 1928 Woods-Mellon

KL#	Fr#		District	Fine	XF	CH CU (63)	Gem CU (65)
2533	2100A		Boston	—	150.	750.	1250.
2533☆	2100A	☆	Boston	500.	1100.	1600.	2750.
2534	2100B		New York	—	125.	600.	1000.
2534☆	2100B	☆	New York	250.	600.	1400.	2500.
2535	2100C		Philadelphia	100.	400.	900.	1400.
2535☆	2100C	☆	Philadelphia	500.	1000.	2500.	3700.
2536	2100D		Cleveland	—	125.	600.	1000.
2536☆	2100D	☆	Cleveland	300.	750.	2400.	4000.
2537	2100E		Richmond	—	150.	750.	1250.
2537☆	2100E	☆	Richmond	250.	650.	2000.	3500.
2538	2100F		Atlanta	—	140.	750.	1250.
2538☆	2100F	☆	Atlanta	250.	650.	2400.	4000.
2539	2100G		Chicago	—	125.	600.	1000.
2539☆	2100G	☆	Chicago	250.	600.	1600.	2750.
2540	2100H		St. Louis	—	150.	750.	1250.
2540☆	2100H	☆	St. Louis	250.	650.	1600.	3000.
2541	2100I		Minneapolis	—	200.	1000.	1750.
2541☆	2100I	☆	Minneapolis	200.	575.	2400.	4000.
2542	2100J		Kansas City	—	150.	800.	1500.
2542☆	2100J	☆	Kansas City	250.	650.	2500.	4500.
2543	2100K		Dallas	—	125.	600.	1000.
2543☆	2100K	☆	Dallas	250.	650.	2500.	4500.
2544	2100L		San Francisco	—	125.	600.	1000.
2544☆	2100L	☆	San Francisco	200.	600.	2500.	4000.

Series 1928A Woods-Mellon

KL#	Fr#	District	Fine	XF	CH CU (63)	Gem CU (65)
2545	2101A	Boston	—	90.00	400.	450.
2546	2101B	New York	—	90.00	375.	400.
2547	2101C	Philadelphia	—	90.00	425.	500.
2548	2101D	Cleveland	—	90.00	400.	450.
2549	2101E	Richmond	—	90.00	500.	550.
2550	2101F	Atlanta	—	120.	450.	500.
2551	2101G	Chicago	—	100.	350.	550.

KL#	Fr#		District	Fine	XF	CH CU (63)	Gem CU (65)
2551☆	2101G	☆	Chicago	1000.	3000.	4500.	7500.
2552	2101H		St. Louis	—	110.	450.	500.
2553	2101I		Minneapolis	—	110.	550.	650.
2554	2101J		Kansas City	—	110.	800.	1000.
2555	2101K		Dallas	—	85.00	700.	800.
2556	2101L		San Francisco	—	95.00	600.	650.

Series 1934 Julian-Morgenthau

KL#	Fr#		District	Fine	XF	CH CU (63)	Gem CU (65)
2557	2102A		Boston	—	60.00	200.	250.
2557☆	2102A	☆	Boston	100.	175.	700.	1000.
2558	2102B		New York	—	60.00	150.	200.
2558☆	2102B	☆	New York	100.	175.	600.	700.
2559	2102C		Philadelphia	—	60.00	150.	200.
2559☆	2102C	☆	Philadelphia	100.	175.	700.	1000.
2560	2102D		Cleveland	—	60.00	150.	200.
2560☆	2102D	☆	Cleveland	100.	175.	700.	1000.
2561	2102E		Richmond	—	60.00	175.	225.
2561☆	2102E	☆	Richmond	100.	175.	800.	1200.
2562	2102F		Atlanta	—	60.00	175.	225.
2562☆	2102F	☆	Atlanta	100.	175.	800.	1200.
2563	2102G		Chicago	—	75.00	175.	300.
2563☆	2102G	☆	Chicago	100.	200.	500.	800.
2564	2102H		St. Louis	—	65.00	175.	225.
2564☆	2102H	☆	St. Louis	100.	200.	800.	1200.
2565	2102I		Minneapolis	—	65.00	200.	275.
2565☆	2102I	☆	Minneapolis	100.	200.	800.	1200.
2566	2102J		Kansas City	—	65.00	175.	200.
2566☆	2102J	☆	Kansas City	100.	200.	750.	1000.
2567	2102K		Dallas	—	65.00	200.	250.
2567☆	2102K	☆	Dallas	100.	200.	900.	1500.
2568	2102L		San Francisco	—	60.00	175.	225.
2568☆	2102L	☆	San Francisco	100.	200.	750.	1500.

Series 1934A Julian-Morgenthau

KL#	Fr#		District	Fine	XF	CH CU (63)	Gem CU (65)
2569	2103A		Boston	—	125.	400.	450.
2569☆	2103A	☆	Boston	125.	500.	1000.	1500.
2570	2103B		New York	65.00	125.	325.	535.
2570☆	2103B	☆	New York	100.	500.	1100.	1700.
2571	2103D		Cleveland	—	100.	275.	325.
2571☆	2103D	☆	Cleveland	125.	500.	1000.	1500.
2572	2103E		Richmond	—	100.	275.	325.
2572☆	2103E	☆	Richmond	250.	500.	1200.	1500.
2573	2103F		Atlanta	—	100.	350.	400.
2573☆	2103F	☆	Atlanta	125.	500.	1000.	1500.
2574	2103G		Chicago	—	95.00	275.	325.

KL#	Fr#		District	Fine	XF	CH CU (63)	Gem CU (65)
2574☆	2103G	☆	Chicago	100.	400.	1100.	1500.
2575	2103H		St. Louis	—	125.	400.	500.
2575☆	2103H	☆	St. Louis	125.	500.	1200.	1500.
2576	2103I		Minneapolis	—	200.	400.	500.
2577	2103J		Kansas City	—	125.	800.	1500.
2578	2103K		Dallas	—	125.	400.	1500.
2579	2103L		San Francisco	—	125.	800.	1500.

Series 1934B Julian-Vinson

KL#	Fr#		District	Fine	XF	CH CU (63)	Gem CU (65)
2580	2104C		Philadelphia	—	125.	350.	400.
2580☆	2104C	☆	Philadelphia	300.	1250.	3500.	4650.
2581	2104D		Cleveland	100.	200.	500.	800.
2581☆	2104D	☆	Cleveland	300.	1000.	3000.	4650.
2582	2104E		Richmond	—	125.	400.	600.
2582☆	2104E	☆	Richmond	300.	1250.	3500.	4650.
2583	2104F		Atlanta	—	125.	400.	600.
2584	2104G		Chicago	—	125.	400.	600.
2585	2104H		St. Louis	—	125.	400.	600.
2586	2104I		Minneapolis	100.	250.	550.	750.
2587	2104J		Kansas City	—	125.	500.	750.
2587☆	2104J	☆	Kansas City	300.	1250.	3500.	4650.
2588	2104K		Dallas	—	135.	550.	750.
2589	2104L		San Francisco	—	125.	450.	650.

Series 1934C Julian-Snyder

KL#	Fr#		District	Fine	XF	CH CU (63)	Gem CU (65)
2590	2105A		Boston	—	125.	300.	500.
2591	2105B		New York	—	110.	220.	350.
2591☆	2105B	☆	New York	250.	600.	1500.	2350.
2592	2105C		Philadelphia	—	125.	300.	450.
2592☆	2105C	☆	Philadelphia	250.	600.	1500.	2350.
2593	2105D		Cleveland	—	100.	250.	425.
2593☆	2105D	☆	Cleveland	250.	750.	1500.	2350.
2594	2105E		Richmond	—	110.	220.	350.
2594☆	2105E	☆	Richmond	250.	600.	1500.	2350.
2595	2105F		Atlanta	—	125.	500.	750.
2596	2105G		Chicago	—	110.	250.	425.
2597	2105H		St. Louis	—	110.	250.	425.
2598	2105I		Minneapolis	—	125.	300.	500.
2598☆	2105I	☆	Minneapolis	250.	600.	1500.	2350.
2599	2105J		Kansas City	—	110.	250.	400.
2600	2105K		Dallas	—	110.	250.	400.
2600☆	2105K	☆	Dallas	250.	600.	1500.	2350.

Series 1934D Clark-Snyder

KL#	Fr#		District	Fine	XF	CH CU (63)	Gem CU (65)
2601	2106A		Boston	125.	—	300.	500.
2601☆	2106A	☆	Boston	1500.	—	4000.	5500.
2602	2106B		New York	85.00	—	400.	550.
2602☆	2106B	☆	New York	1800.	—	4000.	5500.
2603	2106C		Philadelphia	85.00	—	400.	550.
2603☆	2106C	☆	Philadelphia	1200.	—	3000.	4500.
2604	2106E		Richmond	115.	—	500.	750.
2605	2106F		Atlanta	100.	200.	400.	650.
2605☆	2106F	☆	Atlanta	600.	1265.	4000.	6250.
2606	2106G		Chicago	85.00	—	400.	650.
2606☆	2106G	☆	Chicago	1600.	—	2500.	4000.
2607	2106K		Dallas	175.	—	600.	900.

Series 1950 Clark-Snyder

KL#	Fr#		District	Fine	XF	CH CU (63)	Gem CU (65)
2608	2107A		Boston	—	125.	250.	350.
2608☆	2107A	☆	Boston	175.	375.	700.	1000.
2609	2107B		New York	—	125.	250.	350.
2609☆	2107B	☆	New York	175.	375.	700.	1000.
2610	2107C		Philadelphia	—	125.	250.	350.
2610☆	2107C	☆	Philadelphia	175.	400.	700.	1000.
2611	2107D		Cleveland	—	125.	250.	350.
2611☆	2107D	☆	Cleveland	175.	400.	700.	1000.
2612	2107E		Richmond	—	125.	250.	350.
2612☆	2107E	☆	Richmond	175.	400.	700.	1000.
2613	2107F		Atlanta	—	125.	250.	350.
2613☆	2107F	☆	Atlanta	175.	400.	700.	1000.
2614	2107G		Chicago	—	100.	200.	350.
2614☆	2107G	☆	Chicago	200.	400.	800.	1350.
2615	2107H		St. Louis	—	100.	200.	350.
2615☆	2107H	☆	St. Louis	225.	450.	900.	1400.
2616	2107I		Minneapolis	—	250.	500.	650.
2616☆	2107I	☆	Minneapolis	375.	750.	1500.	1800.
2617	2107J		Kansas City	—	100.	200.	350.
2617☆	2107J	☆	Kansas City	300.	600.	1200.	1500.
2618	2107K		Dallas	—	125.	225.	375.
2618☆	2107K	☆	Dallas	225.	450.	900.	1400.
2619	2107L		San Francisco	—	100.	200.	350.
2619☆	2107L	☆	San Francisco	225.	450.	900.	1400.

Series 1950A Priest-Humphrey

KL#	Fr#		District	Fine	XF	CH CU (63)	Gem CU (65)
2620	2108A		Boston	75.00	100.	225.	375.
2620☆	2108A	☆	Boston	125.	350.	700.	950.
2621	2108B		New York	75.00	100.	225.	375.

KL#	Fr#		District	Fine	XF	CH CU (63)	Gem CU (65)
2621☆	2108B	☆	New York	125.	250.	500.	850.
2622	2108C		Philadelphia	75.00	100.	225.	375.
2622☆	2108C	☆	Philadelphia	125.	250.	500.	850.
2623	2108D		Cleveland	75.00	100.	225.	375.
2623☆	2108D	☆	Cleveland	125.	250.	500.	850.
2624	2108E		Richmond	75.00	100.	225.	375.
2624☆	2108E	☆	Richmond	125.	300.	600.	900.
2625	2108F		Atlanta	75.00	125.	250.	400.
2625☆	2108F	☆	Atlanta	125.	300.	600.	900.
2626	2108G		Chicago	75.00	100.	225.	375.
2626☆	2108G	☆	Chicago	125.	250.	500.	850.
2627	2108H		St. Louis	75.00	100.	225.	375.
2627☆	2108H	☆	St. Louis	125.	250.	500.	850.
2628	2108J		Kansas City	75.00	125.	250.	400.
2628☆	2108J	☆	Kansas City	150.	300.	600.	900.
2629	2108K		Dallas	75.00	100.	225.	375.
2629☆	2108K	☆	Dallas	175.	350.	700.	950.
2630	2108L		San Francisco	75.00	100.	225.	375.
2630☆	2108L	☆	San Francisco	175.	350.	700.	950.

Series 1950B Priest-Anderson

KL#	Fr#		District	Fine	XF	CH CU (63)	Gem CU (65)
2631	2109A		Boston	—	80.00	175.	300.
2631☆	2109A	☆	Boston	70.00	200.	400.	500.
2632	2109B		New York	—	80.00	175.	300.
2632☆	2109B	☆	New York	70.00	200.	400.	500.
2633	2109C		Philadelphia	—	80.00	175.	300.
2633☆	2109C	☆	Philadelphia	70.00	200.	400.	500.
2634	2109D		Cleveland	—	80.00	175.	300.
2634☆	2109D	☆	Cleveland	70.00	200.	400.	500.
2635	2109E		Richmond	—	80.00	175.	300.
2635☆	2109E	☆	Richmond	70.00	200.	400.	500.
2636	2109G		Chicago	—	80.00	175.	300.
2636☆	2109G	☆	Chicago	70.00	200.	400.	500.
2637	2109H		St. Louis	—	80.00	175.	300.
2637☆	2109H	☆	St. Louis	70.00	200.	400.	500.
2638	2109J		Kansas City	—	80.00	175.	300.
2638☆	2109J	☆	Kansas City	70.00	200.	400.	500.
2639	2109K		Dallas	—	80.00	175.	300.
2639☆	2109K	☆	Dallas	70.00	200.	400.	500.
2640	2109L		San Francisco	—	80.00	175.	300.
2640☆	2109L	☆	San Francisco	70.00	200.	400.	500.

Series 1950C Smith-Dillon

KL#	Fr#		District	Fine	XF	CH CU (63)	Gem CU (65)
2641	2110A		Boston	—	70.00	175.	300.
2641☆	2110A	☆	Boston	125.	300.	600.	1000.
2642	2110B		New York	—	70.00	175.	300.
2642☆	2110B	☆	New York	125.	300.	600.	1000.
2643	2110C		Philadelphia	—	70.00	175.	300.
2643☆	2110C	☆	Philadelphia	125.	300.	600.	1000.
2644	2110D		Cleveland	—	70.00	175.	300.
2644☆	2110D	☆	Cleveland	125.	300.	600.	1000.
2645	2110E		Richmond	—	70.00	175.	300.
2645☆	2110E	☆	Richmond	125.	300.	700.	1100.
2646	2110G		Chicago	—	70.00	175.	300.
2646☆	2110G	☆	Chicago	125.	300.	600.	1000.
2647	2110H		St. Louis	—	70.00	175.	300.
2647☆	2110H	☆	St. Louis	125.	350.	700.	1100.
2648	2110I		Minneapolis	—	70.00	175.	200.

KL#	Fr#		District	Fine	XF	CH CU (63)	Gem CU (65)
2648☆	2110I	☆	Minneapolis	250.	500.	1000.	1250.
2649	2110J		Kansas City	—	70.00	175.	300.
2649☆	2110J	☆	Kansas City	125.	350.	700.	1100.
2650	2110K		Dallas	—	70.00	175.	300.
2650☆	2110K	☆	Dallas	125.	350.	700.	1100.
2651	2110L		San Francisco	—	70.00	175.	300.
2651☆	2110L	☆	San Francisco	125.	350.	700.	1100.

Series 1950D Granahan-Dillon

KL#	Fr#		District	Fine	XF	CH CU (63)	Gem CU (65)
2652	2111A		Boston	—	100.	225.	375.
2652☆	2111A	☆	Boston	125.	300.	600.	950.
2653	2111B		New York	—	100.	225.	375.
2653☆	2111B	☆	New York	110.	250.	500.	850.
2654	2111C		Philadelphia	—	100.	225.	375.
2654☆	2111C	☆	Philadelphia	110.	250.	500.	850.
2655	2111D		Cleveland	—	100.	200.	350.
2655☆	2111D	☆	Cleveland	110.	250.	500.	850.
2656	2111E		Richmond	—	100.	200.	350.
2656☆	2111E	☆	Richmond	110.	250.	500.	850.
2657	2111F		Atlanta	—	100.	200.	350.
2657☆	2111F	☆	Atlanta	125.	300.	600.	950.
2658	2111G		Chicago	—	100.	200.	350.
2658☆	2111G	☆	Chicago	110.	250.	500.	850.
2659	2111H		St. Louis	65.00	100.	200.	350.
2659☆	2111H	☆	St. Louis	110.	250.	500.	850.
2660	2111I		Minneapolis	—	100.	200.	350.
2660☆	2111I	☆	Minneapolis	150.	350.	700.	1050.
2661	2111J		Kansas City	—	100.	200.	350.
2661☆	2111J	☆	Kansas City	150.	350.	700.	1050.
2662	2111K		Dallas	—	100.	200.	350.
2662☆	2111K	☆	Dallas	150.	350.	700.	1050.
2663	2111L		San Francisco	—	100.	200.	350.
2663☆	2111L	☆	San Francisco	125.	300.	600.	950.

Series 1950E Granahan-Fowler

KL#	Fr#		District	Fine	XF	CH CU (63)	Gem CU (65)
2664	2112B		New York	175.	375.	750.	1275.
2664☆	2112B	☆	New York	300.	650.	1250.	2150.
2665	2112G		Chicago	225.	450.	950.	1400.
2665☆	2112G	☆	Chicago	500.	1000.	21,000.	3000.
2666	2112L		San Francisco	175.	350.	750.	1200.
2666☆	2112L	☆	San Francisco	350.	700.	1400.	2100.

Series 1963A Granahan-Fowler

KL#	Fr#		District	Fine	XF	CH CU (63)	Gem CU (65)
2667	2113A		Boston	—	75.00	200.	250.
2667☆	2113A	☆	Boston	70.00	150.	500.	550.
2668	2113B		New York	—	75.00	200.	250.
2668☆	2113B	☆	New York	70.00	150.	500.	550.
2669	2113C		Philadelphia	—	75.00	200.	250.
2669☆	2113C	☆	Philadelphia	70.00	150.	525.	575.
2670	2113D		Cleveland	—	75.00	200.	250.
2670☆	2113D	☆	Cleveland	70.00	150.	500.	550.
2671	2113E		Richmond	—	75.00	200.	250.
2671☆	2113E	☆	Richmond	70.00	150.	500.	550.
2672	2113F		Atlanta	—	75.00	200.	250.
2672☆	2113F	☆	Atlanta	100.	200.	600.	650.
2673	2113G		Chicago	—	75.00	200.	250.
2673☆	2113G	☆	Chicago	100.	200.	600.	650.
2674	2113H		St. Louis	—	75.00	200.	250.
2674☆	2113H	☆	St. Louis	70.00	150.	500.	550.
2675	2113I		Minneapolis	—	75.00	200.	250.
2675☆	2113I	☆	Minneapolis	70.00	150.	500.	550.
2676	2113J		Kansas City	—	75.00	200.	250.
2676☆	2113J	☆	Kansas City	100.	200.	700.	750.
2677	2113K		Dallas	—	75.00	200.	250.
2677☆	2113K	☆	Dallas	100.	200.	650.	700.
2678	2113L		San Francisco	—	75.00	200.	250.
2678☆	2113L	☆	San Francisco	100.	200.	650.	700.

Series 1969 Elston-Kennedy

KL#	Fr#		District	Fine	XF	CH CU (63)	Gem CU (65)
2679	2114A		Boston	—	60.00	125.	150.
2680	2114B		New York	—	60.00	125.	150.
2680☆	2114B	☆	New York	70.00	125.	250.	275.
2681	2114C		Philadelphia	—	60.00	125.	150.
2681☆	2114C	☆	Philadelphia	125.	225.	450.	500.
2682	2114D		Cleveland	—	60.00	125.	150.
2682☆	2114D	☆	Cleveland	—	60.00	125.	150.
2683	2114E		Richmond	—	60.00	125.	150.
2683☆	2114E	☆	Richmond	125.	275.	550.	600.

KL#	Fr#		District	Fine	XF	CH CU (63)	Gem CU (65)
2684	2114F		Atlanta	70.00	100.	225.	250.
2685	2114G		Chicago	—	60.00	125.	150.
2685☆	2114G	☆	Chicago	75.00	125.	250.	275.
2686	2114H		St. Louis	70.00	100.	225.	250.
2687	2114I		Minneapolis	70.00	100.	200.	225.
2688	2114J		Kansas City	—	75.00	150.	175.
2688☆	2114J	☆	Kansas City	150.	275.	550.	600.
2689	2114K		Dallas	—	75.00	150.	175.
2689☆	2114K	☆	Dallas	150.	275.	550.	600.
2690	2114L		San Francisco	—	75.00	150.	175.
2690☆	2114L	☆	San Francisco	90.00	150.	275.	300.

Series 1969A Kabis-Connally

KL#	Fr#		District	Fine	XF	CH CU (63)	Gem CU (65)
2691	2115A		Boston	—	75.00	150.	175.
2691☆	2115A	☆	Boston	60.00	100.	200.	225.
2692	2115B		New York	—	75.00	150.	175.
2692☆	2115B	☆	New York	60.00	90.00	175.	200.
2693	2115C		Philadelphia	—	75.00	150.	175.
2694	2115D		Cleveland	—	75.00	150.	175.
2695	2115E		Richmond	125.	75.00	150.	175.
2695☆	2115E	☆	Richmond	—	250.	500.	525.
2696	2115F		Atlanta	125.	75.00	150.	175.
2696☆	2115F	☆	Atlanta	—	250.	500.	525.
2697	2115G		Chicago	—	60.00	125.	150.
2697☆	2115G	☆	Chicago	70.00	125.	250.	275.
2698	2115H		St. Louis	—	75.00	150.	175.
2699	2115I		Minneapolis	—	75.00	150.	175.
2700	2115J		Kansas City	—	75.00	150.	175.
2701	2115K		Dallas	—	75.00	150.	175.
2701☆	2115K	☆	Dallas	125.	250.	500.	525.
2702	2115L		San Francisco	—	75.00	150.	175.
2702☆	2115L	☆	San Francisco	85.00	175.	350.	375.

Series 1969B Banuelos-Connally

KL#	Fr#		District	Fine	XF	CH CU (63)	Gem CU (65)
2703	2116A		Boston	300.	700.	1300.	1450.
2704	2116B		New York	300.	600.	850.	1050.
2705	2116E		Richmond	300.	700.	1300.	1450.
2706	2116F		Atlanta	300.	700.	1300.	1450.
2707	2116G		Chicago	300.	700.	1300.	1450.
2708	2116K		Dallas	300.	700.	1300.	1450.
2708☆	2116K	☆	Dallas	600.	1300.	2600.	2850.

Series 1969C Banuelos-Shultz

KL#	Fr#		District	Fine	XF	CH CU (63)	Gem CU (65)
2709	2117A		Boston	—	65.00	100.	110.
2709☆	2117A	☆	Boston	75.00	200.	400.	425.
2710	2117B		New York	—	65.00	100.	110.
2710☆	2117B	☆	New York	75.00	150.	300.	325.
2711	2117C		Philadelphia	—	65.00	100.	110.
2711☆	2117C	☆	Philadelphia	75.00	150.	300.	425.
2712	2117D		Cleveland	—	65.00	90.00	100.
2712☆	2117D	☆	Cleveland	70.00	125.	250.	275.
2713	2117E		Richmond	—	65.00	90.00	100.
2713☆	2117E	☆	Richmond	100.	200.	400.	425.
2714	2117F		Atlanta	—	75.00	150.	175.
2714☆	2117F	☆	Atlanta	125.	250.	500.	550.
2715	2117G		Chicago	—	65.00	90.00	100.
2715☆	2117G	☆	Chicago	75.00	125.	250.	275.
2716	2117H		St. Louis	—	65.00	90.00	100.
2716☆	2117H	☆	St. Louis	100.	200.	400.	425.
2717	2117I		Minneapolis	—	75.00	150.	175.
2717☆	2117I	☆	Minneapolis	100.	200.	400.	425.
2718	2117J		Kansas City	—	75.00	100.	110.
2718☆	2117J	☆	Kansas City	75.00	150.	300.	325.
2719	2117K		Dallas	—	75.00	90.00	100.
2719☆	2117K	☆	Dallas	100.	200.	400.	425.
2720	2117L		San Francisco	—	75.00	90.00	110.
2720☆	2117L	☆	San Francisco	75.00	150.	300.	325.

Series 1974 Neff-Simon

KL#	Fr#		District	Fine	XF	CH CU (63)	Gem CU (65)
2721	2118A		Boston	—	70.00	125.	140.
2721☆	2118A	☆	Boston	70.00	125.	250.	275.
2722	2118B		New York	—	65.00	100.	125.
2722☆	2118B	☆	New York	70.00	125.	250.	275.
2723	2118C		Philadelphia	—	70.00	125.	140.
2723☆	2118C	☆	Philadelphia	70.00	125.	250.	275.
2724	2118D		Cleveland	—	70.00	125.	140.
2724☆	2118D	☆	Cleveland	70.00	125.	250.	275.
2725	2118E		Richmond	—	70.00	125.	140.
2725☆	2118E	☆	Richmond	70.00	125.	250.	275.
2726	2118F		Atlanta	—	70.00	125.	140.
2726☆	2118F	☆	Atlanta	70.00	125.	250.	275.
2727	2118G		Chicago	—	65.00	100.	125.
2727☆	2118G	☆	Chicago	70.00	125.	250.	275.
2728	2118H		St. Louis	—	75.00	150.	175.
2728☆	2118H	☆	St. Louis	70.00	125.	250.	275.
2729	2118I		Minneapolis	—	75.00	150.	175.
2729☆	2118I	☆	Minneapolis	70.00	125.	250.	275.
2730	2118J		Kansas City	—	75.00	150.	175.
2730☆	2118J	☆	Kansas City	70.00	125.	250.	275.
2731	2118K		Dallas	—	75.00	150.	175.
2731☆	2118K	☆	Dallas	70.00	125.	250.	275.
2732	2118L		San Francisco	—	75.00	150.	175.
2732☆	2118L	☆	San Francisco	70.00	125.	350.	400.

Series 1977 Morton-Blumenthal

KL#	Fr#		District	Fine	XF	CH CU (63)	Gem CU (65)
2733	2119A		Boston	—	100.	225.	250.
2733☆	2119A	☆	Boston	75.00	125.	250.	275.
2734	2119B		New York	—	75.00	150.	175.
2734☆	2119B	☆	New York	75.00	100.	200.	225.

KL#	Fr#		District	Fine	XF	CH CU (63)	Gem CU (65)
2735	2119C		Philadelphia	—	100.	225.	250.
2735☆	2119C	☆	Philadelphia	75.00	125.	250.	275.
2736	2119D		Cleveland	—	75.00	175.	200.
2736☆	2119D	☆	Cleveland	75.00	125.	250.	275.
2737	2119E		Richmond	—	85.00	175.	200.
2737☆	2119E	☆	Richmond	75.00	125.	250.	275.
2738	2119F		Atlanta	—	100.	225.	250.
2738☆	2119F	☆	Atlanta	75.00	125.	250.	275.
2739	2119G		Chicago	—	75.00	150.	175.
2739☆	2119G	☆	Chicago	75.00	125.	250.	275.
2740	2119H		St. Louis	—	100.	225.	250.
2740☆	2119H	☆	St. Louis	—	125.	250.	275.
2741	2119I		Minneapolis	—	100.	225.	250.
2742	2119J		Kansas City	—	100.	225.	250.
2742☆	2119J	☆	Kansas City	—	125.	250.	275.
2743	2119K		Dallas	—	100.	225.	250.
2743☆	2119K	☆	Dallas	—	125.	250.	275.
2744	2119L		San Francisco	—	100.	225.	250.
2744☆	2119L	☆	San Francisco	—	125.	250.	275.

Series 1981 Buchanan-Regan

KL#	Fr#		District	Fine	XF	CH CU (63)	Gem CU (65)
3548	2120A		Boston	—	—	200.	—
3549	2120B		New York	—	—	200.	—
3549☆	2120B	☆	New York	—	—	300.	—
3550	2120C		Philadelphia	—	—	200.	—
3551	2120D		Cleveland	—	—	200.	—
3551☆	2120D	☆	Cleveland	—	—	300.	—
3552	2120E		Richmond	—	—	200.	—
3553	2120F		Atlanta	—	—	200.	—
3553☆	2120F	☆	Atlanta	—	—	315.	—
3554	2120G		Chicago	—	70.00	150.	165.
3554☆	2120G	☆	Chicago	75.00	150.	300.	325.
3555	2120H		St. Louis	—	—	200.	—
3556	2120I		Minneapolis	—	—	200.	—
3556☆	2120I	☆	Minneapolis	—	—	315.	—
3557	2120J		Kansas City	—	—	200.	—
3557☆	2120J	☆	Kansas City	—	—	315.	—
3558	2120K		Dallas	—	—	200.	—
3559	2120L		San Francisco	—	—	200.	—
3559☆	2120L	☆	San Francisco	—	—	315.	—

Series 1981A Ortega-Regan

KL#	Fr#		District	Fine	XF	CH CU (63)	Gem CU (65)
3648	2121A		Boston	—	—	225.	—
3649	2121B		New York	—	75.00	150.	165.
3649☆	2121B	☆	New York	100.	175.	350.	375.

KL#	Fr#	District	Fine	XF	CH CU (63)	Gem CU (65)
3651	2121D	Cleveland	—	—	225.	—
3652	2121E	Richmond	—	—	225.	—
3652☆	2121E ☆	Richmond	—	—	350.	—
3653	2121F	Atlanta	—	—	225.	—
3654	2121G	Chicago	—	—	225.	—
3655	2121H	St. Louis	—	—	225.	—
3656	2121I	Minneapolis	—	—	225.	—
3657	2121J	Kansas City	—	—	150.	—
3658	2121K	Dallas	—	—	225.	—
3659	2121L	San Francisco	—	—	225.	—
3659☆	2121L ☆	San Francisco	—	—	350.	—

Series 1985 Ortega-Baker

KL#	Fr#	District	Fine	XF	CH CU (63)	Gem CU (65)
3748	2122A	Boston	—	—	120.	—
3748☆	2122A ☆	Boston	—	—	250.	—
3749	2122B	New York	—	—	120.	—
3749☆	2122B ☆	New York	—	—	250.	—
3750	2122C	Philadelphia	—	—	120.	—
3751	2122D	Cleveland	—	60.00	100.	110.
3751☆	2122D ☆	Cleveland	75.00	100.	250.	275.
3752	2122E	Richmond	—	—	100.	110.
3753	2122F	Atlanta	—	—	100.	110.
3754	2122G	Chicago	—	—	100.	110.
3754☆	2122G ☆	Chicago	75.00	—	250.	275.
3755	2122H	St. Louis	—	—	100.	110.
3756	2122I	Minneapolis	—	—	100.	110.
3757	2122J	Kansas City	—	—	100.	110.
3758	2122K	Dallas	—	—	100.	110.
3759	2122L	San Francisco	—	—	100.	110.

Series 1988 Ortega-Brady

KL#	Fr#	District	Fine	XF	CH CU (63)	Gem CU (65)
3820	2123A	Boston	—	60.00	100.	110.
3821	2123B	New York	—	60.00	100.	110.
3821☆	2123B ☆	New York	—	150.	300.	325.
3823	2123D	Cleveland	—	60.00	100.	110.
3824	2123E	Richmond	—	60.00	100.	110.
3826	2123G	Chicago	—	60.00	100.	110.
3829	2123J	Kansas City	—	60.00	100.	110.
3831	2123L	San Francisco	—	60.00	100.	110.

Series 1990 Villalpando-Brady

KL#	Fr#	District	Fine	XF	CH CU (63)	Gem CU (65)
3964	2124A	Boston	—	—	75.00	78.00
3965	2124B	New York	—	—	70.00	75.00
3965☆	2124B ☆	New York	—	60.00	100.	110.
3966	2124C	Philadelphia	—	—	75.00	78.00
3966☆	2124C ☆	Philadelphia	—	60.00	100.	110.
3967	2124D	Cleveland	—	—	75.00	78.00
3968	2124E	Richmond	—	—	75.00	78.00
3970	2124G	Chicago	—	—	75.00	78.00
3970☆	2124G ☆	Chicago	—	60.00	100.	110.
3971	2124H	St. Louis	—	—	75.00	78.00
3972	2124I	Minneapolis	—	—	75.00	78.00
3973	2124J	Kansas City	—	—	75.00	78.00
3973☆	2124J ☆	Kansas City	—	60.00	100.	110.
3974	2124K	Dallas	—	—	75.00	78.00
3975	2124L	San Francisco	—	—	75.00	78.00

Series 1993 Withrow-Bentsen

KL#	Fr#		District	Fine	XF	CH CU (63)	Gem CU (65)
4060	2125A		Boston	—	—	75.00	78.00
4061	2125B		New York	—	—	75.00	78.00
4061☆	2125B	☆	New York	—	75.00	150.	165.
4063	2125D		Cleveland	—	—	75.00	78.00
4063☆	2125D	☆	Cleveland	—	75.00	150.	165.
4064	2125E		Richmond	—	—	75.00	78.00
4066	2125G		Chicago	—	—	75.00	78.00
4066☆	2125G	☆	Chicago	—	75.00	150.	165.
4067	2125H		St. Louis	—	—	75.00	78.00
4069	2125J		Kansas City	—	—	75.00	78.00
4070	2125K		Dallas	—	—	75.00	78.00

Series 1996 Withrow-Rubin

KL#	Fr#		District	Fine	XF	CH CU (63)	Gem CU (65)
4150	2126A		Boston	—	—	70.00	73.00
4151	2126B		New York	—	—	70.00	73.00
4151☆	2126B	☆	New York	—	70.00	95.00	100.
4152	2126C		Philadelphia	—	—	70.00	73.00
4153	2126D		Cleveland	—	—	70.00	73.00
4154	2126E		Richmond	—	—	70.00	73.00
4155	2126F		Atlanta	—	—	70.00	73.00
4156	2126G		Chicago	—	—	70.00	73.00
4156☆	2126G	☆	Chicago	—	70.00	95.00	100.
4157	2126H		St. Louis	—	—	70.00	73.00
4158	2126I		Minneapolis	—	—	70.00	73.00
4159	2126J		Kansas City	—	—	70.00	73.00
4159☆	2126J	☆	Kansas City	—	70.00	95.00	100.
4160	2126K		Dallas	—	—	70.00	73.00
4161	2126L		San Francisco	—	—	70.00	73.00
4161☆	2126L	☆	San Francisco	—	70.00	95.00	100.

Series 2001 Marin-O'Neill - DC

KL#	Fr#		District	Fine	XF	CH CU (63)	Gem CU (65)
4629	2127A		Boston	—	—	70.00	73.00
4630	2127B		New York	—	—	70.00	73.00
4630☆	2127B	☆	New York	125.	350.	695.	725.
4631	2127C		Philadelphia	—	—	70.00	73.00
4632	2127D		Cleveland	—	—	70.00	73.00
4633	2127E		Richmond	—	—	70.00	73.00
4633☆	2127E	☆	Richmond	75.00	125.	295.	325.
4634	2127F		Atlanta	—	—	70.00	73.00
4635	2127G		Chicago	—	—	70.00	73.00
4636	2127H		St. Louis	—	—	70.00	73.00
4637	2127I		Minneapolis	—	—	70.00	73.00
4638	2127J		Kansas City	—	—	70.00	73.00
4639	2127K		Dallas	—	—	70.00	73.00
4640	2127L		San Francisco	—	—	70.00	73.00

Series 2004 Marin-Snow - FW

Colored underprint.

KL#	Fr#		District	Fine	XF	CH CU (63)	Gem CU (65)
4752	2128A		Boston	—	—	70.00	73.00
4753	2128B		New York	—	—	70.00	73.00
4754	2128C		Philadelphia	—	—	70.00	73.00
4755	2128D		Cleveland	—	—	70.00	73.00
4756	2128E		Richmond	—	—	70.00	73.00
4757	2128F		Atlanta	—	—	70.00	73.00
4758	2128G		Chicago	—	—	70.00	73.00
4758☆	2128G	☆	Chicago	—	—	90.00	95.00
4759	2128H		St. Louis	—	—	70.00	73.00
4760	2128I		Minneapolis	—	—	70.00	73.00
4761	2128J		Kansas City	—	—	70.00	73.00
4762	2128K		Dallas	—	—	70.00	73.00
4762☆	2128K	☆	Dallas	—	—	90.00	95.00
4763	2128L		San Francisco	—	—	70.00	73.00

Series 2006 Cabral-Paulson - FW

KL#	Fr#	District	Fine	XF	CH CU (63)	Gem CU (65)
4825	-	Boston	—	—	70.00	73.00
4826	-	New York	—	—	70.00	73.00
4827	-	Philadelphia	—	—	70.00	73.00
4828	-	Cleveland	—	—	70.00	73.00
4829	-	Richmond	—	—	70.00	73.00
4831	-	Chicago	—	—	70.00	73.00
4832	-	St. Louis	—	—	70.00	73.00
4833	-	Minneapolis	—	—	70.00	73.00
4835	-	Dallas	—	—	70.00	73.00
4836	-	San Francisco	—	—	70.00	73.00

United States Notes

One Hundred Dollars

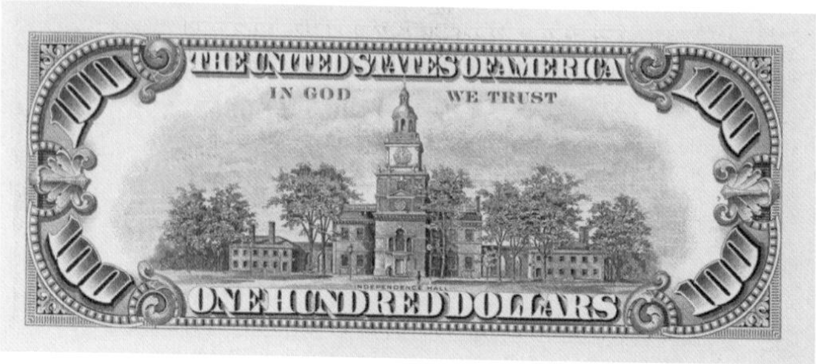

KL#	Fr#	Series	Signatures	Fine	XF	CH CU (63)	Gem CU (65)
2745	1550	1966	Granahan-Fowler	125.	210.	400.	800.
2745☆	1550	1966☆	Granahan-Fowler	400.	800.	2000.	4000.
2746	1551	1966A	Elston-Kennedy	225.	400.	750.	1500.

Gold Certificates

One Hundred Dollars

KL#	Fr#	Series	Signatures	VF	XF	CH CU (63)	Gem CU (65)
2747	2405	1928	Woods-Mellon	—	1250.	3000.	3750.
2747☆	2405	1928☆	Woods-Mellon	3000.	12,500.	19,500.	27,500.
2748	-	1934	Julian-Morgenthau	—	—	—	—

Federal Reserve Bank Notes

KL#	Fr#	Series	District	Fine	XF	CH CU (63)	Gem CU (65)
2749	1890B	1929	New York	130.	165.	400.	575.
2749☆	1890B	1929☆	New York	1100.	3500.	—	—
2751	1890D	1929	Cleveland	125.	175.	350.	600.
2751☆	1890D	1929☆	Cleveland	900.	1725.	—	—

KL#	Fr#	Series	District	Fine	XF	CH CU (63)	Gem CU (65)
2752	1890E	1929	Richmond	150.	300.	700.	825.
2752☆	1890E	1929☆	Richmond	2500.	7500.	10,500.	15,000.
2754	1890G	1929	Chicago	150.	225.	350.	650.
2754☆	1890G	1929☆	Chicago	1000.	2000.	4000.	5750.
2756	1890I	1929	Minneapolis	150.	300.	600.	775.
2756☆	1890I	1929☆	Minneapolis	11,000.	13,000.	—	—
2757	1890J	1929	Kansas City	125.	210.	350.	500.
2757☆	1890J	1929☆	Kansas City	500.	750.	1750.	2000.
2758	1890K	1929	Dallas	400.	1500.	2300.	3300.
2758☆	1890K	1929☆	Dallas	23,000.	—	—	—

Federal Reserve Notes

Series 1928 Woods-Mellon

KL#	Fr#		District	Fine	XF	CH CU (63)	Gem CU (65)
2760	2150A		Boston	—	250.	750.	1000.
2760☆	2150A	☆	Boston	200.	800.	2200.	5000.
2761	2150B		New York	150.	350.	750.	1200.
2761☆	2150B	☆	New York	750.	2000.	3000.	4800.
2762	2150C		Philadelphia	—	225.	750.	800.
2762☆	2150C	☆	Philadelphia	200.	675.	1650.	2000.
2763	2150D		Cleveland	—	225.	600.	700.
2763☆	2150D	☆	Cleveland	200.	600.	1600.	2000.
2764	2150E		Richmond	—	225.	750.	800.
2764☆	2150E	☆	Richmond	200.	700.	2200.	2750.
2765	2150F		Atlanta	—	225.	750.	800.
2765☆	2150F	☆	Atlanta	150.	600.	2200.	2750.
2766	2150G		Chicago	—	225.	600.	800.
2766☆	2150G	☆	Chicago	150.	500.	1550.	2500.
2767	2150H		St. Louis	—	250.	750.	800.
2767☆	2150H	☆	St. Louis	200.	700.	2200.	2800.
2768	2150I		Minneapolis	—	250.	1500.	2000.
2768☆	2150I	☆	Minneapolis	200.	750.	2200.	2800.
2769	2150J		Kansas City	—	225.	750.	1250.
2769☆	2150J	☆	Kansas City	200.	700.	1900.	2250.
2770	2150K		Dallas	—	250.	800.	1250.
2770☆	2150K	☆	Dallas	200.	800.	3000.	4000.
2771	2150L		San Francisco	—	225.	900.	1250.
2771☆	2150L	☆	San Francisco	200.	750.	1900.	2250.

Series 1928A Woods-Mellon

KL#	Fr#		District	Fine	XF	CH CU (63)	Gem CU (65)
2772	2151A		Boston	—	200.	325.	400.
2773	2151B		New York	—	175.	300.	350.
2773☆	2151B	☆	New York	1000.	5000.	10,000.	16,000.
2774	2151C		Philadelphia	—	200.	325.	400.
2775	2151D		Cleveland	—	185.	325.	450.
2776	2151D		Richmond	—	210.	325.	450.
2777	2151E		Atlanta	—	195.	325.	375.
2778	2151G		Chicago	—	175.	300.	375.
2779	2151H		St. Louis	175.	275.	600.	975.
2779☆	2151H	☆	St. Louis	2500.	5000.	10,000.	16,000.
2780	2151I		Minneapolis	—	195.	400.	450.
2781	2151J		Kansas City	—	210.	400.	450.
2782	2151K		Dallas	—	195.	350.	450.
2783	2151L		San Francisco	—	185.	300.	450.

Series 1934 Julian-Morganthau

KL#	Fr#		District	Fine	XF	CH CU (63)	Gem CU (65)
2784	2152A		Boston	—	175.	300.	500.
2784☆	2152A	☆	Boston	—	300.	1000.	1250.
2785	2152B		New York	—	145.	300.	450.
2785☆	2152B	☆	New York	—	500.	1500.	1000.
2786	2152C		Philadelphia	125.	200.	450.	675.
2786☆	2152C	☆	Philadelphia	575.	1275.	2000.	2900.
2787	2152D		Cleveland	—	175.	300.	500.
2787☆	2152D	☆	Cleveland	150.	500.	1200.	1500.
2788	2152E		Richmond	—	175.	300.	500.
2788☆	2152E	☆	Richmond	200.	300.	1500.	2000.
2789	2152F		Atlanta	—	210.	275.	400.
2789☆	2152F	☆	Atlanta	—	300.	1500.	2000.
2790	2152G		Chicago	—	175.	300.	500.
2790☆	2152G	☆	Chicago	150.	200.	1500.	2000.
2791	2152H		St. Louis	—	175.	300.	500.
2791☆	2152H	☆	St. Louis	150.	300.	1000.	1500.
2792	2152I		Minneapolis	—	175.	300.	500.
2792☆	2152I	☆	Minneapolis	150.	400.	1000.	1500.
2793	2152J		Kansas City	—	175.	300.	500.
2793☆	2152J	☆	Kansas City	—	300.	1500.	2000.
2794	2152K		Dallas	—	175.	325.	500.
2794☆	2152K	☆	Dallas	—	300.	1000.	1250.
2795	2152L		San Francisco	—	175.	250.	300.
2795☆	2152L	☆	San Francisco	—	300.	750.	1500.

Series 1934A Julian-Morgenthau

KL#	Fr#		District	Fine	XF	CH CU (63)	Gem CU (65)
2784A	2153A		Boston	—	225.	350.	475.
2784A☆	2153A	☆	Boston	—	500.	650.	900.
2785A	2153B		New York	—	125.	150.	200.
2785A☆	2153B	☆	New York	175.	—	700.	1200.
2786A	2153C		Philadelphia	—	180.	300.	400.
2786A☆	2153C	☆	Philadelphia	200.	500.	650.	900.
2787A	2153D		Cleveland	—	180.	300.	400.
2787A☆	2153D	☆	Cleveland	200.	500.	650.	900.
2788A	2153E		Richmond	—	180.	300.	400.
2788A☆	2153E	☆	Richmond	200.	500.	650.	900.
2789A	2153F		Atlanta	—	180.	300.	400.
2789A☆	2153F	☆	Atlanta	200.	500.	650.	900.
2790A	2153G		Chicago	—	180.	300.	400.
2790A☆	2153G	☆	Chicago	200.	500.	650.	900.
2791A	2153H		St. Louis	—	180.	300.	400.
2791A☆	2153H	☆	St. Louis	200.	500.	650.	900.
2792A	2153I		Minneapolis	—	180.	300.	400.
2792A☆	2153I	☆	Minneapolis	250.	600.	1000.	1250.
2793A	2153J		Kansas City	—	180.	300.	400.
2793A☆	2153J	☆	Kansas City	200.	500.	650.	900.
2794A	2153K		Dallas	—	180.	300.	400.
2794A☆	2153K	☆	Dallas	200.	600.	800.	1000.
2795A	2153L		San Francisco	—	180.	300.	400.
2795A☆	2153L	☆	San Francisco	200.	500.	650.	900.

Series 1934B Julian-Vinson

KL#	Fr#		District	Fine	XF	CH CU (63)	Gem CU (65)
2796	2154A		Boston	—	350.	450.	600.
2797	2154C		Philadelphia	—	350.	450.	600.
2798	2154D		Cleveland	—	350.	450.	600.
2799	2154E		Richmond	150.	225.	450.	675.
2799☆	2154E	☆	Richmond	800.	2200.	4500.	6500.
2800	2154F		Atlanta	—	300.	450.	650.
2800☆	2154F	☆	Atlanta	800.	2200.	4000.	6500.
2801	2154G		Chicago	—	300.	450.	650.
2801☆	2154G	☆	Chicago	800.	2200.	4000.	6500.
2802	2154H		St. Louis	—	300.	450.	650.
2802☆	2154H	☆	St. Louis	800.	2200.	4000.	6500.
2803	2154I		Minneapolis	—	300.	450.	650.
2803☆	2154I	☆	Minneapolis	800.	2200.	4000.	6500.
2804	2154J		Kansas City	—	300.	450.	650.
2804☆	2154J	☆	Kansas City	800.	2200.	4000.	6500.
2805	2154K		Dallas	—	300.	450.	650.
2805☆	2154K	☆	Dallas	800.	2200.	4000.	6500.

Series 1934C Julian-Snyder

KL#	Fr#		District	Fine	XF	CH CU (63)	Gem CU (65)
2806	2155A		Boston	—	175.	500.	700.
2807	2155B		New York	—	250.	1000.	1500.
2808	2155C		Philadelphia	—	200.	500.	750.
2809	2155D		Cleveland	—	180.	300.	450.
2809☆	2155D	☆	Cleveland	500.	2250.	4500.	6500.
2810	2155F		Atlanta	—	200.	400.	550.
2810☆	2155F	☆	Atlanta	500.	1200.	3750.	4500.
2811	2155G		Chicago	—	200.	400.	550.
2811☆	2155G	☆	Chicago	500.	1200.	3000.	4250.
2812	2155H		St. Louis	—	200.	375.	500.
2812☆	2155H	☆	St. Louis	500.	1200.	3750.	5000.

KL#	Fr#		District	Fine	XF	CH CU (63)	Gem CU (65)
2813	2155I		Minneapolis	—	200.	450.	600.
2814	2155J		Kansas City	—	200.	450.	600.
2815	2155K		Dallas	—	200.	450.	600.
2815☆	2155K	☆	Dallas	750.	2500.	5700.	—
2816	2155L		San Francisco	—	200.	450.	600.
2816☆	2155L	☆	San Francisco	750.	2000.	4500.	7500.

Series 1934D Clark-Snyder

KL#	Fr#		District	Fine	XF	CH CU (63)	Gem CU (65)
2817	2156B		New York	750.	2500.	5000.	—
2818	2156C		Philadelphia	—	350.	500.	750.
2818☆	2156C	☆	Philadelphia	750.	3000.	6000.	—
2819	2156F		Atlanta	—	350.	750.	1000.
2819☆	2156F	☆	Atlanta	750.	3000.	6000.	—
2820	2156G		Chicago	175.	375.	750.	1100.
2820☆	2156G	☆	Chicago	1000.	2750.	5500.	8000.
2821	2156H		St. Louis	—	350.	500.	750.
2822	2156K		Dallas	—	350.	500.	750.

Series 1950 Clark-Snyder

KL#	Fr#		District	Fine	XF	CH CU (63)	Gem CU (65)
2823	2157A		Boston	125.	200.	450.	700.
2823☆	2157A	☆	Boston	275.	700.	1200.	1875.
2824	2157B		New York	125.	200.	450.	700.
2824☆	2157B	☆	New York	275.	700.	1200.	1875.
2825	2157C		Philadelphia	125.	200.	450.	700.
2825☆	2157C	☆	Philadelphia	275.	700.	1200.	1875.
2826	2157D		Cleveland	125.	200.	450.	700.
2826☆	2157D	☆	Cleveland	275.	700.	1200.	1875.
2827	2157E		Richmond	125.	200.	450.	700.
2827☆	2157E	☆	Richmond	275.	700.	1200.	1875.
2828	2157F		Atlanta	125.	200.	450.	700.
2829	2157G		Chicago	125.	200.	450.	700.
2830	2157H		St. Louis	125.	200.	450.	700.
2831	2157I		Minneapolis	125.	200.	450.	700.
2832	2157J		Kansas City	125.	200.	450.	700.
2832☆	2157J	☆	Kansas City	275.	750.	1500.	2000.
2833	2157K		Dallas	125.	200.	450.	700.
2834	2157L		San Francisco	125.	200.	450.	700.

Series 1950A Priest-Humphrey

KL#	Fr#		District	Fine	XF	CH CU (63)	Gem CU (65)
2835	2158A		Boston	—	125.	250.	400.
2835☆	2158A	☆	Boston	150.	250.	500.	800.
2836	2158B		New York	—	125.	250.	400.
2836☆	2158B	☆	New York	150.	250.	500.	800.

KL#	Fr#		District	Fine	XF	CH CU (63)	Gem CU (65)
2837	2158C		Philadelphia	—	125.	250.	400.
2837☆	2158C	☆	Philadelphia	150.	250.	500.	800.
2838	2158D		Cleveland	—	125.	250.	400.
2838☆	2158D	☆	Cleveland	150.	250.	500.	800.
2839	2158E		Richmond	—	125.	250.	400.
2839☆	2158E	☆	Richmond	125.	250.	500.	800.
2840	2158F		Atlanta	—	125.	250.	400.
2840☆	2158F	☆	Atlanta	125.	250.	500.	800.
2841	2158G		Chicago	—	125.	250.	400.
2841☆	2158G	☆	Chicago	125.	250.	500.	800.
2842	2158H		St. Louis	—	125.	250.	400.
2842☆	2158H	☆	St. Louis	125.	250.	500.	800.
2843	2158I		Minneapolis	—	125.	250.	400.
2843☆	2158I	☆	Minneapolis	125.	250.	500.	800.
2844	2158J		Kansas City	—	125.	250.	400.
2844☆	2158J	☆	Kansas City	125.	250.	500.	800.
2845	2158K		Dallas	—	125.	250.	400.
2846	2158L		San Francisco	—	125.	250.	400.
2846☆	2158L	☆	San Francisco	125.	250.	500.	800.

Series 1950B Priest-Anderson

KL#	Fr#		District	Fine	XF	CH CU (63)	Gem CU (65)
2847	2159A		Boston	—	185.	300.	475.
2847☆	2159A	☆	Boston	175.	275.	500.	800.
2848	2159B		New York	—	185.	300.	475.
2848☆	2159B	☆	New York	175.	275.	500.	800.
2849	2159C		Philadelphia	—	185.	300.	475.
2849☆	2159C	☆	Philadelphia	200.	300.	550.	900.
2850	2159D		Cleveland	—	185.	300.	475.
2850☆	2159D	☆	Cleveland	200.	300.	550.	900.
2851	2159E		Richmond	—	185.	300.	475.
2851☆	2159E	☆	Richmond	175.	275.	500.	800.
2852	2159F		Atlanta	—	185.	300.	475.
2852☆	2159F	☆	Atlanta	175.	275.	500.	800.
2853	2159G		Chicago	—	185.	300.	475.
2853☆	2159G	☆	Chicago	175.	275.	500.	800.
2854	2159H		St. Louis	—	185.	300.	475.
2854☆	2159H	☆	St. Louis	175.	275.	500.	800.
2855	2159I		Minneapolis	—	185.	300.	475.
2855☆	2159I	☆	Minneapolis	175.	275.	500.	800.
2856	2159J		Kansas City	—	185.	300.	475.
2856☆	2159J	☆	Kansas City	175.	275.	500.	800.
2857	2159K		Dallas	—	185.	300.	475.
2857☆	2159K	☆	Dallas	175.	275.	500.	800.
2858	2159L		San Francisco	—	185.	300.	475.
2858☆	2159L	☆	San Francisco	175.	275.	500.	800.

Series 1950C Smith-Dillon

KL#	Fr#		District	Fine	XF	CH CU (63)	Gem CU (65)
2859	2160A		Boston	—	125.	175.	275.
2859☆	2160A	☆	Boston	150.	300.	700.	1100.
2860	2160B		New York	—	125.	175.	275.
2860☆	2160B	☆	New York	150.	300.	700.	1100.
2861	2160C		Philadelphia	—	125.	175.	275.
2861☆	2160C	☆	Philadelphia	150.	300.	700.	1100.
2862	2160D		Cleveland	—	125.	175.	275.
2862☆	2160D	☆	Cleveland	150.	300.	700.	1100.
2863	2160E		Richmond	—	125.	325.	275.
2863☆	2160E	☆	Richmond	150.	300.	650.	1100.
2864	2160F		Atlanta	—	125.	175.	275.
2864☆	2160F	☆	Atlanta	150.	300.	700.	1100.
2865	2160G		Chicago	—	125.	175.	275.
2865☆	2160G	☆	Chicago	150.	300.	700.	1100.
2866	2160H		St. Louis	—	125.	175.	275.
2866☆	2160H	☆	St. Louis	150.	300.	700.	1100.
2867	2160I		Minneapolis	—	125.	175.	275.
2867☆	2160I	☆	Minneapolis	150.	300.	700.	1100.
2868	2160J		Kansas City	—	125.	175.	275.
2868☆	2160J	☆	Kansas City	150.	300.	700.	1100.
2869	2160K		Dallas	—	125.	175.	275.
2869☆	2160K	☆	Dallas	150.	300.	700.	1100.
2870	2160L		San Francisco	—	125.	175.	275.
2870☆	2160L	☆	San Francisco	150.	300.	700.	1100.

Series 1950D Granahan-Dillon

KL#	Fr#		District	Fine	XF	CH CU (63)	Gem CU (65)
2871	2161A		Boston	—	125.	200.	300.
2871☆	2161A	☆	Boston	175.	275.	575.	900.
2872	2161B		New York	—	125.	175.	300.
2872☆	2161B	☆	New York	175.	275.	575.	900.
2873	2161C		Philadelphia	—	125.	200.	300.
2873☆	2161C	☆	Philadelphia	150.	225.	500.	800.
2874	2161D		Cleveland	—	125.	200.	300.
2874☆	2161D	☆	Cleveland	175.	275.	575.	900.
2875	2161E		Richmond	—	125.	200.	300.
2875☆	2161E	☆	Richmond	175.	275.	575.	900.
2876	2161F		Atlanta	—	125.	200.	300.
2876☆	2161F	☆	Atlanta	175.	275.	575.	900.
2877	2161G		Chicago	—	125.	200.	300.
2877☆	2161G	☆	Chicago	175.	275.	575.	900.
2878	2161H		St. Louis	—	125.	200.	300.
2878☆	2161H	☆	St. Louis	175.	275.	575.	900.
2879	2161I		Minneapolis	—	125.	200.	300.
2879☆	2161I	☆	Minneapolis	175.	275.	575.	900.
2880	2161J		Kansas City	—	125.	200.	300.

KL#	Fr#		District	Fine	XF	CH CU (63)	Gem CU (65)
2880☆	2161J	☆	Kansas City	175.	275.	575.	900.
2881	2161K		Dallas	—	175.	200.	300.
2881☆	2161K	☆	Dallas	150.	225.	575.	900.
2882	2161L		San Francisco	—	175.	225.	325.
2882☆	2161L	☆	San Francisco	150.	225.	575.	900.

Series 1950E Granahan-Fowler

KL#	Fr#		District	Fine	XF	CH CU (63)	Gem CU (65)
2883	2162B		New York	150.	375.	750.	1175.
2883☆	2162B	☆	New York	250.	500.	1200.	1875.
2884	2162G		Chicago	150.	300.	1000.	1250.
2884☆	2162G	☆	Chicago	800.	1200.	4000.	5000.
2885	2162L		San Francisco	200.	300.	750.	825.
2885☆	2162L	☆	San Francisco	600.	800.	3000.	3750.

Series 1963A Granahan-Fowler

KL#	Fr#		District	Fine	XF	CH CU (63)	Gem CU (65)
2886	2163A		Boston	—	125.	175.	200.
2886☆	2163A	☆	Boston	125.	175.	300.	325.
2887	2163B		New York	—	125.	175.	200.
2887☆	2163B	☆	New York	125.	175.	300.	325.
2888	2163C		Philadelphia	—	125.	175.	200.
2888☆	2163C	☆	Philadelphia	125.	175.	300.	325.
2889	2163D		Cleveland	—	125.	175.	200.
2889☆	2163D	☆	Cleveland	125.	175.	300.	325.
2890	2163E		Richmond	—	125.	175.	200.
2890☆	2163E	☆	Richmond	125.	175.	300.	325.
2891	2163F		Atlanta	—	125.	175.	200.
2891☆	2163F	☆	Atlanta	125.	175.	300.	325.
2892	2163G		Chicago	—	125.	175.	200.
2892☆	2163G	☆	Chicago	125.	175.	300.	325.
2893	2163H		St. Louis	—	125.	175.	200.
2893☆	2163H	☆	St. Louis	—	125.	175.	200.
2894	2163I		Minneapolis	—	125.	175.	200.
2894☆	2163I	☆	Minneapolis	125.	175.	300.	325.
2895	2163J		Kansas City	—	125.	175.	200.
2895☆	2163J	☆	Kansas City	125.	175.	300.	325.
2896	2163K		Dallas	—	125.	175.	200.
2896☆	2163K	☆	Dallas	125.	175.	300.	325.
2897	2163L		San Francisco	—	125.	175.	200.
2897☆	2163L	☆	San Francisco	125.	175.	300.	325.

Series 1969 Elston-Kennedy

KL#	Fr#		District	Fine	XF	CH CU (63)	Gem CU (65)
2898	2164A		Boston	—	125.	200.	225.
2898☆	2164A	☆	Boston	125.	200.	400.	450.
2899	2164B		New York	—	125.	200.	225.

KL#	Fr#		District	Fine	XF	CH CU (63)	Gem CU (65)
2899☆	2164B	☆	New York	125.	200.	400.	450.
2900	2164C		Philadelphia	—	125.	200.	225.
2900☆	2164C	☆	Philadelphia	125.	200.	400.	450.
2901	2164D		Cleveland	—	125.	200.	225.
2901☆	2164D	☆	Cleveland	125.	200.	400.	450.
2902	2164E		Richmond	—	125.	200.	225.
2902☆	2164E	☆	Richmond	125.	200.	400.	450.
2903	2164F		Atlanta	—	125.	200.	225.
2903☆	2164F	☆	Atlanta	125.	200.	400.	450.
2904	2164G		Chicago	—	125.	200.	225.
2904☆	2164G	☆	Chicago	125.	200.	400.	450.
2905	2164H		St. Louis	—	125.	200.	225.
2905☆	2164H	☆	St. Louis	125.	200.	400.	450.
2906	2164I		Minneapolis	—	125.	200.	225.
2906☆	2164I	☆	Minneapolis	125.	200.	400.	450.
2907	2164J		Kansas City	—	125.	200.	225.
2907☆	2164J	☆	Kansas City	125.	200.	400.	450.
2908	2164K		Dallas	—	125.	200.	225.
2908☆	2164K	☆	Dallas	125.	200.	400.	450.
2909	2164L		San Francisco	—	125.	200.	225.
2909☆	2164L	☆	San Francisco	125.	200.	400.	450.

Series 1969A Kabis-Connally

KL#	Fr#		District	Fine	XF	CH CU (63)	Gem CU (65)
2909A	2165A		Boston	—	125.	175.	200.
2909A☆	2165A	☆	Boston	—	150.	275.	300.
2909B	2165B		New York	—	125.	175.	200.
2909B☆	2165B	☆	New York	—	150.	275.	300.
2909C	2165C		Philadelphia	—	125.	175.	200.
2909C☆	2165C	☆	Philadelphia	—	150.	275.	300.
2909D	2165D		Cleveland	—	125.	175.	200.
2909D☆	2165D	☆	Cleveland	—	150.	275.	300.
2909E	2165E		Richmond	—	125.	175.	200.
2909E☆	2165E	☆	Richmond	—	150.	275.	300.
2909F	2165F		Atlanta	—	125.	175.	200.
2909F☆	2165F	☆	Atlanta	—	150.	275.	300.
2909G	2165G		Chicago	—	125.	175.	200.
2909G☆	2165G	☆	Chicago	—	150.	275.	300.
2909H	2165H		St. Louis	—	125.	175.	200.
2909H☆	2165H	☆	St. Louis	—	150.	225.	300.
2909I	2165I		Minneapolis	—	125.	175.	200.
2909J	2165J		Kansas City	—	125.	175.	200.
2909K	2165K		Dallas	—	125.	175.	200.
2909K☆	2165K	☆	Dallas	—	150.	225.	300.
2909L	2165L		San Francisco	—	125.	175.	200.
2909L☆	2165L	☆	San Francisco	—	150.	200.	300.

Series 1969C Banuelos-Shultz

KL#	Fr#		District	Fine	XF	CH CU (63)	Gem CU (65)
2910	2166A		Boston	—	125.	200.	225.
2910☆	2166A	☆	Boston	150.	225.	450.	475.
2911	2166B		New York	—	125.	200.	225.
2911☆	2166B	☆	New York	150.	225.	350.	375.
2912	2166C		Philadelphia	—	125.	200.	225.
2912☆	2166C	☆	Philadelphia	150.	225.	450.	475.
2913	2166D		Cleveland	—	125.	200.	225.
2913☆	2166D	☆	Cleveland	150.	225.	450.	475.
2914	2166E		Richmond	—	125.	200.	225.
2914☆	2166E	☆	Richmond	150.	225.	350.	375.

KL#	Fr#		District	Fine	XF	CH CU (63)	Gem CU (65)
2915	2166F		Atlanta	—	125.	200.	225.
2915☆	2166F	☆	Atlanta	150.	225.	350.	375.
2916	2166G		Chicago	—	125.	200.	225.
2916☆	2166G	☆	Chicago	150.	225.	350.	375.
2917	2166H		St. Louis	—	125.	200.	225.
2917☆	2166H	☆	St. Louis	150.	225.	450.	475.
2918	2166I		Minneapolis	—	125.	200.	225.
2918☆	2166I	☆	Minneapolis	150.	225.	450.	475.
2919	2166J		Kansas City	—	125.	200.	225.
2919☆	2166J	☆	Kansas City	150.	225.	350.	375.
2920	2166K		Dallas	—	125.	200.	225.
2920☆	2166K	☆	Dallas	150.	225.	450.	475.
2921	2166L		San Francisco	—	125.	200.	225.
2921☆	2166L	☆	San Francisco	150.	225.	350.	375.

Series 1974 Neff-Simon

KL#	Fr#		District	Fine	XF	CH CU (63)	Gem CU (65)
2922	2167A		Boston	—	—	175.	200.
2922☆	2167A	☆	Boston	125.	200.	325.	350.
2923	2167B		New York	—	—	175.	200.
2923☆	2167B	☆	New York	125.	200.	325.	350.
2924	2167C		Philadelphia	—	—	175.	200.
2924☆	2167C	☆	Philadelphia	125.	200.	325.	350.
2925	2167D		Cleveland	—	—	175.	200.
2925☆	2167D	☆	Cleveland	125.	200.	325.	350.
2926	2167E		Richmond	—	—	175.	200.
2926☆	2167E	☆	Richmond	125.	200.	325.	350.
2927	2167F		Atlanta	—	—	175.	200.
2927☆	2167F	☆	Atlanta	125.	200.	325.	350.
2928	2167G		Chicago	—	—	175.	200.
2928☆	2167G	☆	Chicago	125.	200.	325.	350.
2929	2167H		St. Louis	—	—	175.	200.
2929☆	2167H	☆	St. Louis	125.	200.	325.	350.
2930	2167I		Minneapolis	—	—	175.	200.
2930☆	2167I	☆	Minneapolis	125.	200.	325.	350.
2931	2167J		Kansas City	—	—	175.	200.
2931☆	2167J	☆	Kansas City	125.	200.	325.	350.
2932	2167K		Dallas	—	—	175.	200.
2932☆	2167K	☆	Dallas	125.	200.	325.	350.
2933	2167L		San Francisco	—	—	175.	200.
2933☆	2167L	☆	San Francisco	125.	200.	325.	350.

Series 1977 Morton-Blumenthal

KL#	Fr#		District	Fine	XF	CH CU (63)	Gem CU (65)
2934	2168A		Boston	—	—	150.	175.
2934☆	2168A	☆	Boston	—	175.	300.	340.
2935	2168B		New York	—	—	150.	175.
2935☆	2168B	☆	New York	—	175.	300.	340.
2936	2168C		Philadelphia	—	—	150.	175.
2936☆	2168C	☆	Philadelphia	—	175.	300.	340.
2937	2168D		Cleveland	—	—	150.	175.
2937☆	2168D	☆	Cleveland	—	175.	300.	340.
2938	2168E		Richmond	—	—	150.	175.
2938☆	2168E	☆	Richmond	—	175.	300.	340.
2939	2168F		Atlanta	—	—	150.	175.
2939☆	2168F	☆	Atlanta	—	175.	375.	400.
2940	2168G		Chicago	—	—	150.	175.
2940☆	2168G	☆	Chicago	—	175.	300.	340.
2941	2168H		St. Louis	—	—	150.	175.
2941☆	2168H	☆	St. Louis	—	175.	300.	340.
2942	2168I		Minneapolis	—	—	150.	175.
2942☆	2168I	☆	Minneapolis	—	175.	300.	340.
2943	2168J		Kansas City	—	—	150.	175.
2943☆	2168J	☆	Kansas City	—	175.	300.	340.
2944	2168K		Dallas	—	—	150.	175.
2944☆	2168K	☆	Dallas	—	175.	300.	340.
2944A	2168L		San Francisco	—	—	150.	175.
2944A☆	2168L	☆	San Francisco	—	175.	300.	340.

Series 1981 Buchanan-Regan

KL#	Fr#		District	Fine	XF	CH CU (63)	Gem CU (65)
3560	2169A		Boston	—	125.	200.	225.
3561	2169B		New York	—	125.	200.	225.
3562	2169C		Philadelphia	—	125.	200.	225.
3563	2169D		Cleveland	—	125.	200.	225.
3564	2169E		Richmond	—	125.	200.	225.
3564☆	2169E	☆	Richmond	800.	1700.	3000.	3300.
3565	2169F		Atlanta	—	125.	200.	225.
3566	2169G		Chicago	—	125.	200.	225.
3567	2169H		St. Louis	—	125.	200.	225.
3568	2169I		Minneapolis	—	125.	200.	225.
3569	2169J		Kansas City	—	125.	200.	225.
3570	2169K		Dallas	—	125.	200.	225.
3571	2169L		San Francisco	—	125.	200.	225.

Series 1981A Ortega-Regan

KL#	Fr#		District	Fine	XF	CH CU (63)	Gem CU (65)
3660	2170A		Boston	—	125.	200.	225.
3661	2170B		New York	—	125.	200.	225.
3662	2170C		Philadelphia	—	125.	200.	225.
3663	2170D		Cleveland	—	125.	200.	225.
3664	2170E		Richmond	—	125.	200.	225.
3665	2170F		Atlanta	—	125.	200.	225.
3666	2170G		Chicago	—	125.	200.	225.
3667	2170H		St. Louis	—	125.	200.	225.
3668	2170I		Minneapolis	—	125.	200.	225.
3670	2170K		Dallas	—	125.	200.	225.
3671	2170L		San Francisco	—	125.	200.	225.
3671☆	2170L	☆	San Francisco	375.	750.	1500.	1700.

Series 1985 Ortega-Baker

KL#	Fr#		District	Fine	XF	CH CU (63)	Gem CU (65)
3760	2171A		Boston	—	—	150.	175.
3761	2171B		New York	—	—	150.	175.
3762	2171C		Philadelphia	—	—	150.	175.
3763	2171D		Cleveland	—	—	150.	175.
3763☆	2171D	☆	Cleveland	125.	225.	400.	450.
3764	2171E		Richmond	—	—	150.	175.
3765	2171F		Atlanta	—	—	150.	175.
3766	2171G		Chicago	—	—	150.	175.
3767	2171H		St. Louis	—	—	150.	175.
3768	2171I		Minneapolis	—	—	150.	175.
3769	2171J		Kansas City	—	—	150.	175.
3769☆	2171J	☆	Kansas City	125.	225.	400.	450.
3770	2171K		Dallas	—	—	150.	175.
3770☆	2171K	☆	Dallas	125.	225.	400.	450.
3771	2171L		San Francisco	—	—	150.	175.

Series 1988 Ortega-Brady

KL#	Fr#		District	Fine	XF	CH CU (63)	Gem CU (65)
3832	2172A		Boston	—	125.	175.	200.
3833	2172B		New York	—	125.	175.	200.
3833☆	2172B	☆	New York	150.	250.	500.	575.
3834	2172C		Philadelphia	—	125.	175.	200.
3835	2172D		Cleveland	—	125.	175.	200.
3836	2172E		Richmond	—	125.	175.	200.
3838	2172G		Chicago	—	125.	175.	200.
3839	2172H		St. Louis	—	125.	175.	200.
3841	2172J		Kansas City	—	125.	175.	200.
3843	2172L		San Francisco	—	125.	175.	200.

Series 1990 Villalpando-Brady

KL#	Fr#		District	Fine	XF	CH CU (63)	Gem CU (65)
3976	2173A		Boston	—	—	125.	150.
3977	2173B		New York	—	—	125.	150.
3977☆	2173B	☆	New York	—	175.	195.	225.
3978	2173C		Philadelphia	—	—	125.	150.
3978☆	2173C	☆	Philadelphia	—	175.	195.	225.
3979	2173D		Cleveland	—	—	125.	150.
3980	2173E		Richmond	—	—	125.	150.
3981	2173F		Atlanta	—	—	125.	150.
3982	2173G		Chicago	—	—	125.	150.
3982☆	2173G	☆	Chicago	—	175.	195.	225.
3983	2173H		St. Louis	—	—	125.	150.
3984	2173I		Minneapolis	—	—	125.	150.
3985	2173J		Kansas City	—	—	125.	150.
3985☆	2173J	☆	Kansas City	—	175.	195.	225.
3986	2173K		Dallas	—	—	125.	150.

KL#	Fr#		District	Fine	XF	CH CU (63)	Gem CU (65)
3986☆	2173K	☆	Dallas	—	175.	195.	225.
3987	2173L		San Francisco	—	—	125.	150.
3987☆	2173L	☆	San Francisco	—	175.	195.	225.

Series 1993 Withrow-Bentsen

KL#	Fr#		District	Fine	XF	CH CU (63)	Gem CU (65)
4072	2174A		Boston	—	—	150.	175.
4073	2174B		New York	—	—	150.	175.
4073☆	2174B	☆	New York	—	150.	200.	225.
4074	2174C		Philadelphia	—	—	150.	175.
4074☆	2174C	☆	Philadelphia	—	150.	200.	225.
4075	2174D		Cleveland	—	—	150.	175.
4075☆	2174D	☆	Cleveland	—	150.	200.	225.
4076	2174E		Richmond	—	—	150.	175.
4077	2174F		Atlanta	—	—	150.	175.
4078	2174G		Chicago	—	—	150.	175.
4079	2174H		St. Louis	—	—	150.	175.
4079☆	2174H	☆	St. Louis	—	150.	200.	225.
4080	2174I		Minneapolis	—	—	150.	175.
4081	2174J		Kansas City	—	—	150.	175.
4082	2174K		Dallas	—	—	150.	175.
4083	2174L		San Francisco	—	—	150.	175.
4083☆	2174L	☆	San Francisco	—	—	200.	225.

Series 1996 Withrow-Rubin

KL#	Fr#		District	Fine	XF	CH CU (63)	Gem CU (65)
4132	2175A		Boston	—	—	120.	135.
4132☆	2175A	☆	Boston	—	—	150.	165.
4133	2175B		New York	—	—	120.	135.
4133☆	2175B	☆	New York	—	—	150.	165.
4134	2175C		Philadelphia	—	—	120.	135.
4135	2175D		Cleveland	—	—	120.	135.
4135☆	2175D	☆	Cleveland	—	300.	800.	850.
4136	2175E		Richmond	—	—	120.	135.

KL#	Fr#		District	Fine	XF	CH CU (63)	Gem CU (65)
4136☆	2175E	☆	Richmond	—	—	120.	135.
4137	2175F		Atlanta	—	—	120.	135.
4137☆	2175F	☆	Atlanta	—	—	160.	165.
4138	2175G		Chicago	—	—	120.	135.
4138☆	2175G	☆	Chicago	—	—	160.	185.
4139	2175H		St. Louis	—	—	120.	135.
4140	2175I		Minneapolis	—	—	120.	135.
4141	2175J		Kansas City	—	—	120.	135.
4142	2175K		Dallas	—	—	120.	135.
4142☆	2175K	☆	Dallas	—	—	160.	185.
4143	2175L		San Francisco	—	—	120.	135.

Series 1999 Withrow-Summers - DC

KL#	Fr#		District	Fine	XF	CH CU (63)	Gem CU (65)
4560	2176A		Boston	—	—	125.	150.
4560☆	2176A	☆	Boston	—	—	150.	175.
4561	2176B		New York	—	—	125.	150.
4561☆	2176B	☆	New York	—	—	150.	175.
4562	2176C		Philadelphia	—	—	125.	150.
4563	2176D		Cleveland	—	—	125.	150.
4564	2176E		Richmond	—	—	125.	150.
4565	2176F		Atlanta	—	—	125.	150.
4566	2176G		Chicago	—	—	125.	150.
4567	2176H		St. Louis	—	—	125.	150.
4568	2176I		Minneapolis	—	—	125.	150.
4569	2176J		Kansas City	—	—	125.	150.
4570	2176K		Dallas	—	—	125.	150.

Series 2001 Marin-O'Neill - DC

KL#	Fr#		District	Fine	XF	CH CU (63)	Gem CU (65)
4641	2177A		Boston	—	—	135.	150.
4642	2177B		New York	—	—	135.	150.
4642☆	2177B	☆	New York	—	125.	175.	200.
4643	2177C		Philadelphia	—	—	135.	150.
4644	2177D		Cleveland	—	—	135.	150.
4644☆	2177D	☆	Cleveland	—	125.	175.	200.
4645	2177E		Richmond	—	—	135.	150.
4645☆	2177E	☆	Richmond	—	125.	175.	200.
4646	2177F		Atlanta	—	—	135.	150.
4646☆	2177F	☆	Atlanta	—	125.	175.	200.
4647	2177G		Chicago	—	—	135.	150.
4648	2177H		St. Louis	—	—	135.	150.
4649	2177I		Minneapolis	—	—	135.	150.
4650	2177J		Kansas City	—	—	135.	150.
4651	2177K		Dallas	—	—	135.	150.
4652	2177L		San Francisco	—	—	135.	150.

Series 2003 Marin-Snow - DC

KL#	Fr#		District	Fine	XF	CH CU (63)	Gem CU (65)
4720	2178A		Boston	—	—	135.	150.
4721	2178B		New York	—	—	135.	150.
4721☆	2178B	☆	New York	—	125.	175.	200.
4722	2178C		Philadelphia	—	—	135.	150.
4723	2178D		Cleveland	—	—	135.	150.
4724	2178E		Richmond	—	—	135.	150.
4725	2178F		Atlanta	—	—	135.	150.
4725☆	2178F	☆	Atlanta	—	125.	175.	200.
4726	2178G		Chicago	—	—	135.	150.
4727	2178H		St. Louis	—	—	135.	150.
4728	2178I		Minneapolis	—	—	135.	150.

KL#	Fr#		District	Fine	XF	CH CU (63)	Gem CU (65)
4729	2179J		Kansas City	—	—	135.	150.
4730	2178K		Dallas	—	—	135.	150.
4730☆	2178K	☆	Dallas	—	125.	175.	200.
4731	2178L		San Francisco	—	—	135.	150.

Series 2003A Cabral-Snow - DC

KL#	Fr#	District	Fine	XF	CH CU (63)	Gem CU (65)
4732☆	-	Dallas	—	125.	175.	200.

Series 2006 Cabral-Snow - FW

KL#	Fr#	District	Fine	XF	CH CU (63)	Gem CU (65)
4838	-	New York	—	—	135.	150
4839	-	Philadelphia	—	—	135.	150
4840	-	Cleveland	—	—	135.	150
4841	-	Richmond	—	—	135.	150
4841☆	-	Richmond	—	125.	175.	200.

Gold Certificates

Five Hundred Dollars

KL#	Fr#	Series	Signatures	VF	XF	CH CU (63)	Gem CU (65)
2945	2407	1928	Woods-Mellon	—	10,000.	37,500.	75,000.

Federal Reserve Notes

KL#	Fr#		District	Fine	XF	CH CU (63)	Gem CU (65)
2946	2000A		Boston	—	4000.	12,000.	—
2946☆	2000A	☆	Boston	—	—	—	—
2947	2200B		New York	850.	1600.	3000.	4000.
2947☆	2200B	☆	New York	850.	1600.	3000.	4000.
2948	2200C		Philadelphia	—	1000.	3000.	—
2948☆	2200C	☆	Philadelphia	—	—	—	—
2949	2200D		Cleveland	—	1000.	3000.	—
2949☆	2200D	☆	Cleveland	—	—	—	—
2950	2200E		Richmond	—	1100.	3750.	—
2950☆	2200E	☆	Richmond	—	—	—	—
2951	2200F		Atlanta	—	1100.	3750.	—
2951☆	2200F	☆	Atlanta	—	4000.	—	—
2952	2200G		Chicago	—	1000.	2250.	—
2952☆	2200G	☆	Chicago	—	—	—	—
2953	2200H		St. Louis	—	10,000.	30,000.	—
2953☆	2200H	☆	St. Louis	—	—	—	—
2954	2200I		Minneapolis	—	1100.	4750.	—
2954☆	2200I	☆	Minneapolis	—	—	—	—
2955	2200J		Kansas City	—	1100.	4750.	—
2955☆	2200J	☆	Kansas City	—	—	—	—
2956	2200K		Dallas	—	1100.	4750.	—
2956☆	2200K	☆	Dallas	—	—	—	—
2957	2200L		San Francisco	—	1000.	5000.	—
2957☆	2200L	☆	San Francisco	—	—	—	—

✓ Series 1934 Julian-Morgenthau

KL#	Fr#		District	Fine	XF	CH CU (63)	Gem CU (65)
2958	2201A		Boston	—	850.	1500.	—
2958☆	2201A	☆	Boston	—	—	—	—
2959	2201B		New York	—	850.	1500.	—
2959☆	2201B	☆	New York	—	1800.	6000.	—
2960	2201C		Philadelphia	—	850.	1500.	—
2960☆	2201C	☆	Philadelphia	—	2000.	6000.	—
2961	2201D		Cleveland	—	850.	1500.	—
2961☆	2201D	☆	Cleveland	—	1800.	6000.	—
2962	2201E		Richmond	—	850.	1500.	—
2962☆	2201E	☆	Richmond	—	2000.	6000.	—
2963	2201F		Atlanta	—	850.	1500.	—
2963☆	2201F	☆	Atlanta	—	1800.	6000.	—
2964	2201G		Chicago	—	850.	1500.	—
2964☆	2201G	☆	Chicago	2000.	4000.	9000.	10,800.
2965	2201H		St. Louis	—	850.	1500.	—
2965☆	2201H	☆	St. Louis	—	2200.	6000.	—
2966	2201I		Minneapolis	—	1000.	1900.	—
2966☆	2201I	☆	Minneapolis	—	2000.	6000.	—
2967	2201J		Kansas City	700.	1100.	1800.	2200.
2967☆	2201J	☆	Kansas City	—	1800.	6000.	—
2968	2201K		Dallas	—	850.	1800.	—
2968☆	2201K	☆	Dallas	—	2200.	8000.	—
2969	2201L		San Francisco	—	850.	1500.	—
2969☆	2201L	☆	San Francisco	—	1800.	6000.	—

Series 1934A Julian-Morgenthau

KL#	Fr#		District	Fine	XF	CH CU (63)	Gem CU (65)
2971	2202B		New York	750.	1000.	1750.	1750.
2971☆	2202B	☆	New York	2000.	4500.	9000.	10,800.
2972	2202C		Philadelphia	—	850.	1500.	—
2973	2202D		Cleveland	—	850.	1500.	—
2974	2202E		Richmond	—	850.	1500.	—
2974☆	2202E	☆	Richmond	—	850.	1500.	—

KL#	Fr#	District	Fine	XF	CH CU (63)	Gem CU (65)
2974A	-	Atlanta	—	850.	1500.	—
2975	2202G	Chicago	—	850.	1500.	—
2975☆	2202G ☆	Chicago	—	1800.	8000.	—
2976	2202H	St. Louis	—	850.	1500.	—
2977	2202I	Minneapolis	—	950.	1200.	—
2978	2202J	Kansas City	—	850.	1500.	—
2978☆	2202J ☆	Kansas City	—	2200.	10,000.	—
2979	2202K	Dallas	—	950.	1800.	—
2980	2202L	San Francisco	—	850.	1500.	—
2980☆	2202L ☆	San Francisco	—	1800.	8000.	—

Series 1934B Julian-Vinson

KL#	Fr#	District		Fine	XF	CH CU (63)	Gem CU (65)
2981	2203F	Atlanta	Specimens Only	—	—	—	—

Series 1934C Julian-Snyder

KL#	Fr#	District		Fine	XF	CH CU (63)	Gem CU (65)
2982	2204A	Boston		—	—	—	—
2983	2204B	New York	Specimens Only	—	—	—	—

Gold Certificates

One Thousand Dollars

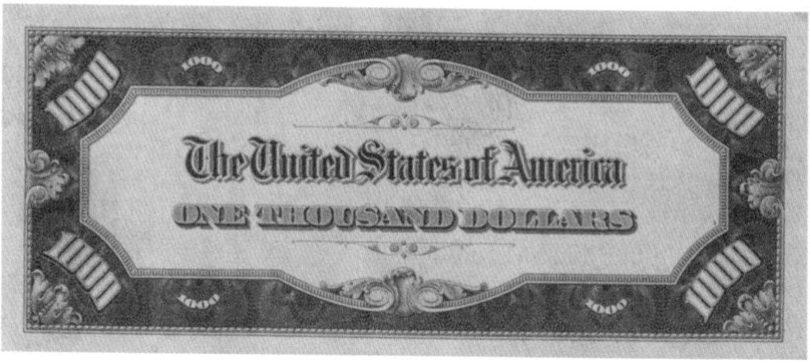

KL#	Fr#	Series	Signatures		VF	XF	CH CU (63)	Gem CU (65)
2984	2408	1928	Woods-Mellon		—	12,500.	35,000.	40,000.
2984A	2408A	1934	Julian-Morgenthau	Extremely Rare.	—	—	—	—

Federal Reserve Notes

Series 1928 Woods-Mellon

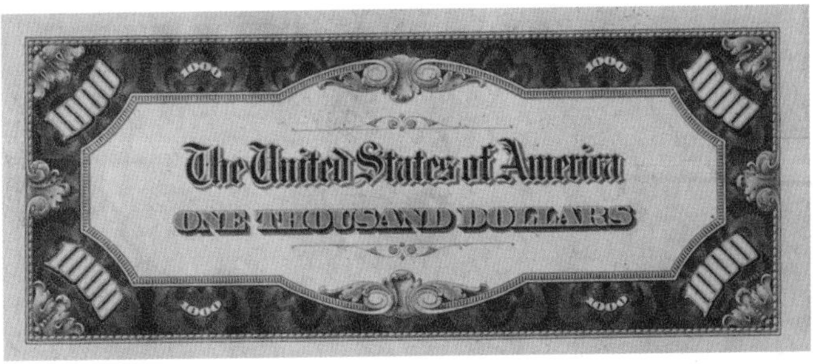

KL#	Fr#		District	Fine	XF	CH CU (63)	Gem CU (65)
2985	2210A		Boston	—	2500.	5000.	—
2985☆	2210A	☆	Boston	—	15,000.	—	—
2986	2210B		New York	—	2250.	3500.	—
2986☆	2210B	☆	New York	—	—	—	—
2987	2210C		Philadelphia	—	2500.	5000.	—
2987☆	2210C	☆	Philadelphia	—	15,000.	—	—
2988	2210D		Cleveland	—	2500.	5000.	—
2988☆	2210D	☆	Cleveland	—	15,000.	—	—
2989	2210E		Richmond	—	2500.	5000.	—
2989☆	2210E	☆	Richmond	—	—	—	—
2990	2210F		Atlanta	—	2500.	5000.	—
2990☆	2210F	☆	Atlanta	—	—	—	—
2991	2210G		Chicago	1250.	2250.	4000.	4900.
2991☆	2210G	☆	Chicago	—	15,000.	—	—
2992	2210H		St. Louis	—	2000.	3000.	—
2992☆	2210H	☆	St. Louis	—	—	39,000.	47,500.
2993	2210I		Minneapolis	—	2500.	15,000.	—
2993☆	2210I	☆	Minneapolis	—	5000.	—	—
2994	2210J		Kansas City	—	2500.	5000.	—
2994☆	2210J	☆	Kansas City	—	—	—	—
2995	2210K		Dallas	—	2500.	15,000.	—
2995☆	2210K	☆	Dallas	—	—	—	—
2996	2210L		San Francisco	—	2500.	5000.	—
2996☆	2210L	☆	San Francisco	—	—	—	—

Series 1934 Julian-Morgenthau

KL#	Fr#		District	Fine	XF	CH CU (63)	Gem CU (65)
2997	2211A		Boston	—	2000.	3500.	—
2997☆	2211A	☆	Boston	—	3000.	15,000.	—
2998	2211B		New York	1750.	2250.	3500.	3800.
2998☆	2211B	☆	New York	12,000.	18,000.	23,000.	25,000.
2999	2211C		Philadelphia	—	2000.	3500.	—
2999☆	2211C	☆	Philadelphia	—	3000.	15,000.	—
3000	2211D		Cleveland	—	2000.	3500.	—
3000☆	2211D	☆	Cleveland	—	2500.	15,000.	—
3001	2211E		Richmond	—	2000.	3000.	—
3001☆	2211E	☆	Richmond	—	—	—	—
3002	2211F		Atlanta	—	2000.	3500.	—
3002☆	2211F	☆	Atlanta	—	3000.	15,000.	—
3003	2211G		Chicago	—	2000.	3000.	—
3003☆	2211G	☆	Chicago	—	2500.	15,000.	—
3004	2211H		St. Louis	—	2000.	3500.	—
3004☆	2211H	☆	St. Louis	—	4000.	15,000.	—
3005	2211I		Minneapolis	—	2000.	6000.	—
3005☆	2211I	☆	Minneapolis	—	3000.	15,000.	—
3006	2211J		Kansas City	—	1650.	3500.	—
3006☆	2211J	☆	Kansas City	—	3000.	15,000.	—
3007	2211K		Dallas	—	2000.	15,000.	—
3007☆	2211K	☆	Dallas	—	—	—	—
3008	2211L		San Francisco	—	1600.	3000.	—
3008☆	2211L	☆	San Francisco	—	2500.	15,000.	—

Series 1934A Julian-Morgenthau

KL#	Fr#		District	Fine	XF	CH CU (63)	Gem CU (65)
3009	2212A		Boston	—	2000.	2500.	—
3009☆	2212A	☆	Boston	—	3000.	10,000.	—
3010	2212B		New York	—	2000.	2000.	—
3010☆	2212B	☆	New York	—	10,000.	—	—
3011	2212C		Philadelphia	—	2000.	2500.	—

KL#	Fr#		District	Fine	XF	CH CU (63)	Gem CU (65)
3011☆	2212C	☆	Philadelphia	—	—	—	—
3012	2212D		Cleveland	—	2000.	2500.	—
3012☆	2212D	☆	Cleveland	—	—	—	—
3013	2212E		Richmond	—	2000.	3000.	—
3013☆	2212E	☆	Richmond	—	—	—	—
3014	2212F		Atlanta	—	2000.	2500.	—
3014☆	2212F	☆	Atlanta	—	—	—	—
3015	2212G		Chicago	1500.	2000.	3000.	3250.
3015☆	2212G	☆	Chicago	3000.	8000.	12,000.	13,200.
3016	2212H		St. Louis	—	2000.	2500.	—
3016☆	2212H	☆	St. Louis	—	—	—	—
3017	2212I		Minneapolis	—	2500.	12,500.	—
3017☆	2212I	☆	Minneapolis	—	—	—	—
3018	2212J		Kansas City	—	2000.	4000.	—
3018☆	2212J	☆	Kansas City	—	—	—	—
3019	2212L		San Francisco	—	2000.	2500.	—
3019☆	2212L	☆	San Francisco	—	—	—	—

Series 1934C Julian-Snyder

KL#	Fr#	District	Fine	XF	CH CU (63)	Gem CU (65)
3020	2213A	Boston	—	—	—	—
3021	2213B	New York Specimens Only	—	—	—	—

Gold Certificates

Five Thousand Dollars

KL#	Fr#	Series	Signatures	VF	XF	CH CU (63)	Gem CU (65)
3022	2410	1928	Woods-Mellon Unique	—	—	—	—

Federal Reserve Notes

Five Thousand Dollars

KL#	Fr#	District	Fine	XF	CH CU (63)	Gem CU (65)
3023	2220A	Boston	20,000.	40,000.	90,000.	135,000.
3024	2220B	New York	—	40,000.	70,000.	—
3025	2220D	Cleveland	—	40,000.	70,000.	—
3026	2220E	Richmond	—	50,000.	80,000.	—
3027	2220F	Atlanta	—	50,000.	80,000.	—
3028	2220G	Chicago	—	50,000.	80,000.	—
3029	2220J	Kansas City	—	50,000.	80,000.	—
3030	2220K	Dallas	—	40,000.	70,000.	—
3031	2220L	San Francisco	—	40,000.	70,000.	—

Series 1934 Julian-Morgenthau

KL#	Fr#	District	Fine	XF	CH CU (63)	Gem CU (65)
3032	2221A	Boston	—	35,000.	55,000.	—
3033	2221B	New York	—	35,000.	55,000.	—
3034	2221C	Philadelphia	—	35,000.	55,000.	—
3035	2221D	Cleveland	—	35,000.	55,000.	—
3036	2221E	Richmond	—	35,000.	55,000.	—
3037	2221F	Atlanta	—	35,000.	55,000.	—
3038	2221G	Chicago	20,000.	34,500.	55,000.	72,000.
3039	2221H	St. Louis	—	35,000.	55,000.	—
3040	2221J	Kansas City	—	35,000.	55,000.	—
3041	2221K	Dallas	—	35,000.	55,000.	—
3042	2221L	San Francisco	—	35,000.	55,000.	—

Series 1934A Julian-Morgenthau

KL#	Fr#	District	Fine	XF	CH CU (63)	Gem CU (65)
3043	2222H	St. Louis	—	—	—	—

Series 1934B Julian-Vinson

KL#	Fr#	District	Fine	XF	CH CU (63)	Gem CU (65)
3044	2223A	Boston	—	—	—	—
3045	2223B	New York	—	—	—	—

Gold Certificates

Ten Thousand Dollars

KL#	Fr#	Series	Signatures		VF	XF	CH CU (63)	Gem CU (65)
3046	2411	1928	Woods-Mellon	Unique	—	—	—	—
3046A	2411A	1934	Julian-Morgenthau	Extremely Rare.	—	—	—	—

Federal Reserve Notes

Series 1928 Woods-Mellon

KL#	Fr#	District	Fine	XF	CH CU (63)	Gem CU (65)
3047	2230A	Boston	—	90,000.	150,000.	—
3048	2230B	New York	—	90,000.	150,000.	—
3049	2230D	Cleveland	—	90,000.	150,000.	—
3050	2230E	Richmond	—	—	240,000.	432,000.
3051	2230F	Atlanta	—	90,000.	150,000.	—
3052	2230G	Chicago	—	90,000.	150,000.	—
3053	2230H	St. Louis	—	90,000.	150,000.	—
3054	2230I	Minneapolis	—	90,000.	150,000.	—
3055	2230J	Kansas City	—	90,000.	150,000.	—
3056	2230K	Dallas	—	90,000.	150,000.	—
3057	2230L	San Francisco	—	90,000.	150,000.	—

Series 1934 Julian-Morgenthau

KL#	Fr#	District	Fine	XF	CH CU (63)	Gem CU (65)
3058	2231A	Boston	—	60,000.	85,000.	—
3059	2231B	New York	—	60,000.	85,000.	—
3060	2231C	Philadelphia	—	60,000.	85,000.	—
3061	2231D	Cleveland	—	60,000.	85,000.	—
3062	2231E	Richmond	—	60,000.	85,000.	—
3063	2231F	Atlanta	—	60,000.	85,000.	—
3064	2231G	Chicago	46,000.	55,000.	75,000.	105,000.
3065	2231H	St. Louis	—	60,000.	85,000.	—
3066	2231J	Kansas City	—	60,000.	85,000.	—
3067	2231K	Dallas	—	60,000.	85,000.	—
3068	2231L	San Francisco	—	50,000.	85,000.	—

Series 1934A Julian-Morgenthau

KL#	Fr#	District	Fine	XF	CH CU (63)	Gem CU (65)
3069	2232G	Chicago Specimens Only	—	—	—	—

Series 1934B Julian-Vinson

KL#	Fr#	District	Fine	XF	CH CU (63)	Gem CU (65)
3070	2233B	New York None in Private Hands	—	—	—	—

National Bank Notes

In the 72 years of their issue more than 14,000 "home town" banks across the United States, the $17,000,000,000 ($17 billion) worth of National Bank Notes issued between December, 1863, and May, 1935, represent a widely collected series of United States paper money.

Their long and historically, as well as financially, interesting life began with the National Currency Act being signed into law by President Abraham Lincoln on Feb. 25, 1863. The dual aim of the legislation was to provide a ready and steady market for the sale of United States bonds issued to finance Federal involvement in the Civil War, and to create a sound bank currency to replace the generally insecure issues of the state banks then in circulation.

While National Bank Notes were only one of seven different types of U.S. paper money in circulation virtually simultaneously during and after the Civil War, they represent more interesting variations and types than any other. For more than half a century, from the implementation of the National Currency Act in 1863 until the creation of the Federal Reserve System in 1914, the National Bank Notes were an important part of the paper money in circulation.

The composition of these notes and the individual histories behind each of the issuing banks and its officers present unlimited fascination for the modern hobbyist.

The National Currency era came to an end in May, 1935, when the Comptroller of the Currency shipped the last National Bank Notes to the issuing bank. The United States bonds which the banks had purchased to secure the value of their Nationals in circulation were called in for payment, ending nearly three-quarters of a century of an important era of "Main Street Banking."

Six distinct series make up the National Bank Note issue; four in large size, two in small size. Large size Nationals are comprised of 1) The Original Series, 2) Series of 1875, 3) Series of 1882 and 4) Series of 1902. In small size, there are the Series of 1929, Type 1 and Type 2. Within each of the large size series, there are several varieties and subtypes.

Alternatively, the Nationals are sometimes grouped according to Charter Period, thus: First Charter, Original Series and Series of 1875; Second Charter, Series of 1882; Third Charter, Series of 1902, and Small Size.

The terms Charter Period and Charter Number are particularly important to National Bank Notes and refer to the issuing authority of each particular bank.

The original National Currency Act of 1863 provided that banks organized under its provisions be chartered as National Banks for a period of 20 years.

In anticipation of the expiration of those first charters in February, 1883, an act was passed on July 12, 1882, extending the banks' existence for another 20 years. A similar extension was granted with an Act of Congress on April 12, 1902, and just before the 1922 expiration date, the National Currency Act was amended to provide 99-year lives for all National banks. This, in turn, was amended five years later, on Feb. 25, 1927, with the endowment of perpetual succession of their corporate identity on National banks.

A better understanding of National Bank Notes as a whole can be gained by a study of the several unique component parts of the National Currency issues.

Charter Number. Upon the approval of its organization as a National Bank, the Comptroller would issue each bank a unique charter number, designating its place on the roster of all such banks. Charter No. 1 was issued to The First National Bank of Philadelphia in June, 1863. Charter No. 14320, the highest to appear on a National Bank Note, was issued in early 1935 to The Liberty National Bank & Trust Company, Louisville, Ky.

The very earliest Original Series National Bank Notes were not required to have their charter number imprinted. However, when it was discovered that notes being presented at the Treasury for redemption could not be quickly sorted, an Act of June 20, 1874, was passed, requiring the charter number be overprinted twice on the face of each note. In the 1882 revision of the National Currency Act, the printing of the charter number as part of the engraved border design in six different places on the face of the note was required; this to facilitate the redemption of partial notes. The 1882 act also required the surcharge of the number on the face, and its printing in the center of the back, giving rise to the popular Series 1882 Brown Back type notes. The Aldrich-Vreeland Act of May 30, 1908, provided for dropping the charter number from the back of the note, thus creating the 1882 Date Back and Value Back series.

The Series of 1902 notes, authorized by the Act of April 12, 1902, again provided for the engraving of the charter number six times on the face border, and overprinting of the number twice on the face.

The small size National Bank Notes which debuted in 1929 were no longer printed from plates specially engraved for each bank. Rather, for the Type 1 notes, the charter number was overprinted twice in black on the face, along with the bank, city and state names, and the officers' signatures. On the Type 2 small size Nationals, the charter number was printed an extra two times on the face, in brown ink, matching the Treasury seal and serial numbers.

Bank Title. Each National bank's title, once approved by the Comptroller of the Currency, was engraved on the face of all currency printing plates for that bank. On large size Nationals, the title, along with city and state of the bank's location, is printed in a variety of bold and interesting type faces in the center of the note. On small size Nationals, the title is printed to the left of the portrait. Prior to May 1, 1886, it took an act of Congress to change the title of a National Bank. Legislation on that date, though, gave the banks authority to change their name upon a vote of the stockholders, and with the approval of the Comptroller of the Currency.

Date. While the engraved date near the title on the face of all large size National Bank Notes remains something of an enigma, it is generally believed to have been chosen by the Comptroller of the Currency to represent the approximate date of issue for the note. This is not an absolute indicator of issue, though, and thus has little significance to the collector.

Treasury Serial Number. From the first issues of National Bank Notes of Dec. 21, 1863, to Aug. 22, 1925, all National Bank Notes carried a U.S. Treasury serial number on the face of the note. On all notes except the $1 and $2, the Treasury serial number appears somewhere in the upper right of the note. On the First Charter $1 and $2 notes, the Treasury number runs vertically at the left end of the note. After Aug. 22, 1925, the Treasury number was replaced by a second impression of the issuing bank's serial number.

Bank Serial Number. Found on all National Bank Notes, except for the small size Type 2 notes, it indicates how many impressions of a particular plate configuration had been printed for a bank. For the Type 2 small size notes, the bank serial number is an indicator of how many notes of a particular denomination had been issued by a bank.

Treasury Signatures. On all National Bank Notes, the engraved signatures of the Register of the Treasury and the Treasurer of the U.S. appear on the face, usually just above center, the Register's to the left of the bank title, and the Treasurer's to the right; though there are exceptions to this placement. The particular combination of these signatures can pinpoint the period in which a plate was engraved for a given bank.

Bank Officers' Signatures. The original National Currency Act of 1863 required that each National Bank Note be signed by the Cashier and the bank's President or Vice President. These signatures, whether pen autographed, rubber stamped, or engraved, always appear at the bottom of the face of the note, the Cashier to the left, the President (or VP) to the right. The signatures gave a local stamp of approval to this type of currency, probably an important consideration when it was first issued and at a time when paper money was often distrusted. The thousands of persons whose signatures appear on National Bank Notes help give each individual note a unique history not found in other forms of U.S. currency.

Treasury Seal. Found on the face of all National Bank Notes, the overprinted Treasury seal was the final Federal authentication of the note, giving each note its validity as circulating currency. Generally found on the right side of the note's face, it varies in color (red, brown, blue), size and embellishment (8 or 12 scallops, 34 or 40 rays).

Geographic Letters. From 1902-1924, large block letters were overprinted with and near the bank's charter number on each National Bank Note to facilitate sorting at central redemption points. Each letter stood for a particular geographic area of the country where the issuing bank was located: N for New England, E for Eastern, S for Southern, M for Midwest, W for Western and P for Pacific.

Plate Position Letters. On all large size National Bank Notes, a letter from A through D appears twice on the face of the note to indicate from which position (top, 2nd, 3rd or bottom) on a printing plate the note had been produced. Because of the great variety of plate configurations used, there is little significance attached by collectors to plate letters, except perhaps in the case of bank serial number 1 notes, in which case the A-position notes might be of greater value.

Among small size Nationals, the plate position letter is part of the serial number. On Series 1929 Nationals, the prefix letter of the serial number is the plate position. Since 1929s were printed six-up in a sheet, the plate positions letters (prefix) run from A through F.

Denominations. National Bank Notes were authorized, over the course of their history, in denominations of $1, $2, $3, $5, $10, $20, $50, $100, $500, $1,000, and $10,000. No notes of the $3 or $10,000 denomination were printed. No surviving $1,000 Nationals are known, although the Treasury still reports 21 outstanding. Only three, of a reported-outstanding 173, $500 Nationals are known in collections. It should also be noted that not all banks issued all denominations in all series.

Circulation. While the original National Banking Act of Feb. 25, 1863, authorized state, as well as National, banks to issue circulating currency upon deposit of U.S. bonds with the Treasury as security, no state banks took advantage of this privilege before it was withdrawn from them by the Act of June 3, 1864, leaving the National banks in a monopoly position as far as bank-issued currency.

The 1863 legislation allowed National banks to issue notes to the total of 90% of the market value of specified series of United States bonds which they had deposited with the Treasurer of the United States. The revision of June 3, 1864, limited the total amount of National Bank Notes in circulation to $300 million; while a provision to apportion that total was added in March 3, 1865, legislation. That act - which also imposed a 10% tax on state bank notes in circulation, effectively killing them off- specified that half of the circulation be apportioned on the basis of population, and half on the basis of banking capital.

In 1870, additional circulation of $54 million was added to the total, and measures taken to more equitably distribute it, while a $500,000 circulation per bank limit was imposed. In 1875, the restrictions on a per bank basis, as well as total circulation, were taken off. In 1900, banks were allowed to issue notes to the full 100% market value of their bond deposits, instead of the 90%.

The circulation privilege was effectively withdrawn in favor of the Federal Reserve Bank System in July, 1935, when the last of the U.S. bonds carrying that privilege were called in. No new bonds of the type have been issued since.

Closing. A National bank could wind up its affairs in one of three manners, as specified by law.

A bank which violated provisions of the current legislation or charter, or which refused to redeem its notes, could be placed in charge of a receiver by order of the Comptroller of the Currency. It may have been allowed to reopen if it could be proved to be sound. If not, the receiver liquidated the bank's assets so as to provide for meeting the greatest amount of the bank's liabilities.

A bank could also go into voluntary liquidation on a two-thirds vote of the stockholders. Such might be done to allow the bank to be absorbed by or to absorb and consolidate with another bank, either National or state.

After Nov. 18, 1918, a National Bank could also close its corporate doors by consolidating with another bank, but not liquidating its assets.

National Bank Note Chronology

Act of Feb. 25, 1863. The original National Currency Act allowed banks with more than $50,000 capital to organize as National banks. Before starting business as such, the bank was required to deposit with the Treasurer of the United States, specified U.S. bonds to the amount of not less than one-third of its capital stock. With that deposit, the Comptroller of the Currency would issue the bank its "Certificate of Authority to Commence Business," its charter. Banks organized under this act were given a corporate life of 20 years from the date of the act.

Act of June 3, 1864. This act provided that any National bank now organized would have a 20-year charter from the date of organization. It also required that bonds deposited against note-issue be registered, interest bearing U.S. bonds.

Act of March 3, 1865. Besides provision mentioned in the earlier text, this allowed state banks with branches to convert to National status. At that time, National banks were not allowed to establish branch banks.

Act of July 12, 1870. This act provided for the organization of National Gold Banks. Subject to greater restrictions than other National Banks, the National Gold Banks could issue currency only to the total of 80% of their deposited bonds, and had to maintain in their vaults gold and silver equal to 25 % of their circulation.

Act of Feb. 14, 1880. The act permitted the conversion of National Gold Banks to regular National banks, and allowed them to keep their original date of organization.

Act of July 12, 1882. This act created the Second Charter Period, allowing National banks to extend their charters for another 20 years.

Act of March 14, 1900. This act greatly increased the number of National banks by allowing the organization of banks with a minimum of $25,000 capital in localities of fewer than 3,000 population.

Act of April 12, 1902. This act created the Third Charter Period by extending the charters of banks chartered or re-chartered under the 1882 act for another 20 years.

Act of May 30, 1908. A response to the financial panic of 1907, this act, known as the Aldrich-Vreeland Act, allowed the formation of voluntary National Currency Associations. To form such an association required at least 10 National banks with a total of at least $50 million in capital and a surplus of at least 2. After formation, such associations could deposit "other securities" against which they could circulate notes to the extent of 75% of their value. These other securities were usually short-term notes, payable within six months. Due to expire on June 30, 1914, the act was extended by the Federal Reserve Act of Dec. 23, 1913, to June 30, 1915, when it did expire.

Act of July 1, 1922. The act provided that all National banks then in existence would have a corporate life of 99 years from the date of the legislation. All National banks organized after this date would have a corporate existence of 99 years from the date of organization.

Act of Feb. 25, 1927. This act provided perpetual corporate life for all National banks then in existence or to be organized in the future. It also allowed National banks to establish branch banks and for the assumption of state banks by National banks.

First Charter Notes

Although the First Charter Period ran from Feb. 25, 1863, through July 11, 1882, notes of the First Charter type were issued until 1902, a 40-year period. This was due to the authorizing legislation which granted a National bank a charter good for 20 years from the date of reorganization, not the date of the National Bank Act (Feb. 25, 1863). Once a bank was chartered in this period, it issued the same type of notes for 20 years, despite the fact that the Second Charter Period may have come into effect (July 12, 1902) during the course of that time. When the bank's original 20-year charter expired, and it was re-chartered under the Second (or even Third) Period, it would begin issue of Second (or Third) Period notes, as appropriate to the date of its charter extension.

During the First Charter period, two different series of notes were issued, Original Series and Series of 1875.

Notes of the Original Series appeared in denominations from $1 through $1,000, and are distinguishable principally by their lack of overprinted charter numbers, although some banks did issue Original Series notes with charter numbers surcharged. The nearly identical Series 1875 notes all have red (or in rare cases, black) charter numbers imprinted, along with the notation at the left of the bank title "Series 1875."

Serial numbers of First Charter notes appear in either red or blue, with the blue variety being the scarcer.

Obligation of the face of the note reads: "This note is secured by bonds of the United States deposited with the U.S. Treasurer in Washington ... The (name and location of bank) will pay the bearer on demand – dollars." On back, there is the inscription: "This note is receivable at par in all parts of the United States, in payment of all taxes and excises and other dues to the United States, except duties on imports, and also for all salaries and other debts and demands owing by the United States to individuals, corporations and associations within the United States except interest on the public debt."

Second Charter Notes

Three distinct note issues make up the National Currency of the Second Charter Period, July 12, 1882, through April 11, 1902. These types differ principally in their back designs for which collectors have evolved the nicknames Brown Back, Date Back and Value Back.

Like the notes of the First Charter Period, the Second Charter Period currency was issued for a span of 40 years, until 1922, when all charters had to be renewed.

The Brown Backs of Series 1882 were placed in circulation that year, and were issued until 1908. The Brown Backs take their name from the large charter number printed on the back in the center of two cartouches of geometric design in brown ink. All other printing on back was also in the brown shades which matched the predominant color of the note's face.

Called Date Backs because of the large 1882-1908 dates on their green-printed backs, the second issue of Series 1882 Nationals was a result of the previously described Aldrich-Vreeland Act. Denominations from $5-$100 were in circulation from June, 1908, to July, 1916, and the $50s and $100s continued current in this type until 1922. Date Back 1882 Nationals were issued only by banks which had issued Brown Backs, and the charter of which were still in force. Those banks whose charter expired in the 1908-1916 period were re-chartered and issued notes of the Third Charter Period.

The expiration of the Aldrich-Vreeland Act in 1915 gave rise to the third type of Series 1882 Nationals, the rare Value Backs (sometimes called Denomination Backs). As implied, the name comes from the large spelled-out indication of value in the center of the back design. As a type, they are the rarest of National Bank Notes, having been issued in the period 1916-1922 by banks which had issued the Date Back type and for which the charter was still in effect. Naturally, this number dwindled each successive year as banks were re-chartered and their note issues switched to the Third Period types.

The Date Back and Value Back notes of Series 1882 were something of emergency issues, produced at a time when it was felt an increase in the supply of currency in circulation was needed to combat hard times. Accordingly, for their issue, the Treasury accepted certain securities other than U.S. bonds on deposit against circulation. This addition is stated on the obligations of these notes.

Third Charter Notes

Passed to extend the life of those National banks whose charters were coming to expiration beginning in 1902, the Currency Act of April 12, 1902, created the Third Charter Period and the three distinct types of National Currency issued thereunder.

In 1922, Congress did away with the need for continual renewing of charters every 20 years by granting National banks perpetual charters to operate.

Issued from 1902 until they were replaced by the small size National Currency in 1929, the Third Charter Nationals represented a change in design to distinguish them from the notes of the Second Charter Period.

The first issue of the Third Charter Period was the popular and often-rare Red Seals. Issued only from 1902-1908, due to the intervention of the Aldrich-Vreeland Emergency Money Act, the Red Seals were issued for a shorter period and by fewer banks than the other two Third Charter types. Their rarity, and the fact that they were issued by every U.S. state and Territory except Hawaii, make them a challenge among collectors who seek to build a state set of this type.

The latter two issues of the Third Charter Period both feature blue Treasury seals, and are principally distinguished by their backs.

The Series 1902 Date Back carries the dates 1902 and 1908 in the white space on the upper back. Like the Second Charter Date Backs, they are something of an emergency issue, having been released during the term of the Aldrich-Vreeland Act, 1908-1915, with the $50s and $100, as in Series 1882, being issued later, until 1926.

Upon expiration of that emergency currency measure, the issues of the Third Charter Period continued with the 1902 Plain Backs, named thus for their lack of the 1902-1908 dates on back. The most plentiful of all National Bank Notes, they were issued from 1915 to 1929, when they were superceded by the small size issue.

Small Size Nationals

When the rest of the currency classes were "down-sized" in July, 1929, the National Bank Notes were included. At the same time, their designs were standardized to fit in with the other types of notes in the same denominations.

Two separate types of small size Nationals were issued. Type 1, current from July, 1929-May, 1933, is distinguished chiefly by the appearance of the bank charter number only twice on the face of the note, in heavy black numerals. Serial numbers of the Type 1 notes consisted of a prefix letter A through F (corresponding to the note's position on the printing plate), six digits and the suffix A (or B, in the case of Ch. No. 2379, The Chase N.B., New York City, the only bank to issue more than six million small size notes in any denomination). The Type 2 Series 1929 Nationals had the same two charter imprints as Type 1, but had an extra pair in brown ink alongside the serial numbers. Serial numbering of the Type 2 notes was also different, being made up of prefix letter A (B only in the case of The Bank of America National Trust and Savings Association of San Francisco) along with six digits.

The obligation was changed on the Series 1929 Nationals, to read "follows: "National Currency secured by United States bonds deposited with the Treasurer of the United States of America ... The (bank name and city/state) will pay to the bearer on demand – dollars." At right, across the brown Treasury seal, was the obligation: "Redeemable in lawful money of the United States at United States Treasury or at the bank of issue."

The calling in of the bonds which secured the National Currency issue ended this Golden Era for U.S. paper money in May, 1935.

Surviving National Bank Notes

Of the approximately $17 billion worth of National Currency issued between 1863-1935, it is estimated that some $50 million worth remain outstanding today, with most knowledgeable observers in agreement that the surviving amount is about equally divided between large and small size issues, representing about 3/10 of 1% of the total issue.

Valuations By Type

Concordia clasping hands before altar. Spiked red seal.
Landing of the Pilgrims at center, state seal at left.

KL#	FR#	Type	Denom.	Signatures	VG	VF	CH CU (63)	Gem CU (65)
1086	380	Orig	$1	Colby-Spinner	1000.	2000.	4250.	5000.
1087	381	Orig	$1	Jeffries-Spinner	2000.	4900.	14,000.	15,000.
1088	382	Orig	$1	Allison-Spinner	1000.	2000.	4250.	5000.

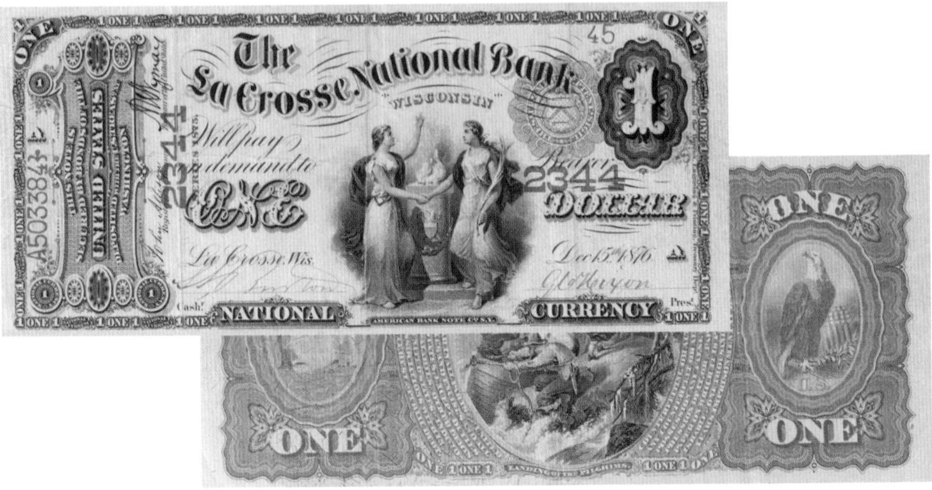

Concordia clasping hands before altar. Scalloped red seal.

KL#	FR#	Type	Denom.	Signatures	VG	VF	CH CU (63)	Gem CU (65)
1089	383	1875	$1	Allison-New	1000.	2000.	4250.	5000.
1090	384	1875	$1	Allison-Wyman	1000.	2000.	4250.	5000.
1091	385	1875	$1	Allison-Gilfillan	1000.	2000.	4250.	5000.
1092	386	1875	$1	Scofield-Gilfillan	1000.	2000.	4250.	5000.

Female seated holding flag at left, large "2" on its side at top right.
Spiked red seal. Sir Walter Raleigh presenting corn and tobacco at center.

KL#	FR#	Type	Denom.	Signatures	VG	VF	CH CU (63)	Gem CU (65)
1093	387	Orig	$2	Colby-Spinner	3000.	5000.	12,000.	15,500.
1094	388	Orig	$2	Jeffries-Spinner	5000.	7000.	18,500.	23,000.
1095	389	Orig	$2	Allison-Spinner	3000.	5000.	12,000.	15,500.

Female seated holding flag at left, large "2" on its side at top right.
Scalloped red seal.

KL#	FR#	Type	Denom.	Signatures	VG	VF	CH CU (63)	Gem CU (65)
1096	390	1875	$2	Allison-New	3000.	5000.	12,000.	15,500.
1097	391	1875	$2	Allison-Wyman	3000.	5000.	12,000.	15,500.
1098	392	1875	$2	Allison-Gilfillan	3000.	5000.	12,000.	15,500.
1099	393	1875	$2	Scofield-Gilfillan	3000.	5000.	12,000.	15,500.

Columbus in sight of land at left,
America presented to the Old World at right.
Spiked red seal. Landing of Columbus at center.

KL#	FR#	Type	Denom.	Signatures	VG	VF	CH CU (63)	Gem CU (65)
1100	394	Orig	$5	Chittenden-Spinner	1300.	2400.	5750.	6750.
1101	397	Orig	$5	Colby-Spinner	1300.	2400.	5750.	6750.
1102	398	Orig	$5	Jeffries-Spinner	6100.	9750.	20,000.	22,750.
1103	399	Orig	$5	Allison-Spinner	1300.	2200.	5750.	6750.

Columbus in sight of land at left,
America presented to the Old World at right. Scalloped red seal.

KL#	FR#	Type	Denom.	Signatures	VG	VF	CH CU (63)	Gem CU (65)
1104	401	1875	$5	Allison-New	-	Rare	-	-
1105	401	1875	$5	Allison-New	1300.	2000.	5750.	6750.

KL#	FR#	Type	Denom.	Signatures	VG	VF	CH CU (63)	Gem CU (65)
1106	402	1875	$5	Allison-Wyman	1300.	2000.	5750.	6750.
1107	403	1875	$5	Allison-Gilfillan	1300.	2000.	5750.	6750.
1108	404	1875	$5	Scofield-Gilfillan	1300.	2000.	5750.	6750.
1109	405	1875	$5	Bruce-Gilfillan	1300.	2000.	5750.	6750.
1110	406	1875	$5	Bruce-Wyman	1300.	2000.	5750.	6750.
1111	406A	1875	$5	Bruce-Jordan	-	Rare	-	-
1112	407	1875	$5	Rosecrans-Huston	1300.	2000.	5750.	6750.
1113	408	1875	$5	Rosecrans-Jordan	1300.	2000.	5750.	6750.

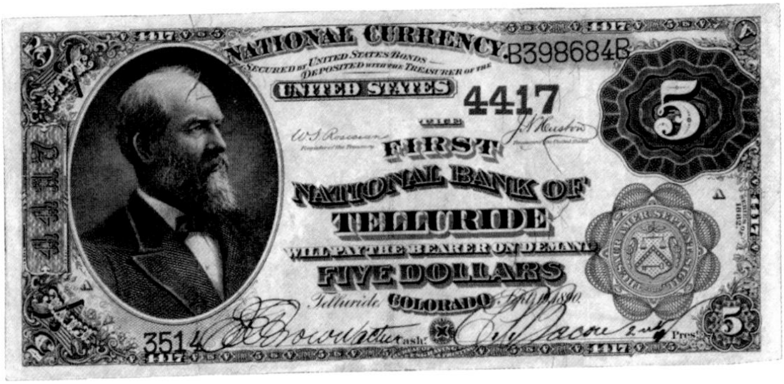

James A. Garfield at left. Charter number in brown field.

KL#	FR#	Type	Denom.	Signatures	VG	VF	CH CU (63)	Gem CU (65)
1114	466	'82BB	$5	Bruce-Gilfillan	700.	1100.	3500.	5250.
1115	467	'82BB	$5	Bruce-Wyman	700.	1100.	3500.	5250.
1116	468	'82BB	$5	Bruce-Jordan	700.	1100.	3500.	5250.
1117	469	'82BB	$5	Rosecrans-Jordan	700.	1100.	3500.	5250.
1118	470	'82BB	$5	Rosecrans-Hyatt	700.	1100.	3500.	5250.
1119	471	'82BB	$5	Rosecrans-Huston	700.	1100.	3500.	5250.
1120	472	'82BB	$5	Rosecrans-Nebeker	700.	1100.	3500.	5250.
1121	473	'82BB	$5	Rosecrans-Morgan	700.	1100.	3500.	5250.
1122	474	'82BB	$5	Tillman-Morgan	700.	1100.	3500.	5250.
1123	475	'82BB	$5	Tillman-Roberts	700.	1100.	3500.	5250.
1124	476	'82BB	$5	Bruce-Roberts	700.	1100.	3500.	5250.
1125	477	'82BB	$5	Lyons-Roberts	700.	1100.	3500.	5250.
1126	478	'82BB	$5	Vernon-Treat	700.	1100.	3500.	5250.

George Washington at left, date in center, Capital Building at right.

KL#	FR#	Type	Denom.	Signatures	VG	VF	CH CU (63)	Gem CU (65)
1127	532	'82DB	$5	Rosecrans-Huston	700.	1100.	3500.	5250.
1128	533	'82DB	$5	Rosecrans-Nebeker	700.	850.	3250.	3500.
1129	533-A	'82DB	$5	Rosecrans-Morgan	850.	1400.	3750.	4250.
1130	534	'82DB	$5	Tillman-Morgan	700.	850.	3250.	3500.
1131	535	'82DB	$5	Tillman-Roberts	700.	850.	3250.	3500.
1132	536	'82DB	$5	Bruce-Roberts	700.	850.	3250.	3500.
1133	537	'82DB	$5	Lyons-Roberts	700.	850.	3250.	3500.
1134	538	'82DB	$5	Vernon-Treat	700.	850.	3250.	3500.
1135	538b	'82DB	$5	Napier-McClung	2200.	3100.	6000.	6500.

George Washington at left, value in center, Capital Building at right.

KL#	FR#	Type	Denom.	Signatures	VG	VF	CH CU (63)	Gem CU (65)
1136	573	'82VB	$5	Tillman-Morgan	800.	1150.	2650.	3500.
1137	573a	'82VB	$5	Tillman-Roberts	800.	1150.	2650.	3500.

KL#	FR#	Type	Denom.	Signatures	VG	VF	CH CU (63)	Gem CU (65)
1138	574	'82VB	$5	Lyons-Roberts	800.	1150.	2650.	3500.
1139	574a	'82VB	$5	Bruce-Roberts	800.	1150.	2650.	3500.
1140	575	'82VB	$5	Vernon-Treat	800.	1150.	2650.	3500.
1141	575a	'82VB	$5	Napier-McClung	800.	1150.	2650.	3500.
1142	575b	'82VB	$5	Teehee-Burke	-	Rare	-	-

Benjamin Harrison at left. Red seal. Landing of the Pilgrims at center.

KL#	FR#	Type	Denom.	Signatures	VG	VF	CH CU (63)	Gem CU (65)
1143	587	'02RS	$5	Lyons-Roberts	700.	1200.	3250.	3750.
1144	588	'02RS	$5	Lyons-Treat	700.	1200.	3250.	3750.
1145	589	'02RS	$5	Vernon-Treat	700.	1200.	3250.	3750.

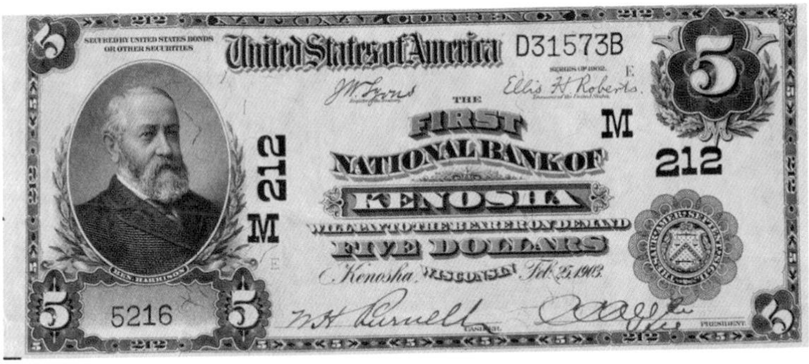

Benjamin Harrison at left. Blue seal.
Dates flanking Landing of the Pilgrims at center.

KL#	FR#	Type	Denom.	Signatures	VG	VF	CH CU (63)	Gem CU (65)
1146	590	'02DB	$5	Lyons-Roberts	275.	375.	850.	975.
1147	591	'02DB	$5	Lyons-Treat	275.	375.	850.	975.
1148	592	'02DB	$5	Vernon-Treat	275.	375.	850.	975.
1149	593	'02DB	$5	Vernon-McClung	275.	375.	850.	975.
1150	594	'02DB	$5	Napier-McClung	275.	375.	850.	975.
1151	595	'02DB	$5	Napier-Thompson	300.	600.	1500.	1750.
1152	596	'02DB	$5	Napier-Burke	275.	375.	850.	975.
1153	597	'02DB	$5	Parker-Burke	275.	375.	850.	975.
1154	597a	'02DB	$5	Teehee-Burke	300.	550.	1500.	1700.

Landing of the Pilgrims at center.

KL#	FR#	Type	Denom.	Signatures	VG	VF	CH CU (63)	Gem CU (65)
1155	598	'02PB	$5	Lyons-Roberts	180.	375.	750.	900.
1156	599	'02PB	$5	Lyons-Treat	180.	375.	750.	900.
1157	600	'02PB	$5	Vernon-McClung	180.	375.	750.	900.
1158	601	'02PB	$5	Vernon-Treat	180.	375.	750.	900.
1159	602	'02PB	$5	Napier-McClung	180.	375.	750.	900.
1160	603	'02PB	$5	Napier-Thompson	180.	375.	750.	900.
1161	604	'02PB	$5	Napier-Burke	180.	375.	750.	900.
1162	605	'02PB	$5	Parker-Burke	180.	375.	750.	900.
1163	606	'02PB	$5	Teehee-Burke	180.	375.	750.	900.
1164	607	'02PB	$5	Elliott-Burke	180.	375.	750.	900.
1165	608	'02PB	$5	Elliott-White	180.	375.	750.	900.
1166	609	'02PB	$5	Speelman-White	180.	375.	750.	900.
1167	610	'02PB	$5	Woods-White	180.	375.	750.	900.
1168	611	'02PB	$5	Woods-Tate	180.	375.	750.	900.
1169	612	'02PB	$5	Jones-Woods	875.	1250.	3150.	3400.

Abraham Lincoln at center. Lincoln Memorial.

KL#	FR#	Type	Denom.	Signatures	VG	VF	CH CU (63)	Gem CU (65)
1170	1800-1	'29T1	$5	Jones-Woods	65.00	100.	300.	375.
1171	1800-2	'29T2	$5	Jones-Woods	90.00	150.	375.	450.

Franklin and Electricity at left, America Seizing Lightning at left. Spiked red seal. DeSoto Discovering the Mississippi at center, state seal at left.

KL#	FR#	Type	Denom.	Signatures	VG	VF	CH CU (63)	Gem CU (65)
1172	409	Orig	$10	Chittenden-Spinner	1950.	2800.	6000.	8000.
1173	412	Orig	$10	Colby-Spinner	2250.	3200.	6375.	8000.
1174	413	Orig	$10	Jeffries-Spinner	-	Rare	-	-
1175	414	Orig	$10	Allison-Spinner	2250.	3299.	6375.	8000.

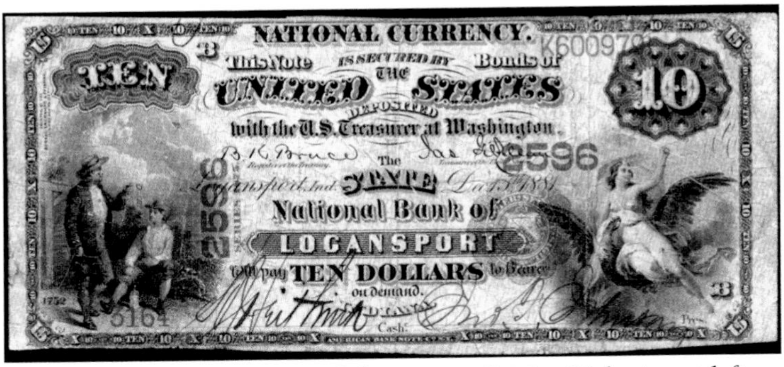

Franklin and Electricity at left, America Seizing Lightning at left. Scalloped red seal.

KL#	FR#	Type	Denom.	Signatures	VG	VF	CH CU (63)	Gem CU (65)
1176	416	1875	$10	Allison-New	2250.	3200.	6375.	8000.
1177	417	1875	$10	Allison-Wyman	2250.	3200.	6375.	8000.
1178	418	1875	$10	Allison-Gilfillan	2250.	3200.	6375.	8000.
1179	419	1875	$10	Scofield-Gilfillan	2250.	3200.	6375.	8000.
1180	420	1875	$10	Bruce-Gilfillan	2250.	3200.	6375.	8000.
1181	421	1875	$10	Bruce-Wyman	2250.	3200.	6375.	8000.
1182	422	1875	$10	Rosecrans-Huston	2250.	3200.	6375.	8000.
1183	423	1875	$10	Rosecrans-Nebeker	2250.	3200.	6375.	8000.
1184	423a	1875	$10	Tillman-Morgan	-	Rare	-	-

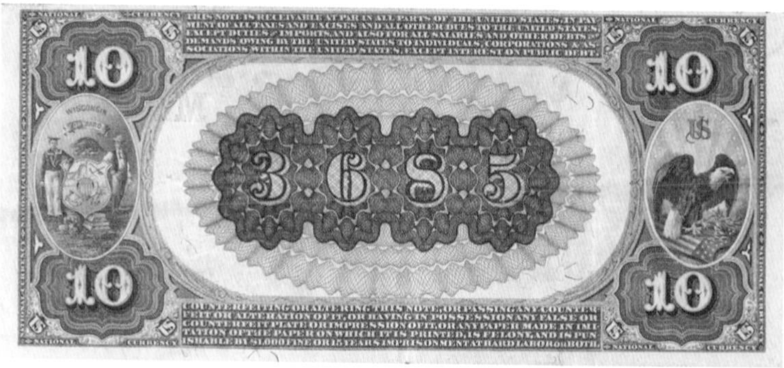

Charter number on brown center, state seal at left.

KL#	FR#	Type	Denom.	Signatures	VG	VF	CH CU (63)	Gem CU (65)
1185	479	'82BB	$10	Bruce-Gilfillan	1150.	1800.	4750.	6000.
1186	480	'82BB	$10	Bruce-Wyman	1150.	1800.	4750.	6000.
1187	481	'82BB	$10	Bruce-Jordan	1150.	1800.	4750.	6000.
1188	482	'82BB	$10	Rosecrans-Jordan	1150.	1800.	4750.	6000.
1189	483	'82BB	$10	Rosecrans-Hyatt	1150.	1800.	4750.	6000.
1190	484	'82BB	$10	Rosecrans-Huston	1150.	1800.	4750.	6000.
1191	485	'82BB	$10	Rosecrans-Nebeker	1150.	1800.	4750.	6000.
1192	486	'82BB	$10	Rosecrans-Morgan	2400.	4000.	9500.	10,000.
1193	487	'82BB	$10	Tillman-Morgan	1150.	1800.	4750.	6000.
1194	488	'82BB	$10	Tillman-Roberts	1150.	1800.	4750.	6000.
1195	489	'82BB	$10	Bruce-Roberts	1150.	1800.	4750.	6000.
1196	490	'82BB	$10	Lyons-Roberts	1150.	1800.	4750.	6000.
1197	491	'82BB	$10	Lyons-Treat	1150.	1800.	4750.	6000.
1198	492	'82BB	$10	Vernon-Treat	1150.	1800.	4750.	6000.

Franklin and Electricity at left, America Seizing Lightning at left. Scalloped blue seal. William P. Fessenden at left, dates at center, Mechanics at right.

KL#	FR#	Type	Denom.	Signatures	VG	VF	CH CU (63)	Gem CU (65)
1199	539	'82DB	$10	Rosecrans-Huston	875.	1250.	3400.	3800.
1200	540	'82DB	$10	Rosecrans-Nebeker	875.	1250.	3400.	3800.
1201	541	'82DB	$10	Rosecrans-Morgan	1700.	3250.	7000.	8000.
1202	542	'82DB	$10	Tillman-Morgan	875.	1250.	3400.	3800.
1203	543	'82DB	$10	Tillman-Roberts	875.	1250.	3400.	3800.
1204	544	'82DB	$10	Bruce-Roberts	875.	1250.	3400.	3800.
1205	545	'82DB	$10	Lyons-Roberts	875.	1250.	3400.	3800.
1206	546	'82DB	$10	Vernon-Treat	875.	1250.	3400.	3800.
1207	547	'82DB	$10	Vernon-McClung	875.	1250.	3400.	3800.
1208	548	'82DB	$10	Napier-McClung	875.	1250.	3400.	3800.

William P. Fessenden at left, value at center, Mechanics at right.

KL#	FR#	Type	Denom.	Signatures	VG	VF	CH CU (63)	Gem CU (65)
1209	576	'82VB	$10	Tillman-Morgan	1000.	1275.	4275.	5500.
1210	576a	'82VB	$10	Tillman-Roberts	1000.	1275.	4275.	5500.
1211	576b	'82VB	$10	Bruce-Roberts	1100.	1500.	5000.	6300.
1212	577	'82VB	$10	Lyons-Roberts	1000.	1275.	4275.	5500.
1213	578	'82VB	$10	Vernon-Treat	1000.	1275.	4275.	5500.
1214	579	'82VB	$10	Napier-McClung	1000.	1275.	4275.	5500.
1215	579b	'82VB	$10	Teehee-Burke	-	Rare	-	-

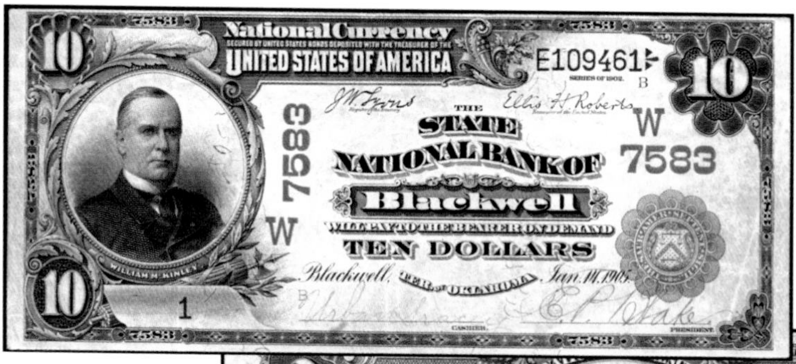

William McKinley at left. Red scalloped seal.
Liberty and Progress standing at center.

KL#	FR#	Type	Denom.	Signatures	VG	VF	CH CU (63)	Gem CU (65)
1216	613	'02RS	$10	Lyons-Roberts	1000.	1250.	5000.	5250.
1217	614	'02RS	$10	Lyons-Treat	1200.	1400.	5250.	5500.
1218	615	'02RS	$10	Vernon-Treat	1300.	1500.	5400.	5650.

William McKinley at left. Blue scalloped seal.
Date flanking top of Liberty and Progress standing at center.

KL#	FR#	Type	Denom.	Signatures	VG	VF	CH CU (63)	Gem CU (65)
1219	616	'02DB	$10	Lyons-Roberts	275.	450.	1200.	1400.
1220	617	'02DB	$10	Lyons-Treat	275.	450.	1200.	1400.
1221	618	'02DB	$10	Vernon-Treat	275.	450.	1200.	1400.
1222	619	'02DB	$10	Vernon-McClung	275.	450.	1200.	1400.
1223	620	'02DB	$10	Napier-McClung	275.	450.	1200.	1400.
1224	621	'02DB	$10	Napier-Thompson	275.	450.	1200.	1400.
1225	622	'02DB	$10	Napier-Burke	275.	450.	1200.	1400.
1226	623	'02DB	$10	Parker-Burke	275.	450.	1200.	1400.
1227	623a	'02DB	$10	Teehee-Burke	275.	450.	1200.	1400.

Liberty and Progress standing at center.

KL#	FR#	Type	Denom.	Signatures	VG	VF	CH CU (63)	Gem CU (65)
1228	624	'02PB	$10	Lyons-Roberts	225.	350.	1000.	975.
1229	625	'02PB	$10	Lyons-Treat	225.	350.	1000.	975.
1230	626	'02PB	$10	Vernon-Treat	225.	350.	1000.	975.
1231	627	'02PB	$10	Vernon-McClung	225.	350.	1000.	975.
1232	628	'02PB	$10	Napier-McClung	225.	350.	1000.	975.
1233	629	'02PB	$10	Napier-Thompson	325.	475.	1350.	1500.
1234	630	'02PB	$10	Napier-Burke	225.	350.	1000.	975.
1235	631	'02PB	$10	Parker-Burke	225.	350.	1000.	975.
1236	632	'02PB	$10	Teehee-Burke	225.	350.	1000.	975.
1237	633	'02PB	$10	Elliott-Burke	225.	350.	800.	975.
1238	634	'02PB	$10	Elliott-White	225.	350.	1000.	975.
1239	635	'02PB	$10	Speelman-White	225.	350.	1000.	975.
1240	636	'02PB	$10	Woods-White	300.	475.	1400.	1650.
1241	637	'02PB	$10	Woods-Tate	300.	475.	1400.	1650.
1242	638	'02PB	$10	Jones-Woods	575.	1250.	2900.	3250.

Alexander Hamilton at center. Treasury Building.

KL#	FR#	Type	Denom.	Signatures	VG	VF	CH CU (63)	Gem CU (65)
1243	1801-1	'29T1	$10	Jones-Woods	75.00	130.	300.	350.

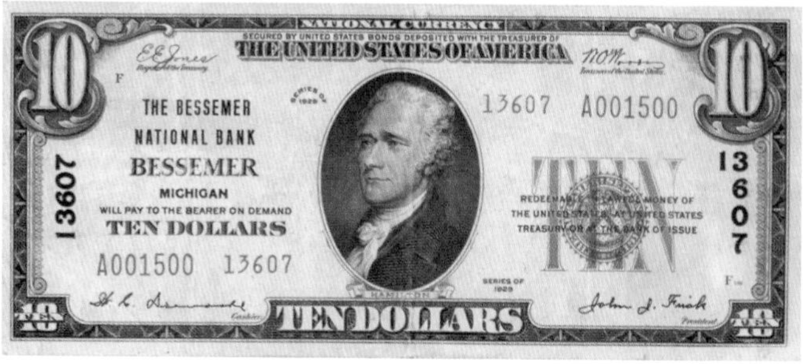

KL#	FR#	Type	Denom.	Signatures	VG	VF	CH CU (63)	Gem CU (65)
1244	1801-2	'29T2	$10	Jones-Woods	85.00	175.	375.	400.

Battle of Lexington at left, Loyalty, female holding flag at right. Spiked red seal. Baptism of Pocahontas.

KL#	FR#	Type	Denom.	Signatures	VG	VF	CH CU (63)	Gem CU (65)
1245	424	Orig	$20	Chittenden-Spinner	2750.	4250.	10,500.	14,000.
1246	427	Orig	$20	Colby-Spinner	2750.	4250.	10,500.	1400.
1247	428	Orig	$20	Jeffries-Spinner	-	Rare	-	-
1248	429	Orig	$20	Allison-Spinner	2750.	4250.	11.00	14,000.

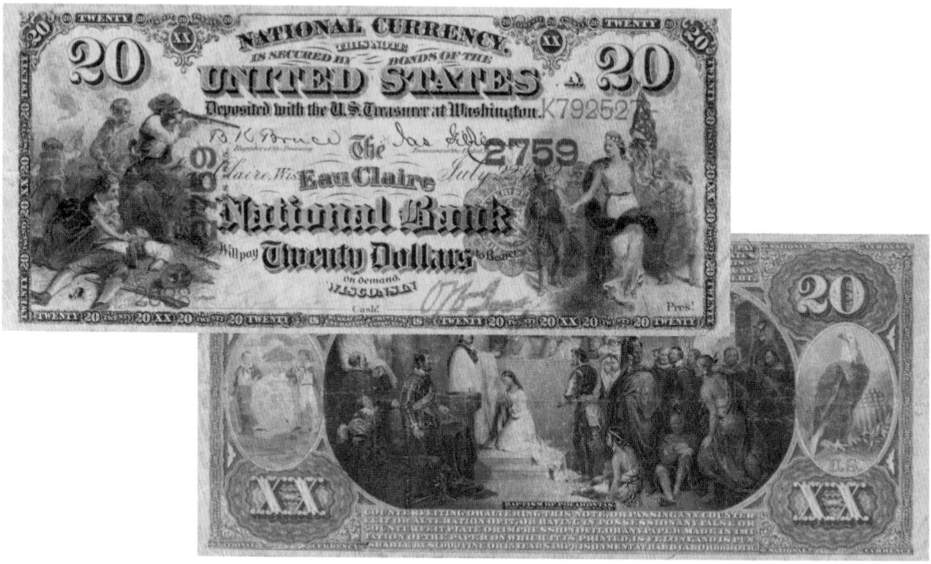

Battle of Lexington at left, Loyalty, female holding flag at right. Scalloped red seal.

KL#	FR#	Type	Denom.	Signatures	VG	VF	CH CU (63)	Gem CU (65)
1249	431	1875	$20	Allison-New	2750.	4000.	10,500.	14,000.
1250	432	1875	$20	Allison-Wyman	2750.	4000.	10,500.	14,000.
1251	433	1875	$20	Allison-Gilfillan	2750.	4000.	10,500.	14,000.
1252	434	1875	$20	Scofield-Gilfillan	2750.	4000.	10,500.	14,000.
1253	435	1875	$20	Bruce-Gilfillan	2750.	4000.	10,500.	14,000.
1254	436	1875	$20	Bruce-Wyman	-	Rare	-	-
1255	437	1875	$20	Rosecrans-Huston	2750.	4000.	10,500.	14,000.
1256	438	1875	$20	Rosecrans-Nebeker	2750.	4000.	10,500.	14,000.
1257	439	1875	$20	Tillman-Morgan	-	Rare	-	-

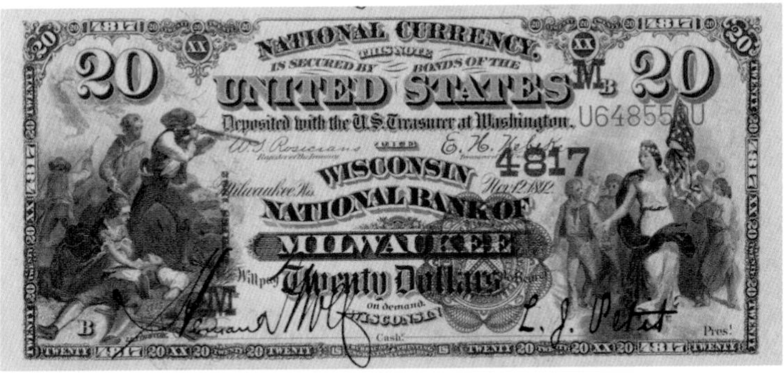

Battle of Lexington at left, Loyalty, female holding flag at right.
Scalloped blue seal. Charter number at center, state seal at left.

KL#	FR#	Type	Denom.	Signatures	VG	VF	CH CU (63)	Gem CU (65)
1258	493	'82BB	$20	Bruce-Gilfillan	1275.	2000.	4375.	5500.
1259	494	'82BB	$20	Bruce-Wyman	1275.	2000.	4375.	5500.
1260	495	'82BB	$20	Bruce-Jordan	1275.	2000.	4375.	5500.
1261	496	'82BB	$20	Rosecrans-Jordan	1275.	2000.	4375.	5500.
1262	497	'82BB	$20	Rosecrans-Hyatt	1275.	2000.	4375.	5500.
1263	498	'82BB	$20	Rosecrans-Huston	1275.	2000.	4375.	5500.
1264	499	'82BB	$20	Rosecrans-Nebeker	1275.	2000.	4375.	5500.
1265	500	'82BB	$20	Rosecrans-Morgan	-	Rare	-	-
1266	501	'82BB	$20	Tillman-Morgan	1275.	2000.	4375.	5500.
1267	502	'82BB	$20	Tillman-Roberts	1275.	2000.	4375.	5500.
1268	503	'82BB	$20	Bruce-Roberts	1275.	2000.	4375.	5500.
1269	504	'82BB	$20	Lyons-Roberts	1275.	2000.	4375.	5500.
1270	505	'82BB	$20	Lyons-Treat	1275.	2000.	4375.	5500.
1271	506	'82BB	$20	Vernon-Treat	1275.	2000.	4375.	5500.

Dates at center, state seal at left.

KL#	FR#	Type	Denom.	Signatures	VG	VF	CH CU (63)	Gem CU (65)
1272	549	'82DB	$20	Rosecrans-Huston	1250.	1750.	4375.	5000.
1273	550	'82DB	$20	Rosecrans-Nebeker	1250.	1750.	4375.	5000.
1274	551	'82DB	$20	Rosecrans-Morgan	-	Rare	-	-
1275	552	'82DB	$20	Tillman-Morgan	1250.	1750.	4375.	5000.
1276	553	'82DB	$20	Tillman-Roberts	1250.	1750.	4375.	5000.
1277	554	'82DB	$20	Bruce-Roberts	1250.	1750.	4375.	5000.
1278	555	'82DB	$20	Lyons-Roberts	1250.	1750.	4375.	5000.
1279	556	'82DB	$20	Vernon-Treat	1250.	1750.	4375.	5000.
1280	557	'82DB	$20	Napier-McClung	1300.	2000.	4600.	5375.

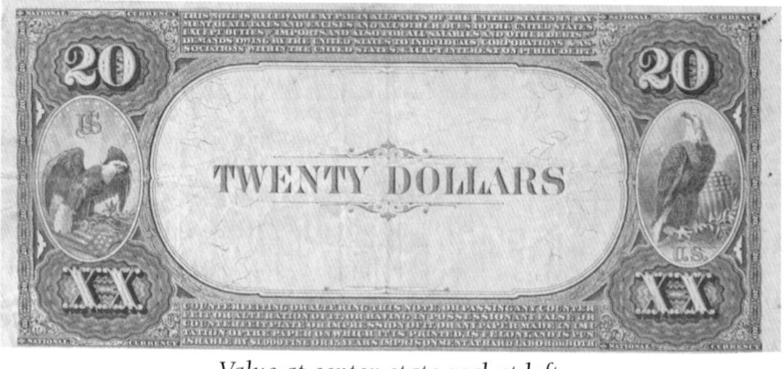

Value at center, state seal at left.

KL#	FR#	Type	Denom.	Signatures	VG	VF	CH CU (63)	Gem CU (65)
1281	580	'82VB	$20	Tillman-Morgan	1200.	1750.	4800.	5750.
1282	580a	'82VB	$20	Tillman-Roberts	-	Rare	-	-
1283	580b	'82VB	$20	Bruce-Roberts	-	Rare	-	-
1284	581	'82VB	$20	Lyons-Roberts	1200.	1750.	4800.	5750.
1285	582	'82VB	$20	Lyons-Treat	1200.	1750.	4800.	5750.
1286	583	'82VB	$20	Vernon-Treat	1200.	1750.	4800.	5750.
1287	584	'82VB	$20	Napier-McClung	1200.	1750.	4800.	5750.
1288	584a	'82VB	$20	Parker-Burke	-	Rare	-	-
1289	585	'82VB	$20	Teehee-Burke	1350.	1900.	5000.	6000.

Hugh McCulloch at left. Red scalloped seal. Union and Civilization at left.

KL#	FR#	Type	Denom.	Signatures	VG	VF	CH CU (63)	Gem CU (65)
1290	639	'02RS	$20	Lyons-Roberts	1200.	1750.	4800.	5750.
1291	640	'02RS	$20	Lyons-Treat	1200.	1750.	5000.	6000.
1292	641	'02RS	$20	Vernon-Treat	1350.	1900.	5000.	6000.

Hugh McCulloch at left. Blue scalloped seal.
Union and Civilization at left, dates at top center.

KL#	FR#	Type	Denom.	Signatures	VG	VF	CH CU (63)	Gem CU (65)
1293	642	'02DB	$20	Lyons-Roberts	275.	450.	1250.	1500.
1294	643	'02DB	$20	Lyons-Treat	275.	450.	1250.	1500.
1295	644	'02DB	$20	Vernon-Treat	275.	450.	1250.	1500.
1296	645	'02DB	$20	Vernon-McClung	275.	450.	1250.	1500.
1297	646	'02DB	$20	Napier-McClung	275.	450.	1250.	1500.
1298	647	'02DB	$20	Napier-Thompson	275.	450.	1250.	1500.
1299	648	'02DB	$20	Napier-Burke	275.	450.	1250.	1500.
1300	649	'02DB	$20	Parker-Burke	275.	450.	1250.	1500.
1301	649a	'02DB	$20	Teehee-Burke	300.	500.	1400.	1650.

Union and Civilization at left.

KL#	FR#	Type	Denom.	Signatures	VG	VF	CH CU (63)	Gem CU (65)
1302	650	'02PB	$20	Lyons-Roberts	250.	425.	1150.	1350.
1303	651	'02PB	$20	Lyons-Treat	250.	425.	1150.	1350.

KL#	FR#	Type	Denom.	Signatures	VG	VF	CH CU (63)	Gem CU (65)
1304	652	'02PB	$20	Vernon-Treat	250.	425.	1150.	1350.
1305	653	'02PB	$20	Vernon-McClung	250.	425.	1150.	1350.
1306	654	'02PB	$20	Napier-McClung	250.	425.	1150.	1350.
1307	655	'02PB	$20	Napier-Thompson	250.	425.	1150.	1350.
1308	656	'02PB	$20	Napier-Burke	250.	425.	1150.	1350.
1309	657	'02PB	$20	Parker-Burke	250.	425.	1150.	1350.
1310	658	'02PB	$20	Teehee-Burke	250.	425.	1150.	1350.
1311	659	'02PB	$20	Elliott-Burke	250.	425.	1150.	1350.
1312	660	'02PB	$20	Elliott-White	250.	425.	1150.	1350.
1313	661	'02PB	$20	Speelman-White	250.	425.	1150.	1350.
1314	662	'02PB	$20	Woods-White	400.	700.	2350.	2650.
1315	663	'02PB	$20	Woods-Tate	400.	700.	2350.	2650.
1316	663a	'02PB	$20	Jones-Woods	-	Rare	-	-

Andrew Jackson at center. White House.

KL#	FR#	Type	Denom.	Signatures	VG	VF	CH CU (63)	Gem CU (65)
1317	1802-1	'29T1	$20	Jones-Woods	65.00	115.	325.	600.

KL#	FR#	Type	Denom.	Signatures	VG	VF	CH CU (63)	Gem CU (65)
1318	1802-2	'29T2	$20	Jones-Woods	75.00	150.	400.	700.

Washington Crossing the Delaware at left, Prayer for Victory at right.
Spiked red seal. Embarkation of the Pilgrims.

KL#	FR#	Type	Denom.	Signatures	VG	VF	CH CU (63)	Gem CU (65)
1319	440	Orig	$50	Chittenden-Spinner	15,000.	20,000.	27,500.	35,000.

KL#	FR#	Type	Denom.	Signatures	VG	VF	CH CU (63)	Gem CU (65)
1320	442	Orig	$50	Colby-Spinner	15,000.	20,000.	27,500.	35,000.
1321	443	Orig	$50	Allison-Spinner	15,000.	20,000.	2750.	35,000.

Washington Crossing the Delaware at left, Prayer for Victory at right. Scalloped red seal.

KL#	FR#	Type	Denom.	Signatures	VG	VF	CH CU (63)	Gem CU (65)
1322	444	1875	$50	Allison-New	15,000.	20,000.	27,500.	35,000.
1323	444a	1875	$50	Allison-Wyman	-	Rare	-	-
1324	445	1875	$50	Allison-Gilfillan	15,000.	20,000.	27,500.	35,000.
1325	446	1875	$50	Scofield-Gilfillan	15,000.	20,000.	27,500.	35,000.
1326	447	1875	$50	Bruce-Gilfillan	15,000.	20,000.	27,500.	35,000.
1327	448	1875	$50	Bruce-Wyman	15,000.	20,000.	27,500.	35,000.
1328	449	1875	$50	Rosecrans-Huston	15,000.	20,000.	27,500.	35,000.
1329	450	1875	$50	Rosecrans-Nebeker	15,000.	20,000.	27,500.	35,000.
1330	451	1875	$50	Tillman-Morgan	15,000.	20,000.	27,500.	35,000.

Washington Crossing the Delaware at left, Prayer for Victory at right. Scalloped brown seal. Large Charter number in center, state seal at left.

KL#	FR#	Type	Denom.	Signatures	VG	VF	CH CU (63)	Gem CU (65)
1331	507	'82BB	$50	Bruce-Gilfillan	5500.	7000.	13,250.	15,000.
1332	508	'82BB	$50	Bruce-Wyman	5500.	7000.	13,250.	15,000.
1333	509	'82BB	$50	Bruce-Jordan	5500.	7000.	13,250.	15,000.
1334	510	'82BB	$50	Rosecrans-Jordan	5500.	7000.	13,250.	15,000.
1335	511	'82BB	$50	Rosecrans-Hyatt	5500.	7000.	13,250.	15,000.
1336	512	'82BB	$50	Rosecrans-Huston	5500.	7000.	13,250.	15,000.
1337	513	'82BB	$50	Rosecrans-Nebeker	5500.	7000.	13,250.	15,000.
1338	514	'82BB	$50	Rosecrans-Morgan	5500.	7000.	13,250.	15,000.
1339	515	'82BB	$50	Tillman-Morgan	5500.	7000.	13,250.	15,000.

KL#	FR#	Type	Denom.	Signatures	VG	VF	CH CU (63)	Gem CU (65)
1340	516	'82BB	$50	Tillman-Roberts	5500.	7000.	13,250.	15,000.
1341	517	'82BB	$50	Bruce-Roberts	5500.	7000.	13,250.	15,000.
1342	518	'82BB	$50	Lyons-Roberts	5500.	7000.	13,250.	15,000.
1343	518a	'82BB	$50	Vernon-Treat	6000.	8500.	16,000.	18,000.

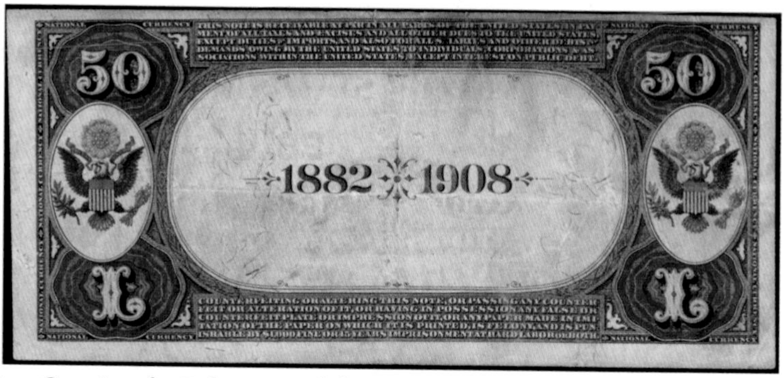

Washington Crossing the Delaware at left, Prayer for Victory at right.
Dates at center, heraldic eagle at each side.

KL#	FR#	Type	Denom.	Signatures	VG	VF	CH CU (63)	Gem CU (65)
1344	558	'82DB	$50	Rosecrans-Huston	5500.	6500.	14,250.	15,675.
1345	559	'82DB	$50	Rosecrans-Nebeker	5500.	6500.	14,250.	15,675.
1346	560	'82DB	$50	Tillman-Morgan	5500.	6500.	14,250.	15,675.
1347	561	'82DB	$50	Tillman-Roberts	5500.	6500.	14,250.	15,675.
1348	562	'82DB	$50	Bruce-Roberts	5500.	6500.	14,250.	15,675.
1349	563	'82DB	$50	Lyons-Roberts	5500.	6500.	14,250.	15,675.
1350	564	'82DB	$50	Vernon-Treat	5500.	6500.	14,250.	15,675.
1351	565	'82DB	$50	Napier-McClung	5500.	6500.	14,250.	15,675.

Value at center, heraldic eagle at each side.

KL#	FR#	Type	Denom.	Signatures	VG	VF	CH CU (63)
1352	586	'82VB	$50	Lyons-Roberts CU:7 known		Rare	

John Sherman at left. Red seal.
Mechanics and Navigation (Steam locomotive at right).

KL#	FR#	Type	Denom.	Signatures	VG	VF	CH CU (63)	Gem CU (65)
1353	664	'02RS	$50	Lyons-Roberts	5750.	6500.	14,000.	19,000.
1354	665	'02RS	$50	Lyons-Treat	5750.	6500.	14,000.	19,000.
1355	666	'02RS	$50	Vernon-Treat	5750.	6500.	14,000.	19,000.

John Sherman at left. Blue seal.
Date at center, Mechanics and Navigation (Steam locomotive at right).

KL#	FR#	Type	Denom.	Signatures	VG	VF	CH CU (63)	Gem CU (65)
1356	667	'02DB	$50	Lyons-Roberts	2000.	2500.	5500.	6000.
1357	668	'02DB	$50	Lyons-Roberts	2000.	2500.	5500.	6000.
1358	669	'02DB	$50	Vernon-Treat	2000.	2500.	5500.	6000.
1359	670	'02DB	$50	Vernon-McClung	2000.	2500.	5500.	6000.
1360	671	'02DB	$50	Napier-McClung	2000.	2500.	5500.	6000.
1361	672	'02DB	$50	Napier-Thompson	2000.	2500.	5500.	6000.
1362	673	'02DB	$50	Napier-Burke	2000.	2500.	5500.	6000.
1363	674	'02DB	$50	Parker-Burke	2000.	2500.	5500.	6000.
1364	674a	'02DB	$50	Teehee-Burke	2000.	2500.	5500.	6000.

Mechanics and Navigation (Steam locomotive at right).

KL#	FR#	Type	Denom.	Signatures	VG	VF	CH CU (63)	Gem CU (65)
1365	675	'02PB	$50	Lyons-Roberts	2000.	3000.	6750.	7500.
1366	676	'02PB	$50	Lyons-Treat	2000.	3000.	6750.	7500.
1367	677	'02PB	$50	Vernon-Treat	2000.	3000.	6750.	7500.
1368	678	'02PB	$50	Vernon-McClung	2000.	3000.	6750.	7500.
1369	679	'02PB	$50	Napier-McClung	2000.	3000.	6750.	7500.
1370	679a	'02PB	$50	Napier-Thompson	2000.	3000.	6750.	7500.
1371	680	'02PB	$50	Napier-Burke	2000.	3000.	6750.	7500.
1372	681	'02PB	$50	Parker-Burke	2000.	3000.	6750.	7500.
1373	682	'02PB	$50	Teehee-Burke	2000.	3000.	6750.	7500.
1374	683	'02PB	$50	Elliott-Burke	2000.	3000.	6750.	7500.
1375	684	'02PB	$50	Elliott-White	2000.	3000.	6750.	7500.
1376	685	'02PB	$50	Speelman-White	2000.	3000.	6750.	7500.
1377	685a	'02PB	$50	Woods-White	2000.	3000.	6750.	7500.

Ulysses S. Grant at center. Capitol Building.

KL#	FR#	Type	Denom.	Signatures	VG	VF	CH CU (63)	Gem CU (65)
1378	1803-1	'29T1	$50	Jones-Woods	3000.	400.	800.	1300.
1379	1803-2	'29T2	$50	Jones-Woods	350.	650.	950.	2900.

Battle of Lake Erie at left, Union at right. Spiked red seal.
Trumbull's Declaration of Independence.

KL#	FR#	Type	Denom.	Signatures	VG	VF	CH CU (63)	Gem CU (65)
1380	452	Orig	$100	Chittenden-Spinner	17,000.	22,500.	47,500.	63,000.
1381	454	Orig	$100	Colby-Spinner	17,000.	22,500.	47,500.	63,000.
1382	455	Orig	$100	Allison-Spinner	17,000.	22,500.	47,500.	63,000.

Battle of Lake Erie at left, Union at right. Scalloped red seal.

KL#	FR#	Type	Denom.	Signatures	VG	VF	CH CU (63)	Gem CU (65)
1383	456	1875	$100	Allison-New	17,000.	22,500.	47,500.	63,000.
1384	457	1875	$100	Allison-Wyman	-	Rare	-	-
1385	458	1875	$100	Allison-Gilfillan	17,000.	22,500.	47,500.	63,000.
1386	459	1875	$100	Scofield-Gilfillan	17,000.	22,500.	47,500.	63,000.
1387	460	1875	$100	Bruce-Gilfillan	17,000.	22,500.	47,500.	63,000.
1388	461	1875	$100	Bruce-Wyman	17,000.	22,500.	47,500.	63,000.
1389	462	1875	$100	Rosecrans-Huston	-	Rare	-	-
1390	462a	1875	$100	Rosecrans-Nebeker	-	Rare	-	-
1391	463	1875	$100	Tillman-Morgan	-	Rare	-	-

Large Charter number at center.

KL#	FR#	Type	Denom.	Signatures	VG	VF	CH CU (63)	Gem CU (65)
1392	519	'82BB	$100	Bruce-Gilfillan	6750.	8000.	16,750.	19,500.
1393	520	'82BB	$100	Bruce-Wyman	6750.	8000.	16,750.	19,500.
1394	521	'82BB	$100	Bruce-Jordan	6750.	8000.	16,750.	19,500.
1395	522	'82BB	$100	Rosecrans-Jordan	6750.	8000.	16,750.	19,500.
1396	523	'82BB	$100	Rosecrans-Hyatt	6750.	8000.	16,750.	19,500.
1397	524	'82BB	$100	Rosecrans-Huston	6750.	8000.	16,750.	19,500.
1398	525	'82BB	$100	Rosecrans-Nebeker	6750.	8000.	16,750.	19,500.
1399	526	'82BB	$100	Rosecrans-Morgan	7500.	8500.	20,000.	25,000.
1400	527	'82BB	$100	Tillman-Morgan	6750.	8000.	16,750.	19,500.
1401	528	'82BB	$100	Tillman-Roberts	6750.	8000.	16,750.	19,500.
1401	529	'82BB	$100	Bruce-Roberts	6750.	8000.	16,750.	19,500.

Battle of Lake Erie at left, Union at right. Scalloped red seal.
Large Charter number at center.

KL#	FR#	Type	Denom.	Signatures	VG	VF	CH CU (63)	Gem CU (65)
1402	530	'82BB	$100	Lyons-Roberts	6750.	8000.	16,750.	19,500.
1403	531	'82BB	$100	Vernon-Treat	-	Rare	-	-

Date at center, eagles at sides.

KL#	FR#	Type	Denom.	Signatures	VG	VF	CH CU (63)	Gem CU (65)
1404	566	'82DB	$100	Rosecrans-Huston	7500.	8250.	18,000.	20,000.
1405	567	'82DB	$100	Rosecrans-Nebeker	7500.	8250.	18,000.	20,000.
1406	568	'82DB	$100	Tillman-Morgan	7500.	8250.	18,000.	20,000.
1407	569	'82DB	$100	Tillman-Roberts	7500.	8250.	18,000.	20,000.
1408	570	'82DB	$100	Bruce-Roberts	7500.	8250.	18,000.	20,000.
1409	571	'82DB	$100	Lyons-Roberts	7500.	8250.	18,000.	20,000.
1410	572	'82DB	$100	Vernon-Treat	7500.	8250.	18,000.	20,000.
1411	572a	'82DB	$100	Napier-McClung	-	Rare	-	-

Value at center, eagles at sides.

KL#	FR#	Type	Denom.	Signatures	VG	VF	CH CU (63)
1412	586-A	'82VB	$100	Lyons-Roberts		CU:5 known	

John Knox at left. Red seal. Eagle on shield flanked by male figures and flags.

KL#	FR#	Type	Denom.	Signatures	VG	VF	CH CU (63)	Gem CU (65)
1413	686	'02RS	$100	Lyons-Roberts	7500.	9500.	18,500.	25,000.
1414	687	'02RS	$100	Lyons-Roberts	7500.	9500.	18,500.	25,000.
1415	688	'02RS	$100	Vernon-Treat	7500.	9500.	18,500.	25,000.

John Knox at left. Blue seal.
Dates above Eagle on shield flanked by male figures and flags.

KL#	FR#	Type	Denom.	Signatures	VG	VF	CH CU (63)	Gem CU (65)
1416	689	'02DB	$100	Lyons-Roberts	2500.	3500.	7750.	8500.
1417	690	'02DB	$100	Lyons-Treat	2500.	3500.	7750.	8500.
1418	691	'02DB	$100	Vernon-Treat	2500.	3500.	7750.	8500.
1419	692	'02DB	$100	Vernon-McClung	2500.	3500.	7750.	8500.
1420	693	'02DB	$100	Napier-McClung	2500.	3500.	7750.	8500.
1421	694	'02DB	$100	Napier-Thompson	2500.	3500.	7750.	8500.
1422	695	'02DB	$100	Napier-Burke	2500.	3500.	7750.	8500.
1423	696	'02DB	$100	Parker-Burke	2500.	3500.	7750.	8500.
1424	697	'02DB	$100	Teehee-Burke	2500.	3500.	7750.	8500.

Eagle on shield flanked by male figures and flags.

KL#	FR#	Type	Denom.	Signatures	VG	VF	CH CU (63)	Gem CU (65)
1425	698	'02PB	$100	Lyons-Roberts	2750.	3750.	8000.	9000.
1426	699	'02PB	$100	Lyons-Treat	2750.	3750.	8000.	9000.
1427	700	'02PB	$100	Vernon-Treat	2750.	3750.	8000.	9000.

KL#	FR#	Type	Denom.	Signatures	VG	VF	CH CU (63)	Gem CU (65)
1428	701	'02PB	$100	Vernon-McClung	2750.	3750.	8000.	9000.
1429	702	'02PB	$100	Napier-McClung	2750.	3750.	8000.	9000.
1430	702a	'02PB	$100	Napier-Thompson	2750.	3750.	8000.	9000.
1431	703	'02PB	$100	Parker-Burke	2750.	3750.	8000.	9000.
1432	704	'02PB	$100	Teehee-Burke	2750.	3750.	8000.	9000.
1433	705	'02PB	$100	Elliott-Burke	2750.	3750.	8000.	9000.
1434	706	'02PB	$100	Elliott-White	2750.	3750.	8000.	9000.
1435	707	'02PB	$100	Speelman-White	2750.	3750.	8000.	9000.
1436	707a	'02PB	$100	Woods-White 2 known	-	Rare	-	-

Benjamin Franklin at center. Independence Hall.

KL#	FR#	Type	Denom.	Signatures	VG	VF	CH CU (63)	Gem CU (65)
1437	1804-1	'29T1	$100	Jones-Woods	400.	600.	700.	900.

KL#	FR#	Type	Denom.	Signatures	VG	VF	CH CU (63)	Gem CU (65)
1438	1804-2	'29T2	$100	Jones-Woods	500.	650.	1000.	1500.

Civilization vignette at left, The Arrival of the Sirius at right.
Spiked red seal. Trumbull's painting:
Surrender of General Burgoyne to General Gates at Saratoga.

KL#	FR#	Type	Denom.	Signatures	VG	VF	CH CU (63)	Gem CU (65)
1439	464	Orig	$500	Colby-Spinner	-	Rare	-	-

Civilization vignette at left, The Arrival of the Sirius at right.
Scalloped red seal.

KL#	FR#	Type	Denom.	Signatures	VG	VF	CH CU (63)	Gem CU (65)
1440	464	1875	$500	Colby-Spinner Unique	-	Rare	-	-
1441	464	1875	$500	Allison-New Unique	-	Rare	-	-

General Scott's entrance into Mexico City at left. U.S. Capitol at right.
Spiked red seal.
Trumbull's painting: Washington resigning his Commission.

KL#	FR#	Type	Denom.	Signatures	VG	VF	CH CU (63)	Gem CU (65)
1442	465	Orig	$1,000	Chittenden-Spinner	Unknown in private hands			

General Scott's entrance into Mexico City at left. U.S. Capitol at right.
Scalloped red seal.

KL#	FR#	Type	Denom.	Signatures	VG	VF	CH CU (63)	Gem CU (65)
1443	465	1875	$1,000	Allison-Wyman	-	-	-	-

Valuations By State

Original Series $1

(KL #1086-1088) (Fr #380-382)

	VG	VF	AU
Alabama	—	Rare	—
Arkansas		Unique	
Colorado Territory	—	Rare	—
Connecticut	450.	1250.	2300.
Dakota Territory	4000.	7000.	9000.
Delaware	—	Rare	—
District of Columbia	—	Rare	—
Georgia	—	Rare	—
Illinois	250.	600.	2500.
Indiana	500.	1100.	2400.
Iowa	450.	100.	2200.
Kansas	375.	900.	1950.
Kentucky	600.	1350.	2775.
Louisiana	—	Rare	—
Maine	400.	1100.	2200.
Maryland	675.	1425.	3000.
Massachusetts	250.	600.	1350.
Michigan	560.	1000.	1800.
Minnesota	560.	1000.	1800.
Missouri	300.	750.	1950.
Montana Territory	—	Rare	—
Nebraska	1250.	2500.	4500.
Nebraska Territory	—	Rare	—
New Hampshire	410.	900.	1800.
New Jersey	340.	710.	1460.
New Mexico Territory	—	Rare	—
New York	250.	600.	1350.
North Carolina	1200.	2700.	5250.
Ohio	300.	675.	1500.
Pennsylvania	375.	900.	2025.
Rhode Island	275.	725.	1300.
South Carolina	—	Rare	—
Tennessee	1950.	3800.	6800.
Texas	3000.	6000.	10,000.
Utah Territory	2500.	5000.	9000.
Vermont	340.	1000.	2475.
West Virginia	—	—	—
Wisconsin	450.	975.	1950.
Wyoming Territory	—	Rare	—

Series 1875 $1

(KL #1089-1092) (Fr #383-386)

	VG	VF	AU
Connecticut	450.	1050.	2300.
Delaware	—	Rare	—
Georgia	—	Rare	—
Idaho Territory	—	—	—
Illinois	260.	600.	1500.
Indiana	375.	825.	1800.
Iowa	340.	750.	1650.
Kansas	375.	900.	1950.
Kentucky	400.	1000.	1850.
Maine	400.	1100.	2200.
Massachusetts	260.	600.	1350.
Michigan	375.	675.	1200.
Minnesota	560.	1000.	1800.
Missouri	300.	750.	2025.
Nebraska	1250.	2500.	4500.
New Hampshire	375.	862.	1800.
New Jersey	300.	710.	1460.
New Mexico Territory	—	Rare	—
New York	260.	600.	1350.
North Carolina	1200.	2700.	5250.
Ohio	300.	675.	1500.
Pennsylvania	375.	900.	2025.
Rhode Island	410.	1085.	1950.
Tennessee	1950.	3800.	6800.
Texas	3000.	6000.	10,000.
Vermont	335.	1010.	2475.
Wisconsin	450.	975.	1950.

Original Series $2

(KL# 1093-1095) (Fr #387-389)

	VG	VF	AU
Connecticut	15,000.	3000.	6750.
Dakota Territory		(Two known)	
Delaware		(Five known)	
District of Columbia		(Two known)	
Idaho Territory		Unique	
Illinois	1125.	3375.	6750.
Indiana	1800.	4050.	8100.
Iowa	1800.	3825.	7650.
Kansas	1575.	4275.	8550.
Kentucky	1875.	4125.	9190.
Louisiana	—	Rare	—
Maine	1950.	4950.	8400.
Maryland	2400.	4200.	9750.
Massachusetts	1460.	3375.	6750.
Michigan	2250.	4500.	9000.
Minnesota	2250.	4500.	9000.
Missouri	1690.	4050.	8550.
Montana Territory		(Two known)	
Nebraska		(Three known)	
Nebraska Territory		(Three known)	
New Hampshire	2700.	5625.	11,700.
New Jersey	1350.	2400.	5100.
New Mexico Territory		(Four known)	
New York	1125.	3375.	6750.
North Carolina	3500.	7500.	12,000.
Ohio	1650.	4800.	10,200.
Pennsylvania	1500.	4500.	9000.
Rhode Island	1460.	2925.	4950.
Tennessee	3750.	6000.	12,000.
Utah Territory		(Four known)	
Vermont	1950.	4200.	8400.
Wisconsin	1050.	3000.	5100.
Wyoming Territory		Unique	

Series 1875 $2

(KL #1096-1099) (Fr #390-393)

	VG	VF	AU
Colorado Territory	4500.	9000.	18,000.
Connecticut	1500.	3000.	6750.
Delaware	—	Rare	—
Georgia	—	Rare	—
Illinois	1125.	3375.	6750.
Indiana	1800.	4050.	8100.
Iowa	1800.	3825.	7650.
Kansas	1575.	4050.	8550.
Kentucky	1875.	4125.	9375.
Maine	1950.	5100.	8700.
Massachusetts	1125.	3375.	6750.
Michigan	2250.	4500.	9000.
Minnesota	2250.	4500.	9000.
Missouri	—	Rare	—
Montana Territory	—	Rare	—
New Hampshire	2700.	5625.	11,700.
New Jersey	2025.	3600.	7762.
New York	750.	2250.	4500.
North Carolina	3500.	7500.	12,000.
Ohio	1100.	3200.	6800.
Pennsylvania	1000.	3000.	6000.
Rhode Island	975.	1950.	3300.
Texas		Unique	
Vermont	1950.	4200.	8400.
Wisconsin	1050.	3000.	5100.

Original Series $5

(KL #1100-1103) (Fr #394-399)

	VG	VF	AU
Alabama	750.	1125.	1800.
Arkansas	—	Rare	—
Colorado Territory	6000.	9000.	13,500.
Connecticut	270.	1000.	2000.
Dakota Territory	—	Rare	—
District of Columbia	1050.	2250.	3450.
Florida	—	Rare	—
Georgia	4500.	7500.	12,000.
Illinois	335.	825.	1950.
Indiana	375.	1200.	2100.
Iowa	450.	1500.	2700.
Kansas	675.	1800.	3300.
Kentucky	675.	1725.	3150.
Louisiana	1650.	2700.	5100.
Maine	1125.	1800.	3375.
Maryland	375.	1425.	2700.
Massachusetts	300.	750.	1800.
Michigan	825.	1350.	2700.
Minnesota	900.	1500.	3000.
Missouri	600.	1050.	2100.
Montana Territory	—	Rare	—
Nebraska	2000.	3200.	6000.
New Hampshire	600.	1650.	4500.
New Jersey	500.	1400.	2800.
New Mexico Territory	—	Rare	—
New York	375.	860.	1875.
North Carolina	2025.	3375.	6750.
Ohio	410.	940.	2625.
Pennsylvania	375.	860.	1875.
Rhode Island	525.	1050.	2025.
South Carolina	2250.	3975.	7875.
Tennessee	1725.	3375.	6750.
Vermont	825.	1725.	3450.
Virginia	1350.	2250.	4500.
West Virginia	1800.	2700.	5300.
Wisconsin	600.	1050.	2100.

Series 1875 $5

(KL #1104-1113) (Fr #401-408)

	VG	VF	AU
Alabama	750.	1125.	1800.
Arizona Territory	—	Rare	—
Arkansas	—	Rare	—
California		Unique	
Colorado	2250.	3975.	7875.
Colorado Territory	6000.	9000.	13,500.
Connecticut	270.	1000.	2000.
Dakota Territory	—	Rare	—
Delaware	—	Rare	—
District of Columbia	1500.	2250.	3450.
Florida	—	Rare	—
Georgia	4500.	7500.	12,000.
Idaho Territory	—	Rare	—
Illinois	335.	825.	1950.
Indiana	375.	1200.	2100.
Iowa	450.	1500.	2700.
Kansas	675.	1800.	3300.
Kentucky	675.	1725.	3150.
Louisiana	1650.	2700.	5100.
Maine	1125.	1800.	3375.
Maryland	375.	1350.	2700.
Massachusetts	375.	940.	2250.
Michigan	825.	1350.	2700.
Minnesota	900.	1500.	3000.
Missouri	600.	975.	1950.
Montana	—	Rare	—
Montana Territory	—	Rare	—
Nebraska	2000.	3200.	6000.
New Hampshire	600.	1650.	4500.
New Jersey	500.	1300.	2600.
New Mexico Territory	—	Rare	—
New York	375.	860.	1875.
North Carolina	2025.	3375.	6750.
North Dakota	—	Rare	—
Ohio	375.	1125.	2475.
Pennsylvania	375.	1125.	2175.
Rhode Island	450.	1425.	3000.
South Carolina	335.	1090.	3000.
South Dakota	—	Rare	—
Tennessee	1725.	3450.	6750.
Texas	5000.	8000.	12,000.
Utah Territory	—	Rare	—
Vermont	675.	1650.	3300.
Virginia	1350.	2250.	4500.
Washington	—	Rare	—
West Virginia	1800.	2700.	5300.

	VG	VF	AU
Wisconsin	600.	1050.	2100.
Wyoming	3750.	6600.	10,500.
Wyoming Territory	—	Rare	—

1882 Brown Back $5

(KL #1114-1126) (Fr #466-478)

	VG	VF	AU
Alabama	525.	1200.	2400.
Arizona Territory	—	Rare	—
Arkansas	1250.	1500.	2700.
California	250.	500.	1000.
Colorado	900.	1725.	3375.
Connecticut	225.	600.	1000.
Dakota Territory	—	Rare	—
Delaware	3000.	5400.	10,800.
District of Columbia	335.	860.	2025.
Florida	1000.	2000.	3500.
Georgia	450.	1125.	2475.
Hawaii	2700.	4500.	6600.
Idaho	—	Rare	—
Idaho Territory	—	Rare	—
Illinois	150.	400.	800.
Indian Territory	3400.	6000.	10,000.
Indiana	200.	550.	1100.
Iowa	200.	500.	1100.
Kansas	250.	550.	1200.
Kentucky	200.	600.	1000.
Louisiana	375.	750.	1350.
Maine	300.	675.	1150.
Maryland	200.	550.	950.
Massachusetts	150.	350.	800.
Michigan	225.	525.	900.
Minnesota	200.	500.	900.
Mississippi	1725.	2850.	5625.
Missouri	150.	425.	900.
Montana	1950.	3600.	6750.
Montana Territory	—	Rare	—
Nebraska	525.	900.	1800.
New Hampshire	335.	1010.	2025.
New Jersey	250.	500.	900.
New Mexico Territory	2700.	4500.	9000.
New York	200.	375.	750.
North Carolina	675.	1350.	2400.
North Dakota	—	Rare	—
Ohio	150.	425.	650.
Oklahoma	—	Rare	—
Oklahoma Territory	3000.	4800.	9000.
Oregon	1200.	2800.	6000.
Pennsylvania	175.	375.	750.
Rhode Island	275.	600.	1200.
South Carolina	600.	1100.	2000.
South Dakota	2025.	3600.	7200.
Tennessee	560.	1125.	2175.
Texas	600.	1200.	2250.
Utah	2400.	4200.	9600.
Utah Territory		Unique	
Vermont	335.	1010.	2025.
Virginia	335.	860.	1725.
Washington	750.	1350.	3000.
Washington Territory	—	Rare	—
West Virginia	335.	1010.	1200.
Wisconsin	300.	675.	1125.
Wyoming	—	Rare	—

1882 Date Back $5

(KL #1127-1135) (Fr #532-538-B)

	VG	VF	AU
Alabama	375.	750.	1500.
Arizona Territory	—	Rare	—
California	375.	600.	1200.
Colorado	750.	1350.	2700.
Connecticut	260.	600.	1275.
Delaware	2400.	4200.	8400.
District of Columbia	410.	900.	1950.
Florida	—	Rare	—
Georgia	450.	900.	1800.
Hawaii	2250.	3600.	6750.
Idaho	—	Rare	—
Illinois	225.	525.	1050.
Indiana	225.	600.	1200.
Iowa	300.	525.	1050.
Kansas	335.	675.	1200.
Kentucky	255.	600.	1275.
Louisiana	600.	1200.	2250.
Maine	525.	1050.	1950.
Maryland	300.	750.	1500.
Massachusetts	260.	525.	1200.
Michigan	375.	750.	1500.
Minnesota	335.	675.	1350.
Mississippi	—	Rare	—
Missouri	300.	600.	1200.
Montana	1500.	2400.	4500.
Nebraska	375.	750.	1350.
New Hampshire	410.	900.	2100.
New Jersey	335.	675.	1200.
New Mexico	1800.	2700.	4950.
New Mexico Territory	3000.	4800.	12,000.
New York	260.	485.	935.
North Carolina	600.	1200.	2250.
North Dakota	750.	1500.	2550.
Ohio	260.	485.	1125.
Oklahoma	410.	785.	1575.
Oregon		Unique	
Pennsylvania	260.	485.	935.
Rhode Island	750.	1310.	2250.
South Carolina	750.	1500.	2700.
South Dakota		Unique	
Tennessee	600.	1200.	3750.
Texas	375.	675.	1350.
Utah	525.	975.	1950.
Vermont	450.	1200.	2400.
Virginia	375.	750.	1500.
Washington	1200.	2250.	4500.
West Virginia	410.	860.	1575.
Wisconsin	260.	560.	900.
Wyoming		Unique	

1882 Value Back $5

(KL #1136-1142) (Fr #573-575-B)

	VG	VF	AU
Alabama	600.	1500.	3400.
California	400.	850.	1900.
Colorado	—	Rare	—
Connecticut	775.	1500.	3800.
District of Columbia	900.	1950.	4350.
Florida	1500.	2250.	4800.
Georgia	900.	1500.	3400.
Hawaii	1650.	4200.	6000.
Idaho		Unique	
Illinois	250.	850.	1900.
Indiana	400.	850.	1950.
Iowa	350.	800.	1700.
Kansas	450.	1000.	2200.
Kentucky	250.	825.	1900.
Maine		Unique	
Maryland	450.	1000.	2000.
Massachusetts	450.	1125.	2250.
Michigan	525.	1050.	2250.
Minnesota	450.	900.	1950.
Missouri		Unique	
Nebraska	600.	1400.	2750.
New Hampshire	—	Rare	—
New Jersey	600.	1200.	2550.
New Mexico	1800.	2900.	6500.
New York	225.	675.	1350.
North Carolina	1000.	1700.	2750.
North Dakota		Unique	
Ohio	250.	900.	1950.
Oklahoma	375.	1200.	2600.
Pennsylvania	525.	900.	1350.
South Dakota		Unique	
Texas	400.	850.	1900.
Utah		Unique	
Virginia	400.	1000.	2200.
Washington		Unique	
West Virginia	525.	1125.	3000.
Wisconsin	350.	850.	1900.

1902 Red Seal $5

(KL #1143-1145) (Fr #587-589)

	VG	VF	AU
Alabama	600.	1200.	2100.
Alaska	6000.	9000.	15,000.
Arkansas	900.	2100.	3150.
California	450.	1000.	1700.
Colorado	900.	1800.	3750.
Connecticut	300.	675.	1350.
Delaware	3000.	7500.	13,500.
District of Columbia	675.	1250.	2400.
Florida	1800.	3000.	5500.
Georgia	1200.	2250.	4500.
Idaho	2000.	3500.	5000.
Illinois	225.	525.	900.
Indian Territory	1500.	2500.	4500.
Indiana	225.	525.	1125.
Iowa	250.	600.	1200.
Kansas	350.	750.	1350.
Kentucky	650.	1250.	2750.
Louisiana	525.	1050.	2100.
Maine	450.	975.	1800.
Maryland	225.	625.	1300.
Massachusetts	190.	450.	950.
Michigan	300.	675.	1350.
Minnesota	250.	600.	1125.
Mississippi	1350.	2400.	4125.
Missouri	190.	450.	950.
Montana	2250.	5500.	11,250.
Nebraska	450.	900.	2000.
Nevada	4500.	8000.	13,500.
New Hampshire	450.	900.	1650.
New Jersey	225.	450.	950.
New York	225.	450.	1050.
North Carolina	2250.	4200.	6600.
North Dakota	1950.	3000.	6000.
Ohio	190.	600.	950.
Oklahoma Territory	1500.	2800.	6000.
Oregon	1500.	3000.	6000.
Pennsylvania	225.	450.	1050.
Rhode Island	450.	900.	1950.
South Carolina	3000.	4800.	7500.
Tennessee	750.	1500.	2700.
Texas	375.	750.	1500.
Vermont	675.	1250.	2400.
Virginia	550.	1000.	2000.
Washington	1350.	2600.	4500.
West Virginia	450.	1100.	2200.
Wisconsin	350.	675.	1400.

1902 Date Back $5

(KL #1146-1154) (Fr #590-597-A)

	VG	VF	AU
Alabama	50.00	195.	325.
Alaska	—	Rare	—
Arizona	1000.	2200.	3600.
Arkansas	100.	300.	500.
California	50.00	135.	225.
Colorado	80.00	240.	400.
Connecticut	60.00	165.	275.
Delaware	350.	725.	1200.
District of Columbia	40.00	140.	235.
Florida	125.	270.	450.
Georgia	40.00	180.	300.
Hawaii	—	Rare	—
Idaho	150.	390.	650.
Illinois	50.00	130.	220.
Indiana	50.00	195.	325.
Iowa	50.00	165.	275.
Kansas	60.00	165.	275.
Kentucky	60.00	210.	350.
Louisiana	75.00	225.	375.
Maine	75.00	180.	300.
Maryland	50.00	195.	325.
Massachusetts	50.00	150.	250.
Michigan	50.00	120.	195.
Minnesota	50.00	150.	250.

	VG	VF	AU
Mississippi	100.	300.	500.
Missouri	50.00	150.	250.
Montana	150.	360.	600.
Nebraska	50.00	120.	200.
Nevada	750.	1600.	2700.
New Hampshire	60.00	180.	300.
New Jersey	50.00	150.	250.
New Mexico	200.	550.	900.
New Mexico Territory	2000.	4000.	6400.
New York	50.00	120.	200.
North Carolina	50.00	180.	300.
North Dakota	100.	300.	500.
Ohio	50.00	150.	250.
Oklahoma	50.00	195.	325.
Oregon	75.00	270.	450.
Pennsylvania	50.00	120.	200.
Rhode Island	60.00	180.	300.
South Carolina	60.00	180.	300.
South Dakota	100.	300.	500.
Tennessee	40.00	135.	225.
Texas	40.00	180.	300.
Utah	75.00	240.	400.
Vermont	75.00	225.	375.
Virginia	40.00	165.	275.
Washington	50.00	180.	300.
West Virginia	40.00	115.	190.
Wisconsin	50.00	115.	250.
Wyoming	250.	725.	1200.

1902 Plain Back $5

(KL #1155-1169) (Fr #598-612)

	VG	VF	AU
Alabama	40.00	180.	300.
Alaska	—	Rare	—
Arizona	900.	1900.	3200.
Arkansas	75.00	275.	450.
California	50.00	120.	200.
Colorado	70.00	225.	375.
Connecticut	40.00	135.	225.
Delaware	300.	700.	1150.
District of Columbia	35.00	130.	220.
Florida	100.	250.	425.
Georgia	30.00	165.	275.
Hawaii	1080.	2350.	3900.
Idaho	135.	360.	600.
Illinois	50.00	120.	200.
Indiana	40.00	180.	300.
Iowa	40.00	180.	200.
Kansas	50.00	150.	250.
Kentucky	50.00	180.	300.
Louisiana	70.00	210.	350.
Maine	65.00	165.	275.
Maryland	40.00	180.	300.
Massachusetts	50.00	120.	200.
Michigan	40.00	100.	175.
Minnesota	50.00	120.	200.
Mississippi	90.00	275.	450.
Missouri	50.00	120.	200.
Montana	135.	330.	550.
Nebraska	30.00	100.	175.
Nevada	675.	1550.	2550.
New Hampshire	60.00	180.	300.
New Jersey	50.00	120.	200.
New Mexico	175.	500.	825.
New York	40.00	100.	180.
North Carolina	45.00	160.	270.
North Dakota	90.00	275.	450.
Ohio	40.00	120.	200.
Oklahoma	40.00	180.	300.
Oregon	50.00	240.	400.
Pennsylvania	40.00	120.	200.
Rhode Island	60.00	180.	300.
South Carolina	55.00	165.	275.
South Dakota	90.00	275.	450.
Tennessee	25.00	120.	200.
Texas	40.00	160.	270.
Utah	70.00	210.	350.
Vermont	70.00	210.	350.
Virginia	40.00	135.	225.
Washington	45.00	165.	275.
West Virginia	35.00	110.	185.
Wisconsin	50.00	120.	200.
Wyoming	250.	660.	1100.

1929 Type 1 $5

(KL #1170) (Fr #1800-1)

	VG	VF	AU
Alabama	—	40.00	80.00
Alaska	—	9000.	15,000.
Arizona	—	350.	700.
Arkansas	—	90.00	180.
California	—	25.00	50.00
Colorado	—	35.00	70.00
Connecticut	—	30.00	60.00
Delaware	—	200.	400.
District of Columbia	—	30.00	60.00
Florida	—	50.00	100.
Georgia	—	35.00	70.00
Hawaii	—	200.	400.
Idaho	—	200.	400.
Illinois	—	25.00	50.00
Indiana	—	25.00	50.00
Iowa	—	25.00	50.00
Kansas	—	25.00	50.00
Kentucky	—	35.00	70.00
Louisiana	—	40.00	80.00
Maine	—	50.00	100.
Maryland	—	35.00	70.00
Massachusetts	—	25.00	50.00
Michigan	—	25.00	50.00
Minnesota	—	25.00	50.00
Mississippi	—	100.	200.
Missouri	—	25.00	50.00
Montana	—	125.	250.
Nebraska	—	30.00	60.00
Nevada	—	300.	600.
New Hampshire	—	40.00	80.00
New Jersey	—	25.00	50.00

	VG	VF	AU
New Mexico	—	125.	250.
New York	—	25.00	50.00
North Carolina	—	45.00	90.00
North Dakota	—	100.	200.
Ohio	—	25.00	50.00
Oklahoma	—	25.00	50.00
Oregon	—	30.00	60.00
Pennsylvania	—	25.00	50.00
Rhode Island	—	40.00	80.00
South Carolina	—	75.00	150.
South Dakota	—	125.	250.
Tennessee	—	35.00	70.00
Texas	—	30.00	60.00
Utah	—	45.00	90.00
Vermont	—	40.00	80.00
Virginia	—	35.00	70.00
Washington	—	35.00	70.00
West Virginia	—	30.00	60.00
Wisconsin	—	25.00	50.00
Wyoming	—	350.	700.

1929 Type 2 $5

(KL #1171) (Fr #1800-2)

	VG	VF	AU
Alabama	—	40.00	80.00
Alaska	—	10,500.	18,000.
Arizona	—	375.	750.
Arkansas	—	120.	240.
California	—	30.00	60.00
Colorado	—	40.00	80.00
Connecticut	—	35.00	70.00
Delaware	—	280.	560.
District of Columbia	—	35.00	70.00
Florida	—	55.00	110.
Georgia	—	40.00	80.00
Hawaii	—	250.	500.
Idaho	—	200.	400.
Illinois	—	30.00	60.00
Indiana	—	30.00	60.00
Iowa	—	30.00	60.00
Kansas	—	30.00	60.00
Kentucky	—	40.00	80.00
Louisiana	—	40.00	80.00
Maine	—	55.00	110.
Maryland	—	40.00	80.00
Massachusetts	—	30.00	60.00
Michigan	—	30.00	60.00
Minnesota	—	30.00	60.00
Mississippi	—	125.	250.
Missouri	—	30.00	60.00
Montana	—	150.	300.
Nebraska	—	35.00	70.00
Nevada	—	325.	650.
New Hampshire	—	45.00	90.00
New Jersey	—	30.00	60.00
New Mexico	—	140.	280.
New York	—	25.00	50.00
North Carolina	—	50.00	100.
North Dakota	—	110.	220.

	VG	VF	AU
Ohio	—	25.00	50.00
Oklahoma	—	30.00	60.00
Oregon	—	40.00	80.00
Pennsylvania	—	25.00	50.00
Rhode Island	—	45.00	90.00
South Carolina	—	80.00	160.
South Dakota	—	140.	280.
Tennessee	—	40.00	80.00
Texas	—	35.00	70.00
Utah	—	50.00	100.
Vermont	—	45.00	90.00
Virginia	—	40.00	80.00
Washington	—	40.00	80.00
West Virginia	—	35.00	70.00
Wisconsin	—	30.00	60.00
Wyoming	—	400.	800.

Original Series $10

(KL #1172-1175) (Fr #409-414)

	VG	VF	AU
Alabama		Unique	
Colorado Territory	6750.	10,500.	21,000.
Connecticut	520.	1750.	4000.
Delaware	2450.	6000.	7500.
District of Columbia	1300.	3600.	5650.
Florida	—	Rare	—
Georgia	2800.	5600.	5650.
Idaho Territory	—	Rare	—
Illinois	700.	1840.	2700.
Indiana	750.	2250.	3000.
Iowa	750.	2250.	3000.
Kansas	1450.	4200.	5400.
Kentucky	1150.	3050.	3750.
Louisiana	3400.	6400.	9000.
Maine	1175.	2150.	3000.
Maryland	825.	2000.	2750.
Massachusetts	600.	1525.	2250.
Michigan	1050.	2400.	3000.
Minnesota	1050.	2400.	2700.
Missouri	725.	1775.	2700.
Montana	—	Rare	—
Nebraska	1950.	3600.	3750.

	VG	VF	AU
Nebraska	1950.	3600.	3750.
New Hampshire	725.	2100.	2800.
New Jersey	750.	1850.	2750.
New York	600.	1400.	2000.
North Carolina	1950.	5450.	6000.
Ohio	650.	1600.	2250.
Pennsylvania	600.	1400.	2000.
Rhode Island	725.	1775.	3000.
South Carolina	1950.	4000.	5000.
Tennessee	1750.	4250.	4500.
Texas	8000.	16,000.	16,000.
Vermont	775.	2400.	3200.
Virginia	1450.	2725.	4000.
West Virginia	1375.	1950.	3150.
Wisconsin	600.	1175.	2050.

Series 1875 $10

(KL #1176-1184) (Fr #416-423-A)

	VG	VF	AU
Alabama		Unique	
Arkansas	—	Rare	—
California	3750.	7500.	12,000.
Colorado	3750.	6000.	10,500.
Colorado Territory	6750.	10,500.	19,500.
Connecticut	400.	1350.	4000.
Dakota Territory	—	Rare	—
Delaware	1900.	3750.	7500.
District of Columbia	1000.	2250.	5650.
Florida	—	Rare	—
Georgia	2150.	3500.	5650.
Idaho Territory	—	Rare	—
Illinois	525.	1150.	2700.
Indiana	575.	1400.	3000.
Iowa	575.	1400.	3000.
Kansas	1100.	2600.	5400.
Kentucky	875.	1900.	3750.
Louisiana	2600.	4000.	9000.
Maine	900.	1350.	3000.
Maryland	625.	1250.	2750.
Massachusetts	450.	950.	2250.
Michigan	800.	1500.	3000.
Minnesota	800.	1500.	2700.
Missouri	550.	1100.	2700.
Montana	—	Rare	—
Nebraska	1500.	2250.	3750.
Nebraska Territory	—	Rare	—
New Hampshire	550.	1300.	2800.
New Jersey	575.	1050.	2750.
New Mexico Territory	—	Rare	—
New York	450.	875.	2000.
North Carolina	1500.	3400.	6000.
North Dakota	—	Rare	—
Ohio	500.	1000.	2250.
Oregon	3500.	5500.	11,000.
Pennsylvania	450.	875.	2000.
Rhode Island	550.	1100.	3000.
South Carolina	1500.	2500.	5000.
South Dakota		Unique	
Tennessee	1350.	2650.	4500.
Texas	6000.	10,000.	16,000.
Vermont	600.	1350.	3200.
Virginia	1100.	1700.	4000.
West Virginia	1050.	1500.	3150.
Wisconsin	450.	900.	2050.
Wyoming	2800.	4900.	3750.
Wyoming Territory	—	Rare	—

1882 Brown Back $10

(KL #1185-1198) (Fr #479-492)

	VG	VF	AU
Alabama	500.	1100.	2200.
Arizona Territory	—	Rare	—
Arkansas	—	Rare	—
California	350.	700.	1350.
Colorado	850.	1500.	3000.
Connecticut	275.	750.	1300.
Dakota Territory		Unique	
Delaware	1350.	2400.	4700.
District of Columbia	350.	750.	1800.
Florida	—	Rare	—
Georgia	475.	1050.	2250.
Hawaii	2500.	4000.	7500.
Idaho	—	Rare	—
Idaho Territory		Unique	
Illinois	250.	625.	1250.
Indian Territory	2200.	3750.	6250.
Indiana	275.	725.	1400.
Iowa	275.	700.	1350.
Kansas	375.	750.	1600.
Kentucky	250.	750.	1300.
Louisiana	550.	1050.	1800.
Maine	450.	900.	1500.
Maryland	275.	750.	1250.
Massachusetts	225.	575.	1100.
Michigan	350.	750.	1200.
Minnesota	250.	700.	1250.
Mississippi	1500.	3500.	5000.
Missouri	225.	575.	1225.
Montana	1750.	3250.	6000.
Montana Territory	—	Rare	—
Nebraska	500.	800.	1650.
Nevada	1250.	3000.	6000.
New Hampshire	350.	950.	1800.
New Jersey	375.	700.	1250.
New Mexico Territory	2400.	4000.	7000.
New York	250.	500.	1050.
North Carolina	625.	1200.	2250.
North Dakota	1200.	2000.	4000.
Ohio	225.	575.	950.
Oklahoma	2100.	3300.	6000.
Oklahoma Territory	2100.	3300.	6000.
Oregon	900.	1900.	4000.
Pennsylvania	190.	375.	800.
Rhode Island	250.	640.	1100.
South Carolina	525.	900.	1650.
South Dakota	750.	1300.	2550.
Tennessee	450.	825.	1500.
Texas	450.	900.	1600.
Utah	900.	1500.	3400.
Utah Territory	3000.	5000.	8250.
Vermont	250.	725.	1450.
Virginia	275.	600.	1200.
Washington	550.	950.	2100.
Washington Territory		Unique	
West Virginia	250.	725.	1450.
Wisconsin	225.	500.	825.
Wyoming	1250.	3000.	6000.
Wyoming Territory		Unique	

1882 Date Back $10

(KL #1199-1208) (Fr #539-548)

	VG	VF	AU
Alabama	390.	715.	1430.
Arizona	—	Rare	—
Arkansas		Unique	
California	390.	650.	1170.
Colorado	715.	1300.	2470.
Connecticut	260.	615.	1200.
Delaware	1755.	2925.	5850.
District of Columbia	290.	650.	1365.
Florida	—	Rare	—
Georgia	455.	875.	1690.
Hawaii	2145.	3250.	5850.
Idaho		Unique	
Illinois	225.	520.	975.
Indiana	260.	585.	1105.
Iowa	260.	520.	975.
Kansas	325.	650.	1170.
Kentucky	260.	615.	1200.
Louisiana	455.	875.	1560.
Maine	520.	975.	1820.
Maryland	225.	550.	1265.
Massachusetts	260.	520.	1170.
Michigan	290.	550.	1070.
Minnesota	260.	485.	975.
Mississippi	1625.	3250.	5850.
Missouri	195.	455.	875.
Montana	1070.	1755.	3120.
Nebraska	390.	715.	1300.
New Hampshire	390.	845.	1950.
New Jersey	325.	650.	1170.
New Mexico	1755.	2535.	4680.
New Mexico Territory	2145.	3510.	6240.
New York	260.	455.	910.
North Carolina	650.	1300.	2080.
North Dakota	780.	1430.	2340.
Ohio	260.	520.	1040.
Oklahoma	260.	520.	975.
Oregon	845.	1690.	2860.
Pennsylvania	260.	455.	910.
Rhode Island	585.	1040.	1820.
South Carolina	715.	1430.	2340.
South Dakota	780.	1430.	2340.
Tennessee	585.	1170.	2210.
Texas	390.	650.	1300.
Utah	485.	910.	1820.
Vermont	455.	1170.	2275.
Virginia	390.	715.	1430.
Washington	585.	1040.	2080.
West Virginia	260.	520.	975.
Wisconsin	260.	552.	975.
Wyoming	2340.	3900.	7800.

1882 Value Back $10

(KL #1209-1215) (Fr #576-579-B)

	VG	VF	AU
Alabama	550.	1500.	3100.
Arizona	—	Rare	—
Arkansas		Unique	
California	400.	800.	1750.
Colorado	1150.	1950.	4300.
Connecticut	525.	1050.	2350.
Georgia	850.	1500.	3100.
Hawaii	1700.	4000.	10,000.
Idaho	1950.	3700.	7800.
Illinois	290.	775.	1700.
Indiana	400.	900.	1750.
Iowa	350.	750.	1550.
Kansas	420.	875.	1950.
Kentucky	250.	775.	1700.
Louisiana	—	Rare	—
Maine	1250.	2700.	5800.
Maryland	400.	975.	1750.
Massachusetts	450.	1100.	2150.
Michigan	400.	750.	1550.
Minnesota	400.	775.	1750.
Mississippi		Unique	
Missouri	525.	1050.	2350.
Montana	2350.	4300.	8500.
Nebraska	360.	750.	1525.
New Hampshire	900.	2150.	4500.
New Jersey	750.	1300.	2900.
New Mexico	1750.	2750.	5850.
New York	325.	900.	1700.
North Carolina	975.	1550.	2250.
North Dakota	775.	1250.	2500.
Ohio	325.	1050.	2200.
Oklahoma	775.	1425.	3100.
Oregon	—	Rare	—
Pennsylvania	325.	775.	1700.
South Carolina	—	Rare	—
South Dakota	775.	1250.	2750.
Tennessee	675.	1175.	3500.
Texas	400.	775.	1700.
Utah	1750.	3500.	6250.
Vermont	—	Rare	—
Virginia	400.	975.	1950.
Washington	1500.	2900.	5200.
West Virginia	325.	690.	1800.
Wisconsin	360.	775.	1700.
Wyoming	2150.	2900.	6250.

1902 Red Seal $10

(KL #1216-1218) (Fr #613-615)

	VG	VF	AU
Alabama	675.	1275.	2250.
Alaska		Unique	
Alaska		Unique	
Arizona Territory	—	Rare	—
Arkansas	800.	1750.	2700.
California	550.	1125.	1800.
Colorado	1050.	2100.	3700.
Connecticut	325.	690.	1500.
Delaware	3375.	7500.	13,500.
District of Columbia	800.	1250.	2700.
Florida	3000.	4800.	9000.
Georgia	2000.	3600.	7200.
Idaho	3375.	5250.	7500.
Illinois	225.	675.	1462.
Indian Territory	1950.	3300.	6700.
Indiana	210.	550.	1400.
Iowa	300.	675.	1350.
Kansas	375.	825.	1425.
Kentucky	675.	1350.	2500.
Louisiana	1200.	2250.	4500.
Maine	525.	1050.	1950.
Maryland	250.	650.	1375.
Massachusetts	200.	450.	1000.
Michigan	335.	750.	2000.
Minnesota	300.	675.	1200.
Mississippi	1500.	2500.	4500.
Missouri	225.	600.	1350.
Montana	2500.	5850.	11,250.
Nebraska	335.	675.	1400.
Nevada	3000.	5250.	9000.
New Hampshire	525.	975.	1800.
New Jersey	250.	675.	1350.
New Mexico Territory	2400.	4800.	7500.
New York	225.	525.	1350.
North Carolina	1800.	3375.	5400.
North Dakota	1050.	1650.	3150.
Ohio	335.	550.	1000.
Oklahoma	—	Rare	—
Oklahoma Territory	1800.	3600.	6750.
Oregon	1650.	3300.	6300.
Pennsylvania	225.	525.	1200.
Puerto Rico	—	Rare	—
Rhode Island	525.	1000.	2000.
South Carolina	1650.	2550.	3900.
South Dakota	1200.	2400.	3750.
Tennessee	825.	1650.	2450.
Texas	400.	825.	1650.
Utah	3375.	6750.	12,750.
Vermont	525.	900.	1750.
Virginia	400.	690.	1500.
Washington	1500.	2700.	4800.
West Virginia	525.	1125.	2475.
Wisconsin	400.	775.	1575.
Wyoming	—	Rare	—

1902 Date Back $10

(KL #1219-1227) (Fr #616-623-A)

	VG	VF	AU
Alabama	105.	225.	440.
Alaska		Unique	
Arizona	1550.	3300.	5250.
Arizona Territory	—	Rare	—
Arkansas	160.	400.	725.
California	75.00	150.	325.
Colorado	100.	225.	490.
Connecticut	75.00	190.	360.
Delaware	325.	750.	1150.
District of Columbia	60.00	150.	320.
Florida	195.	400.	675.
Georgia	75.00	150.	450.
Hawaii	—	Rare	—
Idaho	225.	600.	900.
Illinois	75.00	150.	325.
Indiana	75.00	190.	360.
Iowa	75.00	190.	400.
Kansas	90.00	190.	400.
Kentucky	90.00	225.	490.
Louisiana	90.00	200.	320.
Maine	100.	240.	425.
Maryland	75.00	190.	450.
Massachusetts	75.00	150.	325.
Michigan	90.00	190.	400.
Minnesota	75.00	190.	325.
Mississippi	130.	375.	650.
Missouri	75.00	150.	325.
Montana	225.	490.	850.
Nebraska	90.00	190.	400.
Nevada	1050.	2400.	3700.
New Hampshire	100.	190.	400.
New Jersey	80.00	130.	325.
New Mexico	260.	750.	1250.
New Mexico Territory	2600.	4800.	8300.
New York	75.00	135.	295.
North Carolina	70.00	155.	425.
North Dakota	145.	400.	725.
Ohio	75.00	135.	325.
Oklahoma	100.	225.	450.
Oregon	100.	375.	650.
Pennsylvania	75.00	135.	290.
Puerto Rico		Unique	
Rhode Island	90.00	190.	400.
South Carolina	90.00	250.	450.
South Dakota	145.	400.	725.
Tennessee	60.00	150.	325.
Texas	65.00	190.	450.
Utah	100.	250.	575.
Vermont	115.	225.	490.
Virginia	65.00	190.	400.
Washington	70.00	225.	450.
West Virginia	67.50	150.	250.
Wisconsin	75.00	150.	375.
Wyoming	400.	975.	1700.

1902 Plain Back $10

(KL #1228-1242) (Fr #624-638)

	VG	VF	AU
Alabama	70.00	180.	300.
Alaska	—	Rare	—
Arizona	—	Rare	—
Arkansas	80.00	300.	500.
California	50.00	130.	200.
Colorado	70.00	200.	350.
Connecticut	60.00	140.	225.
Delaware	225.	480.	800.
District of Columbia	35.00	140.	220.
Florida	125.	270.	450.
Georgia	60.00	190.	300.
Hawaii	1200.	2500.	4200.
Idaho	150.	400.	650.
Illinois	50.00	125.	200.
Indiana	60.00	135.	225.
Iowa	50.00	165.	275.
Kansas	60.00	150.	250.
Kentucky	60.00	180.	300.
Louisiana	50.00	180.	220.
Maine	70.00	180.	300.
Maryland	50.00	180.	300.
Massachusetts	50.00	130.	200.
Michigan	60.00	150.	250.
Minnesota	50.00	130.	200.
Mississippi	90.00	270.	450.
Missouri	50.00	130.	200.
Montana	160.	360.	600.
Nebraska	60.00	150.	250.
Nevada	750.	1650.	2700.
New Hampshire	60.00	180.	300.
New Jersey	50.00	130.	200.
New Mexico	200.	550.	900.
New York	50.00	130.	200.
North Carolina	50.00	180.	300.
North Dakota	100.	300.	500.
Ohio	50.00	130.	200.
Oklahoma	70.00	180.	300.
Oregon	50.00	270.	450.
Pennsylvania	50.00	130.	200.
Rhode Island	60.00	180.	300.
South Carolina	60.00	180.	300.
South Dakota	100.	300.	500.
Tennessee	40.00	135.	225.
Texas	50.00	180.	300.
Utah	70.00	250.	400.
Vermont	75.00	210.	350.
Virginia	50.00	135.	225.
Washington	40.00	140.	220.
West Virginia	40.00	110.	185.
Wisconsin	50.00	130.	200.
Wyoming	250.	720.	1200.

1929 Type 1 $10

(KL #1243) (Fr #1801-1)

	VG	VF	AU
Alabama	—	50.00	100.
Alaska	—	11,250.	18,750.
Arizona	—	375.	650.
Arkansas	—	75.00	150.
California	—	30.00	60.00
Colorado	—	40.00	80.00
Connecticut	—	40.00	80.00
Delaware	—	270.	550.
District of Columbia	—	40.00	80.00
Florida	—	50.00	100.
Georgia	—	40.00	80.00
Hawaii	—	200.	400.
Idaho	—	225.	450.
Illinois	—	30.00	60.00
Indiana	—	30.00	60.00
Iowa	—	30.00	60.00
Kansas	—	35.00	70.00
Kentucky	—	35.00	70.00
Louisiana	—	45.00	90.00
Maine	—	50.00	100.
Maryland	—	45.00	90.00
Massachusetts	—	30.00	60.00
Michigan	—	30.00	60.00
Minnesota	—	30.00	60.00
Mississippi	—	100.	200.
Missouri	—	30.00	60.00
Montana	—	125.	250.
Nebraska	—	30.00	60.00
Nevada	—	300.	600.
New Hampshire	—	50.00	100.
New Jersey	—	30.00	60.00
New Mexico	—	125.	250.
New York	—	30.00	60.00
North Carolina	—	45.00	90.00
North Dakota	—	100.	200.
Ohio	—	30.00	60.00
Oklahoma	—	30.00	60.00
Oregon	—	40.00	80.00
Pennsylvania	—	30.00	60.00
Rhode Island	—	50.00	100.
South Carolina	—	75.00	150.
South Dakota	—	125.	250.
Tennessee	—	40.00	80.00
Texas	—	35.00	70.00
Utah	—	50.00	100.
Vermont	—	45.00	90.00
Virginia	—	40.00	80.00
Washington	—	40.00	80.00
West Virginia	—	35.00	70.00
Wisconsin	—	30.00	60.00
Wyoming	—	250.	500.

1929 Type 2 $10

(KL #1244) (Fr #1801-2)

	VG	VF	AU
Alabama	—	55.00	110.
Alaska	—	12,000.	24,000.
Arizona	—	400.	800.
Arkansas	—	80.00	160.
California	—	35.00	70.00
Colorado	—	45.00	90.00
Connecticut	—	45.00	90.00
Delaware	—	270.	550.
District of Columbia	—	45.00	90.00
Florida	—	60.00	120.
Georgia	—	50.00	100.
Hawaii	—	250.	500.
Idaho	—	225.	450.
Illinois	—	35.00	70.00
Indiana	—	35.00	70.00
Iowa	—	35.00	70.00
Kansas	—	40.00	80.00
Kentucky	—	40.00	80.00
Louisiana	—	50.00	100.
Maine	—	60.00	120.
Maryland	—	50.00	100.
Massachusetts	—	35.00	70.00
Michigan	—	35.00	70.00
Minnesota	—	35.00	70.00
Mississippi	—	125.	250.
Missouri	—	35.00	70.00
Montana	—	150.	300.
Nebraska	—	35.00	70.00
Nevada	—	325.	650.
New Hampshire	—	60.00	120.
New Jersey	—	35.00	70.00
New Mexico	—	135.	270.
New York	—	35.00	70.00
North Carolina	—	50.00	100.
North Dakota	—	110.	220.
Ohio	—	35.00	70.00
Oklahoma	—	35.00	70.00
Oregon	—	45.00	90.00
Pennsylvania	—	35.00	70.00
Rhode Island	—	55.00	110.
South Carolina	—	75.00	150.
South Dakota	—	135.	270.
Tennessee	—	45.00	90.00
Texas	—	45.00	90.00
Utah	—	60.00	120.
Vermont	—	50.00	100.
Virginia	—	45.00	90.00
Washington	—	45.00	90.00
West Virginia	—	45.00	90.00
Wisconsin	—	35.00	70.00
Wyoming	—	300.	600.

Original Series $20

(KL #1245-1248) (Fr #424-429)

	VG	VF	AU
Arkansas	—	Rare	—
Connecticut	1800.	4000.	10,500.
Delaware	—	Rare	—
Georgia	—	Rare	—
Illinois	1400.	3600.	6900.
Indiana	1600.	2600.	7200.
Iowa	—	Rare	—
Kentucky	1650.	3800.	7800.
Maine	1950.	4500.	8600.
Maryland	1800.	4200.	9500.
Massachusetts	1050.	2700.	5275.
Michigan	1650.	3600.	6000.
Missouri	1350.	3375.	6000.
Nebraska Territory		Unique	
New Hampshire		Unique	
New Jersey	1350.	3600.	7000.
New York	975.	2500.	4700.
North Carolina	—	Rare	—
Ohio	1050.	2700.	4050.
Pennsylvania	975.	2500.	4700.
Rhode Island	1350.	3150.	8200.
Tennessee	2400.	6000.	8400.
Texas	10,000.	15,000.	25,000.
Vermont	1500.	4000.	8800.
Virginia	1950.	4500.	9750.
West Virginia	2500.	5600.	9750.
Wisconsin	1250.	3375.	6800.

Series 1875 $20

(KL #1249-1257) (Fr #431-439)

	VG	VF	AU
Alabama	—	Rare	—
California	—	Rare	—
Colorado	—	Rare	—
Colorado Territory	—	Rare	—
Connecticut	1600.	2400.	7000.
Dakota Territory	—	Rare	—
Delaware	—	Rare	—
District of Columbia	—	Rare	—
Georgia	—	Rare	—
Illinois	1300.	2200.	4800.
Indiana	1500.	2400.	6800.
Iowa	1500.	2400.	6600.
Kansas	—	Rare	—
Kentucky	1500.	2250.	5400.
Louisiana	—	Rare	—
Maine	1800.	2700.	6000.
Maryland	1600.	2750.	7200.
Massachusetts	975.	1650.	3750.
Michigan	1500.	2250.	4200.
Minnesota		Unique	
Missouri	1200.	2100.	4050.
Montana	—	Rare	—
Montana Territory		Unique	
Nebraska	—	Rare	—
Nevada	—	Rare	—

	VG	VF	AU
New Hampshire	1650.	2700.	6000.
New Jersey	1200.	2250.	5100.
New Mexico Territory	—	Rare	—
New York	900.	1500.	3300.
North Carolina	—	Rare	—
North Dakota	—	Rare	—
Ohio	975.	1650.	3750.
Oregon		(Two known)	
Pennsylvania	900.	1500.	3300.
Rhode Island	1200.	1950.	5700.
South Carolina	—	Rare	—
South Dakota	—	Rare	—
Tennessee	2200.	3600.	6000.
Texas	9000.	13,500.	22,500.
Utah		Unique	
Vermont	1350.	2400.	6000.
Virginia	1800.	2700.	6750.
West Virginia	2250.	3400.	6900.
Wisconsin	1125.	2000.	4750.
Wyoming Territory	—	Rare	—

1882 Brown Back $20

(KL #1258-1271) (Fr #493-506)

	VG	VF	AU
Alabama	900.	1650.	3000.
Arizona Territory	—	Rare	—
Arkansas	—	Rare	—
California	525.	1050.	1750.
Colorado	1250.	2000.	3600.
Connecticut	525.	1050.	1750.
Delaware	1950.	3300.	5500.
District of Columbia	800.	1350.	2250.
Florida	—	Rare	—
Georgia	750.	1350.	2000.
Hawaii	4200.	6600.	11,000.
Idaho	—	Rare	—
Illinois	300.	750.	1350.
Indian Territory	3000.	5250.	8000.
Indiana	350.	900.	1625.
Iowa	375.	975.	1750.
Kansas	525.	1050.	2000.
Kentucky	450.	1050.	1750.
Louisiana	525.	1050.	1800.
Maine	450.	900.	1675.
Maryland	450.	1050.	1750.
Massachusetts	335.	750.	1350.
Michigan	750.	1500.	2450.
Minnesota	525.	1050.	1675.
Mississippi	—	Rare	—
Missouri	400.	825.	1500.
Montana	3000.	4800.	8000.
Nebraska	550.	1000.	1850.
New Hampshire	375.	900.	1675.
New Jersey	450.	850.	1200.
New Mexico Territory	3600.	6000.	8600.
New York	300.	675.	1200.
North Carolina	1125.	1800.	2850.
North Dakota	1800.	3000.	5400.
Ohio	335.	700.	1350.

	VG	VF	AU
Oklahoma	—	Rare	—
Oklahoma Territory	2700.	4800.	7830.
Oregon	1500.	2700.	4700.
Pennsylvania	300.	675.	1200.
Rhode Island	525.	1100.	1700.
South Carolina	1250.	2000.	3000.
South Dakota	1450.	2500.	4250.
Tennessee	600.	1050.	1750.
Texas	675.	1350.	2225.
Utah	1800.	2700.	5500.
Vermont	650.	1250.	2450.
Virginia	550.	950.	2000.
Washington	1050.	1800.	3350.
Washington Territory		Unique	
West Virginia	450.	900.	1675.
Wisconsin	450.	950.	1300.
Wyoming	—	Rare	—

1882 Date Back $20

(KL #1272-1280) (Fr #549-557)

	VG	VF	AU
Alabama	600.	1200.	2100.
Alaska		Unique	
Arizona	—	Rare	—
Arizona Territory		Unique	
Arkansas	—	Rare	—
California	600.	900.	1550.
Colorado	1050.	1800.	3000.
Connecticut	450.	900.	1700.
Delaware	2450.	4000.	7500.
District of Columbia	675.	1125.	1800.
Florida	—	Rare	—
Georgia	650.	1250.	2300.
Hawaii	—	Rare	—
Idaho	—	Rare	—
Illinois	375.	750.	1400.
Indiana	450.	825.	1550.
Iowa	450.	900.	1700.
Kansas	575.	1050.	1950.
Kentucky	450.	900.	1700.
Louisiana	900.	1650.	2800.
Maine	825.	1500.	2500.
Maryland	575.	1050.	2100.
Massachusetts	375.	750.	1400.
Michigan	525.	1050.	1800.
Minnesota	450.	900.	1700.
Mississippi	1250.	2500.	4500.
Missouri	450.	825.	1600.
Montana	1450.	2250.	4200.
Nebraska	525.	1050.	1800.
New Hampshire	600.	1125.	2500.
New Jersey	450.	900.	1700.
New Mexico	2450.	3600.	5800.
New Mexico Territory		Unique	
New York	400.	750.	1400.
North Carolina	1050.	1800.	2800.
North Dakota	1200.	2100.	3300.
Ohio	450.	850.	1600.
Oklahoma	450.	750.	1250.

	VG	VF	AU
Oregon	1200.	2400.	3600.
Pennsylvania	400.	850.	1600.
Rhode Island	—	Rare	—
South Carolina	1200.	1950.	3000.
South Dakota	1200.	2100.	3300.
Tennessee	900.	1650.	2800.
Texas	600.	900.	1700.
Utah	—	Rare	—
Vermont		Unique	
Virginia	600.	1050.	1950.
Washington	900.	1350.	2500.
West Virginia	375.	750.	1250.
Wisconsin	475.	975.	1700.
Wyoming	3600.	4800.	7200.

1882 Value Back $20

(KL #1281-1289) (Fr #580-585)

	VG	VF	AU
Alabama	850.	1700.	3400.
Arizona	—	Rare	—
California	625.	1050.	1800.
Colorado	1750.	2800.	4500.
Connecticut	850.	1700.	3100.
Georgia	1050.	2100.	3900.
Hawaii	—	Rare	—
Idaho		Unique	
Illinois	550.	1100.	2400.
Indiana	700.	1400.	2500.
Iowa	700.	1400.	2400.
Kansas	625.	1250.	2350.
Kentucky	500.	1000.	1800.
Maine	—	Rare	—
Maryland	700.	1400.	2600.
Massachusetts	850.	1700.	3100.
Michigan	600.	1150.	2000.
Minnesota	525.	1050.	1950.
Missouri	525.	1050.	1950.
Montana	—	Rare	—
Nebraska	600.	1150.	2000.
New Hampshire	1250.	2000.	3900.
New Jersey	770.	1500.	2850.
New Mexico	—	Rare	—
New York	550.	1100.	2200.
North Carolina	—	Rare	—
North Dakota	—	Rare	—
Ohio	625.	1250.	2500.
Oklahoma	1250.	2500.	4150.
Oregon	—	Rare	—
Pennsylvania	550.	1100.	2200.
South Carolina	—	Rare	—
South Dakota	1050.	2100.	3450.
Tennessee	1050.	1900.	3100.
Texas	625.	1150.	2150.
Virginia	735.	1450.	2700.
Washington	—	Rare	—
West Virginia	950.	1800.	2900.
Wisconsin	450.	1050.	1950.
Wyoming	—	Rare	—

1902 Red Seal $20

(KL #1290-1292) (Fr #639-641)

	VG	VF	AU
Alabama	800.	1350.	2200.
Alaska		Unique	
Arizona Territory		Unique	
Arkansas	—	Rare	—
California	700.	1200.	1825.
Colorado	1700.	3000.	5300.
Connecticut	375.	750.	850.
District of Columbia	700.	1550.	2800.
Florida	1700.	2700.	5000.
Georgia	1500.	3000.	5000.
Idaho		Unique	
Illinois	325.	675.	1250.
Indian Territory	2150.	3800.	5250.
Indiana	400.	800.	1500.
Iowa	475.	650.	1300.
Kansas	400.	800.	1375.
Kentucky	800.	1550.	2350.
Louisiana	675.	1200.	2250.
Maine	600.	1100.	1875.
Maryland	200.	650.	1400.
Massachusetts	275.	550.	1050.
Michigan	400.	800.	1500.
Minnesota	375.	750.	1250.
Mississippi	2000.	3400.	4700.
Missouri	275.	550.	1050.
Montana	3000.	6000.	11,000.
Nebraska	400.	800.	1375.
Nevada	—	Rare	—
New Hampshire	600.	1100.	1700.
New Jersey	350.	675.	1050.
New Mexico Territory	2700.	5500.	7750.
New York	270.	550.	1100.
North Carolina	2000.	3650.	5000.
North Dakota	1800.	2850.	5350.
Ohio	235.	600.	950.
Oklahoma	—	Rare	—
Oklahoma Territory	2000.	3850.	5800.
Oregon	—	Rare	—
Pennsylvania	270.	550.	1100.
Puerto Rico	—	Rare	—
Rhode Island	600.	1200.	2250.
South Carolina	—	Rare	—
South Dakota	1800.	2850.	4500.
Tennessee	1000.	1750.	2700.
Texas	550.	950.	1600.
Utah		Unique	
Virginia	700.	1200.	2350.
Washington	1550.	2850.	4350.
West Virginia	600.	1200.	2550.
Wisconsin	500.	850.	1600.
Wyoming	4000.	6000.	9500.

1902 Date Back $20

(KL #1293-1301) (Fr #642-649-A)

	VG	VF	AU
Alabama	95.00	195.	450.
Arizona	2000.	3600.	6750.
Arizona Territory	—	Rare	—
Arkansas	225.	475.	825.
California	120.	195.	420.
Colorado	160.	295.	675.
Connecticut	80.00	160.	400.
Delaware	450.	775.	1300.
District of Columbia	80.00	195.	450.
Florida	160.	350.	675.
Georgia	135.	300.	600.
Hawaii		Unique	
Idaho	325.	675.	1150.
Illinois	60.00	115.	250.
Indiana	75.00	140.	300.
Iowa	65.00	130.	290.
Kansas	80.00	160.	330.
Kentucky	75.00	140.	325.
Louisiana	120.	275.	500.
Maine	130.	200.	500.
Maryland	90.00	195.	450.
Massachusetts	80.00	160.	350.
Michigan	65.00	130.	250.
Minnesota	60.00	120.	240.
Mississippi	165.	325.	600.
Missouri	90.00	160.	350.
Montana	300.	575.	1100.
Nebraska	65.00	130.	250.
Nevada	1350.	2300.	4250.
New Hampshire	95.00	200.	480.
New Jersey	90.00	160.	350.
New Mexico	400.	775.	1500.
New Mexico Territory	3800.	5200.	9000.
New York	80.00	160.	290.
North Carolina	130.	230.	500.
North Dakota	195.	450.	900.
Ohio	80.00	160.	350.
Oklahoma	120.	225.	480.
Oregon	130.	325.	650.
Pennsylvania	80.00	160.	290.
Rhode Island	95.00	195.	400.
South Carolina	140.	260.	575.
South Dakota	195.	450.	900.
Tennessee	90.00	180.	400.
Texas	120.	195.	420.
Utah	160.	325.	650.
Vermont	110.	225.	550.
Virginia	80.00	160.	325.
Washington	105.	260.	500.
West Virginia	95.00	195.	400.
Wisconsin	90.00	160.	350.
Wyoming	400.	700.	1500.

1902 Plain Back $20

(KL #1302-1316) (Fr #650-663-A)

	VG	VF	AU
Alabama	80.00	165.	400.
Alaska	—	Rare	—
Arizona	1800.	3000.	5600.
Arkansas	190.	400.	700.
California	100.	160.	400.
Colorado	160.	250.	575.
Connecticut	70.00	140.	330.
Delaware	400.	675.	900.
District of Columbia	70.00	165.	400.
Florida	140.	290.	575.
Georgia	115.	250.	500.
Idaho	290.	550.	950.
Illinois	50.00	100.	225.
Indiana	65.00	120.	270.
Iowa	55.00	115.	250.
Kansas	70.00	140.	290.
Kentucky	65.00	125.	285.
Louisiana	100.	190.	420.
Maine	115.	225.	450.
Maryland	75.00	160.	350.
Massachusetts	75.00	160.	290.
Michigan	55.00	115.	225.
Minnesota	50.00	110.	220.
Mississippi	150.	290.	525.
Missouri	75.00	160.	290.
Montana	250.	500.	950.
Nebraska	55.00	115.	225.
Nevada	1150.	2700.	3700.
New Hampshire	80.00	170.	420.
New Jersey	75.00	160.	290.
New Mexico	350.	675.	1250.
New York	65.00	125.	290.
North Carolina	115.	200.	450.
North Dakota	175.	400.	575.
Ohio	75.00	160.	290.
Oklahoma	115.	190.	450.
Oregon	115.	290.	575.
Pennsylvania	65.00	125.	290.
Rhode Island	80.00	170.	330.
South Carolina	130.	225.	500.
South Dakota	175.	400.	575.
Tennessee	75.00	160.	330.
Texas	100.	190.	400.
Utah	140.	290.	575.
Vermont	95.00	200.	475.
Virginia	70.00	140.	290.
Washington	90.00	275.	450.
West Virginia	80.00	170.	350.
Wisconsin	75.00	160.	290.
Wyoming	350.	675.	1350.

1929 Type 1 $20

(KL #1317) (Fr #1802-1)

	VG	VF	AU
Alabama	—	75.00	150.
Alaska	—	11,250.	22,500.
Arizona	—	400.	800.
Arkansas	—	90.00	180.
California	—	60.00	120.
Colorado	—	60.00	120.
Connecticut	—	50.00	100.
Delaware	—	300.	600.
District of Columbia	—	50.00	100.
Florida	—	65.00	130.
Georgia	—	50.00	100.
Idaho	—	175.	350.
Illinois	—	50.00	100.
Indiana	—	50.00	100.
Iowa	—	50.00	100.
Kansas	—	50.00	100.
Kentucky	—	50.00	100.
Louisiana	—	60.00	120.
Maine	—	80.00	160.
Maryland	—	60.00	120.
Massachusetts	—	50.00	100.
Michigan	—	50.00	100.
Minnesota	—	40.00	80.00
Mississippi	—	125.	250.
Missouri	—	40.00	80.00
Montana	—	150.	300.
Nebraska	—	50.00	100.
Nevada	—	350.	700.
New Hampshire	—	60.00	120.
New Jersey	—	40.00	80.00
New Mexico	—	150.	300.
New York	—	50.00	100.
North Carolina	—	70.00	140.
North Dakota	—	120.	240.
Ohio	—	50.00	100.
Oklahoma	—	50.00	100.
Oregon	—	55.00	110.
Pennsylvania	—	50.00	100.
Rhode Island	—	85.00	170.
South Carolina	—	100.	200.
South Dakota	—	115.	230.
Tennessee	—	50.00	100.
Texas	—	45.00	90.00
Utah	—	55.00	110.
Vermont	—	65.00	130.
Virginia	—	50.00	100.
Washington	—	55.00	110.
West Virginia	—	55.00	110.
Wisconsin	—	50.00	100.
Wyoming	—	350.	700.

1929 Type 2 $20

(KL #1318) (Fr #1802-2)

	VG	VF	AU
Alabama	—	75.00	150.
Alaska	—	12,000.	24,000.
Arizona	—	450.	900.
Arkansas	—	100.	200.
California	—	50.00	100.
Colorado	—	60.00	120.
Connecticut	—	55.00	110.
Delaware	—	300.	600.
District of Columbia	—	55.00	110.
Florida	—	75.00	150.
Georgia	—	65.00	130.
Idaho	—	250.	500.
Illinois	—	50.00	100.
Indiana	—	50.00	100.
Iowa	—	50.00	100.
Kansas	—	55.00	110.
Kentucky	—	50.00	100.
Louisiana	—	55.00	110.
Maine	—	75.00	150.
Maryland	—	75.00	150.
Massachusetts	—	55.00	110.
Michigan	—	55.00	110.
Minnesota	—	55.00	110.
Mississippi	—	125.	250.
Missouri	—	55.00	110.
Montana	—	175.	350.
Nebraska	—	55.00	110.
Nevada	—	375.	750.
New Hampshire	—	80.00	160.
New Jersey	—	55.00	110.
New Mexico	—	170.	340.
New York	—	50.00	100.
North Carolina	—	80.00	160.
North Dakota	—	125.	250.
Ohio	—	50.00	100.
Oklahoma	—	55.00	110.
Oregon	—	75.00	150.
Pennsylvania	—	55.00	110.
Rhode Island	—	90.00	180.
South Carolina	—	85.00	170.
South Dakota	—	125.	250.
Tennessee	—	65.00	130.
Texas	—	60.00	120.
Utah	—	75.00	150.
Vermont	—	100.	200.
Virginia	—	70.00	140.
Washington	—	70.00	140.
West Virginia	—	60.00	120.
Wisconsin	—	50.00	100.
Wyoming	—	400.	800.

Original Series $50

(KL #1319-1321) (Fr #440-443)

	VG	VF	AU
Georgia		(One known)	
Illinois	4000.	10,000.	—
Indiana		(One known)	
Iowa		Unique	
Kentucky		(One known)	
Louisiana	—	Rare	—
Maine		(One known)	
Maryland		(One known)	
Massachusetts		(Nine known)	
Missouri		(One known)	
New York		(Two known)	
Ohio		(Four known)	
Pennsylvania		(Two known)	
Tennessee		(One known)	

Series 1875 $50

(KL #1322-1330) (Fr #444-451)

	VG	VF	AU
Alabama		(One known)	
California		(Two known)	
Colorado Territory		(One known)	
Georgia		Unique	
Illinois		(Six known)	
Indiana		(Two known)	
Iowa		(Five known)	
Kansas		(One known)	
Kentucky		(Five known)	
Louisiana		(One known)	
Maine		(One known)	
Maryland		(Three known)	
Massachusetts		(Three known)	
Michigan		(Two known)	
New Hampshire		(Two known)	
New Jersey		(Two known)	
New York		(Seven known)	
Ohio		(Three known)	
Pennsylvania		(Nine known)	
Tennessee		(Five known)	
Utah Territory		(One known)	
Wisconsin		(One known)	

1882 Brown Back $50

(KL #1331-1343) (Fr #507-518-A)

	VG	VF	AU
Alabama		(Two known)	
Arkansas		(Three known)	
California	5500.	10,250.	16,000.
Colorado		(Six known)	
Connecticut		Unique	
Delaware		(Two known)	
Georgia		(Two known)	
Illinois	2400.	4500.	7700.
Indiana	2900.	6300.	10,500.
Iowa	2650.	5250.	9000.
Kansas	3000.	6500.	10,500.
Kentucky	2800.	6000.	10,000.
Louisiana	4850.	8000.	13,800.
Maryland		(Four known)	
Massachusetts	2800.	5500.	9000.
Michigan		(Three known)	
Minnesota	4500.	8000.	12,000.
Missouri	3250.	6700.	11,300.
Montana		(Four known)	
Nebraska	5000.	9700.	16,200.
New Jersey		(Three known)	
New Mexico Territory		(Two known)	
New Mexico Territory		(Two known)	
New York	2400.	4000.	7000.
North Carolina		(Three known)	
North Dakota		Unique	
Ohio	2400.	4700.	8000.
Oregon		Unique	
Pennsylvania	2400.	4000.	7000.
Rhode Island		Unique	
Tennessee		(Three known)	
Texas	3800.	6500.	9700.
Vermont		(Four known)	
Washington		(Six known)	
Wisconsin		(Three known)	

1882 Date Back $50

(KL #1344-1351) (Fr #558-565)

	VG	VF	AU
Arizona Territory		Unique	
California	3100.	5200.	9000.
Colorado		(Two known)	
Connecticut		Unique	
Delaware		Unique	
Illinois	2000.	4000.	7800.
Indiana	2350.	4400.	8800.
Iowa	2200.	4200.	8800.
Kansas		(Two known)	
Kentucky	1900.	5000.	8800.
Maryland		(Two known)	
Michigan	3400.	7600.	11,000.
Minnesota		(Two known)	
Missouri		(Three known)	
Montana		(Three known)	
Nebraska		(Three known)	
New Mexico	5000.	9750.	14,500.
New Mexico Territory		(Two known)	
New York	1800.	3100.	6500.
Ohio	1600.	2900.	6000.
Oklahoma	2500.	4200.	8000.
Pennsylvania	1350.	2400.	5000.
South Carolina		Unique	
Tennessee		Unique	
Texas	2000.	4200.	6750.
Washington		Unique	

1882 Value Back $50

(KL #1352) (Fr #586)

	VG	VF	AU
Louisiana		Four known	
Ohio		Three known	

1902 Red Seal $50

(KL #1353-1355) (Fr #664-666)

	VG	VF	AU
California		(Two known)	
Colorado		Unique	
Delaware		Unique	
Idaho		Unique	
Illinois	1900.	5500.	11,800.
Indiana		(Two known)	
Indiana		(Two known)	
Iowa		(Two known)	
Iowa		(Two known)	
Kansas	2500.	7600.	12,500.
Louisiana		(Three known)	
Maryland		(Four known)	
Massachusetts		Unique	
Missouri	1900.	5500.	11,800.
New Jersey		(Three known)	
New York	1900.	5500.	11,800.
Ohio	2000.	5600.	12,000.
Oregon		(Two known)	
Pennsylvania	1900.	5500.	11,800.
Puerto Rico		(Two known)	
Rhode Island	2500.	6250.	12,500.
South Dakota		Unique	
Tennessee		(Two known)	
Texas		(Three known)	
Virginia		(Two known)	
Washington	3000.	6500.	12,500.
Wisconsin		(Two known)	

1902 Date Back $50

(KL #1356-1364) (Fr #667-674-A)

	VG	VF	AU
Alabama	—	Rare	—
Arizona Territory	—	Rare	—
California	350.	650.	1350.
Colorado	500.	1000.	2000.
Connecticut	400.	800.	1600.
Delaware	1700.	3400.	5000.
Florida	—	Rare	—
Idaho	450.	900.	1750.
Illinois	350.	650.	1350.
Indiana	375.	750.	1500.
Iowa	375.	750.	1500.
Kansas	400.	800.	1600.
Kentucky	400.	800.	1600.
Louisiana	450.	800.	1750.
Maine	—	Rare	—
Maryland	375.	750.	1500.
Massachusetts	375.	750.	1500.
Michigan	375.	750.	1500.
Minnesota	375.	750.	1500.
Mississippi	—	Rare	—
Missouri	375.	750.	1500.
Montana	2000.	3000.	8000.
Nebraska	350.	650.	1350.
Nevada	2000.	4000.	8000.
New Hampshire	1700.	3400.	6500.
New Jersey	400.	800.	1600.
New York	350.	650.	1350.
North Carolina	—	Rare	—
Ohio	550.	1100.	2100.
Oklahoma	550.	1100.	2100.
Oregon	600.	1200.	2400.
Pennsylvania	350.	650.	1350.
Rhode Island	450.	900.	1750.
South Dakota	600.	1200.	2400.
Tennessee	600.	1200.	2400.
Texas	375.	750.	1500.
Utah	—	Rare	—
Vermont	850.	1700.	3400.
Virginia	—	Rare	—
Washington	450.	900.	1750.
Wisconsin	400.	800.	1600.

1902 Plain Back $50

(KL #1365-1377) (Fr #675-685-A)

	VG	VF	AU
California	350.	675.	1350.
Colorado	475.	950.	1800.
Connecticut	375.	750.	1500.
Delaware	1700.	3400.	6500.
District of Columbia	475.	1000.	1900.
Florida	1700.	3400.	6500.
Idaho	400.	800.	1600.
Illinois	350.	675.	1350.
Indiana	375.	750.	1500.
Iowa	375.	750.	1500.
Kansas	400.	800.	1600.
Kentucky	400.	800.	1600.
Louisiana	400.	800.	1600.
Maryland	375.	750.	1500.
Massachusetts	375.	750.	1500.
Michigan	375.	750.	1500.
Minnesota	375.	750.	1500.
Missouri	375.	750.	1500.
Montana	2000.	4000.	8000.
Nebraska	350.	675.	1350.
Nevada	2000.	4000.	8000.
New Hampshire	1700.	3400.	6500.
New Jersey	400.	800.	1600.
New York	350.	675.	1350.
North Carolina	—	Rare	—
North Dakota	—	Rare	—
Ohio	350.	675.	1350.
Oklahoma	350.	675.	1350.
Oregon	575.	1150.	2300.
Pennsylvania	350.	675.	1350.
Rhode Island	425.	850.	1700.
South Dakota	600.	1200.	2400.

	VG	VF	AU
Tennessee	600.	1200.	2400.
Texas	375.	750.	1500.
Vermont	850.	1700.	3400.
Washington	400.	800.	1600.
West Virginia	1350.	2700.	5000.
Wisconsin	400.	800.	1600.

1929 Type 1 $50

(KL #1378) (Fr #1803-1)

	VG	VF	AU
California	—	130.	260.
Colorado	—	150.	200.
Connecticut	—	275.	550.
Delaware	—	1500.	3000.
Florida	—	300.	600.
Hawaii	—	450.	900.
Idaho	—	300.	600.
Illinois	—	130.	260.
Indiana	—	130.	260.
Iowa	—	130.	260.
Kansas	—	150.	300.
Kentucky	—	150.	300.
Louisiana	—	150.	300.
Maryland	—	150.	300.
Massachusetts	—	150.	300.
Michigan	—	130.	260.
Minnesota	—	130.	260.
Mississippi	—	Rare	—
Missouri	—	130.	260.
Montana	—	450.	900.
Nebraska	—	130.	260.
Nevada	—	750.	1500.
New Hampshire	—	400.	800.
New Jersey	—	130.	260.
New York	—	130.	260.
North Carolina	—	Rare	—
North Dakota	—	350.	700.
Ohio	—	130.	260.
Oklahoma	—	130.	260.
Oregon	—	400.	800.
Pennsylvania	—	130.	260.
Rhode Island	—	300.	600.
South Dakota	—	450.	900.
Tennessee	—	200.	400.
Texas	—	140.	280.
Utah	—	350.	700.
Vermont	—	450.	900.
Washington	—	200.	400.
West Virginia	—	Rare	—
Wisconsin	—	160.	320.
Wyoming	—	Rare	—

1929 Type 2 $50

(KL #1379) (Fr #1803-2)

	VG	VF	AU
Arkansas	—	Rare	—
California	—	400.	800.
Colorado	—	500.	1000.
Hawaii	—	1250.	2500.

	VG	VF	AU
Illinois	—	500.	1000.
Indiana	—	400.	800.
Kansas	—	Rare	—
Kentucky	—	Rare	—
Louisiana	—	400.	800.
Maryland	—	Rare	—
Michigan	—	600.	1200.
Minnesota	—	750.	1500.
Missouri	—	Rare	—
Nebraska	—	600.	1200.
New Jersey	—	Rare	—
New York	—	600.	1200.
Ohio	—	Rare	—
Oklahoma	—	400.	800.
Pennsylvania	—	400.	800.
Rhode Island	—	600.	1200.
Tennessee	—	600.	1200.
Texas	—	400.	800.
Virginia	—	Rare	—
Wisconsin	—	Rare	—

Original Series $100

(KL #1380-1382) (Fr #452-455)

	VG	VF	AU
Connecticut		(One known)	
Illinois	—	—	—
Indiana	—	—	—
Iowa	—	—	—
Louisiana	—	—	—
Maine	—	—	—
Maryland	—	—	—
Massachusetts		(Seven known)	
New York		(Seven known)	
North Carolina		(One known)	
Ohio		(Five known)	
Pennsylvania		(Four known)	
Rhode Island		Unique	
South Carolina		Unique	
Texas		(One known)	
Utah Territory		Unique	

Series 1875 $100

(KL #1383-1391) (Fr #456-463)

	VG	VF	AU
Alabama		(Two known)	
Connecticut		(Two known)	
Illinois		(Two known)	
Indiana		(One known)	
Iowa		(One known)	
Louisiana		(One known)	
Maine		(One known)	
Maryland		(Two known)	
Massachusetts		(Four known)	
New York		(Eleven known)	
Ohio		(Eleven known)	
Pennsylvania		(Rare (Ten known)	
Rhode Island		(One known)	
South Carolina		(One known)	
Utah Territory		(One known)	
Wisconsin		Unique	

1882 Brown Back $100

(KL #1392-1403) (Fr #519-531)

	VG	VF	AU
Alabama		(Five known)	
California	7700.	14,000.	23,000.
Colorado		(Three known)	
Delaware		(Two known)	
Florida		(Three known)	
Georgia		(Four known)	
Illinois	3900.	6500.	11,000.
Indian Territory		(Unique	
Indian Territory		Unique	
Indiana	3400.	6500.	8800.
Iowa	3250.	6000.	9700.
Kansas	3400.	7200.	12,000.
Kentucky	3350.	6700.	11,000.
Louisiana	5500.	8800.	14,000.
Maryland	4000.	7500.	13,500.
Massachusetts	3400.	6300.	10,500.
Michigan		Unique	
Minnesota		(Four known)	
Missouri	3800.	7500.	12,500.
Montana		(Four known)	
Nebraska		(Four known)	
New Hampshire		(Four known)	
New Jersey		(Four known)	
New Mexico Territory		(Three known)	
New York	3900.	6400.	11,200.
North Carolina		(Two known)	
North Dakota		(Two known)	
Ohio	3900.	6400.	11,200.
Oklahoma Territory		(Three known)	
Oregon		Unique	
Pennsylvania	3900.	6400.	11,200.
Rhode Island		Unique	
South Carolina		Unique	
Tennessee		(Three known)	
Texas	6300.	10,500.	17,000.
Utah Territory		Unique	
Vermont		Unique	
Virginia	—	—	—
Washington	7000.	11,200.	14,000.
West Virginia		Unique	

1882 Date Back $100

(KL #1404-1411) (Fr #566-572-A)

	VG	VF	AU
Alabama		Unique	
California	4500.	8750.	14,500.
Colorado		Unique	
Delaware		Unique	
Georgia		Unique	
Hawaii		Unique	
Illinois	3000.	5100.	10,500.
Indiana		(Two known)	
Iowa	3300.	5550.	11,100.
Kansas		Unique	
Kentucky	2700.	5600.	9200.
Maryland		Unique	
Massachusetts	2800.	5200.	8400.
Minnesota		Unique	
Montana		Unique	
New Jersey		Unique	
New Mexico	4800.	7200.	13,600.
New York	3000.	5100.	10,200.
North Carolina	4000.	7500.	14,000.
North Dakota	—	Rare	—
Ohio		(Three known)	
Oklahoma	3900.	6600.	10,800.
Pennsylvania	2000.	3400.	6800.
Texas	3600.	6000.	9000.
Vermont		Unique	
Washington		(Three known)	

1882 Value Back $100

(KL #1412) (Fr #586-A)

	VG	VF	AU
Louisiana		Two known	
Ohio		Three known	

1902 Date Back $100

(KL #1416-1424) (Fr #689-697)

	VG	VF	AU
Alabama		Unique	
California	—	—	—
Colorado	2000.	4000.	8000.
Connecticut	2500.	5000.	10,000.
Delaware		Unique	
Florida		Unique	
Georgia		Unique	
Idaho	900.	1800.	3600.
Illinois	600.	1200.	2400.
Indiana	600.	1200.	2400.
Iowa	600.	1200.	2400.
Kansas	750.	1500.	3000.
Kentucky	750.	1500.	3000.
Louisiana	750.	1500.	3000.
Maine		Unique	
Maryland	750.	1500.	3000.
Massachusetts	750.	1500.	3000.
Michigan	750.	1500.	3000.
Minnesota		Unique	
Mississippi	3000.	6000.	12,000.
Missouri	700.	1400.	2800.
Montana		Unique	
Nebraska	700.	1400.	2800.
Nevada	4000.	8000.	16,000.
New Hampshire	3000.	6000.	12,000.
New Jersey	2600.	4000.	8000.
New York	600.	1200.	2400.
North Carolina	—	Rare	—
North Dakota	—	Rare	—
Ohio	600.	1200.	2400.
Oklahoma	750.	1500.	3000.
Oregon	1000.	2000.	4000.
Pennsylvania	600.	1200.	2400.
Puerto Rico	—	Rare	—
Rhode Island	1000.	2000.	4000.
South Dakota	1250.	2500.	5000.

	VG	VF	AU
Tennessee	1800.	3600.	7200.
Texas	700.	1400.	2800.
Utah		Unique	
Vermont	2000.	4000.	8000.
Virginia	—	Rare	—
Washington	750.	1500.	3000.
Wisconsin	700.	1400.	2800.

1902 Plain Back $100

(KL #1425-1436) (Fr #698-707-A)

	VG	VF	AU
California	300.	600.	1200.
Colorado	1000.	2000.	4000.
Connecticut	1250.	2500.	5000.
Delaware	2000.	4000.	8000.
Idaho	450.	900.	1800.
Illinois	300.	600.	1200.
Indiana	300.	600.	1200.
Iowa	300.	600.	1200.
Kansas	375.	750.	1500.
Kentucky	375.	750.	1500.
Louisiana	375.	750.	1500.
Maryland	375.	750.	1500.
Massachusetts	375.	750.	1500.
Michigan	375.	750.	1500.
Mississippi	1500.	3000.	6000.
Missouri	350.	700.	1400.
Montana	—	Rare	—
Nebraska	350.	700.	1400.
Nevada	2000.	4000.	8000.
New Hampshire	1500.	3000.	6000.
New Jersey	2000.	4000.	8000.
New York	300.	600.	1200.
North Dakota	—	Rare	—
Ohio	300.	600.	1200.
Oklahoma	375.	750.	1500.
Oregon	450.	900.	1800.
Pennsylvania	300.	600.	1200.
Rhode Island	450.	900.	1800.
South Dakota	625.	1250.	2500.
Tennessee	500.	1000.	2000.
Texas	350.	700.	1400.
Vermont	1000.	2000.	4000.
Washington	375.	750.	1500.
West Virginia		Unique	
Wisconsin	350.	700.	1400.

1929 Type 1 $100

(KL #1437) (Fr #1804-1)

	VG	VF	AU
California	—	225.	450.
Colorado	—	250.	500.
Connecticut	—	600.	1200.
Delaware	—	Rare	—
Florida	—	500.	1000.
Hawaii	—	600.	1250.
Idaho	—	500.	1000.
Illinois	—	225.	450.
Indiana	—	225.	450.
Iowa	—	225.	450.
Kansas	—	300.	600.
Kentucky	—	400.	800.
Louisiana	—	300.	600.
Maryland	—	250.	500.
Massachusetts	—	250.	500.
Michigan	—	225.	450.
Minnesota	—	250.	500.
Mississippi	—	Rare	—
Missouri	—	250.	500.
Montana	—	600.	1200.
Nebraska	—	250.	500.
Nevada	—	1500.	3000.
New Hampshire	—	450.	900.
New Jersey	—	250.	500.
New York	—	250.	500.
North Carolina	—	Rare	—
North Dakota	—	550.	1100.
Ohio	—	225.	450.
Oklahoma	—	225.	450.
Oregon	—	900.	1600.
Pennsylvania	—	225.	450.
Rhode Island	—	400.	800.
South Dakota	—	750.	1500.
Tennessee	—	250.	500.
Texas	—	250.	500.
Vermont	—	475.	950.
Washington	—	300.	600.
West Virginia	—	Rare	—
Wisconsin	—	300.	600.
Wyoming	—	Rare	—

1929 Type 2 $100

(KL #1438) (Fr #1804-2)

	VG	VF	AU
Arkansas	—	Rare	—
California	—	500.	1000.
Colorado	—	750.	1500.
Hawaii	—	Rare	—
Illinois	—	650.	1300.
Indiana	—	Rare	—
Kentucky	—	Rare	—
Louisiana	—	750.	1500.
Maryland	—	Rare	—
Michigan	—	Rare	—
Minnesota	—	750.	1500.
New Jersey	—	Rare	—
New York	—	Rare	—
Pennsylvania	—	750.	1500.
Rhode Island	—	900.	1800.
Tennessee	—	Rare	—
Texas	—	650.	1300.
Virginia	—	Rare	—

Pre-Civil War (1812-1861) United States Treasury Notes

Compiled by Russell Rulau

The first paper money issued by the United States government was not, as is often thought, the Interest Bearing Treasury Notes of 1861, these notes were actually the last in the long series of Treasury notes that commenced in 1812 as a consequence of the financial condition of the nation in the War of 1812.

The U.S. Treasury issued five separate series of notes between 1812 and 1815 with denominations ranging from $3 to $1,000. Though originally intended as loans to the government, they soon began to circulate since they were receivable for debts, taxes and duties due the federal government.

Neither the 1812-1815 notes nor later issues until 1861 were ever actually legal tender for all debts, public or private. This is an important distinction between them and the legal tender notes introduced in the Civil War. Compared to private bank notes of the period, however, they were "good as gold".

To provide bridge financing and spot cash, Congress authorized a whole series of interest-bearing Treasury notes – at 5.4% or 1.44 cents per day per $100 by acts of June 30, 1812; Feb. 25, 1813; March 4, 1814, and Feb. 24, 1815. By the 1815 act, Congress for the first time created a true currency with notes of $3 through $50 bearing no interest, but with those of $100 bearing the usual 5.4% annual interest.

Specimen copies of all these notes, punch-canceled but bearing two of the three required signatures, were supplied to the chief customs houses at Baltimore, Boston, Charleston, New York and Philadelphia. Actual issued notes, whether unredeemed or canceled, bring the highest prices, unissued remainder notes sell well. Specimen notes, and printer's proofs, usually in excellent condition, bring slightly lower prices but are often the only notes available.

Of the 1814 issue, only about $40,000 remained outstanding in 1896 out of a total of $8.3 million. Of the 1815 $100 notes, note of the $1.5 million issued was unredeemed in 1896.

The 1815 "small bills" of $3 to $50 were issued to a total of $9,070,386. Some $5.6 million of these were funded into bonds, and in 1896 just $2,061 remained unredeemed.

The panic of 1837-1843 brought out eight more series of Treasury notes. These notes differed from the War of 1812 notes in that they were signed by the Treasurer of the United States and were engraved by Rawdon, Wright & Hatch (RWH) whereas the 1812-1815 notes had been signed by commissioners.

The Mexican War was responsible for the next two series of Treasury notes in 1846 and 1847, also signed by the U.S. Treasurer.

The severe financial conditions of the panic of 1857 resulted in the next three series of Treasury notes, issued form Dec. 1857 through March 1861. These notes were issued at competitive interest rates rather than predetermined rates. Confidence in the federal government was lacking and of the $10 million of 6% notes offered in Dec. 1860 only $70,000 was taken up! The remainder of these notes has to be offered at rates above 6%, with 10, 10.75, 11 and 12% being the largest. (Bids were received as high as 36%, but the Treasury rejected all bids above 12%.) The Acts of July 17 and Aug. 5, 1861 authorized the final issues of Treasury notes.

Most pre-Civil War Treasury notes bear the date of the act that authorized them, and an issue-date (in ink) as well. The catalog section is arranged by authorization (not issue) dates. All pre-Civil War Treasury notes are rare and seldom met with, many are unique.

A famed French politician and numismatist, Alexandre Vattemare, formed one of the largest private collections of the 1812-1815 notes. This collection sold in 1982 by Christie Manson & Woods International, mostly to one person, then re-auctioned in 2000 by R. M. Smtthe & Co.

The largest private collection ever assembled was by John J. Ford, Jr., buyer of much of the Vattemare 2000 offerings to add to his 40-year holds, and Stack's Rare Coins sold this group in late 2004. Heritage Currency Auctions offered another large group, the Taylor family holdings, in early 2005.

This section has been renumbered from previous editions, based on new information that has come to light from these recent offerings.

Bibliography:

Alexandre Vattemare Collection Sale, Christie Manson & Woods International, Sale of Sept., 17, 1982

J. W. Middendorf, II, Sale, Christies, March 22, 1994

John J. Ford, Jr. Sale, Stack's Rare Coins, Oct., 12, 2004

R.M. Smythe Sale. Memphis International Paper Money Show Auction, June 16, 2000.

Taylow Family Holdings Sale. Heritage Currency Auctions, Feb., 18-19, 2005.

Hessler, Gene. "An Illustrated History of U.S. Loans, 1775-1898" BNR Press, 1985 and 1988.

Knox, John Jay. "United States Notes: A history of the Various Issues of Paper Money", NY editions of 1884, 1885 and 1894.

Photos and note data courtesy of Larry Stevens, Eric P. Newman, Christie's, R. M. Smythe & Co., Stack's Rare Coins, and Heritage Currency Auctions.

WAR OF 1812

ACT OF JUNE 30, 1812

1 year notes at 5 2/5% interest. $5,000,000 authorized and issued.
No Issued notes are known to exist.

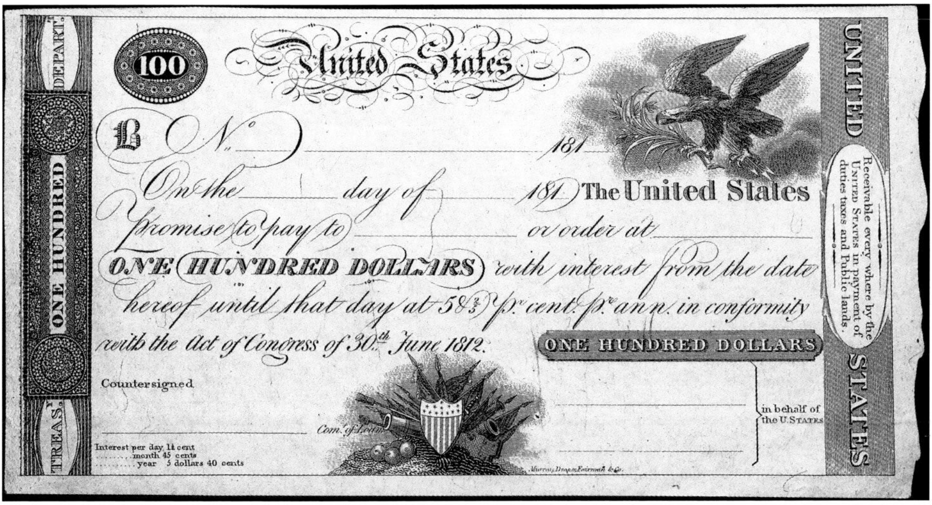

Murray, Draper, Fairman & Company

KL#		Denom.	Description	XF	AU
P1	a	$100	Single remainder.	8050.	17,250.
	b	$100	Remainder, sheet of two.		25,300.
P2		$1,000	Single remainder. (3 known).	21,850.	—

ACT OF FEBRUARY 25, 1813

1 year notes at 5 2/5% interest. $5,000,000 authorized and issued. No issued notes are known.

KL#	Denom.	Description	XF	AU
P3	$100	No description available.	—	—

ACT OF MARCH 4, 1814

1 Year notes at 5 2/5% interest. $10,000,000 authorized and issued. No issued notes are known.

KL#	Denom.	Description	XF	AU
P4	$20	No description available.	—	—
P5	$50	No description available.	—	—

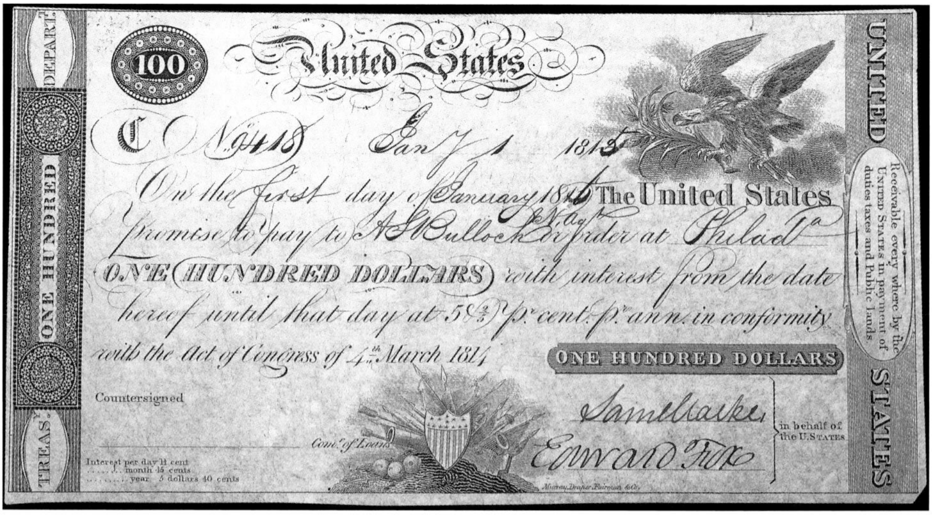

KL#		Denom.	Description	XF	AU
P6		$100	Remainder with 2 signatures. (2 known).	29,900.	—

Murray, Draper, Fairman & Company

ACT OF DECEMBER 26, 1814

1 Year notes at 5 2/5% interest. $8,318,400 issued. No issued notes are known.

KL#		Denom.	Description	XF	AU
P7	a	$20	Remainder with 2 signatures. (About 15 known.)	12,650.	—
	b	$20	Remainder sheet of two.	—	12,650.
	c	$20	Proof on cardstock. (3 known)	—	5000.
P8		$50	No description available.	—	—

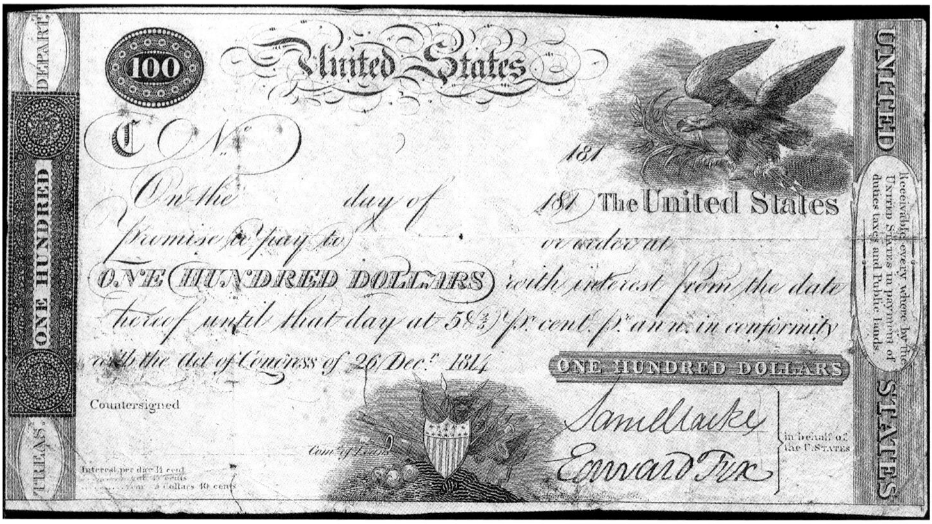

Murray, Draper, Fairman & Company

KL#		Denom.	Description	XF	AU
P9	a	$100	Remainder with 2 signatures. (4 known).	22,425.	—
	b	$100	Proof on card. (2 known).	—	14,950.

ACT OF FEBRUARY 24, 1815

$3 to $50 notes without interest; $100 notes, indefinite interest at 5 2/5% $3,392 issued in $3—50 notes; $4,969,400 issued in $100 notes.

KL#		Denom.	Description	XF	AU
P10	a	$3	Issued note. Signed by Joseph Nourse, F. W. McGeary and C. C. Biddle.	62,500.	—
	b	$3	Single remainder, unsigned. (5 known)	—	8250.
	c	$3	Remainder in sheet of four.	30,000.	—
	d	$3	Proof on cardstock.	—	5750.

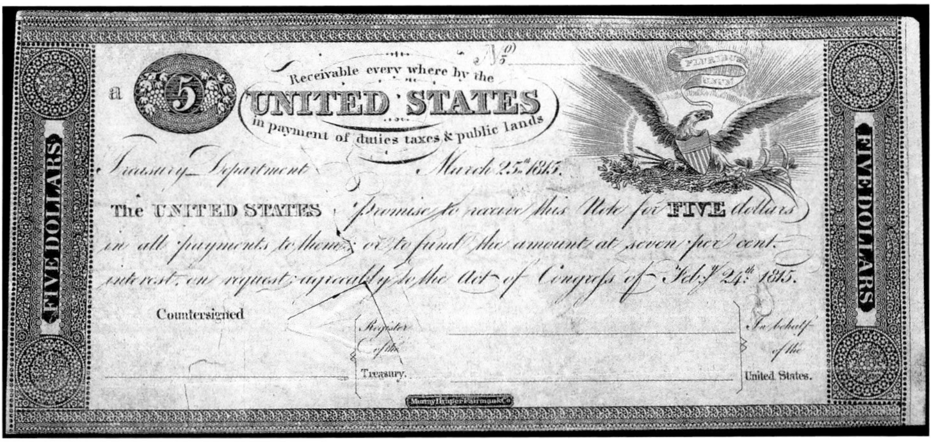

KL#		Denom.	Description	XF	AU
P11	a	$5	Unsigned remainder. (About 13 known)	—	3750.
	b	$5	Two signature remainder sheet of 3.	—	12,750.
	c	$5	Proof on cardstock.	—	5000.

Murray, Draper, Fairman & Company

P12	$10	Remainder with two signatures. (3 known)	5000.	—

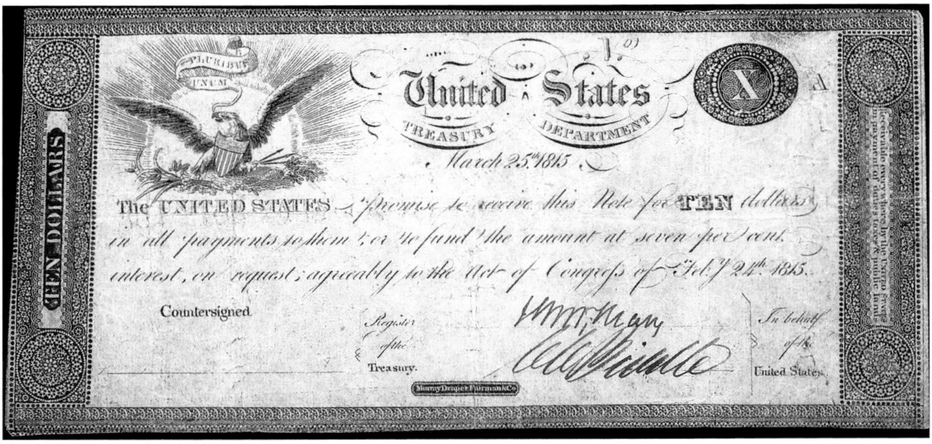

KL#		Denom.	Description	XF	AU
P13	a	$10	Remainder with 2 signatures. (17 known)	5250.	7000.
	b	$10	Remainder sheet of three.	—	10,350.
	c	$10	Single proof on India paper.	—	4000.
	d	$10	Sheet of three proof on India paper.	—	19,000.

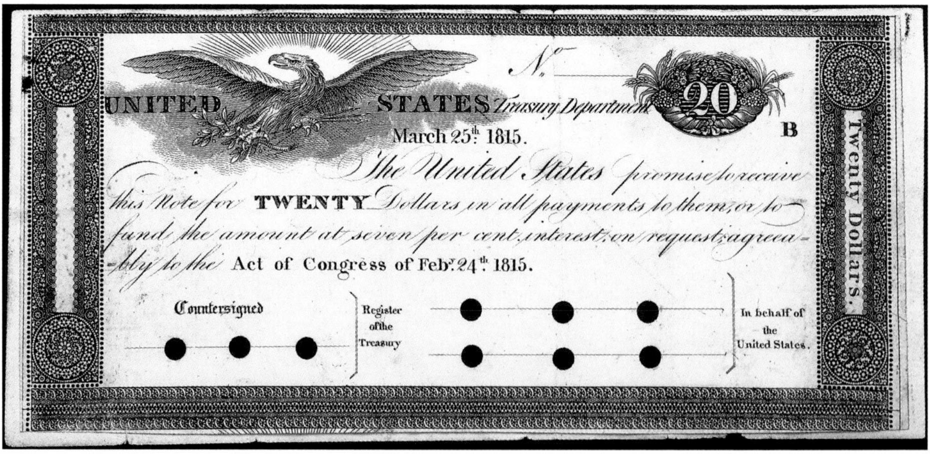

KL#		Denom.	Description	XF	AU
P14	a	$20	Unsigned remainder.	—	—
	b	$20	Sheet of four unsigned remainders.	—	17,250.
	c	$20	Proof on India paper. (3 known)	—	3750.

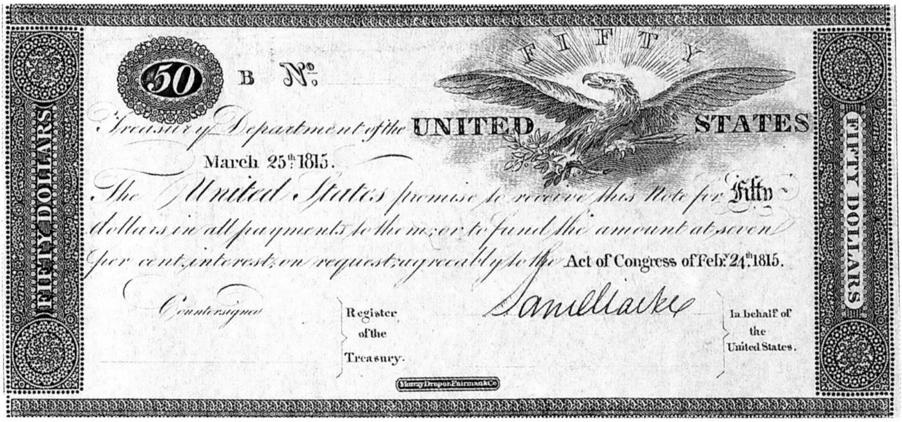

KL#		Denom.	Description	XF	AU
P15	a	$50	Issued, canceled note. Nourse, McGeary, Biddle signatures.	—	3750.
	b	$50	Remainder, sheet of four (one signature).	19,750.	—
	c	$50	Remainder, sheet of three.	—	23,250.

KL#	Denom.	Description	XF	AU
P16 a	$100	Unsigned remainder. (6 known)	8250.	—
b	$100	Unsigned remainder, sheet of three.	—	17,250.
c	$100	Proof on card.	8250.	—
d	$100	Proof, sheet of three.	—	21,000.

PANIC OF 1837
ACT OF OCTOBER 12, 1837

1 year notes issued at four different rates of interest 1 mill, 2%, 5% or 6%, the rate written in by ink at time of issue. The 1—mil rate, which was nominal, was used on notes intended to circulate as currency. $10,000,000 authorize

Face black, back orange. Rawdon, Wright & Hatch. 183 printed.

KL#	Denom.	Description	XF	AU
P17	$50	Unsigned remainder.	8000.	—

Rawdon, Wright & Hatch. Face black, back light orange.

KL#	Denom.	Description	XF	AU
P18	$100	Issued note, canceled.	6100.	—

KL#	Denom.	Description	XF	AU
P19	$500	No description available.	—	—
P20	$1,000	No description available.	—	—

Denomination, date, interest rate to be written in. Back orange. Rawdon, Wright & Hatch.

KL#	Denom.	Description	XF	AU
P20A	(no Denomination)	Unsigned remainder	1950.	—

ACT OF MAY 21, 1838

1 year ntoes at 6% interest. $6,888,809 issued.

KL#	Denom.	Description	XF	AU
P21	$50	No description available.	—	—
P22	$100	No description available.	—	—
P23	$500	No description available.	—	—
P24	$1,000	No description available.	—	—

ACT OF MARCH 2, 1839

1 year notes at 2%, 5%, 5 2/5% or 6% interest, $3,857,276 issued

KL#	Denom.	Description	XF	AU
P25	$50	No description available.	—	—
P26	$100	No description available.	—	—
P27	$500	No description available.	—	—
P28	$1,000	No description available.	—	—

ACT OF MARCH 31, 1840

1 year notes at 2%, 5%, 5 2/5% or 6% interest, the rate written in by ink at time of issuance.

KL#	Denom.	Description	XF	AU
P29	$50	No description available.	—	—

Knox drawing only available.

KL#	Denom.	Description	XF	AU
P30	$100	Specimen.	—	—
P31	$500	No description available.	—	—
P32	$1,000	No description available.	—	—
P33	$10,000	No description available.	—	—

ACT OF JANUARY 31, 1842

1 year notes at 2% or 6% interest, $7,959,994 issued (including reissues).

KL#	Denom.	Description	XF	AU
P34	$50	No description available.	—	—
P35	$100	No description available.	—	—
P36	$500	No description available.	—	—
P37	$1,000	No description available.	—	—

PANIC OF 1837

ACT OF AUGUST 31, 1842

1 year notes at 2% or 6% interest. $3,025,554 issued.

Rawdon, Wright & Hatch.

KL#	Denom.	Description	XF	AU
P38	$50	Unissued remainder.	—	—

KL#	Denom.	Description	XF	AU
P39	$100	Unissued remainder.	—	—
P40	$500	No description available.	—	—

Rawdon, Wright & Hatch.

KL#	Denom.	Description	XF	AU
P41	$1,000	Unissued remainder.	—	—

ACT OF MARCH 3, 1843

1 year notes at 1 mill or 4% interest. $1,806,950 issued.

Rawdon, Wright & Hatch.

KL#	Denom.	Description	XF	AU
P42	$50	Issued note, cancelled. Very Rare.	—	—

Special Note: In 1887 there were only $83,425 outstanding in all Treasury notes issued under acts prior to 1846!

MEXICAN WAR NOTES

ACT OF JULY 22, 1846

1 year notes at 1 mill or 5 2/5% interest. $7,687,800 issued.

Black print, red FIFTY protector near bottom center, blue serial #. One mill.

Rawdon, Wright & Hatch.

KL#	Denom.	Description	XF	AU
P43 a	$50	Specimen.	—	5500.

KL#	Denom.	Description	XF	AU
b	$50	Face proof on India paper.	2500.	—
c	$50	Face proof on India paper, without red FIFTY protector.	2500.	—

Knox drawing only available.

KL#	Denom.	Description	XF	AU
P44	$100		—	—
P45	$500	No description available.	—	—
P46	$1,000	No description available.	—	—

Note: In 1887, only $5,900 was outstanding!

ACT OF JANUARY 28, 1847

60 day or 1 or 2 year notes at 5 2/5% or 6% interest. $26,122,100 issued (including reissues).
Note: In 1887, only $950 or 6% notes were still outstanding!

Black face, orange back. One year note. Rawdon, Wright & Hatch.

KL#	Denom.	Description	XF	AU
P46C	$50	Specimen. Unique.		4250.

MEXICAN WAR WARRANTS

ACT OF AUGUST 10, 1846

5 year warrants, interest not stated.

Blue with red overprint. Rawdon, Wright & Hatch.

KL#	Denom.	Description	XF	AU
P46A	$500	Specimen.	—	—

Black with red overprint. Rawdon, Wright, Hatch & Edson.

KL#	Denom.	Description	XF	AU
P46B	$1,000	Specimen.	—	—

MEXICAN WAR NOTES

ACT OF JANUARY 28, 1847

60 day or 1 or 2 year notes at 5 2/5% or 6% interest. $26,122,100 issued (including reissues).
Note: In 1887, only $950 or 6% notes were still outstanding!

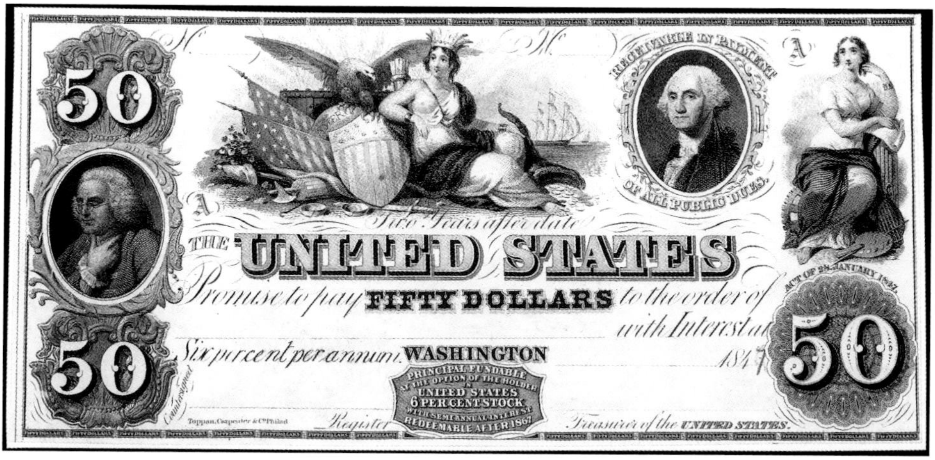

Black face, red back. Toppan, Carpenter & Company. Two year note.

KL#	Denom.	Description	XF	AU
P47 a	$50	Specimen.	—	4750.
b	$50	Proof on card.	4500.	8000.

184 printed. Rawdon, Wright, Hatch & Edson.

KL#	Denom.	Description	XF	AU
P48	$100	Face proof on card.	—	6000.

One year note. Black face, back orange. Rawdon, Wright & Hatch.

KL#	Denom.	Description	XF	AU
P48A	$100	Face and back proof. Unique.	—	5500.

Two year note. 184 printed. Rawdon, Wright, Hatch & Edson.

KL#	Denom.	Description	XF	AU
P48Ba	$100	Face and back proof on card.	—	4500.
b	$100	Face proof on India paper.	—	5000.

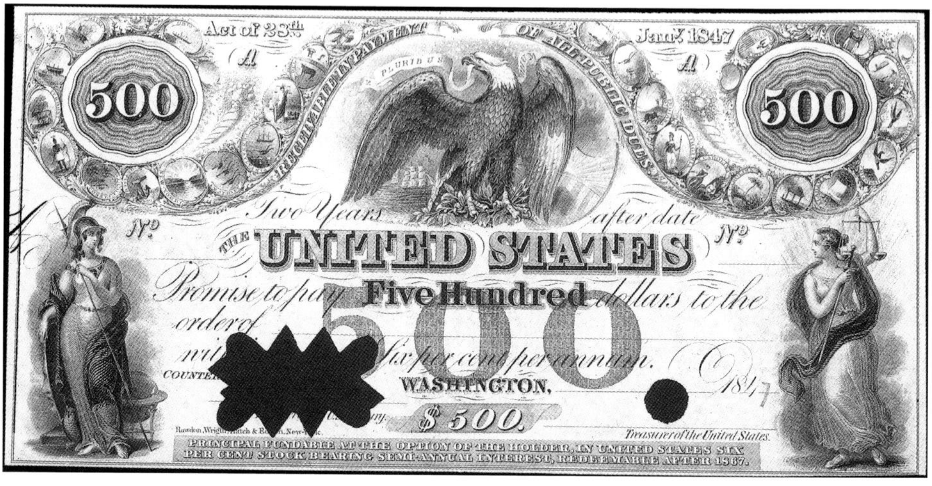

Two year note. Face black with red 500 protector. back brown.
Rawdon, Wright, Hatch & Edson.

KL#	Denom.	Description	XF	AU
P49	$500	Specimen.	—	8500.

One year note. Black face, orange back. Rawdon, Wright & Hatch.

KL#	Denom.	Description	XF	AU
P50	$1,000	Specimen.	—	8500.

Two year note. Toppan, Carpenter & Company.

KL#	Denom.	Description	XF	AU
P50Aa	$1,000	Face proof on India paper.		18,500.
b	$1,000	Face and back proof.		18,500.

Two year note. Rawdon, Wright, Hatch & Edson.

KL#	Denom.	Description	XF	AU
P51	$5,000	Specimen, two sided.	—	—

Face black, back orange. Toppan, Carpenter & Company.

KL#	Denom.	Description	XF	AU
P52	$5,000	Proof on India paper on card.	—	22,000.

PANIC OF 1857

ACT OF DECEMBER 23, 1857

1 year notes at 3% to 6% interest. $20,000,000 authorized.
Note: In 1887, only $700 of all these notes were outstanding!

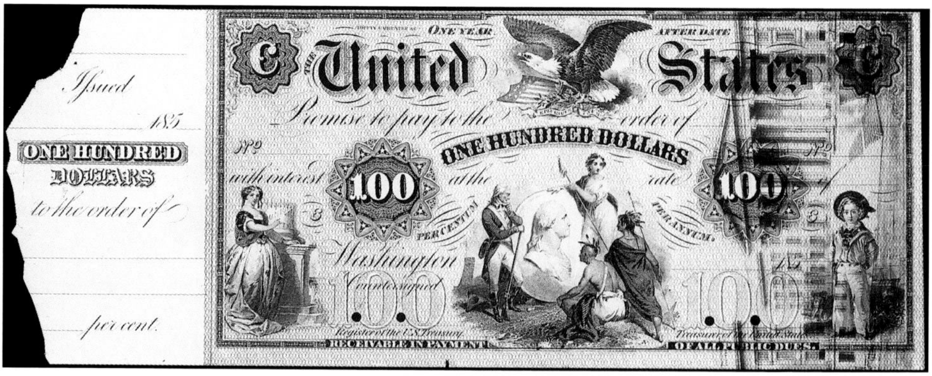

Black print, bronze—gold Treasury building underprint at right.

KL#	Denom.	Description	XF	AU
P53	$100	Face proof with counterfoil at left.	—	5500.
P54	$500	No description available.	—	—

Full green frame and green underprint protectors, black print.
Rawdon, Wright, Hatch & Edson.

KL#	Denom.	Description	XF	AU
P55	$1,000	Face proof on India paper. (3 known)	—	12,750.

ACT OF DECEMBER 17, 1860

1 year notes at 6% to 12% interest. $15,000,000 issued (most at rates of 10 3/4%, 11% or 12%).

KL#	Denom.	Description	XF	AU
P56	$50	No description available.	—	—
P57	$100	No description available.	—	—
P58	$500	No description available.	—	—

Black on green frame and underprint.
Rawdon, Wright, Hatch & Edson and American Bank Note Company.

KL#	Denom.	Description	XF	AU
P59 a	$1,000	Proof. Unique.	—	10,000.
b	$1,000	Two—sided specimen. Back green.	21,000.	—

ACT OF MARCH 2, 1861

1 or 2 year notes at 6% interest. $35,364,450 issued ($22.4 million in 2—year notes).

Black and orange; blue back. National Bank Note Company.

KL#	Denom.	Description	XF	AU
P60 a	$50	Issued note.	375,000.	—
b	$50	Proof.	—	—

Two year, 6%. Black and orange face, blue back. National Bank Note Company.

KL#	Denom.	Description	XF	AU
P60Aa	$50	Face proof on India paper card.		16,250.
b	$50	Two sided proof.		

Black and orange; green back.

KL#	Denom.	Description	XF	AU
P61	$100	Specimen.	—	30,000.

Black print, red 100 protector near bottom center. 60—day note.
Rawdon, Wright, Hatch & Edson.

KL#	Denom.	Description	XF	AU
P62	$100	Face specimen. Unique.	—	16,250.

60—day note, 6% interest. Black, green frame and underprint.
Rawdon, Wright, Hatch & Edson and American Bank Note Company.

KL#	Denom.	Description	XF	AU
P63	$500	Specimen.	—	21,000.

Black & green; brown back. 60—day note.
American Bank Note Company and Rawdon, Wright, Hatch & Edson.

KL#	Denom.	Description	XF	AU
P64	$500	Specimen.	—	—

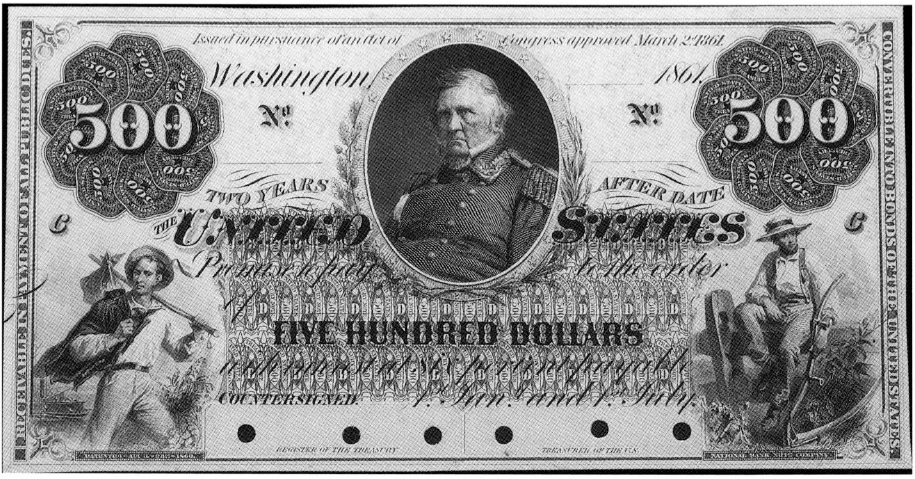

Two—year note, 6% interest. Black on green border and protectors.
National Bank Note Company.

KL#	Denom.	Description	XF	AU
P65 a	$500	Face proof.	—	25,000.
b	$500	Face and back proof.	—	—

Two—year note, 6% interest. Black and green, orange back. National Bank Note Company.

KL#	Denom.	Description	XF	AU
P66 a	$1,000	Specimen.	—	—
b	$1,000	Face proof on India paper on card.	—	30,000.
P67	$5,000	No description available.	—	—
P68	$5,000	No description available.	—	—

CIVIL WAR NOTES

ACT OF JULY 17 AND AUGUST 5, 1861

3 year notes at 7 3/10%. So—called "7—30s". These are the first Treasury notes widely issued for circulation. $800,000,000—plus issued.

Black and green. American Bank Note Company.

KL#	Denom.	Description	XF	AU
P74	$20	Essay on card.	18,000.	—
		Black and green face, back green. American Bank Note Company.		
P75	$50	Issued note, uncancelled.	172,500.	—
P76	$100	Fragment of issued note.	—	—
		Green and black, back green. American Bank Note Company.		
P77 a	$500	Issued note, uncancelled.	300,000.	—
b	$500	Issued note, damaged and cancelled.	—	—
P78	$1,000	Note fragment. No additional description available.	—	—
P79	$5,000	No description available.	—	—

PRINTER ABBREVIATIONS

ABNC	*American Bank Note Company*
NBNC	*National Bank Note Company*
MDF	*Murray, Draper, Fairman & Company*
RW&H	*Rawdon, Wright & Hatch*
RWH&E	*Rawdon, Wright, Hatch & Edson*
TC	*Toppan, Carpenter & Company*

Encased Postage Stamps & Postage Stamp Envelopes

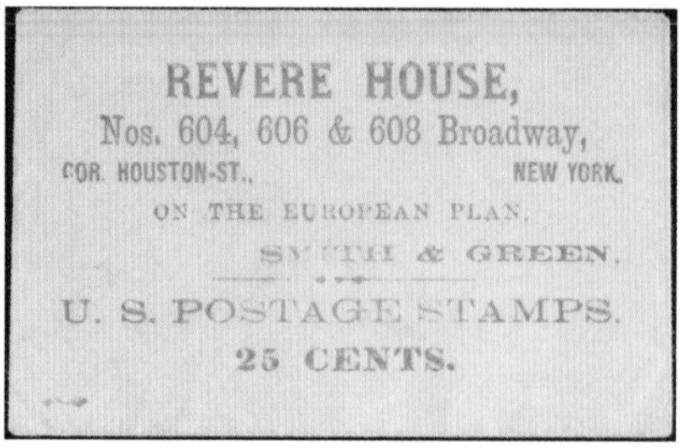

Encased Postage Stamps

By Len Glazer

Encased postage has always been among the most elusive of American numismatic items to collect, and consequently, among the most rewarding. With their natural appeal to numismatists, philatelists, and collectors of antique advertising media, demand has also been strong. This competition for scarce items, especially so in high grades of preservation, has meant a steady upward price progression that also makes Encased Postage Stamps desirable from an investment viewpoint.

While a complete set – by denomination, merchant and major variety – of Encased Postage has never been formed and likely never will be, it is entirely within the grasp of the determined numismatist to assemble a collection that is "complete" within self-set boundaries; that is, 6 denomination, by merchant, by type of merchant (medicinal, dry goods, etc.), by locality of issue, or by any other criteria.

While not generally collected along with the Gault encased postage stamps, the so-called Feuchtwanger rectangular encasement is a contemporary, though unsuccessful, competitor.

Approximately 31x61 mm, with a brass frame and no mica cover for the stamps, this item is generally found with a trio of 3-cent postage stamps; a face value of nine cents. The item is also found with other quantities of 3-cent stamps, though the originality of these other denominations is questionable.

Naturally, since the stamps are easily replaced, their condition has little bearing on the value.

Grading

Three factors must be considered in the grading of Encased Postage Stamps: the case itself, the enclosed stamp and the protective mica.

For the listings which follow, generally accepted standards for coin grading have been used to grade the cases. The accepted standards for grading unused U.S. postage stamps have been considered for that element. For the mica, terminology is that which has been in use since the collecting of Encased Postage Stamps began.

In referring to the price listing that follows, it should be made clear that unlike coins or stamps, which are bought and sold on the basis of generally accepted grading standards, Encased Postage Stamps are sold on the individual merits of the piece involved. This is the result of the many and varied states of preservation of each of the three main elements - case, stamp and mica - of these items.

The valuations quoted refer basically to the condition of the case. If the condition of the stamp and mica are consistent in their own way with that of the case, the valuations can be considered accurate at the time of this catalog's issue. If, however, either the stamp or the mica is significantly better or worse than the case, the value of the item as a whole may be more or less than the figure quoted.

Assume, for example, that a piece with a VF case holds a stamp that is Extremely Fine, protected by a piece of mica which is crazed (see mica grading). The stamp is obviously better than the case, and the crazed mica is also quite nice, though not perfect. The value of such a piece is definitely higher than the quoted VF price, and may be closer to the XF valuation.

Grading of Case

NEW - A condition unknown among Encased Postage Stamps. While there do, indeed, exist specimens which show no wear traces of circulation on the case, the condition of the stamp and/or mica will always contain some imperfection which prevents the accurate description of any Encased Postage Stamp as "New."

ABOUT NEW - The highest grade in which Encased Postage can practically be collected. Just a touch of rubbing on the case, which may or may not still retain some original silvering, if so issued.

EXTREMELY FINE - Higher than average grade, with a bit of noticeable wear on the case; still a very nice piece.

VERY FINE- The average grade for collectible Encased Postage Stamps. The case shows definite wear, but little or no flatness of the embossed lettering. Most catalog values are based on this grade.

FINE - A worn, but acceptable, piece. Generally the lowest undamaged or collectible grade of untampered Encased Postage, since the items did not circulate long enough to attain any greater degree of wear.

Grading of Stamp

In their usage with Encased Postage, stamps are generally described in one of the following degrees of brightness. Since the paper was protected by the mica, the only measurement of the state of preservation of the stamp can be the degree to which it was subjected to the fading effects of sunlight or other causes.

FULLY BRIGHT - A stamp that is 100% as vivid as the day it was issued.

NEAR FULL BRIGHT - Perhaps a spot or two of less than perfect brightness.

BRIGHT - A stamp which has lost some of its original color, but is still sharp and always acceptable.

TONED - A stamp which has darkened with age or exposure to light and other elements.

DULL or FADED - A stamp which has lost much of its color; the lowest generally collectable condition for an undamaged item.

Grading of Mica

Because it is a natural silicate mineral, mica of flawless, perfect quality probably does not exist in connection with its use in Encased Postage Stamps. Collectors are warned that only "perfect" mica generally encountered is acetate which has been used to repair a damaged Encased Postage Stamp. Upon close examination, some flaw can be found on virtually every mica piece used in this manner.

NEARLY PERFECT - The highest degree of preservation for a mica encasement.

CRAZED - Fine cracks in the surface, on the surface, or between the thin natural layers of mica. Separation beginning in its early stages. None of the crazing fully breaks the mica, exposing the stamp.

CRACKED -A break in the mica through to the stamp, but with no piece of the mica missing.

CHIPPED - A breaking of only the upper layer or layers of mica, with the chip or chips missing, though the mica beneath remains intact and the stamp protected.

BROKEN - A break in all layers of the mica, with some missing and the stamp exposed. The degree of broken or missing mica should be described.

Other Terms

Two other terms which the collector of Encased Postage will encounter also bear definition.

RIBBED FRAME - Some varieties of Encased Postage are known with cases which have fine parallel lines on the face (stamp side) of the metal case.

SILVERING - Many Encased Postage Stamps were issued with a thin silver wash on the case, to enhance their resemblance to the disappearing silver coinage of the day. More research is needed to determine which issues came with silvering, which came without and which, if any, were issued both ways. Since the silver wore off very quickly, even many high grade pieces have no traces of the original finish. A piece with a high percentage of silvering remaining is worth a premium, but those with just a trace of silver are not; though it is generally mentioned when describing an item for sale.

Rarity Ratings

When dealing with the relative rarity of Encased Postage Stamps, the collector must realize that all are scarce in terms of numismatic collectibles. Even the most common variety "Take Ayer's Pills" may not be easy to locate on the market at any given time.

Following years of study of major collections and auction offerings, and conversations with other specialists, the following table of rarity lists each piece in what we believe to be its correct order, and broken into six categories of rarity. While there may be some disagreement as to order within category, we believe most knowledgeable specialists will agree with the listing.

VERY RARE

1. Arthur M. Claflin
2. B. F. Miles
3. John W. Norris
4. Pearce, Tolle & Holton

RARE

5. White the Hatter
6. Sands' Ale
7. S. Steinfeld
8. Dougan
9. N.G. Taylor & Co.
10. Ellis McAlpin & Co.
11. L.C. Hopkins & Co.
12. Aerated Bread

VERY SCARCE

13. F. Buhl & Co.
14. Weir & Larminie
15. Lord & Taylor
16. H.A. Cook
17. Bailey & Co.

SCARCE

18. Schapker & Bussing
19. G.G. Evans
20. John Shillito & Co.
21. Mendum's Wine Emporium
22. North America Life Insurance Co.

COMMON

23. Tremont House
24. Joseph L. Bates
25. Kirkpatrick & Gault
26. Irving House
27. Brown's Bronchial Troches
28. Burnett's Cocoaine
29. J. Gault
30. Burnett's Cooking Extracts
31. Drake's Plantation Bitters

MOST COMMON

32. Take Ayer's Pills
33. Ayer's Cathartic Pills
34. Ayer's Sarsaparilla

Aerated Bread Co., New York

KL#	Denom.	Fine	VF	XF	AU
EPS1	1¢	800.	1250.	1500.	2500.

Ayer's Cathartic Pills

(Long Arrows variety)

KL#	Denom.	Fine	VF	XF	AU
EPS2	3¢	100.	175.	250.	500.
EPS3	5¢	125.	275.	350.	600.
EPS4	10¢	250.	500.	650.	1000.

(Short arrows variety)

KL#	Denom.	Fine	VF	XF	AU
EPS5	1¢	150.	225.	300.	975.
EPS6	3¢	100.	175.	250.	500.
EPS7	5¢	125.	275.	350.	600.
EPS8	10¢	200.	350.	500.	1000.
EPS9	12¢	300.	550.	1000.	1500.
EPS10	24¢	1200.	2000.	3000.	4500.
EPS11	30¢	1500.	3000.	4000.	5500.

Take Ayer's Pills

KL#	Denom.	Fine	VF	XF	AU
EPS12	1¢	150.	250.	325.	600.
EPS13	3¢	100.	150.	225.	500.
EPS14	5¢	100.	200.	300.	400.
EPS15	10¢	175.	375.	500.	850.
EPS16	12¢	300.	550.	1000.	1500.
EPS17	90¢	XF:Two known are both suspect as being counterfeit or altered.			

Ayer's Sarsaparilla

(Small Ayer's)

KL#	Denom.	Fine	VF	XF	AU
EPS18	1¢	300.	625.	925.	1000.
EPS19	3¢	350.	550.	750.	900.
EPS20	10¢	300.	625.	925.	1000.
EPS21	12¢	700.	1400.	2000.	3500.

(Medium Ayer's)

KL#	Denom.	Fine	VF	XF	AU
EPS22	1¢	150.	225.	300.	600.
EPS23	3¢	100.	175.	225.	500.
EPS24	5¢	150.	225.	300.	600.
EPS25	10¢	175.	300.	450.	850.
EPS26	12¢	300.	550.	1000.	1500.
EPS27	24¢	1200.	2000.	3000.	4500.
EPS28	30¢	1500.	3000.	4000.	5500.
EPS29	90¢	2500.	5000.	9000.	12,500.

(Large Ayer's)

KL#	Denom.	Fine	VF	XF	AU
EPS30	3¢	275.	400.	750.	1000.
EPS31	10¢	450.	700.	1000.	1500.

Bailey & Co., Philadelphia

KL#	Denom.	Fine	VF	XF	AU
EPS32	1¢	375.	550.	1000.	1500.
EPS33	3¢	375.	550.	1000.	1500.
EPS34	5¢	400.	650.	1300.	1800.
EPS35	10¢	400.	600.	1250.	1750.
EPS36	12¢	1000.	1500.	2500.	4000.

Joseph L. Bates

"Fancy Goods" as two words

KL#	Denom.	Fine	VF	XF	AU
EPS37	1¢	150.	225.	300.	600.
EPS38	3¢	350.	675.	850.	1100.
EPS39	10¢	200.	375.	600.	900.
EPS40	12¢	300.	550.	1000.	1500.

Joseph L. Bates
"Fancy Goods" as one word

KL#	Denom.	Fine	VF	XF	AU
EPS41	1¢	150.	225.	300.	600.
EPS42	3¢	300.	450.	650.	900.
EPS43	10¢	200.	375.	600.	900.

Brown's Bronchial Troches

KL#	Denom.	Fine	VF	XF	AU
EPS44	1¢	225.	375.	550.	700.
EPS45	3¢	175.	300.	400.	500.
EPS46	5¢	175.	300.	400.	600.
EPS47	10¢	250.	375.	500.	850.
EPS48	12¢	600.	1000.	1400.	2000.

F. Buhl & Co., Detroit

KL#	Denom.	Fine	VF	XF	AU
EPS49	1¢	400.	650.	1100.	1500.
EPS50	3¢	400.	700.	1250.	1750.
EPS51	5¢	400.	650.	1100.	1500.
EPS52	10¢	750.	1000.	2000.	2500.
EPS53	12¢	750.	1500.	2000.	3000.

Burnett's Cocoaine Kalliston

KL#	Denom.	Fine	VF	XF	AU
EPS54	1¢	150.	250.	375.	650.
EPS55	3¢	125.	175.	275.	550.
EPS56	5¢	150.	300.	425.	650.
EPS57	10¢	200.	550.	800.	1250.
EPS58	12¢	300.	550.	1000.	1500.
EPS59	24¢	1500.	2000.	3000.	4500.
EPS60	30¢	1750.	3000.	4000.	5500.
EPS61	90¢	2500.	5000.	9000.	12,500.

Burnett's Cooking Extracts
(Plain frame)

KL#	Denom.	Fine	VF	XF	AU
EPS62	1¢	150.	250.	375.	600.
EPS63	3¢	150.	275.	425.	700.
EPS64	5¢	150.	250.	375.	600.
EPS65	10¢	200.	375.	550.	1000.
EPS66	12¢	300.	550.	1000.	1500.
EPS67	24¢	1500.	2000.	3000.	4500.
EPS68	30¢	1750.	3000.	4000.	5500.
EPS69	90¢	2500.	5000.	9000.	10,500.

(Ribbed frame)

KL#	Denom.	Fine	VF	XF	AU
EPS70	10¢	350.	650.	800.	1250.

A.M. Claflin, Hopkinton, R.I.

KL#	Denom.	Fine	VF	XF	AU
EPS71	1¢	3000.	6250.	12,750.	18,000.
EPS72	3¢	3000.	4000.	6000.	10,000.
EPS73	5¢	3000.	4000.	6000.	10,000.
EPS74	12¢	3000.	5000.	7500.	12,500.

H.A. Cook, Evansville, Ind.

KL#	Denom.	Fine	VF	XF	AU
EPS75	5¢	350.	650.	1300.	1500.
EPS76	10¢	600.	1200.	2500.	3500.

Dougan, New York

KL#	Denom.	Fine	VF	XF	AU
EPS77	1¢	800.	1500.	2500.	3500.
EPS78	3¢	800.	1500.	2500.	3500.
EPS79	5¢	600.	1000.	2000.	3000.
EPS80	10¢	1000.	2000.	3000.	4000.

Drake's Plantation Bitters, New York

KL#	Denom.	Fine	VF	XF	AU
EPS81	1¢	175.	225.	300.	600.
EPS82	3¢	125.	275.	400.	650.
EPS83	5¢	200.	300.	400.	650.
EPS84	10¢	225.	375.	550.	850.
EPS85	12¢	300.	550.	1000.	1500.
EPS86	24¢	1500.	2500.	3000.	4500.
EPS87	30¢	2000.	3000.	4000.	5500.
EPS88	90¢	2750.	5500.	9000.	12,500.

Ellis, McAlpin & Co., Cincinnati

KL#	Denom.	Fine	VF	XF	AU
EPS89	1¢	600.	1250.	1850.	2500.
EPS90	3¢	600.	1250.	1750.	2500.
EPS91	5¢	800.	1650.	2300.	3200.
EPS92	10¢	600.	1250.	1750.	2500.
EPS93	12¢	800.	1500.	2250.	3500.
EPS94	24¢	1200.	2000.	3000.	4500.

G.G. Evans, Philadelphia

KL#	Denom.	Fine	VF	XF	AU
EPS95	1¢	300.	600.	900.	1750.
EPS96	3¢	400.	700.	1000.	1750.
EPS97	5¢	450.	750.	1250.	2000.
EPS98	10¢	450.	750.	1250.	2000.

J. Gault
(Plain frame)

KL#	Denom.	Fine	VF	XF	AU
EPS99	1¢	150.	225.	300.	600.
EPS100	2¢	-	12,000.	-	-
EPS101	3¢	150.	250.	350.	600.
EPS102	5¢	150.	250.	375.	700.
EPS103	10¢	200.	300.	500.	850.
EPS104	12¢	300.	550.	1000.	1500.
EPS105	24¢	1250.	2000.	3000.	4500.
EPS106	30¢	1500.	3000.	4000.	5500.
EPS107	90¢	2500.	5000.	9000.	12,500.

(Ribbed frame)

KL#	Denom.	Fine	VF	XF	AU
EPS108	1¢	400.	700.	1000.	1250.

KL#	Denom.	Fine	VF	XF	AU
EPS109	3¢	400.	700.	1000.	1250.
EPS110	5¢	275.	450.	600.	800.
EPS111	10¢	300.	550.	700.	900.
EPS112	12¢	500.	800.	1500.	2000.
EPS113	24¢	1500.	2750.	3500.	5000.
EPS114	30¢	1750.	3000.	4000.	5500.

L. C. Hopkins & Co., Cincinnati

KL#	Denom.	Fine	VF	XF	AU
EPS115	1¢	700.	1250.	1750.	2500.
EPS116	3¢	600.	1150.	1500.	2250.
EPS117	5¢	800.	1500.	2250.	3250.
EPS118	10¢	700.	1250.	1750.	2500.

Irving House, N.Y. (Hunt & Nash)

(Plain frame)

KL#	Denom.	Fine	VF	XF	AU
EPS119	1¢	150.	250.	350.	650.
EPS120	3¢	150.	250.	350.	550.
EPS121	5¢	400.	700.	1000.	1250.
EPS122	10¢	200.	300.	450.	850.
EPS123	12¢	300.	550.	1000.	1500.
EPS124	24¢	1250.	2000.	3000.	4500.
EPS125	30¢	1500.	3000.	4000.	5500.
126	1¢	750.	700.	2500.	1250.

(Ribbed frame)

KL#	Denom.	Fine	VF	XF	AU
EPS127	3¢	400.	700.	1000.	1250.
EPS128	5¢	450.	750.	1500.	2100.
EPS129	10¢	350.	550.	750.	900.
EPS130	12¢	500.	800.	1500.	2000.
EPS131	24¢	1500.	2750.	3500.	5000.

Kirkpatrick & Gault, New York

KL#	Denom.	Fine	VF	XF	AU
EPS132	1¢	150.	225.	300.	600.
EPS133	3¢	125.	200.	275.	550.
EPS134	5¢	175.	350.	500.	750.
EPS135	10¢	200.	300.	500.	850.
EPS136	12¢	300.	550.	1000.	1500.
EPS137	24¢	1250.	2000.	3000.	4500.
EPS138	30¢	1500.	3000.	4000.	5500.
EPS139	90¢	2500.	5000.	9000.	12,500.

Lord & Taylor, New York

KL#	Denom.	Fine	VF	XF	AU
EPS140	1¢	400.	650.	1250.	1750.
EPS141	3¢	400.	650.	1250.	1750.
EPS142	5¢	400.	650.	1250.	1750.
EPS143	10¢	400.	700.	1500.	2250.
EPS144	12¢	800.	1500.	2000.	3500.
EPS145	24¢	1500.	2500.	3500.	5000.
EPS146	30¢	2000.	4000.	5000.	7000.
EPS147	90¢	4000.	7500.	9000.	13,500.

Mendum's Family Wine Emporium, New York
(Plain frame)

KL#	Denom.	Fine	VF	XF	AU
EPS148	1¢	250.	350.	500.	900.
EPS149	3¢	350.	500.	800.	1250.
EPS150	5¢	300.	450.	600.	1200.
EPS151	10¢	300.	450.	700.	1250.
EPS152	12¢	650.	1250.	1750.	2500.

(Ribbed frame)

KL#	Denom.	Fine	VF	XF	AU
EPS153	10¢	400.	700.	1000.	1750.

B. F. Miles, Peoria

KL#	Denom.	Fine	VF	XF	AU
EPS154	5¢	3500.	7000.	9000.	12,000.

John W. Norris, Chicago

KL#	Denom.	Fine	VF	XF	AU
EPS155	1¢	750.	1000.	1700.	2750.
EPS156	3¢	1000.	1750.	3000.	4000.
EPS157	5¢	1000.	1750.	3000.	4000.
EPS158	10¢	1000.	1750.	3000.	4000.

North America Life Insurance Co.,
(Straight "Insurance")

KL#	Denom.	Fine	VF	XF	AU
EPS159	1¢	175.	250.	350.	700.
EPS160	3¢	175.	250.	350.	700.
EPS161	10¢	200.	375.	600.	1000.
EPS162	12¢	450.	1000.	1500.	2250.

(Curved "Insurance", trial piece)

KL#	Denom.	Fine	VF	XF	AU
EPS163	1¢	225.	500.	1000.	1500.
EPS164	10¢	300.	500.	750.	1250.

Pearce, Tolle & Holton, Cincinnati

KL#	Denom.	Fine	VF	XF	AU
EPS165	1¢	1000.	1750.	3000.	4000.
EPS166	3¢	800.	1500.	2500.	3500.
EPS167	5¢	1000.	1750.	3000.	4000.
EPS168	10¢	1100.	2000.	3500.	4750.

Sands' Ale

KL#	Denom.	Fine	VF	XF	AU
EPS169	5¢	800.	1500.	2500.	3500.
EPS170	10¢	1000.	1750.	2750.	4000.
EPS171	30¢	2000.	3500.	5000.	7500.

S. Steinfeld, New York

KL#	Denom.	Fine	VF	XF	AU
EPS182	1¢	1000.	1700.	2500.	3500.
EPS183	10¢	1000.	1600.	2500.	3500.
EPS184	12¢	1000.	1750.	2750.	4500.

Schapker & Bussing, Evansville, Ind.

KL#	Denom.	Fine	VF	XF	AU
EPS172	1¢	400.	700.	1000.	1750.
EPS173	3¢	225.	350.	600.	1000.
EPS174	5¢	450.	750.	1250.	2000.
EPS175	10¢	450.	800.	1250.	2000.
EPS176	12¢	500.	1250.	1750.	2750.

N. G. Taylor & Co., Philadelphia

KL#	Denom.	Fine	VF	XF	AU
EPS185	1¢	800.	1250.	1900.	2500.
EPS186	3¢	800.	1250.	1750.	2500.
EPS187	5¢	800.	1500.	2000.	2750.
EPS188	10¢	800.	1250.	1750.	2500.

John Shillito & Co., Cincinnati

KL#	Denom.	Fine	VF	XF	AU
EPS177	1¢	400.	700.	1000.	1750.
EPS178	3¢	250.	350.	600.	1000.
EPS179	5¢	250.	450.	900.	1250.
EPS180	10¢	275.	425.	750.	1250.
EPS181	12¢	500.	1250.	1750.	2750.

Tremont House (Gage Brothers & Drake), Chicago

KL#	Denom.	Fine	VF	XF	AU
EPS189	1¢	150.	225.	300.	600.
EPS190	5¢	150.	300.	375.	650.
EPS191	10¢	200.	325.	450.	850.
EPS192	12¢	350.	600.	1250.	2000.

Weir & Larminie, Montreal

KL#	Denom.	Fine	VF	XF	AU
EPS193	1¢	450.	750.	1250.	2000.
EPS194	3¢	400.	700.	1000.	1750.
EPS195	5¢	500.	800.	1500.	2250.
EPS196	10¢	600.	900.	1700.	2500.

White the Hatter, New York

KL#	Denom.	Fine	VF	XF	AU
EPS197	1¢	750.	1000.	1900.	3000.
EPS198	3¢	800.	1500.	2500.	3500.
EPS199	5¢	900.	1750.	3000.	4000.
EPS200	10¢	800.	1500.	2500.	3500.

Postage Stamp Envelopes

By R.B. White

The introduction to these pages gives the background of the financial times preceding the introduction of Fractional Currency. In mid-1862, hard money was fast disappearing from circulation and postage stamps were pressed into service as a means of making small change.

The Postmaster General in hi s December report of 1862 said: "In the first quarter of the current year, ending September 20th, the number of stamps issued to postmasters was one hundred and four million dollars; there were calls for about two hundred millions, which would have been nearly sufficient to meet usual demands for the year. This extraordinary demand arose from the temporary use of these stamps as a currency for the public in lieu of the smaller denominations of specie, and ceased with the introduction of the so-called 'postal currency'."

But stamps were ill-suited for the wear and tear of commerce and at least in the early part of this period, the post office refused to exchange them for new issues. Before Gault produced his encased postage or the die-sinkers had produced their "copperheads" (more commonly now known as Civil War Tokens), a few enterprising printers produced small envelopes, approximately 70 x 35 mm in size, labeled with the value of the stamps contained and usually with an advertising message either for themselves or for some local merchant. This was mainly confined to the larger cities of the east. New York City had by far the most pieces, but Brooklyn, Boston, Albany, Cincinnati, Jersey City and Philadelphia are also represented.

The New York Central Railroad, in addition to envelopes, issued a stiff card with two slots by which the stamp or stamps are captured.

Some of these envelopes have the value of the stamps printed on them, others have blank spaces for hand written values. Occasionally the printed values are changed by hand.

The issues of J. Leach, stationer and printer in New York City, are by far the most common. They have been seen in five distinct types with multiple denominations within the types.

The first listing of Civil War postage stamp envelopes was published by Henry Russell Drowne in the *American Journal of Numismatics* in 1918. That article, primarily based on the Moreau hoard of 77 envelopes, reported that these pieces "were variously printed with black, blue, red and green ink on white, amber, lemon, pink, orange, violet, blue pale green, buff, manilla and brown paper." Red and blue ink on white paper was the most popular combination. Wood cuts and electrotypes were employed in the manufacture. One single piece bears a picture of Washington. All of the envelopes show evidence of having been hastily made and printed.

In the listings which follow, spaces have been left in the numbering system to accommodate future finds. No claim is made that the list is complete.

These pieces are all extremely rare. The most common probably having no more than half a dozen extant pieces. The pricing thus reflects the rarity of the firm name and the desirability of the design, legend and value. Drowne reported that the 25cts denomination is "by far the most common, about half as many are for 50cts, and a quarter for 10cts and 75 cts." All prices are for the envelope only; stamps may be included but there is really no way of knowing that they are original with the envelopes. Any stamps will increase the total value by their own philatelic value. Prices are for intact envelopes in very fine condition with no problems. Front-only specimens appear frequently and bring only 15% to 30% of the prices shown. A total of 110 different numbers are listed here; it is doubtful that 500 pieces total of all types still exist.

In the numbering system, a first number is assigned for each firm name or known major design type within that firm. The second number of the system is the stated value of the envelope in cents (blank value shown by 0); "hw" following the second number means the value was hand written. A question mark means that the value of the piece has not been reported. "Vars" means that minor varieties exist.

KL#	Name, address and notations	Value
1	H. Armstrong, Hosiery, Laces, etc 140 6th Ave, (NYC)	700.
3-?	Arthur, Gregory & Co., Stationer 39 Nassau St. NYC	650.
3-50	Arthur, Gregory & Co., Stationer 39 Nassau St. NYC	650.

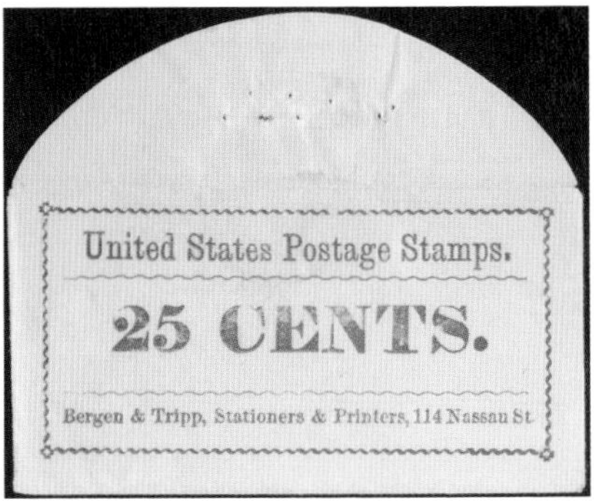

KL#	Name, address and notations	Value
5-25	Bergen & Tripp, Stationer 114 Nassau St, (NYC)	650.
7-25	Berlin & Jones, Stationer 134 William St, NYC	-
9-15	Joseph Bryan, Clothing 214 Fulton St, Brooklyn	650.

KL#	Name, address and notations	Value

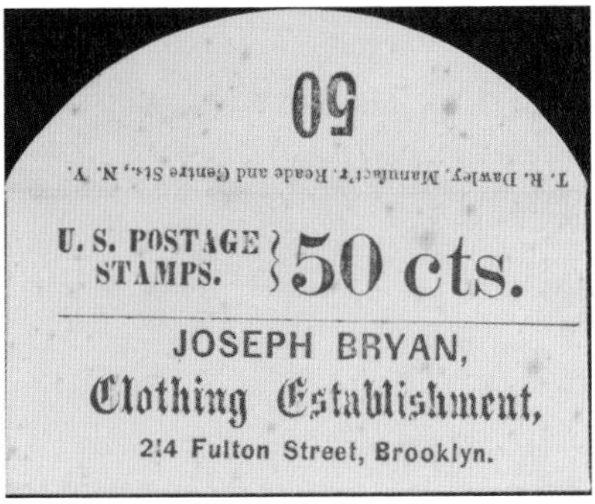

KL#	Name, address and notations	Value
9-50	Joseph Bryan, Clothing 214 Fulton St, Brooklyn	650.
11-25	P.D. Braisted, Jr. Billiards 14-16 4th Ave, NYC	650.
13-50	G.C. Brown, Tobacco 669 Broadway, NYC	650.
15-25	John M. Burnett, Stationer 51 William St, NYC	650.
15-25hw50	John M. Burnett, Stationer 51 William St, NYC	650.
15-50	John M. Burnett, Stationer 51 William St, NYC	650.
17-25	Chas. T. Chickhaus, Tobacco 176 Broadway, NYC	725.

KL#	Name, address and notations	Value
19-?	Clarry & Reilley, Stationer 12-14 Spruce St, NYC	725.
21-50hw25	B.F. Corlies & Macy, Stationer 33 Nassau St, NYC	725.
23-30	Crook & Duff, Bar-Lunch-Dining 39-40 Park Row, (NYC)	800.
25-?	Cutter Tower & Co, Stationer 128 Nassau St, NYC	650.

KL#	Name, address and notations	Value
27-25	Dawley, Stationer & Printer 28, 30 & 32 Center St, NYC	650.

KL#	Name, address and notations	Value
28-50	T.R. Dawley, Printer Cor. Reade & Center Streets, NYC	-
29-0hw25	Mad (Ame) A. Doubet, Importer 697 & 951 Broadway, (NYC)	725.
31-25	Francis Duffy, Oysters & Dining 239-241 8th Ave, (NYC)	-
33-25	Embree, Stationer 130 Grand St, (NYC)	650.
34-50	Jno. C. Force Brooklyn	800.
35-25	Fox's Old Bowery Theatre (NYC)	800.
37-?	German Opera 485 Broadway, NYC	800.
39-75	Gould's Dining Rooms 35 Nassau St, NYC	650.
40-50	Arthur Gregory NYC	800.
41-25	Harlem & NY Navigation Co Sylvan Shore & Sylvan Grove, (NYC) "LEGAL CURRENCY"	850.
43-5	Harpel, Printers Cincinnati	725.
45-10	Irving House, Hotel Broadway & 12th St, NYC	650.
47-25	James, Hatter 525 Broadway, (NYC)	650.
49-0	Hamilton Johnston, Stationer 545 Broadway, (NYC) G. Washington portrait	825.

KL#	Name, address and notations	Value
51-25	C.O. Jones, Stationer 76 Cedar St, NYC	650.
53-25	Kaiser & Waters, Stationer 104 Fulton St, NYC	650.
53-50	Kaiser & Waters, Stationer 104 Fulton St, NYC	650.
55-60	Kavanagh & Freeman, Billards 10th & Broadway, NYC	725.
57-50	Lansingh's Gent's Furnishings Albany	650.
57-25	Lansingh's Gent's Furnishings Albany	650.
57-25	Wm. Murphy, Stationer 438 Canal St, NYC	

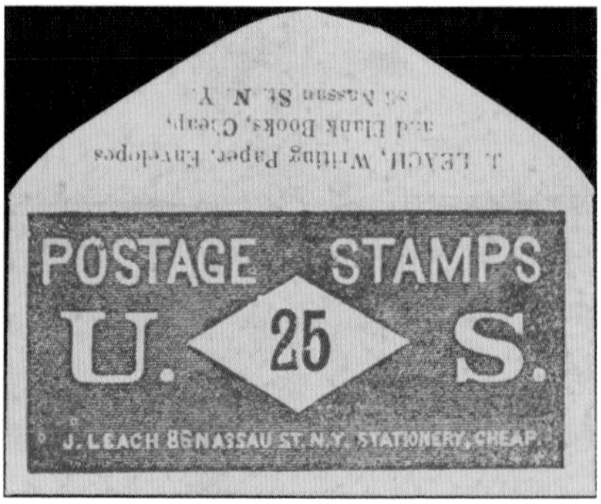

KL#	Name, address and notations	Value
59-25	J. Leach, Stationer 86 Nassau St, NYC Value in central diamond(vars.)	575.
59-10	J. Leach, Stationer 86 Nassau St, NYC Value in central diamond(vars.)	575.
59-15	J. Leach, Stationer 86 Nassau St, NYC Value in central diamond(vars.)	650.

KL#	Name, address and notations	Value
59-20	J. Leach, Stationer 86 Nassau St, NYC Value in central diamond(vars.)	575.

KL#	Name, address and notations	Value
59-50	J. Leach, Stationer 86 Nassau St, NYC Value in central diamond(vars.)	575.

KL#	Name, address and notations	Value
59-30	J. Leach, Stationer 86 Nassau St, NYC Value in central diamond(vars.)	650.

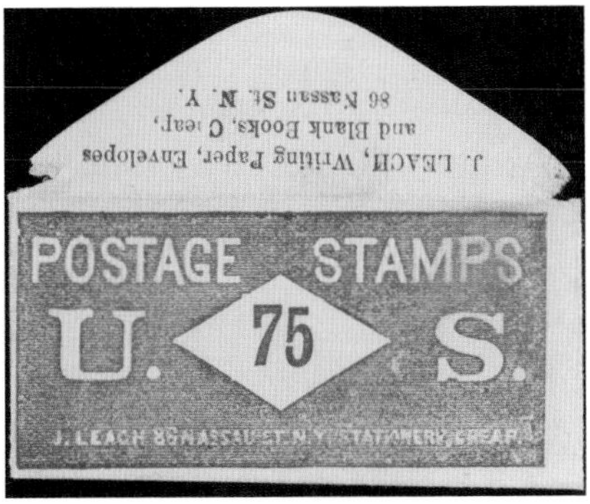

KL#	Name, address and notations	Value
59-75	J. Leach, Stationer 86 Nassau St, NYC Value in central diamond(vars.)	

KL#	Name, address and notations	Value
60-50	J. Leach 86 Nassau St., N.Y. Eagle between "U" and "S" (vars.)	575.

KL#	Name, address and notations	Value
60-15	J. Leach 86 Nassau St., N.Y. Eagle between "U" and "S" (vars.)	575.

KL#	Name, address and notations	Value
60-25	J. Leach 86 Nassau St., N.Y. Eagle between "U" and "S" (vars.)	
61-25	J. Leach 86 Nassau St., N.Y. Large central oval with value (vars.)	575.
61-50	J. Leach 86 Nassau St., N.Y. Large central oval with value (vars.)	575.

KL#	Name, address and notations	Value
62-25	J. Leach 86 Nassau St., N.Y. denomination between flags	575.
63-50	J. Leach 86 Nassau St., N.Y. Denomination in oval, flag left, shield right	-
71-75	D.W. Lee, Stationer 82 Nassau St, NYC	575.
72-0	R. Letson, Mercantile Dining Room, 256 Broadway, NYC	-

KL#	Name, address and notations	Value
73-25	J.W. Lingard, New Bowery Theatre, (NYC)	650.
74-25	Macoy & Herwig, Stationers 112-114 Broadway, (NYC)	650.
75-20	Hy Maillards, Confectionery 621 Broadway, (NYC)	650.

KL#	Name, address and notations	Value
75-25	Hy Maillards, Confectionery 621 Broadway, (NYC)	650.
77-25	Frank McElroy, Stationers 113 Nassau St, (NYC)	650.
81-10	Metropolitan Hotel NYC	650.
83-25	Miller & Grant, Importers, Laces 703 Broadway, NYC	725.
85-50	W.H. Murphy (by D. Murphy's Sons) Stationers, 372 Pearl St, NYC	650.
89-25	National Express Co. 74 Broadway, NYC	800.

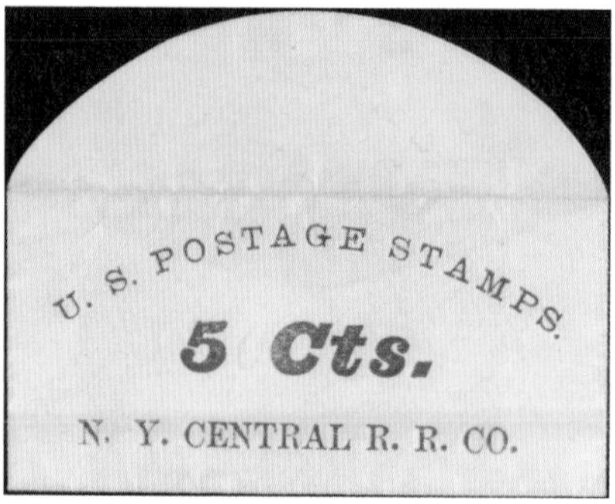

KL#	Name, address and notations	Value
93-05	New York Central Railroad (N.Y.C.R.R.) NYC	-
93-20	New York Central Railroad (N.Y.C.R.R.) NYC	725.
93-25	New York Central Railroad (N.Y.C.R.R.) NYC	700.

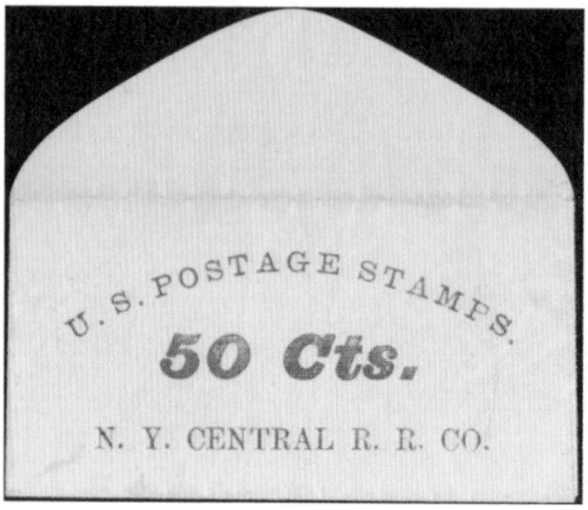

KL#	Name, address and notations	Value
93-50	New York Central Railroad (N.Y.C.R.R.) NYC	700.
95-50	N.Y. Consolidated Stage Co. (NYC)	725.
97-50	Same except Ravel Troupe (NYC)	725.
97-25	Niblos Garden - Wm Wheatley (Edwin Forrest) (NYC)	725.
101-10	Nixon's Cremorne Garden, Palace of Music, 14th and 6th Ave, (NYC)	975.

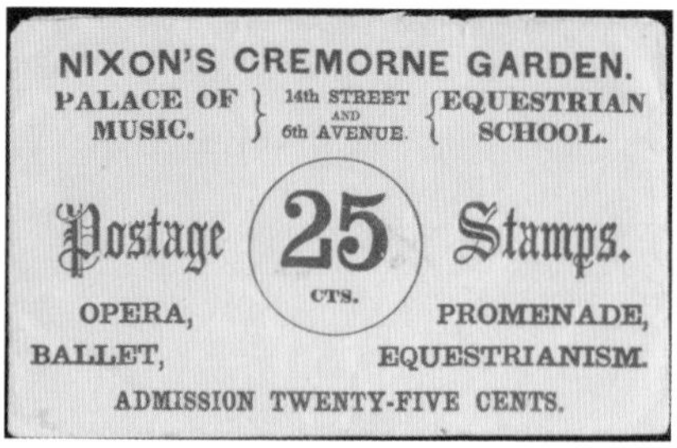

KL#	Name, address and notations	Value
101-25	Hand stamp appears to read "CREMORNE (GARD)EN"	725.
101-25hw10		725.

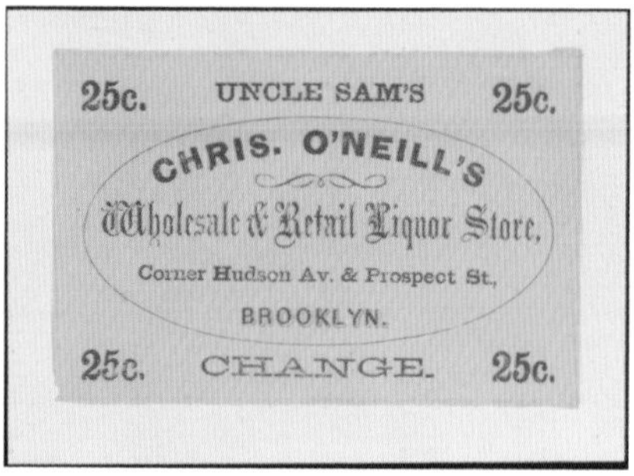

KL#	Name, address and notations	Value
103-25	Chris O'Neills, Liquors Hudson Ave, Brooklyn "UNCLE SAM'S CHANGE"	800.

KL#	Name, address and notations	Value
105-25	Oyster Bay House 553 Broadway, NYC	650.
107-25	The Oyster House 604 Broadway, NYC	650.
108-0hw25	Paulding's Express	-
109-0	Pettit & Crook's Dining Rooms 136 Water St, NYC "UNCLE SAM'S CHANGE"	800.

KL#	Name, address and notations	Value

KL#	Name, address and notations	Value
111-50	Pomroy's 699 Broadway, NYC	650.
113-50	Power, Bogardus & Co., Steamship Line Pier 34, No. River, NYC	700.
115-50	S. Raynor, Envelope Manuf'r 118 William St, NYC	650.

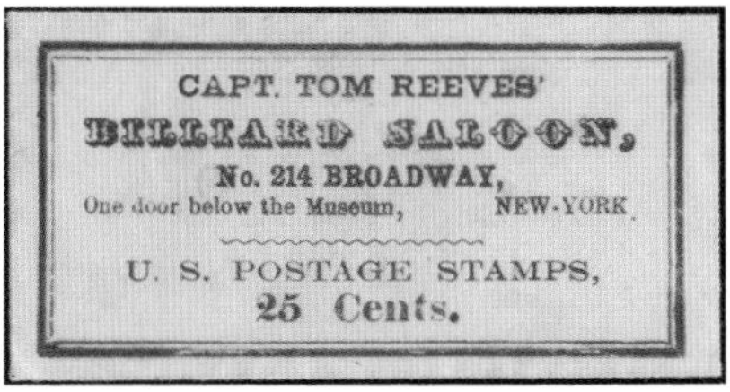

KL#	Name, address and notations	Value
117-25	Capt. Tom Reeves, Billards 214 Broadway, NYC	800.

KL#	Name, address and notations	Value
119-25	Revere House 604-608 Broadway, NYC	650.
121-25	Thomas Richardson, Chop Steak & Oyster House 66 Maiden Lane, NYC	650.
122-50	E.M. Riggin, Sanford House 336 Delaware Ave., Pine St. Wharf, Philadelphia	650.

KL#	Name, address and notations	Value

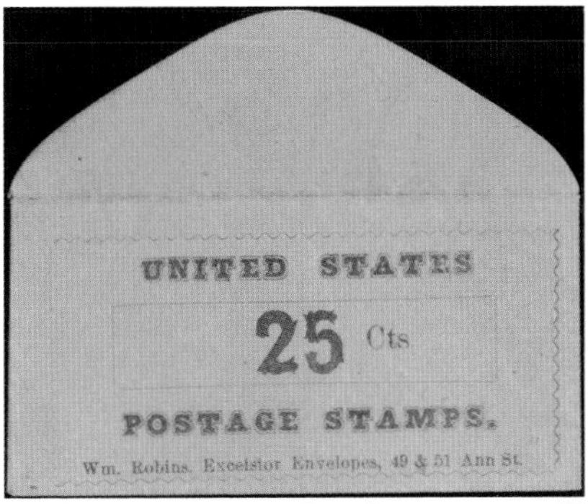

KL#	Name, address and notations	Value
123-25	Wm Robins, Excelsion Envelope Manufactory 51 Ann St, NYC	575.
125-25	R. Scovel, Stationer 26 Nassau St, (NYC)	650.
126-25	Reuben Scovel "GOVERNMENT CURRENCY" 26 Nassau St, (NYC)	650.
126-50	Reuben Scovel "GOVERNMENT CURRENCY" 26 Nassau St, (NYC)	650.

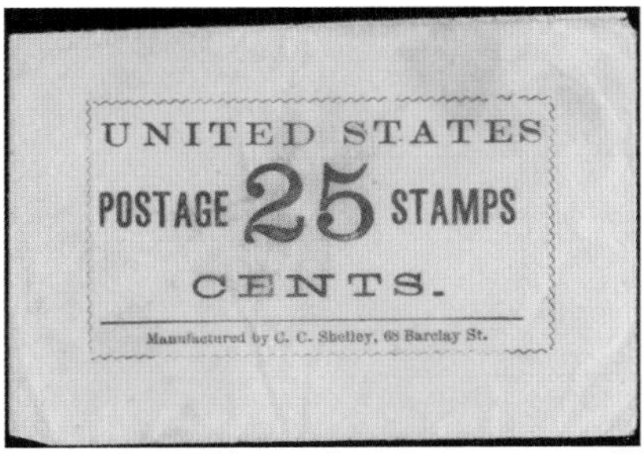

KL#	Name, address and notations	Value
127-25	C.C. Shelley, Stationer 68 Barclay St, NYC	650.
127-50	C.C. Shelley, Stationer 68 Barclay St, NYC	650.
128-13	H. Smith, Stationer 137 Williams St, NYC Denomination in oval, flag left, shield right (vars.)	575.

KL#	Name, address and notations	Value
128-10	H. Smith, Stationer 137 Williams St, NYC Denomination in oval, flag left, shield right (vars.)	-

KL#	Name, address and notations	Value
128-20	H. Smith, Stationer 137 Williams St, NYC Denomination in oval, flag left, shield right (vars.)	650.

KL#	Name, address and notations	Value
128-25	H. Smith, Stationer 137 Williams St, NYC Denomination in oval, flag left, shield right (vars.)	575.

KL#	Name, address and notations	Value
128-50	H. Smith, Stationer 137 Williams St, NYC Denomination in oval, flag left, shield right (vars.)	575.
129-10hw10	H. Smith, Stationer 137 Williams St, NYC Fancy border, no flag, denomination below postage stamps	-

KL#	Name, address and notations	Value
129-15hw50	H. Smith, Stationer 137 Williams St, NYC Fancy border, no flag, denomination below postage stamps	575.
129-50	H. Smith, Stationer 137 Williams St, NYC Fancy border, no flag, denomination below postage stamps	575.
130-0	Snow & Hapgood 22 Court St., Boston (vars.)	700.
130-10	Snow & Hapgood 22 Court St., Boston (vars.)	700.
130-15	Snow & Hapgood 22 Court St., Boston (vars.)	700.

KL#	Name, address and notations	Value
130-25	Snow & Hapgood 22 Court St., Boston (vars.)	700.
130-50	Snow & Hapgood 22 Court St., Boston (vars.)	700.
130-75	Snow & Hapgood 22 Court St., Boston (vars.)	700.
131-25	Sonneborn, Stationer 130 Nassau St., NYC (vars.)	650.
133-25	Taylor's Hotel Exchange Place, Jersey City (vars.)	725.
133-50	Taylor's Hotel Exchange Place, Jersey City (vars.)	725.
135-10	Dion Thomas, Stationer 142 Nassau St, NYC	725.

KL#	Name, address and notations	Value
137-25	R.D. Thompson, Stationer 104 Fulton St, NYC (vars.)	650.
139-25	G.W. & S. Turney 77 Chatham St, NYC	650.
140-0	S.C. Upham 403 Chestnut St., Phil.	650.

KL#	Name, address and notations	Value
141-25	James Wiley, Wines & Liquors 307 Broadway, NYC	650.
141-50	James Wiley, Wines & Liquors 307 Broadway, NYC	650.

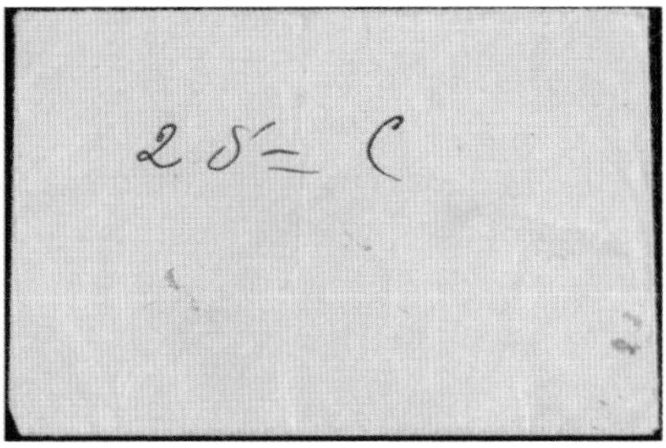

KL#	Name, address and notations	Value
151-25	Blank - marked by hand Envelope was perhaps hand made	500.
152-10	U.S. POSTAGE STAMPS 10 CENTS	-
153-20	U.S. POSTAGE STAMPS 20 CENTS	500.

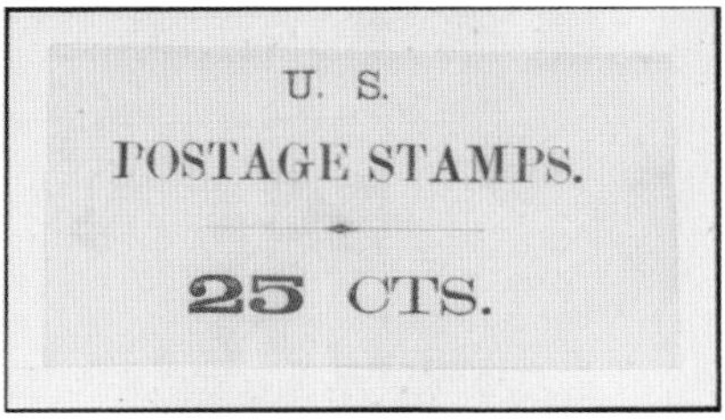

KL#	Name, address and notations	Value
155-25	U.S. POSTAGE STAMPS 25 CENTS (vars.)	500.

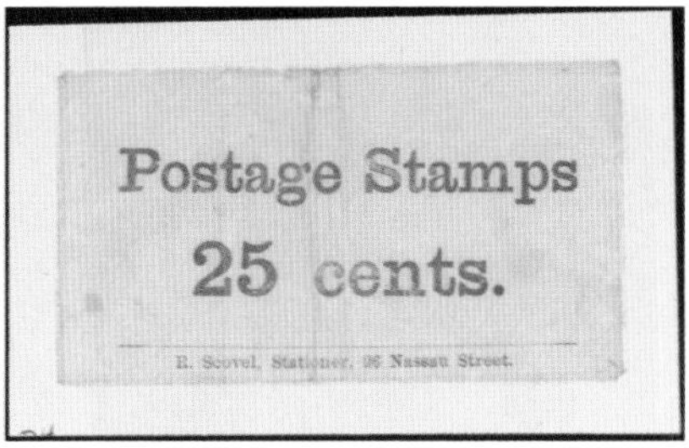

KL#	Name, address and notations	Value
156-25	POSTAGE STAMPS 25 CENTS	500.
157-25	"UNITED STATES POSTAGE STAMPS" in oval	500.
157-30	U.S. POSTAGE STAMPS 30 CENTS	500.

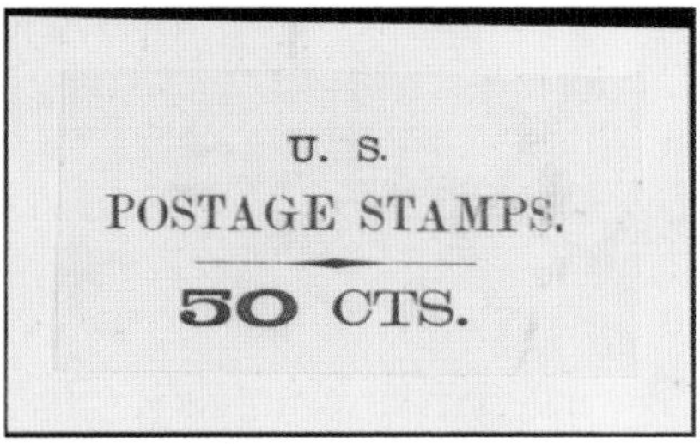

KL#	Name, address and notations	Value
159-50	U.S. POSTAGE STAMPS 50 CENTS (vars.)	500.

KL#	Name, address and notations	Value
161-75	U.S. POSTAGE STAMPS 75 CENTS	500.
163-75hw90	U.S. POSTAGE STAMPS 90 CENTS Hand changed from 75 cents.	650.

Fractional Currency Valuations

Paper Money Substitutes of the Civil War

The collector's first encounter with U.S. Postage and Fractional Currency invariably provokes two questions: What is it? Why was it issued? How was it used?

The first question is easily answered. Postage and Fractional Currency is genuine paper money of the United States issued during the 1862-1875 period in denominations of 3, 5, 10, 15, 25 and 50 cents.

Why paper money in denominations of less than the familiar dollar unit was required in commerce is less easily answered. The causes of this unusual issue of official "paper coins" at a time when people still demanded coins of high intrinsic value can only be found in the jumble of cause and effect that has been the catalyst of numismatic history from time immemorial.

It would be convenient to state, as has frequently been done, that within a few days of the outbreak of the Civil War all of the gold, silver and copper coins in circulation disappeared due to the desire of the timid to save something of universal value from the threatened wreck of the Union, and of the avaricious to hoard something which would possibly increase in value. Undoubtedly, fear and greed acted at once to trigger the hoarding instinct in some individuals, but on the whole, such an observation seems to be overdrawn. Contemporary newspaper accounts make little mention of a serious coin shortage until early in 1862.

It would appear that the initial hoarding of hard money was caused by little more than an ingrained distrust of paper money, an attitude more than justified by the nation's experience with non-metallic currency up to that time. The Yankee worker, whose livelihood was completely bound to the money earned tending the lathes and forges of the industrialized North, simply felt more secure when his paper wages had been converted to gold and silver. Consequently, he gave a cool reception to "Greenbacks," which could not be redeemed for either gold or silver and were suspiciously regarded as "faith paper." The reception grew progressively colder as the flood of paper dollars increased.

This expressed preference for coins inevitably depreciated Greenbacks in terms of the gold standard. Gold coins commanded a premium of three percent over U.S. and state paper money in January, 1862, the month following the general suspension of specie payment by banks and the Federal Treasury; six percent in June, 1862; 15 percent in July, and 32 percent by the end of 1862. Thereafter the depreciation of Greenbacks accelerated, until at one point in 1864 it required $285 in paper to purchase $100 in gold. The distrust of the Government's fiat paper was also maintained by the snowballing national debt, which reached its high-point of the war - $ 2.8 billion - in 1865.

A monetary situation whereby gold commanded a substantial premium over a like face value of paper dollars swiftly drove gold coins from commercial channels, effectively removing the United States from a gold standard. It also created a favorable condition for the exporting of silver coins, which disappeared from the marketplace, but at a less precipitous pace than gold.

In 1858 Canada had adopted a decimal system of coinage with a dollar unit similar to that of the United States. In lieu of a sufficient quantity of decimal coinage of British origin, Canada unofficially adopted the coinage of the United States and used it widely in domestic trade. The West Indies and many Latin American countries also imported large quantities of U.S. silver coinage for domestic use. Disappearance of gold from American trade channels and the willingness of foreign users of U.S. silver coins to pay for them with gold combined to produce a legal and highly profitable bullion trade which speculators and bankers found irresistible.

The discounting of Greenbacks in terms of gold enabled the exchange of paper money for silver coins, which were then exchanged for gold in Canada, the West Indies or Latin America. The gold was then returned to the United States, where it was used to purchase more Greenbacks at the metal's high premium rate. A safer round-robin to riches can hardly be imagined. Even in times of national crisis, pragmatic profit taking will attract more adherents than an idealistic consideration for the national good. During the last week of June and the first week of July, 1862, more than $25 million in subsidiary coins vanished from circulation in the North. The shortage of silver coins, particularly in the eastern United States, would not be relieved until the summer of 1876.

Illogically, the Philadelphia Mint continued a small but steady production of silver coins during the 1861 Although they were of no use to the nation's economy. Bullion dealers obtained them directly from the Mint and . sped them abroad. In 1863, nearly the entire production of silver coins was exported.

The withdrawal of subsidiary silver coins in the summer of 1862 all but paralyzed the institutions and practice of everyday commerce. The smallest denominations of official money available were discounted $5 Legal Tender Notes and the copper-nickel cents which had been fed into circulation in great quantities to retire demonetized Spanish silver coins and the large copper cents.

When first forced upon the public in 1857, the copper-nickel cent, which was intrinsically worth about 60 percent of face value, had been considered a nuisance; it was regularly discounted three percent and more in large transactions. But with the disappearance of silver coins, the ugly duckling became the belle of the ball. The erstwhile nuisance became the only alternative to walking, or going without a newspaper, or buying a pound of pomegranates and receiving change in kumquats and quince. Cents were bundled in bags of 25, 50 and 100 in a hopeless attempt to bridge the gap between the 1-cent piece and the $5 bill. By March 1863, the lowly cent commanded a premium of 20 percent, but few could be found.

The disappearance of nearly all official coinage from trade channels resulted in an outpouring of private emergency monies, some hoary with tradition, others as new and untried as the inspiration which gave them form. State bank notes of $1 and $2 denominations were cut into fractional parts. Other banks issued notes in denominations of $1.25, $1.50 and $1.75. Eastern cities issued their own fractional notes. Merchants, reviving a practice prevalent during the coin shortages of 1837 and 1857, made change in their own promissory notes or "shinplasters," which were notes of small value, redeemable in merchandise at the issuer's place of business. Unscrupulous merchants made change with their own notes even when they had sufficient specie on hand, knowing that the notes were not likely to be presented for redemption by other than their regular neighborhood customers. In like manner, private issues of the eminently collectible Civil War tokens began.

Most novel of the emergency monies called into use was the common postage stamp. The use of postage stamps as a low denomination medium of exchange was not a success, but it led directly to the issuing of the highly successful Postage and Fractional Currency series.

First issued by the Federal Government in 1847, by the time the Civil War began, the adhesive postage stamp had become a well-established part of the public routine. Inasmuch as they were of official origin, had a constant value throughout the country and were easily obtained, consideration of postage stamps as a medium of exchange for coin-deprived people was inevitable. In early July, 1862, Horace Greeley, publisher of the politically influential *New York Tribune,* suggested that stamps pasted on a half sheet of paper, with the other half folded over the stamps to afford them protection from wear, would make an excellent coin substitute. Other newspapers quickly endorsed the proposal, as did the coin-starved public.

Although there were surely those who attempted to do so, fragile, gummed stamps could not be carried loose in pocket or purse without soon becoming a crumpled, stuck-together, totally useless blob of colored paper.

Methods of affording the stamps a degree of protection were quickly devised. They were pasted on sheets of light vellum paper – with or without a protective flap – which also bore an advertising message and a large numeral indicating the total face value of the stamps. Stamps were also encased in small envelopes, on the outside of which was printed the value of the contents and an advertising message.

It soon became apparent that both methods of preparing stamps for the role of emergency money had as many drawbacks as advantages. Pasting the stamps on sheets of paper did not provide them sufficient protection from wear. Those enclosed in envelopes were better protected, but the method of protection provided an opportunity for petty larceny which wasn't neglected. Few recipients had the time to check the contents of each envelope to determine if it contained the proper denominational total of stamps, or if the stamps were unused, or if rectangles of colored paper had been substituted for the stamps.

The method of stamp packaging which best satisfied the dual requirements of visibility and protection was patented on Aug. 12, 1862, by a New England inventor named John Gault, who encased a single postage stamp in a round brass frame (25 mm in diameter) with a clear mica front piece through which the stamp could be viewed. The reverse of this case bore the advertising message of the participating merchant who purchased a quantity of Gault's "encased postage stamps" as a means of giving his customers the precise change required by their purchases.

Stamps encased by Gault were the 1-, 3-, 5-, 10-, 12-, 24-, 30-, and 90-cent denominations of the Series of 1861-1869. That series also contains a 2-cent and a 15-cent stamp, but the 2-cent stamp wasn't issued until July 6, 1863, and the 15-cent value came along on June 17, 1866. But for the eventual authorization of Postage and Fractional Currency, Gault's encased postage stamps would probably have become the chief means of "spending" postage stamps, although they, too, had their disadvantages. The protective mica shield was easily cracked, and the encased stamps cost the distributing merchant the face value of the stamps, plus about two cents per holder. In view of the 20 percent premium existing on official coins, the additional two cents was of little consequence in the instance of the higher denomination stamps, but in the case of the popular one-cent stamp, it meant an expenditure of three cents for every one-cent encased postage stamp obtained from Gault for monetary use.

The timing of the initiation of Gault's encased stamps also worked against their quantity distribution. At the time of their appearance in midsummer of 1862, the Postmaster General, Montgomery Blair, was still not reconciled to the idea of using postage stamps for money, and was doing his utmost to prevent quantity sales of stamps to anyone desiring them for coinage purposes.

All methods of using stamps for money that had been employed prior to July 17, 1862, suffered the ultimate disadvantage of being illegal, with the consequence that the holder of the stamps could neither redeem them at the post office nor exchange them for Treasury notes.

On that date, however, President Lincoln signed into law a measure proposed in self-defense by Treasury Secretary Salmon P. Chase, providing that "postage and other stamps of the United States" were to be received for all dues to the U.S. and were to be redeemable at any "designated depository" in sums less than $5. The law also prohibited the issue by "any private corporation, banking association, firm, or individual" of any note or token for a sum less than $5 – a provision that was widely ignored as the private sector continued its efforts to overcome a coin shortage in the face of which the Government seemed helpless.

The new law was not without its problems of practicality, either. The post office, already facing a stamp shortage before the gummed bits of paper had been declared legal tender, now had the almost impossible task of providing sufficient stamps for postal use as well as "coinage" use.

In addition, there was the problem of who would redeem nearly exhausted specimens of stamps which had been circulating for some time. Blair refused to take them in trade for new stamps and the Treasury would not exchange them for paper money because they hadn't issued them in the first place.

Blair's obstinacy ultimately melted before the heat of public pressure, and he agreed to redeem the masses of soiled and stuck-together stamps, but he continued to insist that the actual intent of the poorly-written law had been for the Treasury Department to print and distribute special stamps that would bear a general resemblance to postage stamps, but would be of a different design. A compromise was finally worked out whereby the Treasury Department would sell and redeem specially marked stamps which the post office would also accept for postage. Blair agreed to print the special stamps for the Treasury.

Before the stamps could be printed, a further decision was made to issue them in a larger, more convenient size, and to print them on a heavier, ungummed paper. Credit for the final form in which Postage Currency appeared is given to Gen. Francis Spinner, Treasurer of the United States. Spinner pasted unused postage stamps on small sheets of Treasury security paper of uniform size, signed his name to some of them and passed them out to his friends as samples of currency. Congress responded to Spinner's suggestion by authorizing the printing of reproductions of postage stamps on Treasury paper in arrangements patterned after Spinner's models. In this form, the "stamps" ceased to be stamps; they became, in effect, fractional Government promissory notes, a development not authorized by the initial enabling legislation of July 17, 1862. Nonetheless, the notes would be issued without legal authorization until passage of the Act of March 3, 1863, which provided for the issuing of fractional notes by the Federal Government.

Five issues of Postage and Fractional Currency in the total amount of $369 million were printed and released to circulation between Aug. 21, 1862, and Feb. 15, 1876, when a flood of silver from the Comstock Lode drove down silver bullion prices, reducing the intrinsic value of silver coins to a point below face, value, thereby insuring that they would remain in circulation. The silver price drop further augmented the supply of circulating silver by triggering a flow back to the United States – where they could be exchanged for their greater face value - of the hundreds of millions of silver coins which had been exported to Canada, the West Indies and Latin America since 1862.

Congressional Acts of Jan. 14, 1875, and April 17, 1876, provided for the redemption of Postage and Fractional Currency in silver coins, and all but about $1.8 million worth was returned to the Treasury for redemption. The outstanding notes remain legal tender and can purchase their face value equivalent in goods and services today.

FIRST ISSUE

August 2, 1862 - May 27,063

Denominations: 5¢, 10¢, 25¢, 50¢

The First Issue of U.S. Government stamp money is the only one of the five issues to be identified by name as Postage Currency. The initial printing of the First Issue was released through Army paymasters on Aug. 1, 1862, and was provided for general circulation a few weeks later.

Although it is a moot point, Postage Currency probably constitutes an illegal issue of fractional notes. Rather than being strictly "postage and other stamps of the United States," and despite being "receivable for postage stamps at any U.S. post office," Postage Currency took the form of reproductions of postage stamps printed on paper which carried the promise of the United States to exchange the currency for United States Notes, which gave Postage Currency the attributes of a promissory note, a development beyond the intent of the enabling Act of July 17, 1862.

The stamps reproduce on Postage Currency are the brown (sometimes buff) five-cent stamp of the Series of 1861, bearing the portrait of Thomas Jefferson, and the green ten-cent stamp of the same series, with George Washington's portrait. The 25- and 50-cent denominations bear multiple reproductions of the appropriate stamp. Various colors of paper were used in printing the four notes of the First Issue, but the color does not influence the collector value of the individual note. Faces of the notes are printed in a color approximating the color of the genuine postage stamp, backs are all printed in black.

An interesting feature of the First Issue is the existence of notes with both perforated and straight edges. Apparently, the idea of perforated Postage Currency was a carry-over from the postage stamp printing process and was discarded when the demand for Postage Currency exceeded the capacity of the perforating machines.

Inasmuch as the Bureau of Engraving and Printing had not yet been established, contracts for printing of the First Issue were awarded to private bank note printing companies. The National Bank Note Company printed the face, the American Bank Note Company, the back. The ABNC monogram appears on the backs of some notes.

Total value of Postage Currency issued was more than $20 million.

SECOND ISSUE

October 10, 1863 - February 23, 1867

Denominations: 5¢, 10¢, 25¢, 50¢

The Second Issue of a fractional currency, authorized by Congress on March 3, 1863, all but discarded the concept of postage stamp money. Notes continued to be "receivable for all United States postage stamps," but the identity of the notes was changed from Postage Currency to Fractional Currency, and the notes of the Second

Issue did not bear a reproduction of a postage stamp, although the portrait of George Washington on all notes of this issue is the same as that appearing on the 24-cent stamp of the Series of 1861. The Second Issue was made necessary by the ease with which notes of the First Issue had been counterfeited.

All Second Issue notes have a slate-colored face with bronze oval surcharge centered on the portrait of Washington. Back of the 5-cent note is brown; the 10-cent, green; the 25-cent, violet, and the 50-cent note, red or reddish-orange. All backs have a large, bronze numerical outline overprinted.

Some specimen notes of this issue (and of the Third Issue) were printed on paper watermarked "C.S.A." in block letters, for Confederate States of America. The paper, made in England for the printing of Confederate States paper money, was contraband seized from a captured blockade runner.

First Issue notes had been printed by the National Bank Note Company and the American Bank Note Company both of New York - which were one concern in all respects but name - at a cost which the Treasury Department thought excessive. The Act of July 11, 1863, instructed the Treasury Department to undertake the printing of its own currency.

Although the primary purpose of Second Issue notes was to retire and replace First Issue notes, they were issued in excess of the requirement, to a total value of $23 million.

THIRD ISSUE

December 5, 1864 - August 16, 1869

Denominations: 3¢, 5¢, 10¢, (15¢ essay), 25¢, 50¢

Authorized by the Act of June 30, 1864, the Third Issue of Fractional Currency was necessitated by an increased demand for the low denomination notes and by the continuing counterfeiting of earlier issues. Counterfeits of the Second Issue were of better quality and even more numerous than those of the First Issue had been.

Third Issue notes provide the greatest number of varieties of any issue of Postage or Fractional Currency. Among these are varieties of paper, different colors of backs, ornamental and numerical value surcharges (or none at all), autographed or printed signatures, no signatures, and multiple designs for a single denomination.

In regard to varieties, the 10-cent note is particularly interesting. Through an oversight, the word CENTS does not appear anywhere on the note. The Third Issue varieties are too extensive to be within the scope of these remarks, but they are indicated and priced in the listing which follows.

The Act of June 30, 1864, contained a provision which, by amending the Act of March 3, 1863, authorized the Secretary of the Treasury to determine the form and denominations of Fractional Currency, the means by which it would be made, and the terms of note redemption. This authority permitted Secretary Chase to issue a 3-cent note to facilitate purchase of the new 3-cent first-class postage stamp. Need for the small note was eventually eliminated by the issue of nickel three-cent coins under the Act of March 3, 1865.

Little events can have lasting repercussions, as exemplified by the story of the 5-cent note of the Third Issue. Without the knowledge or authority of his superiors, Spencer M. Clark, then superintendent of the National Currency Bureau, had his likeness put on the 5-cent note of the Third Issue. Clark's presumptive act so angered Congress that a law was enacted April 7, 1866, prohibiting the placing of the likeness of a living person upon any "bonds, securities, notes, Fractional or Postal Currency of the United States." However, the wording of the law did not prohibit the likeness of a living person if the plate for the intended item had already been prepared. Consequently, Clark's portrait didn't disappear from the nation's currency until the passage of May 17, 1866, legislation which authorized the issue of a nickel 5-cent piece and prohibited the issue of any note with a denomination of less than 10 cents.

Likewise unaffected were the Third Issue 25-cent note bearing the portrait of William Fessenden, and the 50-cent note portraying Francis E. Spinner, "The Father of Fractional Currency." The only note affected by the legislation was a proposed 15-cent denomination bearing the portraits of Generals Grant and Sherman, for which the plate had not yet been completed. This note was printed only as an essay, and in uniface form, with face and back being printed on separate pieces of paper.

All of the Third Issue notes were produced by the Treasury Department. Total face value was in excess of $86 million.

POSTAGE AND FRACTIONAL CURRENCY SHIELD

The Postage and Fractional Currency Shield was one of the measures by which the Treasury Department sought to overcome and prevent the wide-spread counterfeiting of Fractional Currency notes.

The shields consisted of a type set of the first three issues of Postage and Fractional Currency mounted on a heavy cardboard shield surmounted by an eagle and 13 stars. Size of the framed unit was 24 by 28 inches. The shields were made available to banks and other commercial institutions in 1866-67 to provide them with a file of genuine notes to use as a reference when checking suspect notes. Those qualified to receive the shield paid face value for the notes ($4.66), plus a presumed transportation charge, for a total cost believed to be $7.50.

The 39 closely-trimmed notes (20 faces and 19 backs) mounted on the shield are specimen notes printed on one side only. They include the scarce 15-cent Sherman/ Grant essays and the two faces of the 3-cent note, which are distinguished by dark and light backgrounds to Washington's portrait. The shields upon which the notes were pasted are known in gray, pink and green, with gray being the most common.

Although the shields were produced in a quantity believed to be in excess of 4,500, it is presumed that fewer than 200 remain intact, with many of those folded, faded or water-stained. Apparently demand for the shields was less than the Treasury Department had anticipated and the surplus shields were carelessly stored - by common account in an old shed behind the Treasury Building. The number of intact shields was further reduced by early collectors who obtained them solely to secure the scarcer notes, which they removed from the shield.

FOURTH ISSUE

July 14, 1869 - February 16, 1875

Denominations: 10¢, 15¢, *25¢, 50¢*

The Fourth Issue of Fractional Currency continued the refinements evident in the Second and Third Issues, and further diminished the pretense of stamp money with which the five issues of fractional notes were launched. The unaesthetic bronze overprintings were eliminated, and an improved type of paper - containing silk fibers – was used.

Three of the six designs (there are three different 50-cent notes) comprising the Fourth Issue make no mention of "stamps." Allegorical art claimed a greater role in note design than before; the 10-cent note bearing a representation of Liberty, and the

15-cent note, a representation of Columbia. The 25-cent and the trio of 50-cent notes bear definitive male portraits.

The Fourth Issue was produced outside the Treasury Department while the Bureau of Engraving and Printing experimented with new dry-printing operations that only succeeded in destroying nearly every hydraulic press the Government owned. Combined with increased demand for Legal Tender notes, the Treasury was forced to job out the production of the Fourth Issue Fractionals to the National and American Bank Note Companies.

The total value of the Fourth Issue was more than $166 million.

FIFTH ISSUE

February 264874 - February 15, 1876

Denominations: 10¢, 25¢, 50¢

The Fifth Issue of Fractional Currency was short and simple, consisting of but three notes, each of a different design. Why a change of design was thought necessary at that time is unclear, but the decision may reflect the Treasury Department's continuing disenchantment with the cost of notes produced by the two New York bank note firms.

Faces of the Fifth Issue were printed by the Bureau of Engraving and Printing, the backs by the Columbian Bank Note Company of Washington, D.C., and Joseph R. Carpenter of Philadelphia. Printing of this issue was terminated when the appropriations for the printing of Fractional Currency were exhausted.

Noteworthy varieties of the Fifth Issue include the green seal 10-cent note and the "long key" and "short key" 10- and 25-cent notes. All notes have faces printed in black, with green backs. All carry printed signatures.

Fifth Issue notes were printed to the total value of nearly $63 million, bringing the total value of all Postage and Fractional Currency issued to about $369 million, of which an estimated $1.8 million remains outstanding.

FIRST ISSUE "POSTAGE CURRENCY"

5 Cents

KL#	Fr#	Date Description	Fine	XF	CU
3209	1228	17.7.1862. Brown. Perforated edges. Face, One 5 cent Jefferson stamp at center flanked by 5's. Back, Large 5 at center with ABNC's monogram.	65.00	125.	250.
3210	1229	Perforated edges. Face, One 5 cent Jefferson stamp at center flanked by 5's. Back, Large 5 at center without ABNC's monogram.	100.	170.	325.
3211	1230	Straight edges. Face, One 5 cent Jefferson stamp at center flanked by 5's. Back, Large 5 at center with ABNC's monogram.	50.00	75.00	125.
3212	1231	Straight edges. Face, One 5 cent Jefferson stamp at center flanked by 5's. Back, Large 5 at center without ABNC's monogram.	65.00	125.	395.

10 Cents

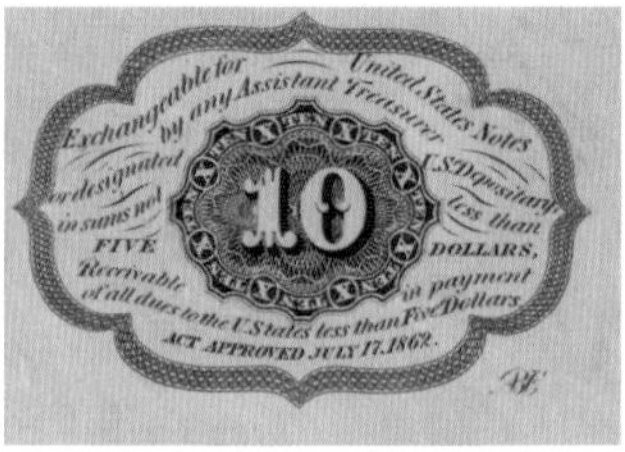

KL#	Fr#	Date Description	Fine	XF	CU
3213	1240	17.7.1862. Green. Perforated edges. Face, One 10 cent Washington stamp at center flanked by 10's. Back, Large 10 at center with ABNC's monogram.	65.00	125.	395.
3214	1241	Perforated edges. Face, One 10 cent Washington stamp at center flanked by 10's. Back, Large 10 at center without ABNC's monogram.	65.00	125.	395.
3215	1242	Straight edges. Face, One 10 cent Washington stamp at center flanked by 10's. Back, Large 10 at center with ABNC's monogram.	50.00	75.00	125.
3216	1243	Straight edges. Face, One 10 cent Washington stamp at center flanked by 10's. Back, Large 10 at center without ABNC's monogram.	65.00	125.	300.

25 Cents

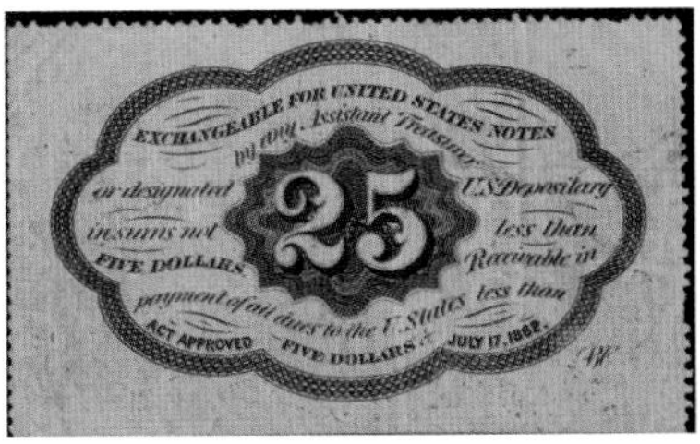

KL#	Fr#	Date Description	Fine	XF	CU
3217	1279	17.7.1862. Brown. Perforated edges. Face, Horizontal row of five 5 cent Jefferson stamps. Back, Large 25 at center with ABNC's monogram.	65.00	125.	300.
3218	1280	Perforated edges. Face, Horizontal row of five 5 cent Jefferson stamps. Back, Large 25 at center without ABNC's monogram.	175.	300.	500.
3219	1281	Straight edges. Face, Horizontal row of five 5 cent Jefferson stamps. Back, Large 25 at center with ABNC's monogram.	55.00	100.	200.
3220	1282	Straight edges. Face, Horizontal row of five 5 cent Jefferson stamps. Back, Large 25 at center without ABNC's monogram.	125.	200.	500.

50 Cents

KL#	Fr#	Date Description	Fine	XF	CU
3221	1310	17.7.1862. Green. #12 perforated edges. Face, Horizontal row of five 10 cent Washington stamps. Back, Large 50 at center with ABNC's monogram.	100.	175.	400.
3222	1310A	#14 perforated edges. Face, Horizontal row of five 10 cent Washington stamps. Back, Large 50 at center with ABNC's monogram.	—	—	—
3223	1311	Perforated edges. Face, Horizontal row of five 10 cent Washington stamps. Back, Large 50 at center without ABNC's monogram.	200.	350.	600.
3224	1312	Straight edges. Face, Horizontal row of five 10 cent Washington stamps. Back, Large 50 at center with ABNC's monogram.	60.00	100.	200.
3225	1313	Straight edges. Face, Horizontal row of five 10 cent Washington stamps. Back, Large 50 at center without ABNC's monogram.	245.	400.	700.

SECOND ISSUE

5 Cents

All notes have oval bronze ovpt. on face around head of Washington at center and large bronze outlined denomination numeral(s) on back.

KL#	Fr#	Date Description	Fine	XF	CU
3226	1232	3.3.1863. Face, George Washington at center flanked by 5's. Back, Large outlined 5 over smaller 5 on shield without overprint.	40.00	65.00	100.
3227	1233	Face, George Washington at center flanked by 5's. Back, Large outlined 5 over smaller 5 on shield with overprint: "18—63".	45.00	70.00	125.
3228	1234	Face, George Washington at center flanked by 5's. Back, Large outlined 5 over smaller 5 on shield with overprint: "18—63" and "S".	55.00	90.00	200.
3229	1235	Fiber paper. Face, George Washington at center flanked by 5's. Back, Large outlined 5 over smaller 5 on shield with overprint: "18—63" and "R—1".	125.	200.	500.

10 Cents

KL#	Fr#	Date Description	Fine	XF	CU
3230	1244	Face, George Washington at center flanked by 10's. Back, Large outlined 10 over smaller 10 on shield without overprint.	45.00	70.00	125.
3231	1245	Face, George Washington at center flanked by 10's. Back, Large outlined 10 over smaller 10 on shield with overprint: "18—63".	50.00	75.00	155.
3232	1246	Face, George Washington at center flanked by 10's. Back, Large outlined 10 over smaller 10 on shield with overprint: "18—63" and "S".	60.00	100.	225.
3233	1247	Face, George Washington at center flanked by 10's. Back, Large outlined 10 over smaller 10 on shield with overprint: "18—63" and "1".	65.00	125.	325.
3234	1248	Face, George Washington at center flanked by 10's. Back, Large outlined 10 over smaller 10 on shield with overprint: "0—63".	725.	1200.	2300.
3235	1249	Fiber paper. Face, George Washington at center flanked by 10's. Back, Large outlined 10 over smaller 10 on shield with overprint: "18—63" and "T—1".	125.	200.	575.

25 Cents

KL#	Fr#	Date Description	Fine	XF	CU
3236	1283	3.3.1863. Face, George Washington at center flanked by 25's. Back, Large outlined 25 over smaller 25 on shield without overprint.	60.00	100.	225.
3237	1284	Face, George Washington at center flanked by 25's. Back, Large outlined 25 over smaller 25 on shield with overprint: "18—63".	75.00	125.	275.
3238	1285	Face, George Washington at center flanked by 25's. Back, Large outlined 25 over smaller 25 on shield with overprint: "18—63"and "A".	60.00	100.	225.
3239	1286	Face, George Washington at center flanked by 25's. Back, Large outlined 25 over smaller 25 on shield with overprint: "18—63" and "S".	60.00	100.	250.
3240	—	Face, George Washington at center flanked by 25's. Back, Large outlined 25 over smaller 25 on shield with overprint: "18—63" and "1". Reported, not confirmed	—	—	—
3241	1288	Face, George Washington at center flanked by 25's. Back, Large outlined 25 over smaller 25 on shield with overprint: "18—63" and "2".	65.00	125.	275.
3242	1289	Fiber paper. Face, George Washington at center flanked by 25's. Back, Large outlined 25 over smaller 25 on shield with overprint: "18—63" and "T—1".	125.	200.	700.
3243	1290	Fiber paper. Face, George Washington at center flanked by 25's. Back, Large outlined 25 over smaller 25 on shield with overprint: "18—63" and "T—2".	125.	200.	500.
3244	—	Face, George Washington at center flanked by 25's. Back, Large outlined 25 over smaller 25 on shield with overprint: "18—63" and "S—2". Reported, not confirmed	—	—	—

50 Cents

KL#	Fr#	Date Description	Fine	XF	CU
3245	1316	3.3.1863. Face, George Washington at center flanked by 50's. Back, Large outlined 50 over smaller 50 on shield with overprint: "18—63".	60.00	100.	325.
3246	1317	Face, George Washington at center flanked by 50's. Back, Large outlined 50 over smaller 50 on shield with overprint: "18—63" and "A".	60.00	100.	325.
3247	1318	Face, George Washington at center flanked by 50's. Back, Large outlined 50 over smaller 50 on shield with overprint: "18—63" and "I".	65.00	125.	350.

KL#	Fr#	Date Description	Fine	XF	CU
3248	1320	Fiber paper. Face, George Washington at center flanked by 50's. Back, Large outlined 50 over smaller 50 on shield with overprint: "18—63" and "0—1".	100.	175.	450.
3249	1321	Fiber paper. Face, George Washington at center flanked by 50's. Back, Large outlined 50 over smaller 50 on shield with overprint: "18—63" and "R—2".	185.	300.	900.
3250	1322	Fiber paper. Face, George Washington at center flanked by 50's. Back, Large outlined 50 over smaller 50 on shield with overprint: "18—63" and "T—1".	100.	175.	450.

THIRD ISSUE

3 Cents

KL#	Fr#	Date Description	Fine	XF	CU
3252	1226	3.3.1863. Face, Portrait of Washington at center with light background. Back, Large 3 at center.	60.00	100.	200.
3253	1227	Face, Portrait of Washington at center with dark background. Back, Large 3 at center.	65.00	125.	250.

5 Cents

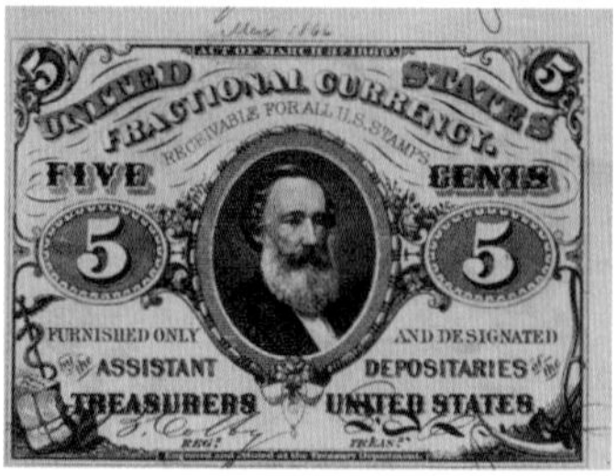

KL#	Fr#	Date Description	Fine	XF	CU
3254	1236	3.3.1863. Red back. Face, Portrait of Clark at center. Back, 5 in each corner.	65.00	125.	300.
3255	1237	Red back. Face, Portrait of Clark at center with "a". Back, 5 in each corner.	70.00	150.	400.
3256	1238	Green back. Face, Portrait of Clark at center. Back, 5 in each corner.	55.00	100.	155.
3257	1239	Green back. Face, Portrait of Clark at center with "a". Back, 5 in each corner.	60.00	105.	175.

10 Cents

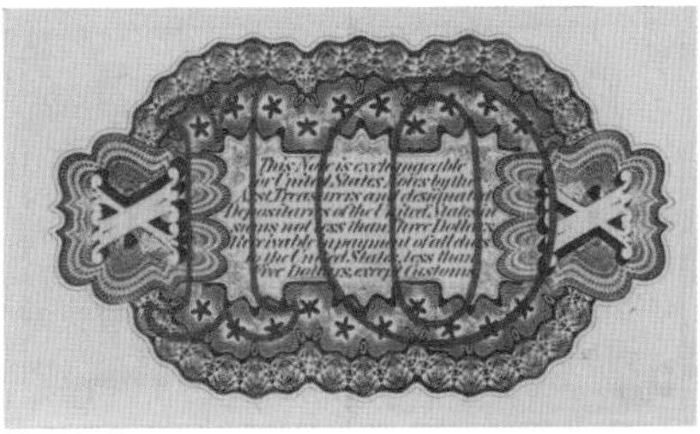

KL#	Fr#	Date Description	Fine	XF	CU
3258	1251	3.3.1863. Small signature. Red back. Face, Portrait of Washington at center; bronze 10's in each corner. Back, Large outlined 10 at center.	60.00	100.	250.
3259	1252	Red back. Face, Portrait of Washington at center with one "1"; bronze 10's in each corner. Back, Large outlined 10 at center.	65.00	125.	400.
3260	1253	Large autographed signature. Face, Portrait of Washington at center; bronze 10's in each corner. Back, Large outlined 10 at center.	100.	175.	300.
3261	1254	Large autographed signature. Face, Portrait of Washington at center; bronze 10's in each corner. Back, Large outlined 10 at center.	125.	200.	450.
3262	1255	Green back. Printed signature. Face, Portrait of Washington at center; bronze 10's in each corner. Back, Large outlined 10 at center.	40.00	65.00	100.
3263	1255A	Green back. Large autographed signature. Face, Portrait of Washington at center; bronze 10's in each corner. Back, Large outlined 10 at center.	—	—	—
3264	1256	Large printed. Green back. Face, Portrait of Washington at center with one "1"; bronze 10's in each corner. Back, Large outlined 10 at center.	50.00	75.00	200.

25 Cents

KL#	Fr#	Date Description	Fine	XF	CU
3265	1291	3.3.1863. Red back. (No "a"). Face, Portrait of Fessenden at center. Back, Large outlined 25 at center.	75.00	120.	300.
3266	1292	Red back. Face, Portrait of Fessenden at center with small "a". Back, Large outlined 25 at center.	95.00	155.	300.
3268	1294	Green back. (No "a"). Face, Portrait of Fessenden at center. Back, Large outlined 25 at center.	45.00	70.00	120.

KL#	Fr#	Date Description	Fine	XF	CU
3269	1295	Green back. Face, Portrait of Fessenden at center with small "a". Back, Large outlined 25 at center.	60.00	100.	200.
3270	1296	Green back. "a" is 7mm to the right and down from normal location. (Very large "a"). Face, Portrait of Fessenden at center with large "a". Back, Large outlined 25 at center.	1200.	2000.	3900.
3271	1297	Fiber paper. Face, Portrait of Fessenden at center. Back, Large outlined 25 at center with overprint: "M—2—6—5".	60.00	100.	395.
3272	1298	Fiber paper. Face, Portrait of Fessenden at center with "a". Back, Large outlined 25 at center with overprint: "M—2—6—5".	100.	175.	425.
3273	1299	Fiber paper. Face, Portrait of Fessenden at center with solid bronze ornamental overprint. Back, Large outlined 25 at center.	850.	1400.	2100.
3274	1300	Fiber paper. Face, Portrait of Fessenden at center with solid bronze ornamental overprint and "a". Back, Large outlined 25 at center.	1750.	2900.	5000.

50 Cents

KL#	Fr#	Date Description	Fine	XF	CU
3275	1324	3.3.1863. Small printed signature. Red back. Face, Portrait of General Spinner at center. Back, Large 50 at ends with overprint: "A—2—6—5" and 50.	100.	170.	450.
3276	1325	Printed signature. Red back. Face, Portrait of General Spinner at center with "1" and "a". Back, Large 50 at ends.	250.	425.	975.
3277	1326	Printed signature. Red back. Face, Portrait of General Spinner at center with "1". Back, Large 50 at ends.	125.	195.	325.
3278	1327	Printed signature. Red back. Face, Portrait of General Spinner at center with "a". Back, Large 50 at ends.	125.	195.	395.
3279	1328	Large autograph signature. Red back. Face, Portrait of General Spinner at center. Back, Large 50 at ends.	130.	200.	495.
3281	1329	Autograph signature. Red back. Face, Portrait of General Spinner at center. Back, Large 50 at ends.	175.	300.	700.
3282	1330	Autograph signature. Red back. Face, Portrait of General Spinner at center. Back, Large 50 at ends.	1500.	2500.	4300.
3283	1331	Green back. Face, Portrait of General Spinner at center. Back, Multiple 50's.	65.00	125.	400.
3284	1332	Green back. Face, Portrait of General Spinner at center with "1" and "a". Back, Multiple 50's.	100.	175.	425.
3285	1333	Green back. Face, Portrait of General Spinner at center with "1". Back, Multiple 50's.	70.00	135.	295.
3286	1334	Green back. Face, Portrait of General Spinner at center with "a". Back, Multiple 50's.	65.00	110.	375.
3287	1335	Green back. Face, Portrait of General Spinner at center. Back, Multiple 50's with overprint: "A—2—6—5".	65.00	125.	350.
3288	1336	Green back. Face, Portrait of General Spinner at center with "1" and "a". Back, Multiple 50's.	1075.	1800.	2900.
3289	1337	Green back. Face, Portrait of General Spinner at center with "1". Back, Multiple 50's.	150.	250.	700.
3290	1338	Green back. Face, Portrait of General Spinner at center with "a". Back, Multiple 50's.	120.	195.	595.
3291	1339	Redesigned green back. Face, Portrait of General Spinner at center.	110.	155.	325.
3292	1340	Redesigned green back. Face, Portrait of General Spinner at center with "1" and "a".	180.	300.	900.

KL#	Fr#	Date Description	Fine	XF	CU
3293	1341	Redesigned green back. Face, Portrait of General Spinner at center with "1".	100.	175.	400.
3294	1342	Redesigned green back. Face, Portrait of General Spinner at center with "a".	125.	225.	550.

KL#	Fr#	Date Description	Fine	XF	CU
3295	1343	3.3.1863. Red back. Small printed signature. Face, Justice seated at center.	125.	200.	500.
3296	1344	Printed signature. Red back. Face, Justice seated at center with "1" and "a".	725.	1200.	3500.
3297	1345	Printed signature. Red back. Face, Justice seated at center with "1".	125.	200.	450.
3298	1346	Printed signature. Red back. Face, Justice seated at center with "a".	125.	200.	495.
3299	1347	Red back. Face, Justice seated at center. Back, Overprint: "A—2—6—5".	125.	200.	495.
3300	1348	Red back. Face, Justice seated at center with "1" and "a".	1025.	1695.	3000.
3301	1349	Red back. Face, Justice seated at center with "1".	200.	350.	600.
3302	1350	Red back. Face, Justice seated at center with "a".	245.	400.	800.
3303	1351	Red back. Fiber paper. Small printed signature. Face, Justice seated at center. Back, Overprint: "S—2—6—4".	600.	1000.	19,000.
3304	1352	Red back. Fiber paper. Only 3 known. CAA 5/7/05 Fine $32,000. Stack's 5/04 AU $115,000. Face, Justice seated at center with "1" and "a".	25,000.	39,000.	—
3305	1353	Red back. Fiber paper. CAA 5/7/05 O'Mara Sale AU $15,000. Face, Justice seated at center with "1".	8000.	12,900.	21,000.
3306	1354	Red back. Fiber paper. CAA 5/7/05 O'Mara Sale AU $20,000. Face, Justice seated at center with "a".	10,000.	16,000.	23,000.
3307	1355	Red back. Large autographed signature. Face, Justice seated at center.	175.	300.	500.
3308	1356	Large autographed signature. Red back. Face, Justice seated at center. Back, Overprint: "A—2—6—5".	200.	325.	600.
3309	1357	Large autographed signature. Fiber paper. Red back. Face, Justice seated at center. Back, Overprint: "S—2—6—4".	500.	800.	1600.
3310	1358	Green back. Face, Justice seated at center.	125.	195.	450.
3311	1359	Green back. Face, Justice seated at center with "1" and "a".	850.	1400.	2300.
3312	1360	Green back. Face, Justice seated at center with "1".	125.	200.	500.
3313	1361	Green back. Face, Justice seated at center with "a".	135.	225.	550.
3314	1362	Green back. Face, Justice seated at center. Back, Overprint: "A—2—6—5" compactly spaced. (92mm x 30mm).	135.	225.	475.

KL#	Fr#	Date Description	Fine	XF	CU
3315	1363	Green back. Face, Justice seated at center with "1" and "a". Back, Overprint: "A—2—6—5" compactly spaced. (92mm x 30mm).	250.	425.	825.
3316	1364	Green back. Face, Justice seated at center with "1". Back, Overprint: "A—2—6—5" compactly spaced. (92mm x 30mm).	125.	175.	475.
3317	1365	Green back. Face, Justice seated at center with "a". Back, Overprint: "A—2—6—5" compactly spaced. (92mm x 30mm).	120.	200.	500.
3318	1366	Green back. Face, Justice seated at center. Back, Overprint: "A—2—6—5" widely spaced (98mm x 34mm).	185.	300.	550.
3319	1367	Green back. Face, Justice seated at center with "1" and "a". Back, Overprint: "A—2—6—5" widely spaced (98mm x 34mm).	1200.	2000.	5000.
3320	1368	Green back. Face, Justice seated at center with "1". Back, Overprint: "A—2—6—5" widely spaced (98mm x 34mm).	300.	500.	900.
3321	1369	Green back. Face, Justice seated at center with "a". Back, Overprint: "A—2—6—5" widely spaced (98mm x 34mm).	400.	650.	900.
3322	1370	Fiber paper. Green back. Face, Justice seated at center. Back, Overprint: "A—2—6—5".	225.	375.	900.
3323	1371	Fiber paper. Green back. Face, Justice seated at center with "1" and "a". Back, Overprint: "A—2—6—5".	1200.	2000.	4500.
3324	1372	Fiber paper. Green back. Face, Justice seated at center with "1". Back, Overprint: "A—2—6—5".	245.	400.	1000.
3325	1373	Fiber paper. Green back. Face, Justice seated at center with "a". Back, Overprint: "A—2—6—5".	250.	425.	1000.
3326	1373A	Fiber paper. Green back. CAA O'Mara Sale 5/7/05 AU $46,000. Face, Justice seated at center. Back, Overprint: "S—2—6—4".	—	—	—

FOURTH ISSUE

10 Cents

KL#	Fr#	Date Description	Fine	XF	CU
3327	1257	3.3.1863. Watermarked paper with pink silk fibers Face, Bust of Liberty at left; 40mm red seal. Back, Large 10 at left and right.	50.00	75.00	125.
3328	1258	Unwatermarked paper with pink silk fibers. Face, Bust of Liberty at left. Back, Large 10 at left and right.	60.00	100.	175.
3329	1259	Paper with violet silk fibers. Face, Bust of Liberty at left with bluish right side of face. Back, Large 10 at left and right.	45.00	75.00	145.
3331	1261	Face, Bust of Liberty at left; 38mm red seal; bluish right side of face. Back, Large 10 at left and right.	60.00	100.	175.

15 Cents

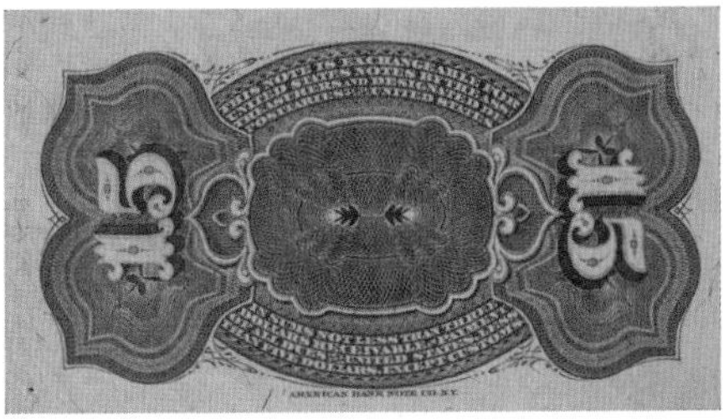

KL#	Fr#	Date Description	Fine	XF	CU
3332	1267	3.3.1863. Watermarked paper with pink silk fibers. Face, Bust of Columbia at left; 40mm red seal. Back, Large 15 at left and right.	75.00	125.	250.
3333	1268	Unwatermarked paper with pink silk fibers. Face, Bust of Columbia at left. Back, Large 15 at left and right.	425.	700.	1200.
3334	1269	Paper with violet silk fibers. Face, Bust of Columbia with bluish right side of face. Back, Large 15 at left and right.	85.00	150.	275.
3336	1271	Face, Bust of Columbia at left. 38mm red seal; bluish right side of face. Back, Large 15 at left and right.	100.	175.	300.

25 Cents

KL#	Fr#	Date Description	Fine	XF	CU
3337	1301	3.3.1863. Watermarked paper with pink silk fibers. Face, Portrait of Washington at left; 40mm red seal.	50.00	75.00	125.
3338	1302	Unwatermarked paper with pink silk fibers. Face, Portrait of Washington at left; 40 mm seal.	60.00	100.	175.
3340	1303	Paper with violet silk fibers. Face, Portrait of Washington at left. Bluish right side of face.	65.00	125.	200.
3342	1307	Face, Portrait of Washington at left. 38mm red seal; bluish right side of face.	60.00	100.	195.

50 Cents

The brown seal was believed to have been caused by the sizing chemicals in the early stages of printing and must be between a rich chocolate brown to a rich purple brown.

KL#	Fr#	Date Description	Fine	XF	CU
3343	1374	3.3.1863. Watermarked paper with silk fibers. Face, Portrait of Lincoln at right.	150.	250.	525.
3345	1376	3.3.1863. Face, Portrait of Stanton at left; red seal.	75.00	145.	250.
3347	1379	3.3.1863. Face, Portrait of Dexter at left; green seal.	70.00	125.	225.

FIFTH ISSUE, SERIES OF 1874/1875

Shield Varieties

10 Cents

KL#	Fr#	Date Description	Fine	XF	CU
3348	1264	Face, Portrait of Meredith at left. Green seal with long key. Back, Small 10 at top right and bottom right.	50.00	75.00	155.
3349	1265	Face, Portrait of Meredith at left. Red seal with long key. Back, Small 10 at top right and bottom right.	30.00	45.00	80.00
3350	1266	Face, Portrait of Meredith at left. Red seal with short key. Back, Small 10 at top right and bottom right.	30.00	45.00	80.00

25 Cents

KL#	Fr#	Date Description	Fine	XF	CU
3351	1308	1874. Face, Portrait of Walker at left. Red seal with long key. Back, Large 25 cents at right.	30.00	45.00	85.00
3352	1309	Face, Portrait of Walker at left. Red seal with short key. Back, Large 25 cents at right.	50.00	75.00	125.

FIFTH ISSUE, SERIES OF 1874/1875

Shield Varieties

50 Cents

The brown seal was believed to have been caused by the sizing chemicals in the early stages of printing and must be between a rich chocolate brown to a rich purple brown.

KL#	Fr#	Date	Description	Fine	XF	CU
3357	1381		White paper. Face, Portrait of Crawford at left.	25.00	75.00	125.

Fractional Currency Shield

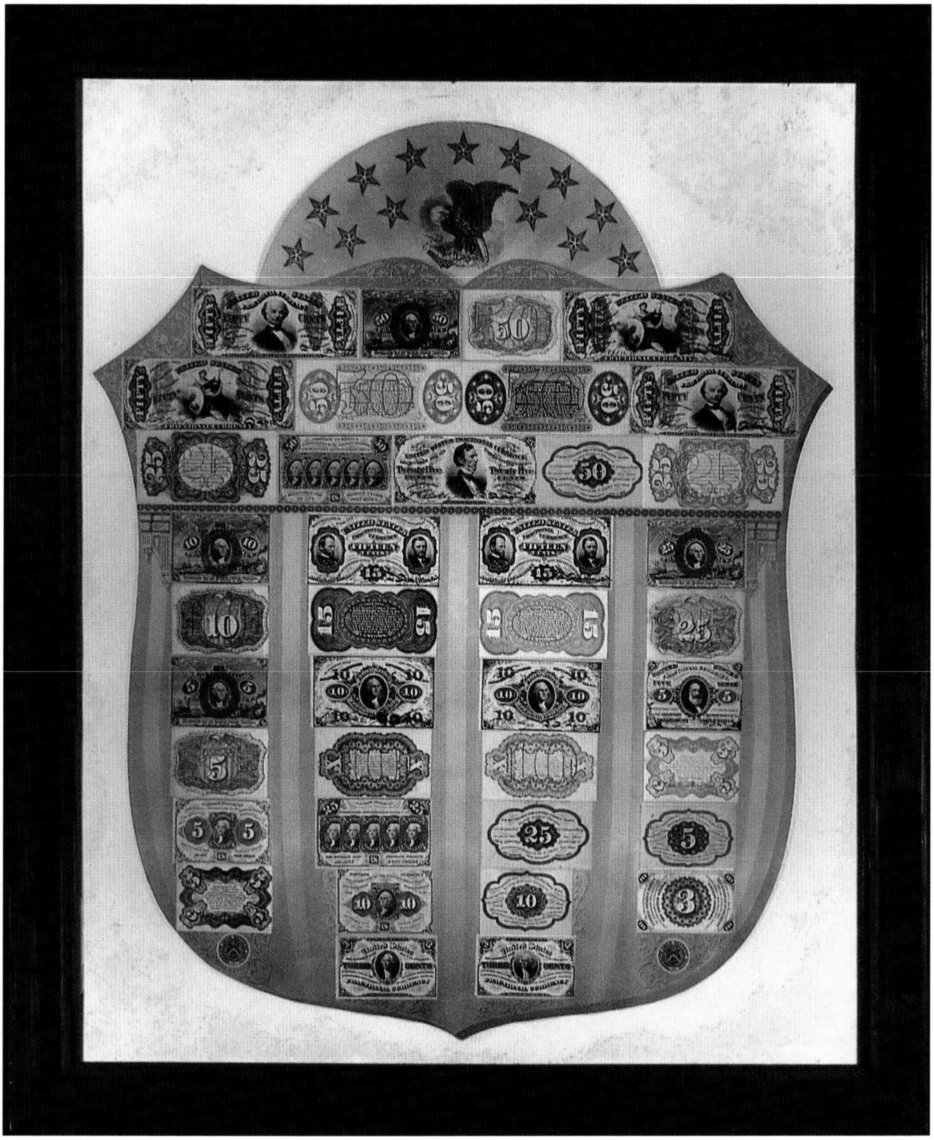

KL#	Fr#	Description	Fine	XF	CU
3354	—	Grey background	—	—	8,500
3355	—	Pink background	—	—	15,000
3356	—	Green background	—	—	20,000

Specimens

FIRST ISSUE "POSTAGE CURRENCY"

5 Cents

KL#	Fr#	Date	Description	Fine	XF	CU
3212SP a	—		Face with narrow margins.	—	—	125.
3212SP b	—		Face with wide margins.	—	—	300.
3212SP c	—		Back with narro margins.	—	—	125.
3212SP d	—		Back with wide margins.	—	—	600.

10 Cents

KL#	Fr#	Date	Description	Fine	XF	CU
3216SP a	—		Face with narrow margins.	—	—	125.
3216SP b	—		Face with wide margins.	—	—	300.
3216SP c	—		Back with narrow margins.	—	—	125.
3216SP d	—		Back with wide margins.	—	—	300.

25 Cents

KL#	Fr#	Date	Description	Fine	XF	CU
3220SP a	—		Face with narrow margins.	—	—	125.
3220SP b	—		Face with wide margins.	—	—	300.
3220SP c	—		Back with narrow margins.	—	—	125.
3220SP d	—		Back with wide margins.	—	—	300.

50 Cents

KL#	Fr#	Date	Description	Fine	XF	CU
3225SP a	—		Face with narrow margins.	—	—	125.
3225SP b	—		Face with wide margins.	—	—	425.
3225SP c	—		Back with narrow margins.	—	—	125.
3225SP d	—		Back with wide margins.	—	—	300.

SECOND ISSUE

5 Cents

KL#	Fr#	Date	Description	Fine	XF	CU
3226SP a	—		Face with narrow margins.	—	—	175.
3226SP b	—		Face with wide margins.	—	—	300.
3226SP c	—		Back with narrow margins.	—	—	175.
3226SP d	—		Back with wide margins.	—	—	300.

10 Cents

KL#	Fr#	Date Description	Fine	XF	CU
3230SP a	—	Face with narrow margins.	—	—	125.
3230SP b	—	Face with wide margins.	—	—	300.
3230SP c	—	Back with narrow margins.	—	—	125.
3230SP d	—	Back with wide margins.	—	—	300.

25 Cents

KL#	Fr#	Date Description	Fine	XF	CU
3236SP a	—	Face with narrow margins.	—	—	125.
3236SP b	—	Face with wide margins.	—	—	300.
3236SP c	—	Back with narrow margins.	—	—	125.
3236SP d	—	Back with wide margins.	—	—	300.

50 Cents

KL#	Fr#	Date Description	Fine	XF	CU
3245SP a	—	Face with narrow margins.	—	—	125.
3245SP b	—	Face with wide margins.	—	—	350.
3245SP c	—	Back with narrow margins.	—	—	125.
3245SP d	—	Back with wide margins.	—	—	500.

THIRD ISSUE

3 Cents

KL#	Fr#	Date Description	Fine	XF	CU
3252SP a	—	Face with narrow margins, light background.	—	—	125.
3252SP b	—	Face with wide margins, light background. Rare.	—	—	7000.
3252SP c	—	Back with narrow margins.	—	—	195.
3252SP d	—	Back with wide margins.	—	—	350.
3253SP a	—	Face with narrow margins, dark background.	—	—	125.
3253SP b	—	Face with wide margins, dark dark background.	—	—	450.

5 Cents

KL#	Fr#	Date Description	Fine	XF	CU
3254SP a	—	Face with narrow margins.	—	—	195.
3254SP b	—	Face with wide margins.	—	—	350.
3254SP c	—	Red back with narrow margins.	—	—	195.
3254SP d	—	Red back with wide margins.	—	—	395.
3256SP c	—	Green back with narrow margins.	—	—	125.

KL#	Fr#	Date	Description	Fine	XF	CU
3256SP d	—		Green back with wide margins.	—	—	295.

10 Cents

KL#	Fr#	Date	Description	Fine	XF	CU
3258SP a	—		Face with narrow margins.	—	—	125.
3258SP b	—		Face with wide margins.	—	—	325.
3258SP c	—		Red back with narrow margins.	—	—	150.
3258SP d	—		Red back with wide margins.	—	—	395.
3260SP a	—		Face with narrow margins.	—	—	190.
3260SP b	—		Face with wide margins.	—	—	350.
3261SP a	—		Face with narrow margins.	—	—	395.
3261SP b	—		Face with wide margins.	—	—	3900.
3262SP c	—		Green back ith narrow margins.	—	—	150.
3262SP d	—		Green back with wide margins.	—	—	325.

25 Cents

KL#	Fr#	Date	Description	Fine	XF	CU
3265SP a	—		Face with narrow margins.	—	—	125.
3265SP b	—		Face with wide margins.	—	—	325.
3265SP c	—		Red back with narrow margins.	—	—	150.
3265SP d	—		Red back with wide margins.	—	—	350.
3268SP c	—		Green back with narrow margins.	—	—	125.
3268SP d	—		Green back with wide margins.	—	—	350.

50 Cents

KL#	Fr#	Date	Description	Fine	XF	CU
3275SP a	—		Face with narrow margins.	—	—	200.
3275SP b	—		Face with wide margins.	—	—	350.
3275SP c	—		Red back with narrow margins.	—	—	250.
3275SP d	—		Red back with wide margin.	—	—	450.
3279SP a	—		Face with narrow margins.	—	—	250.
3279SP b	—		Face with wide margins.	—	—	495.
3281SP a	—		Face with narrow margins. Rare.	—	—	4500.
3281SP b	—		Face with wide margins. Rare.	—	—	14,500.
3282SP a	—		Face with narrow margins.	—	—	395.
3282SP b	—		Face with wide margins. Rare.	—	—	7000.
3283SP c	—		Green back with narrow margins.	—	—	125.
3283SP d	—		Green back with wide margins.	—	—	350.

KL#	Fr#	Date Description	Fine	XF	CU
3291SP c	—	Green back with narrow margins.	—	—	4500.
3291SP d	—	Green back with wide margins.	—	—	5500.
3295SP a	—	Face with narrow margins.	—	—	125.
3295SP b	—	Face with wide margins.	—	—	350.
3307SP a	—	Face with narrow margins.	—	—	250.
3307SP b	—	Face with wide margins.	—	—	395.
3309SP a	—	Face with narrow margins.	—	—	395.
3309SP b	—	Face with wide margins. Rare.	—	—	9000.

15 Cents

KL#	Fr#	Date Description	Fine	XF	CU
3453SP a	—	Face with narrow margins.	—	—	750.
3453SP b	—	Face with wide margins.	—	—	750.
3453SP c	—	Green back with narrow margins.	—	—	300.
3453SP d	—	Green back wih wide margins.	—	—	350.
3454SP a	—	Face with narrow margins.	—	—	2500.
3455SP a	—	Face with narrow margins.	—	—	495.
3455SP b	—	Face with wide margins.	—	—	895.
3455SP c	—	Red back with narrow margins.	—	—	395.
3455SP d	—	Red back with wide margins.	—	—	700.
3456SP a	—	Face with narrow margins.	—	—	700.
3456SP b	—	Face with wide margins.	—	—	995.
3457SP a	—	Face with narrow margins. Rare.	—	—	—

Military Payment Certificates

Military Payment Certificates (MPC) were special currency issued by the U.S. Armed Forces between the end of World War II and 1973.

Their issue to and use by the military and certain civilian personnel in lieu of regular U.S. currency was designed to minimize black market trafficking in occupied areas and around U.S. military installations. The various series of MPC replaced each other with no advanced warning, and the scrip, exchangeable only by those to whom its issue was authorized, could become worthless overnight. This discouraged its acceptance by unauthorized local civilians.

Given the low rate of military pay during most of this period and the fact that no MPC retains any redemption value, it is no wonder that high denomination notes in uncirculated condition are rare in many of the series.

MPC replacement notes, analogous to star notes in regular U.S. currency, are designated by the lack of a suffix letter in the serial number. They are especially sought-after by collectors.

SERIES 461

Issued: European Theater, Sept. 16, 1946; Pacific Theater, Sept. 30, 1946
Withdrawn: March 10, 1947 **Areas of Use:** Austria, Belgium, England, France, Germany, Greece, Hungary, Iceland, Italy, Japan, Korea, Morocco, Philippines, Ryukyus, Scotland, Trieste, Yugoslavia.

KL#	Denomination	Fine	VF	XF	Unc
M1	5 Cents	4.00	7.50	20.00	65.00
M1r	5 Cents Replacement A-	150.	400.	750.	1000.
M2	10 Cents	4.00	7.50	20.00	65.00
M2r	10 Cents Replacement A-	150.	400.	750.	1000.
M3	25 Cents	13.00	25.00	45.00	250.
M3r	25 Cents Replacement A-	950.	1100.	—	—
M4	50 Cents	14.00	25.00	70.00	250.
M4r	50 Cents Replacement A-	950.	1100.	—	—
M5	1 Dollar	5.50	10.00	30.00	185.
M5r	One Dollar Replacement A-	200.	500.	900.	1300.
M6	5 Dollars	30.00	85.00	125.	325.
M6r	Five Dollars Replacement A-	1100.	1750.	—	—
M7	10 Dollars	25.00	45.00	75.00	300.
M7r	Ten Dollars Replacement A-	350.	1000.	1600.	—

SERIES 471

Issued: March 10, 1947

Withdrawn: March 22, 1948 **Areas of Use:** Austria, Belgium, England, France, Germany, Greece, Hungary, Iceland, Italy, Japan, Korea, Morocco, Philippines, Ryukyus, Scotland, Trieste, Yugoslavia

KL#	Denomination	Fine	VF	XF	Unc
M8	5 Cents	7.50	15.00	30.00	90.00
M8r	5 Cents Replacement B-	750.	950.	2000.	—
M9	10 Cents	6.00	12.00	30.00	90.00
M9r	10 Cents Replacement B-	800.	1000.	1800.	—
M10	25 Cents	15.00	25.00	75.00	300.
M10r	25 Cents Replacement B-	750.	1250.	—	—
M11	50 Cents	20.00	50.00	110.	325.
M11r	50 Cents Replacement B-	—	Rare	—	—
M12	1 Dollar	15.00	35.00	85.00	275.
M12r	1 Dollar Replacement B-	700.	1000.	1500.	—
M13	5 Dollars	775.	1000.	2375.	20,000.
M13r	5 Dollars Replacement B-	—	Rare	—	—

KL#	Denomination	Fine	VF	XF	Unc
M14	10 Dollars	200.	350.	600.	2400.
M14r	10 Dollars Replacement B-	—	Rare	—	—

SERIES 472

Issued: March 22, 1948 **Withdrawn:** June 20, 1951 **Areas of Use:** Austria, Belgium, England, France, Germany, Greece, Hungary, Iceland, Italy, Japan, Korea, Morocco, Philippines, Ryukyus, Scotland, Trieste, Yugoslavia

KL#	Denomination	Fine	VF	XF	Unc
M15	5 Cents	1.00	2.00	4.00	12.50
M15r	5 Cents Replacement C-	50.00	75.00	300.	750.
M16	10 Cents	2.25	6.50	18.00	70.00
M16r	10 Cents Replacement C-	110.	175.	375.	675.

KL#	Denomination	Fine	VF	XF	Unc
M17	25 Cents	8.00	17.50	65.00	225.
M17r	25 Cents Replacement C-	—	Rare	—	—
M18	50 Cents	10.00	28.00	75.00	275.
M18r	50 Cents Replacement C-	600.	900.	—	—

KL#	Denomination	Fine	VF	XF	Unc
M19	1 Dollar	12.00	18.00	85.00	250.
M19r	1 Dollar Replacement C-	225.	400.	750.	2400.
M20	5 Dollars	125.	250.	900.	2750.
M20r	5 Dollars Replacement C-	—	Rare	—	—
M21	10 Dollars	50.00	130.	275.	2000.
M21r	10 Dollars Replacement C-	—	Rare	—	—

SERIES 481

Issued: June 20, 1951 **Withdrawn:** May 25, 1954 **Areas of Use:** Austria, Belgium, England, France, Germany, Greece, Hungary, Iceland, Italy, Japan, Korea, Morocco, Philippines, Ryukyus, Scotland, Trieste, Yugoslavia

KL#	Denomination	Fine	VF	XF	Unc
M22	5 Cents	2.00	4.00	9.00	27.50
M22r	5 Cents Replacement D-	75.00	125.	300.	600.
M23	10 Cents	2.50	4.50	15.00	35.00
M23r	10 Cents Replacement D-	85.00	150.	300.	450.
M24	25 Cents	10.00	18.50	25.00	60.00
M24r	25 Cents Replacement D-	225.	400.	450.	800.
M25	50 Cents	10.00	25.00	55.00	275.
M25r	50 Cents Replacement D-	—	Rare	—	—
M26	1 Dollar	20.00	45.00	95.00	295.
M26r	1 Dollar Replacement D-	450.	475.	600.	1000.
M27	5 Dollars	80.00	175.	550.	3000.
M27r	5 Dollars Replacement D-	—	Rare	—	—
M28	10 Dollars	35.00	85.00	300.	1750.
M28r	10 Dollars Replacement D-	900.	Rare	—	—

SERIES 521

Issued: May 25, 1954 **Withdrawn:** May 27, 1958 **Areas of Use:** Austria, Belgium, England, France, Germany, Greece, Hungary, Iceland, Italy, Japan, Korea, Morocco, Philippines, Ryukyus, Scotland, Trieste, Yugoslavia

KL#	Denomination	Fine	VF	XF	Unc
M29	5 Cents	2.00	5.00	9.00	30.00
M29r	5 Cents Replacement E-	300.	500.	900.	1500.
M30	10 Cents	3.00	6.00	12.50	32.50
M30r	10 Cents Replacement E-	300.	500.	1000.	2000.

KL#	Denomination	Fine	VF	XF	Unc
M31	25 Cents	8.00	15.00	27.50	85.00
M31r	25 Cents Replacement E-	500.	1000.	1500.	2250.
M32	50 Cents	10.00	25.00	75.00	150.
M32r	50 Cents Replacement E-	600.	800.	1600.	2500.
M33	1 Dollar	9.50	20.00	50.00	175.
M33r	1 Dollar Replacement E-	300.	500.	1200.	2250.
M34	5 Dollars	300.	550.	1300.	3000.
M34r	5 Dollars Replacement E-	1600.	2250.	—	—

KL#	Denomination	Fine	VF	XF	Unc
M35	10 Dollars	100.	165.	650.	1800.
M35r	10 Dollars Replacement E-	1900.	3000.	3600.	—

SERIES 541

Issued: May 27, 1958 **Withdrawn:** May 26, 1961

Areas of Use: Cyprus, England, France, Germany, Iceland, Northern Ireland, Italy, Japan, Korea, Morocco, Philippines, Ryukyus, Scotland

KL#	Denomination	Fine	VF	XF	Unc
M36	5 Cents	1.50	3.00	6.00	17.50
M36r	5 Cents Replacement E-	50.00	75.00	175.	350.

KL#	Denomination	Fine	VF	XF	Unc
M37	10 Cents	5.00	10.00	20.00	50.00
M37r	10 Cents Replacement F-	50.00	75.00	175.	350.
M38	25 Cents	9.00	15.00	30.00	80.00
M38r	25 Cents Replacement F-	75.00	125.	225.	600.
M39	50 Cents	30.00	55.00	100.	325.
M39r	50 Cents Replacement F-	40.00	50.00	150.	300.
M40	1 Dollar	30.00	50.00	100.	400.
M40r	1 Dollar Replacement F-	250.	375.	1000.	1500.
M41	5 Dollars	1250.	2250.	3750.	15,000.
M41r	5 Dollars Replacement F-	—	Rare	—	—

KL#	Denomination	Fine	VF	XF	Unc
M42	10 Dollars	300.	500.	1500.	3500.
M42r	10 Dollars Replacement F-	2375.	3750.	—	—

SERIES 591

Issued: May 26, 1961 **Withdrawn:** Pacific, Jan. 6, 1964; Europe, Jan. 14, 1946
Areas of Use: Cyprus, Iceland, Japan, Korea, Philippines

KL#	Denomination	Fine	VF	XF	Unc
M43	5 Cents	3.50	7.00	12.50	55.00
M43r	5 Cents Replacement G-	225.	400.	800.	1250.
M44	10 Cents	4.00	10.00	15.00	65.00
M44r	10 Cents Replacement G-	1200.	1400.	1600.	2500.
M45	25 Cents	17.50	35.00	55.00	140.
M45r	25 Cents Replacement G-	—	Rare	—	—

KL#	Denomination	Fine	VF	XF	Unc
M46	50 Cents	35.00	60.00	85.00	240.
M46r	50 Cents Replacement G-	600.	700.	800.	1200.

KL#	Denomination	Fine	VF	XF	Unc
M47	1 Dollar	25.00	40.00	90.00	275.
M47r	1 Dollar Replacement G-	800.	1000.	1600.	2500.
M48	5 Dollars	550.	850.	1750.	4500.
M48r	5 Dollars Replacement G-	—	Rare	—	—
M49	10 Dollars	200.	300.	350.	2000.
M49r	10 Dollars Replacement G-	1250.	2500.	3500.	—

SERIES 611

Issued: Jan. 6, 1964 **Withdrawn:** April 28, 1969

Areas of Use: Cyprus, Japan, Korea, Libya

KL#	Denomination	Fine	VF	XF	Unc
M50	5 Cents	5.00	7.50	19.00	40.00
M50r	5 Cents Replacement H-	45.00	60.00	90.00	125.

KL#	Denomination	Fine	VF	XF	Unc
M51	10 Cents	5.00	8.00	20.00	45.00
M51r	10 Cents Replacement H-	45.00	60.00	90.00	125.
M52	25 Cents	30.00	75.00	110.	275.
M52r	25 Cents Replacement H-	1000.	1250.	—	—
M53	50 Cents	30.00	75.00	100.	275.
M53r	50 Cents Replacement H-	—	Rare	—	—

KL#	Denomination	Fine	VF	XF	Unc
M54	1 Dollar	5.00	10.00	17.50	100.
M54r	1 Dollar Replacement H-	60.00	90.00	120.	250.
M55	5 Dollars	125.	175.	375.	2000.
M55r	5 Dollars Replacement H-	900.	1200.	1875.	3000.

KL#	Denomination	Fine	VF	XF	Unc
M56	10 Dollars	130.	225.	375.	1400.
M56r	10 Dollars Replacement H-	750.	1100.	1275.	2100.

SERIES 641

Issued: Aug. 31, 1965 **Withdrawn:** Oct. 21, 1968 **Areas of Use:** Vietnam

KL#	Denomination	Fine	VF	XF	Unc
M57	5 Cents	1.00	2.00	3.50	13.50
M57r	5 Cents Replacement J-	75.00	125.	200.	300.
M58	10 Cents	1.00	2.00	4.00	18.50
M58r	10 Cents Replacement J-	75.00	120.	200.	450.
M59	25 Cents	2.50	4.00	10.00	23.00
M59r	25 Cents Replacemetn J-	75.00	120.	200.	450.
M60	50 Cents	3.50	7.00	15.00	35.00
M60r	50 Cents Replacement J-	120.	200.	450.	750.
M61	1 Dollar	4.00	9.00	17.50	45.00
M61r	1 Dollar Replacement J-	450.	750.	1000.	1250.

KL#	Denomination	Fine	VF	XF	Unc
M62	5 Dollars	17.50	30.00	75.00	250.
M62r	5 Dollars Replacement J-	900.	1100.	2750.	3750.

KL#	Denomination	Fine	VF	XF	Unc
M63	10 Dollars	10.00	17.50	30.00	250.
M63r	10 Dollars Replacement J-	325.	425.	600.	1500.

SERIES 651

Issued: April 28, 1969 **Withdrawn:** Japan, May 19, 1969; Libya, June 11, 1969; Korea, Nov. 19, 1973 **Areas of Use:** Japan, Korea, Libya

KL#	Denomination	Fine	VF	XF	Unc
M72A	5 Cents	—	—	—	700.
M72B	10 Cents	—	—	—	700.
M72C	25 Cents	—	—	—	700.

KL#	Denomination	Fine	VF	XF	Unc
M72D	50 Cents	—	—	—	275.
M72E	1 Dollar	6.00	15.00	25.00	45.00
M72Er	One Dollar Replacement A-	—	Rare	—	—
M73	5 Dollars	50.00	85.00	150.	275.
M73r	5 Dollars Replacement A-	—	Rare	—	—
M74	10 Dollars	50.00	85.00	150.	275.
M74r	Ten Dollars Replacement A-	2000.	2500.	—	—

SERIES 661

Issued: Oct. 21, 1968 **Withdrawn:** Aug. 11, 1969 **Areas of Use:** Vietnam

KL#	Denomination	Fine	VF	XF	Unc
M64	5 Cents	—	1.50	3.00	10.00
M64r	5 Cents Replacement B-	400.	500.	600.	800.
M65	10 Cents	—	1.50	3.00	10.00
M65r	10 Cents Replacement B-	75.00	120.	200.	375.
M66	25 Cents	2.00	5.00	12.50	27.50
M66r	50 Cents Replacement B-	100.	150.	250.	600.
M67	50 Cents	2.00	5.00	10.00	23.00
M67r	50 Cents Replacement B-	—	Rare	—	—

KL#	Denomination	Fine	VF	XF	Unc
M68	1 Dollar	5.00	8.00	12.50	24.00
M68r	1 Dollar Replacement B-	125.	225.	450.	750.
M69	5 Dollars	5.00	8.00	15.00	30.00
M69r	5 Dollars Replacement B-	300.	500.	600.	800.

KL#	Denomination	Fine	VF	XF	Unc
M70	10 Dollars	200.	325.	750.	1850.
M70r	10 Dollars Replacement B-	800.	1200.	3500.	5000.
M71	20 Dollars	125.	200.	350.	1450.
M71r	20 Dollars Replacement B-	700.	1000.	1600.	3000.

SERIES 681

Issued: Aug. 11, 1969 **Withdrawn:** Oct. 7, 1970 **Areas of Use:** Vietnam

KL#	Denomination	Fine	VF	XF	Unc
M75	5 Cents	—	2.00	5.00	12.00
M75r	5 Cents Replacement C-	75.00	100.	150.	250.
M76	10 Cents	—	2.00	5.00	16.00
M76r	10 Cents Replacement C-	60.00	90.00	125.	250.
M77	25 Cents	2.00	5.00	10.00	27.50
M77r	25 Cents Replacement C-	—	Rare	—	—

KL#	Denomination	Fine	VF	XF	Unc
M78	50 Cents	3.00	10.00	15.00	24.00
M78r	50 Cents Replacement C-	90.00	150.	300.	450.
M79	1 Dollar	3.00	10.00	15.00	25.00
M79r	1 Dollar Replacement C-	75.00	125.	275.	400.

KL#	Denomination	Fine	VF	XF	Unc
M80	5 Dollars	10.00	20.00	50.00	125.
M80r	5 Dollars Replacement C-	475.	750.	1250.	2250.

KL#	Denomination	Fine	VF	XF	Unc
M81	10 Dollars	30.00	60.00	125.	300.
M81r	5 Dollars Replacement C-	—	Rare	—	—
M82	20 Dollars	30.00	70.00	100.	1100.

KL#	Denomination	Fine	VF	XF	Unc
M82	20 Dollars	30.00	70.00	100.	1100.
M82r	20 Dollars Replacement C-	—	Rare	—	—

SERIES 691

Printed but not released.

KL#	Denomination	Fine	VF	XF	Unc
M87	1 Dollar	—	—	—	250.

KL#	Denomination	Fine	VF	XF	Unc
M88	5 Dollars	—	—	—	—

KL#	Denomination	Fine	VF	XF	Unc
M93	10 Dollars	—	—	—	—
M94	20 Dollars	—	—	—	300.

SERIES 692

Issued: Oct. 7, 1970

Withdrawn: Fractional denominations, June 1, 1971; dollar denominations, March 15, 1973 **Areas of Use:** Vietnam

KL#	Denomination	Fine	VF	XF	Unc
M83	5 Cents	1.00	3.00	8.00	16.50
M83r	5 Cents Replacement E-	50.00	75.00	125.	200.
M84	10 Cents	1.00	3.00	8.00	17.50
M84r	10 Cents Replacement E-	60.00	90.00	125.	250.
M85	25 Cents	3.00	7.00	15.00	29.50
M85r	25 Cents Replacement E-	225.	300.	450.	750.
M86	50 Cents	4.00	8.00	16.50	40.00
M86r	50 Cents Replacement E-	225.	300.	450.	750.
M87	1 Dollar	8.00	20.00	35.00	95.00
M87r	1 Dollar Replacement E-	80.00	120.	200.	450.
M88	5 Dollars	50.00	95.00	200.	1000.

KL#	Denomination	Fine	VF	XF	Unc
M89	10 Dollars	75.00	150.	275.	1150.

KL#	Denomination	Fine	VF	XF	Unc
M90	20 Dollars	30.00	75.00	200.	1200.
M92r	5 Dollars Replacement E-	—	Rare	—	—
M93r	10 Dollars Replacement E-	—	Rare	—	—
M94r	20 Dollars Replacement E-	325.	600.	1000.	1800.

SERIES 701

Printed but not released.

KL#	Denomination	Fine	VF	XF	Unc
M103	1 Dollar	—	—	—	750.
M104	5 Dollars	—	—	—	750.
M105	10 Dollars	—	—	—	750.
M106	20 Dollars	—	—	—	750.

Philippines

The catalog numbers shown here are those from the Standard Catalog of World Paper Money, Volume 2, General Issues.

UNITED STATES ADMINISTRATION

BANCO ESPAÑOL FILIPINO

1904 Issue

#A31-A36 Denominations w/o *FUERTES*.

		Good	Fine	XF
A31	**5 Pesos** 1.1.1904. Black. Bank arms at upper center. Paper: Pink. Printer: BFL. Rare.	—	—	—
A32	**10 Pesos** 1.1.1904. Black. Bank arms at upper center. Paper: Green. Printer: BFL. Rare.	—	—	—
A33	**25 Pesos** 1.1.1904. Black. Bank arms at upper center. Paper: Light purple. Printer: BFL. Rare.	—	—	—
A34	**50 Pesos** 1.1.1904. Black. Bank arms at upper center. Paper: Green. Printer: BFL. Rare.	—	—	—
A35	**100 Pesos** 1.1.1904. Black. Bank arms at upper center. Paper: Yellowish brown. Printer: BFL. Rare.	—	—	—
A36	**200 Pesos** 1.1.1904. Black. Bank arms at upper center. Back: Multicolor. Paper: Yellowish brown. Printer: BFL. Rare.	—	—	—

1908 Issue

#1 and 2 w/1 stamped sign. (at l.) and 2 printed sign. #4-6 w/only 2 printed sign.

		Good	Fine	XF
1	**5 Pesos** 1.1.1908. Black on red underprint. Woman seated at left. Signature *J. Serrano* at left. Back: Red. Printer: USBEP (without imprint).	75.00	150.	325.

No.	Description	Good	Fine	XF
2	**10 Pesos**			
	1.1.1908. Black on brown underprint. Woman with flowers at center. Back: Brown. Printer: USBEP (without imprint).			
	a. Signature *Julian Serrano* at left. Rare.	—	—	—
	b. Signature *J. Serrano* at left.	175.	500.	—
3	**20 Pesos**			
	1.1.1908. Black on lilac underprint. Woman at left. Back: Tan. Printer: USBEP (without imprint).			
	a. Signature Julian Serrano at left. Rare.	—	—	—
	b. Signature J. Serrano at left.	500.	1000.	—

No.	Description	Good	Fine	XF
4	**50 Pesos**			
	1.1.1908. Black on blue underprint. Woman standing with flower at left. Back: Red. Printer: USBEP (without imprint).	250.	650.	—

		Good	Fine	XF
5	**100 Pesos**			
	1.1.1908. Black on green underprint. Woman seated with scroll and globe at left. Back: Olive. Printer: USBEP (without imprint).	350.	700.	—
6	**200 Pesos**			
	1.1.1908. Black on tan underprint. Justice with scales and shield at center. Back: Orange. Printer: USBEP (without imprint). Rare.	—	—	—

BANK OF THE PHILIPPINE ISLANDS

1912 Issue

#7-12 designs like previous issue. Printer: USBEP (w/o imprint). Replacement notes of b. varieties: Star prefix.

		Good	Fine	XF
7	**5 Pesos**			
	1.1.1912. Black on red underprint. Woman seated at left. Similar to #1. Back: Light red. Printer: USBEP (without imprint).			
	a. Signature D. Garcia and Jno. S. Hord.	5.00	35.00	75.00
	b. Signature D. Garcia and E. Sendres.	7.50	40.00	85.00
8	**10 Pesos**			
	1.1.1912. Black on brown underprint. Woman with flowers at center. Similar to #2. Printer: USBEP (without imprint).			
	a. Signature D. Garcia and Jno. S. Hord.	5.00	25.00	75.00
	b. Signature D. Garcia and E. Sendres.	5.00	25.00	75.00

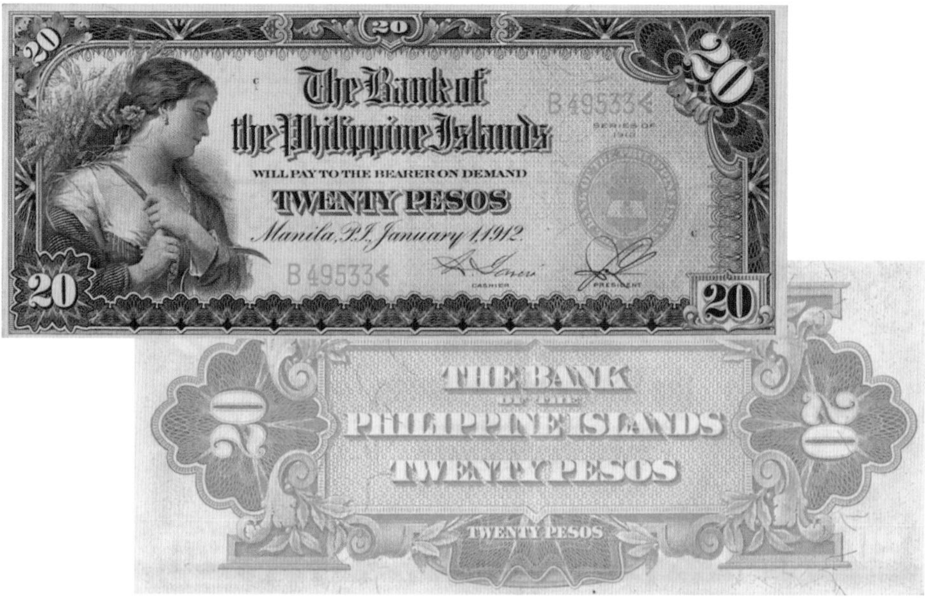

9	20 Pesos	Good	Fine	XF
	1.1.1912. Black on lilac underprint. Woman at left. Similar to #3. Printer: USBEP (without imprint).			
	a. Signature D. Garcia and Jno. S. Hord.	7.50	40.00	100.
	b. Signature D. Garcia and E. Sendres.	7.50	35.00	90.00

10	50 Pesos	Good	Fine	XF
	1.1.1912. Black on blue underprint. Woman standing with flower at left. Similar to #4. Printer: USBEP (without imprint).			
	a. Signature D. Garcia and Jno. S. Hord.	25.00	125.	300.
	b. Signature D. Garcia and E. Sendres.	20.00	100.	250.

		Good	Fine	XF
11	**100 Pesos**			
	1.1.1912. Black on green underprint. Woman seated with scroll and globe at left. Similar to #5. Printer: USBEP (without imprint).			
	a. Signature D. Garcia and Jno. S. Hord.	100.	300.	550.
	b. Signature D. Garcia and E. Sendres.	75.00	250.	500.
12	**200 Pesos**			
	1.1.1912. Black on tan underprint. Justice with scales and shield at center. Similar to #6. Signature D. Garcia and Jno. S. Hord. Printer: USBEP (without imprint).	300.	800.	—

1920 Issue

#13-15 like #7b-9b except for date and serial # prefix-suffix. Replacement notes: Star prefix.

		Good	Fine	XF
13	**5 Pesos** 1.1.1920. Black on red underprint. Woman seated at left. Like #7b. Signature D. Garcia and E. Sendres. Back: Orange. Printer: USBEP (without imprint).	5.00	12.50	50.00
14	**10 Pesos** 1.1.1920. Black on brown underprint. Woman with flowers at center. Like #8b. Signature D. Garcia and E. Sendres. Printer: USBEP (without imprint).	5.00	20.00	75.00
15	**20 Pesos** 1.1.1920. Black on lilac underprint. Woman at left. Like #9b. Signature D. Garcia and E. Sendres. Printer: USBEP (without imprint).	5.00	30.00	85.00

1928 Issue

#16-21 designs like #7-12 but w/o unpt. Replacement notes: Star prefix.

		Good	Fine	XF
16	**5 Pesos** 1.1.1928. Black. Woman seated at left. Like #7. Signature D. Garcia and Fulg. Borromeo. Back: Orange. Printer: USBEP (without imprint).	2.00	10.00	50.00
17	**10 Pesos** 1.1.1928. Black. Woman with flowers at center. Like #8. Signature D. Garcia and Fulg. Borromeo. Printer: USBEP (without imprint).	5.00	20.00	60.00
18	**20 Pesos** 1.1.1928. Black. Woman at left. Like #9. Signature D. Garcia and Fulg. Borromeo. Printer: USBEP (without imprint).	5.00	25.00	80.00
19	**50 Pesos** 1.1.1928. Black. Woman standing with flower at left. Like #10. Signature D. Garcia and Fulg. Borromeo. Printer: USBEP (without imprint).	25.00	80.00	190.
20	**100 Pesos** 1.1.1928. Black. Woman seated with scroll and globe at left. Like #11. Signature D. Garcia and Fulg. Borromeo. Printer: USBEP (without imprint).	60.00	200.	500.
21	**200 Pesos** 1.1.1928. Black. Justice with scales and shield at center. Like #12. Signature D. Garcia and Fulg. Borromeo. Printer: USBEP (without imprint).	175.	400.	850.

1933 Issue

#22-24 like #16-18 except for date and serial # prefix-suffix. Replacement notes: Star prefix.

No.	Description	Good	Fine	XF
22	**5 Pesos** 1.1.1933. Black. Woman seated at left. Like #16. Signature D. Garcia and P.J. Campos. Printer: USBEP (without imprint).	3.00	10.00	50.00
23	**10 Pesos** 1.1.1933. Black. Woman with flowers at center. Like #17. Signature D. Garcia and P.J. Campos. Printer: USBEP (without imprint).	6.00	15.00	50.00
24	**20 Pesos** 1.1.1933. Black. Woman at left. Like #18. Signature D. Garcia and P.J. Campos. Printer: USBEP (without imprint).	7.50	25.00	85.00

PHILIPPINE ISLANDS

1903 Issue

		Good	Fine	XF
25	2 Pesos			
	1903. Black on blue underprint. Portrait José Rizal at upper left. Back: Blue. Printer: USBEP (without imprint).			
	a. Signature William H. Taft and Frank A. Branagan.	100.	300.	650.
	b. Signature Luke E. Wright and Frank A. Branagan.	200.	600.	1000.

		Good	Fine	XF
26	**5 Pesos**			
	1903. Black on red underprint. Portrait President William McKinley at left. Back: Red. Printer: USBEP (without imprint).			
	a. Signature William H. Taft and Frank A. Branagan.	100.	450.	1400.
	b. Signature Luke E. Wright and Frank A. Branagan.	200.	550.	1500.

		Good	Fine	XF
27	**10 Pesos**			
	1903. Black on brown underprint. Portrait George Washington at lower center. Back: Brown. Printer: USBEP (without imprint).			
	a. Signature William H. Taft and Frank A. Branagan.	175.	650.	1500.
	b. Signature Luke E. Wright and Frank A. Branagan.	250.	1000.	2000.
27A	**10 Pesos**			
	1903. Black on brown underprint. Portrait George Washington at lower center. Like #27. Signature Henry C. Ide with title: *Governor General* and Frank A. Branagan. Back: Brown. Printer: USBEP (without imprint).	1500.	3250.	—

Note: The chief executive's title before 1905 was: Civil Governor.

1905 Issue

#28-31 issued w/ovpt. like #27A. Sign. Luke E. Wright w/title: *Governor General*

		Good	Fine	XF
28	**20 Pesos**			
	1905. Black on yellow underprint. Mt. Mayon at center. Signature Luke E. Wright and Frank A. Branagan. Back: Tan. Rare.	—	—	—
29	**50 Pesos**			
	1905. Black on red underprint. Portrait Gen. Henry W. Lawton at left. Signature Luke E. Wright and Frank A. Branagan. Back: Red. Rare.	—	—	—
30	**100 Pesos**			
	1905. Black on green underprint. Portrait Ferdinand Magellan at center. Signature Luke E. Wright and Frank A. Branagan. Back: Olive. Rare.	—	—	—
31	**500 Pesos**			
	1905. Black. Portrait Miguel Lopez de Legazpi at center. Signature Luke E. Wright and Frank A. Branagan. Back: Purple. Rare.	—	—	—

1906 Issue

		Good	Fine	XF
32	**2 Pesos**			
	1906. Black on blue underprint. Portrait José Rizal at upper left. Similar to #25 but payable in silver or gold. Back: Blue.			
	a. Signature James F. Smith and Frank A. Branagan.	60.00	150.	325.
	b. Signature W. Cameron Forbes and J. L. Barrett.	80.00	300.	—
	c. Signature W. Cameron Forbes and J. L. Manning.	90.00	400.	550.
	d. Signature Francis Burton Harrison and J. L. Manning.	60.00	175.	350.
	e. Signature like d., but without blue underprint. (error).	50.00	175.	—
	f. Signature Francis Burton Harrison and A. P. Fitzsimmons.	30.00	75.00	175.
33	**500 Pesos**			
	1906. Black. Portrait Miguel Lopez de Legazpi at center. Similar to #31. Back: Purple.			
	a. Signature James F. Smith and Frank A. Branagan. Rare.		30,000.	
	b. Signature W. Cameron Forbes and J. L. Barrett. Rare.	—	—	—
	c. Signature Francis Burton Harrison and A. P. Fitzsimmons. Rare.	—	—	—

1908 Issue

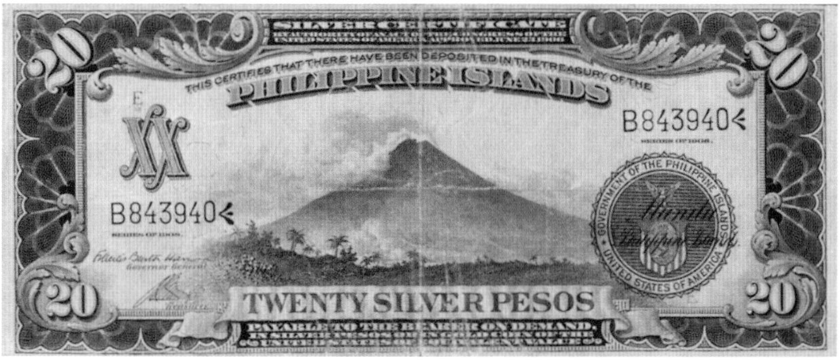

		Good	Fine	XF
34	**20 Pesos**			
	1908. Black on yellow underprint. Mt. Mayon at center. Similar to #28. Back: Tan.			
	a. Signature James F. Smith and Frank A. Branagan.	100.	350.	—
	b. Signature W. Cameron Forbes and J. L. Barrett.	125.	400.	800.
	c. Signature W. Cameron Forbes and J. L. Manning.	125.	400.	—
	d. Signature Francis Burton Harrison and J. L. Manning.	125.	350.	—
	e. Signature Francis Burton Harrison and A. P. Fitzsimmons.	75.00	325.	—

1910 Issue

35	5 Pesos	Good	Fine	XF
	1910. Black on red underprint. Portrait President William McKinley at left. Similar to #26. Back: Red.			
	a. Signature W. Cameron Forbes and J. L. Barrett.	75.00	200.	550.
	b. Signature W. Cameron Forbes and J. L. Manning.	75.00	200.	—
	c. Signature Francis Burton Harrison and J. L. Manning.	75.00	200.	—
	d. Signature Francis Burton Harrison and A. P. Fitzsimmons.	40.00	150.	400.

1912 Issue

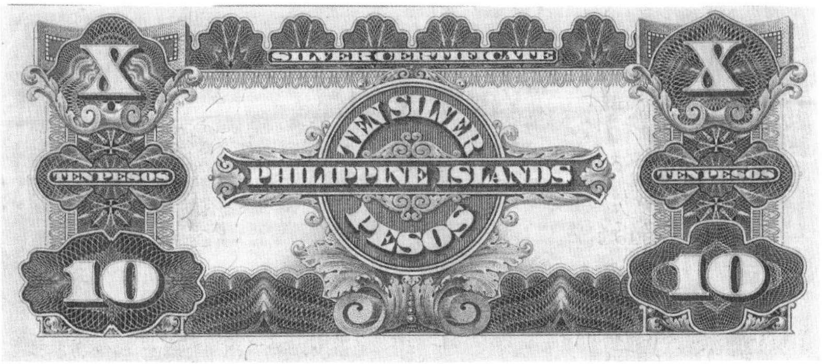

		Good	Fine	XF
36	**10 Pesos**			
	1912. Black on brown underprint. Portrait George Washington at lower center. Similar to #27. Back: Brown.			
	a. Signature W. Cameron Forbes and J. L. Barrett.	85.00	275.	—
	b. Signature W. Cameron Forbes and J. L. Manning.	85.00	275.	—
	c. Signature Francis Burton Harrison and J. L. Manning.	85.00	275.	—
	d. Signature Francis Burton Harrison and A. P. Fitzsimmons.	40.00	175.	450.

1916 Issue

		Good	Fine	XF
37	**50 Pesos**			
	1916. Black on red underprint. Portrait Gen. Henry W. Lawton at left. Similar to #29. Back: Red. Rare.	—	—	—
38	**100 Pesos**			
	1916. Black on green underprint. Portrait Ferdinand Magellan at center. Similar to #30. Back: Olive. Rare.	—	—	—

PHILIPPINE NATIONAL BANK

1917 Emergency WW I Issue

#39-42 Local printing.

		VG	VF	UNC
39	**10 Centavos** 20.11.1917. Gold on yellow underprint. Back: Yellow. American bald eagle.	—	20.00	50.00
40	**20 Centavos** 20.11.1917. Blue on yellow underprint. Back: Blue. American bald eagle.	—	20.00	50.00

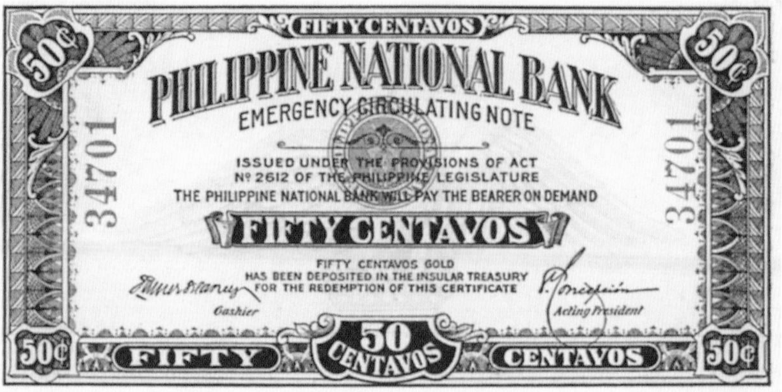

		VG	VF	UNC
41	**50 Centavos** 22.9.1917. Black on green underprint. Back: Green. American bald eagle.	5.00	25.00	65.00
42	**1 Peso** 22.9.1917. Black on red underprint. Back: Red. American bald eagle.	10.00	40.00	125.

1919 ND Emergency Issue

#43-43B new bank name, seal, sign. ovpt on Bank of the Philippine Islands notes.

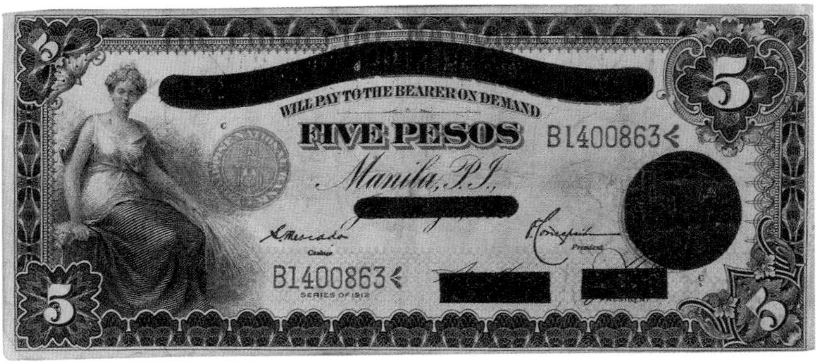

		VG	VF	UNC
43	**5 Pesos** ND (1919 - old date 1912). Black on red underprint. Woman seated at left. Back: Light red. Rare.	2000.	6000.	—
43A	**10 Pesos** ND (1919 - old date 1912). Black on brown underprint. Woman with flowers at center. Back: Brown. Rare.	—	8000.	
43B	**20 Pesos** ND (1919 - old date 1912). Black on lilac underprint. Woman at left. Back: Tan. Rare.	5500.	—	—

1916-20 Regular Issue

#44-50 Replacement notes: Star prefix.

		Good	Fine	XF
44	**1 Peso**			
	1918. Black on orange underprint. Portrait Charles A. Conant at left. Back: Green. Printer: USBEP (without imprint).	45.00	150.	450.
45	**2 Pesos**			
	1916. Black on blue underprint. Portrait José Rizal at left (similar to Silver and Treasury Certificates). Back: Blue. Printer: USBEP (without imprint).	65.00	225.	400.
46	**5 Pesos**			
	1916. Black on red underprint. Portrait Pres. William McKinley at left (similar to Silver and Treasury Certificates). Back: Red-orange. Printer: USBEP (without imprint).			
	a. Signature S. Ferguson and H. Parker Willis.	125.	400.	—
	b. Signature S. Mercado and V. Concepcion.	1.50	5.00	20.00

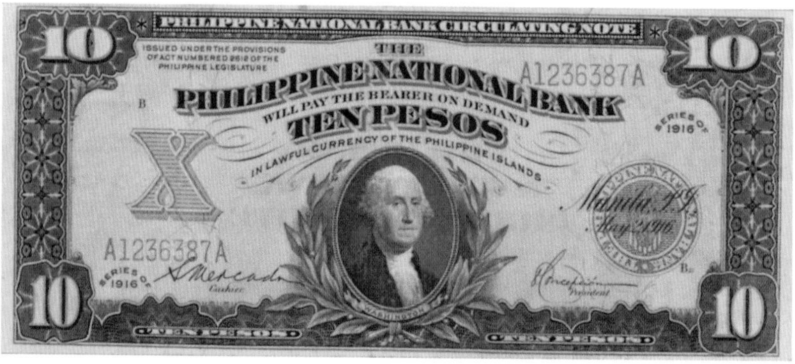

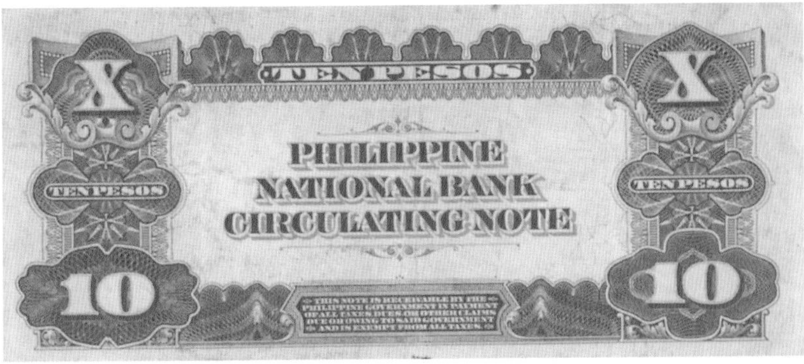

		Good	Fine	XF
47	**10 Pesos**			
	1916. Black on brown underprint. Portrait George Washington at center (similar to Silver and Treasury Certificates). Back: Brown. Printer: USBEP (without imprint).			
	a. Signature S. Ferguson and H. Parker Willis.	125.	400.	—
	b. Signature S. Mercado and V. Concepcion.	4.00	20.00	100.

		Good	Fine	XF
48	**20 Pesos**			
	1919. Black on yellow underprint. Portrait Congressman William A. Jones at lower center. Back: Tan. Printer: USBEP (without imprint).	100.	400.	—

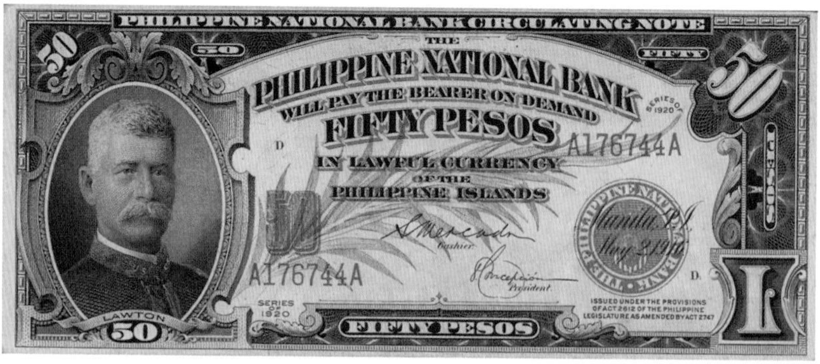

49	50 Pesos	Good	Fine	XF
	1920. Black on green underprint. Portrait Gen. Henry W. Lawton at left. Back: Red. Printer: USBEP (without imprint).	6.00	25.00	90.00

Note: #49 was never officially issued. 10,000 pieces were captured and issued during WW II by the Japanese (serial #90001-100000). The others were looted by Moros in the province of Mindanao who sold them at one-tenth of their face value. This accounts for their relative availability.

		Good	Fine	XF
50	**100 Pesos** 1920. Green on red underprint. Portrait Ferdinand Magellan at center. Back: Olive. Printer: USBEP (without imprint). Rare.	—	3000.	—

1921 Issue

#51-55 designs like previous issue but notes w/o unpt. Replacemnet notes: Star prefix.

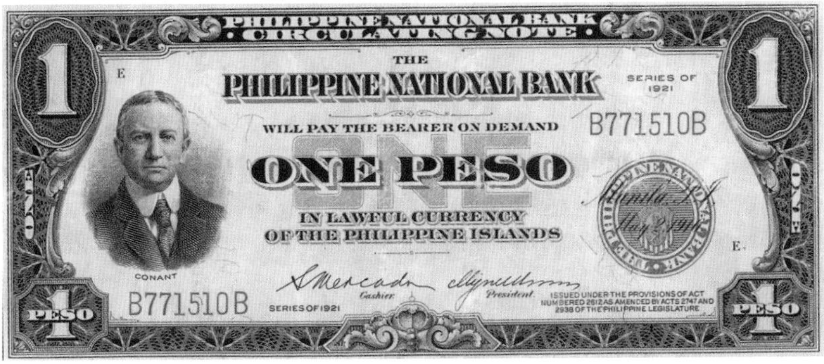

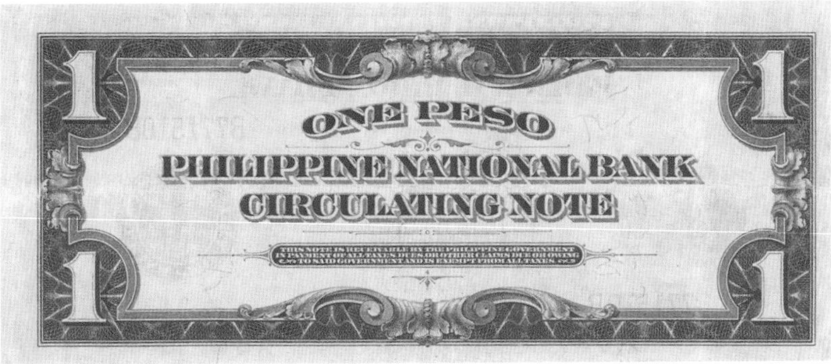

		Good	Fine	XF
51	**1 Peso** 1921. Black on orange underprint. Portrait Charles A. Conant at left. Like #44. Back: Green. Printer: USBEP (without imprint).	40.00	125.	300.

No.	Description	Good	Fine	XF
52	**2 Pesos** 1921. Black on blue underprint. Portrait José Rizal at left. Like #45. Back: Blue. Printer: USBEP (without imprint).	50.00	150.	375.

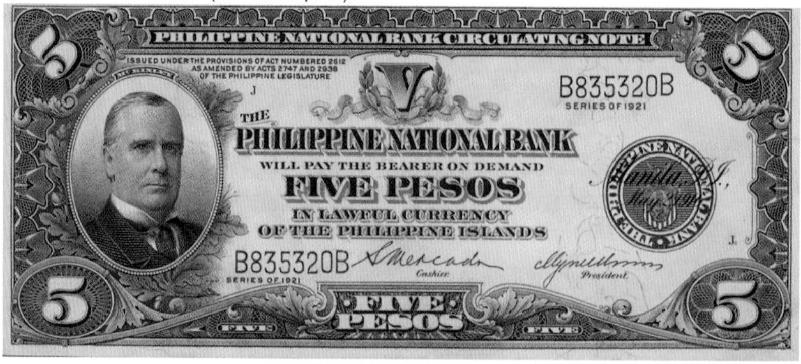

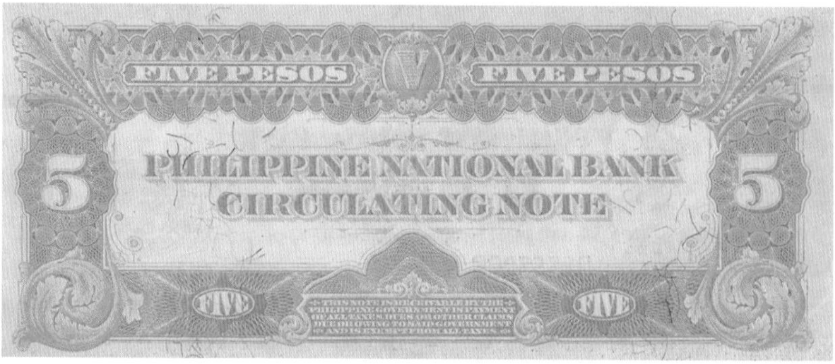

No.	Description	Good	Fine	XF
53	**5 Pesos** 1921. Black on red underprint. Portrait Pres. William McKinley at left. Like #46. Back: Red-orange. Printer: USBEP (without imprint).	1.50	4.00	15.00
54	**10 Pesos** 1921. Black on brown underprint. Portrait George Washington at center. Like #47. Back: Brown. Printer: USBEP (without imprint).	5.00	25.00	75.00
55	**20 Pesos** 1921. Black on yellow underprint. Portrait Congressman William A. Jones at lower center. Like #48. Back: Tan. Printer: USBEP (without imprint).	10.00	50.00	350.

1924 Issue

#56, replacement notes: Star prefix.

No.	Description	Good	Fine	XF
56	**1 Peso** 1924. Black on orange underprint. Portrait Charles A. Conant at left. Like #51. Back: Green.	10.00	65.00	150.

1937 Issue

#57-59 Replacement notes: Star prefix.

No.	Description	VG	VF	UNC
57	**5 Pesos** 1937. Black on red underprint. Portrait Pres. McKinley at left. Similar to #53. Text reads: PHILIPPINES insted of PHILIPPINE ISLANDS. Back: Red-orange. Printer: USBEP.	5.00	20.00	60.00

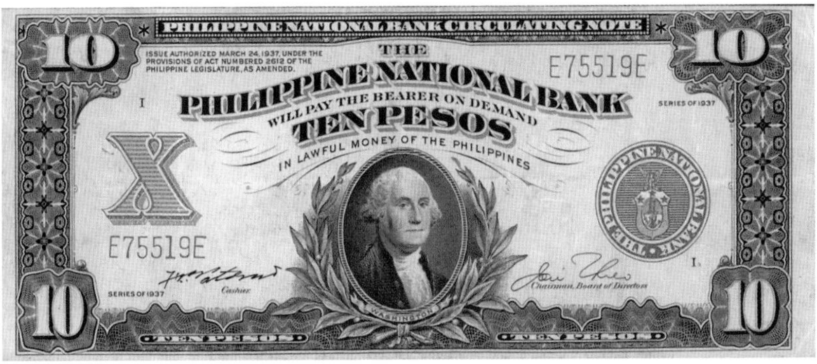

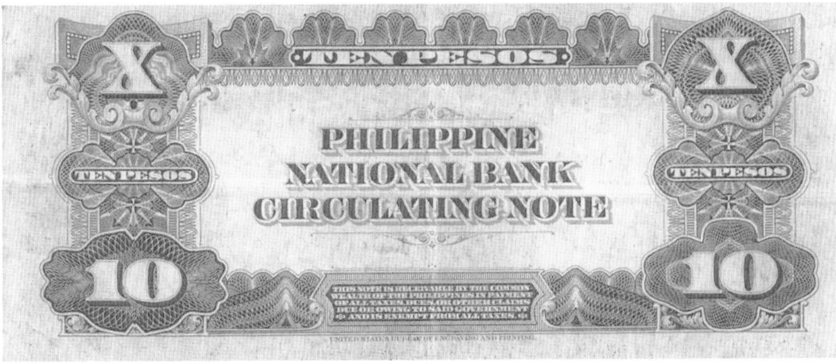

		VG	VF	UNC
58	**10 Pesos** 1937. Black on brown underprint. Portrait George Washington at center. Similar to #54. Text reads: PHILIPPINES insted of PHILIPPINE ISLANDS. Back: Brown. Printer: USBEP.	10.00	40.00	125.
59	**20 Pesos** 1937. Black on yellow underprint. Portrait Congressman William A. Jones at lower center. Similar to #55. Text reads: PHILIPPINES insted of PHILIPPINE ISLANDS. Back: Tan. Printer: USBEP.	65.00	175.	600.

PHILIPPINE ISLANDS

1918 Issue

#60-67 Replacement notes: Star prefix.

		Good	Fine	XF
60	**1 Peso** 1918. Black on green underprint. Portrait A. Mabini at left. Back: Green. Printer: USBEP (without imprint).			
	a. Signature Francis Burton Harrison and A. P. Fitzsimmons.	8.50	50.00	200.
	b. Signature Francis Burton Harrison and V. Carmona.	10.00	75.00	250.
61	**2 Pesos** 1918. Black on blue underprint. Portrait J. Rizal at left. Back: Blue. Printer: USBEP (without imprint).	35.00	200.	350.
62	**5 Pesos** 1918. Black on light red underprint. Portrait President William McKinley at left. Back: Red-orange. Printer: USBEP (without imprint).	60.00	200.	—

63 **10 Pesos** | **Good** 200. | **Fine** 700. | **XF** —

1918. Black on brown underprint. Portrait George Washington at center. Back: Brown.. Printer: USBEP (without imprint).

63A **20 Pesos** | **Good** 60.00 | **Fine** 250. | **XF** 550.

1918. Black on yellow underprint. Mayon volcano at center. Ornate blue *XX* at upper left. Signature Francis Burton Harrison and A. P. Fitzsimmons. Back: Tan. Printer: USBEP (without imprint).

No.	Description	Good	Fine	XF
64	**20 Pesos**			
	1918. Black on yellow underprint. Mayon volcano at center. Like #63A. Signature Francis Burton Harrison and V. Carmona. Back: Tan. Printer: USBEP (without imprint).	60.00	225.	550.
65	**50 Pesos**			
	1918. Black on green underprint. Portrait Gen. Lawton at left. Back: Red. Printer: USBEP (without imprint).			
	a. Signature Francis Burton Harrison and A. P. Fitzsimmons.	200.	600.	—
	b. Signature Francis Burton Harrison and V. Carmona.	200.	600.	—
66	**100 Pesos**			
	1918. Black on green underprint. Portrait Ferdinand Magellan at center. Back: Olive. Printer: USBEP (without imprint).			
	a. Signature Francis Burton Harrison and A. P. Fitzsimmons. Rare.	—	—	—
	b. Signature Francis Burton Harrison and V. Carmona. Rare.	—	—	—
67	**500 Pesos**			
	1918. Black on orange underprint. Portrait Legazpi at center. Back: Purple. Printer: USBEP (without imprint). Rare.	—	—	—

1924 Issue

#68-72 w/o unpt. Replacement notes: Star prefix.

No.	Description	Good	Fine	XF
68	**1 Peso**			
	1924. Black. Portrait A. Mabini at left. Like #60. Back: Green. Printer: USBEP (without imprint).			
	a. Signature Leonard Wood and Salv. Lagdameo with title: *Acting Treasurer.*	8.00	50.00	150.
	b. Signature Leonard Wood and Salv. Lagdameo with title: *Treasurer.*	15.00	70.00	200.
	c. Signature H. L. Stimson and Salv. Lagdameo.	7.50	40.00	140.
69	**2 Pesos**			
	1924. Black. Portrait J. Rizal at left. Like #61, but large denomination numeral added in red at lower left center. Back: Blue. Printer: USBEP (without imprint).			

	Good	Fine	XF
a. Signature Leonard Wood and Salv. Lagdameo with title: *Acting Treasurer.*	20.00	100.	250.
b. Signature Leonard Wood and Salv. Lagdameo with title: *Treasurer.*	25.00	110.	260.
c. Signature Henry L. Stimson and Salv. Lagdameo.	10.00	75.00	175.

		Good	Fine	XF
70	**5 Pesos**			
	1924. Black. Portrait President William McKinley at left. Like #62. Printer: USBEP (without imprint).	20.00	80.00	300.
71	**10 Pesos**			
	1924. Black. Portrait George Washington at center. Like #63. Back: Brown. Printer: USBEP (without imprint).	15.00	70.00	250.

		Good	Fine	XF
72	**500 Pesos**			
	1924. Black on blue underprint. Portrait Legazpi at center. Blue numeral. Like #67. Printer: USBEP (without imprint).			

	Good	Fine	XF
a. Back light green.	1500.	5000.	—
p. Back purple. Proof.	—	—	—

Note: Though official records indicate that the backs of #72 were printed in purple, the only issued notes seen in collections have light green backs. Further reports are needed.

1929 Issue

#73-80 Replacement notes: Star prefix. Many changes were effected on US-Philippine currency with the 1929 Issue, as the United States changed from the large to small size formats. Significant design alterations were introduced as well as some color changes.

		Good	Fine	XF
73	**1 Peso**			
	1929. Black on orange underprint. Portrait A. Mabini at left. Similar to #60 but several minor alterations in plate. Back: Orange. Printer: USBEP (without imprint).			
	a. Signature Dwight F. Davis and Salv. Lagdameo.	5.00	40.00	125.
	b. Signature Theodore Roosevelt and Salv. Lagdameo.	15.00	75.00	225.
	c. Signature Frank Murphy and Salv. Lagdameo.	3.00	15.00	800.
74	**2 Pesos**			
	1929. Black on blue underprint. Portrait J. Rizal at left. Similar to #61 but several minor alterations in plate. Back: Blue. Printer: USBEP (without imprint).			
	a. Signature Theodore Roosevelt and Salv. Lagdameo.	6.00	50.00	150.
	b. Signature Frank Murphy and Salv. Lagdameo.	3.00	15.00	80.00
75	**5 Pesos**			
	1929. Black on yellow underprint. Portrait William McKinley at left, Adm. Dewey at right. Back: Yellow. Printer: USBEP (without imprint).	10.00	50.00	325.

No.	Description	Good	Fine	XF
76	**10 Pesos** 1929. Black on brown underprint. Portrait George Washington at left. Back: Brown. Printer: USBEP (without imprint).	15.00	60.00	325.
77	**20 Pesos** 1929. Black on yellow underprint. Mayon volcano at center. Similar to #64 but several minor alterations in plate. Back: Tan. Printer: USBEP (without imprint).	20.00	100.	350.
78	**50 Pesos** 1929. Black on pink underprint. Portrait Gen. Lawton at left. Back: Dark red. Printer: USBEP (without imprint).	125.	500.	—

No.	Description	Good	Fine	XF
79	**100 Pesos** 1929. Black on green underprint. Portrait Ferdinand Magellan at left. Back: Green. Printer: USBEP (without imprint). Rare.	—	2500.	—
80	**500 Pesos** 1929. Black on orange underprint. Portrait Legazpi at left. Back: Purple. Printer: USBEP (without imprint). Rare.	—	—	—

COMMONWEALTH

PHILIPPINES

1936 Issue

#81-88 Title reads: *PHILIPPINES* instead of *PHILIPPINE ISLANDS*.
Replacement notes: Star prefix.

		VG	VF	UNC
81	**1 Peso** 1936. Black on orange underprint. Portrait A. Mabini at left. Similar to #73. New red Commonwealth seal. Signature Manuel Quezon and Antonio Ramos. Back: Orange. Printer: USBEP (without imprint).	1.50	4.00	25.00

		VG	VF	UNC
82	**2 Pesos** 1936. Black on blue underprint. Portrait J. Rizal at left. Similar to #74. New red Commonwealth seal. Signature Manuel Quezon and Antonio Ramos. Back: Blue. Printer: USBEP (without imprint).	3.00	10.00	55.00
83	**5 Pesos** 1936. Black on yellow underprint. Portrait William McKinley at left, Adm. Dewey at right. Similar to #75. New red Commonwealth seal. Signature Manuel Quezon and Antonio Ramos. Back: Yellow. Printer: USBEP (without imprint).			
	a. Regular issue. Serial # D1D to D3 244 000D.	3.00	10.00	50.00
	b. U.S.A. War Department issue (1944). D3 244 001D to D3 544 000D.	50.00	150.	350.

		VG	VF	UNC
84	**10 Pesos** 1936. Black on brown underprint. Portrait George Washington at left. Similar to #76. New red Commonwealth seal. Signature Manuel Quezon and Antonio Ramos. Printer: USBEP (without imprint).			
	a. Regular issue. Serial # D1D to D2 024 000D.	5.00	50.00	375.
	b. U.S.A. War Department issue (1944). D2 024 001D to D2 174 000D.	75.00	275.	600.
85	**20 Pesos** 1936. Black on yellow underprint. Mayon volcano at center. Similar to #77. New red Commonwealth seal. Signature Manuel Quezon and Antonio Ramos. Back: Tan. Printer: USBEP (without imprint).			
	a. Regular issue. D1D to D1 664 000D.	15.00	60.00	300.
	b. U.S.A. War Department issue (1944). D1 664 001D to D1 739 000D.	75.00	350.	1500.
86	**50 Pesos** 1936. Black on pink underprint. Portrait Gen. Lawton at left. Similar to #78. New red Commonwealth seal. Signature Manuel Quezon and Antonio Ramos. Back: Dark red. Printer: USBEP (without imprint).	125.	300.	600.
87	**100 Pesos** 1936. Black on green underprint. Portrait Ferdinand Magellan at left. Similar to #79. New red Commonwealth seal. Signature Manuel Quezon and Antonio Ramos. Back: Green. Printer: USBEP (without imprint).			
	a. Regular issue. Serial # D1D to D41 000D.	200.	500.	—
	b. U.S.A. War Department issue (1944). D41 001D to D56 000D. Rare.	600.	—	—
88	**500 Pesos** 1936. Black on orange underprint. Portrait Legazpi at left. Similar to #80. New red Commonwealth seal. Signature Manuel Quezon and Antonio Ramos. Back: Purple. Printer: USBEP (without imprint). Rare.	—	—	—

Note: #83b, 84b, 85b and 87b were made at the request of Army Headquarters, Brisbane, Australia in 1944 for use in military operations.

1941 Issue

#89-93 like previous issue. Replacement notes: Star prefix.

		VG	VF	UNC
89	**1 Peso** 1941. Black on orange underprint. Portrait A. Mabini at left. Like #81. Signature Manuel Quezon and A.S. de Leon. Back: Orange. Printer: USBEP (without imprint).			
	a. Regular issue. Serial # E1E to E6 000 000E.	1.50	3.50	12.50
	b. Processed to simulate used currency at Bureau of Standards (1943). #E6 008 001E to E6 056 000E; E6 064 001E to E6 072 000E; E6 080 001E to E6 324 000E. Total 300,000 notes.	150.	200.	—
	c. Naval Aviators' Emergency Money Packet notes (1944). E6 324 001E to E6 524 000E.	5.00	15.00	50.00
90	**2 Pesos** 1941. Black on blue underprint. Portrait J. Rizal at left. Like #82. Signature Manuel Quezon and A.S. de Leon. Back: Blue. Printer: USBEP (without imprint).	4.00	25.00	100.
91	**5 Pesos** 1941. Black on yellow underprint. Portrait William McKinley at left, Adm. Dewey at right. Like #83. Signature Manuel Quezon and A.S. de Leon. Back: Yellow. Printer: USBEP (without imprint).			
	a. Regular issue. Serial #E1E to E1 188 000E.	10.00	35.00	100.
	b. Processed like #89b (1943). #E1 208 001E to E1 328 000E.	350.	—	—
	c. Packet notes like #89c (1944). #E1 328 001E to E1 348 000E.	15.00	75.00	300.

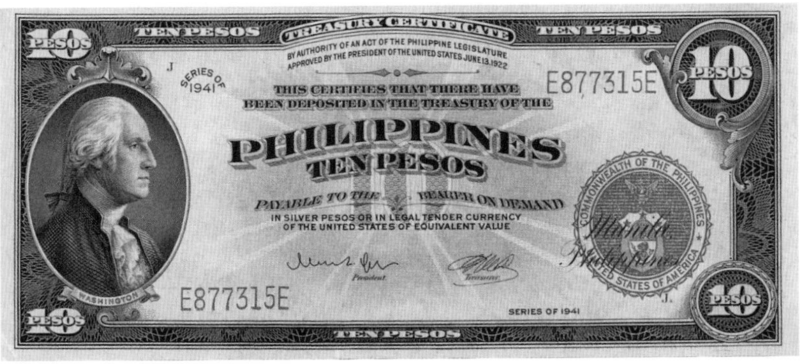

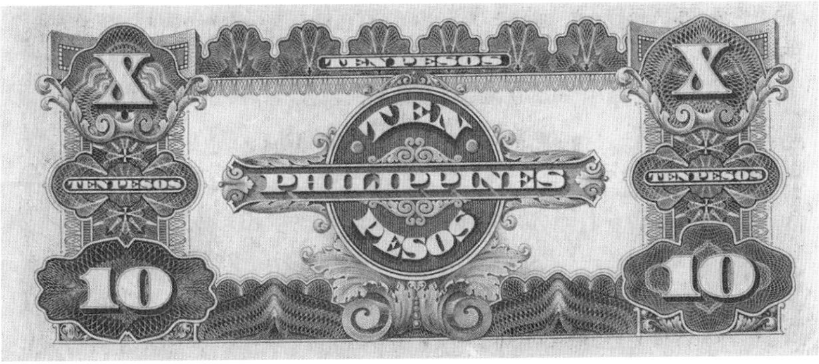

		VG	VF	UNC
92	**10 Pesos**			
	1941. Black on brown underprint. Portrait George Washington at left. Like #84. Signature Manuel Quezon and A.S. de Leon. Back: Brown. Printer: USBEP (without imprint).			
	a. Regular issue. Serial #E1E to E800 000E.	10.00	75.00	350.
	b. Processed like #89b (1943). E810 001E to E870 000E.	400.	—	—
	c. Packet notes like #89c (1944). #E870 001E to E890 000E.	20.00	85.00	400.
93	**20 Pesos**			
	1941. Black on yellow underprint. Mayon volcano at center. Like #85. Signature Manuel Quezon and A.S. de Leon. Back: Tan. Printer: USBEP (without imprint).	75.00	325.	—

Note: 50, 100 and 500 Pesos notes Series of 1941 were printed but never shipped because of the outbreak of World War II. All were destroyed in 1949, leaving extant only proof impressions and specimen sheets.

1944 ND Victory Issue

#94-101 Black ovpt: *VICTORY* in large letters. Replacement notes: Star suffix.

		VG	VF	UNC
94	**1 Peso**			
	ND (1944). Black on orange underprint. Portrait A. Mabini at left. Like #89. Text: VICTORY Series No. 66 twice instead of date, with blue seal. Signature Sergio Osmeña and J. Hernandez. Back: Orange. Printer: USBEP (without imprint).	.75	2.00	6.00

		VG	VF	UNC
95	**2 Pesos**			
	ND (1944). Black on blue underprint. Portrait J. Rizal at left. Like #90. Text: VICTORY Series No. 66 twice instead of date, with blue seal. Back: Blue. Printer: USBEP (without imprint).			
	a. Signature Sergio Osmeña and J. Hernandez with title: *Auditor General.*	1.00	3.00	15.00
	b. Signature Manuel Roxas and M. Guevara with title: *Treasurer.*	5.00	20.00	75.00
96	**5 Pesos**			
	ND (1944). Black on yellow underprint. Portrait William McKinley at left, Adm. Dewey at right. Like #91. Text: VICTORY Series No. 66 twice instead of date, with blue seal. Signature Sergio Osmeña and J. Hernandez. Back: Yellow. Printer: USBEP (without imprint).	2.50	10.00	65.00
97	**10 Pesos**			
	ND (1944). Black on brown underprint. Portrait George Washington at left. Like #92. Text: VICTORY Series No. 66 twice instead of date, with blue seal. Signature Sergio Osmeña and J. Hernandez. Back: Brown. Printer: USBEP (without imprint).	5.00	20.00	125.
98	**20 Pesos**			
	ND (1944). Black on yellow underprint. Mayon volcano at center. Like #93. Text: VICTORY Series No. 66 twice instead of date, with blue seal. Back: Tan. Printer: USBEP (without imprint).			
	a. Signature Sergio Osmeña and J. Hernandez with title: *Auditor General.*	5.00	35.00	85.00
	b. Signature Manuel Roxas and M. Guevara with title: *Treasurer.*	20.00	75.00	300.
99	**50 Pesos**			
	ND (1944). Black on pink underprint. Portrait Gen. Lawton at left. Like #86. Text: VICTORY Series No. 66 twice instead of date, with blue seal. Back: Dark red. Printer: USBEP (without imprint).			
	a. Signature Sergio Osmeña and J. Hernandez with title: *Auditor General.*	30.00	120.	400.
	b. Signature Manuel Roxas and M. Guevara with title: *Treasurer.*	30.00	150.	575.

		VG	VF	UNC
101	**500 Pesos** ND (1944). Black on orange underprint. Portrait Legazpi at left. Like #88. Text: VICTORY Series No. 66 twice instead of date, with blue seal. Back: Purple. Printer: USBEP (without imprint).			
	a. Signature Sergio Osmeña and J. Hernandez with title: *Auditor General.*	500.	1000.	2500.
	b. Signature Sergio Osmeña and M. Guevara with title: *Treasurer.*	250.	850.	2000.
	c. Signature Manuel Roxas and M. Guevara.	350.	900.	2200.

Error Notes

by Frederick J. Bart and Doris A. Bart

United States Paper Money Production

Paper money is produced at Bureau of Engraving and Printing (BEP) in Washington, D.C. with a satellite facility in Fort Worth Texas. Federal Reserve Notes are printed via the dry intaglio method and finished on the currency overprinting and processing equipment (COPE).

First Printing (back). Back designs are produced on a 32 subject printing plate. Each plate has the back design along with the same back plate check number. The sheet passes between the engraved plate and the impression cylinder under tremendous pressure. The sheet is then allowed to dry before advancing to the next stage of printing.

Second Printing (face). The second printing consists of the portrait, outer borders, series, and engraved signatures of the Treasurer of the United States and the Secretary of the Treasury. The second printing is accomplished in black ink. After the printing, the sheets are cut vertically into sixteen subject panes and then piled into stacks of 10,000 half sheets to advance to the third stage of printing

Third Printing (overprint). The last stage includes the serial numbers and seals. However, in some cases the treasury seal may be applied independently of the serial numbers. The currency overprinting and processing equipment contains built in electronic and photoelectric sensors that interrupt the operation when a mistake is found. Otherwise, the sheets are stacked into piles of one hundred consecutively numbered bills, strapped together and sealed into a "brick" with plastic shrink-wrap. The bricks are then sent to 12 Federal Reserve banks or one of the 24 Federal Reserve Bank branches.

With literally billions of notes produced on an annual basis, it becomes impossible for even experienced inspectors within the BEP to catch every mistake. This chapter presents a smattering of errors that have escaped the watchful eyes of government personnel. This format is based upon the book,

United States Paper Money: A Comprehensive Catalog & Price Guide, 2nd Edition, Frederick J. Bart, Krause Publications, 2003.

Numerous factors influence the price of error currency. These include: the state of preservation or grade, the type of paper money, the series, the denomination, the rarity, and eye-appeal.

DOUBLE DENOMINATIONS

The dual denomination oddity is aptly titled "The King of Errors". It reigns supreme among paper money mistakes. The double denomination note has the face of one value and the back of another. Large size double denominations are found in more different varieties than those on small size notes. The authors speculate that as many as two hundred double-denomination notes exist. The value of both large and small size double denomination notes are about the same.

Fine $17,500 EF $25,000 CU $27,500

FAULTY ALIGNMENTS

Faulty alignments are caused by from improper relationship between the printed designs on one side of the note relative to the other side. One side of the note is well centered while the other side appears "shifted". Faulty alignments are a common error and range from just a small "shift" to a major mis-position showing portions of the adjacent note. Collectors of all levels seek examples of faulty alignments.

Minor faulty alignments value;
Fine $75 EF $150 CU $250

More dramatic faulty alignments value;
Fine $500 EF $1000 CU $2000

INSUFFICIENT INKINGS

Insufficient inking occurs when the ink fountain fails to fully charge or fill the printing plate. This causes the image to be faint or incomplete. The insufficient inking error may involve all or part of the design, depending on the amount of the plate which is affected. Most insufficient inking occurs on the 1st or 2nd printings.

Minor insufficient ink value;
Fine $50 EF $100 CU $200

More dramatic insufficient ink;
Fine $100 EF $200 CU $400

INVERTED BACKS

The inverted back error is caused when a stack of currency sheets, after receiving the first printing, is rotated 180 degrees and enters the printing press. In actuality, because the back is printed first the error should be called an "inverted face". One might anticipate that the inverted back error would be rather common, as there is no visible error for the BEP inspectors to notice; however, this is one of the most difficult errors to find.

Small size inverted backs value;
Fine $500 EF $1000 CU $2000

Large size inverted back value;
Fine $1500 EF $3000 CU $7500

BLANK BACKS

Missing printing errors are readily identified because the back of the note is entirely missing. There are other types of missing printing that occur during the 2nd and 3rd printing which will be covered in this chapter. Most common cause of this error is due to two uncut sheets being fed into the press at the same time, with one sheet accepting an impression and the other sheet passing through protected and leaving the press blank.

Fine $150 EF $250 CU $350

MULTIPLE ERRORS

The scarcity of multiple errors cannot be overstated. Multiple errors arise independently of each other either during the printing or cutting process. The value of these errors remains a matter of negotiation and agreement between the seller and the buyer. Therefore it is impractical to attempt to provide any guide to values of these elusive multiple mistakes.

MULTIPLE PRINTINGS

Multiple printing errors go through the normal three printing stages. There are several causes for this error: a loose impression cylinders or the press operator stops the machinery, keeps the sheet in position, and then re-starts the press. However, the most common cause of the multiple printing error is a sheet which is re-run through the same printing press for a second or subsequent time. If the note is re-fed thru the 1st or 2nd printing stages, one often finds different plate check numbers on the finished product. Value varies depending on the eye-appeal of the error.

Fine $750 EF $1250 CU $2000

OBSTRUCTED PRINTINGS

Whenever stray material comes between the currency paper and the printing plate an obstruction error occurs. The intervening material causes a portion of the note to be left blank. Several causes are paper, cellophane, fiber threads, adhesive bandage backing, masking tape and cardboard, to mention a few. If the obstructing item is recovered along with the affected note, the value of the error increases significantly.

Obstructed print without fragment value;
Fine $100 EF $250 CU $500

Obstructed print with fragment value;
Fine $2500 EF $5000 CU $7500

OFFSET PRINTINGS

Offset errors look like one side of the note "bled through" to the other. However, the offset is a mirror image of the note's opposite side. This error occurs when a sheet of currency fails to enter the press. As such, the plate contacts the impression cylinder. When the next currency sheet is inserted it receives not only the intended printing on the correct side, but a transfer or offset printing on the opposite side as well. The ink lightens with each sheet that is fed. Not surprisingly, the amount of the design imprinted onto the impression cylinder dictates the size and shape of the offset. Offsets occur front to back or back to front. The rich, bold offsets demand the highest price; with the first and second impressions being desirable.

Minor partial offset value
Fine $15 EF $25 CU $35

Complete offset value

Fine $100	EF $200	CU $400

OVERPRINTS (3RD print) ON BACK

The serial number, Treasury seal and, if applicable, the Federal Reserve bank or universal seal and district numbers appear on the wrong side of the bill. Overprint on back errors occur when the sheet is fed into the press with the back side towards the overprinting press instead of the front. Inverted overprinted errors on back occur the same way, except the sheet is not only fed on the wrong side but rotated 180 degrees causing the 3rd printing to be inverted as well.. Mistakes appear on both sides of the note. There is a lack of information on the face while the back appears quite crowded.

Overprint on back

Fine $100	EF $175	CU $350

Overprint on back inverted value;
Fine $750 EF $1500 CU $3500

INVERTED OVERPRINTS

Inverted overprints demonstrate the seal and serial numbers upside down relative to the face printing. These errors occur when the ∫ sheet is fed into the press 180 degrees from the proper alignment before and during the 3rd printing.

Inverted Overprint value;
Fine $150 EF $355 CU $750

MISALIGNED OVERPRINTS

Misaligned overprint errors are easily spotted by the shift in the 3rd printing causing the serial numbers and seals to be off center. This occurs when the paper is improperly fed either at a angle or with unequal amounts of paper on the right and left sides. For a misalignment to qualify as an error, a portion of the overprint must rest atop a portion of the design it was not intended to cover. These errors can range from hardly noticeable—and, therefore only minimally desirable-- to incredibly dramatic and the object of great desire.

Minor Misaligned Overprint value
Fine $30 EF $45 CU $65

Major Misaligned Overprint value
Fine $250 EF $500 CU $800

MISSING OVERPRINTS

Missing overprint error lacks the application of the 3rd printing. An example of this mistake is missing the serial numbers and seals. The error occurs from any of several different causes. The most frequent occurrence involves two sheets being fed through the overprinting press at the same time. This results in the top sheet accept a normal imprint while the bottom sheet misses the 3rd printing. Another cause of the missing overprint error develops when the sheet is fed properly, but the press fails to engage and does not make contact with the sheet. Alternatively, there may be a large obstruction blocking the sheet.

Fine $200 EF $500 CU $1000

MISSING 2ND PRINTINGS

This error occurs again when 2 sheets are fed at the same time, with the top sheet receiving the second printing and the bottom sheet missing all of the second printing. Another explanation for this visually dramatic mistake is the accidental advancement of a stack of sheets from the 1st printing presses to the overprinting presses without the intervening stop for the face printing. These are among the most dramatic of mistakes encountered.

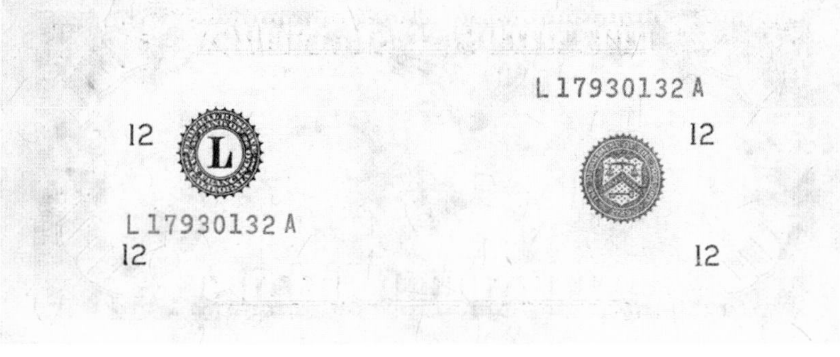

Fine $250 EF $500 CU $850

MISMATCHED SERIAL NUMBERS

Mismatched serial numbers occur when a press operator fails to set the same sequence of numbers on the two different numbering wheels prior to initiating the printing. Mismatched errors will also occur when the numbering machine sticks at a particular serial number, while the other continues to advance normally. Prefix and suffix letters also are subject to be mismatched. Mismatched prefix or suffix letters result from human error during the press set-up. Mismatched characters are actually scarcer than mismatched numbers.

Single Digit Mismatch value

Fine $250 EF $500 CU $1000

Mismatch Prefix value

Fine $250 EF $500 CU $750

STUCK DIGITS

Stuck digit errors and partially turned digits occur from a clogging of the numbering wheel on the cylinder that imprints the serial numbers. If the wheel freezes in place it will print a partially turned digit. Once it advances a stuck digit may result

Stuck Digit value;
Fine $40 EF $75 CU $125

CUTTING ERRORS

Cutting errors occur during the terminal stage of production. The 16-subject half-sheets are separated into 2-subject blocks and then into individual notes. A cutting error is generated by misalignment of the uncut sheet upon meeting the knives. Unlike faulty alignments, which occur on only one side of the note. The cutting error shows a shift or misalignment on both sides from being cut incorrectly. There are various types of cutting errors from minor to dramatic.

Minor Cutting Error
Fine $5 EF $15 CU $45

Major Cutting Error value;
Fine $750 EF $3000 CU $5500

GUTTER OR INTERIOR FOLDS

Gutter fold or interior folds occur when a wrinkle occurs in the currency paper as it receives a printed image. The appearance is an unprinted, blank, white channel interrupting the back, face, or over printing.

Occasionally, the paper will wrinkle several times causing multiple gutters. Gutters are the second most common type of errors found on United States paper money.

Single Gutter Fold value;
Fine $30 EF $40 CU $50

Multiple Gutter Fold value;
Fine $75 EF $150 CU $300

PRINTED OR EXTERIOR FOLDS

Printed folds may occur prior to or during any stage of the production process. As the name implies, the currency sheet folds over and remains folded during the printing. The ultimate shape of the note depends upon whether the sheet unfolds before cutting. The fold may be minor with just a corner tip being folded or more dramatic with a large portion of the note being folded. Occasionally a tear occurs in the paper with a similar effect in the final product.

Printed Fold value;

Fine $500 EF $1500 CU $2500

Printed Tear value
Fine $500 EF $1500 CU $2500

INK SMEARS

Ink smears occur from the printing plates being cleaned inadequately. The amount of residual ink left on the surface of the plate determines the size and shape of the smear. This can range from a small spot or fine line to a large portion of the note covered with ink. The term "solvent smear" is solvent, which smears. This occurs when the ink is heavily diluted with a solvent solution. The excessive amount of solvent reaches the printing plate causing the ink to be blurry and watery.

Minor Ink Smear value;
Fine $10 EF $25 CU $40

Major Ink Smear value;
Fine $150 EF $300 CU $500

Solvent Smear value;
Fine $150 EF $300 CU $500

FAKE ERRORS

Collectors need to be aware of the existence of fake errors. Trickery and greed are everywhere. Unscrupulous sellers go to great lengths to fool collectors. Internet auction sites are overrun with bogus mistakes. Some of the most frequently encountered alterations include: the backs of notes which are yellow or orange, seals or serial numbers which have been erased, removed, or changed color, spurious addition of a design, and cutting errors created from uncut sheets sold directly to the public. numbers and seals. And one of the most dramatic is the cutting error. On Federal Reserve notes from 1981 or later with the serial numbers beginning with 96000000, most of these notes were released in uncut sheet form and are especially subject to alteration.

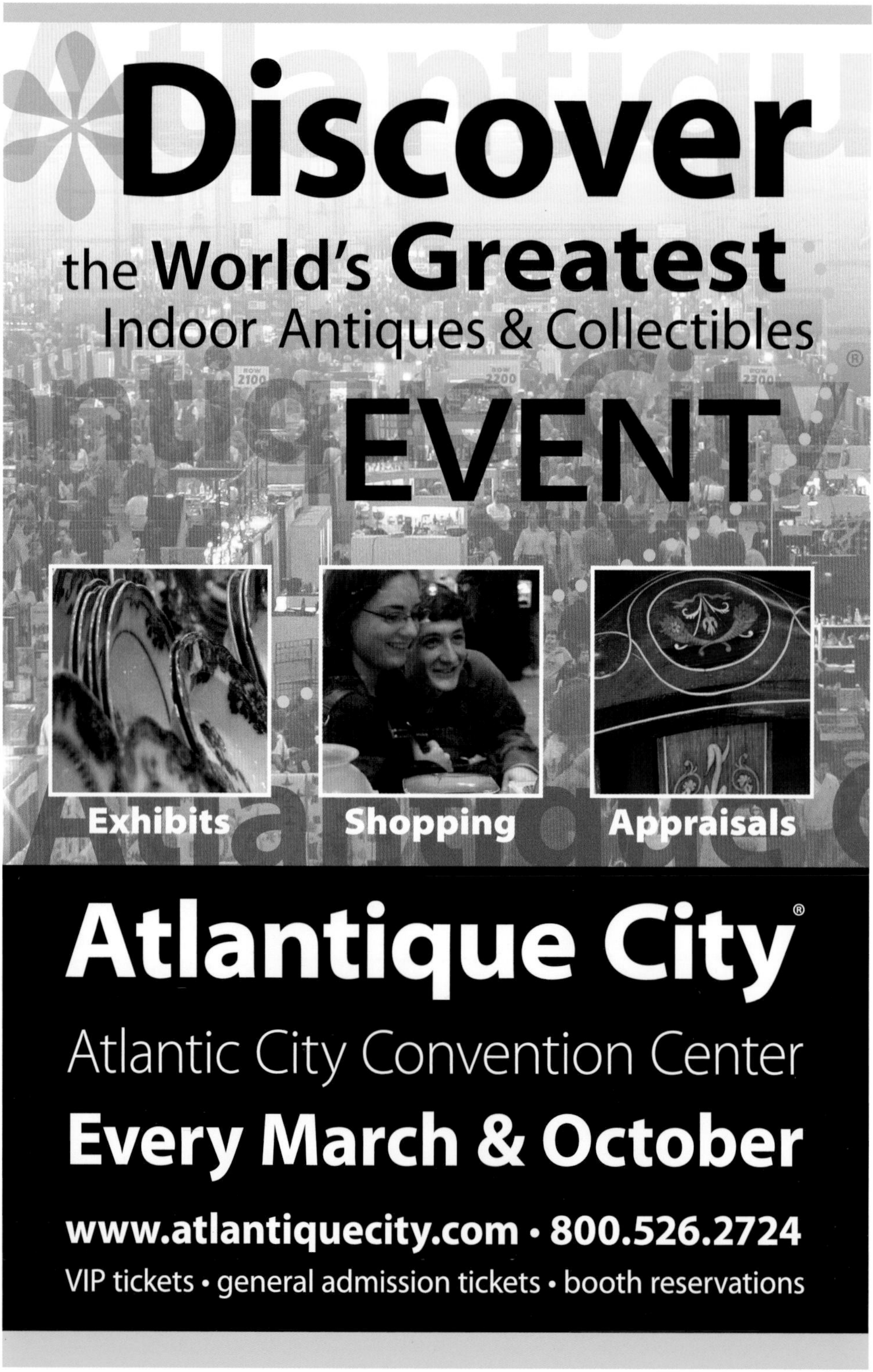